SECOND EDITION
VOLUME B

Worlds Together, WORLDS APART

NORTH POLAR
REGION

NORTH
AMERICA

ARCTIC
OCEAN

ASIA

North Magnetic Pole ★

North Pole ★

GREENLAND

ARCTIC

GREENLAND

Iceland

NORTH
AMERICA

NORTH

AMERICA

NORTH
PACIFIC
OCEAN

NORTH

ATLANTIC

OCEAN

Hudson
Bay

Gulf of
Mexico

TROPIC OF CANCER

Hawaii

CENTRAL
AMERICA

MID-ATLANTIC RIDGE

EQUATOR

Amazon
Basin

SOUTH

AMERICA

SOUTH
PACIFIC

OCEAN

TROPIC OF CAPRICORN

SOUTH

ATLANTIC

OCEAN

Falkland Islands

Cape Horn

Drake Passage

ANTARCTIC CIRCLE

ANTARCTIC
PENINSULA

WEDDELL
SEA

Ellsworth Land

Marie Byrd Land

ANTAR

GLOBAL SATELLITE MOSAIC

The beauty and complexity of Earth's landscapes—above and below the oceans—is revealed with the Global Satellite Mosaic. The mosaic, produced for the National Geographic Society by NASA's Jet Propulsion Laboratory, uses more than 500 satellite images from the National Oceanic and Atmospheric Administration. The cloud-free images show Earth in its natural colors as it might be seen from space. One can easily identify the world's major glaciers, deserts, mountain ranges, and rain forests. For example, follow the green ribbon of lush vegetation from the Nile into the stark, dry Sahara. The mountain ranges seem to rise off the map thanks to digital elevation databases from the Department of Defense. The deepest areas of ocean realm are colored dark blue in contrast to the light blue areas, highlighting continental shelves, submarine ridges, and undersea mountains.

BIOSPHERE

Thousands of satellite images combined to show a picture of biological productivity. In the oceans, red, yellow, and green indicate waters rich in phytoplankton. On land, green areas show high potential plant productivity, tan areas suffer from productivity limitations due to aridity and temperature.

THE W

SATELL

NAT
GEO
M

OCEAN

SIBERIA

EUROPE

ASIA

NORTH

PACIFIC

OCEAN

AFRICA

ARABIAN
PENINSULA

INDIA

SOUTH
CHINA
SEA

PHILIPPINE
SEA

Congo
Basin

MICRONESIA

INDONESIA

MELANESIA

INDIAN

OCEAN

AUSTRALIA

SOUTH
PACIFIC
OCEAN

Madagascar

Kalahari
Desert

Cape of Good Hope

SOUTHWEST INDIAN RIDGE

SOUTHEAST INDIAN RIDGE

TASMAN
SEA

NEW
ZEALAND

North Island

South Island

KERGUELEN
PLATEAU

SOUTH POLAR REGION

ANTARCTICA

WEST
ANTARCTICA

EAST
ANTARCTICA

Weddell
Sea

Queen Maud Land

Antarctic
Peninsula

Ross
Ice
Shelf

Marie Byrd Land

Wilkes Land

South Pole

South
Magnetic Pole

ANTARCTIC CIRCLE

THE NEED FOR SATELLITES

This Global Satellite Mosaic along with the biosphere image (lower left) and the surface temperature image (lower right) provides an integrated view of our world. The very high elevations of the Himalaya and Tibet show up as a cold area (blue temperature image) and as a plant-poor area (tan, biosphere image). Temperature, plant life, and landscape are interrelated. The need to understand the forces shaping environmental change has led to a space race among various countries. In 1997 alone some 60 rockets launched more than 140 satellites—mostly from China, Europe, Japan, Russia, and the United States. Some satellites provide vital communication links propelling economic development, other satellites supply data on patterns and trends associated with agricultural productivity, pollution monitoring, weather forecasting, and many other environmental concerns.

Wilkes
Land

ANTARCTICA

Winkel Tripel Projection, Central Meridian 0°
SCALE 1:38,931,000
1 CENTIMETER = 389 KILOMETERS; 1 INCH = 614 MILES AT THE EQUATOR

SURFACE TEMPERATURE
Reddish colors vividly show average high temperatures on the two largest continents, Africa and Asia, from the Sahara to Central Asia. Latitude, mountains, and oceans influence land temperatures.

WORLD
E MAP

WORLD · POLITICAL

NATIONAL BOUNDARIES

While man's impact is quite evident, and even striking, on many remotely sensed scenes, sometimes, as in the case with most political boundaries, it is invisible. State, provincial, and national boundaries can follow natural features, such as mountain ridges, rivers, or coastlines. Artificial constructs that possess no physical reality—for example, lines of latitude and longitude—can also determine political borders. The world political map (right) represents man's imaginary lines as they slice and divide Earth.

The National Geographic Society recognizes 192 independent states in the world as represented here. Of those nations, 185 are members of the United Nations.

Winkel Tripel Projection

ROBERT TIGNOR

JEREMY ADELMAN

STEPHEN ARON

PETER BROWN

BENJAMIN ELMAN

STEPHEN KOTKIN

XINRU LIU

SUZANNE MARCHAND

HOLLY PITTMAN

GYAN PRAKASH

BRENT SHAW

MICHAEL TSIN

SECOND EDITION
VOLUME B
600 TO 1850

Worlds Together, WORLDS APART

A HISTORY OF THE WORLD FROM THE BEGINNINGS OF HUMANKIND TO THE PRESENT

W · W · NORTON & COMPANY
NEW YORK · LONDON

W. W. Norton & Company has been independent since its founding in 1923, when William Warder Norton and Mary D. Herter Norton first published lectures delivered at the People's Institute, the adult education division of New York City's Cooper Union. The Nortons soon expanded their program beyond the Institute, publishing books by celebrated academics from America and abroad. By mid-century, the two major pillars of Norton's publishing program—trade books and college texts— were firmly established. In the 1950s, the Norton family transferred control of the company to its employees, and today—with a staff of four hundred and a comparable number of trade, college, and professional titles published each year—W. W. Norton & Company stands as the largest and oldest publishing house owned wholly by its employees.

Editor: Jon Durbin
Developmental Editors: Sandy Lifland, Alice Falk
Copy Editors: Alice Falk, Ellen Lohman
Project Editor: Rebecca Homiski
Photo Researchers: Stephanie Romeo, Jennie Bright, Julie Tesser
Production Manager: Roy Tedoff
Managing Editor, College: Marian Johnson
Emedia Editor: Steve Hoge
Book Designer: Rubina Yeh
Ancillary Editors: Matthew Arnold, Alexis Hilts
Layout Artist: Brad Walrod
Editorial Assistants: Rob Haber, Alexis Hilts
Cartographer: Carto-Graphics

About the Cover Image: Objects such as this jade vessel crowned by a king's likeness, found in a royal tomb, testify to the Maya's artistic skills and far-flung commerce, as they reveal features from neighboring cultures. Luxuries, including jade, exotic pelts, and feathers, were traded throughout Mesoamerica.

ISBN: 978-0-393-93209-6

W. W. Norton & Company, Inc., 500 Fifth Avenue, New York, NY 10110
wwnorton.com

W. W. Norton & Company Ltd., Castle House, 75/76 Wells Street, London W1T 3QT

1 2 3 4 5 6 7 8 9

Contents in Brief

Contents

Chapter 10 Becoming "The World," 1000–1300 CE 417

CHAPTER 11 CRISES AND RECOVERY IN AFRO-EURASIA, 1300s–1500s 473

CHAPTER 13   WORLDS ENTANGLED, 1600–1750   553

CHAPTER 14   CULTURES OF SPLENDOR AND POWER, 1500–1780   599

CHAPTER 15   REORDERING THE WORLD, 1750–1850 639

Global Connections
& Disconnections Features

Primary Source Documents

Maps

THE MAKING OF *Worlds Together, Worlds Apart*

*M*ost books have a back story, though authors often hesitate to trot out the truly revealing details. In this case, however, some details should be disclosed because they illuminate the shape and substance of the narrative. The story begins nearly twenty years ago, when the Princeton University history department established its first course in world history. Called "The World and the West," the course surveyed the major developments in the history of the modern world from 1500 to the present. Although the importance of the course for students of an increasingly globalized era was immediately recognized, the course placed immense demands on teachers and students. The greatest challenge was how to treat the many regions of the world and the many centuries in an integrated way and in a single semester. The instructors searched in vain for a textbook that would provide both coverage and integrated analysis. Some of the books available at the time were written by a single author; these tended to have a clear narrative framework but to suffer from the limitations that a single individual, no matter how well read, necessarily encountered when dealing with the immensity of world history. Others were written by a team of regional experts and had authoritative treatments of regions but lacked integration and balance.

With the full support of Princeton University, a small group of modern historians in the Princeton history department decided to try our hand at world history, agreeing to meet on a regular basis to plan a text that addressed the weaknesses in the other books. Each of us had a regional specialization as well as an interest in how our regions fitted into larger cross-regional relationships. For an entire year we met to discuss the ways in which we would craft a modern world history and the global themes we wanted to stress. After intensive and sometimes contentious discussions, we decided on an overarching framework, the chapter divisions, and the global themes and regional variations. During these meetings, we also settled on the all-important idea of building each chapter around a turning point or central story in world history, such as the spread of the Black Death or the rise of the nation-state, that would enable us to integrate all the regions of the world into most chapters. Then we began to write. We wrote a lot—and a lot of what we wrote ended up in recycling bins. We all wrote sections in each of the chapters, shared them with one another, and then gave one of our group the assignment of integrating each chapter. All this meant that every one of us wrote something for each of the chapters. Different individuals coordinated the chapters, after which the drafts circulated to everyone once again for additional thoughts and revisions. The general editor then wrote the final draft to ensure that a strong, single voice would emerge and that the level of presentation would be consistent throughout. *Worlds Together, Worlds Apart: A History of the Modern World* (WTWA), the final product, was truly a collaborative work. No section, no matter how seemingly specialized, was the product of just one author.

We were pleased to discover, very soon after publication, that teachers and students liked WTWA. The original text (now Volume Two) was adopted widely in its first year of publication and has gone on to be used at over 200 colleges and universities worldwide and has sold over 40,000 copies. Then, instructors began to ask, Why not apply the WTWA model to the early period of world history? In 2003 we set out to do just that, with Robert Tignor and Jeremy Adelman from the modern volume joining forces with a distinguished group of historians of the earlier periods. In crafting the stories and chapters that would cover the earlier periods of world history, we have used the same highly collaborative writing model that proved so successful with the original volume, and we have built the chapters covering the earlier periods around turning points and central stories in world history, such as the formation of the Silk Road and the rise of universal religions, just as we did the chapters in the original volume. While we were hard at work writing the chapters covering the earlier periods, the authors of the modern chapters set about revising them so that all the chapters would fit seamlessly together. Ten years after we began our work, we are very pleased to offer *Worlds Together, Worlds Apart: A History of the World from the Beginnings of Humankind to the Present.*

Over the ten-year period of work on this book, world history has gained even more prominence in college classrooms and historical studies. Courses in the history of the world now abound, often replacing the standard surveys of European history and western civilization overviews. Graduate history students receive training in world history, and journals routinely publish studies in this field. A new generation of textbooks is needed to help students and instructors make sense of this vast, complex, and rapidly evolving field. WTWA hopes to be the first to plot this new course and to inspire its readers to continue their studies in this increasingly critical field.

OUR GUIDING PRINCIPLES

Five principles inform this book, guiding its framework and the organization of its individual chapters. The first is that **world history is global history**. There are many fine histories of the individual regions of the world, which we have endeavored to make good use of. But unlike the authors of many other so-called world histories, we have chosen not to deal with the great regions and cultures of the world as separate units, reserving individual chapters to East Asia, South Asia,

Southwest Asia, Europe, Africa, and the Americas. Our goal is to place each of these regions in its largest geographical context. It would be misleading to say that the context is the world, because none of these regions, even the most highly developed commercially, enjoyed commercial or cultural contact with peoples all over the globe before Columbus's voyage to the Americas and the sixteenth century. But the peoples living in the Afro-Eurasian landmass, probably the single most important building block for our study, were deeply influenced by one another, as were the more scattered peoples living in the Americas and in Africa below the Sahara. Products, ideas, and persons traveled widely across the large land units of Eurasia, Africa, and the Americas. Indeed, Afro-Eurasia was not divided or thought of as divided into separate landmasses until recent times. It is in this sense that our world history is global.

The second principle informing this work is **the importance of chronology in framing world history**. Rather than telling the story of world history by analyzing separate geographical areas, we have elected to frame the chapters around significant historical turning points or periods that transcended regional and cultural boundaries—moments or periods of meaningful changes in the way that human beings organized their lives. Some of these changes were dramatic and affected many people. Environments changed; the earth became drier and warmer; humans learned to domesticate plants and animals; technological innovations in warfare, political organization, and commercial activities occurred; and the appeal of new religious and cultural beliefs spread far and wide. These changes swept across large landmasses, paying scant heed to preexisting cultural and geographical unity. They affected peoples living in widely dispersed societies. In other cases, changes occurred in only one locality while other places retained their traditions or took alternative routes. Chronology helps us understand the ways in which the world has, and has not, shared a common history. Chapter headings give a clue to the turning points or periods that paid no heed to geography and culture. At the outset of human existence, after *Homo sapiens* populated the world and became truly human (Chapter 1), men and women established the first cities and hierarchical polities and societies in the riverine basins of the Near East and northwest India (4000–2000 BCE; Chapter 2). Several millennia later, nomadic invaders provided a stimulus to re-create powerful territorial polities, employing horse-drawn chariots to undermine the old polities and to fashion new ones (2000–1200 BCE; Chapter 3). During the next millennium, powerful Asian monarchs established the first large-scale kingdoms that even aspired to world domination (1200 BCE–250 CE; Chapters 4 through 6). In more modern times, the spread of the bubonic plague across the Afro-Eurasian landmass brought great loss of life and undermined existing polities, preparing the groundwork for a new set of political organizations that proved to be long-lived (Chapter 11). The discovery of large silver mines in Spanish America in the sixteenth century provided a precious metal that brought the economies of the world into closer contact (Chapter 12). In the nineteenth century, ideas of freedom swept across the world, propelled by the American and French revolutions, only to be superseded by European imperial ambitions (Chapters 16 through 18). Two world wars linked the entire international community on battlefields and in great loss of life (Chapters 19 and 20).

The third principle is **historical and geographical balance**. Ours is not a history focused on the rise of the West. We seek to pay attention to the global histories of all peoples and not to privilege those developments that led directly into European history as if the rest of the history of the world was but a prelude to the rise of western civilization. We deal with peoples living outside Europe on their own terms and try to see world history from their perspective. Even more significantly, while we describe societies that obviously influenced Europe's historical development, we do so in a context very different from that which western historians have stressed. Rather than simply viewing these cultures in terms of their role in western development, we seek to understand them in their own terms and to illuminate the ways they influenced other parts of the world. From our perspective, it is historically inaccurate to annex Mesopotamia and Egypt to western civilization, because these territories lay well outside Europe and had a large influence on Africa, South Asia, and East Asia as well as on Europe. Indeed, our presentation of Europe in the period leading up to and including the founding of the Roman Empire is different from many of the standard treatments. The Europeans we describe are rather rough, wild-living, warring peoples living on the fringes of the settled parts of the world and looked down on by more politically stable communities. They hardly seem to be made of the stuff that will catapult Europeans to world leadership a millennium later—indeed, they were very different people from those who, as the result of myriad intervening and contingent events, founded the nineteenth- and twentieth-century empires whose ruins are still all around us.

Our fourth principle is **an emphasis on connections and what we call disconnections across societal and cultural boundaries**. World history is not the history of separate regions of the world at different periods of time. It is the history of the connections among peoples living often at great distances from one another, and it is also the history of the resistances of peoples living within and outside societies to connections that threatened to put them in subordinate positions or to rob them of their independence.

A stress on connections inevitably foregrounds those elements within societies that promoted long-distance ties. Merchants are important, as are military men and political potentates seeking to expand their polities. So are scholars and religious leaders, particularly those who believed that they had universalistic messages with which to convert others to their visions. Perhaps most important of all in premodern world history, certainly the most understudied, are the nomadic pastoral peoples, who were often the agents for the transmission of products, peoples, and ideas across long and harsh distances. They exploded onto the scene of settled societies at critical junctures, erasing old cultural and geographical barriers and producing new unities, as the Arabs did in the seventh century CE and the Mongols in the thirteenth century. *Worlds Together, Worlds Apart* is not intended to convey the message that the history of the world is a story of increasing integration. What for one ruling group brought benefits in the form of increased workforces, material prosperity, and political stability often meant enslavement, political subordination, and loss of territory for other groups. The historian's task, then, is not only to represent the different experiences of increased connectedness, describing worlds that came together, but also to be attentive to the opposite trends, describing peoples and communities that remained apart.

The fifth and final principle is that **world history is a narrative of big themes and high-level comparisons**. *Worlds Together, Worlds Apart* is not a book of record. Indeed, in a work that covers the whole of the historical record of humankind from the beginnings of history to the present, the notion that no event or individual worthy of attention would be excluded is the height of folly. We have sought to offer clear themes and interpretations in order to synthesize the vast body of data that often overwhelms histories of the world. Our aspiration is to identify the main historical forces that have moved history, to highlight those monumental innovations that have changed the way humans lived, and to describe the creation and evolution of those bedrock institutions, many of which, of course, endure. In this regard, self-conscious cross-cultural comparisons of developments, institutions, and even founding figures receive attention to make students aware that some common institutions, such as slavery, did not have the same features in every society. Or, in the opposite fashion, the seemingly diverse terms that were used, say, to describe learned and religious men in different parts of the world—monks in Europe, ulama in Islam, Brahmans in India, and scholar-gentries in China—often meant much the same thing in very different settings. We have constructed *Worlds Together, Worlds Apart* around big ideas, stories, and themes rather than filling the book with names and dates that encourage students only to memorize rather than understand world history concepts.

OUR MAJOR THEMES

The primary organizing framework of *Worlds Together, Worlds Apart*—one that runs through the chapters and connects the different parts of the volume—is the theme of **interconnection and divergence**. While describing movements that facilitated global connectedness, this book also shows how different regions developed their own ways of handling or resisting connections and change. Throughout history, different regions and different population groups often stood apart from the rest of the world until touched by traders or explorers or missionaries or soldiers. Some of these regions welcomed global connections. Others sought to change the nature of their connections with the outside world, and yet others resisted efforts to bring them into the larger world. All, however, were somehow affected by their experience of connection. Yet, the history of the world is not simply one of increasing globalization, in which all societies eventually join a common path to the present. Rather, it is a history of the ways in which, as people became linked, their experience of these global connections diverged.

Besides the central theme of interconnection and divergence, other themes also stand out in WTWA. First, the book discusses **how the recurring efforts of people to cross religious, political, and cultural borders brought the world together**. Merchants and educated men and women traded goods and ideas. Whole communities, in addition to select groups, moved to safer or more promising environments. **The transregional crossings of ideas, goods, and peoples produced transformations and conflicts**—a second important theme. Finally, the movement of ideas, peoples, products, and germs over long distances upset the balance of power across the world and within individual societies. Such movements changed the relationship of different population groups with other peoples and areas of the world and led over time to dramatic shifts in the ascendancy of regions. **Changes in power arrangements within and between regions explain which parts of the world and regional groups benefited from integration and which resisted it.** These three themes (exchange and migration, conflict and resistance, and alterations in the balance of power) weave themselves through every chapter of this work.

In *Worlds Together, Worlds Apart,* we tell the stories of people caught in these currents of exchange, conflict, and changing power relations. We describe those historical actors, such as Roman legionnaires, early Christian and Muslim proselytizers, Indian Ocean merchants in the sixteenth century, and late-nineteenth-century European imperialists, who sought a more closely integrated world economy and polity. But we also describe those individuals who led movements in defense of cherished historical and cultural heritages. Jewish prophets under Roman rule, the Indian prophet Tenskwatawa in North America, and the religious cleric al-Wahhab on the Arabian Peninsula all urged their people to return to traditional identities. Others, such as Shiite clerics under Umayyad rule in the seventh and eighth centuries CE, Indian rebels in 1857, and advocates of a third way after World War II, sought a less unified world and used their historical and cultural traditions to favor new arrangements of world power.

From the beginnings of humanity to the present, in examining the forces that brought peoples and cultures together and those that kept them apart, this book explores not only the changing power relations between societies but also those within societies. Chief among these have been the divisions between rulers and subjects, between commoners and nobles,

and between men and women. The **gender divide** has been one of the most important factors in shaping the evolution of societies, and this theme receives attention in Volume One and fresh accenting in the revised chapters of Volume Two.

Women and men lived in small-scale, relatively egalitarian societies until about 8,000 years ago, when hierarchical, urbanized, and centralized societies sprang up in three of the major river basins of Afro-Eurasia. One of the primary divides across all societies was the difference between men and women. If there was a world apart, from the time of the early agrarian breakthrough, it was within the family itself, as divisions of labor sharpened between men and women. Not all societies stratified themselves along gender lines in the same way. Indeed, many left open the possibility of women exercising influence and authority. But what underlay so many of the world's first civilizations was the way in which societies defined some traits as virtuous (such as the ability to fight) or created new social roles for rulers but restricted them mainly to men (such as scribes or priests). In this fashion, the social order took on gendered features from the very start. This was a long-term legacy that evolved over the ensuing centuries of human history.

By the same token, over the sweep of the millennia people acquired more and more skills and aptitudes for changing the environment to suit their needs and wants. They went from adapting to nature to controlling it, though this was hardly a linear process. There was plenty of backsliding. As with gender, not all societies related to their environments in the same way. To a very large extent, the differences in habitat were influential. In arid steppe lands, nomads followed their food around, while in large river basins, urban zones and complex, stratified societies emerged because water helped with transportation and settled agriculture. Similarly, societies coped with nature's vagaries in different ways. Some learned from experience, such as when China developed vast hydraulics to control flooding. Others could not cope with shocks, such as when the bubonic plague ravaged Afro-Eurasian populations in the fourteenth century and, most devastatingly, Old World diseases were introduced to the New World after 1492. A recurring theme, however, is **the way in which adaptation to environmental constraints was the source of large-scale unintended consequences that often brought societies face to face with similar plights**. In this sense, environmental history was a force that divided and united world societies.

OVERVIEW OF VOLUME ONE

Volume One of *Worlds Together, Worlds Apart* deals with the period from the beginnings of human history through the Mongol invasions of the thirteenth century and the spread of the Black Death across Afro-Eurasia. It is divided into eleven chapters, each of which marks a distinct historical period. Hence, each chapter has an overarching theme or small set of themes that hold otherwise highly diverse material together.

Chapter 1, "Becoming Human," presents biological and cultural perspectives on the way that early hominoids became truly human. World history books now have a nearly mandatory opening chapter on prehistory. We believe that this chapter is important in establishing the global context of world history. We believe too that our chapter is unique in its focus on how humans became humans, so we discuss how early humans became bipedal and how they developed complex cognitive processes such as language and artistic abilities. Recent research indicates that *Homo sapiens* originated in Africa, probably no more than 200,000 years ago. These early men and women walked out of the African landmass sometime between 120,000 and 50,000 years ago, gradually populating all regions of the world. What is significant in this story is that the different population groups around the world, the so-called races of humankind, have only recently broken off from one another. Also in this chapter, we describe the domestication of plants and animals and the founding of the first village settlements around the globe.

In **Chapter 2, "Rivers, Cities, and First States, 4000–2000 BCE,"** we focus on five of the great river basins where extraordinary breakthroughs in human activity occurred. On the flood plains of the Tigris and Euphrates in Mesopotamia, the Nile in Egypt, the Indus valley in modern-day northern India and Pakistan, and the Yellow and Yangzi rivers in China, men and women mastered annual floods and became expert in seeding and cultivating foodstuffs. In these areas, populations became dense. Riverine cultures had much in common. They had highly developed hierarchical political, social, and cultural systems, priestly and bureaucratic classes, and organized religious and cultural systems. But they also differed greatly, and these differences were passed from generation to generation. Compare ancient Egypt, which had a dearth of large cities, with Mesopotamia, which was the heartland of urban development. Consider as well the Chinese ruling elites, who early on displayed a talent for organizing large swaths of territories with heavy population densities and gradually imposing on them a unified culture. The development of these major complex societies certainly is a turning point in world history.

In **Chapter 3, "Nomads, Territorial States, and Microsocieties, 2000–1200 BCE,"** extensive climatic and technological changes serve as major turning points. Drought, environmental degradation, and political instability brought the first riverine societies to a crashing end around 2000 BCE. When aridity forced tribal and nomadic peoples living on the fringes of the settled populations to move closer to settled areas, they brought with them an insurmountable military advantage. They had become adept at yoking horses to war chariots, and hence they were in a position to subjugate or intermarry with the peoples in the settled polities in the river basins. Around 2000 BCE these peoples established new territorial kingdoms in Mesopotamia, Egypt, the Indus valley, and China, which gave way a millennium later (1000 BCE) to even larger, militarily and politically more powerful states. In the Americas, the Mediterranean, sub-Saharan Africa, and the Pacific worlds, microsocieties arose as an alternative form of polity in which peoples lived in much smaller-scale societies that showcased their own unique and compelling features.

Chapter 4, "First Empires and Common Cultures in Afro-Eurasia, 1200–350 BCE," describes the different ways in which larger-scale societies grew and became unified. In the case of the world's first empires, the neo-Assyrian and Persian, political power was the main unifying element. Both states established different models that future empires would emulate. The Assyrians used brutal force to intimidate and subjugate different groups within their societies and neighboring states. The Persians followed a pattern that relied less on coercion and more on tributary relationships, while reveling in cultural diversity. The Zhou state in China offered yet a third way of political unity, basing its rule on the doctrine of the mandate of heaven, which legitimated its rulers' succession as long as they were able to maintain stability and order. Vedic society in South Asia offers a dramatically different model in which religion and culture are the main unifying forces. Religion moves to the forefront of the narrative in other ways in this chapter. The birth of monotheism occurred in the Zoroastrian and Hebrew faiths and the beginnings of Buddhism—all three religions endure today.

During the last millennium before the common era, the worlds surrounding these centralized, riverine polities emerged as major players on the historical stage just as these first empires were declining. As **Chapter 5, "Worlds Turned Inside Out, 1000–350 BCE,"** demonstrates, these worlds took advantage of the small-scale and more intimate relationships to create highly individualistic cultures, even in some cases to experiment with a democratic polity. They also developed new strategies for understanding the natural world and humankind. The Greek city-states were the most dynamic of these new cultures, and they spread their Hellenistic culture far and wide. In China, Confucians and Daoists debated how best to create a well-ruled and stable society during the Warring States period. Similar debates occurred in South Asia, where early Buddhists and Brahmin priests in Vedic society strove to provide a more spiritually compelling belief system for their followers. In Greece, Plato, Socrates, and the Sophists discussed nature and humanity. In Africa, the Bantu peoples spread across sub-Saharan Africa, and the Sudanic peoples of Meroe created a society that blended Egyptian and sub-Saharan influences. These were all dynamic hybrid societies building on existing knowledge. Equally dramatic transformations occurred in the Americas, where the Olmec and Chavín peoples were creating hierarchical societies of the like never before seen in their part of the world.

Chapter 6, "Shrinking the Afro-Eurasian World, 350 BCE–250 CE," describes three major forces that simultaneously integrated large segments of the Afro-Eurasian landmass culturally and economically. First, Alexander and his armies changed the political and cultural landscape of North Africa and Southwest and South Asia. Culturally, Alexander spread Hellenism through North Africa and Southwest and central Asia, making it the first cultural system to achieve a transregional scope. Hellenism's appeal to peoples with varying historical and cultural backgrounds was irresistible. Alexander and his men followed existing pathways across Southwest Asia on their way to South Asia, but it was in the post-Alexander world that these commercial roads were stabilized and intensified. For the first time, a trading network, known as the Silk Road, stretching from Palmyra in the West to Central Asia in the East, came into being. Buddhism was the first religion to seize on the Silk Road's more formal existence as its followers moved quickly with the support of the Mauryan Empire to spread their ideas into central Asia. Finally, we witness the growth of a "silk road of the seas" as new technologies and bigger ships allowed for a dramatic expansion in maritime trade from South Asia all the way to Egypt and East Africa.

Chapter 7, "Han Dynasty China and Imperial Rome, 300 BCE–300 CE," describes Han China and the Roman Empire. The world's first empires appeared in Chapter 4, and developments introduced in previous chapters paved the way for the massive Roman and Han empires, which provided two political, economic, and cultural systems that dominated much of the Afro-Eurasian landmass from 200 BCE to 200 CE. Both the Han Dynasty and the Roman Empire ruled effectively in their own way, providing an instructive comparative case study. Both left their imprint on Afro-Eurasia, and rulers for centuries afterward tried to revive these glorious polities and use them as models of greatness. This chapter also discusses the effect of state sponsorship on religion, as Christianity came into existence in the context of the late Roman Empire and Buddhism was introduced to China during the decline of the Han.

Chapter 8, "The Rise of Universal Religions, 300–600 CE," describes how out of the crumbling Roman Empire new polities and a new religion emerged. The Byzantine Empire, claiming to be the successor state to the Roman Empire, embraced Christianity as its state religion. The Tang rulers patronized Buddhism to such a degree that Confucian statesmen feared it had become the state religion. Both Buddhism and Christianity enjoyed spectacular success in the politically fragmented post-Han era in China and in the feudal world of western Europe. These dynamic religions represent a decisive turning point in world history. Christianity enjoyed its eventual successes through state sponsorship via the Roman and Byzantine empires and by providing spiritual comfort and hope during the chaotic years of Rome's decline. Buddhism grew through imperial sponsorship and significant changes to its fundamental beliefs, when adherents to the faith deified Buddha and created notions of an afterlife. In Africa we see a wide range of significant developments and a myriad of cultural practices, yet we also witness the ongoing development of large common cultures. The Bantu peoples spread throughout the southern half of the landmass, spoke closely related languages, and developed similar political institutions based on the prestige of individuals of high achievement. In the Americas the Olmecs established their own form of the city-state, while the Mayans owed their success to a decentralized common culture built around a strong religious belief system and a series of spiritual centers.

In **Chapter 9, "New Empires and Common Cultures, 600–1000 CE,"** we look at how from a relatively remote corner of the Arabian Peninsula arose another world religion, Islam, which enjoyed unanticipated political, military, cultural, and economic successes. The rise of Islam, clearly another turning point in world history, provides a contrast to the way in which universalizing religions and political empires interacted. Islam and empire arose in a fashion quite different from Christianity and the Roman Empire. Christianity took over an already existing empire—the Roman—after suffering persecution at its hands for several centuries. In contrast, Islam created an empire almost at the moment of its emergence. Toward the end of his life, the Prophet Muhammad was already establishing the rudiments of an empire as he contemplated taking control of the whole Arabian Peninsula and extending his influence to Syria and Iraq. By the time the Abbasid Empire came into being in the middle of the eighth century, Islamic armies, political leaders, and clerics exercised power over much of the Afro-Eurasian landmass from southern Spain, across North Africa, all the way to Central Asia. Islam worked its way into West and East Africa, as Muslim clerics and traders crossed the Sahara and the Indian Ocean. They reached far into the interior of the sub-Saharan region. The Tang Empire in China, however, served as a counterweight to Islam's power both politically and intellectually. Confucianism enjoyed a spectacular recovery in this period. With the Tang rulers, Confucianism slowed the spread of Buddhism and further reinforced China's development along different, more secular pathways. Japan and Korea also enter world history at this time, as tributary states to Tang China and as hybrid cultures that mixed Chinese customs and practices with their own. The Vikings highlight the role that nomadic peoples played in developing trade in Afro-Eurasia. The Christian world split in this period between the western Latin church and the eastern Byzantine church. Both branches of Christianity played a role in unifying societies, especially in western Europe, which lacked strong political rule.

Chapter 10, "Becoming 'The World,' 1000–1300 CE," looks at the increase of prosperity and population across most of Afro-Eurasia and into West and East Africa. Just as importantly, the world in this period divided into regional zones that are recognizable today. And trade grew rapidly.

A look at the major trading cities of this time demonstrates how commerce transformed cultures. Sub-Saharan Africa also underwent intense regional integration via the spread of the Mande-speaking peoples and the Mali Empire. The Americas witness their first empire in the form of the Chimu peoples in the Andes. This chapter ends with the Mongol conquests of the twelfth and thirteenth centuries, which brought massive destruction. The Mongol Empire, however, once in place, promoted long-distance commerce, scholarly exchange, and travel on an unprecedented scale. The Mongols brought Eurasia and North Africa and many parts of sub-Saharan Africa into a new connectedness. The Mongol story also underscores the important role that nomads played throughout the history of the early world.

Finally, **Chapter 11, "Crises and Recovery in Afro-Eurasia, 1300s–1500s,"** brings into relief the turning point of the Black Death, which turned this period into one where many traditional institutions and polities gave way and peoples were compelled to rebuild their cultures. The polities that came into being at this time and the intense religious experimentation that took place effected a sharp break with the past. The bubonic plague wiped out as much as two-thirds of the population in many of the densely settled locations of Afro-Eurasia. Societies were brought to their knees by the Mongols' depredations as well as by biological pathogens. In the face of one of humanity's grimmest periods, peoples and societies demonstrated tremendous resilience as they looked for new ways to rebuild their communities, some turning inward and others seeking inspiration, conquests, and riches elsewhere. Volume One concludes on the eve of the "Columbian Exchange," the moment when "old" worlds discovered "new" ones and a vast series of global interconnections and divergences commenced.

OVERVIEW OF VOLUME TWO

The organizational structure for Volume Two reaffirms the commitment to write a decentered, global history of the world. Christopher Columbus is not the starting point, as he is in so many modern world histories. Rather, we begin in the eleventh and twelfth centuries with two major developments in world history. The first, set forth in **Chapter 10, "Becoming 'The World,' 1000–1300 CE,"** describes a world that was divided for the first time into regions that are recognizable today. This world experienced rapid population growth, as is shown by a simple look at the major trading cities from Asia in the East to the Mediterranean in the West. Yet nomadic peoples remain a force as revealed in the Mongol invasions of Afro-Eurasia. **Chapter 11, "Crises and Recovery in Afro-Eurasia, 1300s–1500s,"** describes how the Mongol warriors, through

their conquests and the integration of the Afro-Eurasian world, spread the bubonic plague, which brought death and depopulation to much of Afro-Eurasia. Both these stories set the stage for the modern world and are clear-cut turning points in world history. The primary agents of world connection described in this chapter were dynasts, soldiers, clerics, merchants, and adventurers who rebuilt the societies that disease and political collapse had destroyed. They joined the two hemispheres, as we describe in **Chapter 12, "Contact, Commerce, and Colonization, 1450s–1600,"** bringing the peoples and products of the Western Hemisphere into contact and conflict with Eurasia and Africa. It is the collision between the Eastern and Western Hemispheres that sets in motion modern world history and marks a distinct divide or turning point between the premodern and the modern. Here, too, disease and increasing trade linkages were vital. Unprepared for the advanced military technology and the disease pool of European and African peoples, the Amerindian population experienced a population decline even more devastating than that caused by the Black Death.

Europeans sailed across the Atlantic Ocean to find a more direct, less encumbered route to Asia and came upon lands, peoples, and products that they had not expected. One item, however, that they had sought in every part of the world and that they found in abundance in the Americas was precious metal. In **Chapter 13, "Worlds Entangled, 1600–1750,"** we discuss how New World silver from Mexico and Peru became the major currency of global commerce, oiling the long-distance trading networks that had been revived after the Black Death. The effect of New World silver on the world economy was so great that it, even more than the Iberian explorations of the New World, brought the hemispheres together and marks the true genesis of modern world history. We also discuss the importance of sugar, which linked the economies and polities of western Europe, Africa, and the Americas in a triangular trade centered on the Atlantic Ocean. Sugar, silver, spices, and other products sparked and expanded commercial exchanges and led to cultural flourishing around the world.

Chapter 14, "Cultures of Splendor and Power, 1500–1780," discusses the Ottoman scientists, Safavid and Mughal artists, and Chinese literati, as well as European thinkers, whose notable achievements were rooted in their own cultures but tempered by awareness of the intellectual activities of others. In this chapter, we look closely at how culture is created as a historical process and describe how the massive growth in wealth during this period, growing out of global trade, led to one of the great periods of cultural flourishing in world history.

Around 1800, transformations reverberated outward from the Atlantic world and altered economic and political relationships in the rest of the world. In **Chapter 15, "Reordering the World, 1750–1850,"** we discuss how political revolutions in the Americas and Europe, new ideas about how to trade and organize labor, and a powerful rhetoric of freedom and universal rights underlay the beginning of "a great divide" between peoples of European descent and those who were not. These forces of laissez-faire capitalism, industrialization, the nation-state, and republicanism not only attracted diverse groups around the world; they also threatened groups that put forth alternative visions. Ideas of freedom, as manifested in trading relations, labor, and political activities, clashed with a traditional world based on inherited rights and statuses and further challenged the way men and women had lived in earlier times. These political, intellectual, and economic reorderings changed the way people around the world saw themselves and thus represent something quite novel in world history. But these new ways of envisioning the world did not go unchallenged, as **Chapter 16, "Alternative Visions of the Nineteenth Century,"** makes clear. Here, intense resistance to evolving modernity reflected the diversity of peoples and their hopes for the future. This chapter looks at Wahabbism in Islam, the strongman movement in Africa, Indian resistance in America and Mexico, socialism and communism in Europe, the Taiping Rebellion in China, and the Indian Mutiny in South Asia. Prophets and leaders had visions that often drew on earlier traditions and that led these individuals to resist rapid change.

Chapter 17, "Nations and Empires, 1850–1914," discusses the political, economic, military, and ideological power that thrust Europe and North America to the fore of global events and led to an era of nationalism and modern imperialism, new forces in world history. Yet this period of seeming European supremacy was to prove short-lived. **Chapter 18, "An Unsettled World, 1890–1914,"** demonstrates that even before World War I shattered Europe's moral certitude, many groups at home (feminists, Marxists, and unfulfilled nationalists) and abroad (anticolonial nationalists) had raised a chorus of complaints about European and North American dominance. As in Chapter 14, we look at the processes by which specific cultural movements arise and reflect the concerns of individual societies. Yet here, too, syncretistic movements emerged in many cultures and reflected the sway of global imperialism, which by then had become a dominant force.

Chapter 19, "Of Masses and Visions of the Modern, 1910–1939," briefly covers World War I and then discusses how, from the end of World War I until World War II, different visions of being modern competed around the world. It is the development of modernism and its effects on multiple cultures that integrate the diverse developments discussed in this chapter. In the decades between the world wars, proponents of liberal democracy struggled to defend their views and often to impose their will on authoritarian rulers and anticolonial nationalists.

Chapter 20, "The Three-World Order, 1940–1975," presents World War II and describes how new adversaries arose after the war. A three-world order came into being— the First World, led by the United States and extolling capitalism, the nation-state, and democratic government; the Second World, led by the Soviet Union and favoring authoritarian polities and economies; and the Third World, made up of former colonies seeking an independent status for themselves in world affairs. The rise of this three-world order dominates the second half of the twentieth century and constitutes another major theme of world history.

In **Chapter 21, "Globalization, 1970–2000,"** we explain that, at the end of the cold war, the modern world, while clearly more unified than before, still had profound cultural differences and political divisions. At the beginning of the twenty-first century, capital, commodities, peoples, and ideas move rapidly over long distances. But cultural tensions and political impasses continue to exist. It is the rise of this form of globalism that represents a vital new element as humankind heads into a new century and millennium. We close with an **Epilogue,** which tracks developments since the turn of the millennium. These last few years have brought profound changes to the world order, yet we hope readers of *Worlds Together, Worlds Apart* will see more clearly how this most recent history is, in fact, entwined with trends of much longer duration that are the chief focus of this book.

The history of the world is not a single, sweeping narrative. On the contrary, the last 5,000 years have produced multiple histories, moving along many paths and trajectories. Sometimes these histories merge, intertwining themselves in substantial ways. Sometimes they disentangle themselves and simply stand apart. Much of the time, however, they are simultaneously together and apart. In place of a single narrative, the usual one being the rise of the West, this book maps the many forks in the road that confronted the world's societies at different times and the surprising turns and unintended consequences that marked the choices that peoples and societies made, including the unanticipated and dramatic rise of the West in the nineteenth century. Formulated in this way, world history is the unfolding of many possible histories, and readers of this book should come away with a reinforced sense of the unpredictability of the past, the instability of the present, and the uncertainty of the future.

Let us begin our story!

PEDAGOGICAL PROGRAM

Worlds Together, Worlds Apart is designed for maximum readability. The crisp, clear narrative, built around stories, themes, and concepts, is accompanied by a highly useful pedagogical program designed to help students study while engaging them in the subject matter. Highlights of this innovative program are described below.

STELLAR MAP PROGRAM WITH ENHANCED CAPTIONS

The book's more than 120 beautiful maps are designed to reinforce the main stories and concepts in each chapter.

Every chapter opens with a two-page map of the world designed to highlight the main story line of the chapter. Within the chapter appear four to five more maps that focus on the regions covered. Enhanced captions encourage more interaction with the map program. Each caption provides contextual information and then asks three types of questions:

- *Factual.* Understanding basic geography
- *Analytical.* Understanding patterns and trends on the map
- *Interpretive.* Thinking beyond the map

Focus-Question System

The focus-question system helps the reader remain alert to key concepts and questions on every page of the text. Focus questions guide students' reading in three ways: (1) a focus-question box at the beginning of the chapter previews the chapter's contents, (2) relevant questions reappear at the start of the section where they are discussed, and (3) running heads on right-hand pages keep these questions in view throughout the chapter.

Primary Source Documents

The authors have selected three to five primary source documents for each chapter. Unlike the primary sources found in other books, which are designed to cover only the greatest hits, our selections reinforce the book's main themes and provide colorful material to augment the chapter's main story line. Perhaps most importantly, many of them challenge students to see world history through the eyes of others and from different perspectives. Each excerpt is accompanied by at least two study questions. Additional primary sources are available on the Digital History Reader, which is part of the Norton StudySpace website.

Global Connections & Disconnections Features

Each chapter contains one thematic feature built around key individuals or phenomena that exemplify the main emphasis of the text. Among the many topics included are how historians use technology to date bones and objects from early history, the use of ritual funeral objects in the contexts of religion and trade, the role of libraries in early world history, the travels of Marco Polo and Ibn Battuta, coffee drinking and coffeehouses in different parts of the world, cartography and maps as expressions of different worldviews, the growth of universities around the world, and Che Guevera as a radical visionary who tried to export revolution throughout the Third World.

New Chapter Chronologies

With the Second Edition come new chronologies that are organized regionally rather than temporally. Each chapter ends with a chronology. The chronologies allow students to track unifying concepts and to see influences across cultures and societies within a given time period.

Study Questions

Following each chapter's conclusion is a series of study questions to help ensure that students have grasped the major concepts and ideas.

Further Readings

Each chapter includes an ample list of suggested further readings, annotated so that students can see what each book or article covers.

Acknowledgments

Worlds Together, Worlds Apart would never have happened without the full support of Princeton University. In a highly unusual move, and one for which we are truly grateful, the university helped underwrite this project with financial support from its 250th Anniversary Fund for undergraduate teaching and by allowing release time for the authors from campus commitments.

The history department's support of the effort over many years has been exceptional. Two chairs—Daniel Rodgers and Philip Nord—made funds and departmental support available, including the department's incomparable administrative talents. We would be remiss if we did not single out the department manager, Judith Hanson, who provided us with assistance whenever we needed it. We also thank Eileen Kane, who provided help in tracking down references and illustrations and in integrating changes into the manuscript. We also would like to thank Pamela Long, who made all of the complicated arrangements for ensuring that we were able to discuss matters in a leisurely and attractive setting. Sometimes that meant arranging for long-distance conference calls. She went even further and proofread the entire manuscript, finding many errors that we had all overlooked.

We drew shamelessly on the expertise of the departmental faculty, and although it might be wise simply to include a roster of the Princeton history department, that would do an injustice to those of whom we took most advantage. So here they are: Robert Darnton, Sheldon Garon, Anthony Grafton, Molly Greene, David Howell, Harold James, William Jordan, Emmanuel Kreike, Michael Mahoney, Arno Mayer, Kenneth Mills, John Murrin, Susan Naquin, Willard Peterson, Theodore Rabb, Stanley Stein, and Richard Turits. When necessary, we went outside the history department, getting help from L. Carl Brown, Michael Cook, Norman Itzkowitz, Martin Kern, Thomas Leisten, and Heath Lowry. Two departmental colleagues—Natalie Z. Davis and Elizabeth Lunbeck—were part of the original team but had to withdraw because of other commitments. Their contributions were vital, and we want to express our thanks to them. David Gordon, now at the University of Maryland, used portions of the text while teaching an undergraduate course at the University of Durban in South Africa and shared comments with us. Shamil Jeppie, like

David Gordon a graduate of the Princeton history department, now teaching at the University of Cape Town in South Africa, read and commented on various chapters.

Beyond Princeton, we have also benefited from exceptionally gifted and giving colleagues who have assisted this book in many ways. Colleagues at Louisiana State University, the University of Florida, the University of North Carolina, the University of Pennsylvania, and the University of California at Los Angeles, where Suzanne Marchand, Michael Tsin, Holly Pittman, and Stephen Aron, respectively, are now teaching, pitched in whenever we turned to them. Especially helpful have been the contributions of James Gelvin, Naomi Lamoreaux, Gary Nash, and Joyce Appleby at UCLA; Michael Bernstein at the University of California at San Diego; and Maribel Dietz, John Henderson, Christine Kooi, David Lindenfeld, Reza Pirbhai, and Victor Stater at Lousiana State University. It goes without saying that none of these individuals bears any responsibility for factual or interpretive errors that the text may contain. Xinru Liu would like to thank her Indian mentor, Romila Thapar, who changed the way we think about Indian history.

The quality and range of reviews on this project were truly exceptional. The final version of the manuscript was greatly influenced by the thoughts and ideas of numerous instructors. We wish to particularly thank our consulting reviewers, who read multiple versions of the manuscript from start to finish.

First Edition Consultants
Hugh Clark, Ursinus College
Jonathan Lee, San Antonio College
Pamela McVay, Ursuline College
Tom Sanders, United States Naval Academy

Second Edition Consultants
Jonathan Lee, San Antonio College
Pamela McVay, Ursuline College
Steve Rapp, Georgia State University
Cliff Rosenberg, City University of New York

We are also indebted to the many other reviewers from whom we benefited greatly.

First Edition Reviewers
Lauren Benton, New Jersey Institute of Technology
Ida Blom, University of Bergen, Norway
Ricardo Duchesne, University of New Brunswick
Major Bradley T. Gericke, United States Military Academy
John Gillis, Rutgers University
David Kenley, Marshall University
John Kicza, Washington State University
Matthew Levinger, Lewis and Clark College
James Long, Colorado State University
Adam McKeown, Columbia University
Mark McLeod, University of Delaware

John Mears, Southern Methodist University
Michael Murdock, Brigham Young University
David Newberry, University of North Carolina, Chapel Hill
Tom Pearcy, Slippery Rock State University
Oliver B. Pollak, University of Nebraska, Omaha
Ken Pomeranz, University of California, Irvine
Major David L. Ruffley, United States Air Force Academy
William Schell, Murray State University
Major Deborah Schmitt, United States Air Force Academy
Sarah Shields, University of North Carolina, Chapel Hill
Mary Watrous-Schlesinger, Washington State University

Second Edition Reviewers
William Atwell, Hobart and William Smith Colleges
Susan Besse, City University of New York
Tithi Bhattacharya, Purdue University
Mauricio Borrerero, St. John's University
Charlie Briggs, Georgia Southern University
Antoinne Burton, University of Illinois, Urbana-Champaign
Jim Cameron, St. Francis Xavier University
Kathleen Comerford, Georgia Southern University
Duane Corpis, Georgia State University
Denise Davidson, Georgia State University
Ross Doughty, Ursinus College
Alison Fletcher, Kent State University
Phillip Gavitt, Saint Louis University
Brent Geary, Ohio University
Henda Gilli-Elewy, California State Polytechnic University, Pomona
Fritz Gumbach, John Jay College
William Hagen, University of California, Davis
Laura Hilton, Muskingum College
Jeff Johnson, Villanova University
David Kammerling Smith, Eastern Illinois University
Jonathan Lee, San Antonio College
Dorothea Martin, Appalachian State University
Don McGuire, State University of New York, Buffalo
Pamela McVay, Ursuline College
Joel Migdal, University of Washington
Anthony Parent, Wake Forest University
Sandra Peacock, Georgia Southern University
David Pietz, Washington State University
Jared Poley, Georgia State University
John Quist, Shippensburg State University
Steve Rapp, Georgia State University
Paul Rodell, Georgia Southern University
Ariel Salzman, Queen's University
Bill Schell, Murray State University
Claire Schen, State University of New York, Buffalo
Jonathan Skaff, Shippensburg State University
David Smith, California State Polytechnic University, Pomona
Neva Specht, Appalachian State University
Ramya Sreeniva, State University of New York, Buffalo
Charles Stewart, University of Illinois, Urbana-Champaign

Rachel Stocking, Southern Illinois University, Carbondale
Heather Streets, Washington State University
Tim Teeter, Georgia Southern University
Charlie Wheeler, University of California, Irvine
Owen White, University of Delaware
James Wilson, Wake Forest University

We do want to pay special thanks to our most ardent supporter of the *Worlds Together, Worlds Apart* enterprise. Jon Lee, San Antonio College, has played many important roles on this project. He has served as a super reviewer on both editions, reading the draft manuscripts multiple times. He also created many of the original support materials that accompanied the First Edition. With the Second Edition, he was the primary force behind the map and pedagogy program for Volume One. He also has taken on the responsibilities for creating the digital history reader that accompanies the text. We are ever grateful to him for his ongoing support and contributions. We also want to thank Nancy Khalek (Ph.D. Princeton University), who has just taken her first tenure-track job, at Franklin and Marshall College. Nancy was our jack-of-all-trades who helped in any way she could. She attended all the monthly meetings during the development of the early volume. She provided critiques of the manuscript, helped with primary research, worked on the photo program and the Global Connections and Disconnections features, and contributed content to the student website. She was invaluable.

Our association with the publisher of this volume, W. W. Norton & Company, has been everything we could have asked for. Jon Durbin took us under the wing of the Norton firm. He attended all of our monthly meetings spanning the better part of four years across the creation of both volumes. How he put up with some of our interminable discussions will always be a mystery, but his enthusiasm for the endeavor never flagged, even when we seemed to grow weary. Sandy Lifland was the ever-watchful and ever-careful development editor for each volume. She let us know when we were making sense and when we needed to explain ourselves more fully. We also want to thank newcomers to the project Alice Falk and Rebecca Homiski. Alice Falk was our talented and insightful co-developmental editor and copyeditor on Volume One. Between the efforts of Sandy and Alice, we couldn't have asked for more from our manuscript editors. Rebecca Homiski did a fabulous job as our project editor, co-ordinating the responses of up to twelve authors on both volumes combined and locking down all the details on the project. We also want to thank Ellen Lohman for copyediting the Volume Two manuscript ably and with just the right touch under a very tight schedule and Sarah England for providing comments on our Volume Two revisions in a timely and thoughtful fashion. Stephanie Romeo, Jennifer Bright, and Julie Tesser shared duties in finding wonderful photos for both volumes. Rubina Yeh created a beautiful design. Roy Tedoff guided the manuscripts through the production process under a very tight schedule. On the media front, we want to thank Steve Hoge for creating the Norton Study-Space website, which includes the impressive Norton Digital History Reader. On the print ancillary front, we'd like to thank Matt Arnold for finding an excellent group of authors to create the instructor's manual, test bank, and study guide. We also want to thank Alexis Hilts, the most recent newcomer to the project, for helping to pull together many loose ends during the copyediting and production stages.

Finally, we must recognize that while this project often kept us apart from family members, their support held our personal worlds together.

About the Authors

ROBERT TIGNOR (Ph.D. Yale University) is Professor Emeritus and the Rosengarten Professor of Modern and Contemporary History at Princeton University and the three-time chair of the history department. With Gyan Prakash, he introduced Princeton's first course in world history nearly twenty years ago. Professor Tignor has taught graduate and undergraduate courses in African history and world history and written extensively on the history of twentieth-century Egypt, Nigeria, and Kenya. Besides his many research trips to Africa, Professor Tignor has taught at the University of Ibadan in Nigeria and the University of Nairobi in Kenya.

JEREMY ADELMAN (D.Phil. Oxford University) is currently the chair of the history department at Princeton University and the Walter S. Carpenter III Professor of Spanish Civilization and Culture. He has written and edited five books, including *Republic of Capital: Buenos Aires and the Legal Transformation of the Atlantic World*, which won the best book prize in Atlantic history from the American Historical Association. Professor Adelman is the recent recipient of a Guggenheim Memorial Foundation Fellowship and the Frederick Burkhardt Award from the American Council of Learned Societies.

STEPHEN ARON (Ph.D. University of California, Berkeley) is professor of history at the University of California, Los Angeles, and executive director of the Institute for the Study of the American West, Autry National Center. A specialist in frontier and Western American history, Aron is the author of *How the West Was Lost: The Transformation of Kentucky from Daniel Boone to Henry Clay* and *American Confluence: The Missouri Frontier from Borderland to Border State*. He has also published articles in a variety of books and journals, including the *American Historical Review*, the *Pacific Historical Review*, and the *Western Historical Quarterly*.

PETER BROWN (Ph.D. Oxford University) is the Rollins Professor of History at Princeton University. He previously taught at London University and the University of California, Berkeley. He has written on the rise of Christianity and the end of the Roman Empire. His works include *Augustine of Hippo, The World of Late Antiquity, The Cult of the Saints, Body and Society, The Rise of Western Christendom*, and *Poverty and Leadership in the Later Roman Empire*. He is presently working on issues of wealth and poverty in the late Roman and early medieval Christian worlds.

BENJAMIN ELMAN (Ph.D. University of Pennsylvania) is professor of East Asian studies and history at Princeton University. He is currently serving as the director of the Princeton Program in East Asian Studies. He taught at the University of California, Los Angeles, for over fifteen years. His teaching and research fields include Chinese intellectual and cultural history, 1000–1900; the history of science in China, 1600–1930; the history of education in late imperial China; and Sino-Japanese cultural history, 1600–1850. He is the author of five books: *From Philosophy to Philology: Intellectual and Social Aspects of Change in Late Imperial China; Classicism, Politics, and Kinship: The Ch'ang-chou School of New Text Confucianism in Late Imperial China; A Cultural History of Civil Examinations in Late Imperial China; On Their Own Terms: Science in China, 1550–1900*; and *A Cultural History of Modern Science in China*. He is the creator of Classical Historiography for Chinese History at www.princeton.edu/~classbib/, a bibliography and teaching website published since 1996.

STEPHEN KOTKIN (Ph.D. University of California, Berkeley) is professor of history and teaches European and Asian history at Princeton University, where he also serves as director of Russian studies. He is the author of *Armageddon Averted: The Soviet Collapse, 1970–2000* and *Magnetic Mountain: Stalinism as a Civilization* and is a coeditor of *Mongolia in the Twentieth Century: Landlocked Cosmopolitan.* He is currently finishing a book entitled *Lost in Siberia: Dreamworlds of Eurasia,* which is a study of the Ob River valley over the last seven centuries. Professor Kotkin has twice been a visiting professor in Japan.

XINRU LIU (Ph.D. University of Pennsylvania) is assistant professor of early Indian history and world history at the College of New Jersey. She is associated with the Institute of World History and the Chinese Academy of Social Sciences. She is the author of *Ancient India and Ancient China, Trade and Religious Exchanges,* AD *1–600; Silk and Religion, an Exploration of Material Life and the Thought of People,* AD *600–1200; Connections across Eurasia, Transportation, Communication, and Cultural Exchange on the Silk Roads,* co-authored with Lynda Norene Shaffer; and *A Social History of Ancient India* (in Chinese). Professor Liu promotes South Asian studies and world history studies in both the United States and the People's Republic of China.

SUZANNE MARCHAND (Ph.D. University of Chicago) is associate professor of European and intellectual history at Louisiana State University, Baton Rouge. Professor Marchand also spent a number of years teaching at Princeton University. She is the author of *Down from Olympus: Archaeology and Philhellenism in Germany, 1750–1970* and is currently writing a book on German "orientalism."

HOLLY PITTMAN (Ph.D. Columbia University) is professor of art history at the University of Pennsylvania, where she teaches art and archaeology of Mesopotamia and the Iranian Plateau. She also serves as curator in the Near East Section of the University of Pennsylvania Museum of Archaeology and Anthropology. Previously she served as a curator in the Ancient Near Eastern Art Department of the Metropolitan Museum of Art. She has written extensively on the art and culture of the Bronze Age in the Middle East and has participated in excavations in Cyprus, Turkey, Syria, Iraq, and Iran, where she currently works. Her research investigates works of art as media through which patterns of thought, cultural development, and historical interactions of ancient cultures of the Near East are reconstructed.

GYAN PRAKASH (Ph.D. University of Pennsylvania) is professor of modern Indian history at Princeton University and a member of the Subaltern Studies Editorial Collective. He is the author of *Bonded Histories: Genealogies of Labor Servitude in Colonial India* and *Another Reason: Science and the Imagination of Modern India.* Professor Prakash edited *After Colonialism: Imperial Histories and Postcolonial Displacements* and has written a number of articles on colonialism and history writing. He is currently working on a history of the city of Bombay. With Robert Tignor, he introduced the modern world history course at Princeton University.

BRENT SHAW (Ph.D. Cambridge University) is the Andrew Fleming West Professor of Classics at Princeton University, where he is director of the Program in the Ancient World. He was previously at the University of Pennsylvania, where he chaired the Graduate Group in Ancient History. His principal areas of specialization as a Roman historian are Roman family history and demography, sectarian violence and conflict in Late Antiquity, and the regional history of Africa as part of the Roman Empire. He has published *Spartacus and the Slaves Wars;* edited the papers of Sir Moses Finley, *Economy and Society in Ancient Greece;* and published in a variety of books and journals, including the *Journal of Roman Studies,* the *American Historical Review,* the *Journal of Early Christian Studies,* and *Past & Present.*

MICHAEL TSIN (Ph.D. Princeton) is associate professor of history and international studies at the University of North Carolina at Chapel Hill. He previously taught at the University of Illinois at Chicago, Princeton University, Columbia University, and the University of Florida. Professor Tsin's primary interests include the histories of modern China and colonialism. He is the author of *Nation, Governance, and Modernity in China: Canton, 1900–1927.* His current research explores the politics of cultural translation with regard to the refashioning of social and institutional practices in China since the mid-nineteenth century.

NORTH
AMERICA

ATLANTIC
OCEAN

SAHARA

Niger R.

Rhine R.

PACIFIC
OCEAN

SOUTH
AMERICA

| 0 | | 1000 | | 2000 Miles |
| 0 | 1000 | | 2000 Kilometers | |

THE GEOGRAPHY OF THE ANCIENT AND MODERN WORLDS

Today, we believe the world to be divided into continents, and most of us think that it was always so. Geographers usually identify six inhabited continents: Africa, North America, South America, Europe, Asia, and Australia. Inside these continents they locate a vast number of subcontinental units, such as East Asia, South Asia, Southeast Asia, the Middle East, North Africa, and sub-Saharan Africa. Yet this geographical understanding would have been completely alien to premodern men and women, who did not think that they inhabited continents bounded by large bodies of water. Lacking a firm command of the seas,

they saw themselves living on contiguous landmasses, and they thought these territorial bodies were the main geographical units of their lives. Hence, in this volume we have chosen to use a set of geographical terms, the main one being *Afro-Eurasia*, that more accurately reflect the world that the premoderns believed that they inhabited.

The most interconnected and populous landmass of premodern times was Afro-Eurasia. The term *Eurasia* is widely used in general histories, but we think it is in its own ways inadequate. The preferred term from our perspective must be *Afro-Eurasia*, for the intercon-

ARCTIC OCEAN

A F R O - E U R A S I A

EUROPE

INNER EURASIA

Danube R.

BLACK SEA

CASPIAN SEA

ARAL SEA

CENTRAL ASIA

TAKLAMAKAN DESERT

Yellow R.

YELLOW SEA

AEGEAN SEA

Tigris R.

IRANIAN PLATEAU

TAURUS MTS.

Indus R.

HIMALAYA MTS.

Yangzi R.

EAST ASIA

MEDITERRANEAN SEA

SOUTHWEST ASIA

Euphrates R.

Pearl R.

PACIFIC OCEAN

DESERT

RED SEA

ARABIAN SEA

SOUTH ASIA

SOUTH CHINA SEA

Lake Chad

Nile R.

SOUTHEAST ASIA

Congo R.

Lake Victoria

SUB-SAHARAN AFRICA

INDIAN OCEAN

AUSTRALIA

nected landmass of premodern and indeed much of modern times included large parts of Europe and Asia and significant regions in Africa. The major African territories that were regularly joined to Europe and Asia were Egypt, North Africa, and even parts of sub-Saharan Africa.

Only gradually and fitfully did the divisions of the world that we take for granted today take shape. The peoples inhabiting the northwestern part of the Afro-Eurasian landmass did not see themselves as European Christians, and hence as a distinctive cultural entity, until the Middle Ages drew to a close in the twelfth and thirteenth centuries. Islam did not arise and extend its influence throughout the middle zone of the Afro-Eurasian landmass until the eighth and ninth

centuries. And, finally, the peoples living in what we today term the *Indian subcontinent* did not feel a strong sense of their own cultural and political unity until the Delhi Sultanate of the thirteenth and fourteenth centuries and the Mughal Empire, which emerged at the beginning of the sixteenth century, brought political unity to that vast region. As a result, we use the terms *South Asia, Vedic society,* and *India* in place of *Indian subcontinent* for the premodern part of our narrative, and we use *Southwest Asia* and *North Africa* to refer to what today is designated as the *Middle East.* In fact, it is only in the period from 1000 to 1300 that some of the major cultural areas that are familiar to us today truly crystallized.

SECOND EDITION
VOLUME B

Worlds Together, WORLDS APART

9

NEW EMPIRES AND COMMON CULTURES, 600–1000 CE

*I*n 754 CE, when the Muslim caliph al-Mansur (ruled 754–775 CE) began his search for a new capital city, Islam was already more than a century old and into its second dynasty, the Abbasids. Al-Mansur wanted to relocate his primary city from Damascus, the capital of Islam's first dynasty, in order to shift the center of imperial power toward the Iranian plateau, the Abbasids' home region. Traveling the length and breadth of the Tigris and Euphrates rivers, the caliph eventually decided to build near a small, unimposing village called Baghdad, located along the west bank of the Tigris.

He had good reasons for his selection. The site lay between Mesopotamia's two great rivers, where they were only twenty-five miles apart and were linked by canals. As one contemporary observer noted, the area was "surrounded by palm trees and near water so that if one district suffers from drought or fails to yield its harvest in due season, there will be relief from another" (Hodges, *Mohammed*, p. 126). Al-Mansur also knew that his metropolis would arise close to the illustrious ancient capital of the Sasanian Empire, Ctesiphon, where the old Arch of Khusro was still standing. This was also the site of earlier Sumerian and

Babylonian imperial power. Rulers decided to build at Baghdad with the intention of reaffirming Mesopo- tamia's centrality in the Afro-Eurasian world, and in so doing exalting the universalizing ambitions of Islam. Al-Mansur proceeded with the vigor that characterized the new Abbasid regime. He laid the first brick in 762 CE; within five years, a set of towering inner city walls surrounded what soon became known as the "round city."

Al-Mansur's choice was inspired. As the new capital of Islam, Baghdad also became a crossroads for Africa and Eurasian commerce; as the nexus of a universalizing faith, it also became an economic point of world convergences. Overnight, this city turned into a bustling world emporium. Chinese merchants supplied it with silk, paper, and porcelain. Indian traders shipped it pepper, and East Africa was its source for gold, ivory, and slaves. While Chinese goods arrived by land and sea, commodities originating in Inner Eurasia came via the well-traveled Silk Road from Khurasan. Large camel caravans wound across Baghdad's western desert, linking the capital with Syria, Egypt, North Africa, and even southern Spain. In effect, the unity that the Abbasids imposed with their impressive capital at Baghdad redoubled the movement of peoples, ideas, innovations, and commodities. Baghdad's reputation quickly spread. Seen as the "navel of the earth," Baghdad attracted people "from all countries far and near, and people from every side have preferred Baghdad to their own homelands." To its inhabitants and visitors, Iraq was "the most elegant country," from which goods "can be procured so readily and so certainly that it is as if all the good things of the world were sent there, all the treasures of the earth assembled there, and all the blessings of creation reflected there" (Yaqubi and Muqaddasi, in Lewis, p. 70).

These were the words of the ninth-century Arab Muslim intellectuals Yaqubi and Muqaddasi. For them, Baghdad's eminence and prosperity needed no explanation. After all, the city was the center of the Islamic world, which in turn was

God's gift to his believers. The transformation was remarkable. Here was a tribal people from a distant and remote part of the Arabian Peninsula, founders of a religion that by 762 CE had sliced through the territory of the once dominant Christian Byzantine Empire and totally absorbed the Zoroastrian Sasanian Empire. Here was an empire that replaced the eastern and southern regions of the old Roman Empire and that represented a polity as powerful as the Tang empire in China. The rise of Islam is yet another example of how religion and empire entwined to create the foundations of the world's modern social geography.

RELIGIONS, EMPIRES, AND AGRICULTURAL REVOLUTIONS

> → *How did the growth of Islamic empires lead to a revolution in agriculture across Afro-Eurasia?*

But Islam's origins illustrate how the entwinings of religion and empire were not all the same. Islam alters the pattern displayed by the ascent of Christianity and Buddhism. As we saw in Chapter 8, empire served as the main vehicle for the growth of those two universalizing religions. Moreover, they played significant political and spiritual roles in societies weakened by the breakdown of the Roman, Mauryan, and Han empires. In the case of Islam, in contrast, it was religion that led to the creation of empires. Having swept aside their predecessors in Southwest Asia, Muslim leaders had to form their own imperial system. Although they borrowed liberally from the Byzantines and Persians, their underlying reason for

Focus Questions NEW EMPIRES AND COMMON CULTURES

> → *How did the growth of Islamic empires lead to a revolution in agriculture across Afro-Eurasia?*
>
> → *What factors created a common cultural outlook among Muslim communities in Afro-Eurasia during this era?*
>
> → *How did the Tang state balance its desire to restore Confucian principles to China with the growth of new universal religions in East Asia?*
>
> → *To what extent did Japanese and Korean states and societies emulate Tang China during this era?*
>
> → *How did two Christianities come to exist in western Eurasia?*

 WWNORTON.COM/STUDYSPACE

establishing an imperial system was new: to secure, defend, and spread their religion. Christianity and Zoroastrianism converted empires to their own views; Islam created its empire from scratch.

When we consider how religions had pervaded the lives of the Afro-Eurasian populations in the previous three centuries, we should not be surprised that a charismatic and prophetic figure would arise among the Arabs, proclaiming new religious precepts. By this time, religions had become the currency of life. Christianity and Buddhism were now laying claim to universal truths, and groups seeking to compete with them in making a mark on the Afro-Eurasian landmass at the end of the sixth century had to speak their language of universal religion. The Tang dynasty in China alone withstood the universalizing claims of religion that swept across the region in this period, as Confucianism and Daoism responded to the upsurge of Chinese Buddhism—proving again that China would follow a somewhat different path from the other Afro-Eurasian empires by maintaining its commitments to its past traditions and customs.

At the same time that Islam was spreading, the Muslim world was experiencing significant developments in agriculture. Islam may well have been a crucial factor in this transformation. As a syncretic culture, it assimilated the ideas, institutions, and beliefs of many different peoples and geographical zones—a feature that was as fully apparent in the agricultural realm as in other areas of culture. Farmers in the early Muslim empire became agricultural innovators, introducing a host of new crops and employing new agrarian techniques that made possible rapid population growth, rising standards of living, and urbanization.

By the dawn of the Common Era, India had replaced Mesopotamia as the source of a wide range of new crops. In fact, most of the new cultigens in Afro-Eurasia in the first millennium CE had their origins in Southeast Asia, made their way only gradually to India, and dispersed from there throughout the Muslim world. Southeast Asia provided Indian cultivators with rice, taro, sour oranges, lemons, limes, and most likely coconut palm trees, sugarcane, bananas, plantains, and mangoes. Sorghum and quite possibly cotton and watermelons arrived from Africa. Only the eggplant was indigenous to India. Although many of these crops spread quickly and easily to East Asia, where they became staples in the Chinese diet, their movement westward was not so rapid. A few crops made their way into Sasanian Persia and the Arabian Peninsula, but it was not until the Muslim conquest of Sindh in the lower Indus region of northern India in 711 CE that the territories to the west were fully opened up to the crop innovations pioneered in South Asia.

Most of the new cultigens had their origins in Southeast Asia, made their way only gradually to India, and dispersed from there throughout the Muslim world.

Writing in the fourteenth century, the Arab historian Ibn Khaldun once observed about his peoples that "all of their customary activities lead to travel and movement" (Ibn Khaldun, *Prologomena*). India fascinated them, and their travelers, merchants, scholars, and landed gentry exploited the new agriculture of India to the hilt. Between 700 and 1000 CE nothing less than a revolution in cultigens and diet swept through the Muslim world. Sorghum supplanted millet and the other grains of antiquity because it was hardier, had higher yields, and required a shorter growing season. Citrus trees added flavor to the diet and provided refreshing drinks during the heat of the summer, and the spread of cotton cultivation led to increased demand for textiles.

During the first three and half centuries after the appearance of Islam, farmers from northwest India in the east to Spain, Morocco, and West Africa in the west used these new cultigens to expand the area under cultivation; they increased agricultural output, became a more productive workforce, slashed fallow periods, and grew two and sometimes even three crops on lands that had previously yielded only one. (See Map 9-1.) The results were impressive. Farmers could feed larger urban communities and offer consumers more diversified and healthier diets. We lack population figures for this period, but the evidence from Arab travelers and geographers is incontrovertible. Cities grew, and the countryside became more densely populated and more productive. According to one writer, the Fayyum region of Egypt had no fewer than 360 villages, each of which, by his account, was so productive that its cultivators could provision the whole of Egypt for a day. Once Islam began to consolidate its command over much of the region spanning North Africa to the edges of India, it acted as a massive conveyor belt of these agrarian breakthroughs, with dramatic repercussions for the peripheries of Eurasia and Africa. In the long run, the Afro-Eurasian world was set on a path of population increase and ever-larger cities; its growth accelerated after 1000 CE and was not interrupted until the fourteenth century, when the Black Death produced dying and suffering on a scale that few had seen before.

The transformation also swept through East Asia. China, too, experienced an agricultural surge between 600 and 1000 CE, receiving—often directly from Southeast Asia rather than through India—the same crops that Islamic cultivators were carrying westward. Rice was critical. New varieties entered China from the south; as populations migrated down from the north, fleeing the political turmoil that followed the collapse of the Han empire, they eagerly took up the new crops. By the eleventh century, Chinese farmers had become the world's most intensive wet-field rice cultivators. Early- and

MAP 9-1(A & B)   THE SPREAD OF ISLAM AND AGRICULTURAL DIFFUSION IN THE FIRST MILLENNIUM

The second half of the first millennium saw a revolution in agriculture throughout Afro-Eurasia. As the map on page 371 demonstrates, agriculturalists across the landmass increasingly cultivated similar crops. How does the map suggest these cultigens diffused across a wider geographic area? What role did the spread of Islam and the growth of Islamic empires play in this process? How did the spread of this new religion act as a massive conveyor belt for crop diffusion? How did this process shape the history of Afro-Eurasia?

late-ripening seeds made it possible to harvest two or three plantings during a single year. Champa rice, introduced from central Vietnam, was the most widely used. It was drought resistant, had low gluten content, and ripened faster than the older strains.

The introduction of new grains and new technologies opened vast new arable lands in China's south to feed an expanding populace. In 742 CE, 60 percent of China's 80 million people lived in the wheat- and millet-producing areas of the Yellow and Wei rivers in the north and northwest. By 980, only 38 percent of China's 100 million people still lived in the north. This shift was made possible by improvements in irrigation techniques and the expansion of the road and water transportation system. Rice needs ample supplies of water, and Chinese hydraulic engineers designed water-lifting devices while peasant farmers built more canals linking lakes and rivers and drained swamps, alleviating the malaria that had long troubled the region. These developments created a booming and constantly moving rice frontier. (See Map 9-2.)

Europe was the exception to these agricultural breakthroughs. Most of the new crops were tropical and semi-tropical cultigens, suited only to the Mediterranean basin. Moreover, cultivators in northern Europe were still in the early stages of clearing the primeval forest. The critical ingredients for agricultural growth in Europe were the axe, the steel plow, and the harnessed horse; in China they were new seeds, dams, sluice gates, and sophisticated hydraulic devices. In Europe, agrarian innovation lagged and took longer to flourish, but it, too, would soon come, as the next chapter will illustrate.

So it was that a vibrant new universalizing faith erupted onto the Afro-Eurasian stage just as an agrarian transformation was about to spread across the middle latitudes of the landmass. The two movements—the diffusion of a rural revolution and a spiritual riptide—reinforced each other and heightened the potential of each to change the cultural, political, and economic geography of the world. They did so in league with new imperial formations in the heartlands, integrating the dis-

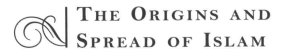

Trade routes

Original Source Areas of Staple Crops | Spread of Staple Crops | Areas to Which Crops Had Spread by 1500

Bananas · Bananas · Bananas
Sugarcane · Sugarcane · Sugarcane
Cotton · Cotton · Cotton
Sorghum · Sorghum · Sorghum

---

persed peoples of the middle of Southwest Asia and North and East Africa into an increasingly common cultural system. The long-term effect was to strengthen the linkages across even longer distances, from China to Africa. These linkages were the interlocking effects of three significant changes: an agrarian revolution (which fostered more commerce and denser populations), the resurgence of empires in the wake of Roman and Han collapses (which created institutional structures with greater unity to facilitate some stability within polities), and the appearance of a new, vibrant universalizing faith in the region straddling western and eastern Afro-Eurasia. It was the ascent of Islam out of Arabia, its unifying effects on the territories between the two other spreading universal faiths—Christianity and Buddhism—and its provision of the spiritual foundations for a new empire in Southwest Asia and Africa that brought the world together in historically unprecedented ways. It also laid the basis for a new set of divisions that would drive worlds apart, as a politicized Islam created internal and external sources of conflict across these regions.

THE ORIGINS AND SPREAD OF ISLAM

> → *What factors created a common cultural outlook among Muslim communities in Afro-Eurasia during this era?*

Any explanation of Islam's emergence as a universalizing religion that sowed the seeds for a widespread common culture must begin where Islam's story began: inside Arabia. Despite its remoteness and sparse population, by the sixth century CE Arabia was feeling the influence of outside currents of long-distance trade, religious disputation, and imperial politics. Toward the end of the sixth century, as we learned in Chapter 8, Byzantine and Sasanian imperial pressures had intruded deeply into Arabia. Commodities from Egypt, Syria,

MAP 9-2   THE SUI DYNASTY CANALS

China, like the Islamic world, experienced an explosion in population during this period (see the discussion on page 370). What role did the building of the Sui dynasty canals play in this growth? What role might the canals have played in fostering massive internal migrations in China? What other advantages might the presence of these canals provide to the Chinese state and its peoples?

and Iraq circulated in local markets, and learned men debated the doctrinal tenets of Christianity and Judaism. The Hijaz, the western region of Arabia bordering the Red Sea, was connected to the outside world by trading routes that led all the way up the coast to the Mediterranean. Yet without the actions of a deeply inspired and powerful religious leader, the Prophet Muhammad, it is doubtful that the peoples of Arabia would have entered the mainstream of world history so forcefully.

Mecca, in the Hijaz, was not an imposing place. A pre-Islamic poet wrote of it that "winter and summer are equally intolerable. No waters flow . . . [and there is] not a blade of grass on which to rest the eye; no, nor hunting. [Here there are] only merchants, the most despicable of professions" (Peters, p. 23). Hardly more than a village, Mecca was composed of simple mud huts whose inhabitants sustained themselves less as traders than as caretakers of a revered sanctuary, the kaaba, an otherwise unprepossessing collection of unmortared rocks piled one on top of the other that local peoples regarded as the dwelling place of deities. But it was here that a great prophet was born.

A VISION, A TEXT

Born in Mecca around 570 CE into a well-respected tribal family, Muhammad enjoyed only moderate success in his career as a trader. Little in his early life suggested the momentous events that were in the offing. Then came a revelation, one that would convert this broker of commodities into a proselytizer of a new faith. In the year 610 CE, while he was on a monthlong spiritual retreat in a cave on Mount Hira (near Mecca), God himself, or possibly the angel Gabriel, came to him in a vision and commanded him to recite the following words, which eventually became Sura 96 of the Quran:

> Recite in the Name of the Lord who createth,
> Createth man from a clot
> Recite: And thy Lord is the most Bounteous who
>   teacheth by the pen
> Teacheth man that which he knew not.

Further revelations followed. The early ones were like the first: short, powerful, and full of instructions for his fellow Meccans. Note in particular the injunction to teach, to carry the message to nonbelievers. They were eminently memorable, an important feature in an oral culture where no art form was more highly prized than poetry recitation. Muhammad's early preaching had a sharp and clear message. He enjoined his followers to act righteously, to set aside false deities, to submit themselves to the one and only true God, and to care for the less fortunate, for the Day of Judgment was imminent. Muhammad's most insistent message was the oneness of God, a belief that has remained at the core of the faith ever since.

When finally compiled into a single authoritative version sometime around 650 CE, more than a decade after the Prophet's death, the Quran consisted of 114 chapters, known as suras, which were arranged in descending order of length; the longest ran to 300 verses and the shortest, a mere three. According to Arab historians, the verses were at first written down on "bits of parchment, thin white stones, leafless palm branches, and the bosoms of men" (Arberry, p. viii). Accepted as the very word of God, they were transmitted without flaw through God's perfect instrument, thee Prophet Muhammad.

Like basic works described in earlier chapters, such as the Jewish Torah, the Christian Bible, and other foundational texts, this was one meant to inscribe the tenets of a faith to unite a people and to convey a set of stable messages to other cultures, to expand the frontiers of the new faith. Here was one God, one set of lessons, one text, and a providential purpose to spread the word.

Muhammad saw himself as the last of the long line of prophets—or, as he said, the seal of the prophets. He believed that he was in the tradition of Moses, other Hebrew prophets, and Jesus and that he communicated with the same God that they did. As we have seen, Christian and Jewish religious ideas and communities existed in the Arabian peninsula at the time of Muhammad. A substantial Jewish community resided in the city of Yathrib (later called Medina). Just how deeply Muhammad understood the tenets of Judaism and Christianity is difficult to determine, but his professed

Mecca. At the great mosque at Mecca, which many consider the most sacred site in Islam, hundreds of thousands of worshippers gather for Friday prayers. Many are performing their religious duty to go on a pilgrimage to the holy places in the Arabian Peninsula.

THE QURAN

These two suras from the Quran are relatively short ones, but they provide some of the essence of Muhammad's message and the faith of Islam. The Quran opens with a sura known as the fatiha, *which in its powerful prayerlike quality lends itself to frequent recitation. Sura 87, "The Most High," provides a deeper insight into the nature of humanity's relationship with God.*

THE EXORDIUM

IN THE NAME OF GOD THE COMPASSIONATE THE MERCIFUL

Praise be to God, Lord of the Universe,
The Compassionate, the Merciful,
Sovereign of the Day of Judgement!
You alone we worship, and to You alone we turn for help.
Guide us to the straight path,
The path of those whom You have favoured,
Not of those who have incurred Your wrath,
Nor of those who have gone astray   (1.1–1.7)

THE MOST HIGH

IN THE NAME OF GOD, THE COMPASSIONATE, THE MERCIFUL

Praise the Name of your Lord, the Most High, who has
    created all things and proportioned them; who has
    ordained their destinies and guided them; who brings

forth the green pasture, then turns it to withered
    grass.
'We shall make you recite Our revelations, so that you
    shall forget none of them except as God pleases. He
    has knowledge of all that is manifest, and all that is
    hidden.
We shall guide you to the smoothest path. Therefore give
    warning, if warning will avail. He that fears God will
    heed it, but the wicked sinner will flout it. He shall
    burn in the gigantic Fire, where he shall neither die
    nor live. Happy shall be the man who purifies him-
    self, who remembers the name of his Lord and prays.
Yet you prefer this life, although the life to come is better
    and more lasting.
All this is written in earlier scriptures; the scriptures of
    Abraham and Moses.   (87.1–87.19)

→ *What themes can you glean from these passages about humanity's relationship to God?*
→ *Do you find any similarities to the tenets of Judaism and Christianity as you have encountered them in this volume?*

SOURCE: *The Koran*, trans. with notes by N. J. Dawood (London: Penguin, 1993), pp. 9, 424.

---

indebtedness to and affiliation with their tradition is a part of Islamic belief.

THE MOVE TO MEDINA, 622 CE

Muslims date the beginning of the Muslim era from the year 622 CE, when Muhammad and a small group of followers, persecuted by the leaders of Mecca, escaped to Yathrib (later renamed Medina)—an event known as the Hegira (in Arabic *Hijra,* "breaking off of relations" or "departure"). The perilous 200-mile journey accomplished more than a flight. It yielded an entirely new form of communal unity: the *umma*

(band of the faithful), which supplanted traditional family, clan, and tribal affiliations with loyalty to Muhammad as the one and true Prophet of God. Medina became the birthplace of a new faith, called Islam, which means "submission" (to the will of God), and a new collectivity, called Muslims (literally, "those who submit"). Its believers accepted the prophecy of Muhammad. From Medina Muhammad's adherents broadcast their new faith and their new mission, first to the recalcitrants of Mecca and then, after Mecca had been converted, to all inhabitants of Arabia and even beyond—to the larger world of Asia, Africa, and Europe. In this way, Islam joined Christianity in seeking to bring the whole known world under its authority—asserting a logic of world integration,

→ *What factors created a common cultural outlook among Muslim communities in Afro-Eurasia during this era?*

The Battle of Badr. This image depicts the battle of Badr, which took place in 624 and marked the beginning of Muhammad's reconquest of Mecca from his new base in the city of Medina.

but also laying out a fundamental new division between the worlds of believers and nonbelievers.

CONQUESTS, 632–661 CE

In 632, in his early sixties, the Prophet passed away. Islam could easily have withered. What kept the new religious movement moving forward were the inspiration of the founder himself and the energy of the early leaders—especially the first four successors to Muhammad, referred to in later Muslim accounts as the "rightly guided caliphs." The word caliph, or *khalīfa,* means "successor" in Arabic, and in this context it referred to the successors to Muhammad as political rulers over the Muslim peoples and the expanding state.

The expansive spiritual force of Islam galvanized its imperial political authority. Muhammad's successors decided to implement the Prophet's plans to send Arab-Muslim armies into Syria and Iraq. Spurred on by religious fervor and a desire to enrich their growing empire with the wealth of conquered territories, Muslim soldiers embarked on military conquests; this expansion of the Islamic state was one aspect of the struggle that they referred to as *jihad* (another aspect focuses on the daily personal struggle for faith). Within a decade and a half they had control over Syria, Egypt, and Iraq. These centerpieces of the Byzantine and Sasanian empires then became the pillars of an even larger new Islamic empire. Mastery of desert warfare and inspired military leadership help explain these astonishing exploits, but equally important was the exhaustion of the Byzantine and Sasanian empires after generations of continuous warfare. The Byzantines saved the core of their empire by pulling most of their troops back to highlands of Anatolia, where they had more defensible frontiers, and conceding the more distant and discontented parts of their territories. In contrast, Sasanian rulers gambled all on a final effort: they hurled their remaining military resources against the armies of the Muslim believers, only to be crushed and then to collapse. Having lost Iraq and unable to defend the Iranian plateau, the Sasanian Empire passed out of existence, its remnants absorbed into a new imperial regime.

AN EMPIRE OF ARABS, 661–750 CE

When the last of the first four caliphs, Ali, was assassinated in 661 CE, new men took over. A political vacuum had opened, and a branch of one of the Meccan clans, the Umayyads, seized the opportunity to lay claim to Ali's legacy. As the governors of the province of Syria under Ali, this first dynasty moved the core of Islam out of Arabia and introduced the principle of a hereditary monarchy to resolve leadership disputes. Cosmopolitan traders who were adaptable in their outlook, they ruled from the city of Damascus until they were overthrown by the Abbasids in 750 CE.

By then, the core practices and beliefs of every Muslim had already crystallized and were known early on as the five "pillars" of Islam. These tenets built on long-standing practices. In addition to a declaration of a belief in one God and in the role of Muhammad as Messenger, ritual prayer, fasting, pilgrimage, and alms were prescribed in the text of the Quran, and were similar to either familiar Jewish practices or old Arabian customs. They became solid parts of Islamic practice in the first decades of Muhammad's career as a prophet.

In its early days, converting to Islam was a simple affair. The religion was also open to blending with older belief systems, an openness that enhanced its ability to spread by adaptation. Rather than insisting that followers abandon all of their former ways of life, the new faith called on them to add adherence to its key beliefs, which involved allegiance to Muslim authorities and payment of alms. Another major incentive to convert was a reduction in the *jizra,* or "toleration tax." The simplicity of these core doctrines, especially the first and essential pillar affirming a belief in one God and the prophecy of Muhammad, may have attracted early converts, but Islam in fact made many demands on its faithful, particularly after the full elaboration of its legal system, the sharia, a century after Muhammad's death.

There was, however, a political limit to Islam's ability to integrate others. Although tolerant of conquered populations, the ruling groups during the Umayyad dynasty did not permit non-Arabic-speaking converts to rise to high political offices. The overthrow of Umayyad rule ended the "Arabs only" empire, paving the way for the incorporation of non-Arab populations into the Islamic core. This changed the nature of the incipient empire. For as the political center of Islam moved out of Arabia to Syria, and then with the Abbasids to Mesopotamia, it sacrificed ethnic purity for geographic expansion. So while this universalizing religion spread the word to create a more common spiritual world, it became more and more diverse within the Islamic world. To be sure, obstacles to converts' acceptance still existed, and the pace of conversion was often slow—fastest in Persia, sluggish in Egypt. By the middle of the eighth century, probably less than 20 percent of the peoples residing in the Islamic empire were Muslims.

THE ABBASID REVOLUTION

As the Umayyad dynasty spread Islam beyond Arabia to integrate more people and provinces, it created resistance to its authority. The province of Khurasan in central Asia contained many who had accepted the Islamic faith and resented discrimination at the hands of the Arab peoples. Here, religious reformers and political dissidents stressed doctrines of religious purity and depicted the Umayyads as irreligious and politically repressive. A coalition emerged led by the Abbasi family, which claimed descent from the Prophet's family. Disgruntled provincial authorities and their military allies joined the Abbasid movement, which also found strong support among the non-Arab converts to Islam—individuals known as *Mawali,* or freedmen, who had made themselves clients to Muslim Arabs, embraced Islam, and learned Arabic, only to discover that they were still regarded as second-class citizens. This coalition amassed a sizable military force and trounced the Umayyad ruler in 750 CE. The Abbasid triumph in turn shifted the center of the caliphate to Iraq, signifying the eastward sprawl of the faith and of its empire. It also represented a success for non-Arab ethnic groups within Islam without entirely eliminating Arab influence at the center of the new dynasty, as indicated by the Abbasids' decision to make Baghdad in Arabic-speaking Iraq the capital of their empire.

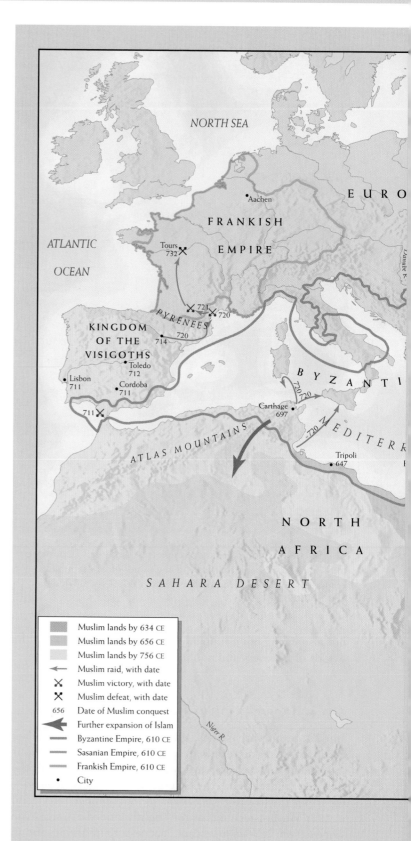

→ *What factors created a common cultural outlook among Muslim communities in Afro-Eurasia during this era?*

MAP 9-3 THE SPREAD OF ISLAM DURING THE FIRST MILLENNIUM

Islam emerged in the Arabian Peninsula in the seventh century. Within 150 years, leaders of this religious community had conquered a vast amount of territory. Identify the areas that came under Islamic armies' control by the eighth century. How were Arab armies able to defeat their Byzantine and Sasanian counterparts? To what extent did Islamic conquests lead to widespread conversion to the religion among those they conquered during this era? How did Islam expand beyond these areas of conquest?

But conversion to Islam rested on the zeal of evangelizers and the appeal of the new faith to converts. Some turned to it for practical reasons, seeking a reduction in their taxes or aspiring to exercise power. Others were impressed with the message of Islam. They regarded the new way of life as offering superior answers to a range of secular and spiritual questions. Not only did the Abbasids move aggressively to open Islam to Persian peoples, they also encouraged the Islamic world to embrace Greek and Hellenistic learning, Indian science, and Chinese innovations. No doubt the origins of the Abbasid dynasty broadened their worldview, as peoples along the Silk Road in central Asia were exposed to elements from all major cultures. The result was to make Islam in the Abbasid period truly cosmopolitan. It successfully merged the contributions of peoples from vastly different geographical expanses and widely different intellectual backgrounds into a rich yet unified culture.

> *Not only did the Abbasids move aggressively to open Islam to Persian peoples, they also encouraged the Islamic world to embrace Greek and Hellenistic learning, Indian science, and Chinese innovations.*

RALLYING POINTS: THE CALIPHATE One of the first questions that the Abbasid rulers had to answer was how traditional or "Arab" they could be and still rule over so vast an empire. They chose to retain the bedrock political institution of the early Islamic state—the caliphate, a political and spiritual head of the Islamic community—which the early Islamic community had recognized as the successor to the incandescent leadership of Muhammad. Although from the outset the caliphs exercised temporal and spiritual authority over the Muslim community, Muhammad's successors did not inherit his prophetic powers. Nor were they expected to exercise authority in the realm of religious doctrines: that power was reserved to specialist religious scholars, called *ulama* (the Arabic plural of *alim,* meaning "scholar"). But the Abbasid caliphs differed from their predecessors, the Umayyads and the first four Meccan caliphs, in leadership style. The new approach revealed how syncretic imperial Islam had become. Exposure to Byzantine and Persian political influences significantly altered what the community of believers expected of their rulers and how they were chosen. The Persians stressed the leader's absolute authority, such as that wielded by the rulers of the Achaemenid Empire. And like Byzantine rulers, Abbasid caliphs lived in secluded palaces, cut off from their subjects and protected by eunuchs and professional bodyguards.

The rulers of imperial Islam mingled practices of absolute authority with decentralized exercise of power through their envoys in the provinces. It was a delicate and ultimately unsustainable balancing act. As the empire grew it became increasingly decentralized, making it possible for regional governors and even counter-caliphates in Spain and Egypt to take hold. The political result was an Islamic world characterized by multiple nodes of power, nominally led by a weakened Abbasid caliphate. But as its political center shifted in the coming centuries, the spiritual center of the faith always remained fixed in Mecca.

RALLYING POINTS: THE ARMY The Abbasids, like all rulers, relied on force to integrate their empire; and for imperial Islam, as was true of the Romans, the exercise of military power necessitated the involvements of warriors and soldiers from different ethnic backgrounds from across Afro-Eurasia. How "Arab" should the Muslim armies be? In the early stages of conquest, leaders had conscripted their military forces from local Arab populations, creating, in effect, citizen armies. But as Arab populations settled down in new garrison cities, the rulers turned to professional soldiers. The Abbasids looked to the peripheries of the empire for their military forces, recruiting from the Turkish-speaking communities in central Asia and from Berbers and black Africans in the West. Their reliance on these foreign (non-Arab) groups as the core of their military, much like that of the second- and third-century Romans on the Germanic peoples and Goths, represented a major historical shift in the Islamic world. Not only did the change bring new populations into the empire, but by the ninth and tenth centuries these groups had begun to wield decisive political authority, just as the "barbarians" had done in the last centuries of the Roman Empire. Having begun as an Arab state and then incorporated strong Persian influence, the Islamic empire now embraced Turkish elements from the pastoral belts of Inner and central Asia. So, as the universalizing religion spread, it became increasingly multicultural while uniting diverse peoples into a single community of believers. Like other universalizing religions, this faith brought people together in more integrated political and religious structures, and in doing so created polities that were more ethnically and culturally diverse. The presence of the nomadic Turkish warriors in particular reminds us of the important role that pastoral peoples continued to play throughout the history of the early world. Ultimately, the Ottoman Turks would become the successor state to the Umayyad dynasty and rule over stretches of southern Europe and Southeast Asia for more than eight centuries.

RALLYING POINTS: ISLAMIC LAW (THE SHARIA) AND THEOLOGY In the Abbasid period, not just the caliphate but also a crucial foundation of Islam—Islamic law, known as the *sharia*—took shape. Sharia law covers all aspects of practical as well as spiritual life, providing legal principles for marriage contracts, trade regulations, and religious prescriptions such as prayer, pilgrimage rites, and ritual fasting. It was the work of generations of religious scholars, rather than of men of the sword, courtiers, and bureaucrats— and its life has continued until today all over the Muslim world, independent of empires.

The early Muslim communities prepared the ground for the sharia, endeavoring (guided by the Quran) to handle legal matters in ways that they thought Muhammad would have wanted. But because the Quran dealt mainly with family concerns, religious beliefs, and social relations—not legal questions—local judges exercised their own judgment where the Quran was silent. The most influential of these early legal scholars was an eighth-century Iraqi, al-Shafi'i, who was determined to make the laws of the empire entirely Islamic. He insisted that the laws that Muhammad had laid out in the Quran, with the addition of the Prophet's sayings and actions that were written down in later reports known as *hadith,* provided all the legal guidance that Islamic judges needed.

The triumph of scholars such as Shafi'i marked an important development in the Muslim world. It placed the ulama, the Muslim scholars, at the heart of Islam. Ulama, not princes and kings, became the lawmakers, insisting that the caliphs could not define or make religious law. Only the scholarly class had the right to interpret the Quran and determine which hadith were authentic. The emergence of the ulama opened a sharp division within Islam between the secular realm, where the caliphs and their representatives exercised power, and the religious sphere, where a wide range of religious officials and scholars—judges (*qudah,* or qadis), experts on Islamic jurisprudence or *fiqh,* teachers, and holy men (*a'immah,* or imams)—held forth.

RALLYING POINTS: GENDER IN EARLY ISLAM An area in which early Islam adapted new rules to older arrangements was its handling of the relations between men and women. Pre-Islamic Arabia was one of the last regions in Southwest Asia where patriarchy had not triumphed. Instead, men still married into women's families and moved to their wives' locations, as was common in tribal communities. Some women were known to engage in a variety of occupations and even, if they became wealthy, to marry more than one husband. But here, too, the status of women was changing, as the communities of Arabia became more settled and entered into closer contact with the rest of Southwest Asia.

Muhammad's own personal biography and his evolving relations with women reflected the changes that were occurring around him. As a young man, he married a woman fifteen years his senior—Khadija, an independent trader—and took no other wives before she died. During some of the crucial battles between Mecca and Medina, he allowed women to fight at his side. Later in life, however, he took younger wives and insisted on their veiling. He married his favorite wife, Aisha, when she was only nine or ten.

Hence, by the time that Islam spread through Southwest Asia and North Africa, where strict gender rules existed and where women had already become deeply subordinated to men, the new faith had already begun to accommodate itself to the already-established patriarchal way of life. Muslim men could divorce freely; women could not. A man could take four wives and numerous concubines, while a woman could have only a single husband. Well-to-do women were veiled and lived secluded from male society. Still, the Quran did offer women some protections. Men were required to treat each wife with respect if they took more than one. Women could inherit property, although only a half of what a man received. Infanticide was prohibited. Marriage dowries were paid directly to the bride rather than to the bride's guardian, indicating that women had independent legal standing; and while a woman's adultery was harshly punished, its proof required eyewitness testimony. The result was a legal system that helped reinforce the dominance of men over women but gave to magistrates superior powers to oversee the definition of male honor and proper behavior.

THE BLOSSOMING OF ABBASID CULTURE

The arts flourished during the Abbasid period, a blossoming that left its imprint throughout society. Within a century, Arabic had superseded Greek as the world's most widely used language in poetry, literature, medicine, science, and philosophy. Like Greek, it spread beyond its native speakers to become the language of the educated classes. Arabic scholarship made many important contributions to the world of learning, including the preservation and extension of Greek and Roman thought and the transmission of Greek and Latin treatises to Europe. Scholars at Baghdad translated the principal works of Aristotle; essays by Plato's followers; many works by Hippocrates, Ptolemy, and Archimedes; and above all the medical treatises of Galen, the second-century CE court physician. This extensive borrowing exemplified the most substantial effort by one culture to assimilate the learning of other peoples since the Roman conquest of Greece. To house these and other scholarly manuscripts, the patrons of the arts and sciences, including the caliphs themselves, opened massive—and magnificent—libraries.

The acts of borrowing, translating, storing, and diffusing written works helped bring worlds together. The Muslim world in this period absorbed the scientific breakthroughs of China and other areas and circulated them throughout thee Islamic world and beyond, incorporating into its societies the use of paper from China, siege warfare from China and Byzantium, and knowledge of plants from the old Greek texts. From Indian sources, scholars borrowed a numbering system based on the concept of zero and units of ten—what we today call Arabic numerals. Arab mathematicians were pioneers in

Global Connections & Disconnections

PREMODERN LIBRARIES: FROM ROYAL ARCHIVES TO REPOSITORIES OF UNIVERSAL KNOWLEDGE

Libraries invariably accompanied urbanization, centralized governments, and writing. Not surprisingly, in the ninth and tenth centuries the biggest, most carefully organized, and most actively used were found in the Islamic and Chinese empires. These were the great centers of learning and government; their cultures extolled the written word. Respect for books and libraries was especially plentiful in the Islamic world, for in the Quran Muhammad had brought the very words of God to his followers. Later generations added to Islam's religious traditions by collecting sayings attributed to the Prophet and the Prophet's companions and the early caliphs (hadith), writing treatises on religious law (the sharia), and assimilating the knowledge of the Greeks, Persians, Indians, and Chinese when they overran their territories or came into contact with their merchants, travelers, and scholars. Moreover, since Egypt and Southwest Asia had seen the world's earliest writing, these areas—the heartland of Islam—already had strong literary and library traditions in place.

The world's very first libraries arose, predictably, in Mesopotamia, where writing itself first appeared. These libraries were quite different from modern repositories of learning. They did house literary masterpieces, like the Sumerian *Epic of Gilgamesh,* but their principal function was to serve as government archives, holding the important records of the kings and the state to which future rulers and government bureaucrats might need to refer. The library often considered to be the first storehouse of written materials was that created by King Ashurbanipal II of Assyria, who ruled over the Assyrian Empire from his capital city at Nineveh in the seventh century BCE. Like other monarchs aspiring to universal sway, he set about to collect all significant literary works. His library, which numbered perhaps as many as 25,000 tablets, contained omens, incantations, and hymns; it also held the literatures of the many Mesopotamian languages, including Assyrian, Sumerian, Ugaritic, and Aramaic.

Because the "books" of King Ashurbanipal II's library were clay tablets etched in cuneiform, hardened through baking in kilns, they were safe from the destroyer of many later libraries—fire. Those in its famous successor in Alexandria were not so fortunate. That magnificent library was established by Ptolemy I and Ptolemy II (ruled 323–285, 285–246 BCE), two enlightened kings who believed that the arts, sciences, and literature of the Greeks were unmatched in the world and had to be preserved for future generations. They set their administrators the task of collecting anything written in Greek. Though the size of Alexandria's holdings (housed in several buildings) is unknown, it was by all estimates almost unimaginably large for this period, whether as little as 40,000 scrolls or, at the other extreme, half a million separate works. But beginning in the first century BCE, these collections were repeatedly subject to burning and looting. By the fourth century CE, an immense body of literature had been almost wiped out, and the peoples of this region in Afro-Eurasia were forced to start over again.

The Muslims led the way, as impressive and large libraries arose in the heartland of Islam. They appeared first in the early mosques, including those in Cairo, Damascus, and Baghdad. But book and manuscript collecting spread rapidly to the outskirts of the Islamic world, where libraries

arithmetic, geometry, and algebra, and they expanded the frontiers of plane and spherical trigonometry.

ISLAM IN A WIDER WORLD

As Islam spread and became more decentralized, it gave rise to a series of dazzling and often competitive dynasties in Spain, North Africa, and points further east in central Asia. Each of these dynastic states put on display the Muslim talent for achieving high levels of artistry in locations far from the political and cultural heartland. Spreading the message brought more and more peoples under the roof provided by the Quran, its priests, and its scholarly interpreters. Such expansion invigorated a world of Islamic learning and science. But the growing diversity of peoples gave rise to a problem: the political structures Islam invented could not hold its widely dispersed believers under a single regime. Many legal elements were shared, especially those controlled by Islamic texts and its enforcers. But when it came to secular power, Islam was deeply divided—and remains so to this day. (See Map 9-4.)

in Timbuktu in West Africa, Samarkand in central Asia, and Jakarta in Southeast Asia earned deservedly high reputations for their extraordinary collections of religious and scientific treatises.

Compared with those in Christian Europe, the Muslim libraries were immense. The library at Cordova in Muslim Spain at the end of the tenth century was reported to hold 600,000 books, or more than two books for every household in the city. Ibn Sina, the great Muslim scholar of the eleventh century, marveled at the library holdings at the Saminid court in Persia. There he found Greek books that he had not seen anywhere else and that most of the best Muslim scholars barely knew of. Probably the largest collection of them all was Cairo's vast library, known as the House of Learning, assembled over time by the Fatimid caliphs. At its height at the beginning of the eleventh century, when the caliph al-Hakim merged his collection with that of one of his predecessors, the caliph al-Aziz, the collection was said to number 1.5 million books. By contrast, Germany's Reichenau, one of the largest monastic libraries in Christian Europe, the West, had only 450 volumes in parchment—almost one-third of them prayer books. It did, however, have a catalog and a system of interlibrary loans that served monasteries spread across Germany, northern Italy, and France.

As befit another empire that had a strong literary tradition and relied on written records for administrative purposes, China was very much the equal of the Islamic world in its wealth of libraries. Indeed, the Chinese had many advantages over the western neighbors with whom they shared the Afro-Eurasian landmass. They had invented paper during the Western Han Dynasty and printing during the Tang era. As a result, scholarship, book production, and libraries became vital ingredients of the cultural fabric of China. Accompanying the highbrow classical works printed for literati during the Tang and Song dynasties were lowbrow works of popular literature and primers that circulated more widely among a commoner audience.

The Chinese infatuation with the printed word and book collecting led to the emergence of a small, elite class of bibliophiles. These individuals located source materials and created the reference works necessary to found coherent scholarly disciplines. Although Chinese libraries housed printed books, unpublished manuscripts formed a more substantial portion of many collections.

During the Han, private libraries did not exceed 10,000 "rolls" (each holding about a chapter) of books or manuscripts. But in the Tang era, many Buddhist monasteries accumulated thousands of books and religious sutras. Some 30,000 rolls, for example, survived in the precious Buddhist grottoes of Dunhuang along the Silk Road, which were made public in 1907. The largest collection was gathered at the emperor's command to form the imperial library in the capital. Bibliophiles played an important role in creating the Tang imperial library, which was staffed by tens of scholars who as collators and editors recompiled the Confucian classics and dynastic histories for the examination system and for posterity. The Tang imperial catalog indicates that by the early eighth century, the imperial library contained some 54,000 unique titles and, including duplicates, about 200,000 rolls. Then as now, libraries were crucial repositories of knowledge and culture.

SPAIN One such Muslim state that vied with the others arose in Spain under that region's most dynamic ruler, Abd al-Rahman III, al-Nasir (the Victorious), who reigned from 912 until 961 CE. The Muslim kingdom in Iberia had been founded at the time of the Abbasid revolution of 750 CE, when a member of the defeated Umayyad family fled Damascus and established an independent kingdom in Spain. Abd al-Rahman brought peace and stability to a frontier region whose commerce and intellectual exchanges had been disrupted by civil conflict and much violence. His evenhanded approach to governance facilitated amicable relations among the Muslims, Christians, and Jews, and his extensive diplomatic relations with Christian potentates as far away as France, Germany, and Scandinavia promoted prosperity among all of the communities of western Europe and North Africa. He expanded and beautified the capital city of Cordova, and his successor, al-Hakim II, made the Great Mosque of Cordova one of Spain's most stunning sites. With room for 20,000 worshippers, it could have comfortably held the total population of Paris in the mid–tenth century!

As in the Mediterranean lands and Southwest Asia after Alexander the Great, competition between rival rulers spurred

MAP 9-4 POLITICAL FRAGMENTATION IN THE ISLAMIC WORLD, 750–1000

By 1000, the Islamic world was politically fractured and decentralized. The Abbasid caliphs still reigned in Baghdad, but they wielded very limited political authority. Why were Abbasid caliphs unable to create and sustain political unity in the Islamic world? In what regions, according to the map, did other Islamic powers emerge? How did the Sunni-Shiite schism among the Islamic faithful contribute to political decentralization?

creativity in the arts. By the tenth century, the Islamic world resembled a series of dazzling lanterns, each vying to exceed the brightness of the others as each powerful center strove to outdo the others in glory. Abd al-Rahman built an extravagant city, Madinat al-Zahra, next to Cordova; it was intended to overshadow the splendor of Islam's most fabled cities, including Baghdad and al-Qayrawān, the great North African city in northeast Tunisia. He surrounded the main administrative offices and mosque of its city center with gardens, pools, fountains, and aqueducts. Madinat al-Zahra was meant to be paradise on earth.

A CENTRAL ASIAN GALAXY OF TALENT At the other end of the Islamic empire, 8,000 miles east of Spain, the region beyond the Oxus River in central Asia experienced an equally spectacular cultural flowering in the eighth and ninth

centuries. In a territory where Greek culture had once sparkled and where Sogdians had emerged as the leading intellectuals, Islam now became the dominant faith and the source of intellectual ferment. The Abbasid rulers in Baghdad delighted in surrounding themselves with learned men from this region in whose accomplishments they took great pride. The famous Barmaki family, who for several generations held high administrative offices during the Abbasid caliphate, came from the central Asian city of Balkh. They had been Buddhists living close to the great carved Buddhas of Bamiyan (see Chapter 8). The Barmakis prospered under Islam and enjoyed remarkable influence in Baghdad. According to the tenth-century Arab historian Ali al-Mas'udi, the Barmaki family was responsible for building the Abbasid bureaucratic system and opening the Islamic world to many inventions from Central Asia, including papermaking. Loyal

The Great Mosque of Cordova. The great mosque of Cordova was built in the tenth century by the caliph al-Hakim II, who succeeded Abd al-Rahman III, considered by many historians to have been the most powerful and effective of the Spanish Umayyad caliphs.

servants of the caliph, they ensured that all the wealth and talent from the crossroads of Asia made their way to Baghdad, as they themselves had done.

In turn, the Barmakis aided their native region as patrons of the arts. They collected and had Arabic translations made of Persian, Greek, and Sanskrit manuscripts, and they encouraged scholars from central Asia to enhance their learning by moving to Baghdad. One of their protégés, the highly regarded Islamic cleric al-Bukhari (d. 870 CE), from Bukhara, was Islam's most dedicated collector of hadith, which provided vital knowledge about the Prophet's life.

Others from the area made notable contributions to science and mathematics. Al-Khwarizmi (c. 780–850 CE) modified the Indian digits into Arabic numerals, wrote the first book on algebra, and through the Latinized version of his name is the source of the word *algorithm*. He became one of the most valued members of Baghdad's famous translation center, the House of Knowledge, using his deep familiarity with the geography of the regions described by the Alexandrian polymath Ptolemy (fl. 127–148 CE) to correct many of Ptolemy's mistakes. The renowned Abbasid philosopher al-Farabi (d. 950 CE), from a Turkish military family, also made his way to Baghdad, where he studied Hellenistic Christian teachings. Although he regarded himself as a Muslim, he thought formal religions were for the common people, not

Materia Medica. A page from an Arabic translation of the classical text of Dioscorides, *Materia Medica.* The translated text is dated to 1224 and comes from Iraq, which was one of the centers for the translation of classical Greek and Roman works into Arabic.

the intellectual elite. In his view, good societies would naturally embrace the idea of a single God, but they would succeed only if their rulers implemented the political tenets espoused in Plato's *Republic*. He championed a virtuous "first chief" to rule over an Islamic commonwealth in much the same way that Plato had favored a philosopher-king.

As the power of the Abbasid caliphate began to decline in the eleventh century because of the same problems that had faced the Roman Empire—overextension and the influx of outsider groups—scholars from central Asia no longer made the trek to the caliph's court at Baghdad. Yet the intellectual vitality of central Asia did not suffer, for young men of learning began to find patrons among local rulers. Consider Ibn Sina, known in the West as Avicenna (980–1037 CE). He never made it to Baghdad; he grew to adulthood in Bukhara, practiced medicine in the courts of various Islamic rulers, and spent the last fifteen years of his life in Isfahan, in central Persia. Schooled in the Quran, the Arabic secular literature known as *adab,* philosophy, geometry, and Indian and Euclidean mathematics, Ibn Sina had mastery over many disciplines. His *Canon of Medicine* was the standard medical text in both Southwest Asia and Europe for centuries.

ISLAM IN SUB-SAHARAN AFRICA Islam also crossed the Sahara and entered Africa, carried by traders and scholars rather than by soldiers. (See Map 9-5.) Its movement depended largely on camels, which were domesticated well before the Common Era but were not used for crossing the Sahara Desert until the third century CE; these animals, able to carry heavy loads and to go weeks without water, enabled long-distance traders to traverse the deserts with almost as much ease as they traveled through settled areas and across seas. By the seventh and eighth centuries, large numbers of Islamic adventurers were arriving in sub-Saharan West Africa, where in exchange for weapons and textiles they received gold, salt, and slaves. The lively trading networks included the old city of Jenne in modern-day Mali, whose archaeological remains can be dated to around 400 BCE. Four centuries later, it had become a bustling entrepôt, with residences and town buildings taking up about 100 acres and surrounded by a large protective wall.

Trade did more than join West Africa to North Africa. It also generated wealth, which in turn facilitated the creation of centralized political kingdoms in West Africa. The most celebrated of these kingdoms was Ghana, located north and east of the modern country of that name, in the eastern region of modern Mauritania. It lay at the terminus of North Africa's major trading routes.

Of Ghana, we know little. The first to mention it was the Baghdadi scholar al-Fazari, who in the eighth century described Ghana as "the land of gold." A century later, the Arab traveler and geographer al-Yaqubi wrote of "the kingdom of Ghana, the king of which is very powerful. In his country there are gold mines. Under his authority are other kingdoms

Ibn Sina. Ibn Sina was a versatile scholar, most famous for his *Canon of Medicine,* which was for centuries the standard medical text in Southwest Asia and Europe.

. . . and gold is found in all of these regions" (Fage, p. 15). Although Muslim traders frequented the state, its rulers were not Muslims. Still, the pomp and power of the state impressed visitors; in 1067–1068, the Andalusian geographer al-Bakri wrote of a powerful and resplendent king who heard "grievances against officials in a domed pavilion around which stand ten horses covered with gold-embroidered materials.

→ *What factors created a common cultural outlook among Muslim communities in Afro-Eurasia during this era?*

Direction of trade
Trade route
Extent of the Ghana Empire, c. 1050 CE
Swahili settlement in the 14th century

Commodities
△ Salt
⬭ Gold
⬭⬭ Slaves
✕ Weapons
⬗ Textiles

▨ Gold source
▲ Major salt source

MAP 9-5   ISLAM AND TRADE IN SUB-SAHARAN AFRICA, 700–1000

Islamic merchants and scholars, not Islamic armies, carried Islam into sub-Saharan Africa soon after their religion emerged. According to the map, what kinds of goods were Islamic merchants seeking below the Sahara? How did increased trade with the broader Afro-Eurasian world affect societies below the Sahara? How did trade and commerce lead to the further geographic expansion of the Islamic faith?

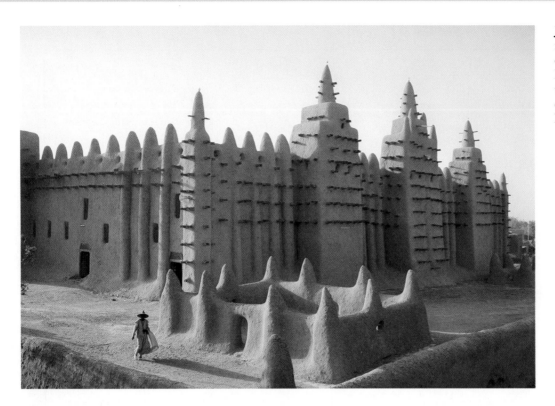

Jenne Mosque. This fabulous mosque arose in the kingdom of Mali when it was at the height of its power. It speaks to the depth and importance of Islam's roots in the Malian kingdom.

Behind the king stand ten pages holding shields and swords decorated with gold and on his right are the sons of the (vassal) kings of his country wearing splendid garments and their hair plaited with gold" (Levtzion and Spaulding, p. 16).

Seafaring Muslim traders carried Islam into East Africa as Islam became a dominant mercantile force in the Indian Ocean. A small Islamic trading community had come into being in the eighth century at Lamu, along the northern coast of present-day Kenya. By the middle of the ninth century, other East African coastal trading communities had sprung up. On the island of Pate, off the coast of Kenya, the inhabitants of Shanga constructed the region's first mosque, a simple structure replaced 200 years later by a mosque capable of holding all of the adult members of the community when they gathered for their Friday prayers. These communities, an amalgam of African and Arab populations, exported ivory and possibly slaves. Already by the tenth century, the East African coast featured a mixed African-Arab culture. The evolving Bantu language of the region took in Arabic loanwords—at first a few and later, especially after the fifteenth century, many more—and before long was given a new name, Swahili (derived from the Arabic plural of the word meaning "coast").

OPPOSITION WITHIN ISLAM, SHIISM, AND THE RISE OF THE FATIMIDS

Islam's whirlwind rise generated internal tensions from the start. Such a powerful religious movement fostered a shared reverence for a basic text and a single God. But there was not much else that was shared. The divisions were apparent from the time of Muhammad's proselytizing campaigns, and only grew deeper as Islam spread into new corners of Eurasia and Africa. Once the charismatic Prophet died, in 632 CE, the latent fissures came to the surface as believers disagreed over who should take his place and how to preserve some authority. Strains associated with the selection of the first four caliphs after Muhammad's death left a legacy of protest; to this day, they represent the greatest challenge facing Islam in its efforts to create a unified culture.

Early and spirited opposition originated during the seventh century among a group calling itself the Kharijites, who came together in Arabia during the dispute over the succession to Muhammad. Spurning all of the conservatives' choices for caliphs, the Kharijites believed that the rulers of Islam should only be individuals of impeccable religious credentials—individuals who most resembled Muhammad himself. The doctrine found support especially among those peoples who felt deprived of power, appealing to the highlander Berber peoples of North Africa and the inhabitants of lower Iraq, who complained that the leaders of the faith discriminated against them, despite the teaching that all Muslims belonged equally to the community of believers.

The Kharijite movement died out. It was too individualistic to challenge the authority of established political elites. But another, more powerful, movement of opposition arose in many of the same areas where Kharijism had been influential. In North Africa, lower Iraq, and the Iranian plateau, the mat-

GHANA AS SEEN BY A MUSLIM OBSERVER IN THE ELEVENTH CENTURY

The following excerpt is taken from a manuscript written in the eleventh century by a Muslim serving under the Umayyad regime in Spain. Its author, Abdullah Abu Ubayd al-Bakri, produced a massive general geography and history of the known world, as did many of the most accomplished Muslim scholars of this period. This manuscript has special value because it provides information about West Africa, a region in which the Spanish rulers had a great interest and into which Islam had been spreading for several centuries.

Ghana is the title of the king of the people. The name of the country is Aoukar. The ruler who governs the people at the present time—the year 460 AH (after the Hijra and 1067–68 CE)—is called Tenkamein. He came to the throne in 455 AH. His predecessor, who was named Beci, began his reign at the age of 85. He was a prince worthy of great praise as much for his personal conduct as for his zeal in the pursuit of justice and his friendship to Muslims. . . .

Ghana is composed of two towns situated in a plain. The one inhabited by Muslims is large and contains twelve mosques, in which the congregants celebrate the Friday prayer. All of these mosques have their imams, their muezzins, and their salaried readers. The city possesses judges and men of great erudition. . . . The city where the king resides is six miles away and carries the name el-Ghaba, meaning "the forest." The territory separating these two locations is covered with dwellings, constructed out of rocks and the wood of the acacia tree. The dwelling of the king consists of a chateau and several surrounding huts, all of which are enclosed by a wall-like structure. In the ruler's town, close to the royal tribunal, is a mosque where Muslims come when they have business with the ruler in order to carry out their prayers. . . . The royal interpreters are chosen from the Muslim population, as was the state treasurer and the majority of the state ministers. . . .

The opening of a royal meeting is announced by the noise of a drum, which they call a *deba*, and which is formed from a long piece of dug-out wood. Upon hearing the drumming, the inhabitants assemble. When the king's coreligionists appear before him, they genuflect and throw dust on their heads. Such is the way in which they salute their sovereign. The Muslims show their respect for the king by clapping their hands. The religion of the Negroes is paganism and fetishism. . . . The land of Ghana is not healthy and has few people. Travelers who pass through the area during the height of the agricultural season are rarely able to avoid becoming sick. When the grains are at their fullest and are ready for harvesting is the time when mortality affects visitors.

The best gold in the land comes from Ghiarou, a town located eighteen days journey from the capital. All of the gold found in the mines of the empire belongs to the sovereign, but the sovereign allows the people to take gold dust. Without this precaution, the gold would become so abundant that it would lose much of its value. . . . It is claimed that the king owns a piece of gold as large as an enormous rock.

→ *From this excerpt, how much can you learn about the kingdom of Ghana?*
→ *What influence did Islam have in the empire?*
→ *What elements of Ghana most interested the author, al-Bakri?*

SOURCE: Abou-Obeïd-el-Bekri, *Description de l'Afrique septentrionale*, revised and corrected edition, translated by [William] Mac Guckin de Slane (Paris: A. Maisonneuve, 1965), pp. 327–31; translated from the French by Robert Tignor.

ter of who should succeed the Prophet and how the succession should take place was a source of fundamental disagreement from the outset. Some repudiated the Umayyad and Abbasid rulers and the claims to succession defended by those who came to be known as Sunnis (from the Arabic word meaning "tradition"). Among the earliest dissidents were the Shiites (literally, members of the party of Ali), who believed that the proper successors to the Prophet should have been Ali, who had married the Prophet's daughter Fatima, and his descendants. Shiites also believed that Ali's descendants, whom they called imams, had religious and prophetic power as well as political authority and should enjoy spiritual primacy even over

Muslim scholars with more extensive religious training. Like Kharijism, Shiism appealed to groups whom the Umayyads and Abbasids had excluded from power; it became Islam's most potent dissident force and created a permanent divide within Islam. Shiism was well established in the first century of Islam's existence.

But not until the tenth century, after nearly 300 years of struggling, did the Shiites finally seize power. Repressed in Iraq and Iran, Shiite activists made their way to North Africa, where they joined with dissident Berber groups to bring down several rulers. In 909 CE, a Shiite religious and military leader, Abu Abdallah, overthrew the Sunni ruler in North Africa. Thus began the Fatimid regime; after conquering Egypt in 969 CE, it set itself against the Abbasid caliphs of Baghdad, refusing to acknowledge their legitimacy and claiming authority to speak for the whole of the Islamic world. The Fatimid rulers established their capital in a new city that arose alongside al-Fustat, the old Umayyad capital. They called this place al-Qahira (or Cairo), "the Victorious." Although intended simply as a royal refuge, Cairo soon overshadowed al-Fustat, and the Fatimid rulers promoted its beauty. One of their first acts was the founding of a place of worship and learning, the Azhar mosque, which attracted scholars from all over Afro-Eurasia and spread Islamic learning outward from Egypt; they also built other elegant mosques and centers of learning. The Fatimid regime remained in power until the end of the twelfth century, though its rulers made little headway in persuading the Egyptian population to embrace their Shiite beliefs.

By 1000 CE Islam had become the dominant political and cultural force in the middle regions of the Afro-Eurasian landmass. At Afro-Eurasia's peripheries, its armies, merchants, and scholars had finally run out of energy, leaving much of western Europe and China outside the Islamic domain. Moreover, by the beginning of the new millennium Muslims were ceasing to be a minority within their own lands. A rapidly increasing rate of conversions reduced the Christian, Jewish, and other non-Muslim populations living in polities ruled by Muslim kings and princes. Yet the political unification of the whole Muslim world had not followed. Although the Abbasid caliphate made claims to universal political power, breakaway regimes disputed these claims. Powerful separatist Muslim states emerged in Spain and North Africa.

THE TANG STATE

> → *How did the Tang state balance its desire to restore Confucian principles to China with the growth of new universal religions in East Asia?*

The rise of the Sui (581–618 CE) and Tang (618–907 CE) empires in China and their pervasive impact on Korea and Japan paralleled Islam's explosion out of Arabia in the seventh cen-

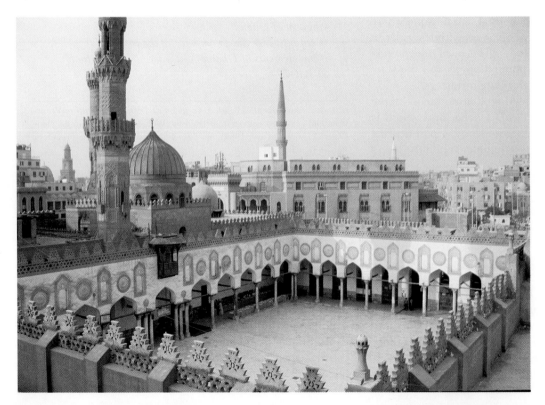

Al-Azhar Mosque. The mosque of al-Azhar is Cairo's most important ancient mosque. Built in the tenth century by the Fatimid conquerors and rulers of Egypt, it quickly became a leading center for worship and learning, frequented by Muslim clerics and admired in Europe.

tury and its rise to prominence throughout Afro-Eurasia in the eighth, ninth, and tenth centuries. Once again, the Afro-Eurasian landmass had two centers of power. Islam, stretching to Africa and Iberia, replaced the Roman Empire in providing a counterbalance to the power and wealth of China.

But in one fundamental way, this bipolar world differed from that of the Roman and Han empires: in the centuries since their waning, Eurasian and African worlds had been brought much closer together by trade, conversion, and more regular political contacts. The two most powerful political and cultural systems of Afro-Eurasia now had common borders. They converged and then competed for dominance in central Asia, were influenced by one another and even shared populations, admired features of the other, and encouraged travelers and traders to share information about the other society. The world had, indeed, become smaller. Peoples, ideas (especially technological innovations), and commodities moved rapidly across political boundaries.

Yet in China, religion did not play the role in shaping the formation of states and empires seen in the rest of Afro-Eurasia. Instead, its religious and political histories ran on separate but not parallel rails. China's political fortunes did not rest nearly as much on sacred foundations as did the smaller dynasties of India or Europe, or the powerhouse of the caliphate and Islam. Underneath a single dynastic and imperial culture in China lay a plurality of religions and sects—an amalgamation of belief systems rather than a single integrated culture functioning as the polity's bulwark. In this regard, China exemplifies the many ways in which Eurasian and African worlds balanced the forces of integration and diversity as they neared the end of the first millennium.

China was both at the receiving end of foreign influences and a source of influences on its neighbors. Indeed, it was becoming the hub of East Asian integration. Like the Umayyads and the Abbasids, the Tang promoted a cosmopolitan culture that absorbed and digested many new cultural elements arising at a great distance. Buddhism, medicine, and mathematics from India via central Asia gave China's chief cities an international flavor. Buddhist monks from Bactria; Greeks, Armenians, and Jews from Constantinople; Muslim envoys from Samarkand and Persia; Vietnamese tributary missions from Annam; chieftains of nomadic tribes from the Siberian plains; officials and students from Korea; and monkish visitors from Japan rubbed elbows in the streets of the dual Tang capitals at Chang'an and Luoyang, previously the Qin and Han capitals. Ideas floated to the east as well—notably in the middle of the first millennium CE, when the early societies and states in Korea and Japan emerged in the shadow of China. Even when China was disunited politically after the fall of the Han, the impact of Chinese religions, particularly Daoism and Buddhism, in Korea and then Japan was marked. Similarly, Chinese statecraft—as enunciated principally through the Confucian classics—seemed to the early Korean and Japanese scholars and courtiers to provide the best and most universally applicable model for their own state building.

Yet conversely, even during the Tang dynasty (608–907 CE), when the Chinese empire revived as never before, China's impact on Korea and Japan was limited. The latter never became "little Chinas." Each culture adapted and appropriated Chinese institutions, values, and religions in ways that suited its own political and social conditions. To be sure, for the sake of trade relations each paid lip service to the Middle Kingdom's efforts to define them as subordinate states that had to pay tribute in their economic and diplomatic exchanges with China. But each maintained cultural autonomy and often turned Chinese learning and cultural and political concepts to its own purposes, sometimes with unexpected consequences.

Throughout its history, China was the "Middle Kingdom" (*Zhongguo*), but this name mainly differentiated between those who considered themselves Chinese and those who were seen as outsiders. During the Warring States era (see Chapter 5), the key states were referred to in aggregate as "Zhongguo," that is, the "middle states." Under the Tang, the name differentiated the "Middle Kingdom" of China proper from her non-Chinese provinces. During the Song and thereafter, the term demarcated the Middle Kingdom (and its Han civilization) from the steppe barbarians (and their allegedly uncivilized ways). The Mongol and Manchu conquests of China made this last distinction moot, as they both equated their dynasties with the Middle Kingdom.

CHINESE TERRITORIAL EXPANSION UNDER THE SUI AND TANG DYNASTIES

After the fall of the Han in 220 CE, China faced a long period of political instability (see Chapter 8). But it was only a matter of time before a new set of the rulers (the Sui and Tang) took advantage of military weaknesses and political fragmentation to restore Han models of empire building. Their claims that a big imperial system could outperform small states found a receptive audience in a populace fatigued by internal chaos. Both dynasties expanded the boundaries of the Chinese state and reestablished China's dominance in East and central Asia.

Leading the way back to empire was Yang Jian, who had served as an official of the militarily strong Northern Zhou dynasty (557–580 CE). His struggles for unification ended in the Sui dynasty, which heralded the revival of Han imperial ideals. The Sui reunification continued reforms begun at the Northern Zhou court that were aimed at enhancing the state's power over the aristocracy. The two emperors of Sui, Wendi (ruled 581–604 CE) and Yangdi (ruled 605–616 CE), father and son, championed the notion that bigger is better as they channeled the state's domestic energy into territorial expansion into Korea, Vietnam, Manchuria, Tibet, and central Asia. Yet those efforts, particularly the costly and disastrous military campaigns undertaken against Silla Korea in the early seventh century, fatally weakened the dynasty. In addition, as so often occurred throughout Chinese history (e.g., see Chapter 7), a precipitous change in the course of the Yellow River, causing extensive flooding on the North China plain, led to popular revolts; they set the stage for Li Yuan, a Sui general, to march on Chang'an and take the throne for himself. Li Yuan promptly established the new Tang dynasty in 618 CE and began building a powerful central government. He increased the number of prefectures and counties and expanded the bureaucracy. By doubling the number of government offices, the emperor tightened his control over individual governors. By 624 CE the initial steps needed to found the new Tang dynasty had been completed. (See Map 9-6.)

THE ARMY AND IMPERIAL CAMPAIGNING

An expanding Tang state required a large and professionally trained army, capable of defending far-flung frontiers and squelching recalcitrant populations. The military organization created by the Tang emperors consisted of aristocratic cavalry and peasant soldiers. The aristocrats were used primarily on the northern steppes in Inner Eurasia to deal with nomadic peoples, who similarly fought mounted; at its height the Tang military had some 700,000 horses. At the same time, between 1 and 2 million peasant soldiers garrisoned the south and were also used for public work projects.

MAP 9-6   THE TANG STATE IN EAST ASIA

The Tang dynasty, at its territorial peak in 750, was the most powerful, most advanced, and best administered empire in the world. It controlled a state that extended from central Asia to the East China Sea. How did Tang rulers promote order and stability in such a diverse realm? In particular, how did they foster and try to control the growth and spread of religious communities? According to the map, how did Tang policies promote an economic revolution in China? To what extent did the empire influence other peoples in Afro-Eurasia not ruled directly ruled by the Tang state?

Much like the Islamic forces, the Tang's frontier armies, especially those that operated beyond the Great Wall—newly repaired now that China was reunified—became increasingly reliant on pastoral nomadic soldiers from the Inner Eurasian steppe. Notable among them were the Uighurs, Turkish-speaking steppe peoples who had moved into the Tarim basin in western China and who by 750 CE had become the most potent military force in the empire. The Tang military also enabled the westward expansion of the state, which brought the first Chinese penetration of parts of Tibet, then emerging as a powerful centralized kingdom in the southwest and along the Silk Road. The Red River valley in northern Vietnam and Manchuria in the north came under Chinese suzerainty as well. Briefly, Tang authority stretched from Tibet and central Asia to Korea.

Though it rested on earlier imperial foundations, the Tang's spread into East and central Asia was no less dramatic than the expansion of Islam. By 650 CE, as Islamic armies were moving toward central Asia, the Tang were already the new colossus of the region, claiming to have surpassed even the Han in scope and scale. At this empire's height, Tang armies controlled more than 4 million square miles of territory—an area that was as large as and was much more centrally administered than the whole of the Islamic world in the ninth and tenth centuries. The Tang population of more than 80 million surpassed the Han peak of 60 million and was far greater than the populations under Islamic rulers in the eighth and ninth centuries. Once the Tang administrators had brought the rich farmlands of South China under cultivation—draining swamps, building an intricate network of canals and channels to complement those in the north, and connecting lakes and rivers to the rice lands—the state was able to collect taxes from no fewer than 10 million families in agricultural labor, representing 57 million individuals.

In spite of the Abbasid Empire's precocious spread, China in 750 CE was the most powerful, most advanced, and best administered empire in the world. Korea and Japan, its neighbors in East Asia, recognized its superiority in every material aspect of life. Muslims were among the people who arrived from the four corners of the world to pay homage. Persians, Armenians, and Turks brought tribute and merchandise via the busy Silk Road or by sea, and other travelers and traders came from Southeast Asia and Japan.

This was the peak of Chinese power—at the very moment that the Abbasids were expanding into the Tang portions of central Asia. The map of Afro-Eurasia was now connected by bordering empires on the east and west, filling in the political landscape with powerful states, some of them bursting with religious energy. The rivalry for Afro-Eurasian supremacy brought the worlds together, but not peaceably. Muslim forces drove the Tang from Turkistan in 751 CE at the battle of Talas, and their success emboldened new groups such as the Sogdians and Tibetans to challenge the Tang in the west. As a result, the Tang were forced to retreat from central Asia

and mainland Southeast Asia into the old heartlands of China along the Yellow and Yangzi rivers. Even in the Wei River valley, Chinese rulers saw their capital in Chang'an fall to invading Tibetans and Sogdians in the middle of the eighth century. Misrule, court intrigues, economic exploitation, and popular rebellions weakened the empire, but the dynasty held on for over a century more until northern invaders brought an end to it in 907 CE. The next half century saw the fragmentation of China into five northern dynasties and ten southern kingdoms, a brief repeat of the era of disunity after the fall of the Han dynasty in 220 CE. Wars and rebellions devastated the population.

ORGANIZING AN EMPIRE

The Tang empire was a worthy successor to the Han and deservedly ranks as one of China's great dynastic polities. In its nearly 300-year tenure, it was exceeded only by the Han (202 BCE–220 CE) and it surpassed the Ming (1368–1644) and Qing (1644–1912) dynasties, China's other long-lasting empires. Although Tang rulers emulated the Han in many ways, including the compilation of their own legal code (which drew heavily on that of the Han) in 624 CE, they also introduced new institutions, the most significant and enduring of which was the imperial examination system. Moreover, as an empire in an age of universalistic and proselytizing religions, the Tang had to deal with the arrival of global religions inside their borders and accommodate these new religious institutions and agents within their imperial framework. Its methods for achieving and maintaining power often differed from those employed by the Abbasid Empire, Afro-Eurasia's other superpower at this time.

CONFUCIAN ADMINISTRATORS Even though the Tang ultimately relied on military force, their day-to-day control of

China Trade. In this seventh-century silk painting, we see envoys from the busy Silk Road bearing tribute to gain access to the lucrative China trade.

the empire depended on an efficient and loyal civil service. Unlike the multilingual, multiethnic, and even multireligious Islamic empire, which was held together by a shared spiritual commitment to Islam, the Tang had to devise other formulas for integrating their remote territories and diverse ethnicities and linguistic groups. Instead of a single universalizing faith, the Tang provided the political framework for a spiritual mosaic of Buddhism, Confucianism, and Daoism. In some areas, local deities continued to flourish. Rather than relying on a world religion to anchor their empire, to maintain order the Tang created a formidable and unifying political culture based on Confucian teachings composed in the classical written language that was mastered by Mandarin-speaking officials and China's educated elites.

Chinese integration began at the top. To enter the ruling group required knowing the ideas of Confucius and all of the subsequent commentaries on the classics that he had transmitted to his disciples. It also entailed handling the intricacies of the classical Chinese language, in which all such literature was written. These skills were as powerful in forging cultural and political solidarity as Islam was for the Abbasid state or Christianity for Europe and the Byzantine Empire. Thus a common written language (classical Chinese) and a common philosophy (Confucianism) served as a surrogate for the universalistic religions that created common cultures elsewhere in Eurasia and Africa. Confucian thought, learned and embraced by a privileged group of individuals from elite families, provided a set of common characteristics for the rulers and administrators of Tang society. Indeed, we have seen that the adoption of a common language—Latin, Greek, Arabic—at least among elites, can be a powerful element unifying an empire.

Of the highest importance in exalting the powers of the Tang state was the world's first written civil service examination system. Examinations now became the mechanism for making knowledge of a specific language and the Confucian classics the only route to power and the means of uniting the Chinese state, and no innovation was more significant for promoting the obedience and loyalty of state appointees. Candidates for office, whom local elites recommended, gathered in the capital to take qualifying examinations that required them to know the classics and display highly developed literary skills. Those who were successful underwent further trials to evaluate their character and determine the level of their appointments. New officials were selected from the pool of examination graduates on the basis of deportment, eloquence, skill in calligraphy and mathematics, and legal knowledge. When Emperor Li Shimin (ruled 627–649 CE) first observed the new officials obediently parading out of the examination hall, he slyly noted, "The heroes of the empire are all in my pocket!" (Miyazaki, *China's Examination Hell*, 13).

Having assumed the mandate of heaven (see Chapter 4), the Tang rulers and their supporters were intent on estab-

Tang Official. Tang officials were selected through competitive civil examinations in order to limit the power of Buddhist and Daoist clerics. This painted clay figure of a Tang official c. 717 was excavated in 1972.

lishing a common code of moral values for the whole empire. Building on Han models, they expanded the state school in the capital into an empire-wide hierarchy of select state schools that prepared those who had already mastered the required Confucian texts for the civil examinations. But Tang rulers and officials also favored the continued use of the Daoist classics as texts for the examinations, because the rulers and many elites still regarded the early Daoists as an important stream of ancient wisdom. What the Tang managed to do was to amalgamate this range of texts, codes, and

Primary Source

INTEGRATING EMPIRE BY EXAMINATION

The young and old competed equally in the Tang examination market, bringing different experiences into the examination halls. The rituals of success looked alluring to youths, while the tortures of failure were common among their older competitors still seeking an elusive degree. For all, however, the emotional tensions they felt when the list of successful candidates was posted—following years of preparation for young boys, and even more years of defeat for old men—were the private, human response to success or failure. The few that passed would look back on that day with relief and pride.

In the Southern Court they posted the list. (The Southern Court was where the Board of Rites ran the administration and accepted documents. All prescribed forms together with the stipulations for each [degree] category were usually publicized here.) The wall for hanging the list was by the eastern wall of the Southern Court. In a separate building a screen was erected which stood over ten feet tall, and it was surrounded with a fence. Before dawn they took the list from the Northern Court to the Southern Court where it was hung for display.

In the sixth year of Yuanhe [AD 811] a student at the University, Guo Dongli, broke through the thorn hedge. (The thorn hedge was below the fence. There was another outside the main gate of the Southern Court.) He then ripped up the ornamental list [*wenbang*]. It was because of this that afterwards they often came out of the gateway of the Department [of State Affairs] with a mock list. The real list was displayed a little later.

→ *Why were the stakes so high in the civil examinations?*
→ *Was the Tang civil examination system an open system that tested talent—that is, a meritocracy?*
→ *What happened to those that failed?*

SOURCE: Wang Dingbao (870–940), quoted in Oliver J. Moore, *Rituals of Recruitment in Tang China* (Leiden: Brill, 2004), p. 175.

tests into a common intellectual and cultural credo for the governing classes.

CHINA'S FIRST FEMALE EMPEROR Not all Tang power brokers were men. Women also played influential roles in the court, usually behind the scenes—but sometimes publicly. Consider the example of Empress Wu, who dominated the Tang court in the late seventh and early eighth centuries. She deftly used the examination system to check the power of aristocratic families and helped consolidate courtly authority by creating cadres of loyal bureaucrats, who in turn preserved loyalty to the dynasty at the local level.

Born into a rich and noble family, Wu Zhao (626–706 CE) played music and mastered the Chinese classics as a young girl. By thirteen, because she was witty, intelligent, and beautiful, Wu was recruited to Li Shimin's court, where she soon became his favorite concubine. She also became enamored of his son. When Li Shimin died, his son assumed power and became the Emperor Gaozong (ruled 649–683 CE). Wu quickly became the new emperor's favorite concubine as well and gave birth to the sons he required to succeed him. As the mother of the future emperor, Wu's prestige in court was heightened, and her political power grew. Subsequently, she took the place of Gaozong's Empress Wang by accusing her—falsely—of killing Wu's newborn daughter. Gaozong believed Wu and married her.

When Emperor Gaozong suffered a stroke in 660 CE, Wu Zhao became administrator of the court, a position equal to the emperor's. She created a secret police force to spy on her opposition, and she jailed or killed those who stood in her way, including the unfortunate Empress Wang. Upon the emperor's death, Wu outmaneuvered her eldest sons and placed her youngest son in power; she named herself as his regent. Shortly afterward she seized power in her own right as Empress Wu (ruled 684–705 CE), becoming the first and only female ruler in Chinese history, though initially reigning in the name of her son. She expanded the military and recruited her administrators from the civil examination candidates to oppose her enemies at court.

Challenging Confucian beliefs that subordinated women, Wu elevated their position. She ordered scholars to write biographies of famous women, and she empowered her mother's clan by giving her relatives by marriage high political posts. Later, she moved her court away from the seat of traditional power in Chang'an to Luoyang, where she tried to establish a new "Zhou dynasty" in imitation of the time of Confucius.

Despite the ruthlessness of her climb to power, her rule proved to be benign and competent. During her reign, Empress Wu elevated Buddhism over Daoism as the favored state religion. She invited the most gifted Buddhist religious scholars to her capital at Luoyang, built Buddhist temples, and subsidized the building of spectacular cave sculptures, particularly in northwest China. Chinese Buddhism achieved its highest officially sponsored development in this period.

As she grew older, Empress Wu lessened the power of her secret police, but she became superstitious and fearful. Sor-

Empress Wu. When she seized power in her own right as Empress Wu, Wu Zetian became the first and only female ruler in Chinese history. Although ruthless toward her court enemies, she expanded the military and recruited administrators from the civil examination candidates. She also challenged Confucian beliefs that subordinated women.

cerers and corrupt court favorites flattered her. Finally, in 705 CE, she gave up the throne in favor of her third son. Later that year, she died in retirement at age eighty.

Although official careers were in theory open to anyone of talent, in practice members of many groups were excluded. Despite Empress Wu's prominence, women were not permitted to serve, nor were sons of merchants and those who could not afford a classical education. The Tang restored the Han dynasty state school in the capital, but because there were still no public schools, initially many candidates—as in Zhou and Han times—still came from aristocratic families. Tang civil examinations over time forced aristocrats to compete with rising southern families, commoners whose economic wealth and new educational resources made them the equals of the old elites. Under the banner of a classical meritocracy that Empress Wu enforced, a new aristocracy of academic ability emerged in the upper echelons of the Tang government. Through examinations, this new elite of southern commoners eventually outdistanced the sons of the landed northern aristocracy in the Tang government.

The system also indirectly benefited the poor by impressing on them the value of an education as the primary avenue for entering the ruling elite. Even poor families sought the best classical education they could for their sons. Although few from the ranks of the less well-off succeeded in the civil service examinations, many boys and even some girls learned the fundamentals of reading and writing. The Buddhists played a crucial role in extending education across society, for their temple schools introduced many children to primers based on classical texts as part of their charitable empire-wide mission. Relatively few of these students became fully literate in classical Chinese, but in a society containing nearly 16 million families and 80 million people in 750 CE, many were at least functionally literate.

EUNUCHS Abbasid and Tang rulers alike defended themselves and their most valued possessions, including their womenfolk, from opponents and enemies by surrounding themselves with loyal and well-compensated men. The caliphs in Baghdad chose young male slaves, frequently Turks, as their personal guards, although males known as eunuchs, who were surgically castrated as youths to perform a specific social function, also protected the harem. Similarly, Tang emperors in Chang'an and Luoyang relied on castrated males from the lower classes to guard the harem and protect the royal family because they were rendered sexually impotent. By the late eighth century, however, eunuchs in China were fully integrated into the empire's institutions, wielding a great deal more court power than those of the male slaves in Baghdad.

The numbers provide a sense of their growing power: in 820 CE the Tang government included 4,618 eunuchs, and 1,696 of them served at the highest administrative grade. The Chief Eunuch controlled the military, and through him the military power of court eunuchs extended to every province

Eunuchs. Castrated males, known as eunuchs, guarded the harem and protected the royal family of Tang emperors. By the late eighth century, eunuchs were fully integrated into the government and wielded a great deal of military and political power.

Tang Court Women. This tenth-century painting of elegant ladies of the Tang imperial court enjoying a feast and music tells us a great deal about the aesthetic tastes of elite women in this era. It also shows the secluded "inner quarters," where court ladies passed their daily lives far from the hurly-burly of imperial politics.

and garrison station in the empire, forming an all-encompassing network. In effect, the eunuch bureaucracy mediated between the emperor and provincial governments.

Under Emperor Xianzong (ruled 806–820 CE), eunuchs acted as a third pillar of the government, working alongside the official bureaucracy and the imperial court. By establishing clear career patterns for eunuchs that paralleled those in the civil service, Xianzong empowered them and sparked a striking rise in their levels of literacy and their cultural attainments. More eunuchs acquired enough classical training to handle imperial documents and official reports. Yet by 838 CE, the delicate balance of power that had existed between the throne, eunuchs, and civil officials had evaporated. Eunuchs became an unruly political force in late Tang politics, and their machinations equaled those of the slaves guarding the Abbasid caliph and his harem.

AN ECONOMIC REVOLUTION

In the Abbasid caliphate and in Tang China, political stability fueled remarkable economic achievements. Rising agricultural production based on an egalitarian land allotment system for peasant farmers, an increasingly fine handicrafts industry, a diverse commodity market, and dynamic urban life highlighted China's dramatic successes. The Sui had started this

economic progress by building canals—especially the Grand Canal linking North and South China—throughout the country (see Map 9-2). The Tang continued the canal-building endeavor, centering their efforts on the Grand Canal and the Yangzi River, which flows from west to east. These new waterways aided communication and transport to all parts of the empire and helped raise living standards. Granaries built along the canals enabled the Tang to transport rice from the south to the north. The south grew richer, largely through the hard work of northern immigrants. Fertile land along the Yangzi became China's new granary, and areas south of the Yangzi became the demographic center of the Chinese empire.

Chinese merchants took full advantage of the Silk Road to trade with India and the Islamic world; but when mid-eighth-century rebellions in northwest China and the rise of Islam in central Asia jeopardized the land route, the "silk road by sea" blossomed. From all over Asia and Africa, merchant ships arrived in South China ports bearing cargos of spices, medicines, and jewelry; they left carrying Chinese silks and porcelain. The capital, Chang'an, became the richest and arguably the most populous city in the world. Its million or so residents included minorities from many countries. Fortified with a wall and moat, the city was divided into government and residential quarters; in its two main markets full of shops and stores, more than 200 types of businesses sold a wide variety of domestic and international goods.

Tang Tripod Jar. Tricolor glazed stoneware was all the rage in the early and middle Tang court and among elites in Chang'an, Loyang, and the provinces. This glazed jar from the eighth century imitated ancient Zhou bronzes (see Chapter 4). Such stoneware was displaced in the late Tang by the exquisite jadelike porcelains made in high-fired kilns.

In the larger cities of the Yangzi delta—debatably the world's first industrial heartland—workshops proliferated; they were admired far and wide for the elegance of their wares, which included brocades, fine paper, printed woodblocks, iron casts, and high-fired porcelains. Chinese industrialists used locally grown cotton to produce clothing of the highest quality. The textile industry prospered as painting and dyeing technology improved, and superb silk products were a major source of tax revenue. Asian art collectors valued what became known as Tang "tricolor porcelain," decorated with brilliant hues of yellow, green, white, brown, and blue. Many of these pieces moved through the river and lake systems of the middle Yangzi region to major urban centers and then on to Chang'an and Luoyang in the northwest. Conspicuous consumption of manufactured fineries stimulated Tang producers of high-value textiles and porcelain. Chinese luxuries dominated the domestic and international trading networks that reached Southwest Asia, Europe, and Africa via the Silk Road and Arab ships from the Indian Ocean.

DEALING WITH WORLD RELIGIONS

The Confucian ideology at heart was secular. Although it posited a heaven from which the ruling dynasty claimed the authority to govern, it did not hold out the promise of an afterlife or threaten unbelievers with eternal damnation. Not surprisingly, therefore, the early Tang emperors tolerated a remarkable amount of religious diversity. Nestorian Christianity (originally based in the old Persian capital of Ctesiphon), Zoroastrianism, and Manichaeanism (a radical Christian sect) had entered China through central Asia from Persia at the time of the Sasanian Empire. Islam came later. These—together with Buddhism and the indigenous teachings of Daoism and Confucianism—spread throughout the empire and were not at first viewed as conflicting with state power.

THE GROWTH OF BUDDHISM Buddhism, in particular, thrived under Tang rule. Many foreign students from Korea and Japan journeyed to China in the early years of the dynasty to study it.

Emperor Li Shimin distrusted Buddhist monks because they avoided serving the government and paying taxes. Yet once Buddhism was accepted as one of the "three ways" of learning—joining Daoism and Confucianism—Li endowed monasteries, sent emissaries to India to collect texts and relics, and commissioned Buddhist paintings and statuary. To provide devotional sites where the people could practice Buddhism through good works and prayer, huge monasteries were built with imperial patronage. Giant carvings of the Buddha in northwestern temple sanctuaries dotted the trading routes to central Asia, and less monumental temples filled with ornate statuary provided sites for religious refuge throughout South China. Such temples provided shelter, and gave some measure of autonomy to commoners and women burdened by the rigid Tang social hierarchy. Chinese pilgrims braved the Silk Road and the heights of the Pamirs to travel to India, where they learned Sanskrit; when they returned, they brought back Buddhist texts. One of these pilgrims was Xuanzang, whose story was told in Chapter 8. On returning, Xuanzang won many followers in Japan as well as in China. His life inspired the widely read novel *Journey to the West* (c. 1590), a classic of the Ming dynasty.

ANTI-BUDDHIST CAMPAIGNS By the middle of the ninth century, the Tang empire contained nearly 50,000 monasteries and hundreds of thousands of Buddhist monks and nuns. By comparison, the Carolingian Empire under Charlemagne in France had only 700 major monasteries (see the following section). Such success by a foreign religion, in conjunction with the beginning of the decline of the Tang dynasty in the mid–eighth century, threatened the Confucian and Daoist leaders. They therefore attacked Buddhism, arguing that its values were at variance with Confucian and Daoist traditions.

One example of a Confucian response comes from the scholar-official Han Yu (768–824 CE). Han Yu represented the rising literati from the south, who championed ancient writing forms based on Confucian classics. Han Yu's Memorial of 819 protested the emperor's plan to bring a relic of the Buddha to the capital for exhibition. Striking a xenophobic note that would have been inconceivable during the cosmopolitanism of the early Tang, Han Yu attacked Buddhism as a foreign doctrine of barbarian peoples who were different in language, culture, and knowledge. For raising these objections, Han was exiled to the southern province of Guangdong. Yet, two decades later, the state began suppressing Buddhist monasteries and confiscating their wealth.

Secular rulers grew more and more concerned that religious loyalties would undermine political ones. Increasingly intolerant Confucian scholar-administrators argued that the Buddhist monastic establishment threatened the imperial order. They accused Buddhists of undercutting kinship values and undermining the cardinal family relations of father and son, husband and wife, and so on. They claimed that the clergy were conspiring to destroy the state, the family, and the body—a conspiracy that they labeled the "Three Destructions" of Buddhism.

Piecemeal measures against the monastic orders gave way in the 840s CE to open persecution. Emperor Wuzong (ruled 841–847 CE) closed more than 4,600 monasteries and destroyed 40,000 temples and shrines. More than 260,000 Buddhist monks and nuns were forced to return to secular life, and the state parceled out monastery lands to taxpaying landlords and peasant farmers. Two important points can be made about the persecution of Buddhism in this period. First, in China the Tang government brought the Buddhist monastic communities under its control; in Latin Europe, in contrast, the Christian church dominated feudal states. Second, because the Chinese bureaucracy was steeped in the traditions of Confucianism and Daoism, its traditions had a power base that Buddhism lacked. China's most prominent universalizing religion was thus vulnerable once Emperor Wuzong began to persecute it.

To expunge the cultural impact of Buddhism, classically trained literati emphasized the revival of ancient prose styles and the teachings of Confucius and his followers. Linking classical scholarship, ancient literature, and Confucian morality, they constructed a cultural fortress that reversed the early Buddhist successes in China. Scholars such as Liu Zongyuan (773–819 CE) claimed that skill in writing ancient prose verse forms was still the best measure of talent and should remain the core of the civil examinations. The Tang poets Li Bai (701–761 CE), Du Fu (c. 712–c. 770 CE), and Bo Juyi (772–846 CE) extolled verse, always popular with the literate population, as the most effective genre for expressing moral concerns and personal emotions, thereby obviating the need to turn to the Buddhist religion for solace.

Among the many remarkable feats of the Tang era was the triumph of the homegrown ideologies of Confucianism and Daoism over the universalistic ethos of Buddhism. The result was persistent religious pluralism within China. Tang China stands out in this age of world religions as the one cultural zone that remained committed to a secular common culture and that resisted the pressures to embrace universalistic religions.

THE FALL OF TANG CHINA

China's deteriorating economic conditions in the ninth century resulted in peasant uprisings, some led by failed examination candidates. These revolts, which began in 859 CE, ultimately brought down the dynasty. In the tenth century, China fragmented into as many as ten regional states. The result was a new era of decentralization, which even the Song dynasty that emerged in 960 CE could not overcome. Only the Mongols, invading steppe peoples, were later able to restore the glory of the Han and Tang empires.

EARLY KOREA AND JAPAN

> → *To what extent did Japanese and Korean states and societies emulate Tang China during this era?*

At the same time that China was opening up to the cultures of its western regions, such as Chinese Turkestan, versions of its culture colored by Buddhism (and thereby rendered more flexible and less distinctly Chinese) reached out to the east— to Korea and, eventually, to Japan. (See Map 9-7.) To comprehend Korean and Japanese history of this era, we need to gain some understanding of the developments that predated the Koryo kingdom and the Japanese experience of the ninth and tenth centuries.

EARLY KOREA

Chinese cultural influences in Korea can be documented as early as the third century BCE, when Chinese immigrants from the northeast helped locals set up a small state called Lelang (also called Lolang) at the present-day site of Pyongyang. By the fourth century CE, three independent states had emerged on the peninsula that jutted into the Yellow Sea: Koguryo in the north, Paekche in the southwest, and Silla in the southeast. Koguryo subsequently expanded its influence northward into Manchuria. By contrast, because of its location on the southwest coast facing the Yellow Sea and Shandong province in China, Paekche had close ties with North China. This division into what was known as the "Three Kingdoms" of Korea lasted until 668 CE, when the southeastern kingdom of Silla gained control over the entire peninsula and unified it for the first time. During this period, Japan also maintained a small enclave on Korea's southern coast at Kaya (also called Mimana).

Extent of Silla power, 670–935 CE
Extent of Nara state by 600 CE
⊙ Capital
• City
⌂ Buddhist temple
⊛ Shinto shrine
▲ Holy mountain
Bohai

MAP 9-7   BORDERLANDS: KOREA AND JAPAN, 600–1000

The Tang dynasty held great sway and power over emerging Korean and Japanese states in East Asia, although it never directly ruled either region. Study the map above. How did state formation evolve in Korea and Japan between 600 and 900? What connections existed between these states and the Tang empire during this era? To what extent did Korean and Japanese states adapt Tang traditions and customs during this time?

Silla's unification of Korea after 670 CE enabled the Koreans to establish a unified government modeled on the Tang Chinese imperial state. Silla dispatched annual embassies to the Chinese capital at Chang'an, as well as regularly sending students and monks to China. Like Latin among diverse populations in Europe, literary Chinese became the written language of Korean elites. Koreans later devised a phonetic system for writing their own language that simplified Chinese characters, but most official writing remained in Chinese. Early Korean society, like China's, was based on a hereditary aristocracy who monopolized official posts. But like Japan, Korea initially resisted the classical meritocracy that would be introduced into Tang China through the civil service examinations.

Silla's own fortunes were entwined with those of the Tang. In the wake of the Tang decline, the state of Silla also began to fragment. In 936 CE, Wang Kon, a rebel leader, absorbed Silla into the northern-based Koryo kingdom (918–1392 CE), an act that tenuously reunified the country. The Koryo dynasty, from which the country's modern name derives, began to construct a new cultural identity for itself by enacting an unprecedented bureaucratic system aimed at replacing the archaic tribal system that had continued under the Silla. Unlike in Japan, Tang dynasty–style civil service examinations to select the most capable officials to govern at court and in the provinces were successfully put in place in Korea. Wang Kon's heirs consolidated control over the peninsula and strengthened its political and economic foundations by more closely following the bureaucratic and land allotment systems of Tang China.

Yet during this period, Korea, like Tang China itself, was harassed continuously by northern tribes such as the Khitan people. As we will see in Chapter 10, the Khitan also took advantage of the fall of the Tang dynasty to control northern Chinese lands after 907 CE, establishing the rival Liao dynasty (907–1126 CE) in northeast China. During this troubled period, Korean artisans anxiously carved wooden printing blocks for 81,258 scriptures from the Buddhist canon as an offering to the Buddha to protect them from invading enemies—but in vain. After being overwhelmed by the Khitan in 1010, the Koryo dynasty revived, only to be invaded by the Mongols in 1231 (see Chapter 10). Despite these temporary invasions, the dynasty managed to last until 1392.

EARLY JAPAN

Beginning in the Ice Age, tribal groups known as the Jomon (from 10,000 years ago to 400 BCE; see Chapter 2) and succeeding Yayoi peoples (400 BCE–250 CE) dominated prehistoric Japan. Subsequently, in the middle of the third century, a warlike group from northeast Asia arrived by sea from Korea and aggressively imposed their military and social power on southern Japan. These conquerors, known today as the "Tomb Culture" because of their elevated necropolises near present-day Osaka, unified Japan by extolling their imperial ancestors and maintaining the social hierarchy that they had brought with them from Korea and Manchuria. They also brought with them a belief in the power of female shamans, who married into the imperial clans; like Himiko, discussed below, these women became de facto rulers of early Japanese kinship groups, combining religious and political power.

Chinese dynastic records describe the early Japanese, with whom imperial China had contact in this period, as a "dwarf" people who maintained a rice and fishing economy. The Japanese farmers had also mastered Chinese-style sericulture. According to the Chinese, the Japanese were united under a shaman-queen, Himiko, who sent an envoy in 239 CE to the state of Wei—one of the Three Kingdoms in China after the fall of the Han. The complex aristocratic society that developed under the leaders of the Tomb Culture became the basis of an emerging Yamato Japanese state, which in successive waves incorporated many natives and Korean migrants. The rise of the Japanese state coincided with the Three Kingdoms era in Korea; they were linked for a long time and at least until 688 CE, when Silla, with Tang military help, occupied the Japanese enclave of Kaya on the Korean peninsula. Many Koreans, along with Japanese who had fought on the side of Paekche, crossed the straits and settled in the island kingdom.

THE YAMATO EMPEROR AND THE ORIGINS OF JAPANESE SACRED IDENTITY Ancestor worship, though influenced by China, was native to Japan and lay at the heart of a belief system that emerged after the fourth century. Ancestral rites that predated the influx of Buddhism and Confucianism from Paekche in the sixth century underwent significant transformation in the hands of the early Japanese aristocratic clans. For the early Japanese, a person's *tamashii*, his or her soul or spirit, became a *kami* or local deity when it was fully nourished and purified through the proper rituals and festivals after death. Before the imperial Yamato clan

Tomb Culture. Daisenryo Kofun, in Osaka, is allegedly the tomb of Emperor Nintoku, dating from the fifth century.

Creation Myth. Tsukioka Yoshitoshi (1839–1892) depicted Japan's creation myth in "Amaterasu Appearing from the Cave." To entice Amaterasu, the goddess of the sun, out so that light would be returned to the world, the other gods performed a ribald dance.

became dominant, each clan had its own pantheon of ancestral deities; but after 500 CE, the ancestors of the Yamato clan were increasingly worshipped by all Japanese. Other regional ancestral deities were later subordinated to the Yamato deities, who claimed direct lineage from Amaterasu, the Sun Goddess and creator of the sacred islands of Japan.

After 587 CE, the Soga kinship group—originally from Korea—became Japan's leading family and controlled the Japanese court. The Soga were particularly sympathetic to the Buddhist religion of the southwestern kingdom of Paekche, which also faced China, and sympathy flowed the other way as well. From the polity's inception, aristocratic birth and kinship, tied to descent lines from the *kami,* were the overriding qualification for social status and advancement within the Yamato imperial clan. The imperial line justified it-

self by embracing a tradition that used both Buddhism and Shinto to sacralize the Japanese state and Japanese society.

The political developments in Japan differed strikingly from those in China or Korea, where a more secular state took hold: the Yamato scribes wove together a unique historical blend that presented their emperor as the living embodiment of Japan and its peoples. They created a sacred past in which the divine and human realms coalesced in the imperial state to form the "way of the deities" (Shinto). Its divine characteristics placed the Yamato aristocratic families at the top of the Japanese state and its aristocratic society.

PRINCE SHOTOKU AND THE TAIKA POLITICAL REFORMS By 600 CE, just as the new Sui dynasty (581–618 CE) was bringing together North and South China under a single ruler for the first time in 300 years, the Japanese had gained a sense of themselves as a distinct and unified people. Looking back on this era a century later, and eager to believe that they owed little or nothing to outside influences, the Soga kinship group attributed everything that was innovative in the culture of the early Japanese Yamato state to their own creative young Prince Shotoku (574–622 CE). Contemporary Japanese scribes claimed that Prince Shotoku rather than Korean immigrants had introduced Buddhism to Japan and that his illustrious reign had touched off Japan's rise as an exceptional and powerful island kingdom in East Asia. Indeed, the Japanese Buddhists saw in Prince Shotoku what the Christians of the Roman Empire saw in Constantine: the founding religious figure and chief political icon. But Shotoku's actual historical role remains, at the very least, overstated.

When the Sui dynasty took power, Prince Shotoku allegedly sent envoys to China to inquire about their strengths, and Chinese artists, craftsmen, and clerks were brought to help Japan reshape its institutions. In addition, Shotoku was given credit for preparing a seventeen-article treatise in 1604 that promoted governmental reforms along the Chinese lines; then, the model was the Sui dynasty. At the end of Prince Shotoku's regency, Japan's neighbor underwent a momentous change, as the Sui dynasty quickly gave way to the Tang. For Korea and Japan, such success transformed the Tang empire into a model for up-to-date statecraft, culture, religion, the arts, and society in East Asia.

As in China, Japanese rulers tolerated, and even promoted, a mosaic of religions. Increasing political integration was cover for growing religious pluralism. Shotoku promoted Buddhism and Confucianism; though the groundwork for their growth had been laid by Korean immigrants the century before, he was given credit for introducing them into a native religious culture, Shintoism, which had been wholly Japanese. The prince's prestige has also been associated with several Buddhist temples modeled on Tang pagodas and massive halls; one of these, built in Nara (near present-day Kyoto and Osaka), was the Horyuji Temple; it is still extant, the oldest surviving wooden structure in the world. Its frescoes include figures derived directly from the art of Iran and central Asia. They are a reminder that within two centuries, Buddhism had dispersed its visual culture along the full length of the Silk Road, from Afghanistan to China, and then on to Korea and the island kingdom of Japan in the Pacific Ocean. In Japan, it contributed to the variety of religions.

Political integration was not necessarily the same as political stability. In 645 CE, another leading kinship group known as the Nakatomi came to power via a violent coup d'état that eliminated the Soga and their allies. The leader of the coup, Nakatomi no Kamatari (614–669 CE), and his family used their power over the throne to enact the Taika Reform edicts, which were based on Confucian principles of government allegedly first enunciated by Prince Shotoku in

Taishi. Prince Shotoku Taishi was instrumental in the establishment of Buddhism in Japan, although his actual historical role was overstated. In this hanging scroll painting from the early fourteenth century, he is idealized as a sixteen-year-old son, holding an incense censer and praying for the recovery of his sick father, the Emperor Yomei (r. 585–87).

604 CE. These reforms were sponsored by Nakatomi courtiers in the Yamato court who advanced a new Japanese imperial ideology. According to these edicts, the ruler was no longer simply an ancestral kinship group leader. Instead he became an exalted "emperor" (*tenno*) who ruled by the mandate of heaven, as in China, and exercised absolute authority.

By adapting the Chinese notion of the mandate of heaven, the Yamato court elevated the religious prestige of the Japanese emperor. But not all aspects of Chinese culture were welcomed. Even when Tang institutions of governance were introduced during the Taika reforms of 645, the Japanese court refused to institute the Chinese civil service examination system for fear that doing so would destabilize the aristocrats in power. In the early eighth century, the imperial court at the first Japanese capital of Nara prepared a political narrative about themselves, written in classical Chinese. They linked religious reverence for earlier imperial Yamato ancestors with legitimate political power in Japan.

MAHAYANA BUDDHISM AND THE SANCTITY OF THE JAPANESE STATE Religious influences continued to flow into Japan, contributing to spiritual pluralism while bolstering its rulers. Although Prince Shotoku and later Japanese emperors turned to Confucian models for government, they also dabbled in the occult arts and in Daoist purification rituals. In addition, the Taika edicts under the Nakatomi promoted Buddhism as the state religion of Japan, following Shotoku's lead. Though the imperial family did not cease to support native Shinto traditions, association with Buddhism gave the Japanese state extra status by affiliating it with a universal religion whose appeal stretched to Korea, China, and India.

State-sponsored spiritual diversity led native religions to formalize credos of their own. The introduction of Confucianism and Buddhism to Japan motivated the adherents of native Shinto cults to organize what had been an amorphous body of religious practices into something comparable to these two well-organized belief systems—much as Buddhism had spurred a transformation of Vedic religion in distant India a few centuries earlier. Shinto priests now collected ancient liturgies, and Shinto rituals were incorporated into the official Department of Religion.

The Japanese did not fully accept the traditional Buddhist view of the state as purely a vehicle to protect and propagate moral and social justice for both the ruler and his subjects. The Japanese emperor was the object of more explicit worship as the sacred ruler, one in a line of luminous Shinto gods. He was not simply the temporal ruler who turned the wheel of the law (*dharmaraja*) and patronized the Buddhist monasteries from afar. Unlike rulers in Korea and China, the Japanese emperor was a supreme *kami*—a divine force in his own right. Buddhism as a universal religion imported from China and Paekche was adapted and spread in Japan to also serve the interests of the state, much as Christianity would be used by

European monarchs and Islam by the various Islamic dynasties. But in one respect Japan fundamentally differed from Christianity and Islam. Whereas a single faith—splintered and fractious, to be sure—integrated the latter, Shinto and Buddhism became symbiotically intertwined in the political and religious life of the Japanese. Moreover, unlike in China, emperors in Japan rarely wielded direct power themselves. We will see in Chapter 10 that other individuals, whether next of kin or warrior elites, usually invoked the religious aura of the emperor to legitimate their own political protection of the imperial line.

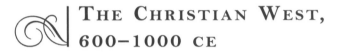

THE CHRISTIAN WEST, 600–1000 CE

→ *How did two Christianities come to exist in western Eurasia?*

Seen from the Mediterranean and the Islamic world, post-Roman Europe during the period from 600 to 1000 CE seemed little more than a warrior-dominated world. In the fifth century, the mighty Roman military machine gave way to a multitude of warrior leaders whose principal allegiances were local affiliations. Indeed, ever since the days of the ancient Celts, small societies of farmers and herders (living in scattered homesteads or in villages with populations rarely larger than 300) had been dominated by warlords. Yet, here, too, major innovations were under way. The leading force was Christianity, and the leading agents of the Christianization of the European peoples were missionaries and monks. The political ideal of the Roman Empire cast a vast shadow over the western Europeans, but the inheritor of the mantle of Rome was increasingly a spiritual institution—the Roman Catholic Church—whose powerful head, the pope, was based in Rome.

CHARLEMAGNE'S FLEDGLING EMPIRE

In 802 CE, Harun al-Rashid, the ruler of Baghdad, sent the gift of an elephant to Charlemagne, the king of the Franks, in northern Europe. The elephant, named Abuldabaz—after Abu Abbas, Harun's ancestor and the founder of the Abbasid dynasty—caused a sensation among the Franks, who saw the gift as an acknowledgment of Charlemagne's power. In fact, Harun, like the Sasanian King of Kings centuries before him, often sent rare beasts to distant rulers as a gracious reminder of his own formidable power. In his eyes, Charlemagne's "empire" was a minor principality. Indeed, the region would have struck those accompanying the elephant from Baghdad as

profoundly underdeveloped. Northern Europe contained few cities—the largest, Paris, had only 20,000 inhabitants—and they were smaller than the long-deserted Roman settlements now in ruins.

This was an empire that Charlemagne ruled with tireless energy from 768 to 814 CE, often traveling 2,000 miles a year on campaigns of plunder and conquest. By 802 CE, he controlled much of western Europe, lands reaching across the Pyrenees Mountains as far south as Catalonia in modern-day Spain, as far east as across the Alps, and as far south as Naples in modern-day Italy. Yet, compared with the rulers of the Islamic world, he was a political lightweight. His empire had a population of less than 15 million; he rarely commanded armies larger than 5,000; and he had only the most rudimentary tax system. At a time when the palace quarters of the caliph at Baghdad covered nearly 250 acres, Charlemagne's newly built palace at Aachen was merely 330 by 655 feet. (Baghdad itself was almost 40 square miles in area, whereas there was virtually no "town" outside the palace at Aachen.) Constructed in 796 CE (only a generation after the foundation of Baghdad), it was little more than a large country house set in the middle of open countryside, close to the

Charlemagne's Throne. From this raised throne, Charlemagne presided over services performed by the clergy. Constructed of slabs of marble transported all the way from Rome to Aachen, the throne showed that Charlemagne was the "new" emperor of the West and heir of the emperors of Rome.

Charlemagne's Palace and Chapel. Though not large by Byzantine or Islamic standards, Charlemagne's palace and chapel were heavy with symbolic meaning. A royal hall for banqueting in Frankish, "barbarian" style was linked by a covered walkway to the imperial domed chapel, which was meant to look like a miniature version of the Hagia Sophia of Constantinople. Outside the chapel was a courtyard, like that outside the shrine of Saint Peter at Rome.

woods of the Ardennes where Charlemagne and his Franks loved to hunt wild boar on horseback.

He and his men were representatives of the warrior class that had come to dominate post-Roman western Europe. Set against the broader history of northern and western Europe, there was nothing unusual about the Franks. Roman rule, which inaugurated a period when large towns were privileged over the countryside and educated civilians valued over warriors, had briefly imposed an alien way of life. That Mediterranean empire had withdrawn, and from 500 CE onward, war became, once again, the duty and the joy of the aristocrat: buoyed up by their chieftains' mead—a heavy beer made with honey, "yellow, sweet and ensnaring"—young men were expected to follow their lords into battle, "among the war horses and the blood-stained armor" (Aneirin, *Y Gododin*, ll. 102, 840).

And though the Franks vigorously engaged in trade, that trade was based on war: Europe's principal export at this time was Europeans. The Frankish empire was financed by the massive sale of prisoners of war. From Venice, which grew rich from its role as middleman in human trafficking, the captives were sent across the sea to Alexandria, Tunis, and southern Spain. The main victims of this trade were Slavic-speaking peoples, tribal communities of hunters and cultivators whose populations had slowly grown in eastern Europe. Their long oppression is preserved in the English language,

for the medieval Latin *sclavus* (which originally meant "Slavic") replaced the classical Latin *servus* to denote "slave"; *servus*, by contrast, was applied to those who stayed at home and became the English word "serf"—a peasant tied for life to the estates of the aristocracy.

Yet in this seemingly uncivilized and inhospitable zone, a religion with universalistic aspirations—Christianity—began to sink down roots. Although its worldwide expansion did not occur for centuries, its spiritual conquest of the European peoples established institutions and fired enthusiasms that would later drive believers to carry its message to faraway lands.

A CHRISTIANITY FOR THE NORTH

Charlemagne's empire was unquestionably primitive when compared with the Islamic empire or the Tang empire of China. But what mattered most about it was *where*, not what, it was. Far removed from the old centers of high culture, it had left the Roman Mediterranean behind. Charlemagne's empire was a polity of the borderlands. It was also based on an expansionist and proselytizing Christianity that drew energy from its rough frontier mentality. (See Map 9-8.)

As the fuzzy frontier lines between the Roman Empire and the territories to its north vanished forever, Christianity was pulled into a new world profoundly different from the Mediterranean cities in which it had taken form.

Through its evangelizing efforts, the Christianity of the West bridged the ancient gulf between the Mediterranean world and the non-Roman world of the north. As a result, Christians felt that theirs was the only truly universal religion. It could bring hitherto opposed groups into a single "catholic" church that, as we have seen, had begun to replace a political unity lost in western Europe when the Roman Empire fell.

As far back as 410 CE, reacting to the Visigothic sack of Rome, the great Christian bishop Augustine of Hippo (a seaport in modern Algeria) had laid down the outlines of this belief. Of Augustine's many books, the most important for future centuries was his *City of God*. He wrote it to persuade contemporary Christians that the barbarian takeover already happening around them was not the end of the world. The "city of God" was represented on earth by the Catholic Church, and the Catholic Church was not for Romans only— it was for all times and for all peoples, "in a wide world which has always been inhabited by many differing peoples, that have so many different customs and languages, so many different forms of organization and so many languages, and who have had so many different religions" (Augustine, *The City of God*, 14.1). Nonetheless, only one organization would bring them all to paradise: the Catholic Church.

Such confidence may appear paradoxical. After all, around 800 CE barely 25 percent of the Christians in the

MAP 9-8   CHRISTENDOM, 600–1000

The end of the first millennium saw much of Europe divided between two versions of Christianity, each with different traditions and histories. Identify the regions where each version of Christianity held sway. Why do you think the Catholic Church based in Rome was successful in expanding its influence in the west, but not the east? Why did the Orthodox version of Christianity based in Constantinople expand into eastern Europe, but not the west? How influential was Charlemagne's empire in promoting this division?

world were found in western Europe. Most lived in the richer and more populous Byzantine Empire—the eastern Roman empire of Constantinople—or in the large and sophisticated Christian communities that were thriving under a relatively tolerant Muslim rule. Independent Christian kingdoms still flourished in Africa, in Nubia on the Upper Nile and in the highlands of Ethiopia. Beyond the Islamic lands, to the east, Nestorian Christianity was a major presence on the Silk Road. Yet none of these offshoots of Christianity felt quite the certainty of being truly, and exclusively, the one universal

Primary Source

CHRISTENDOM ON THE EDGE: A VIEW OF EMPIRE IN IRELAND

A young Christian Briton of Roman citizenship who lived near Hadrian's Wall experienced the pull of Christianity around 400. In his teens, Patricius was captured by Irish slave raiders and spent six years herding pigs on the Atlantic coast of Mayo. He escaped and years later decided to return in order to convert his former captors to Christianity. He believed that in making the fierce Irish Christians, he also made them "Romans." He thus brought Christianity to the Atlantic edge of the known world. Patricius, who died around 460, is remembered today as Saint Patrick.

16 But after I reached Ireland, well, I pastured the flocks every day. . . . I would even stay in the forests and on the mountain and would wake to pray before dawn in all weathers, snow, frost, rain. . . .

17 And it was in fact there that one night while asleep I heard a voice saying to me: 'You do well to fast, since you will soon be going to your home country;' and again, very shortly after, I heard this prophecy: 'See, your ship is ready.' And it was not near at hand but was perhaps two hundred miles away, and I had never been there and did not know a living soul there. And then I soon ran away and abandoned the man with whom I had been for six years. . . . till I reached the ship.

23 And again a few years later I was in Britain with my kinsfolk. . . . And it was there that I saw one night in a vision a man coming as it were from Ireland . . .

with countless letters, and he gave me one of them, and I read the heading of the letter, 'The Voice of the Irish,' and as I read these opening words aloud, I imagined at that very instant that I heard the voice of those who were beside the forest of Foclut which is near the western sea; and thus they cried, as though with one voice: 'We beg you, holy boy, to come and walk again among us.'

→ *What does this passage tell us about life in the Celtic worlds?*

→ *What does this passage reveal to us about how St. Patrick's spiritual experiences compare to those of priests in the older Christian communities in the Mediterranean worlds of Rome and Constantinople?*

SOURCE: *St. Patrick: His Writings and Muirchu's Life*, edited and translated by A. B. E. Hood (London: Phillimore, 1978), pp. 41, 44–46, 50.

church that was enjoyed by the Catholic Church of Europe in the age of Charlemagne.

Several developments helped give rise to this attitude. First, the arrival of Christianity in northern Europe had provoked a cultural revolution. Preliterate societies made contact, for the first time, with a sacred text in a language that seemed utterly strange to them. Latin became a sacred language, and books themselves became charged vehicles of the holy. As we saw in Chapter 8, Roman Christians had already moved from the clumsy scroll to the bound codex, but it was still a messy object. Written on papyrus, the codex had none of the features that Europeans today associate with a modern book—no divisions between the words, no punctuation, no paragraphs, and no chapter headings. The reader was assumed to know Latin well enough (as a spoken language) that no further aids to understanding were needed. The same assumption could not be made of an Irishman, a Saxon, or a Frank who had never spoken Latin but wished to read and understand the Bible. Hence the care lavished in the new Christian north on the Latin scriptures. The few parchment texts that circulated in northern Europe were carefully prepared, with the words in them separated, the sentences correctly punctuated and introduced by uppercase letters, and chapter headings provided: they were far more like the book you are reading now than anything available to Romans at the height of the empire.

Celtic Bible. Unlike the simple codex of early Christian times, the Bible came to be presented in Ireland and elsewhere in the northern world as a magical book. Its pages were filled with mysterious, intricate patterns, which imitated on parchment the jewelry and treasure for which early medieval warlords yearned.

Second, those who produced the new Bibles were starkly different from ordinary men and women. They were monks and nuns. Monasticism, which had been a feature of Mediterranean Christianity since 300 CE, had originated in Egypt, and its technical terms underscore its eastern source. The root of "monastic" (and of "monk") is the Greek *monos*, "alone": a man or a woman who chose to live alone, without the support of marriage or family. And "hermit" derives from the Greek *herēmos*, "man of the desert," for zealous Christians had retired to the desert to find solitude.

Monasticism had been immensely popular in Egypt, Syria, and elsewhere, but it also suited the missionary tendencies of Christianity in northern Europe particularly well. It placed small, well-organized groups of men and women in the middle of societies with which they had nothing in common.

Monasticism rapidly took hold because it appealed to a deep sense that precisely the men and women who had least in common with those whose lives were "normal" were best able to mediate between the believer and God. Just as in Buddhism, in the monastic Christianity of western Europe the relation between the members of religious orders and the laity was grounded in religious "merit," or spiritual credit. Lay persons gave gifts to the monasteries and offered their protection. In return for these righteous acts, they gained the prayers of the monks and nuns and the very real reassurance that although they themselves were warriors and men of blood, the monks' and nuns' intercessions would keep them from going to hell.

With the spread of monasticism, the Christianity of the north took a decisive turn. In Muslim (as in Jewish) societies, religious leaders tended to emphasize their commonalities with those around them: many of the greatest scholars, theologians, and mystics of Islam were married men, including merchants and courtiers. In the Christian West, the opposite was true: preliterate warrior societies honored small groups of men and women who were utterly unlike themselves— unmarried, unfit for warfare, and intensely literate in an incomprehensible tongue. Even their hair looked different. Unlike warriors, these men were close-shaven; by contrast, the Orthodox clergy of the eastern Roman empire sported long, silvery beards (signifying wisdom and maturity and not, as in the West, the warrior's masculine strength). The heads of Catholic monks and priests were shaved as well, in a rite known as "tonsure." Such deliberate differentiation shows that the Catholic Church of northern Europe owed its ambitious horizons, as a missionary religion, to the same principles that explained the spread of Buddhism in central and Inner Asia (and later in Japan): it was a religion of monks, whose communities represented an otherworldly alternative to the warrior societies in which they found themselves. By the year 800 CE, few regions of northern Europe were without great monasteries, many of which held more than 300 monks or nuns (they were larger, that is, than the local villages). Supported by thousands of serfs donated to them by kings and local warlords, these were powerhouses of prayer, which kept the regions safe.

Northern Christianity also gained new ties to an old imaginative center. As the cleric leading the gigantic former capital of the empire, the Christian bishop of Rome had always enjoyed much prestige around the Mediterranean. But he was only one bishop among many. He was often overshadowed and contradicted by his peers in Carthage, Alexandria, Antioch, and Constantinople. Though he was spoken of with respect as *papa*, as "the grand old man," many others shared that title.

By the year 800 CE, this picture had dramatically changed. As believers looked down into the Mediterranean from the distant north, they saw only one *papa* left in western Europe: Rome's pope. The papacy as we know it rose because of the

→ *How did two Christianities come to exist in western Eurasia?*

St. Gallen Monastery. The great monasteries of the age of Charlemagne were like Roman legionary settlements. Placed on the frontiers of Germany, they were vast, stone buildings, around which entire towns would gather. Their libraries, the largest in Europe, were filled with parchment volumes, carefully written out and often lavishly decorated in a "northern," Celtic style. Though dwarfed by the Islamic libraries of the same time, they were the places where Latin literature was preserved. All Latin "classical" texts known to us survive because they were copied by monks in such monasteries at this time.

fervor with which the Catholic Church of western Europe united to support a single and exclusive symbolic center, represented by the popes at Rome. This movement had begun at the time of the collapse of the Roman Empire in the west, and sometime after 750 CE it achieved its goal. The popes owed their position in the Christian West to two developments: the Arab conquests, which had removed Rome's competition by abruptly slicing the Mediterranean in two, and the increased need of new Christians who had grown up in the northern borderlands to create a more vibrant, more exclusively religious focus for their hopes.

Charlemagne recognized this need very well. In 800 CE, he went out of his way to celebrate Christmas Day by visiting the shrine of Saint Peter at Rome. There, Pope Leo III acclaimed him as the new "emperor" of the West. The hurried ceremony added nothing to his power, but it ratified the aspirations of an age. A "modern" Rome—inhabited by popes, famous for the shrines of the martyrs, and protected by a "modern" Christian monarch from the north—and not the "ancient" Rome of pagan emperors was what his subjects wanted.

Stone Beehive Huts. Monasticism was also about the lonely search for God at the very end of the world, which took place in these Irish monasteries on the Atlantic coast. The cells, made of loose stones piled in round domes, are called "beehives." Beyond, in the ocean, is the rock of Saint Michael (Skellig Michál), a place of total isolation for monks known as "hermits"—men of the deep desert. Having no deserts, the Irish turned to offshore rocks and islands to find a place to be alone with God.

THE AGE OF THE VIKINGS, 800–1000 CE

Harun's elephant died in 813—one year before Charlemagne himself. Abuldabaz's death was recorded because the Franks viewed it as an omen of coming disasters. The great beast keeled over when he was marched out to confront the army

The Coronation of Charlemagne. This is how the coronation of Charlemagne at Rome in 800 was remembered in medieval western Europe. This painting stresses the fact that it was the pope who placed the crown on Charlemagne's head, thereby claiming him as a ruler set up by the Catholic Church for the Catholic Church. But in 800 contemporaries saw the pope as recognizing the fact that Charlemagne had already deserved to be emperor. The rise of the papacy to greater prominence and power in later medieval Europe caused this significant "re-remembering" of the event.

of a Viking king from Denmark. In the next half century, the Vikings from Scandinavia exposed the weakness of Charlemagne's self-confident regime. His once powerful empire of borderland peoples met its match on the widest border of all: that between the European landmass and the mighty Atlantic. (See Map 9-9.)

The motives of the Vikings were simple and announced in their name, which is derived from the Old Norse *vik*, "to be on the warpath." The Vikings sought to loot the now wealthy Franks and replace them as the dominant warrior class of northern Europe. It was their turn to extract plunder and to

Oseberg Ship. The Viking ship was a triumph of design. It could be rowed up the great rivers of Europe, and, at the same time, its sail could take it across the Atlantic.

sell droves of slaves across the water. They succeeded because of a deadly technological advantage: ships of unparalleled sophistication, developed by Scandinavian sailors in the Baltic Sea and the long fjords of Norway. Light and agile, with a shallow draft, they could be rowed up the rivers of northern Europe and even carried overland from one river system to another. Under sail, the same boats could tackle open water and cross the hitherto unexplored wastes of the North Atlantic.

In the ninth century, the Vikings set their ships on both courses. They emptied northern Europe of its treasure, sacking the great monasteries that had sprung up in precisely those places most vulnerable to attack from the sea—along the Atlantic and North Sea coasts of Ireland and Britain and on the banks of the Rhine and the Seine, great, slow rivers that led into the very heart of Charlemagne's Frankish empire. At the same time, Norwegian adventurers colonized first the hitherto uninhabited island of Iceland, and then Greenland. By 982 CE, they had even reached the New World and established a substantial settlement at L'Anse aux Meadows on the coast of Labrador. Viking goods have been found as far west as the Inuit settlements of Baffin Island to the north of Hudson Bay, carried there along intricate trading routes by Native Americans.

The consequences of this spectacular reach across the ocean to the coast of America were short-lived, but the penetration of eastern Europe by Viking ships had lasting effects. Ruthless and supremely well equipped to penetrate long river systems, the Vikings sailed east along the Baltic and then turned south, edging up the rivers that flowed into the Baltic to cross the watershed of central Russia, where the Dnieper, the Don, and the Volga begin to flow south into the Black Sea and the Caspian. By opening this link between the Baltic and what is now Kiev in modern Ukraine, they created an av-

MAP 9-9   THE AGE OF VIKINGS AND THE SLAVE TRADE, 800–1000

Vikings from Scandinavia dramatically altered the history of Christendom in the late first millennium. What impact did Viking raiders have on western Christendom during this era? Was their influence on the communities of eastern Europe similar or different? What influence did Vikings have on people beyond the Afro-Eurasian world? What role did the Vikings and the Holy Roman emperors play in expanding the slave trade during this period?

enue of commerce that, for the first time, linked Scandinavia and the Baltic directly to Constantinople and Baghdad. What they added was yet more slaves; Muslim geographers bluntly called this newly opened route "The Highway of the Slaves." The fortified trading posts of the Scandinavians would eventually form the spine of medieval Russia.

THE SURVIVAL OF THE CHRISTIAN EMPIRE OF THE EAST

On reaching the Black Sea, the Vikings made straight for Constantinople. In 860 CE, more than 200 of their long ships gathered ominously in the straits of the Bosporus, beneath the walls of the city. What they found was not Charlemagne's rustic Aachen but a proud city with a population exceeding 100,000, surrounded by well-engineered late Roman walls.

The Vikings had come up against a state hardened by battle. For two centuries on end, the empire of East Rome, centered on Constantinople, had held Islamic armies at bay. Once Southwest Asia as a whole had fallen to the Islamic empire of Baghdad, the East Romans fought across Anatolia and the eastern Mediterranean for their own survival. From 640 to 840 CE they faced almost yearly campaigns launched by an empire that grew to be ten times greater in extent than their own, with a budget fifteen times greater. For years on end, Muslim armies and navies came within striking distance of Constantinople. Each time they failed, outmaneuvered by highly professional generals and unable to prevail against a skillfully constructed line of fortresses that controlled the roads across Anatolia. Muslim writers took the Christian empire of East Rome—Rûm—seriously, as they never took the Franks. The Christian empire of East Rome fought the caliphs of Baghdad to a draw.

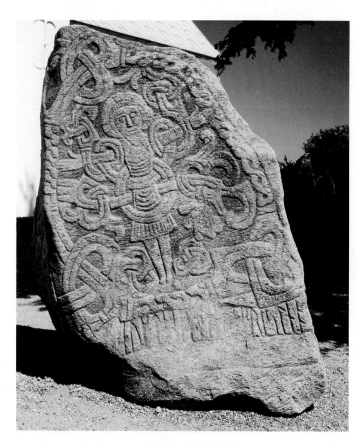

Jelling Stone. Carved on the side of this great stone, Christ appears to be almost swallowed up in an intricate pattern of lines. For the Vikings, complicated interweaving like serpents or twisted gold jewelry was a sign of majesty: hence, in this, the first Christian monument in Denmark, Christ is part of an ancient pattern of carving, which brought good luck and victory to the king.

Moreover, this empire had its own technological advantage, one used to deadly effect in naval warfare: Greek fire, a combination of petroleum and potassium that, when sprayed from siphons, would explode in a great sheet of flame on the water. In 717 CE, the emperor Leo III used it for the first time to destroy the Muslim fleet as it lay at anchor within sight of the imperial palace of Constantinople. A century and a half later, the experience and weaponry of East Rome were too much for the Vikings, and their raid was a spectacular failure.

In the long run, the sense of having outlasted an endless series of military emergencies bolstered the morale of East Roman Christianity and led to its unexpected flowering in distant lands. Not just Constantinople but Justinian's glorious church, the Hagia Sophia, its heart, had survived. That great building and the solemn Greek liturgy that was performed in it might not impress Catholic Franks. But Scandinavian adventurers from the new slave markets of Kiev and the Volga—like their medieval Russian successors—were prepared to be immensely impressed. Here was the central church of a Christian empire that for half a millennium had represented

all that was most dignified and venerable in the Christian tradition. In the tenth century, as Charlemagne's empire collapsed in western Europe, large areas of eastern Europe became Greek Orthodox, not Catholic. As a result, Greek Christianity gained a spiritual empire that eventually offset the losses of the eastern Roman empire in Southwest Asia.

The conversion of Russian peoples and the Balkan Slavs to Orthodox Christianity was a complex process. But it was based on an admiration for Constantinople, on the part of Russians, Bulgarians, and other Slav princes, as intense as that of any Western Catholic for the Roman popes. This admiration amounted to awe, as shown by the famous story, preserved in a Russian chronicle, of the conversion to Greek Christianity in 987 CE of the rulers of Kiev (descendants of Viking adventurers from the Baltic):

> The envoys reported[,] . . . "We went among the Germans [the Catholic Franks] and we saw them performing many ceremonies in their churches; but we beheld no glory there. Then we went to Greece [in fact, to Constantinople and Hagia Sophia], and the Greeks led us to the edifices where they worship their God, and we knew not whether we were in heaven or on earth. For on earth there is no such splendor or such beauty, and we are at a loss to describe it. We only know that God dwells there among men, and their service is fairer than the ceremonies of other nations. For we can not forget that beauty. (Cross and Sherbowitz-Westor, *The Russian Primary Chronicle*, 111)

By 1000, two Christianities existed: one was the new and confident "borderland" Catholicism of western Europe, and the other was an ancient Greek Orthodoxy, protected against constant threat of extinction by the iron framework of a "Roman" state inherited directly from Constantine and Justinian. Western Catholics believed that their church was destined to expand everywhere. East Romans were less euphoric but more tenacious. They believed that their Christian empire would, somehow, forever survive the regular ravages of invasion. It was a significant difference in attitudes, and neither side liked the other. East Romans considered the Franks barbarous and grasping: "no one deserves to have a Frank as their neighbor" was an East Roman proverb of the age of Charlemagne. For their part, Western Catholics contemptuously called the East Romans "Greeks" and condemned them for "Byzantine" cunning—failing to recognize that the generals and diplomats of Constantinople managed for centuries to fend off Baghdad's aggression largely by living by their wits. And locked in this confrontation, both Catholics and Orthodox tended to forget the sizable Christian communities to the east and south of them, from Ethiopia to Armenia, who continued under Muslim rule or on the frontiers of the Islamic empire, largely unaffected by what happened in either Europe or Byzantium.

Thus, like Islam, the Christian world was divided, though in this case the main division was into just two distinct entities—Western and eastern Christianity. Their differences

Viking Longhouse. A simple turf bunker was built by the Vikings on the coast of Canada. Low-lying for protection against wind and snow, it was built as a permanent settlement and trading post with the Eskimos. Viking trade goods appear far to the north in Baffin Island.

at that time were not doctrinal, like those of Shia and Sunni Islam. They were differences in heritage, customs, and levels of civilization. At that time, the orthodox world was considerably more ancient and more cultured than that of the Catholic west. Both encountered the expansionist ambitions of Muslim warriors, but they dealt with Islam differently. At Constantinople, capital of eastern Christianity and heir to the eastern part of the Roman Empire, Christianity held off Muslim forces that constantly threatened the integrity of the great city and its Christian hinterlands. In the west, on the other hand, Muslim expansionism ran its course confined to the Iberian Peninsula, behind the Pyrenees Mountains. Western Christendom, led by the Roman papacy, did not feel the same degree of political and cultural intimidation from Islam. It set about the task of spreading Christianity to the pagan tribes to the north, and as the period drew to a close it began to contemplate retaking lands from the Muslims.

Also like Islam, western Christianity expanded its geographic reach into new frontiers by harnessing faith to empire. (Byzantine Christianity tended to keep within its own frontiers and used the religion only for matters of interstate diplomacy.) In this fashion, universalizing religions reinforced the claims to power of aspiring rulers; but they also relied on rulers' armies to subdue or incorporate nonbelievers into the expanding circle of common spirituality. But much more than in Islam, where conquering armies more effectively centered the faith in Baghdad, Christendom was cleaved between east and west, and within the west it was splintered among rivalrous warrior provinces with only nominal allegiance to popes and other central authorities. Religion adapted itself to the localized political structures. And in contrast to China, where new rulers rebuilt integrated empires using traditional means

of rulership while accommodating and even promoting growing religious pluralism, in Christendom, especially in the west, we see increasing religious homogeneity and common faith, but no recovery of the bygone power of Rome—to which ambitious pretenders continued to aspire.

 # CONCLUSION

The four centuries from 600 to 1000 CE were marked both by extraordinary fluidities and by striking rigidities. Eurasian and North African societies witnessed a radical reordering of their political and cultural maps that encouraged movement across cultural boundaries and over long distances while at the same time insisting on the distinctiveness and often the superiority of individual political and cultural systems. Commodities, technological innovations, ideas, travelers, merchants, adventurers, and scholars moved with unusual rapidity from one end of Afro-Eurasia to the other, and up and down coastal Africa. This mercantile activity was accompanied by missionizing into new frontiers. The proximity and relatively porous boundaries of the two great political and cultural units of this period—Abbasid Islam and Tang China—abetted the movement of people and commodities; in this regard, the two empires stood in glaring contrast to their two powerful predecessors, Han China and Rome, which had occupied the far corners of the Afro-Eurasian landmass and were separated by great distances. The Silk Road was now even more widely traveled than in the previous centuries. And the agrarian revolution that swept much of middle Afro-Eurasia only fueled the bounty and population growth.

Yet in spite of the circulation of peoples and ideas throughout Eurasia and Africa, a new set of political and cultural boundaries were developing that would split this landmass in ways that it had not known before. The most important of these dividing forces was the new universalistic religion, Islam, which emerged in the first half of the seventh century and immediately challenged and slowed the spread of an equally determined universalistic religion, Christianity. As a consequence, Afro-Eurasia's highly differentiated major cultural zones now began to compete with one another in their universalistic religious and cultural doctrines. The Abbasid empire pushed back the borders of the Tang empire. But the intensity of interimperial conflict grew particularly high between the Islamic and Christian worlds, where the clash involved faith as well as frontiers.

The Sui and Tang empires revived Confucianism, insisting on its primacy within the Chinese political and moral system as the foundation of a new imperial order; and they embraced the classical written language as another unifying element in a new common culture. They thereby successfully counteracted the powerful global forces that brought foreign religions, notably Buddhism but also Islam, into the Chinese state. The same adaptive strategies, promoting religious amalgamation of new and old belief systems while elevating the powers of centralizing dynasties, also influenced the creation of new systems on the Korean Peninsula and in Japan.

Chronology

MAJOR TRENDS	200 CE	300 CE	400 CE	500 CE
THE ISLAMIC WORLD	*Afro-Eurasian agricultural revolution begins*			
EAST ASIA		▋ *Three Kingdoms dominate Korea from the 3rd century*		*Yamato clan becomes dominant in Japan, 500* ▋
EUROPE				

There were, therefore, many ways to cope with the emergence and spread of universalizing religions across Eurasia and Africa, but all were linked to empire. In some circumstances, faith followed empire and relied on rulers' support or tolerance, as well as some measure of political stability, to spread the word. This was the case especially in East Asia. At the opposite extreme, empire followed faith, as in the case of Islam, whose believers imagined an empire out of new cloth. To be sure, emerging dynasts exploited older symbolic resources, like the allure of a "restored" Mesopotamian centrality. But for the most part, the Islamic empire—and its successors—represented a new force on the world stage: expanding political power backed by one God whose instructions to believers was to spread his message. In the worlds of Christianity, a common faith yielded to elements of a common culture (shared books, a language for learned classes), but in the west only in name did rulers overcome the intense allegiance to local sources of political authority.

While this was an age in which universalizing religions expanded and common cultures grew, especially among literati and learned groups who aligned themselves with state power, there was also enormous debate and dissent within each religion over basic principles. In spite of the diffusion of basic texts inscribed in "official" languages, many variations of Christianity, Islam, and Buddhism existed, proliferating even more as each of these belief systems spread into new

600 CE	700 CE	800 CE	900 CE	1000 CE

■ *Muhammad born in Mecca, 570*

■ *Muhammad and small group of followers flee Mecca for Medina, 622*

■ *Death of Muhammad, 632*

■ *Arab armies conquer Southwest Asia, North Africa, Spain, Central Asia, and parts of South Asia, 650–750*

■ *Ummayad caliphate rules from Damascus, 661–750*

■ *Shiism emerges as major dissident force within Islam, late 7th century*

■ *Abbasid caliphate rules from Baghdad, 750–1258*

■ *Al-Khwarizmi (c. 780–850) writes first book on algebra*

Fatimid Shiite regime forms, based in Egypt, 969 ■

Ibn Sina (980–1037) produces Canon of Medicine ■

■ *Prince Shotoku (574–622) initiates Taika political reforms*

■ *Sui state unites much of China, 581–618*

■ *Tang state emerges in China, 618*

■ *Tang dynasty establishes strong influence on Central Asia by 650*

■ *Silla state unifies Korea, 668*

■ *Empress Wu reigns over Tang state, 690–705*

■ *Tang army loses battle of Talas in 751 to Islamic forces, beginning Tang retreat from Central Asia*

■ *Tang state embarks on anti-Buddhist campaigns*

■ *Peasant uprising begins, 859*

■ *Tang dynasty disintegrates, 906*

Koryo kingdom assumes control of Korea, 918 ■

■ *Khitan invasion*

■ *Arab armies conquer much of Byzantine Empire's lands in Southwest Asia, but the empire survives, 632–661*

■ *Missionaries and monastic orders begin converting much of northern Europe into Christian communities loyal to the popes in Rome (had been converted by 800)*

■ *Catholic Church based in Rome dominates Christian West*

■ *Charlemagne (768–814) unites much of western Europe into a short-lived kingdom*

■ *Vikings plunder northern Europe, 9th century*

■ *Vikings establish strong commercial links across eastern Europe to Constantinople*

Vikings reach North America, 982 ■

Russian leaders convert to Orthodox Christianity, 987 ■

regions. As the first millennium drew to a close, religion, reinforced by prosperity and imperial resources, was a means to bring peoples together in unprecedented ways. But it was also, as the next chapter will illustrate, a new means to drive them apart in bloodcurdling confrontations.

STUDY QUESTIONS

 WWNORTON.COM/STUDYSPACE

1. Analyze the impact of the spread of Islam on the various societies of Afro-Eurasia. How did the emergence of a large Islamic empire shape the movement of peoples, ideas, innovations, and commodities across the vast landmass?

2. Describe the process through which the spread of Islam fostered an agricultural revolution in Afro-Eurasia. What crops and cultivation techniques were involved in this process?

3. Compare and contrast the spread of Islam, Christianity, and Buddhism between 600 and 1000. What was the geographic range of each religious community? Through which methods did each religion gain new converts?

4. Explain the origins and basic concepts of Islam. How similar to and different from other religions that began in Southwest Asia, such as Judaism, Christianity, and Zoroastrianism, was this new religious outlook?

5. Analyze the successes and failures of Islamic leaders in creating one large empire to govern Islamic communities. What opponents emerged to challenge this goal?

6. Describe the Tang dynasty's attempts to restore political unity to East Asia. How did Tang leaders react to the growth of universal religions within their realm?

7. Explain the significance of the year 751 in world history. How did the battle of Talas shape the history of Afro-Eurasia?

8. Describe the state structure that emerged in Korea and Japan during this era. How were these new states shaped by other developments in Afro-Eurasia, such as the growth of universal religions?

9. Compare and contrast Christian communities in western Europe to those in eastern Europe and the Byzantine Empire. What factors contributed to each region's distinctiveness?

10. Analyze the impact of Viking communities on world history during this era. How did Vikings shape developments in the Christian world especially?

FURTHER READINGS

Ahmed, Leila, *Women and Gender in Islam* (1992). A superb overview of the relations between men and women throughout the history of Islam.

Aneirin, *Y Gododdin: Britain's Oldest Heroic Poem*, ed. and trans. A. O. H. Jarman (1988). A sixth-century Welsh text that describes the battle of the last Britons against the invading Anglo-Saxons.

Arberry, Arthur J., introduction to *The Koran Interpreted: A Translation,* trans. Arthur J. Arberry (1986). One of the most eloquent appreciations of this classical work of religion.

Augustine, *The City of God*, trans. H. Bettenson (1976). An excellent translation of Augustine's monumental work of history, philosophy, and religion.

Berkey, Jonathan P., *The Formation of Islam: Religion and Society in the Near East, 600–1800* (2005). A recent overview of the history of Islam before the modern era. It is particularly sensitive to the influence of external elements on the history of the Muslim peoples.

Bol, Peter, *This Culture of Ours: Intellectual Transitions in T'ang and Sung China* (1994). A study tracing the transformation of the shared culture of the Chinese learned elite from the seventh to the twelfth centuries.

Brown, Peter, *The Rise of Western Christendom: Triumph and Diversity, AD 200–1000*, 2nd ed. (2003). A description of the changes in Christianity in northern Europe and the emergence of the new cultures and political structures that coincided with this development.

Bulliet, Richard W., *Conversion to Islam in the Medieval Period: An Essay in Quantitative History* (1979). A determined and largely successful effort to measure the rate at which the populations overrun by Arab conquerors in the seventh century CE embraced the religion of their rulers.

Cook, Michael, *The Koran: A Very Short Introduction* (2000). A useful overview of Islam's holy book.

———, *Muhammad* (1983). A brief but careful life of the Prophet that takes full account of the prolific and often controversial preexisting scholarship.

Cross, S. H., and O. P. Sherbowitz-Westor, trans., *The Russian Primary Chronicle* (1953).

Donner, Fred M., *The Early Islamic Conquests* (1981). The best account of the Arab conquests in the Persian and Byzantine empires in the seventh century.

Fage, J. D., *Ghaua: A Historical Introduction* (1966). A brief but authoritative history of Ghaua from earliest times to the present.

Fisher, Humphrey J., *Slavery in the History of Muslim Black Africa* (2001). A general history of the relations between North Africa and black Africa, focusing on one of the most important aspects of contact—the slave trade.

Graham-Campbell, James, *Cultural Atlas of the Viking World* (1994). A positioning of the Vikings against their wider background in both western and eastern Europe.

Hawting, G. R., *The First Dynasty of Islam: The Umayyad Caliphate, A.D. 661–750* (2000). The essential scholarly treatment of Islam's first dynasty.

Herrmann, Georgina, *Iranian Revival* (1977). The structure and horizons of the Sasanian Empire as revealed in its monuments.

Hillgarth, J. N. (ed.), *Christianity and Paganism, 350–750: The Conversion of Western Europe*, rev. ed. (1986). A collection of contemporary sources.

Hodges, Richard and David Whitehouse, *Mohammed, Charlemagne, and the Origins of Europe* (1983). A spirited comparison of Islam and the rise of Europe.

Hodgson, Marshall G. S., *The Venture of Islam: Conscience and History in a World Civilization* (1977), 3 vols. A magnificent history of the Islamic peoples. Its first volume, *The Classical Age of Islam*, is basic reading for anyone interested in the history of the Muslim world.

Holdsworth, May, *Women of the Tang Dynasty* (1999). An account of women's lives during the Tang dynasty.

Hourani, Albert, *History of the Arab Peoples* (2002). The best overview of Arab history.

Jones, Gwynn, *The Norse Atlantic Saga* (1986). The Viking discovery of America.

Kennedy, Hugh, *The Prophet and the Age of the Caliphate: The Islamic Near East from the Sixth to the Eleventh Century* (2004). A very good recent synthesis.

Lee, Peter, et al. (eds.), *Sources of Korean Tradition*, vol. 1 (1996). A unique view of Korean history through the eyes and words of the participants or witnesses themselves, as provided in translations of official documents, letters, and policies.

Levtzion, Nehemia, *Ancient Ghana and Mali* (1980). The best introduction to the kingdoms of West Africa.

Levtzion, Nehemia, and Jay Spaulding, *Medieval West Africa: Views from Arab Scholars and Merchants* (2003). An indispensable source book on early West African history.

Lewis, Bernard, *The Middle East: Two Thousand Years of History from the Rise of Christianity to the Present Day* (1995). A stimulating introduction to an area that has seen the emergence of three of the great world religions.

——— (trans.), *Islam from the Prophet Muhammad to the Caphre of Constantinople* (1974). Vol. 2: Religion and Society. A fine collection of original sources that portray various aspects of classical Islamic society.

Middleton, John, *The Swahili: The Social Landscape of a Mercantile Community* (2000). An exciting synthesis of the Swahili culture of East Africa.

Miyazaki, Ichisada, *China's Examination Hell* (1981).

Nurse, Derek, and Thomas Spear, *The Swahili: Reconstructing the History and Language of an African Society, 800–1500* (1984). A work laying out what we know at present about the history of the Muslim peoples who lived along the coast of East Africa.

Peters, F. E., *Muhammad and the Origins of Islam* (1994). A work that explores the early history of Islam and highlights the critical role that Muhammad played in promoting a new religion and a powerful Arab identity.

Schirokauer, Conrad, et al., *A Brief History of Japanese Civilization*, 2nd ed. (2005). A balanced account; chapters focus on developments in art, religion, literature, and thought as well as on Japan's economic, political, and social history in medieval times.

Smith, Julia, *Europe after Rome: A New Cultural History, 500–1000* (2005). A vivid analysis of society and culture in so-called Dark Age Europe.

Twitchett, Denis, *The Birth of the Chinese Meritocracy: Bureaucrats and Examinations in Tang China* (1976). A description of the role of the written civil examinations that began during the Tang dynasty.

———, *Financial Administration under the Tang Dynasty* (1970). A pioneering account—based on rare Dunhuang documents that survived from medieval times in Buddhist grottoes in central Asia—of the political and economic system undergirding the Chinese imperial state.

Whittow, Mark, *The Making of Byzantium, 600–1025* (1996). A study on the survival and revival of the eastern Roman empire as a major power in eastern Europe and Southwest Asia.

Wood, Ian, *The Missionary Life: Saints and the Evangelization of Europe, 400–1050* (2001). The horizons of Christians on the frontiers of Europe.

Chapter

10

BECOMING "THE WORLD," 1000–1300 CE

In the late 1270s, two Christian monks, Bar Sāwmā and Markōs, voyaged into the heart of Islam. They were not Europeans. They were Uighurs, a Turkish people of central Asia, among whom the Nestorian Christians had established churches in the seventh century CE. Sent by the mighty Mongol ruler Kubilai Khan on the eve of his becoming the first emperor of China's Yuan dynasty (1280–1368), the monks were supposed to worship at the temple in Jerusalem. But the Great Khan also had political ambitions—he had his eyes on conquering Jerusalem, held by the Muslims. Accordingly, he dispatched the monks to help make alliances with Christian kings of western Afro-Eurasia and to gather intelligence on his potential enemy's readiness in Palestine.

By 1280, conflict and conquest had transformed many parts of the world. But friction was simply one manifestation of cultures around the world brushing up against each other. Another had become more important: trade. Indeed, Bar Sāwmā and Markōs were delayed at the magnificent trading hub of Kashgar in what is now far western China, where caravan routes of Afro-Eurasia converged in a market for jade, exotic spices, and precious

417

silks. They were following the pathways of traders and migrants who were bringing Afro-Eurasian worlds into greater contact with each other. The monks detoured to Baghdad, and from there they parted ways. Bar Sāwmā himself visited Constantinople (where the king gave him gold and silver), Rome (where he met with the pope at the shrine of Saint Peter), and Paris (where he saw that city's university, teeming with students), before deciding to return to China, where the Christians of the East awaited his reports. In the end, neither monk ever returned. Yet their voyages exemplified the crisscrossing of people, money, and goods along the trade routes and sea-lanes that connected the world's parts. For just as religious conflict was a hallmark of this age, so too was a surge in trade, migration, and global exchange.

During the period from 1000 to 1300, people from distant regions often borrowed ideas, tools, and norms from other cultures. It was an era of great population growth, rising wealth, and social transformation, which propelled the world's cultures into heightened cross-cultural contact—a far cry from the common view that the world moved in slow motion before 1500 and the advent of modern institutions and technologies. But it was equally an age of conflict, carnage, and colonization, in which warfare fractured old states and created militarized new ones. Economic splendor, social change, and political upheaval entwined in the first three centuries of the second millennium in the Common Era. Commerce, conflict, and conquest did not make the world's people at the beginning of the second millennium more alike, however. To the contrary: contact and exchange reinforced the sense of difference across cultures and created a feeling of apartness, of living within bounded cultural worlds that would soon come to be called "Europe," or "China," or "India." Even the minimal contact with other cultures experienced by the more separate areas of the world, such as sub-Saharan Africa, Japan, and the Americas, strengthened their identities. The paradoxical result was that the world was becoming more interconnected, while its regions became more clearly differentiated. The more geographical boundaries were crossed, the more they were reinforced by distinct cultural identities—which began to map out the world's regions as we recognize them today.

COMMERCIAL CONNECTIONS

> → *What factors led to the explosion of global trading activity between 1000 and 1300?*

The pace of economic change started to gather speed during this period. The effects of the agrarian and commercial breakthroughs of earlier periods began to make themselves felt in hitherto remote regions of Afro-Eurasia, drawing them closer together and making them more and more interdependent. The Americas, a region truly apart from the structures of

Focus Questions BECOMING "THE WORLD"

→ *What factors led to the explosion of global trading activity between 1000 and 1300?*

→ *How did trade and migration affect sub-Saharan Africa between 1000 and 1300?*

→ *How did trade and migration affect the Islamic world between 1000 and 1300?*

→ *In what ways did India remain a cultural mosaic?*

→ *What transformations in communication, education, and commerce contributed to the emergence of a distinct Chinese identity during this era?*

→ *How were Southeast Asia, Japan, and Korea influenced by sustained contact with other regions in this era?*

→ *How did Christianity produce a distinct identity among the diverse peoples of Europe?*

→ *Where did societies in the Americas demonstrate strong commercial expansionist impulses?*

→ *How did Mongol conquests affect cross-cultural contacts and regional development in Afro-Eurasia?*

WWNORTON.COM/STUDYSPACE

long-distance trade and migration, also saw greater regional trade, urbanization, and population growth. The most visible sign of these prosperous times was the global explosion of trading activity.

REVOLUTIONS AT SEA

In the centuries after 1000 CE, traders took to the seas. By the tenth century, sea routes were eclipsing old land-based trading networks for long-distance trade. The combination of improved navigational aids, refinements in shipbuilding, better mapmaking, and breakthroughs in commercial laws and accounting practices made shipping easier and slashed the costs of seaborne long-distance trading. The numbers testify to the power of the maritime revolution: while a porter could carry about 10 pounds of commodities over long distances, and animal-drawn wagons could move 100 pounds of goods, the large Arab dhows that plied the Indian Ocean were capable of transporting as many as 5 tons of cargo. The result was that some small coastal ports, like Mogadishu in present-day Somalia, on the east coast of Africa, became in the eleventh century vast transshipment centers for a thriving trade across the Indian Ocean.

A new instrument made available to navigators was crucial in this boom: the needle compass. This Chinese invention was initially intended to find auspicious locations and orientations for houses and tombs, but it was also employed by sailors from Canton in the eleventh century to help guide them on the high seas. Use of the device spread rapidly from there. By the early thirteenth century, the compass was a vital tool on all vessels plying the sea-lanes between Southeast Asian and Indian trading hubs. Not only did it make sailing under cloudy skies possible—thus opening up the Mediterranean, which in Roman times had been too dangerous to travel from November to March, to year-round travel—but it made mapmaking less arduous and more accurate. And, of course, it made all the oceans, including the Atlantic, easier to navigate.

Shipping became less dangerous. Navigators relied on their trusty vessels—lateen-rigged dhows between the Indian Ocean and the Red Sea, heavy junks in the South China seas. They could also rely on the protection of political authorities, such as the Song dynasts in China, in guiding the trading fleets in and out of harbors. The Fatimid caliphate (909–1171 CE) in Egypt, for instance, profited from the maritime trade and therefore agreed to defend merchant fleets from pirates. Armed convoys of five or three ships escorted com-

Dhow. This modern dhow in the harbor of Zanzibar displays the characteristic triangle sail. The triangle sail can make good use of the trade monsoon and thus has guided dhows on the Arabian Sea since ancient times.

mercial fleets, a system called *karim* that regularized the traffic on the Indian Ocean and Red Sea. Because of its success, the system soon spread west to North Africa and southern Spain. *Karimi* firms were often family-based, and they sent young men of the family, sometimes servants or even slaves, to work in India. Housewives in Cairo could expect gifts from their husbands to arrive with the *karim* fleet.

Antique Chinese Compass. Chinese sailors from Canton started to use needle compasses in the eleventh century. By the thirteenth century, needle compasses were widely used on ships in the Indian Ocean and were starting to appear in the Mediterranean.

The needle compass and changes in navigation ushered in the slow demise of the overland routes. Just as the merchants of the Silk Road had adapted by moving to southern routes in earlier centuries, so they eventually pulled up their stakes from the camel trains, fragrant caravansaries, and oasis hubs as they abandoned the road for the sea-lanes. It took centuries for the shift to be completed, but overland routes and camels were no commercial match for multiple-masted cargo ships laden with tons of silks, spices, and even more basic tradable staples. As the end of the first millennium drew near, a new interregional and increasingly global set of connections emerged on the high seas, bringing the parts of the world together, and thereby also creating new divisions.

COMMERCIAL CONTACTS

The opening of the sea-lanes sparked a commercial transformation. It also tapped into changes occurring in world agriculture. Agricultural development in Afro-Eurasia, and especially in western Europe, altered the nature of trade and transportation. (See Map 10-1.)

For a long time it was thought that agriculture remained primitive, not much more advanced than in Neolithic times, until the introduction of modern husbandry and the application of science. This view, we now know, misses the gradual and fundamental shifts occurring by 1000. The centuries of great irrigation works began to yield their enormous returns.

MAP 10-1   AFRO-EURASIAN TRADE, 1000–1300

During the early second millennium, Afro-Eurasian merchants increasingly turned to the Indian Ocean to transport their goods. Larger commercial flows profoundly shaped the history of the region. What revolutions in maritime travel facilitated this development? Why were ocean-based commercial routes more lucrative than land-based routes? Identify Quilon, Alexandria, Cairo, and Guangzhou. What role did they play in connecting the peoples of Afro-Eurasia?

Farmers learned how to rotate their crops to preserve soil fertility. The development of new strains of cereals, especially of barleys, ryes, and oats, and in the Americas the refinement of maize, enabled the cultivation of grains in vast areas that had formerly been too cold and arid to sustain them. Clover, alfalfa, and newly domesticated grasses of other sorts became fodder for grazing healthier, stronger, and fatter animals. Agriculture pushed into new regions, buoying population growth and yielding surpluses in many provinces—surpluses that now could be shipped great distances.

The Silk Road had conveyed luxuries, such as gemstones, fragrances and spices, silk textiles, woolen rugs, and tapestries. Their value was high, and they were light and easily carried. But now rice and other agrarian staples joined manufactured goods such as porcelains and silks in the long-distance trading systems. Ships made it feasible and lucrative to transport bulky and lower-value commodities—goods whose shipment was impossible or impractical when technologies of distribution were less developed: tea, rice, palm oil, woolen linen, and cotton textiles. Some goods, like the popular celadon porcelain ware, were not only heavy but fragile; they often shattered when carried on the backs of camels. Ships were a better means of conveying such delicate commodities to distant markets. In addition, the weight of porcelain added ballast necessary for long-distance sailing vessels.

GLOBAL COMMERCIAL HUBS

Long-distance trade spawned a new kind of metropolis: the commercial city. These hubs, the meeting points between distant cultures that we call entrepôts, became cosmopolitan nerve centers of an increasingly integrated world. Beginning in the late tenth century, three places emerged as the major anchorages of the maritime trade linking the landmasses of Afro-Eurasia, including the islands of Southeast Asia and Africa. In the west, the city of Cairo-Fustat (old Cairo) was a commanding headquarters for commerce between the Mediterranean and the Indian Ocean through the Red Sea. In the east, Quanzhou was the major port handling China's international trade. And Quilon, a port near the tip of Indian peninsula, which pushed deeply into the Indian Ocean's shipping lanes, functioned as the way station for voyages between the South China Sea and the Red Sea. All of these great trading centers thrived, in part because the free-for-all of trade and market life flourished under the political stability provided by big, powerful dynasts who recognized that the wealth created by trade would benefit their regimes.

THE EGYPTIAN ANCHORAGE The Egyptian cities of Cairo and Alexandria were Europe's main maritime commercial centers with ties to the Indian Ocean and beyond. Cairo, some 100 miles up the Nile, was home to numerous Muslim and Jewish trading firms, and Alexandria was their lookout

Persian Book. Books, such as this hand-copied one written in Kufic style, were traded in the Afro-Eurasian market starting in the tenth century.

post on the Mediterranean. These trading firms were kin-based, made up of family members, servants, and even slaves; they therefore took form within a single religion and conducted business according to rules set by their respective religious authority. Yet Jews, Muslims, and Christians were close partners in trade. On the Indian Ocean, Muslim firms owned most of the ships ferrying cargoes of Jewish traders to India.

Silk yarn and textiles were the most commonly traded commodities. It was through Alexandria that Europeans acquired silks from China, especially the coveted *zaytuni* (satin) fabric from Quanzhou. Spanish silks also passed through Alexandria on their way to eastern Mediterranean markets. But the entrepôts handled much more. Traditional goods from the Mediterranean included olive oil, glassware, flax, corals, and various metals. Gemstones and aromatic perfumes made from plants and animals poured in from India. Long-distance traders also shipped many staples such as minerals and chemicals for dying textiles or tanning skins, and raw materials such as timber and bamboo. The real novelties were paper and books. Hand-copied Bibles, Talmuds, works of legal and moral instruction, grammars in various languages, and Arabic books became the first best sellers of the Mediterranean.

Cairo and Alexandria prospered because Islamic leaders created sophisticated commercial institutions. Success began with the states that took seriously their obligation to protect merchants from predators. As noted above, the powerful Fatimid caliphate began regularly dispatching armed convoys to escort commercial fleets in the Mediterranean and the Red Sea, enabling the *karimi* firms and their family members to send goods and information on schedule. So regular were these fleets that they soon became the basis of an effective postal system. Thus, when an Egyptian trader who had traveled to Quilon around 1100 was delayed on his journey home, he could send a consoling message to his wife in Cairo. He could also send tokens of his love. In his letter he apologized for his absence from home but promised several gifts, including pearl bracelets, garments of red silk, a bronze basin, a ewer, and a six-year-old slave girl: "I shall send them, if God wills it, with somebody who is traveling home in the *Karim*" (Goitein, "New Light," 179).

The Islamic legal system also was involved in creating an environment favorable to conducting business. Those efforts are perhaps best exemplified in the techniques that specialists in law employed to get around the rule that would probably have brought commerce to a halt—the injunction in the sharia against usury, which prohibited earning any interest on loans. With the blessing of the clerics, Muslim traders formed partnerships, called *commenda* in medieval Europe, between those who had capital to lend and those who needed money to expand their businesses. These partnerships enabled owners of capital or merchandise to entrust their money or commodities to agents who, after their work was done, returned the initial investment and a share of the profits to the owners, keeping the rest as their reward. The English word "risk" derives from the Arabic *rizq*, the extra allowance paid to merchants in lieu of interest.

> *The English word "risk" derives from the Arabic* rizq, *the extra allowance paid to merchants in lieu of interest.*

THE ANCHORAGE OF QUANZHOU At the other end of Afro-Eurasia, in China, Quanzhou was as busy as the cities of Cairo and Alexandria, although trade there was not a free-for-all. The Song government set up offices of Seafaring Affairs in its three major ports: Canton, Quanzhou, and an area near present-day Shanghai in the Yangzi delta. In return for taking a portion of the taxes, these offices registered and examined cargoes, sailors, and traders, while archers employed as guards kept a keen eye on the traffic.

All foreign traders were guests of the governor, who doubled as the Chief of Seafaring Affairs. Part of his mandate was to host an annual ritual intended to summon favorable winds for ships. Unlike in the Arabian Sea, where monsoons make the wind direction predictable, winds in the Taiwan Strait do not fall into regular seasonal patterns. Every year, the governor took his place on a high perch facing the harbor, in front of a rock cliff filled with inscriptions that recorded the wind-calling rituals. Traders of every origin witnessed the rite, then joined the governor and local dignitaries for a large banquet. Quanzhou sailors, foreigners as well as Chinese, also frequently sought protection at the shrine of the goddess Mazu. According to the local legend, before assuming godhood Mazu had lived from 960 to 987 and had performed many miracles. Her temple became prominent after 1123, when the governor of Quanzhou survived a bad storm at sea while returning home from Korea. Ever since then, sailors as well as their wives and mothers regularly burned incense for the goddess and prayed for her aid in keeping them safe at sea.

Ships departing from Quanzhou and other Chinese ports were junks—large flat-bottomed ships with internal sealed bulkheads and stern-mounted rudders. Those from Quanzhou headed for Srivijaya, or Java, in the Malay Archipelago, navigating through the Strait of Melaka, a choke point between the South China Sea and the Indian Ocean. The final destination was Quilon, on the Malabar Coast of southwest India. Traders wishing to go further west unloaded their cargo and boarded small Arabian dhows, to make passage in Arab-dominated seas. Conversely, traders from Islamic countries arriving at Quilon in dhows and wishing to travel further east had to change to big Chinese ships.

Chinese traders had the best ships in the world. Multiple watertight compartments increased their stability and seaworthiness, and the larger ships contained as many as four decks, six masts, and a dozen sails and could carry 500 men. Navigators used up-to-date charts and compasses to reach foreign ports.

The traders who arrived at Chinese ports on junks were not all Chinese. Arabs, Persians, Jews, and Indians traded at Quanzhou, and quite a few stayed on to manage their businesses. Perhaps as many as 100,000 Muslims lived in Quanzhou's trading communities during the Song dynasty. Foreign traders could become power brokers in their own right. Consider the Pu family, which owned several hundred ships that plied the routes between India and Islamic countries. To promote good relationships in the community, it made large donations over several generations for public projects such as bridges, and the contributions even garnered official positions for some male family members. After the Mongols conquered the Southern Song in the late thirteenth century, Pu Shougeng, the patriarch of the family, turned over all the ships and the city of Quanzhou. The new emperor, Kubilai, was pleased with his services—and granted him the position of administrating the port's overseas trade.

Foreign merchants did not stay in isolated neighborhoods, apart from the rest of the city. Indeed, their residences and graves were scattered throughout Quanzhou. However, they had their own buildings for religious worship and indicated their faith on their gravestones. A well-built mosque from this period is still standing on a busy street. Hindu traders who lived in Quanzhou worshipped in a Buddhist shrine, Kaiyuan Si, where statues of the Hindu deities Hanuman and Krishna stand beside Buddhist gods. Like so many of the new global entrepôts, Quanzhou was simultaneously a power base in its own state and a home for world traders and travelers.

THE TIP OF INDIA In the tenth century, the Chola dynasty in modern Tamil Nadu rose as a major power in south India. It supplied the political support and protection for a new commercial nerve center for maritime trade between

China and the Red Sea and the Mediterranean. As the Chola dynasts profited from their commercial ventures, they expanded their reach. Following their conquest of Sri Lanka, they moved on to extend their influence over key ports on the southern Malay Peninsula, Sumatra, and eventually to the all-important Strait of Malacca, the seagoing gateway to Southeast and East Asia (see more on the islands of Southeast Asia below).

A commercial revolution swept the Indian Ocean as networks of Chola traders fanned out to establish entrepôts around the sea's rim. Indian merchant ships benefited from the Chola patronage to sail to Chinese ports. However, the Chola golden age lasted only about two generations. Indian Ocean trade continued to flourish after the Chola hegemony. Beginning in the mid–eleventh century, Islamic traders, both Arabs and Iranians, made adjustments to their trading arrangements. Many Muslim traders settled in Malabar, on the southwest coast of the Indian peninsula, and Quilon became a major hub. Dhows arrived, laden with goods from the Red Sea and Africa, and unloaded their cargoes. Passengers, traders, sojourners, and fugitives also disembarked and made Quilon into a cosmopolitan city. Big Chinese junks entered the port to unload their wares of silks and porcelain, and to pick up passengers and commodities for East Asian markets. Sailors and traders strictly observed the customs of this entrepôt; as they knew well, it was good business to respect others' norms and values while engaging in commerce with them.

Muslims constituted the largest foreign community, living in their own neighborhoods. They shipped horses from Arab countries to India and southeast islands. Kings of the tropical countries viewed horses as symbols of royalty, and because the animals could not survive long in those climates the demand was constant. Elephants and cattle from tropical countries were also sold in Quilon, though the bulk of the goods traded were spices, perfumes, and textiles. Traders who frequented Quilon knew each other well, and personal relationships were key in their transactions. When trying to strike a deal with a local merchant, a Chinese trader would mention his Indian neighbor in Quanzhou and the residence of that family in Quilon. Global commercial hubs relied on friendship and family to keep their businesses humming across religious and regional divides.

SUB-SAHARAN AFRICA COMES TOGETHER

> → *How did trade and migration affect sub-Saharan Africa between 1000 and 1300?*

The dawn of the new millennium produced dramatic transformations in sub-Saharan Africa's relationship to the rest of the world, while heightening North Africa's integration into an emerging global economy. Before 1000 CE, sub-Saharan Africa had never been a world truly apart, but after this date its integration became firmer. Africans and outsiders now became more determined to overcome the sea, river, and desert barriers that had blocked the peoples who lived below the Sahara Desert from participating in long-distance trade and intellectual exchanges. (See Map 10-2.) During this period, hardly a region within Africa escaped the effects of the outside world, though many inhabitants who lived far away from the new routes bearing trade and culture were unaware of how events outside of Africa were now altering their lives.

WEST AFRICA AND THE MANDE-SPEAKING PEOPLES

Ever since the camel had bridged the great Sahara Desert (see Chapter 9), trade, commodities, and ideas linked Africa south of the Sahara to the Muslim world of North Africa and Southwest Asia. As the savanna region of West Africa became increasingly connected to Afro-Eurasian developments, the mobile Mande-speaking peoples emerged as the primary agents for integration within and beyond West Africa, using their expertise in commerce and political organization to edge out other groups living in the area. The Mande languages are a branch of the large Niger-Congo family, which contains most of the African languages below the Sahara (including those in the Bantu branch). But Mande was more than a linguistic category. It was also associated with a way of life, as its speakers shared a common culture.

The home to the Mande or Mandinka peoples was, and continues to be, the vast area between the bend in the Senegal River to the west and the bend of the Niger River to the east (1,000 miles wide), a territory stretching from the Senegal River in the north to the Bandama River in the south (a distance of more than 2,000 miles). This was the locale in which the kingdom of Ghana had come into being around the eighth century and where Ghana's successor state—the Mandinka state of Mali, discussed below—emerged around 1100 CE.

The Mande-speaking peoples were constantly on the go, and they were marvelously adaptable. By the eleventh century they were spreading their cultural, commercial, and political hegemony from the high grasslands of the West African savanna southward into the woodlands and the tropical rainforests that stretched to the Atlantic Ocean. Those who lived in the rain forests of West Africa organized themselves into small-scale societies led by local councils, while those who occupied the savanna lands of the interior of West Africa became adept at centralized forms of government. It was in these high grasslands that the Mande and other groups developed an institution that marked the centralized polities of West Africa: sacred kingships. The inhabitants of these polities believed that their kings had descended from the gods

MAP 10-2   SUB-SAHARAN AFRICA, 1300

Increased commercial contacts continued to influence the religious and political geography of sub-Saharan Africa between 1000 and 1300. Compare this map to Map 9-5 (p. 385). Where had strong Islamic communities emerged by 1300 and what factors facilitated their growth? How did Mande speakers heighten the cultural integration of sub-Saharan societies? To what extent had sub-Saharan Africa "come together"?

and that they enjoyed the blessing of the gods. As the Mande broadened their territory from the interior of West Africa all the way to the Atlantic coast, they gained access to the tradable items much sought after in the interior, notably kola nuts and malaguetta peppers, for which they exchanged iron products and textile manufactures. By 1300, the Mandinka merchants had followed the Senegal River to its outlet on the northern coast of present-day Senegal, and then pushed their commercial frontiers further inland and down the coast. Thus, even before the arrival of European explorers and traders in the middle of the fifteenth century, West African peoples had created dynamic trading networks that linked the African hinterlands with coastal trading hubs.

In the period from the eleventh century to the end of the fifteenth century, the most vigorous and profitable businesses were those that stretched across the Sahara Desert. The Mande-speaking peoples, with their far-flung commercial networks and highly dispersed populations, dominated this trade as well. Here one of the most prized items of trade was salt, mined in the northern Sahel, around the city of Taghaza; it was in demand on both sides of the Sahara. Another highly valued commodity was gold, mined within the Mande homeland itself and borne by camel caravans to the northern societies on the far side of the Sahara, where it was exchanged for a variety of manufactures. Equally important in West African commerce were slaves, who were shipped to the settled Muslim communities of North Africa and Egypt.

THE EMPIRE OF MALI

Booming trade spawned new political organizations. The empire of Mali was the Mande successor state to the kingdom of Ghana. Founded during the first half of the twelfth century, it exercised political sway over a vast area up until the fifteenth century, when it gave way to yet another sprawling Muslim state, Songhai, whose center was based further to the east. The Mali Empire represented the triumph of horse warriors, and its origins have long been enshrined in an epic involving the dynasty's founder, the legendary Sundiata. According to *The Epic of Sundiata,* a powerful but deformed youngster eventually overcame unjust and irreligious rulers to install a righteous Islamic state in the new capital city of Niamey. Many historians believe that an individual named Sundiata actually existed, noting that the famed Arab historian Ibn Khaldun referred to him by name a full century later and reported that he was "their [Mali's] greatest king. He overcame the Susu, conquered their country, and seized the power from their hands" (Levtzion, p. 64). He—or if not he, then someone very much like him—lived in the early part of the thirteenth century, and his triumph, as narrated in *The Epic,* marked the victory of the new cavalry forces over traditional foot soldiers. Henceforth, horses—which had always existed in some parts of Africa—became prestige objects of the savanna peoples, the essential symbols of state power.

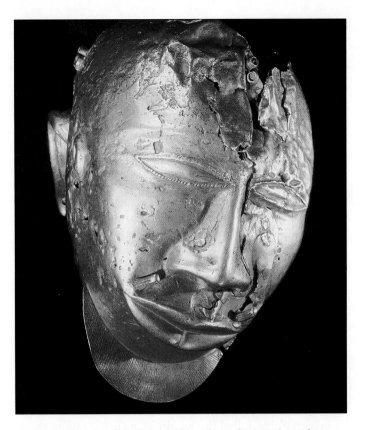

Asanti Gold. Although this gold head from the kingdom of Asante was made in the eighteenth century, it nicely shows the artistic abilities of the West African peoples. The head probably belonged to the Asante ruler, known as the Asantehene, and symbolized his power and wealth.

The Mali Empire was a thriving polity, and its commerce was in full swing in the fourteenth century. Because Mande trade routes ran through the rain forests to the Atlantic Ocean and crossed the Sahara Desert, West Africa was no longer a distant, isolated periphery of the central Muslim lands. The noted Arab traveler Ibn Battuta, who visited Mali in the early thirteenth century, praised the Muslims of the area for their punctuality in carrying out the five daily prayers required of the faithful. Mali's most famous sovereign, Mansa Musa, who ruled from 1312 until 1332, made a celebrated hajj, the pilgrimage to Mecca, in 1325–1326, traveling through Cairo and impressing crowds of merchants and clerics with the size of his retinue and with his displays of wealth, which usually featured items made from gold.

The Mali Empire boasted two of West Africa's largest cities. Jenne, an ancient northern commercial entrepôt, was a vital assembly point for caravans of salt, gold, and slaves about to set out on their long journeys west to the Atlantic Ocean coastal area and north over the Sahara. An urban settlement first appeared here around 200 BCE, and from that time on it became an important gathering place for traders. The town itself arose as the area became more arid and was no longer subject to annual Niger River flooding. The first

Primary Source

AN AFRICAN EPIC

The traditional story of the founding of the kingdom of Mali is long and complex; it was passed down orally from generation to generation by griots, counselors, and other official historians to the royal family. Only in 1960 was it finally written down in French. Because the narrative involves many complicated stories as it recounts the life of Sundiata, the heroic founder of the Mali state, no single excerpt can fully capture its flavor. The following short passage provides some insight into the role of the narrator (the griot) in the Malian kingdom and identifies the qualities of good and bad rulers.

We are now coming to the great moments in the life of Sundiata. The exile will end and another sun will arise. It is the sun of Sundiata. Griots know the history of kings and kingdoms and that is why they are the best counsellors of kings. Every king wants to have a singer to perpetuate his memory, for it is the griot who rescues the memories of kings from oblivion, as men have short memories.

Kings have prescribed destinies just like men, and seers who probe the future know it. They have knowledge of the future, whereas we griots are depositories of the knowledge of the past. But whoever knows the history of a country can read its future.

Other peoples use writing to record the past, but this invention has killed the faculty of memory among them. They do not feel the past any more, for writing lacks the warmth of the human voice. With them everybody thinks he knows, whereas learning should be a secret. The prophets did not write and their words have been all the more vivid as a result. What paltry learning is that which is congealed in dumb books!

I, Djeli Mamoudou Kouyaté, am the result of a long tradition. For generations we have passed on the history of kings from father to son. The narrative was passed on to me without alteration and I deliver it without alteration, for I received it free from all untruth.

Listen now to the story of Sundiata, the Na'Kamma, the man who had a mission to accomplish.

At the time when Sundiata was preparing to assert his claim over the kingdom of his fathers, Soumaoro was the king of kings, the most powerful king in all the lands of the setting sun. The fortified town of Sosso was the bulwark of fetishism against the word of Allah. For a long time Soumaoro defied the whole world. Since his accession to the throne of Sosso he had defeated nine kings whose heads served him as fetishes in his macabre chamber. Their skins served as seats and he cut his footwear from human skin. Soumaoro was not like other men, for the jinn had revealed themselves to him and his power was beyond measure. So his countless sofas [soldiers] were very brave since they believed their king to be invincible. But Soumaoro was an evil demon and his reign had produced nothing but bloodshed. Nothing was taboo for him. His greatest pleasure was publicly to flog venerable old men. He had defiled every family and everywhere in his vast empire there were villages populated by girls whom he had forcibly abducted from their families without marrying them.

→ *Are you able to understand the function of the griot after reading this passage?*

→ *How reliable do you think this kind of oral history is?*

→ *Soumaoro was the adversary of Sundiata and exemplified the characteristics of a bad ruler. Sundiata, in contrast, prevailed because he embodied good kingly qualities. What were they?*

→ *Comment on the role of religion in the founding of this empire.*

SOURCE: *Sundiata: An Epic of Old Mali*, translated by D. T. Niane (Harlow: Longman Group, 1965), pp. 40–41.

houses were made of mud, but most of these had been replaced by 1000 CE with more substantial brick structures. Around the city, running for more than a mile, was an impressive wall more than eleven feet thick at its base. Even more spectacular than Jenne was the city of Timbuktu; founded around 1100 as a seasonal camp for nomads, it grew in size and importance under the patronage of different Malian kings. By the fourteenth century the city was a thriving commercial and religious center, famed for its two large mosques, which are still standing. In addition to being a

King of Mali. This 1375 picture shows the king of Mali on his throne, surrounded by images of gold. The Europeans considered the interior of West Africa to be an important source of gold.

booming commercial center, it was also renowned for its intellectual vitality. Here, West African Muslim scholars congregated to debate the tenets of Islam and to ensure that Islam even when distant from the Muslim heartland was rigorously practiced, with no taint of pagan observances. These clerics acquired learned treatises on Islam from all over the world for their personal libraries, remnants of which remain to this day.

EAST AFRICA AND THE INDIAN OCEAN

Eastern and southern African regions were also integrated into long-distance trading systems. The monsoon winds, blowing from the southwest in January and the northeast in July, had made East Africa a logical end point for much of the Indian Ocean trade; Swahili peoples living along that coast became active brokers intermediating between the peoples of the Arabian Peninsula, the Persian Gulf territories, and the west coast of India. The city of Kilwa soon caught up with the booming port of Mogadishu as a great entrepôt. Merchants in Kilwa, along the coast of present-day Tanzania, brought ivory, slaves, gold, and other items from the African interior and shipped them to destinations around the Indian Ocean.

The most valued commodity for Swahili traders was gold. It was the key to the commercial revolution along the East African coast—and fueled the extravagant success of the In-

dian Ocean trading system. Located in the highlands between the Limpopo and Zambezi rivers, gold was mined by Shona-speaking peoples, who had established their dominance in the region around 500 CE. By the beginning of the new millennium, the Shona had already founded as many as fifty small centers of religious and political significance; each was dominated by stone structures that displayed its political and religious power and was surrounded by many small peasant villages. Around 1100 one of these centers, Great Zimbabwe, emerged as supreme among the Shona peoples. It was built on the fortunes made from gold, and its most impressive landmark was a massive elliptical building—32 feet high, 17 feet thick in parts, and stretching for more than 800 feet—made of stone so expertly that its fittings needed no grouting. The buildings of Great Zimbabwe were probably intended to house the king, known as *monomotapas*, whose religious and political powers were greatly extolled and feared. They probably also contained the smelters for melting down the gold that had been mined or panned nearby.

The commercial integration of the Swahili and Shona peoples enabled gold and other products to flow from the interior of eastern and southern Africa across the Indian Ocean. Before Europeans accidentally happened upon the Americas, Africa was the world's largest source of precious metals.

One of the great meeting grounds of the Indian Ocean trading system was the island of Madagascar—the fourth-largest island of the world, lying just 150 miles off the coast of East Africa. Indeed, during this period so intense was the point, as well as an import-export market, for traders crossing the Indian Ocean.

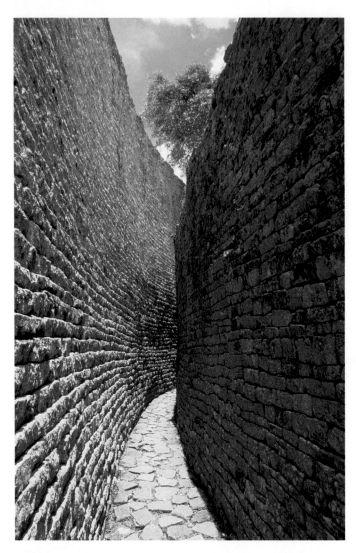

Great Zimbabwe. These walls surrounded the city of Great Zimbabwe, which was a center of the gold trade between the East African coastal peoples and traders plying the Indian Ocean. Great Zimbabwe flourished during the thirteenth, fourteenth, and fifteenth centuries.

interchange of peoples, plants, and animals from mainland Africa and around the rest of the Indian Ocean that Madagascar became one of the most intermixed and multicultural places in the world. The minority population came from Bantu-speaking peoples, who by then dominated the southern part of the African landmass (see Chapter 8); the majority were of Malay-Indonesian origin. Early seafarers from Indonesia, plying large, seaworthy outrigger canoes, hugged the shores of the Indian Ocean as they sailed from their homes past Sri Lanka and South Asia, and were carried by the monsoon winds to the African coast. Then they sailed south, perhaps picking up Bantu-speaking peoples along the way, and finally arrived at the island of Madagascar. The first evidence of human settlement does not occur until the eighth century CE. Thereafter, the island became a regular stopover

THE TRANS-SAHARAN AND INDIAN OCEAN SLAVE TRADE

African slaves were as valuable as African gold in shipments to the Mediterranean and Indian Ocean markets. Unlike gold, slave populations left a permanent imprint, since they eventually merged into the North African and Indian Ocean communities. There had been a busy trade in African slaves, mainly from Nubia, into pharaonic Egypt well before the Common Era. After Islam spread into Africa and sailing techniques improved, the slave trade across the Sahara and Indian Ocean boomed. As noted above, slaves were an important component of West African commerce.

This slave system was unlike the chattel slavery found much later in the Americas (the form of slavery most familiar to us today). The Prophet Muhammad had found slavery to be a well-established institution in the Arabian Peninsula when he was promulgating his message in the seventh century. The Quran attempted to mitigate its severity, requiring Muslim slave owners to treat their slaves with kindness and generosity and praising the manumission of slaves as an act of piety. Nonetheless, the African slave trade flourished under Islam, and slaves filled a great variety of roles in the slave-importing societies.

African slaves were obtained in this period much as they were later on: some were taken in wars; others were judged to be criminals and sold into slavery as punishment. Their duties in slave-importing societies were quite varied. Some slaves were pressed into military duties, rising in a few instances to positions of high authority. Others were valued for their seafaring skills and were used as crewmen on dhows or dockworkers servicing dhows in the Indian Ocean's port cities. Still others, mainly women, were domestic servants, and not a few African slave women became concubines of powerful Muslim political figures and businessmen. African slaves were also used on plantations, the most notorious and oppressive being the agricultural estates of lower Iraq—very early forerunners of the plantations of the antebellum South in the United States; there slaves worked under fearsome discipline and carried out a revolt in the ninth century. Yet in this era, such labor was more the exception than the rule. Slaves were more prized as adjuncts to family labor or as status symbols for their owners. Although the precise numbers are not known, the Arab Muslim slave traders transported many millions of Africans across the Sahara or the Indian Ocean from the beginning of the seventh century until the end of the nineteenth century. Slavery was therefore widespread. But in the words of the American historian Ira Berlin, these were societies with many slaves rather than slave societies—that is, societies whose basic economic fortunes and social structures rested on the widespread ownership of human beings as a source of labor.

١٠٩

Slave Market. Slaves were a common commodity in the marketplaces of the Islamic world. Turkish conquests during the years from 1000 to 1300 put many prisoners into the slave market.

ISLAM IN A TIME OF POLITICAL FRAGMENTATION

→ *How did trade and migration affect the Islamic world between 1000 and 1300?*

Islam underwent the same burst of expansion, prosperity, and cultural diversification that swept through the rest of the Afro-Eurasian world in the three centuries after 1000. (See Map 10-3.) However, in contrast to many other regions, where prosperity fostered greater integration, the peoples of Islam remained politically fractured despite sharing a common faith and culture. The Islamic empire's population at the turn of the millennium (excluding India and Africa below the Sahara) was well below that of China and India at this time—a mere 34 million, just slightly less than that of Europe (including European Russia). This was a paradoxical age, in which the dream of a unified Islam became precisely that: a dream nurtured in a bountiful present by the sense of a glorious past. As in China, efforts to unite under a common rulership failed, giving way to defeats by marauding outsiders. The attempt to uphold centralized rule ended cataclysmically in 1258 with the Mongol sacking of Baghdad and the execution of the last Abbasid caliph.

Islam responded to its political fragmentation not by turning inward but by undergoing major changes, many prompted by contacts (and conflicts) with neighbors. Commercial networks, sustained by active Muslim merchants, carried the word of the Quran far and wide. As Islam spread, it attracted more converts. But new converts often carried on many traditions that the ulama and other Islamic leaders condemned as incompatible with the religion. This conflict between orthodox Muslims and newer converts threatened to divide the wider Islamic community. At the same time (as discussed below), many Sufi orders emerged that blended orthodox and unorthodox practices in a fashion that held broad appeal and linked diverse communities. Also, as the commercial revolution driven by the dramatic expansion of Afro-Eurasian trade within the old Islamic heartlands brought urban and peasant masses into trading relations, it introduced them to a faith that previously had been shared mainly by political, commercial, and scholarly elites. In these three centuries, Islam became an even more open and accommodating religious system, embracing Persian literature, Turkish ruling skills, and Arabic language contributions in the fields of law, religion, literature, and science. In this way the world acquired another "core" region centered in what we now call the Middle East—the lands between the "Far East" of China and Japan and the "Near East," or the countries of the eastern Mediterranean—united by a shared faith and pulsating with frenetic commercial energies.

But by the thirteenth century, India and China, rather than the Islamic world, were the most technologically advanced and prosperous agrarian societies. Cultivation in Islamic societies began to stagnate and, in some places, even decline. Trade became the main source of prosperity when the agrarian innovations that Islam had so dynamically spread across Afro-Eurasia stalled. Muslim merchants became the world's premier traders in this era; the old Islamic heartland became the crossroads for Afro-Eurasian commercial networks.

AFRO-EURASIAN MERCHANTS

The peoples most responsible for integrating the sprawling Islamic worlds were long-distance merchants. They also were the main cultural brokers mediating between Islamic peoples and the rest of the world. Afro-Eurasia's expanding populations and rising material prosperity offered unprecedented opportunities for the merchants of Islam to enrich themselves; Southwest Asia was poised at the center of the Afro-Eurasian landmass, its merchants settled in key nodal points.

These merchants were as diverse as their businesses. Islam's lack of violent turmoil, the spread of the Arabic

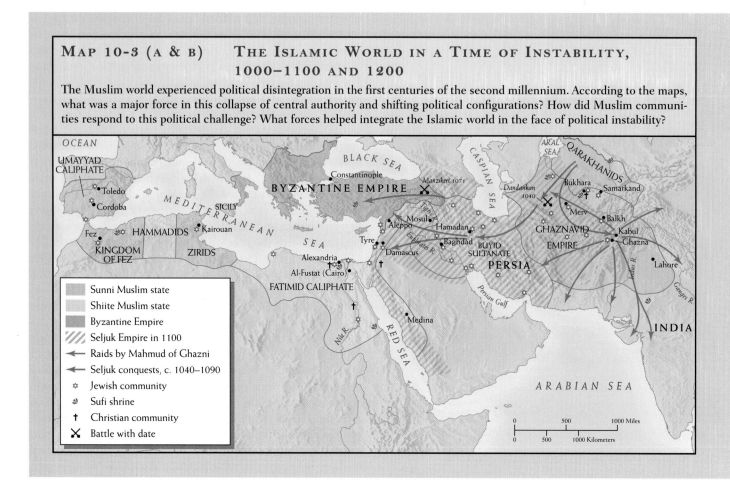

MAP 10-3 (A & B)　THE ISLAMIC WORLD IN A TIME OF INSTABILITY, 1000–1100 AND 1200

The Muslim world experienced political disintegration in the first centuries of the second millennium. According to the maps, what was a major force in this collapse of central authority and shifting political configurations? How did Muslim communities respond to this political challenge? What forces helped integrate the Islamic world in the face of political instability?

language, and Islamic law enabled entrepreneurs of many different ethnic and religious backgrounds to flourish. While Muslims played a major part in the brisk long-distance trading of this period, Armenian, Indian, and Jewish traders who were based in Islam's major cities and connected with families in North Africa and Central Asia also expanded their commercial networks. Documents discovered in a Jewish synagogue in Cairo that date back to this era reveal how voluminous and far-reaching this trade was. Jewish merchants, residing in major cities from Morocco to India, oversaw a booming trade from intermediate points such as Aden.

Long-distance trade surged because it was supported by a highly sophisticated legal framework. Traders drew up elaborate contracts; and when the contracts were breached, merchants took their cases to the courts. Although disputes involving Jewish, Armenian, or Christian coreligionists were often resolved by local religious tribunals, many merchants appeared before Islamic *qadis* (judges), who presided over the Islamic courts and whose expertise in commercial matters was greatly admired. Yet, in truth, merchants rarely needed to seek legal recourse. The mercantile community was self-policing; its members severely punished those who violated trust, sometimes ending their careers. Relying on partner-

ships, using letters of credit, and possessing knowledge of local trading customs and currencies, traders and their customers were confident that agreements made in India would be honored in Southeast Asia, Egypt, and North Africa.

DIVERSITY AND UNIFORMITY IN ISLAM

Not until the ninth and tenth centuries did Muslims become a majority within their own recently ascendant Abbasid Empire. From the outset, Muslim rulers and clerics had to deal with large non-Muslim populations, even as these populations were gradually converting to Islam. Borrowing freely from subject peoples and regarding those with their own scriptures as fellow "peoples of the book," Muslim rulers accorded non-Muslims religious toleration as long as they accepted Islam's political dominion. Jewish, Christian, and Zoroastrian communities were permitted to choose their own religious leaders and to settle internal disputes in their own religious courts. They were, however, obligated to pay a special tax, called the *jizya,* and to be properly deferential to their rulers. Especially in times of heightened religious tension, such deference could entail wearing special clothing and dis-

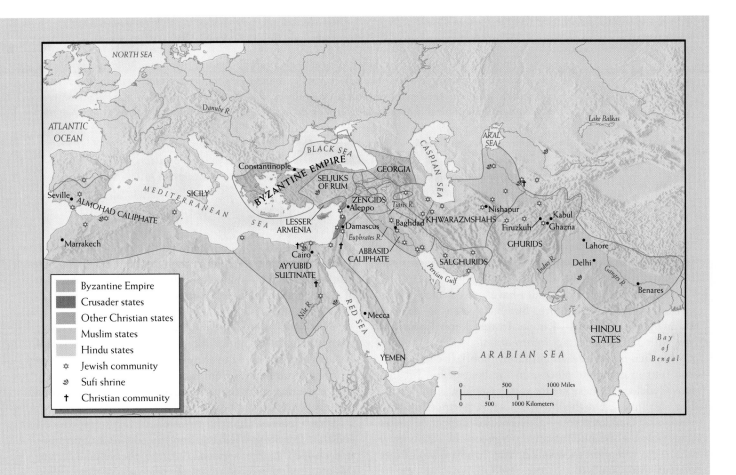

mounting from horses when they passed important Muslim personages.

These regulations, which shaped what was known as the *dhimma* system, granted protections to religious minorities. They therefore spared the Islamic world some of the religious conflict that afflicted other areas. Non-Muslims were free to worship in their traditional ways and were encouraged to make significant contributions to the economic and political well-being of Islamic lands. Such tolerance helped make Islamic cities hospitable environments for traders from around the world.

Still, Islam was an expansionist faith. Some intense proselytizing carried the sacred word to new frontiers, and in the process reinforced the spread of Islamic institutions that supported more commercial exchanges. There were also moments of intense religious passion within Islam's frontiers, especially when Muslim rulers feared that Christian minorities would make common cause with the Europeans who were pressing on their borders. Ugly incidents erupted, and some churches were burned. Pressures to convert to Islam were unremitting at this time; after a surge of conversions to Islam from the ninth century onward, the Christian Copts of Egypt shrank to a small community and never recovered their numbers.

Islam was hardly uniform. One strong element was the mystical movement known as Sufism, a name derived from the wool garments (*suf* in Arabic) that many of its adherents wore. By performing such ecstatic rituals as repeating over and over again the name of God, dancing, and most notably whirling, they sought to liberate the soul from the body and even to come face to face with God. It was inside the Sufi brotherhoods (*turuq* in Arabic) that Islam truly became a religion for the people. Indeed, Sufi orders brought about mass conversions from Christianity to Islam.

The formalizing of Sufi brotherhoods did little to lessen mystics' desire to experience the love of God. Some expressed that desire in poetry, and several of Islam's most highly regarded mystical love poets belonged to Sufi orders. The most admired of all, Jalal al-Din Rumi (1207–1273), was the spiritual founder of the Mevlevi Sufi order, famed for the ceremonial dancing of its whirling dervishes. Rumi, who wrote in Persian, celebrated all forms of love, spiritual and sexual, and preached a universalistic religious message:

> What is to be done of Muslims? For I do not recognize myself,
> I am neither Christian, nor Jew, nor Gabr [Zoroastrian], nor Muslim.

THE MERCHANTS OF EGYPT

The most comprehensive collection of eleventh- and twelfth-century commercial materials from the Islamic world comes from a repository originally connected to the Jewish synagogue in Cairo. It was the custom of the Jewish community to preserve all texts that mention God in a special storeroom called a geniza. *A huge collection of such documents came to light just before 1890 when the Cairo Geniza became known to the outside world. Most of these papers, which are a rich source of information about the Jewish community in Egypt at that time, were purchased for the University Library of Cambridge University. The documents touch on all manner of activities: cultural, religious, judicial, political, and commercial. The following letter is addressed to Joseph ibn 'Awkal, one of Egypt's leading merchants in the eleventh century.*

Dear and beloved elder and leader, may God prolong your life, never take away your rank, and increase his favors and benefactions to you.

I inform you, my elder, that I have arrived safely. I have written you a letter before, but have seen no answer. Happy preoccupations—I hope. In that letter I provided you with all the necessary information.

I loaded nine pieces of antimony (kohl), five in baskets and four in complete pieces, on the boat of Ibn Jubār—may God keep it; these are for you personally, sent by Mūsā Ibn al-Majjānī. On this boat, I have in partnership with you—may God keep you—a load of cast copper, a basket with (copper) fragments, and two pieces of antimony. I hope God will grant their safe arrival. Kindly take delivery of everything, my lord.

I have also sent with Banāna a camel load for you from Ibn al-Majjānī and a camel load for me in partnership with you—may God keep you. He also carries another partnership of mine, namely, with 'Ammār Ibn Yijū, four small jugs (of oil).

With Abū Zayd I have a shipload of tin in partnership with Salāma al-Mahdawī. Your share in this partnership with him is fifty pounds. I also have seventeen small jugs of s[oap]. I hope they arrive safely. They belong to a man [called . . .]r b. Salmūn, who entrusted them to me at his own risk. Also a bundle of hammered copper, belonging to [a Muslim] man from the Maghreb, called Abū Bakr Ibn Rizq Allah. Two other bundles, on one is written Abraham,

on the other M[. . .]. I agreed with the shipowner that he would transport the goods to their destination. I wish my brother Abū Nasr—may God preserve him—to take care of all the goods and carry them to his place until I shall arrive, if God wills.

Please sell the tin for me at whatever price God may grant and leave its "purse" (the money received for it) until my arrival. I am ready to travel, but must stay until I can unload the tar and oil from the ships.

I have no doubt that you have sent me a letter containing all the quotations.

I have learned that the government has seized the oil and that Ibn al-Naffāt has taken the payment upon himself. I hope that this is indeed the case. Please take care of this matter and take from him the price of five skins (filled with oil). The account is with Salāma.

Al-Sabbāgh of Tripoli has bribed Bu 'l-'Alā the agent, and I shall unload my goods soon.

Kindest regards to your noble self and to my master [. . . and] Abu 'l-Fadl, may God keep them.

→ *What can you learn from the letter about the commodities traded?*
→ *What does the letter tell us about the ties among merchants, and about how they conducted their business?*

SOURCE: *Letters of Medieval Jewish Traders,* translated with introductions and notes by S. D. Goitein (Princeton, NJ: Princeton University Press, 1973), pp. 85–87.

Another Sufi mystic and advocate of the universality of religions, the Spanish Muslim poet Ibn Arabi (1165–1240), wrote in Arabic:

My heart has been of every form; it is a pasture for gazelles and a convent for Christian monks.
And a temple for idols and the pilgrim's kaaba, and the tables of the Torah and the book of the Quran.

Dervishes. Today, the whirling dance of dervishes is almost a tourist attraction, as shown in this picture from the Jerash Cultural Festival in Jordan. Though Sufis in the early second millennium CE were not this neatly dressed, the whirling dance was an important means of reaching union with God.

POLITICAL INTEGRATION AND DISINTEGRATION, 1050–1300

Just as the Islamic faith was increasing its global reach from Africa to India and ultimately into Southeast Asia, its political bulwarks collapsed. Islam's religious and cultural influences transcended its political powers. For a century, from 950 to 1050, it appeared that Shiism would be the vehicle for uniting the whole of the Islamic world. While the Fatimid Shiites established their authority over Egypt and much of North Africa (see Chapter 9), the Abbasid state in Baghdad fell under the sway of the Shiite Buyid family. Each created universities—in Cairo and Baghdad, respectively—thereby ensuring that Islam's two leading centers of higher learning in the eleventh century were Shiite. But the divisions also sapped Shiism; Sunni Muslims began to challenge Shiite power and to establish their own strongholds. The last of the Shiite Fatimid rulers gave way to a new Sunni regime in Egypt. In Baghdad, the Shiite Buyid family surrendered to an unrelated group of Sunni strongmen.

Those strongmen were mainly Turks, who had been migrating into the Islamic central core from the steppe lands of Asia since the eighth century, bringing with them superior military skills and an intense devotion to Sunni Islam. Ensconced in Baghdad, they established outposts in Syria and Palestine, and then moved into Anatolia after defeating Byzantine forces at the battle of Manzikert in 1071. But this Turkish state also crumbled, as Turkish-speaking tribesmen quarreled with one another for preeminence. Thus, by the thirteenth century the Islamic core area, stretching from Morocco in the west to the Oxus River in the east, was fractured into three distinctive regions. In the east (central Asia, Iran,

and eastern Iraq), the remnants of the old Abbasid state persevered. Here, caliphs succeeded one another, still claiming to speak for all of Islam yet lacking the ability to enforce their directives. They deferred without fail to their Turkish military commanders. Even in the central core of the Islamic world (Egypt, Syria, and the Arabian Peninsula), where Arabic was the primary tongue, military men of non-Arab origin held the reins of power. Further west, in the Maghreb, Arab rulers prevailed—but there the influence of Berbers, some from the northern Saharan region, was extensive. Islam was a vibrant faith, but its polities were splintered.

WHAT WAS ISLAM?

Buoyed by Arab dhows on the high seas and carried on the backs of camels, following commercial networks, Islam evolved from Muhammad's original goal of creating a religion for Arab peoples. By 1300, its influence was spreading across Eurasia and Africa. It lacked only an American toehold. It attracted urbanites and rural peasants alike, as well as its original audience, desert nomads. Its extraordinary appeal to such diverse populations generated an intense Islamic cultural flowering at the turn of the millennium in 1000 CE.

Some worried about the preservation of Islam's true nature. The Arabic language ceased to be the idiom of Islamic believers. True, the devout read and recited the Quran in its original tongue, as the religion mandated. But Persian was now often employed in Muslim philosophy and art, and Turkish in law and administration. Moreover, Jerusalem and Baghdad no longer stood alone as Islamic cultural capitals. There were now many important cities, and consequently many universities and centers of learning, boasting alternative, vernacular versions of Islam. In fact, some of the most dynamic thought came from Islam's fringes. To confront the question of Islam's identity meant dealing with its great—and ever growing—heterogeneity.

At the same time, heterogeneity fostered cultural efflorescence, as was apparent in all fields of high learning. Arabic remained a preeminent language of science, literature, and religion in 1300. Indicative of Islam's and Arabic's prominence in thought was the culture's most influential and versatile thinker—the legendary Ibn Rushd (1126–1198). Known as Averroës in the Western world, where scholars pored over his writings, he wrestled with the same theological issues that troubled Western scholars. Steeped in the writings of Aristotle, Ibn Rushd became Islam's most thoroughgoing rationalist. His knowledge of Aristotle was so great that it influenced the thinking of the Christian world's leading philosopher and theologian, Thomas of Aquino (Thomas Aquinas, 1225–1274). Above all, Ibn Rushd believed that faith and reason could be compatible. He also argued for a new kind of social hierarchy, in which learned men would command influence akin to Confucian scholars in China or Greek philosophers in Athens. Ibn Rushd believed that the proper forms of reasoning had to be entrusted to the educated class—in the case of Islam, the ulama—who would serve the common folk.

Equally powerful works were produced in Persian, which by the eleventh century was seen as a language capable of expressing the most sophisticated ideas of culture and religion. The intellectual who best represented the new Persian ethnic pride was Abu al-Qasim Firdawsi (920–1020), a devout Muslim who also believed in the importance of pre-Islamic Sasanian traditions. In the long epic poem *Shah Namah,* or *Book of Kings,* he celebrated the origins of Persian culture and narrated the history of the peoples of the Iranian highlands from the dawn of time to the Muslim conquest. As part of his effort to extol a pure Persian culture, Firdawsi attempted to compose the whole of his poem in Persian unblemished by other languages, avoiding Arabic loanwords.

By the fourteenth century, Islam had achieved what early converts would have considered unthinkable. No longer a religion of a minority of peoples living amid larger Christian, Zoroastrian, and Jewish communities, it had become the people's faith. The agents of conversion were mainly Sufi saints and Sufi brotherhoods and not the ulama, whose exhortations and knowledge of legal and philosophic texts had little impact on common people. The Sufis had carried their faith to the Berbers of North Africa, to villagers living on the plateaus of Anatolia, and to West African animists. Indeed, Ibn Rushd worried about the growing influence and appeal of what he considered an "irrational" piety. But his message failed, because he did not appreciate that Islam's expansionist powers rested on its appeal to common folk. While the sharia was the core of Islam for the educated and scholarly classes, Sufism spoke to the religious beliefs and experiences of ordinary men and women.

INDIA UP FOR GRABS

> → *In what ways did India remain a cultural mosaic?*

Trade and migration affected India, just as it did the rest of Asia and Africa. As in the case of Islam, however, prosperity led to growing social and cultural interconnections; but there was little political continuity or integration. Under the large canopy of Hinduism, India remained a cultural mosaic; in fact, in this period the Islamic faith joined with others in South Asia to make the region even more of a cultural mosaic. (See Map 10-4.) India, in this sense, was a crossroads of various parts of Eurasia and Africa; it illustrates how integration into long-distance, cross-cultural networks can just as easily preserve diversity as promote internal unity.

Turks spilled into India as they had the Islamic heartlands, carrying with them their newfound Islamic beliefs. But in India, these newcomers, like all previous invaders, encountered an existing ethnic and religious mix to which they would add something new without greatly upsetting the balance. India became an intersection for the trade, migration, and culture of Afro-Eurasian peoples—a vital nerve center of the world. Moreover, with 80 million inhabitants in 1000,

Hindu Temple. When Buddhism started to decline in India, Hinduism was on the rise. Numerous Hindu temples were built, many of them adorned with ornate carvings like this small tenth-century temple in Bhubaneshwar, east India.

MAP 10-4   SOUTH ASIA IN 1300

As the fourteenth century began, India was a blend of many cultures. Politically, Muslim Turks dominated the region. To what extent did the rulers of the Delhi Sultanate integrate India into the broader Islamic world during this era? What factors accounted for Hinduism's continued appeal despite the political power of Muslim leaders? How did Muslim communities integrate themselves into the larger cultural mosaic in South Asia?

India had the second-largest population in Afro-Eurasia at the time, not far behind China's 100 million but well ahead of Islamic Southwest Asia and North Africa (34 million) as well as Christian Europe (36 million).

India was rich, but it remained splintered into the rivalrous chiefs called *rajas*. By the end of the tenth century, their constant struggles had left them all exhausted. So, when northern invaders began encroaching on their frontiers, both the will and the resources to put up a fight were scarce. Before large-scale invasions by the Turks, central Asian invaders to India did not seek to conquer all the rajas; instead they accommodated and reinforced local rajas' power bases. Claiming *kshatriya* (warrior) status, the invaders cemented an alliance with the local rajas through marriages. Meanwhile, rajas old and new solicited support from high-caste Brahmans by making land concessions to them. Much of the land was not under cultivation. Brahmans took the leadership in reclaiming the wastelands. First they built temples, and then they converted the indigenous hunter-gatherer peoples to the Hindu faith. Then they showed the new converts how to cultivate the land. The Brahmans simultaneously spread their faith and greatly expanded the agrarian tax base for themselves and the rajas. Brahmans reciprocated for their good fortunes by compiling elaborate genealogies for the rajas, endowing them with a lengthy (and therefore legitimizing) ancestry. For their part, the rajas demonstrated that they were well-versed in Sanskrit culture, including equestrian skills and courtly etiquette, and they became the patrons of artists and poets. Ultimately, many of the warriors and their heirs became Indian rajas. However, Turkish invaders were armed with Islam, so the conquerors remained sultans instead of becoming rajas.

INVASIONS AND CONSOLIDATIONS

Turkish warlords entered India in a series of waves that began in the tenth century, introducing their customs into the fertile lands between the Indus and Ganges basins, while also accepting many of the existing political structures. Concerned to uphold their image as promoters of Islamic culture, they constructed grandiose mosques and built impressive libraries where scholars could toil and share their wisdom with the court. The first wave of invaders did not intend to stay in India. Mahmud of Ghazna (971–1030), who launched many expeditions from the Afghan heartland into the wealthy northern provinces of India, was one such conqueror, seeking to make his capital, Ghazni, a great center of Islamic learning in order to win status within Islam. The booty of his invasions—especially the jewels and precious goods plundered from the Hindu temples—also helped boost his status. Worse than Mahmud, Muhammad Ghuri in the 1180s led another wave of Islamic Turkish invasions from Afghanistan and dispersed across the Delhi region in north India. Wars over the control of the plains between the Indus and Ganges rivers raged until one by one, all the way to the lower Ganges valley, the fractured kingdoms toppled.

The now land-bound Turkish Muslim regime of northern India was known as the Delhi Sultanate (1206–1526), and its rulers strengthened the cultural diversity and tolerance that had already become a hallmark of the Indian social order. Although the Delhi sultans knew how to exploit a rich agricultural society, they had little knowledge of or interest in the flourishing commercial life that had sprung up along the Indian coast. They therefore permitted these areas to develop on their own. Persian Zoroastrian traders settled on the Konkan coast in the northwest, around modern-day Mumbai (Bombay). The Malabar Coast to the south became the preserve of Arab traders, who further developed the trade that their ancestors had started. The Delhi Sultanate was a rich and powerful regime that brought political integration but did not enforce cultural homogeneity.

WHAT WAS INDIA?

The entry of Islam into India made the region more of a cultural mosaic, not less. The local Hindu population treated the arrival of the Turks in India as they had done earlier invaders from central Asia: they expected to assimilate their conquerors. The Turks cooperated, but only up to a point. They became Indians but retained their Islamic beliefs and their steppe ways. They behaved as they had in their highland redoubts, wearing their distinctive trousers and robes and riding their horses. The Turks also did not eliminate all the rajas. Some rajas continued to rule certain areas under the sultans.

Although the sultans spoke Turkish languages, they regarded Persian literature as a high cultural achievement and made Persian the sultanate's courtly and administrative language. Meanwhile, most of their Hindu subjects continued to speak local languages that had evolved out of Sanskrit and to

Lodi Gardens. The Lodi Dynasty was the last Delhi sultan dynasty. Lodi Gardens, the cemetery of Lodi sultans, places Central Asian Islamic architecture in the Indian landscape, thereby creating a scene of "heaven on the earth."

follow their caste regulations in daily life. Moreover, they adhered to their local adaptations of the Hindu faith. The sultans did not meddle with the beliefs and cultures of the conquered but merely collected the special *jizya* tax that they paid.

Despite the reluctance of most people in India to embrace Islam, the faith flourished. Islam did not have to be a conquering religion to prosper. As rulers, sultans granted lands to Islamic scholars, the ulama, and Sufi saints, much as Hindu rajas had earlier granted lands to Brahmans. Prestigious scholars and saints in turn attracted followers to their large estates and forests to enjoy the benefits of membership in this community of believers.

The Delhi sultans built strongholds to defend their conquests. Every new sultanate built a fortress in the Delhi region, employing both local workers and foreign artisans from central Asia and Iran. The curves of domes and arches on mosques, tombs, and palaces, formed in the shape of the lotus flower, were uniquely South Asian in flavor. As expenditures at court attracted traders and artisans of all sorts, the palaces and fortresses quickly evolved into prosperous cities.

Although newcomers and locals lived in separate worlds, their customs began to merge. Delhi sultans maintained their steppe lifestyle and equestrian culture, and they were delighted when conquered peoples adopted nomadic customs and artifacts. They realized, however, that they had to learn the local language to rule the country effectively. Court scholars and Sufi holymen started to use local dialects to write and teach. Hindustani, an Indian language full of Persian and Arabic words, was taking shape and became the ancestral language of both Hindi and Urdu. Foreign artisans who arrived with their rulers produced the silk textiles, rugs, and appliances to irrigate gardens that the leading families of Delhi so cherished. Their talents spread beyond the palaces and influenced the manufacturing techniques of the local population. Before long, Indians had learned from the Muslim workers how to extract long filaments from silk cocoons and were themselves weaving fine silk textiles. The merging of cultures became even more apparent when the common people began to wear Turkish–style trousers and robes and when the Persian wheel, a water-lifting device, became widely used by farmers.

By this period, Buddhism in India had already been in decline for centuries. When Vedic Brahmanism evolved into Hinduism (see Chapter 8), it absorbed many doctrines and practices from Buddhism, such as the doctrine of *ahimsa* (non-killling) and the practice of vegetarianism. The two religions became so similar that Hindus simply considered the Buddha to be one of their deities—specifically, an incarnation of the great god Vishnu. Many Buddhist moral teachings were mixed and became Hindu stories. Artistic motifs were similarly adopted and adapted. Following the onslaught of the Turkish invaders, who destroyed many monasteries in the thirteenth century, several leading Buddhist scholars re-

Vishnu. With Buddhism disappearing from India, Buddha was absorbed by the cult of Vishnu and became one of the incarnations of the Hindu god. This late-twelfth-century Angkor Wat style sculpture from Cambodia shows Vishnu asleep; from his nostril sprouts the lotus that will give birth to Buddha.

treated to Tibet, where they helped lead a flowering of Buddhism on the plateau. Bereft of local spiritual leaders and lacking dynastic support, Buddhists in India were assimilated into the Hindu population or converted to Islam.

SONG CHINA, 960–1279

> → *What transformations in communication, education, and commerce contributed to the emergence of a distinct Chinese identity during this era?*

The preeminent world power in 1000 CE was still China, despite its recent experience of turmoil. That turbulence would give rise to a long era of stability and splendor—a combination that made China one of the main regional engines of Afro-Eurasian prosperity. After the end of the Tang dynasty (907 CE), China entered the Five Dynasties period. For two centuries the Tang dynasty's power had waned until North and South China broke into a series of regional kingdoms, usually led by military generals. But one of those generals, Zhao Kuangyin, put a stop to the fragmentation in 960 CE. Overthrowing the boy emperor of his own kingdom, Zhao moved quickly to reunify China by conquering three more of the seven major regional kingdoms between 963 and 975 CE. He was succeeded after his death in 976 CE by his younger brother, who finished the reunification effort by annexing the last three kingdoms. Thus, the Song dynasty took over the mandate of heaven.

The three centuries of Song rule in China would witness many economic and political successes, but powerful nomadic tribes in the far northern stretches of China kept the Song from completely securing their reign. (See Map 10-5.) Their efforts to fight off or pay off these warriors from the north would ultimately prove unsuccessful, and in 1127, the Song finally would lose control of northern China to the nomadic Jurchen, the ancestors of the Manchu. After reconsti-

tuting their dynasty in southern China, the most populous and economically robust region of their empire, they would enjoy another century and a half of rule before falling to the Mongols in 1276.

A Chinese Commercial Revolution

China's commercial revolution during this period had agrarian roots. Without vast fields of rice, the population would never have reached 120 million in the twelfth century—doubling its size from the previous millennium. Agriculture

Map 10-5 (a & b)   East Asia, 1000–1300

Several states emerged in East Asia between 1000 and 1300, but none as strong as the Song dynasty in China. What geographic and political factors contributed to the Song state's economic dynamism? What factors contributed to the Song state's loss of territory to the Jurchen Jin dynasty? How did the Jin state demonstrate the continued impact of pastoral groups on East Asian history in this era?

benefited from breakthroughs in metalworking. China's farmers were able to employ new and stronger iron ploughs, which they harnessed to sturdy water buffalo, to break the tough soil in the south, and to extend the farming frontier. In 1078, for example, total Song iron production peaked somewhere between 75,000 and 150,000 tons, roughly the equivalent of European iron production at the start of the eighteenth century. The Chinese piston bellows were a marvel of the age, of a size unsurpassed anywhere in the world until the nineteenth century.

Manufacturing flourished. In the early years of the tenth century, Chinese alchemists were mixing saltpeter with sulfur and charcoal to produce a product that would burn and could be deployed on the battlefield. By 1040, the first gunpowder recipes were being written down. Over the next 200 years, Song entrepreneurs invented a remarkable array of incendiary devices that flowed from their mastery of techniques for controlling explosions. Song Chinese also devised an "eruptor," a weapon that functioned like a cannon, and it was quickly emulated by their enemies. This was not the only manufacturing breakthrough to astonish the world. Building on their predecessors' techniques, Song artisans produced lighter, more durable, and stunningly more beautiful porcelains. Before long, Song porcelain (now called "china") had become the envy of all Afro-Eurasia. China's artisans also produced vast amounts of clothing and handicrafts from the hemp, mulberry, and cotton that its farmers were growing in great abundance. In effect, the Song Chinese brought about the world's first manufacturing revolution, producing finished goods on a large scale for consumption far and wide.

The growth of commerce transformed the role of money and its worldwide circulation. By the middle of the eleventh century, the Song government was annually minting nearly two million strings of currency—each string containing 1,000 copper coins—far in excess of the Tang maximum of about 300,000 strings. Indeed, the inability of the supply of metal currency to keep pace with demand fueled East Asia's thirst for East African gold in this era. At the same time, merchants began to tinker with printed paper certificates; their guilds in northwestern Shanxi developed the first letters of exchange, which were called "flying cash." These letters linked northern traders with their colleagues in the south. The paper habit spread, and by the thirteenth century printed money had eclipsed coins. Even the government became heavily dependent on paper currency, as it found itself now able to collect more than half of its tax revenues in cash rather than in grain and cloth. The government also turned to its own printing presses to issue more and more notes to pay its bills—a practice that ultimately contributed to the world's first case of runaway inflation, which destabilized the Song and later the Yuan regimes.

NEW ELITES

The commercial revolutions enabled the early Song emperors to champion civilian rule over military values and to usher in a period of social and cultural vitality. The Song undercut the powers of the hereditary aristocratic elites, establishing instead a society governed by a central bureaucracy of scholar-officials chosen through competitive civil service examinations whose scope exceeded that of the Tang. The shift of loyalties from aristocratic clans to the ruling house solidified during the reign of Zhao Kuangyin, also known as Emperor Taizu (ruled 960–976 CE), who in 973 himself administered the final test for all those who had passed the highest-level palace examination. In subsequent dynasties, the emperor became the nation's premier examiner, symbolically demanding oaths of allegiance from successful candidates for public office. Civil officials were now drawn almost exclusively from the ranks of learned men, and by 1100 they had accumulated sufficient power to become China's new ruling elite.

NEGOTIATING WITH NEIGHBORS

As the Song flourished, nomads on the outskirts eyed Chinese successes closely. At the dynasty's northern borders, Khitan, Tungusic, Tangut, and Jurchen nomadic societies formed their own dynasties and adapted Chinese techniques to their

Song Civil Service. Song emperors championed civilian rule to undercut the remaining Tang aristocratic elites. A civil service composed of scholar-officials selected through competitive examinations in both the provinces and the capital took hold. Here we see a painting of an examination being administered during Emperor Renzong's reign (1023–1031).

own advantage. Located within the boundaries of the "greater China" established by the Han and Tang dynasties, these non-Chinese polities watched with envy as China's core amassed extraordinary wealth and prestige. It was only a matter of time before nomadic armies such as those of the Khitan and Jurchen saw China proper as an object of conquest.

In one important way the Song dynasts were weak: they had limited military power, despite their sophisticated weapons. Steel tips increased the effectiveness of Song arrows used with crossbows, and Song armies also boasted flamethrowers and "crouching tiger catapults" for lobbing incendiary bombs at their enemies. But none of these breakthroughs was secret. Warrior neighbors on the steppe, such as the Khitan tribal confederation and Jurchen, mastered the new arts of war more fully than did the Song dynasts themselves.

China's strength as a manufacturing powerhouse made economic diplomacy an option. To keep borderlanders at bay, the Song relied on "gifts" and generous trade agreements with the peoples on the fringes. Defeated militarily by the Liao dy-

Trebuchet. Derived from the sling, the trebuchet served as a siege engine to smash masonry walls or throw flaming projectiles over them. Trebuchets were invented in China in about the fourth century BCE and came to Europe in the sixth century CE. All trebuchets were made of wood and could fling a three hundred–pound (140 kg) projectile at high speed. The illustration here shows a Song Dynasty naval river ship c. 1044 equipped with a traction trebuchet catapult.

nasty in 1004, the Song agreed to make annual payments of 100,000 ounces of silver and 200,000 bolts of silk. The treaty enabled the Song to live in relative peace for more than a century. Another Inner Asian tribal confederation, the Tangut, pressed on the Song's northwestern border. The Tangut state also received an annual subsidy from the Song when an agreement was reached in 1044. Securing peace meant emptying the state coffers—and thus the state turned to its printing presses to make more paper money. The resulting runaway inflation added economic instability to military weakness, making the Song an easy target when the Jurchen invaders made their final assault.

WHAT WAS CHINA?

Paradoxically, the increasing contact and exchange between outsiders and insiders within China hardened the lines that divided them. This was a pattern displayed centuries earlier, in the entanglements of the nomadic Northern Wei rulers with the Han people in China proper (see Chapter 8). The exchanges that did take place, and there were many, wound up nurturing a "Chinese" identity for those who considered themselves true insiders and referred to themselves as Han.

Thus, transformations in communications and education intensified the sense among the Han Chinese that they were authentically Chinese, and that outsiders were radically different. Driven from their ancient homeland in the north beginning in the eleventh century, the Han Chinese grew increasingly suspicious and resentful toward the outsiders living in their midst. They once again called them "barbarians" and treated them accordingly, drawing a dividing line between the nomadic warrior cultures of the Eurasian steppe and their own society based on the large-scale cultivation of grain and rice. Yet these identities were not completely fixed: Han Chinese and non-Han barbarians, insiders and outsiders, were in fact mutually dependent. For long periods, the two groups had easily coexisted, particularly in northwestern and northern China, with much interchange of cultures and technologies. But despite the nomadic borrowing of Chinese ways, and the assimilation of warrior elites to Han Chinese ways, the differences between civilized "China" and the barbarian "other" became a durable stereotype. To be authentically Chinese, even if ruled by outsiders, meant valuing civilian mores, especially for those educated Chinese who were steeped in the civil examination system. It meant being literate—able to read, write, and live by codes inscribed in foundational texts.

Of all the Afro-Eurasian societies in 1300, the Chinese had created the most advanced print culture. The Song government published a wide variety of works, using its plentiful supply of paper to print books, especially medical texts, and to distribute calendars. The private publishing industry also expanded, and printing houses sprang up throughout the country. They produced the Confucian classics, works on

Chinese and Barbarian. After losing the north, the Han Chinese grew resentful of outsiders. They drew a dividing line between their own agrarian society and the nomadic warriors, calling them "barbarians." Such identities were not fixed, however. Chinese and so-called barbarians were mutually dependent.

history, philosophical treatises, and literature, all of which were employed in the civil examinations, which were administered not just centrally but in provincial capitals throughout the country. In Fujian province alone, some 17,000 to 18,000 candidates gathered in the coastal capital city triennially to take the provincial examination. Buddhist publications were also available everywhere. Song printing directly influenced the precocious Koryo dynasty (918–1392) in Korea, which also made great headway in printing by developing movable metal type in 1234, about two centuries before its independent invention in Europe.

CHINA'S NEIGHBORS, 1000–1300

> → *How were Southeast Asia, Japan, and Korea influenced by sustained contact with other regions in this era?*

Under its Song rulers, China became the most populous and wealthiest of the world's regions. Its population of more than 120 million in 1100 projected the influence of Chinese culture, through trade and migration, across all of Afro-Eurasia, especially into Korea, Japan, and Southeast Asia. Chinese commodities found ready markets in neighboring cultures, as local elites had a growing appetite for manufactured textiles, porcelains, and other luxuries. In return, they shipped staples to Chinese cities along the coast, both foodstuffs and industrial inputs. The Koryo rulers in Korea, for example, actively imitated Song culture, religions, and technology, which they passed on to Japan. Their capital, Kaesong, was one of the world's most impressive cities. Koryo rulers ordered the construction of hundreds of Buddhist temples in the Tang-Song style, as well as the creation of countless religious artworks.

THE RISE OF WARRIORS IN JAPAN

As China became an economic and political powerhouse, the cultures around its rim were forced to adapt. They could not help but feel the gravitational pull of China. Often these neighbors responded by consolidating internal political authority to resist being swallowed up, while increasing their participation in commercial transactions. In Japan, rulers had to resolve some endemic problems to create a stable regime out of feuding warrior factions. Their solution was to amalgamate the Heian court's imperial authority with the military power of the more rusticated provincial warriors in the east.

The pattern of regents ruling in the name of the sacred emperor was repeated many times in Japanese history, but it

began in the Heian period (794–1185). First court nobles—an entrenched aristocracy—in the new capital of Heian (today's Kyoto) dominated Japan, and later rough-and-ready warriors followed their model in literally winning possession of the throne to "protect" its sanctity as an object of popular veneration. They captured it to gain the symbolic power of the emperor, which was transferred to his protectors.

By intermarrying with and ruling through the Heian imperial family for two centuries, the influential Fujiwara family added considerably to the power of their ancestors, the powerful Nakatomi kinship group in Nara (described in Chapter 9). The Fujiwara nobles presided over a refined Heian culture of flower and tea ceremonies. They also exchanged poetry written in classical Chinese and their native language and dressed in the elegant costumes that have influenced Japanese public life and private taste up to this day.

Political marriages enabled the Fujiwara to control the throne, but the rise of large private estates (called *shōen*) outside the capital shifted the balance of power from the court to the regional elites in the provinces. A hierarchy of land tenures emerged in the countryside: peasant cultivators were at the bottom, managers and estate officials in the middle, and absentee patrons at the top. By 1100 more than half of Japan's rice land was controlled by these large estates, and the revenue and power of the state fell considerably. In the midst of such privatization, Heian became for aristocrats a theater state—politically weak but culturally influential—while the hinterlands provided their economic wealth.

Heian aristocrats ruled through political stealth and artistic style and disdained the military. In 792—even before Heian became the capital—the conscription system to raise imperial armies was abolished. In the provinces, however, trained warriors affiliated with specific kinship groups gathered strength. The rural elites were expert horsemen who fought in armor, and they defended their private estates by relying on their skill with the bow and sword. As incipient samurai, they formed local warrior organizations in the outlying regions, particularly on Kantō Plain (where today's Kamakura and Tokyo are located), well to the east of the capital.

Japan became the home to multiple sources of power: an aristocracy, an imperial family, and local warriors (known as samurai). It was a combustible mix, a recipe for intrigue and double-dealing. Although the sanctity of the Japanese emperor and the Heian aristocracy remained intact, outside warrior groups such as the Minamoto and Taira families provided a new bridge between the elites of the capital and the nouveaux riches in the provinces. Using native Japanese script developed in the Heian era, Lady Murasaki Shikibu (c. 976–c. 1031) described the elegant lives and sordid affairs of the courtiers and their women in *The Tale of Genji*, Japan's—and possibly the world's—first novel. Neither nobles nor warriors refrained from political intrigue, as they grasped at any and all possible alliances that would propel them into power. First, beginning in 1168, the Taira kinship group ruled as

Heiji Rebellion. This illustration from the Kamakura period depicts a battle during the Heiji Rebellion, which was fought between rival subjects of the cloistered emperor Go-Shirakawa in 1159. Riding in full armor on horseback, the fighters on both sides are armed with devastating long bows.

samurai elites in the name of the emperor. Next General Yoritomo (1147–1199) led his Minamoto kin (also called the Genji) to a dramatic victory over the Taira at the sea battle of Dan no Ura off the southern island of Shikoku in 1185. Ultimately, it was the alliance of local potentates and military commanders under the Kamakura shoguns (1192–1333)—generalissimos who served as military "protectors" of the ruler in Heian—that brought more stable rule to Japan. The Kamakura age thus provided the fierce warriors who successfully fended off the Mongol naval invasions of 1274 and 1281. Moreover, the shogunate form of military government remained intact under the theoretical sovereignty of the Japanese emperor in Heian until 1868.

THE CULTURAL MOSAIC OF SOUTHEAST ASIA

Southeast Asia, like India, became a crossroads of Afro-Eurasian influences. (See Map 10-6.) Its population was still relatively low (probably not more than 10 million in 1000), especially when compared with that of its nearest neighbors, China and India. Certainly, the dominance of island life and island culture, particularly as developed on the lands that were to become Indonesia in modern times, set the peoples of this unique geographical area off from others. But the Southeast Asian communities were not immune to the influences of the peoples that flocked into this region. Like India,

the archipelago became a cultural mosaic, its sea-lanes (and peoples) connecting China with Asia and Africa. The elongated Malay Peninsula became the home to many trading ports and stopovers for traders shuttling between India and China, and thus connected the Bay of Bengal and the Indian Ocean with the South China Sea.

Indian influence had been prominent both on the Asian mainland and in island portions of Southeast Asia since 800 CE. Islamic expansion into the islands that comprised maritime Southeast Asia after 1200 gradually superseded these cultural influences. Only Bali and a few other outlying islands located far to the east of the Malayan crossroads, for example, were able to preserve their Vedic religious origins relatively intact. Elsewhere in Java and Sumatra, Islam irrevocably became the universalistic religion of the islands. In Vietnam and northern portions of mainland Southeast Asia, Chinese cultural influences and northern schools of Mahayana Buddhism were especially prominent.

The prosperity and cultural vitality of the heavily populated regions of China and India spilled over into the maritime and Asian mainland worlds of Southeast Asia, especially benefiting the Thai, Vietnamese, and Burmese peoples who gradually emerged as the largest population groups on the mainland. Island residents of the Malay Archipelago—especially of Java and Sumatra—controlled much of the region's maritime activity. Each population group adjusted as Chinese and Indian influences rose and fell, selecting those aspects of "Indo-Chinese" civilization that they found compatible with local

THE TALE OF GENJI

Lacking a written language of their own, Heian aristocrats adopted classical Chinese as the official written language while continuing to speak Japanese. Men at the court took great pains to master the Chinese literary forms imported from the Tang dynasty via the Heian tributary missions periodically sent to Chang'an. Japanese court ladies, however, were not expected to master Chinese writing. For example, Lady Murasaki, the author of The Tale of Genji, *went to great pains to hide her knowledge of Chinese, fearing that she would be criticized for being unladylike. In the meantime, the Japanese developed a syllabary for their own language by simplifying Chinese written graphs and tying them directly to native sounds. Using this syllabary, Lady Murasaki began a diary in Japanese that she kept up for two years. In it she gave vivid accounts of Heian court life, whose frivolity she herself disliked. Lady Murasaki noted that some might also view writing fiction as frivolous, but she made clear that fiction could be as truthful as a work of history in capturing human life and its historical significance.*

So saying she pushed away from her the book which she had been copying. Genji continued: "So you see as a matter of fact I think far better of this art than I have led you to suppose. Even its practical value is immense. Without it what should we know of how people lived in the past, from the Age of the Gods down to the present day? For history-books such as the *Chronicles of Japan* show us only one small corner of life; whereas these diaries and romances which I see piled around you contain, I am sure, the most minute information about all sorts of people's private affairs. . . ." He smiled, and went on: "But I have a theory of my own about what this art of the novel is, and how it came into being. To begin with, it does not simply consist in the author's telling a story about the adventures of some other person. On the contrary, it happens because the storyteller's own experience of men and things, whether for good or ill— not only what he has passed through himself, but even events which he has only witnessed or been told of—has moved him to an emotion so passionate that he can no longer keep it shut up in his heart. Again and again something in his own life or in that around him will seem to the writer so important that he cannot bear to let it pass into oblivion. There must never come a time, he feels, when men do not know about it. That is my view of how this art arose.

"Clearly then, it is no part of the storyteller's craft to describe only what is good or beautiful. Sometimes, of course, virtue will be his theme, and he may then make such play with it as he will. But he is just as likely to have been struck by numerous examples of vice and folly in the world around him, and about them he has exactly the same feelings as about the pre-eminently good deeds which he encounters: they are more important and must all be garnered in. Thus anything whatsoever may become the subject of a novel, provided only that it happens in this mundane life and not in some fairyland beyond our human ken.

"The outward forms of this art will not of course be everywhere the same. At the court of China and in other foreign lands both the genius of the writers and their ac-

tual methods of composition are necessarily very different from ours; and even here in Japan the art of storytelling has in course of time undergone great changes. There will, too, always be a distinction between the lighter and the more serious forms of fiction. . . . Well, I have said enough to show that when at the beginning of our conversation I spoke of romances as though they were mere frivolous fabrications, I was only teasing you. Some people have taken exception on moral grounds to an art in which the perfect and imperfect are set side by side. But even in the discourses which Buddha in his bounty allowed to be recorded, certain passages contain what the learned call *Upāya* or 'Adapted Truth'—a fact that has led some superficial persons to doubt whether a doctrine so inconsistent with itself could possibly command our credence. Even in the scriptures of the Greater Vehicle there are, I confess, many such instances. We may indeed go so far as to say there is an actual mixture of Truth and Error. But the purpose of these holy writings, namely the compassing of our Salvation, remains always the same. So too, I think, may it be said that the art of fiction must not lose our allegiance because, in the pursuit of the main purpose to which I have alluded above, it sets virtue by the side of vice, or mingles wisdom with folly. Viewed in this light the novel is seen to be not, as is usually supposed, a mixture of useful truth with idle invention, but something which at every stage and in every part has a definite and serious purpose."

→ *What does this account tell us about the relation between historical fact and fictional romance?*

→ *How are "truth and error" displayed in religious writings, which, like novels, use stories in pursuit of their didactic purpose?*

SOURCE: *Sources of Japanese Tradition,* compiled by Ryūsaku Tsunoda, Wm. Theodore de Bary, and Donald Keene (New York: Columbia University Press, 1964), vol. 1, pp. 177–79.

→ *How were Southeast Asia, Japan, and Korea influenced by sustained contact with other regions in this era?*

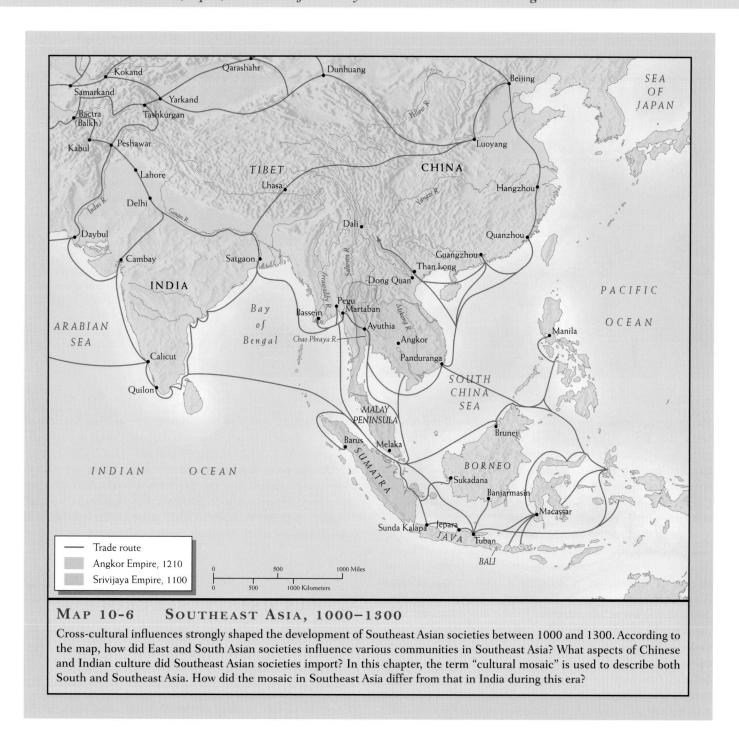

MAP 10-6 SOUTHEAST ASIA, 1000–1300

Cross-cultural influences strongly shaped the development of Southeast Asian societies between 1000 and 1300. According to the map, how did East and South Asian societies influence various communities in Southeast Asia? What aspects of Chinese and Indian culture did Southeast Asian societies import? In this chapter, the term "cultural mosaic" is used to describe both South and Southeast Asia. How did the mosaic in Southeast Asia differ from that in India during this era?

state formation and cultural activities. Chinese and Indian peoples also became part of the new trading milieu.

Cambodian, Burmese, and Thai peoples founded powerful mixed polities along the Mekong, Salween, Chaophraya, and Irriwaddy river basins of the Asian mainland. The important Vedic and Buddhist kingdoms of the Khmer (today's Cambodia), Pagan (today's Burma), and Siam (today's Thailand) emerged as political buffers between the strong states in China and India. These Southeast Asian kingdoms were

soon robust enough to consolidate their hold on these borderlands, thereby bringing stability and furthering the commercial prosperity of the region.

Consider the great kingdom that ruled Angkor in present-day Cambodia. With their capital in Angkor, the Khmers (889–1431) created the most powerful and wealthy empire in Southeast Asia between the tenth and thirteenth centuries. Countless water reservoirs enabled the Khmers to flourish on the great plain to the west of the Mekong River. Public works

Aerial View of Angkor Wat. Mistaken by later European explorers as a remnant of Alexander the Great's conquests, the enormous temple complexes built by the Khmer people in Angkor borrowed their intricate layout and stupa architecture from the Brahmanist Indian temples of the time. As the capital, Angkor was a microcosm of the world for the Khmer, who aspired to represent the macrocosm of the universe in the magnificence of Angkor's buildings and their geometric-astronomic layout.

and magnificent temples dedicated to the glory of the revived Vedic gods from India went hand in hand with the earlier influence of Indian Buddhism in mainland Southeast Asia. Eventually the Khmer kings gathered enough military strength to unite adjacent kingdoms and extend Khmer influence to the Thai and Burmese states along the Chaophraya and Irriwaddy rivers.

One of the greatest temple complexes in Angkor exemplified the heavy borrowing by the Khmer peoples from Indian temples and architecture. By this time, the Brahmanist revival of Vedic religion in India circa 1000 CE had eclipsed Buddhism there, except on the island of Ceylon. Angkor aspired to represent the universe in the magnificence of its buildings. As signs of the ruler's power, the pagodas, pyramids, and terra-cotta friezes presented the life of the gods on earth. The royal palace alone extended 1,970 feet east to west and 820 feet north to south; it was crowned by the magnificent Vaishnavite temple of Angkor Wat, measuring about a mile square and probably the largest religious structure ever built. The buildings and statues represented the revival of the Hindu pantheon of gods in the Khmer royal state, such as Shiva and Vishnu, in great detail and with great artistry, but far less Buddhist influence is visible.

Because of its strategic location and proximity to Malayan tropical produce, Melaka became perhaps the most international city in the world. Indian, Javanese, and Chinese merchants and sailors spent months at a time in such ports selling their goods, purchasing a return cargo, and waiting for the winds to change so that they might reach their next destination. Seasonal shifts in the monsoon winds across the Bay of Bengal, the South China Sea, and the Java Sea al-

lowed Chinese and Japanese ships to arrive from January to March and then return home in August. Ships from India came from May to early October and sailed back west in winter. During peak season, Southeast Asian ports were filled with foreign sailors and traders from all over Asia who accompanied their own merchandise. They gathered in large numbers at crossroads where agriculture sustained the local population and maritime trade routes converged.

CHRISTIAN EUROPE

> → *How did Christianity produce a distinct identity among the diverse peoples of Europe?*

In the far western corner of the Afro-Eurasian landmass, a people were building a culture revealingly different. (See Map 10-7.) Although their numbers were still relatively small compared with the rest of Afro-Eurasia in 1000 (36 million in Europe, compared to 80 million in India and 100 million in China), their population was rapidly rising and would soar to 80 million before the arrival of the Black Death at the beginning of the fourteenth century.

This was a region of contrasts. On the one hand, the first three centuries of the second millennium witnessed an intense localization of politics. There was no successor to the Roman or Carolingian empires (see Chapter 9). On the other hand, the territory was ever more united by a progressively

MAP 10-7   LATIN CHRISTENDOM IN 1300

Catholic Europe expanded geographically and integrated culturally during this era. According to this map, into what areas did Western Christendom successfully expand? What factors contributed to the growth of a widespread common culture and shared ideas? How did long-distance trade shape the history of the region during this time?

greater shared sense of its place in the world. Indeed, in these years some even began for the first time to believe in the existence of something called "Europe," whose inhabitants were increasingly referring to themselves as "Europeans."

A WORLD OF KNIGHTS

The collapse of the Carolingian empire (768–814 CE) had exposed much of northern Europe to invasion, principally from the Vikings, and left the region's peasantry with no central authority to protect them from the power of local warlords. These warlords collected taxes and imposed forced labor. Armed with new and more deadly weapons, the warrior class came to stand out as the unchallenged rulers of society. In this growth of a warrior aristocracy, northern France led the way. The Franks (who gradually came to be called "Frenchmen" in this period) were the self-proclaimed trendsetters of eleventh- and twelfth-century western Europe.

The most important change was the subjugation of the peasantry to the knightly class. Previously, well-to-do peasants

The Bayeux Tapestry. This tapestry was prepared by a queen and her ladies to celebrate the victories of William the Conqueror. It shows the fascination of the entire "feudal" class, even women, with the sinews of war on which they depended—great horses, tightly meshed chain mail, long shields, and the stirrups that made such cavalry warfare possible.

had carried arms, and doing so had marked themselves as "free" men. The moment the farmers lost their right to carry arms, they were no longer free. They slipped back to being mere agricultural laborers. Each peasant was under the authority of a lord, who controlled every detail of his or her life. This was the basis of a system known as feudalism.

Assured of control of the peasantry, feudal lords watched over an agrarian breakthrough—which formed the basis of a commercial transformation that would link Europe to the rest of the global trading networks. This breakthrough was largely due to massive deforestation, which, in turn, implied more advanced use of metal tools (axes and ploughs) and heavier livestock to pull the ploughs that turned the heavy, root-infested sods of northern Europe. Above this stood the castle—a threatening presence that ensured that (unlike many other regions of the world) the peasantry did not simply vanish into the woods that they had cleared. They stayed within range of the collector of rents and services for the lords and of tithes for the Church. In this blunt way, "feudalism" harnessed agrarian energy to its own needs. The population of western Europe as a whole leaped forward, most spectacularly in the north. By 1300, northern Europe contained almost half of Europe's inhabitants. As a result, northern Europe (from England to Poland) finally ceased to be an underdeveloped barbarian appendage of the Mediterranean.

EASTERN EUROPE

Nowhere did pioneering peasants develop more land than in the wide-open spaces of eastern Europe, the region's land of opportunity. Between 1100 and 1200, some 200,000 farmers emigrated from Flanders (modern Belgium), Holland, and northern Germany into eastern frontiers. Well-watered landscapes, covered with vast forests, in what are now Poland,

the Czech Republic, Hungary, and the Baltic states filled up. "Little Europes," whose castles, churches, and towns echoed the landscape of France, sprang up to replace economies that had been based on gathering honey, hunting, and the slave trade. In Silesia (western Poland), for instance, 1,200 villages were founded within a century. For a thousand miles along the Baltic Sea, from the city of Lübeck in Germany to Riga in present-day Latvia, forest clearings dotted with new farmsteads and small towns edged inward from the coast up the river systems.

The social structure in eastern Europe was a marriage of convenience between migrating peasants and local elites. Western European peasants sought to enjoy, in a different land, some of the freedoms that had been lost to their feudal overlords. Eastern Europe offered the promise of freedom from arbitrary justice and from the imposition of forced labor.

Olavinilinna Castle. This castle in Finland was the easternmost extension of a "western," feudal style of rule through great castles. It was built at the very end of the Baltic, to keep away the Russians of Novgorod.

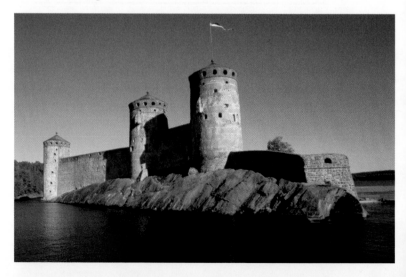

Even the harsh landscape of the eastern Baltic (where the sea froze every year and vast forests blocked the way of settlers from the coast) was preferable to life in the feudal west. For their part, the elites of eastern Europe—the nobility of Poland, Bohemia, and Hungary and the princes of the Baltic—wished to live well, in the "French" style. But they could do so only if they attracted manpower to their vast lands by offering peasants and townspeople a liberty that they had no hope of enjoying in the west.

THE RUSSIAN LANDS

In Russian lands, western settlers and knights met an eastern brand of Christian devotion. This was a world that had chosen to look toward Byzantium. Russia was a giant borderland between the interior steppe lands of Afro-Eurasia and the booming feudalisms of Europe, bridging east and west. Its cities lay at the crossroads of overland trade and migration, and Kiev became one of the greatest cities of Europe. Standing on a bluff above the Dnieper River, it straddled newly opened trade routes. With a population of well over 20,000, partly made up of merchants drawn from all over eastern Europe, western Europe, and the Middle East, Kiev was larger than Paris—larger even than the much-diminished city of Rome.

Kiev looked south to the Black Sea and to Byzantium. Under Iaroslav the Wise (1016–1054), it was carefully re-built so as to become a small-scale Constantinople on the Dnieper. A stone church called St. Sophia was placed (as in Constantinople) beside the imperial palace. Indeed, with its distinctive "Byzantine" domes, it was a miniature Hagia Sophia. Almost a hundred feet high from the floor to the top of the dome, it was at its completion the largest structure ever built in Europe east of the Elbe. Splendid mosaics covered the walls with images of Byzantine saints, which faithfully echoed the religious art of Constantinople. But the message was political as well as religious, for the ruler of Kiev similarly was cast in the mold of the emperor of Constantinople. He was now called *tsar* from the ancient Roman name given to the emperor, Caesar. From this time onward, *tsar* was the title of rulers in Russia.

The Russian form of Christianity embraced the Byzantine style of churches and replicated them up the great rivers leading to the largely independent trading cities of the north and northeast. These were not centers of growing agrarian settlement and dense populations but entrepôts, the hubs of expanding long-distance trade across Afro-Eurasia. Each city became a small-scale Kiev, and thus became a smaller-scale echo of the Great City—Constantinople. The Orthodox religion associated with Byzantium's Hagia Sophia, and not the Catholic religion associated with the popes in Rome, was their form of Christianity. Russian Christianity remained the Christianity of a borderland—a series of vivid oases of high culture, set against the backdrop of vast forests and widely

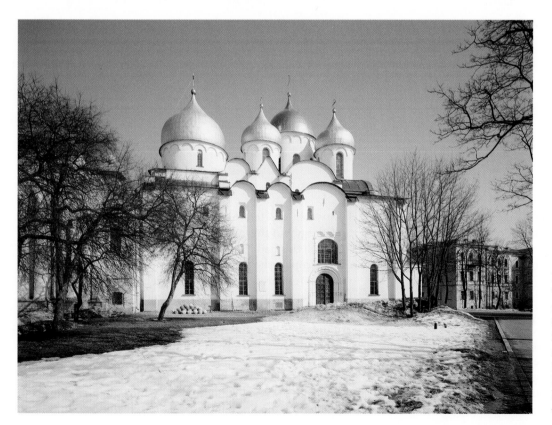

Hagia Sophia, Novgorod. The cathedral of Novgorod (as that of Kiev) was called Hagia Sophia. It was a deliberate imitation of the Hagia Sophia of Constantinople, showing Russia's roots in a glorious Roman/Byzantine past that had nothing to do with western Europe.

Primary Source

VOICES FROM THE PAST: THE BIRCH BARK LETTERS OF NOVGOROD

From 1951 onward, the excavations of Russian archaeologists in Novgorod have revealed almost a thousand letters and accounts scratched on birch bark. Written on wood, they were preserved in the sodden, frequently frozen ground. Reading them we realize what a remarkable place Novgorod must have been in the twelfth and thirteenth centuries.

First, we meet the merchants. Many letters are notes by creditors of the debts owed to them by trading partners. The sums are often expressed in precious animal furs. They contain advice to relatives or to partners in other cities:

> Giorgii sends his respects to his father and mother: Sell the house and come here to Smolensk or to Kiev: for the bread is cheap there.

Then we meet neighborhood disputes:

> From Anna to Klemiata: Help me, my lord brother, in my matter with Konstantin. . . . [For I asked him,] "Why have you been so angry with my sister and her daughter. You called her a cow and her daughter a whore. And now Fedor has thrown them both out of the house."

There are even glimpses of real love. A secret marriage is planned:

> Mikiti to Ulianitza: Come to me. I love you, and you me. Ignato will act as witness.

And a poignant note from a woman was discovered in 1993:

> I have written to you three times. What is it that you hold against me, that you did not come to see me this Sunday? I regarded you as I would my own brother. Did I really offend you by that which I sent to you? If you had been pleased you would have torn yourself away from company and come to me. Write to me. If in my clumsiness I have offended you and you should spurn me, then let God be my judge. I love you.

→ *What does the range of people writing on birch bark tell us about these people?*

→ *What does the final note tell us about the expression of love among the peoples from the northern stretches of Afro-Eurasia?*

SOURCE: A. V. Artsikhovskii and V. I. Borkovski, *Novgorodskie Gramoty na Bereste*, 11 vols. (Moscow: Izd-vo Akademii nauk SSSR, 1951–2004), document nos. 424, 531, 377, and 752.

---

scattered settlements. As the settlement frontier pushed outward, it merged with the shamanistic cultures of the Arctic and Siberia, and, in the south, with the nomad corridor that linked Europe to central Asia along the coast of the Black Sea.

WHAT WAS CHRISTIAN EUROPE?

In this era, Catholicism became a mass faith, a transformation that shaped the emergence of the region then coming to be known by some as "Europe." The Christianity of post-Roman Europe had been a religion of monks, and its most dynamic centers were great monasteries. Members of the laity were expected to revere and support their monks, nuns, and clergy, but they were not encouraged to imitate them. By 1200, all this had changed. The internal colonization of western Europe—the clearing of woods and the founding of villages—ensured that parish churches arose in all but the wildest landscapes. Their spires could be seen and their bells could be heard from one valley to the next. The graveyards around the churches were the only places where a good Christian could be buried; criminals and outlaws were piled into "heathen" graves outside the cemetery walls. Even the bones of the believers helped make Europe Christian.

The clergy reached more deeply into the private lives of the laity. For the first time in Christian history, marriage and

Amiens Cathedral. The cathedrals of northern France and elsewhere in Europe were built largely by local townsmen with the wealth that came to them through trade and industry. Each town strove to build its own cathedral ever higher and higher. No building was as high in Roman times. Even the Hagia Sophia was dwarfed by these light and lofty marvels of engineering.

UNIVERSITIES AND INTELLECTUALS During this era, Europe acquired its first class of intellectuals. Since the end of the twelfth century, scholars had tended to come together in Paris. There they formed a *universitas*—a term borrowed from the merchant communities, where it denoted the equivalent of the modern "union." Those who belonged to the *universitas* were protected by their fellows and were allowed to continue their trade. Similarly protected by their union, the scholars of Paris set about wrestling with the new learning from Arab lands. And when in 1212 the bishop of Paris forbade this undertaking, they simply moved to the Left Bank of the Seine, so as to place the river between themselves and the officials of the bishop, who lived around the cathedral of Notre Dame.

The ability of the scholars to organize themselves gave them an advantage not enjoyed by their Arab contemporaries, despite the latter's immense cultural resources. For all his genius, Ibn Rushd had to spend his life courting the favor of

Medieval Lecture. Crowded lecture halls, open to a wide audience, were a creation of the medieval university. Previously, learning had taken place in small groups over long periods of time.

divorce (which had been treated, by aristocrats and peasants alike, as family matters over which the clergy had no jurisdiction) became a full-time preoccupation of the church. Sin, for instance, was no longer dealt with as an offense that just happened to the laity. It was a matter that the laity could do something about, preferably on a day-to-day basis. After 1215, for the first time ever, regular confession to a priest was made obligatory for all Catholic, western Christians. The followers of Francis of Assisi (1182–1226)—a man from a merchant background, whose father traded wool in northern France—emerged as an order of preachers who brought to the towns a message of repentance. They did not tell their audiences to enter the monastery (as would have been the case in the early Middle Ages). Instead, the listeners were to weep, to confess their sins to their local priests, and to try to be better Christians. Franciscans instilled in the hearts of all believers a new, Europe-wide Catholicism, based on daily remorse and on the daily contemplation of the sufferings of Christ and his mother, Mary. From Ireland to Riga and Budapest, Catholic Christians shared a common piety.

individual monarchs to protect him from conservative fellow Muslims. Frequently his books were burned. Ironically, European scholars congregating in the Schools of Paris could quietly absorb the most persuasive elements of Arabic thought, like Ibn Rushd's. Yet, at the same time, they endeavored to show that everything gradually converged to prove that Christianity was the only religion that fully met the aspirations of all rational human beings. Such was the message of the great teacher and intellectual Thomas Aquinas, born in southern Italy, whose *Summa contra Gentiles* (*Summary of Christian Belief against Non-Christians*) was written in 1264.

The Europe of 1300 was more culturally unified than it had been in previous centuries. It was more fully permeated by a version of its dominant Catholicism, made more accessible than ever before to the laity of the new towns through preachers such as Saint Francis and through stunning monuments such as the new Gothic cathedrals of northern France. Its leading intellectuals extolled the virtues of Christian learning and thought. Such a confident region was not, however, a happy place for heretics, Jews, or Muslims.

TRADERS Western Europeans were expanding frontiers around the Mediterranean and pushing beyond it. Great trading hubs emerged, most famously Venice and Genoa, as the nodes of commerce and finance linking Europe, Africa, and Asia. Powerful families commanded trading fleets and used their deep pockets to influence dealings far and wide. They also possessed the means to meddle in political affairs. Indeed, both Venice and Genoa set their sights on the waning power of Constantinople and on its eastern trade, vying for access to Asia Minor, the Black Sea, and the thriving commercial hinterlands of Afro-Eurasia. The Genoese showed, on a worldwide stage, what urban magnates could do when they combined sea power with a zest for organization. By 1300, Genoese ships had linked the Mediterranean to the coast of Flanders through regular sailings along the Atlantic coast of Spain, Portugal, and France. In 1291, some ventured as far as the Azores in the Atlantic, only to be lost as they pushed further southwest. Genoese maps displayed the entire coast of West Africa—including the kingdom of Mali, ruled by Mansa Musa (see above), which was the source of the gold dust that was now carried across the Sahara to the coast of North Africa.

CRUSADERS By the tenth and eleventh centuries, Europe had gained a strong enough sense of its separate identity that its elites and even many of its common folk regarded the area as a distinct region. Western Christianity was on the move. It spread into Scandinavia, southern Italy, the Baltic, and eastern Europe. Its ambitions to reconquer Spain and Portugal, which had been under Islamic control since the eighth century, demonstrated one of the effects of the flourishing of feudal power: the self-confidence of lords, their belief in their

military capability, and their pious sense of manifest destiny were all inflated. Besides, the wealth of the east, fueled by the prosperity of trading cities, was irresistible to those whose piety was entwined with an appetite for plunder. Nor were feudal lords alone in mixing opportunism and a passion for sacred causes. The leaders of the eastern and western churches were keen to recover or gain strength. Rome and Byzantium both sought to gain the upper hand in the scramble for religious command in Europe; each considered a blow to the "infidel" a cunning ploy to out-do the other. Yet the two Christendoms formed an uneasy alliance to roll back the expanding frontiers of Islam.

Crusader. Kneeling, this Crusader promises to serve God (as he would serve a feudal lord) by going to fight on a crusade (as he would fight for any lord to whom he had sworn loyalty). The two kinds of loyalty—to God and to one's lord—were deliberately confused in Crusader ideology. Both were about war. But fighting for God was unambiguously good, while fighting for a lord was not always so clearcut.

THE CRUSADES FROM DUAL PERSPECTIVES

In 1095, at the Council of Clermont, Pope Urban II called for the First Crusade in the following words:

> Oh, race of Franks, race from across the mountains, race chosen and beloved by God, as shines forth in very many of your works, set apart from all nations by the situation of your country, as well as by your Catholic faith and the honor of the Holy Church! To you our discourse is addressed, and for you our exhortation is intended. We wish you to know what a grievous cause has led us to your country, what peril, threatening you and all the faithful, has brought us.

The "grievous cause" was the occupation of the Holy City of Jerusalem by the Islamic empire. Formed within the complex relationship between the Byzantine Empire and the western Christian papacy and kingdoms of Europe, the religious motivation behind the Crusades became the subject of many literary renditions of the tumultuous events. It also generated emotionally stirring and polemical writing, depicting either a Muslim or Christian enemy (depending on the work's author).

Polemics are often passionate, harsh, and emotional. They are also often meant to inspire and reinforce the conviction of fellow believers, with little concern for the accuracy of their portrayals. Thus authors of polemic in the time of the Crusades were usually too biased, too distant from the events or people they described, or simply too misinformed to present accurate portraits of the enemies against whom they were pitting themselves. But occasionally, firsthand accounts in the form of chronicles and histories offer us unique glimpses into Christian-Muslim relations in the age of the Crusades.

Consider Usāmah ibn Munqidh (1095–1188), the deeply learned ruler of the city of Shaizar on the Orontes River in western Syria. Skirmishes, truces, and the ransoming of prisoners were part of his daily life, and Usāmah socialized with his Frankish neighbors quite as much as he fought with them. He offers a dismissive opinion of his enemies. Basically, they struck him as "animals possessing the virtues of courage and fighting, but nothing else." In particular, their medical practice appalled him. More strange yet, the Franks allowed their wives to walk about freely and to talk to strangers unaccompanied by male guardians. How could men be at once so brave and yet so lacking in a proper, Arab sense of honor, which would lead a man to protect his women? In fact, sexual laxity seemed to be one of the aspects of Frankish life that most appalled Usāmah, who claimed that the Franks were "void of all zeal and jealousy," meaning that they were unconcerned with relatively loose sexual mores. Unlike other Muslim authors of his time, however, Usāmah does not refer to the Franks in derogatory terms such as "infidels" or "devils." In fact, he occasionally refers to some of them as his companions, and writes in one case of a Frank who used to call him "my brother" (*An Arab-Syrian Gentleman and Warrior in the Time of the Crusades*, 16).

Christian authors had similar interests in documenting the habits and customs of their enemies in battle. Jean de Joinville (1224/1225–1317) was a chronicler of medieval France. He also composed a biography of King Louis II, at the request of Jeanne of Navarre, the queen. In 1309 Joinville completed his work on the *Histoire de Saint Louis*, which documents how he himself had been in the service of the king. During the crusade launched from 1248 to 1254, Joinville, one of the king's confidants, had occasion to note the social behavior of the Muslims:

> Whenever the Sultan was in the camp, the men of the personal Guard were quartered all round his lodging, and appointed to guard his person. At the door of the Sultan's lodging there was a little tent for the Sultan's door-keepers, and for his musicians, who had Arabian horns and drums and kettledrums; and they used to make such a din at daybreak and at nightfall that people near them could not hear one another speak, and that they could be heard plainly all through the camp. The musicians never dared sound their instruments in the daytime unless by the order of the Chief of the Guard. Thus it was, that whenever the Sultan had a proclamation to make he used to send for the Chief of the Guard, and give him the order; and then the Chief would cause all the Sultan's instruments to be sounded; and thereupon all the host would come to hear the Sultan's commands.

Although we should regard literary renditions of the events described with a certain degree of caution, they are useful for gleaning personal details that may be left out of other types of works. The colorful accounts by authors such as Usāmah ibn Munqidh and Joinville have proven invaluable as resources for the social and cultural history of the Crusader era.

The result was that Europeans took war outside their own borders on a mass scale. In the late eleventh century, western Europeans launched the wave of attacks that we now know as the Crusades. The First Crusade began in 1095, when Pope Urban II appealed to the warrior nobility of France to put their violence to good use. They should combine their role as pilgrims to Jerusalem with that of soldiers and free Jerusalem from Muslim rule. What the pope and clergy proposed, in effect, was a novel kind of war. Previously, the clergy had regarded war as a dirty business and a source of sin (not unlike sex). Now the clergy told the knights that good and just wars were possible. Such wars could cancel out the sins of those who waged them.

Starting in 1097, an armed host of around 60,000 men—a force larger than any "barbarian" wave at the end of the Roman Empire—moved all the way from northwestern Europe to Jerusalem. In all, there would be four "crusades," over the course of two centuries. They cannot be described as successful. Only a small proportion of Crusaders stayed behind to guard the territories they had won. No more than 1,200 knights remained to defend the Kingdom of Jerusalem after the First Crusade. Most knights returned home, their epic pilgrimage completed. The fragile network of small Crusader lordships could only occasionally pose a threat to the true heartlands of the Islamic world. On July 4, 1187, the Frankish heavy cavalry was lured on to the dry plateau above the Sea of Galilee, where they were slaughtered in the blazing heat by Saladin (Salah ad-Din, "Righteous in Faith"), the Kurdish commander who had made himself ruler over Egypt. Subsequent forays were equally disastrous. Stretched thin, with feeble supply lines, the dwindling forces of Christian occupiers (or "liberators," depending on one's perspective) were too easy to pick off, surround and besiege, or simply overrun. Against such odds, western Christian forces took out their frustrations against other Christians and allies. In one infamous "crusade" Frankish armies went on a rampage in the Byzantine capital and sacked Constantinople in 1204. According to one Byzantine monk, "nothing worse than this has happened nor will happen." When news reached the far-off Scandinavian world, Christian I, king of Norway and Denmark, saw it as a signal of the forthcoming apocalypse, when the beast would rise from the waters, as described in the New Testament.

Muslim leaders did not see the Frankish knights as much of a threat to their heartland. From the point of view of the Muslim Middle East, the Crusades were largely irrelevant. As far as the average Muslim of the region was concerned, the Crusaders had blundered into a no-man's-land of little importance. The principal long-term effect of these assaults was to harden Muslim feelings against the *Ferangi* (Franks) of the West and to bring about a worsening of the condition of many millions of non-Western Christians who had previously lived peacefully in Egypt and Syria.

Other Crusade-like campaigns of Christian expansion undertaken around this time were considerably more successful. Rather than being overseas ventures, these were launched from a secure home base. In this period, the Spanish Reconquista got under way. Beginning with the capture of Toledo in 1061, the Christian kings of northern Spain (who could count on support from their immediate Christian neighbors across the Pyrenees) slowly but surely pushed back the Muslims. Eventually, they reached the rich heart of Andalusia and in 1248 they conquered Seville, a victory that permanently added more than 100,000 square miles of territory to Christian Europe. Another force from northern France crossed Italy to conquer Muslim-held Sicily in 1091, thereby ensuring that a rich island only seventy-five miles away from the coast of Africa and in a position to control the middle of the Mediterranean was subject to Christian rule. These two conquests accomplished in less than a century, and not the fragile foothold of the Crusaders on the edge of the Middle East, were the events that truly turned the tide in the relations between Christian and Muslim power in the Mediterranean.

THE AMERICAS

> → *Where did societies in the Americas demonstrate strong commercial expansionist impulses?*

Alone in the world, untouched by the increasing connections across the Afro-Eurasian regions, were the Americas. Simply put, the revolution in communications did not enable Asian, African, or European navigators to cross the large oceans that separated the Americas from other lands. However, isolation did not mean that the Americas were stagnant. Many of the commercial and expansionist impulses that swept the rest of the world occurred independently in the Western Hemisphere and similarly brought the peoples of the Americas into closer contact with each other.

ANDEAN STATES

Growth and prosperity in the Andean region led to the formation of South America's first empire. Known as the Chimú Empire, it developed during the first century of the second millennium in the fertile Moche Valley, bordering the Pacific Ocean. (See Map 10-8.) At its height, the Moche people had expanded their influence across a number of valleys—and thus incorporated a wide number of ecological zones, from pastoral highlands to rich valley floodplains to the fecund fishing grounds of the Pacific Coast. As their geographical reach grew, so did their wealth. The Chimú regime lasted until Incan armies invaded the coastal strongholds in the 1460s and incorporated the Pacific state into its own immense empire.

The Chimú economy was successful because it was highly commercialized. Agriculture was its base, and complex irrigation systems turned the arid coast into a string of fertile oases capable of feeding an expanding and far dispersed population. Cotton became a lucrative export to distant markets along the Andes. Parades of llamas and porters lugged these commodities up and down the steep mountain chains that are the spine of South America. As in China, a large, well-trained bureaucracy was responsible for constructing and maintaining canals, with a hierarchy of provincial administrators to watch over commercial hinterlands.

Between 850 and 900 CE, the Moche peoples founded their biggest city, Chan Chan, with a core population of 30,000 inhabitants. A sprawling metropolis surrounded by twenty-six-foot-high walls, covering nearly ten square miles with extensive roads circulating through adobe neighborhoods, it had ten huge palaces at its center. These were residence halls, protected by thick walls thirty feet high, whose prestige and opulence demonstrated the rulers' power over other Moche subjects. Within the compound, emperors erected mortuary monuments, which became stores for their accumulated riches. In them archaeologists have found

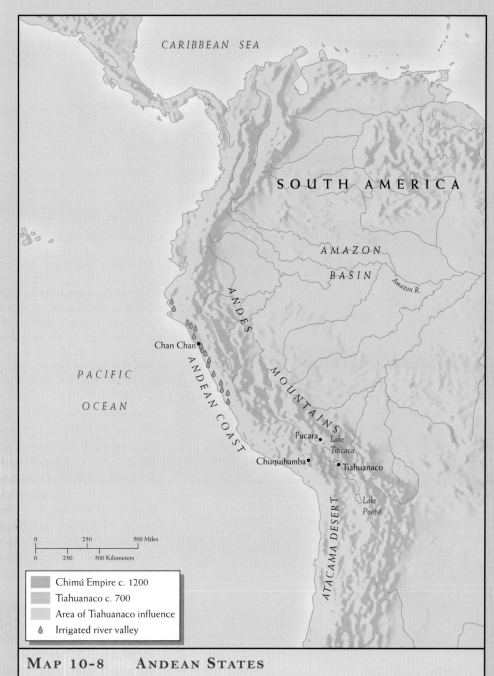

MAP 10-8 ANDEAN STATES

Although the Andes region of South America was isolated from Afro-Eurasian developments before 1500, it was not a stagnant region. Indeed, political and cultural integration brought the peoples of this region closer together. What kind of empire was the Chimú? What kinds of ecological niches did it govern? How did each polity encourage greater cultural and economic integration?

Chan Chan. This is what is left of Chan Chan. The city covered fifteen square miles and was divided into distinct neighborhoods for nobles, artisans, and commoners, with the elites living closest to the hub of governmental and spiritual power. Adobe was the basic construction material; it held up well in the arid conditions of the Peruvian coast.

Tihuanaco Buildings. The buildings of Tihuanaco were made of giant, hand-hewn stones assembled without mortar. Engineers had not discovered the principle of curved arches and keystones and instead relied on massive slabs atop gateways. Gateways were important symbolic features, for they were places where people acknowledged the importance of sun and moon gods. In this building, a giant monolith stood in the gateway that looked out over the Andean horizon.

treasures of fine cloth, gold and silver objects, splendid *Spondylus* shells, and piles of other high-status goods. Around the emperors' compound were neighborhoods for nobles and artisans; in the further reaches of the city stood small rows of houses for Moche commoners.

The Andes also saw its first highland empires during this period. On the shores of the high plateau lake Titicaca, the people of Tiahuanaco forged a high-altitude state. Though neither as large nor as wealthy as the Chimú Empire, it was complex, and it converted the seemingly inhospitable highlands into an environment where farmers and herders thrived. There is, moreover, extensive evidence of long-distance trade between the highland peoples and neighbors in semitropical valleys, and even signs of highlanders migrating down to the lowlands to set up agrarian colonies to produce staples for their kin in the mountains. Dried fish and cotton came from the coast; fruits and vegetables came from lowland valleys. Trade was active enough to sustain an enormous urban population of up to 115,000 people. Looming over the skyline of

Lake Titicaca. This is the setting for the first great Andean polity of Tihuanaco (Tiwanaku). Surrounded by the glacial peaks of the Andes, Tihuanaco grew up near the shores of Lake Titicaca, a source of water, fish, and legends about the birth of gods. To cultivate the steep mountainsides, farmers developed complex terrace systems. Most settlements were nestled, like these ruins, on valley floors or by the shores of the lake.

Tiahuanaco was an imposing pyramid of massive sandstone blocks; its advanced engineering system conveyed water to the summit, from which the liquid flowed in an imitation of rainfall down the carefully carved sides—an awesome spectacle of engineering prowess in such an arid region.

NORTH AMERICAN CONNECTIONS

By 1000 CE, Mesoamerica had seen the rise and fall of several complex societies. Caravans of porters worked the intricate roads that connected the coast of the Gulf of Mexico and the Pacific, and the southern lowlands of Central America to the arid regions of modern Texas. (See Map 10-9.) Its heartland was the rich valley of central Mexico. The Toltecs rose to power with great rapidity because they were able to fill the political vacuum left by the decline of the great city of Teotihuacán (see Chapter 8) and tap into the commercial network that radiated from the valley.

The Toltecs themselves were hybrids—a combination of migrant groups, refugees from the south, and farmers from the north—who settled northwest of Teotihuacán as the city waned. Their capital was Tula, growing in the shadow of the Mesoamerican metropolis. The Toltecs relied on a maize-based economy, supplemented by beans, squash, and dog, deer, and rabbit meat, as local agrarian production covered the population's needs. Rulers, however, relied on the enterprise of merchants to provide them with status goods such as ornamental pottery, rare shells and stones, and precious skins and feathers.

Tula was a commercial hub. But it was also a political capital and a ceremonial center. While the city's layout differed from Teotihuacán's, many features revealed borrowings from other Mesoamerican peoples. Temples were made of giant pyramids topped by colossal stone soldiers, and the ball courts where subjects and conquered peoples alike played their ritual sport were ubiquitous. The architecture and monumental art bespoke the mixed and migratory origins of the Toltecs: a combination of Mayan and Teotihuanacu influences decorated the city's great public works. At its height, the Toltec capital was home to around 60,000 people—a huge metropolis by contemporary European standards.

Cities at the hubs of trading networks could be found all across North America. North of Tula, the largest was Cahokia, by the shores of the Mississippi River (near modern-day East St. Louis), a city of about 15,000 (which would make it about the size of London at the time). Farmers and hunters settled in the region around 600 CE, attracted by the combination of good soil, availability of woodlands for fuel and game, and access to the trading artery of the mighty Mississippi. Eventually, fields planted with rows of maize (their main staple) and other crops fanned out into the horizon. The hoe replaced the trusty digging stick, increasing yields, and smaller satellite towns put up granaries to hold foodstuffs.

Cahokia became a commercial center for regional and long-distance trade. The hinterlands produced staples for urban consumers. In return, Cahokia's crafts were exported, carried inland on the backs of porters and to distant North American markets in canoes. The city's woven fabrics and ceramics were desired by faraway consumers. In exchange, traders brought to the rich city mica from the Appalachian Mountains, seashells and sharks' teeth from the Gulf of Mexico, and copper from the upper Great Lakes. Indeed, Cahokia became more than an importer and exporter: it was the

Toltec Temple. Tula, the capital of the Toltec Empire, carried on the Mesoamerican tradition of locating ceremonial architecture at the center of the city. The Pyramid of the Morning Star cast its shadow over all other buildings. And above them stood columns of the Atlantes, carved Toltec god-warriors, the figurative pillars of the empire itself. The walls of this pyramid were likely embellished with images of snakes and skulls. The north face of the pyramid has the image of a snake devouring a human.

MAP 10-9   COMMERCIAL HUBS IN MESOAMERICA AND NORTH AMERICA, 1000

Both Cahokia and Tula, shown on the map above, represented commercial hubs of vibrant regional trade networks between 1000 and 1300. What kinds of goods do your readings suggest circulated through these cities? How much political influence on the surrounding region do you think each city maintained? Do you think that the trade networks anchored by each city ever interacted with each other during this time?

entrepôt for an entire regional commercial network, containing many trading nodes where salt, tools, pottery, woven stuffs, jewelry, and ceremonial goods could be procured from traders from other places.

Cahokia's urban landscape was dominated by mounds, really big mounds (which is one reason Cahokians are often known as "mound people"). These earth monuments were delicately maintained: Cahokians enveloped their shells with layers of sand and clay to prevent their foundations from drying and then cracking. It was from these great artificial hills that Cahokians paid homage to spiritual forces. Of course, building this kind of infrastructure without draft animals, hy-

draulic tools, or even wheels was labor-intensive. To solve this problem, Cahokians recruited other North Americans to serve in working brigades. Around the city was an endless palisade made from neighboring forests, to protect the metropolis from marauders and enemies.

In the end, the city outgrew its environment. The woodlands were cleared and arable soil began to lose nutrients. Timber and food became scarce. Because the city lacked a means of transportation to ship bulky items over long distances, Cahokia's success bred its downfall. When the creeks that fed its water system could not keep up with demand, engineers changed their course, to no avail. By 1350, the city

Cahokia Mounds. This is all that is left of what was once a large city organized around temple mounds in what today is Illinois. The largest of the temples, known as Monks' Mound, was likely a burial site, with four separate terraces for crowds to gather. Centuries of neglect and erosion have taken their toll on what was once the largest human-made earthen mound in North America.

was practically empty. Nevertheless, Cahokia represented the growing networks of trade and migration across North America, and it demonstrated the ability of North Americans to organize vibrant commercial societies and powerful states.

THE MONGOL TRANSFORMATION OF AFRO-EURASIA

> → *How did Mongol conquests affect cross-cultural contacts and regional development in Afro-Eurasia?*

The world's sea-lanes grew crowded with ships; ports buzzed with activity. Commercial networks were clearly one way to integrate the world. But just as long-distance trade connected people, so could conquerors—as we have seen throughout the history of the early world. In this instance, these transformative conquerors came from the inner Eurasian steppe lands, the same place where horse-riding warriors such as the Xiongnu originated centuries earlier (see Chapters 6 and 7). Like the Xiongnu and the Kushans before them, the Mongols would both conquer peoples and intensify trade and cultural exchange. By setting up a latticework of states across northern and central Asia, the Mongols created a new empire that straddled the east and west. (See Map 10-10.) It was unstable, and not as durable as other dynasties. It did

not even have a shared faith; the mother of the conquering emperors, Hulagu and Kubilai Khan, was a devout Christian, reflecting the success of Nestorian missionaries who had been laboring for centuries to bring about conversions among the animistic nomads. Many Europeans hoped and prayed that the entire empire would convert. But it did not; the Mongols were a religious patchwork of Afro-Eurasian belief systems. Yet the Mongols succeeded in bringing parts of the world together.

Who were these conquerors of territories so much larger than their own? The Mongols were a combination of forest and prairie peoples. Residing in circular, felt-covered tents, which they shared with some of their animals, the Mongols lived by a combination of hunting and livestock herding. A mobile society, they changed campgrounds with the seasons, hunting game and herding livestock south in winter and north in summer. Life on the steppes was a constant struggle, which meant that only the strong survived. Their food, consisting primarily of animal products from their herds or from game they hunted, provided high levels of protein, which built up their muscle mass and added to their strength. Always on the march, the Mongols created a society that resembled a perpetual standing army. Their bands were organized into strictly disciplined military units led by commanders chosen for their skill. Mongol archers, using a heavy compound bow, made of sinew, wood, and horns, could fire an arrow more than 200 yards at full gallop with accuracy. Mongol horses were stocky, and capable of withstanding extreme cold. Their saddles had high supports in front and back, enabling the warriors to ride and maneuver at high speeds. Iron stirrups permitted the riders to rise in their saddles to shoot their arrows without stopping. The Mongols were expert horsemen, who could remain in the saddle all day and night, even sleeping while their horses continued on the move. Each warrior kept many horses, enabling Mongol armies to travel as many as sixty or seventy miles per day. Between military campaigns, soldiers kept sharp by engaging in winter hunting.

Mongol tribes were imperialists in a special way: while they conquered they also adjoined their conquests by extending kinship networks. In this fashion, the empire was made of a confederation of familial tribes. The tents (households) were interrelated mostly by marriage; that is, they were alliances sealed by exchange of daughters. Conquest involved marrying conquering men to the women of the conquered, and selecting conquered men to marry the conqueror's women. Chinggis Khan is said to have had more than 500 wives, most of them daughters of tribes that he conquered or that sought alliance with him. As a result a great proportion of steppe chiefs were kin. Patrimony was king, but empire was achieved through the exchange of women.

Women in Mongol society were responsible for child-rearing as well as shearing and milking livestock and processing their pelts for clothing. But women also took part in

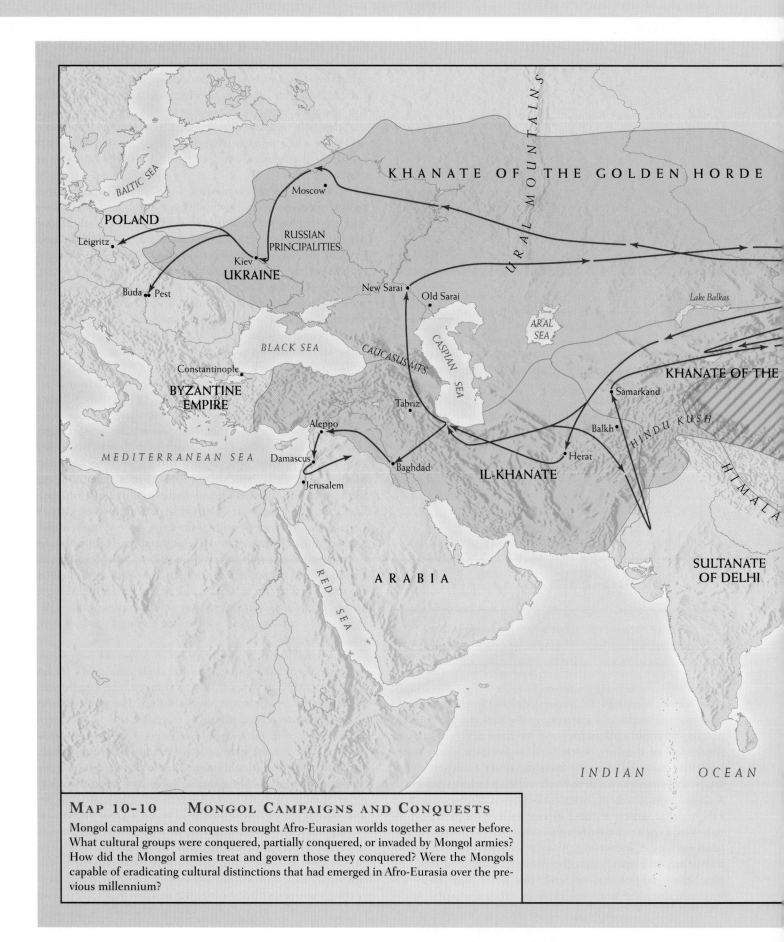

MAP 10-10 MONGOL CAMPAIGNS AND CONQUESTS

Mongol campaigns and conquests brought Afro-Eurasian worlds together as never before. What cultural groups were conquered, partially conquered, or invaded by Mongol armies? How did the Mongol armies treat and govern those they conquered? Were the Mongols capable of eradicating cultural distinctions that had emerged in Afro-Eurasia over the previous millennium?

→ *How did Mongol conquests affect cross-cultural contacts and regional development in Afro-Eurasia?*

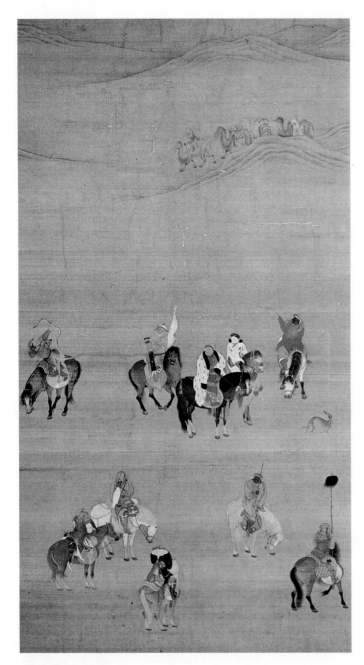

Mongols on Horseback. Even after the Mongols became the rulers of China, the emperors remembered their steppe origin and maintained the skills of horse-riding nomads. This detail from a thirteenth/fourteenth-century silk painting shows Kubilai Khan at hunting.

that each son acquired a different second language that would aid in administrating conquered lands. She gathered Confucian scholars to prepare Kubilai Khan to rule China. Chabi, Kubilai's senior wife, followed a similar pattern, offering patronage to Tibetan monks who set about converting the Mongol elite in China to Tibetan Buddhism.

At least initially, the nomads' desire for conquests may have been fueled by their need for grazing lands. Then, as the Mongols moved into new lands, they were able to increase their wealth enormously by extracting taxes through their tributary system. Trade disputes were also a powerful spur to their expeditions. The Mongols were dependent on trade with settled peoples, seeking especially grain but also manufactured goods (including iron for tools, wagons, weapons, bridles, and stirrups), and their first expansionist forays followed caravan routes. Here were opportunities to raid instead of trade.

The nomads' expansionist thrust began in 1206, when a cluster of tribes joined into a united force. A large gathering of clan heads acclaimed one of those present as Chinggis (Genghis) Khan, or Supreme Ruler. Chinggis (c. 1155–1227) subsequently launched a series of conquests southward across the Great Wall of China, and westward through central Asia to Afghanistan and Persia. The Mongols also launched a massive invasion of Korea in 1231. Although the Korean armies fiercely resisted, the Koryo state was no match for the well-organized horsemen from the northern steppe. The armies of Chinggis's son and first successor reached both the Pacific Ocean and the Adriatic Sea. His grandsons founded dynasties in China, Persia, and on the southern Eurasian steppes east of Europe. One of them, Kubilai Khan, enlisted thousands of Koryo men and ships for ill-fated invasions of Japan in 1274 and 1281. Thus, a realm took shape that was more than 6,000 miles wide and touched all four of Afro-Eurasia's main worlds.

Mongol raiders built a permanent empire by incorporating conquered peoples and by absorbing some of their ways. By stretching their power across the northern arch of Afro-Eurasia, horsemen bypassed the Pamir watershed, which divides central Asia into eastern and western portions. This unification was far more surprising and sudden than the ties developed incrementally by traders and travelers on ships. Now, Afro-Eurasian regions were connected by land and by sea, in historically unparalleled ways.

battles. Kubilai Khan's niece Khutulun became famous for besting men in wrestling matches and claiming their horses as spoils. Although women were often bought and sold, Mongol wives had the right to own property and even to divorce. Elite Mongol women played important political roles. Sorghaghtani Beki, Kubilai Khan's birth mother, helped to engineer the rule of her sons. Illiterate herself, she made sure

MONGOLS IN CHINA

In 1200, the north of China was still under the control of the Jin dynasty (1115–1234), which was led by Jurchen, who had driven the Song into the south. The Song court and its Chinese followers had regrouped in the south and called themselves the "Southern Song." As the political and military upheaval continued in the north, much of the economic ac-

Mongolian Warriors. This miniature painting is one of the illustrations for *History* by Rashid al Din, the most outstanding scholar under the Mongol regimes. Note the relatively small horses and strong bows used by the Mongol soldiers.

tivity of trade and finance moved southward and focused on their new capital, Hangzhou. This former provincial seaport became the political center of the Chinese people in their ongoing struggles with northern steppe nomads. It also became one of China's gateways to the rest of the world via the South China Sea. Agrarian staples and precious manufactures poured out of southern China to feed and clothe people in distant markets, as Chinese precious goods were coveted by elites far and wide.

The Jin fell fairly quickly in 1234 because of the Mongols' superiority in cavalry on the North China Plain. But below the Yangzi River, the climate and weather changed, no longer favoring the Mongol horsemen against Southern Song forces. They grew ill from diseases such as malaria, and their horses perished from the heat. To conquer the semitropical south, the Mongols increasingly took to boats and fought along rivers and canals, as Chinese had done since the Three Kingdoms period and during the Sui and Tang reunifications. Kubilai, Chinggis's grandson, completed the conquest of the grandest prize of all—southern China—after 1260. His generals marched their cavalries through the higher plateaus of Sichuan and Yunnan in southwest China, and then attacked South China's economic heartland from the west. The Southern Song army, composed of hired mercenaries, proved unable to withstand the onslaught of warriors who were armed with the latest gunpowder-based weapons (developed from a technology originally invented by the Chinese themselves).

Still, Mongol armies pressed south until they reached the outskirts of Hangzhou; this last Song capital succumbed to the invaders in 1276. Rather than see the invaders pillage the city and the tombs of the emperors, they bowed to the inevitable. The Song court was in disarray: the young emperor had died suddenly in 1274, and all his heirs were minors. The new regents for the successor and the Empress Dowager were unable to handle the internal chaos and the advancing army. Meanwhile, Kubilai Khan's most trusted and able commander, Bayan, led his crack Mongol forces as they seized town after town, ever closer to the capital. The Empress Dowager tried to buy off the invaders, as the Chinese had often done in the past, proposing regular and substantial tribute payments—250,000 taels of silver and 250,000 bolts of silk—but Bayan had his eye on the prize: Hangzhou.

On the eve of the city's fall in 1276, the Empress Dowager presented Bayan with the Song dynasty's seal, the sign that she had given up. Later the Song emperor appeared in person and submitted to the new masters of the city. Bayan was magnanimous in his victory. He ordered his men to conduct a census of Hangzhou and register its granaries and treasury. He also prohibited his men from plundering the suburban tombs of the Southern Song emperors—in contrast to the Jin conquerors, who in 1127 had pillaged the Northern Song tombs outside Kaifeng. Bayan also escorted the Song emperor and the Empress Dowager to Beijing, where Kubilai treated them with honor. Pockets of resistance persisted after 1276, but within three years Song China's defeat was complete. Having extended their military sway over all of South China, the Mongols established the Yuan dynasty (1280–1368) with a new capital at Dadu ("Great Capital," present-day Beijing).

THE TRAVELS OF MARCO POLO AND IBN BATTUTA

Although no traveler crossed the Atlantic or Pacific oceans, an increasing number ventured through the lands of Africa, Europe, and Asia. The most famous of these thirteenth- and fourteenth-century travelers, Marco Polo and Ibn Battuta, encountered a world tied together by trade routes that crossed the Afro-Eurasian landmass and the Indian Ocean that often had as their ultimate destination the imperial court of the Great Khan in China. These two men and similar, though less-celebrated travelers, observed worlds that were both highly localized and yet had culturally unifying features.

In 1271, Marco Polo (1254–1324), the son of an enterprising Venetian merchant, set out with his father and uncle on a journey to East Asia. Making their way along the fabled silk route across central Asia, the Polos arrived in Xanadu, the summer capital of the Mongol empire, after a three-and-a-half year journey. There they remained for more than two decades. When they returned to their home in Venice in 1295, fellow townsmen greeted them with astonishment, so sure were they that the Polos had perished years before. So, too, Marco Polo's published account of his travels generated an incredulous reaction. Some of his European readers considered his tales of Eastern wonders to be mere fantasy, yet others found their appetites for Asian splendor whetted by Polo's descriptions.

A half-century after Polo commenced his travels, the Moroccan-born scholar Muhammad ibn Abdullah ibn Battuta (1304–1369) embarked on a journey of his own. Then just twenty-one, Ibn Battuta vowed to visit the whole of the Islamic world without traveling the same road twice. It was an ambitious assignment, for Islam's domain extended from one end of the Eurasian landmass to the other and far into Africa as well. On his journey, Ibn Battuta eventually covered some 75,000 miles and traveled through West and East Africa, across the interior of Asia, and beyond the realm of Islam to China. Along his way, he claimed to have met at least sixty rulers, and in his book he recorded the names of more than 2,000 persons whom he knew personally.

Marco Polo and Ibn Battuta provide a wealth of information on the well-traversed lands of Africa, Europe, and Asia. What they and other travelers observed was the extreme diversity that characterized the peoples living in Afro-Eurasia, where numerous ethnicities, many political formations, and varied religious faiths and practices prevailed. In addition, they observed that the vast majority of people lived deeply localized lives, the primary goal of which was to obtain the basic necessities of everyday living. Yet, they were also aware that these very same societies, however local their orientations, welcomed and even encouraged contact, trade, and cultural exchange over long distances and between regions. In fact, they wrote most eloquently about the way in which each of the four major cultural systems of the Afro-Eurasian landmass—Christian, Muslim, Indian, and Chinese—struggled to articulate definitions of themselves. Interestingly, if Ibn Battuta and Marco Polo had been able to travel in the "unknown" worlds—the African hinterlands, the Americas, and Oceania—they would have witnessed to varying degrees similar phenomena and challenges.

The exploits of Marco Polo and Ibn Battuta suggest that a few men and women, mainly merchants and scholars, routinely traversed immense distances. These travelers used and strengthened existing trade routes between regions and fostered contacts across cultural boundaries. Their journeys revealed a Eurasian world linked from the Mediterranean in the west to China in the east. Along the trade routes, merchants, travelers, commodities, and ideas circulated freely through great port cities such as Surat and Calicut along the Malabar coast in India; Zanzibar and Kilwa in East Africa; and Genoa, Venice, and Alexandria along the northern and southern shores of the Mediterranean Sea.

Although it fell in 1276, Hangzhou survived the Mongol conquest reasonably intact. However, the tombs of the Song royal family were ransacked for valuables in 1285 to raise funds for the construction and renovation of Buddhist monasteries and temples. It was still, when the Venetian traveler Marco Polo visited it in the 1280s and the Muslim traveler Ibn Battuta in the 1340s, one of the greatest cities in the world. They both agreed that neither Europe nor the Islamic world had anything like it.

After defeating the Jin in northern China in 1234 and the Southern Song by 1280, the Mongol conquest changed the political and social landscape. The population in the north, especially in Kaifeng, already had begun to drop precipitously under the Jin. When the demand for iron ores and coal dried up, steel production declined; it came to almost a total halt after the Yellow River shifted south in 1194, severing Kaifeng, as the key industrial city in the north, from its iron mines and smelters. By 1330, now under the Mongols, the once magnificent Kaifeng, with a population once exceeding a million, had become a ramshackle town of fewer than 90,000 inhabitants.

Mongol rule did not involve the imposition of rough ways of the steppe lands on "civilized" urbanite Chinese (though such was the view of Han ideologues). True, China acquired a new ruling hierarchy. Chinese Confucian insiders were relegated to a subordinate station—and withdrew to exercise power, to the extent they were permitted, at the local level. Outsiders, non-Chinese known as the *semu* (categorized peoples), took over political control. They themselves were a heterogeneous group of Afro-Eurasian peoples—Mongols, Tanguts, Khitan, Jurchen, Muslims, Tibetans, Persians, Turks, Nestorians, Jews, Armenians—a new conquering elite that ruled over a vast Han majority. The result was a segmented ruling system, in which incumbent Chinese elites governed locally while newcomers who came from around Afro-Eurasia handled the levers of the central dynastic polity and collected taxes for the Mongols.

MONGOL REVERBERATIONS IN SOUTHEAST ASIA

Southeast Asia was also whiplashed by the Mongol conquests. Circling Song defenses along the rivers and lakes in South China, the Mongols marched into the southwest and conquered the states of Dali and Pyu in Yunnan and Burma. From there, in the 1270s, the armies turned back to China, heading directly east into the soft underbelly of the Song state. In this sweep, portions of mainland Southeast Asia became part of the Mongol empire and thus were annexed to China for the first time. As the kingdom of Dali and other polities became prefectures of Mongol-ruled China, the autonomy that the southwest had enjoyed since the Han and Tang dynasties came to an end. Even the distant Khmer regime felt the consequences of the Mongol conquest of the Song dynasty when

the Mongol fleet passed by on the way to attack and take Java—unsuccessfully, as it turned out—in 1293.

THE FALL OF BAGHDAD

As in China, in Islamic lands the brunt of foreign invasions was borne by the empire's core. By this time Baghdad had become a mere shadow of its former glorious self, though caliphs continued to sit on the throne, proclaiming their dominion over all the Islamic world. From their earlier attacks on the Islamic borderlands of central Asia, Mongol raiding parties learned of the weaknesses and divisions of Islamic rulers in the heartlands.

In the thirteenth century, Mongol tribesmen streamed west out of the eastern steppes, crossing the whole of Asia and entering into the eastern parts of Europe. Mongke Khan, a grandson of the great Mongol unifier and war leader Chinggis, made clear the Mongol aspiration for world domination, appointing his brother Kubilai to rule over China, Tibet, and the northern parts of India and commanding another brother, Hulagu, to add the western territories of Iran, Syria, Egypt, Byzantium, and Armenia to the Mongol imperium.

When Hulagu reached Baghdad in 1258, he encountered a feeble foe: merely 10,000 horsemen faced his army of 200,000 soldiers, who were eager to acquire the booty of a wealthy city at the crossroads of Afro-Eurasian commerce. Even before the battle had taken place, Baghdadis knew the fate that awaited them. Poets were composing elegies for the dead and mourning the defeat of Islam.

The slaughter was vast, and few were spared. Hulagu himself boasted to one of the European kings that he had taken the lives of at least 200,000 people. The Mongols gave no quarter, pursuing their adversaries everywhere. They hunted them in wells, latrines, and sewers and followed them into the upper floors of buildings, killing them on rooftops until, as the Iraqi Arab historian Ibn Kathir observed, "blood poured from the gutters into the streets. . . . The same happened in the mosques and . . . Baghdad, which had been the most civilized of all cities, became a ruin with only a few inhabitants" (Lewis, pp. 82–83). In a few weeks of sheer terror, the venerable Abbasid caliphate was demolished. Hulagu's forces showed no mercy to the caliph himself, who was rolled up in a carpet and trampled to death by horses, his blood soaked up by the rug so it would leave no mark on the ground. With Baghdad crushed, the Mongol armies pushed on to Syria, slaughtering Muslims along the way. A succession crisis in the Mongol heartland pulled Hulagu away from the front, however.

In the end, the Egyptian Mamluks, an Islamic regime built by slave-soldiers, stemmed the advance of the Mongol armies in 1261, thereby preventing Egypt from falling into Mongol hands. The Mongol empire had reached its outer limits. Better at conquering than controlling, defeating rather than governing, the Mongols struggled to rule their vast possessions in makeshift states. But bit by bit, and with gathering speed, they ceded control to local administrators and dynasties who promised to govern as their surrogates. There was also chronic feuding among the Mongol dynasts, especially between jealous sons. In China and in Persia, Mongol rule collapsed in the fourteenth century.

Mongol conquest reshaped the social landscape of Afro-Eurasia. Islam was decisively transformed: never again would it have a unifying authority like the caliphate or a powerful center like Baghdad. Though not sundered in quite the way Islam's heartland was, China was divided and changed in other ways. The Mongols introduced many Persian, Islamic, and Byzantine influences on China's architecture, art, science, and medicine. The Yuan policy of benign tolerance for foreign creeds and consistent contacts with western Asia also brought elements from Christianity, Judaism, Zoroastrianism, and Islam into the Chinese mix. The Mongol thrust into China thus led to a flowering and great opening, as fine goods, traders, and technology would flow unstintingly from China to the rest of the world in the ensuing centuries. Finally, the Mongol state, after its bloody conquests, settled down and promoted an Afro-Eurasian interconnectedness that this huge territorial landmass had not known before and would not experience again for many centuries. Out of conquest and translandmass warfare would come centuries of trade, migration, and increasing contacts among Africa, Europe, and Asia.

Chronology

	700 CE	800 CE	900 CE	1000 CE
SUB-SAHARAN AFRICA				
THE AMERICAS		Moche people found Chan Chan, c. 900 Toltec Empire in Mexico Valley, c. 900–1100	Cahokia flourishes as a commercial hub in Mississippi River valley, c. 1000 Chimú Empire, 1000–1460	
THE ISLAMIC WORLD			Muslims become a majority in Abassid caliphate	
SOUTH ASIA			Turkish invasions from Central Asia begin	
EAST ASIA		Heian period in Japan, 794–1185	Song dynasty founded, 960 Koryo dynasty rules, 918–1392 Lady Shikibu (c. 976–c. 1031) writes The Tale of Genji Gunpowder invented	
SOUTHEAST ASIA		Khmer kingdom, 899–1431		
CHRISTIAN EUROPE			Iaroslav the Wise (1016–1054) rebuilds Kiev as a small scale Constantinople	

CONCLUSION

Between 1000 and 1300, the world of Afro-Eurasia was being divided into large cultural spheres. At the same time, as people traded and migrated across longer distances, the regions of Afro-Eurasia prospered and became more integrated. In the center of Afro-Eurasia, Islam was firmly ensconced, its merchants, scholars, and travelers taking full advantage of their location to serve as commercial and cultural intermediaries joining the entire landmass together. As Indian Ocean seaborne trade expanded, India, too, became a commercial crossroads. Merchants set up businesses in the Indian port cities and welcomed traders who arrived from the Arab lands to the west, from China, and from Southeast Asia. China also boomed, pouring its manufactures into trading networks that encompassed all of Afro-Eurasia and reached into African frontiers.

Trade helped delineate the parts of the world. The prosperity it brought also helped create new classes of peoples—thinkers, writers, and naturalists—who more clearly defined what it meant to belong to the regions of Afro-Eurasia. By 1300, learned priests and writers had begun to reimagine each of the world's regions as more than just territories: they were ideas that were now maturing into cultures with definable—and defensible—geographic boundaries. More and more these intellectuals sought to deliver their messages to commoners as well as to rulers.

1100 CE	1200 CE	1300 CE	1400 CE
Kingdom of Mali emerges	Swahili emerges as a distinct language linking the coast of East Africa		
Great Zimbabwe	Mandinka merchants establish vast commercial networks linking West Africa		
	King Mansa Musa of Mali (ruled 1312–1332) completes the hajj, 1325–1326		
Turkish forces defeat Byzantine armies at Manzikert, 1071			
Ibn Rushd (1126–1198) refines rationalist philosophy			
	Jalal al-Din Rumi (1207–1273) spreads Sufi ideas		
	Mongol forces sack Baghdad, end Abassid caliphate, 1258		
	Turkish warriors found Delhi Sultanate in northern India, 1206–1526		
	Buddhism loses almost all influence in India		
		Japan fends off Mongol invasions, 1274–1281	
Song iron production peaks, 1078		Mongols conquer Southern Song dynasty, 1279	
Song dynasty loses North China to Jurchen Jin dynasty, 1127		Mongol invasions of Korea	
Kamakura shogunate, 1192–1333		Yuan dynasty, 1280–1368	
	Islamic influence increases in city-states		
	Mongols invade southwestern China and Burma		
		Mongol fleet attacks Java, 1293	
	Francis of Assisi (1182–1226) preaches message of repentance		
	Genoese ships link northern and southern Europe by sea		
Spanish Reconquista, 1061–1492	Half of Europe's population lives in its west		
Crusades, 1095–1272			
Roman Catholic farmers migrate from the western to central and eastern European frontier zones			

While Afro-Eurasia was increasingly carved up into large cultural blocs with more rigid identities and boundaries, neither the Americas nor sub-Saharan Africa saw quite the same degree of integration. But trade and migration in these areas of the world did have profound effects. Great African cultures flourished as they came into contact with the commercial energy of trade on the Indian Ocean. Indeed, Africans' trade with one another grew, bringing together coastal and interior regions into an ever-more integrated world. American peoples also built great cities that dominated large cultural areas and thrived through long-distance and regional trade. American cultures shared significant common features—reliance on trade, maize, and the exchange of similar status goods, such as shells and precious feathers. And larger and larger areas honored the same spiritual centers.

By 1300, trade, migration, and conflict were making the Afro-Eurasian regional worlds interconnected in unprecedented ways. When Mongol armies swept into China, into Southeast Asia, and into the heart of Islam, they applied a veneer of political integration to these dispersed parts and built on strong commercial links that already existed. But it is worth reminding ourselves that most people lived local lives, governed by the perennial need for subsistence and by the micro-level powers of spiritual and governmental agents who acted at the behest of distant and very remote authorities. Still, locals could see and hear the evidence of cross-cultural exchanges everywhere—in the clothing styles of provincial elites, such as Chinese silks in Paris or Quetzal plumes in northern Mexico; in enticements to move (and forced removals) to new frontiers; in the news of faraway conquests or advancing armies. In these ways, worlds were coming together within themselves and across their territorial boundaries, while remaining apart as they sought to maintain their own identity and traditions. In Afro-Eurasia especially, as the movement and goods and peoples shifted from ancient land routes to sea-lanes, these long-distance contacts were more frequent and far-reaching. Never before had the world seen so much activity that connected its parts. Nor within those parts had it ever seen so much shared cultural affinity—linguistic, religious, legal, and military. Indeed, by the time of the rise of the Mongol empire, the regions that composed the globe were those that we now recognize as the cultural spheres of today's world.

STUDY QUESTIONS

WWNORTON.COM/STUDYSPACE

1. List the major cultural regions that existed in the thirteenth century that are explored in this chapter and explain where they were. Which of these regions were "together" and which were "apart"? How were regions connected?

2. List the four major cultural regions in Afro-Eurasia and briefly explain the defining characteristics of each. What did the various people and groups in these geographic areas all have in common that distinguished them from others?

3. Explain the role of global commercial hubs in India, China, and Egypt in fostering global commercial contacts across Afro-Eurasia. How did they reflect revolutions in maritime transportation?

4. Explain which areas of sub-Saharan Africa were parts of the larger Afro-Eurasian world by 1300. How did contact with other regions shape political and cultural developments in sub-Saharan Africa?

5. Describe the cultural diversity within the Islamic world during this era. How were these diverse communities integrated into a uniform regional identity?

6. Analyze the impact of Muslim Turkish invaders on India between 1000 and 1300. To what extent did India remain distinct from the Islamic world in this era?

7. Describe how the Song dynasty reacted to the military strength of its pastoral neighbors. How did these relationships foster a separate and distinct Chinese identity during this era?

8. Compare and contrast cultural and political developments in Korea, Japan, and Southeast Asia during this era. How were these societies influenced by other regional cultures?

9. Describe how Christianity expanded its geographic reach during this era. How did this expansion affect Latin Christianity in western Europe and Orthodox Christianity in eastern Europe?

10. Analyze the extent to which peoples in the Americas established closer contact with each other during this era. How extensive were these contacts compared with those in the Afro-Eurasian world?

11. Describe the empire created by the Mongols in the thirteenth century. How did Mongol policies bring the various regions of Afro-Eurasia into greater contact with each other?

FURTHER READINGS

Allsen, Thomas, *Commodity and Exchange in the Mongol Empire: A Cultural History of Islamic Textiles* (1997). A study that uses golden brocade, the textile most treasured by Mongol rulers, as a lens through which to analyze the vast commercial networks facilitated by the Mongol conquests and control.

———, *Culture and Conquest in Mongol Eurasia* (2001). A work that emphasizes the cultural and scientific exchanges that took place across Afro-Eurasia as a result of the Mongol conquest.

Bartlett, Robert, *The Making of Europe: Conquest, Colonization and Cultural Change, 950–1350* (1993). The modes of cultural, political, and demographic expansion of feudal Europe along its frontiers, especially in eastern Europe.

Bay, Edna G., *Wives of the Leopards: Gender, Politics, and Culture in the Kingdom of Dahomey* (1998). A work that stresses the role of women in an important West African society and dips into the early history of this area.

Beach, D. N., *Shona and Zimbabwe, 900–1850: An Outline of Shona History* (1980). A good place to start for exploring the history of Great Zimbabwe.

Brooks, George E., *Landlords and Strangers: Ecology, Society, and Trade in Western Africa, 1000–1630* (1993). A survey assembled from primary sources of early West African history that stresses transregional connections.

Buzurg ibn Shahriyar of Ramhormuz, *The Book of the Wonders of India: Mainland, Sea and Islands*, ed. and trans. G. S. P. Freeman-Greenville (1981). A collection of stories told by sailors, both true and fantastic; they help us imagine the lives of sailors of the era.

Chappell, Sally A. Kitt, *Cahokia: Mirror of the Cosmos* (2002). A thorough and vivid account of the "mound people"; it explores not just what we know of Cahokia but how we know it.

Christian, David, *A Short History of Russia, Central Asia, and Mongolia*, vol. 1, *Inner Eurasia from Prehistory to the Mongol Empire* (1998). Essential reading for students interested in interconnections across the Afro-Eurasian landmass.

Curtin, Philip, *Cross-Cultural Trade in World History* (1984). A groundbreaking book on intercultural trade with a primary focus on Africa, especially the cross-Saharan trade and Swahili coastal trade.

Dawson, Christopher, *Mission to Asia* (1980). Accounts of China and the Mongol Empire brought back by Catholic missionaries and diplomats after 1240 CE.

Foltz, Richard C., *Religions of the Silk Road: Overland Trade and Cultural Exchange from Antiquity to the Fifteenth Century* (1999). A study of the populations and the cities of the Silk Road as transmitters of culture across long distances.

Franklin, Simon, and Jonathan Shepherd, *The Emergence of Rus: 750–1200* (1996). The formation of medieval Russia between the Baltic and the Black Sea.

Gibb, Hamilton A. R., *Saladin: Studies in Islamic History*, ed. Yusuf Ibish (1974). A sympathetic portrait of one of Islam's leading political and military figures.

Goitein, S. D., *Letters of Medieval Jewish Traders* (1973). The classic study of medieval Jewish trading communities based on the commercial papers deposited in the Cairo Geniza (a synagogue storeroom) during the tenth and eleventh centuries; it explores not only commercial activities but also the personal lives of the traders around the Indian Ocean basin.

———, *A Mediterranean Society: An Abridgment in One Volume*, rev. and ed. Jacob Lassner (1999). A portrait of the Jewish merchant community with ties across the Afro-Eurasian landmass, based largely on the documents from the Cairo Geniza (of which Goitein was the primary researcher and interpreter).

———, "New Light on the Beginnings of the Karim Merchant," *The Journal of Social and Economic History of the Orient* 1 (1958). Goiten's description of Egyptian trade.

Harris, Joseph E., *The African Presence in Asia: Consequences of the East African Slave Trade* (1971). One of the few books that looks broadly at the impact of Africans and African slavery on the societies of Asia.

Hartwell, Robert, "Demographic, Political, and Social Transformations of China, 750–1550," *Harvard Journal of Asiatic Studies* 42 (1982): 365–442. A pioneering study of the demographic changes that overtook China during the Tang and Song dynasties, which are described in light of political reform movements and social changes in this seminal era.

Historical Relations across the Indian Ocean: Report and Papers of the Meeting of Experts Organized by UNESCO at Port Louis, Mauritius, from 15 to 19 July, 1974 (1980). Excellent essays on the connections of Africa with Asia across the Indian Ocean.

Hitti, Philip, *An Arab-Syrian Gentleman and Warrior in the Period of the Crusades: Memoirs of Usāmah ibn-Munqidh* (1929). The Crusaders seen through Muslim eyes.

Holt, P. M., *The Age of the Crusades: The Near East from the Eleventh Century to 1517* (1984). The Crusades period as seen from the eastern Mediterranean and through the lens of a leading British scholar of the area.

Hymes, Robert, and Conrad Schirokauer (eds.), *Ordering the World: Approaches to State and Society in Sung Dynasty China* (1993). A collection of essays that traces the intellectual, social, and political movements that shaped the Song state and its elites.

Ibn Battuta, *The Travels of Ibn Battuta*, trans. H.A.R. Gibb (2002). A readable translation of the classic book, originally published in 1929.

Ibn Fadlan, Ahmad, *Ibn Fadlan's Journey to Russia: A Tenth Century Traveler from Baghdad to the Volga River*, trans. with commentary by Richard Frye (2005). A coherent summary of the firsthand observations by an envoy who traveled from Baghdad to Russia.

Irwin, Robert, *The Middle East in the Middle Ages: The Early Mamluk Sultanate, 1250–1582* (1986). Egypt under Mamluk rule.

Lancaster, Lewis, Kikun Suh, and Chai-shin Yu (eds.), *Buddhism in Koryo: A Royal Religion* (1996). A description of Buddhism at its height in the Koryo period, when the religion made significant contributions to the development of Korean culture and monasteries of great beauty were constructed.

Levtzion, Nehemia, and Randall L. Pouwels (eds.), *The History of Islam in Africa* (2000). A useful general survey of the place of Islam in African history.

Lewis, Bernard (trans.), *Islam from the Prophet Muhammad to the Caphre of Constantinople* (1974). Vol. 2: Religion and Society. A fine collection of original sources that portray various aspects of classical Islamic society.

Lopez, Robert S., *The Commercial Revolution of the Middle Ages, 950–1350* (1976). An account focusing on the development around the Mediterranean of commercial practices such as the use of currency, accounting, and credit.

Maalouf, Amin, *The Crusades through Muslim Eyes*, trans. Jon Rothschild (1984). The European Crusaders as seen by the Muslim world.

Marcus, Harold G., *A History of Ethiopia* (2002). An authoritative overview of the history of this great culture.

Mass, Jeffrey, *Yoritomo and the Founding of the First Bakufu: The Origins of Dual Government in Japan* (1999). A revisionist account of how the Kamakura military leader Minamoto Yoritomo established the "dual polity" of court and warrior government in Japan.

McDermott, Joseph, *A Social History of the Chinese Book: Books and Literati Culture in Late Imperial China* (2006). The history of the book in China traced since the Song dynasty, with comparisons to the role of books in other civilizations, particularly the European.

McIntosh, Roderik, *The Peoples of the Middle Niger: The Island of Gold* (1988). A historical survey of an area often omitted from other textbooks.

Moore, Jerry D., *Cultural Landscapes in the Ancient Andes: Archaeologies of Place* (2005). The most recent and up-to-date analysis of findings based on recent archaeological evidence, emphasizing the importance of local cultures and diversity in the Andes.

Niane, D. T. (ed.), *Africa from the Twelfth to the Sixteenth Century*, vol. 4 of *General History of Africa* (1984). The general UNESCO history of Africa's volume on four centuries of African history. This work features the scholarship of Africans.

Oliver, Roland (ed.), *From c. 1050 to c. 1600*, vol. 3 of *The Cambridge History of Africa*, ed. J. D. Fage and Roland Oliver (1977). Another general survey of African history. This volume draws heavily on the work of British scholars.

Parry, J. H., *The Age of Reconnaissance: Discovery, Exploration and Settlement, 1450–1650* (1981). This book connects intellectual and technological developments of the Renaissance to the explorations of the new world.

Peters, Edward, *The First Crusade* (1971). The Crusaders as seen through their own eyes.

Petry, Carl F. (ed.), *Islamic Egypt, 640–1517*, vol. 1 of *The Cambridge History of Egypt*, ed. M. W. Daly (1998). A solid overview of the history of Islamic Egypt up to the Ottoman conquest.

Polo, Marco, *The Travels of Marco Polo*, ed. Manuel Komroff (1926). A solid translation of Marco Polo's famous account.

Popovic, Alexandre, *The Revolt of African Slaves in Iraq in the 3rd/9th Century*, trans. Leon King (1999). The account of a massive revolt against their slave masters by African slaves taken to labor in Iraq's mines and fields.

Scott, Robert, *Gothic Enterprise: A Guide to Understanding the Medieval Cathedral* (2003). The meaning and social function of religious building in medieval cities in northern Europe.

Shaffer, Lynda Norene, *Maritime Southeast Asia to 1500* (1996). A history of the peoples of the southeast fringe of the Eastern Hemisphere, up to the time that they became connected to the global commercial networks of the world.

Shimada, Izumi, "Evolution of Andean Diversity: Regional Formations (500 BCE–CE 600)," in Frank Salomon and Stuart Schwartz (eds.), *South America*, vol. 3 of *The Cambridge History of the Native Peoples of the Americas* (1999), part 1, pp. 350–517. A splendid overview that contrasts the varieties of lowland and highland cultures.

Steinberg, David Joel, et al., *In Search of Southeast Asia: A Modern History* (1987). An account of the emergence of the modern Southeast Asian polities of Cambodia, Burma, Thailand, and Indonesia.

Tyerman, Christopher, *God's War: A New History of the Crusades* (2006). The balance of religious and nonreligious motivations in the Crusades.

Waley, Daniel, *The Italian City-Republics*, 3rd ed. (1988). The structures and culture of the new cities of medieval Italy.

Watson, Andrew, *Agricultural Innovation in the Early Islamic World: The Diffusion of Crops and Farming Techniques, 700–1100* (1983). An impressive study of the spread of new crops throughout the Muslim world.

11

CRISES AND RECOVERY IN AFRO-EURASIA, 1300S–1500S

W hen Mongol armies besieged the Genoese trading outpost of Caffa on the Black Sea in 1346, they not only damaged old trading links between East Asia and the Mediterranean, they also unleashed an even more devastating, invisible force. Mongol troops entered the city and brought with them a disease picked up in the Gobi Desert: the bubonic plague. Defeated Genoese merchants and soldiers withdrew, inadvertently taking the germs with them aboard their ships. By the time they arrived in Messina, Sicily, half the passengers were dead. The rest were dying. Those who waited eagerly on shore were horrified at the sight and turned the ship away. Desperately, the ship's captain went to the next port, only to face the same fate. Despite this, the Europeans were unable to keep the plague (referred to as the Black Death) from reaching their shores. As it spread from port to port, it eventually contaminated all of Europe, killing about one-third of its population.

This story exemplifies one of the many disruptive effects of the Mongol invasions on societies across the Afro-Eurasian landmass. These invasions ushered in an age in which people of dispersed worlds engaged in greater communication and contact

473

across cultural and political borders. But in establishing and extending channels of exchange, the Mongols unwittingly created conduits for the flow of microbes to follow the land trails and sea lanes of human voyagers. These germs devastated societies even more decisively than did the Mongols. They were the real "murderous hordes" of world history, infecting people from every community, class, and culture they encountered. So staggering was the magnitude of the Black Death's toll that Afro-Eurasia did not regain the population densities of the thirteenth century for another 200 years. It shook many communities to their very cores. The interconnectedness that the Mongols had fostered fell apart. The most severely affected were those regions and populations that the Mongols had brought together. Settlements and commercial hubs along the old Silk Road and around the Mediterranean Sea and the South China Sea became places of dying. While segments of the Indian Ocean trading world experienced death and disruption, South Asian societies, which had escaped the Mongol conquest, were also spared the wholesale dying and political disruptions associated with the Black Death.

During the fourteenth and fifteenth centuries, following population loss, political crises, and widespread social disorders often caused by the plague, many Afro-Eurasian societies recovered their political vitality. They improved new means to rebuild their communities and attempted to build new dynasties—rule by royal hereditary households—to restore order and stability. The new rulers, merchants, and scholar-bureaucrats not only revived the old links between communities but also pioneered new commercial networks. In so doing, they created new polities, economic institutions, and social hierarchies across Afro-Eurasia—a world in which imperial dynasties became ever more important.

This chapter explores how Afro-Eurasian societies coped with and responded to the long-term impact of the Mongol invasions and the Black Death. We leave for subsequent chapters the discussions of political changes beyond Afro-Eurasia. Here, we focus on how Afro-Eurasian societies rebuilt their political orders, creating centralized power struc-

tures that lasted for centuries and that shaped their encounters with peoples and polities in Africa, the Americas, and Oceania. Here, too, we highlight several defining events and decisions that had far-reaching, if hardly predictable, consequences for reshaping the power relations between different parts of the world.

COLLAPSE AND INTEGRATION

> → *What were the key factors in rebuilding political societies?*

While the Mongol invasions overturned political systems, the plague devastated society itself. Afro-Eurasia's rulers could explain the assaults of outside "barbarians" to their people, but it was much harder for them to make sense of the invisible enemy. Many concluded fatalistically that mass death was God's wish. The upheaval wrought by the plague, however, provided rulers the opportunity to consolidate and centralize their power by making dynastic matches, putting in place new armies and taxes to support them, and establishing new systems to administer their states.

THE BLACK DEATH

The spread of the Black Death out of Mongolia in East Asia and other adjoining parts of central Asia was the single most significant historical development for much of the Afro-Eurasian world in the fourteenth century. The disease stemmed from a combination of bubonic, pneumonic, and septicaemic plague strains and resulted in a frightening loss of life. Among infected populations, death rates ranged from 25 to 50 percent.

Focus Questions   CRISES AND RECOVERY IN AFRO-EURASIA

→ *What were the key factors in rebuilding political societies?*

→ *What were the major differences among the three Islamic dynasties?*

→ *Why did Europe remain disunited (and have difficulty recovering from the Black Death)?*

→ *How did the Ming centralize their authority?*

 WWNORTON.COM/STUDYSPACE

How did the Black Death spread so far? One explanation seems to have been the climatic changes of this period. A drying up of the central Asian steppe borderlands may have forced rodents out of their usual dwelling places and also pressed the pastoral peoples who carried the strains, to move south into closer proximity to settled, agricultural communities. So, it is thought, began the migration of microbes. But what spread germs across Afro-Eurasia was the Mongols' economic and political grid. Breaking out first around the 1320s in the Yunnan province of southwestern China, the plague spread throughout China and then traversed the major Afro-Eurasian trade routes (see Map 11-1). The main avenue of transmission was across central Asia to the Crimea and the Black Sea, and from there by ship to the Mediterranean Sea and the Italian city-states. Secondary routes were by sea, one from China to the Red Sea and another across the Indian Ocean, through the Persian Gulf, and into the Fertile Crescent and Iraq. All routes terminated at the Italian port cities, where ships with dead and dying men aboard arrived in October 1347. From there, what Europeans at the time called the Pestilence or the Great Mortality spread across the western end of the Afro-Eurasian landmass.

The Black Death struck an expanding Afro-Eurasian population, made vulnerable because its members had no immunities to the disease and because its major cultural realms were now connected through more intensively used trading networks. Rodents, mainly rats, carried the plague bacilli that caused the disease. Fleas transmitted the bacilli from rodent to rodent, as well as to humans. The epidemic was terrifying, for the disease had not been seen for centuries and its causes were unknown at the time. The infected died quickly, sometimes overnight, and with great suffering, coughing up blood and oozing pus and blood from ugly black sores the size of eggs. Some European wise men attributed the ravaging of their societies to astrological forces; they suspected an unusual alignment of the planets Saturn, Jupiter, and Mars as the cause. Many believed that God was angry with man. The Florentine historian Matteo Villani compared the plague to the biblical Flood and believed that the end of mankind was imminent.

The Black Death wrought devastation throughout much of the Afro-Eurasian landmass. Entire populations perished. The Chinese population plunged from around 120 million to 80 million over the course of a century. Europe saw its numbers reduced by one-third. When farmers were afflicted, food production collapsed. As a result, famine often followed the disease, thereby killing off the weak survivors. But the worst afflicted were those in the crowded cities, especially in the ports along the Afro-Eurasian coast, which had been the hubs of trade and migration and where settlement was most dense. Some cities lost up to two-thirds of their population. Refugees from the cities fled their homes, seeking security and food in the countryside. The shortage of food and other necessities led to rapidly rising prices, strikes, and unrest across Afro-

Plague Victim. The plague was highly contagious and quickly led to death. Here the physician and his helper cover their noses to avoid the unbearable stench emanating from the patient; they can do little to help the victim as they do not understand what causes the boils, internal bleeding, or violent coughing that afflict him.

Eurasia. Political leaders added to their unpopularity by repressing unrest. The great Arab historian Ibn Khaldun (1332–1406), who lost his mother and father and a number of his teachers to the Black Death in Tunis, underscored the sense of desolation in the wake of the plague: "Cities and buildings were laid waste, roads and way signs were obliterated, settlements and mansions became empty, dynasties and tribes grew weak," he wrote. "The entire world changed."

REBUILDING STATES

Starting in the late fourteenth century, Afro-Eurasians began the task of rebuilding their political order and reconstructing their trading networks. Rebuilding military and tax administrations could not be tackled without political legitimacy.

SCANDINAVIA
• 1349

NORTH SEA

BALTIC SEA

Novgorod

Edinburgh
(1350)

Moscow
•
MUSCOVY
• 1351

Dublin
(1349)
BRITAIN

Oxford
(1348)
London
(1348)

Lübeck
(1349)

Danzig

Bremen
(1349)
Cologne
(1349)

Amiens
(1348)
Paris
(1348)

EUROPE

Cracow

Kiev

KHANATE OF THE
GOLDEN HORDE

Rostov

New Sarai

ARAL
SEA

Bordeaux
(1348)

Venice
(1347)

Buda
(1349)

Avignon
(1347)
Genoa
(1347)
Florence
(1347)
Pisa
(1347)
Siena
(1347)

Caffa
(1346)

CASPIAN
SEA

Barcelona
(1348)
Marseille

BLACK
SEA

Constantinople
(1347)

Trebizond

Bukhara

Madrid
•

Naples

Lisbon
(1349)
SPAIN
• 1348

Palermo
(1347)

Messina
(1347)

Athens
(1347)

Tabriz

Silk route

Ceuta
Fez

Algiers

Tunis

MEDITERRANEAN

SEA

Aleppo
(1347)

Damascus
(1347)

Baghdad
(1347)

PERSIA

Isfahan
•

IL-KHANATE

Marrakesh
(1349)

Tripoli
(1348)

Alexandria
(1347)

Cairo
(1347)

Basra
•

Shiraz
•

Persian Gulf

Hormuz
•

RED SEA

Mecca
(1348)

ARABIA

AFRICA

ARABIAN

Aden
(1351)

Mogadishu

INDIA

ATLANTIC

OCEAN

> Progress of bubonic plague
> —— Trade routes
> • Known areas of major outbreaks
> * Modern Chinese provincial names for
>   regions affected by outbreak of plague

MAP 11-1   THE SPREAD OF THE BLACK DEATH

The Black Death was an Afro-Eurasian pandemic of the fourteenth century. Use the map to identify its place of origin. Can you explain why certain parts of Afro-Eurasia were more severely affected than others? Why were its major places of outbreak located in China and western Europe? The Black Death spread across the whole of the Mongol Empire. Can you offer any explanation why the Mongol states were so involved?

Lake Baikal

MONGOL

ANCESTRAL

HOMELAND

Karakorum

Shangdu

Silk route

Tashkent

Samarkand

Kashgar

(1354)
Beijing

1351
1352

1331
HEBEI*

Balkh

SHANDONG*   1345

Kabul

1353
1351

1354   1353   1346

1335   Kaifeng

TIBET

1332   1321

KHANATE OF THE

HUBEI*   1323

Delhi

Lhasa

1320

Hangzhou

GREAT KHAN

1351

Nagasaki

JAPAN

SEA
OF
JAPAN

Nanchang
(1352)   Fuzhou

1356

1353   FUJIAN*

DELHI

YUNNAN*   1354   1345

SULTANATE

1320

BURMA

Guangzhou
(1354)

Pagan
(before 1320)

PACIFIC

SOUTH

OCEAN

CHINA

SEA   Angkor

SEA

Calicut

Brunei

OCEAN

Melaka

BORNEO

SUMATRA

JAVA

0		500		1000 Miles

0	500	1000 Kilometers

In much of Afro-Eurasia, this was the challenge of the fourteenth century. In the wake of disease, rulers needed to revive confidence in themselves and their polities, which they did by fostering beliefs and rituals that confirmed their legitimacy and by increasing their control over subject peoples.

The basis for power was the dynasty—the hereditary ruling family that passed power from one generation to the next. Dynasties sought to establish their legitimacy in three fundamental ways: First, the ruling families insisted that they belonged in power as a calling from above. The Ming emperors in China traditionally claimed a "mandate of heaven," while European monarchs claimed to rule by "divine right." Either way, ruling households claimed to be closer to the gods than to commoners. Second, leaders attempted to prevent squabbling and fighting among potential heirs by promulgating clear rules about succession to the throne. Clear-cut succession made it difficult for contenders to challenge the authority of the heir to the throne; many European nations tried to standardize succession by passing titles down to the eldest male heir, but in practice there were many complications and quarrels over the right to the throne. In the Islamic world, successors could be designated by the incumbent or elected by the community; but here too, struggles over succession occurred regularly. Third, ruling families elevated their power through conquest or alliance—sending armies to extend their domains or having princes and princesses marry the rulers of other states or members of other elite households. Once it established its legitimacy, the royal family would seek to consolidate its power by enacting coercive laws and punishments and sending royal emissaries to govern far-flung territories. It would also establish standing armies and set up new administrative structures to collect taxes and to oversee building projects that would proclaim royal power.

State-building in the wake of great devastation varied across Afro-Eurasia but usually drew upon older traditions. Some areas, like South Asia, had been spared the ravages of the Black Death, and some, like western Europe, had avoided conquest by the Mongols. In China, the Ming renounced the Mongol legacy, extolling their pure Han Chinese identity and repudiating the Mongol eagerness to expand. Two of the successor Islamic states, the Ottoman Empire and the Safavid state, had to deal with a large influx of Turkish-speaking peoples stemming from the Mongol invasion of the Islamic world; the third Islamic state, the Mughal Empire in South Asia, replaced the Delhi Sultanate, which had been seriously weakened, not by a Mongol army, but by Turkish warriors. Many of these regimes lasted for centuries; their political institutions and cultural values became deeply embedded in

> *Many of these regimes lasted for centuries; their political institutions and cultural values became deeply embedded in the fabric of their societies.*

the fabric of their societies and influenced the actions of rulers and subjects at home and abroad.

ISLAMIC DYNASTIES

> → *What were the major differences among the three Islamic dynasties?*

In 1258 the Mongols sacked the great city of Baghdad, capital of the Abbasid Empire.

In doing so the Mongols had effectively destroyed older Islamic political regimes, but they failed to establish enduring dynasties. Part of their problem was that they were unable to shed their military orientation. The original Mongol state was organized for military action; economic advancement and cultural development occupied a decidedly secondary status in the minds of these military men, who were unwilling to share power with other groups. The Persian Il-khans made Maraghah in Azerbaijan their capital, even though it was little more than an enlarged military encampment, in preference to the great administrative center of Baghdad. They continued to employ terrorizing military tactics in dealing with their opponents, leveling recalcitrant villages and intimidating their subjects by parading the heads of their enemies on pikes before sullen resisters. Mongol rule was doomed because the Mongol rulers were unsuccessful at unifying warriors and pastoral peoples—and their enormous herds—with settled farmers.

Although they did not leave behind them institutional foundations for a new order, the Mongols did clear the political slate of the old order in much of the Islamic world. And then came an even more devastating killer: the Black Death. It reached Baghdad by 1347, carried there, perhaps, by an Azerbaijani army that besieged the city in that year. By the next year, the plague had come to Egypt, Syria, and Cyprus; one report from Tunis in June 1348 records the deaths of more than 1,000 people a day in the North African city. Animals too were heavily afflicted; one Egyptian writer commented: "The country was not far from being ruined. . . . One found in the desert the bodies of savage animals with the bubos under their arms. It was the same with horses, camels, asses, and all the beasts in general, including birds, even the ostriches." In the eastern Mediterranean, too, the Black Death left much of the Islamic world in a state of near political and economic collapse.

As new polities emerged from this economic and demographic crisis, they had to build from the ground floor. Warrior chiefs and charismatic religious leaders vied with one another to fill the political vacuum. The new rulers who appeared as Mongol power waned in the fourteenth century, notably the Ottomans in Anatolia and the Safavids in western Persia, operated out of strategic locations in the Islamic heartland. These new rulers gradually rebuilt state institutions.

Through migration, warfare, and eventually the consolidation of post-Mongol states, the boundaries of Islam's domain spread. Prior to the Mongol incursions, the political, economic, and cultural centers of the Islamic world were to be found in Egypt, Syria, and Iraq. The majority of the inhabitants of these regions spoke Arabic, the language of the Prophet, and hence the language of Islamic devotion and theology. These areas, along with the Arabian peninsula, contained Islam's most holy cities: Mecca, Medina, Jerusalem, Damascus, Cairo, and various religious cities in Iraq. Even before the Mongol invasions, Turks had begun to migrate into these regions, and Persian had started to emerge as a rival language of Islamic poetry and philosophy. Yet, it was the Mongol invasions of the thirteenth century, with the devastation that they brought to Persia and Iraq and the influx of nomadic peoples, which opened the door for a new Islamic world to appear. The new world of Islam, based now to a much larger extent than before on Turkish- and Persian-speaking populations, emerged in a vast geographical triangle that stretched from Anatolia in the west to Khurasan in the east and to the southern apex at Baghdad. Of course, the old Arabic-speaking Islamic world did not die out, but it had to cede some of its hegemony to the new rulers and the new religious men who now came to the fore.

At the beginning of the sixteenth century, three new and powerful dynasties dominated much of the old Islamic world. Eventually, they grew powerful enough to become empires. Between them, the Ottoman, Safavid, and Mughal empires used and developed the rich agrarian resources of the regions of the Indian Ocean and the Mediterranean Sea basin and benefited from a brisk seaborne and overland trade. Of these three, the Ottomans were in full flourish at the beginning of the sixteenth century; the Safavids and Mughals were just beginning to emerge.

By the middle of the sixteenth century, the Mughals dominated the northern Indus River valley, the Safavids Persia, and the Ottomans Anatolia, the Arab world, and large parts of southern and eastern Europe. Sharing core Islamic beliefs, each empire had unique political features. The most centralized and powerful, the Ottoman Empire, occupied the pivotal expanse between Europe and Asia. The Ottomans embraced a Sunni, or orthodox, view of Islam, while adopting pre-existing Byzantine ways of ruling and finding innovative ways to integrate the many new peoples who inhabited their ever-expanding territories. The Safavids were adherents

of Shiism and ardently devoted to the pre-Islamic traditions of Persia (present-day Iran). While the Safavids were an internally cohesive Turkish people, Safavid rulers were less effective at expanding their mission beyond their Persian base. The Mughals ruled over the wealthy but divided realm that is much of today's India, Pakistan, and Bangladesh and carried even further the already well-developed South Asian religious and political traditions of assimilating Islamic and pre-Islamic Indian ways. Their very wealth and the decentralization of their domain made the Mughals constant targets for internal dissent and eventually for external aggression.

THE RISE OF THE OTTOMAN EMPIRE

Although the Mongols had little interest in Anatolia, a borderland region of little economic importance to them, their military forays against the Anatolian Seljuk Turkish state opened the region up to new political forces in the late thirteenth century. The ultimate victors in Anatolia proved to be the Ottoman Turks, who succeeded in transforming themselves from Islamic warrior bands operating on the borderlands between the Islamic and Christian worlds into rulers of a settled state and finally into sovereigns of a far-flung, highly bureaucratic empire.

Under their chief, Osman (ruled 1299–1326), the Turkish Ottomans developed a stern and disciplined warrior ethos, and they triumphed over other warrior bands because, unlike their rivals, they succeeded in mastering the techniques of settled administration. Other warrior bands, composed of young men who lived off the land and fought for booty under the leadership of charismatic military leaders, typically had little place in their societies for artisans, merchants, bureaucrats, and clerics. By contrast, the Ottomans, based in the city of Bursa in western Anatolia, realized that their consolidation of power depended on attracting just these groups. This they did with great skill, and in time, not only did the Ottoman state win the favor of Islamic clerics, but it also became the champion of Sunni, orthodox Islam throughout the entire Islamic world.

By the middle of the fourteenth century, the Ottomans had expanded beyond their regional base in Anatolia and moved into the Balkans, becoming the most powerful force in the eastern Mediterranean and western Asia. The state controlled a vast territory, stretching in the west to the Moroccan border, in the north to Hungary and Moldavia, in the south through the Arabian peninsula, and in the east to the Iraqi-Persian border (see Map 11-2). At the top of the Ottomans' elaborate hierarchy sat the sultan. Below him was a military and civilian bureaucracy, whose task was to exact obedience and revenue from subjects. The Ottoman bureaucracy allowed the sultan to expand his realm, which in turn forced him to invest in a larger bureaucracy.

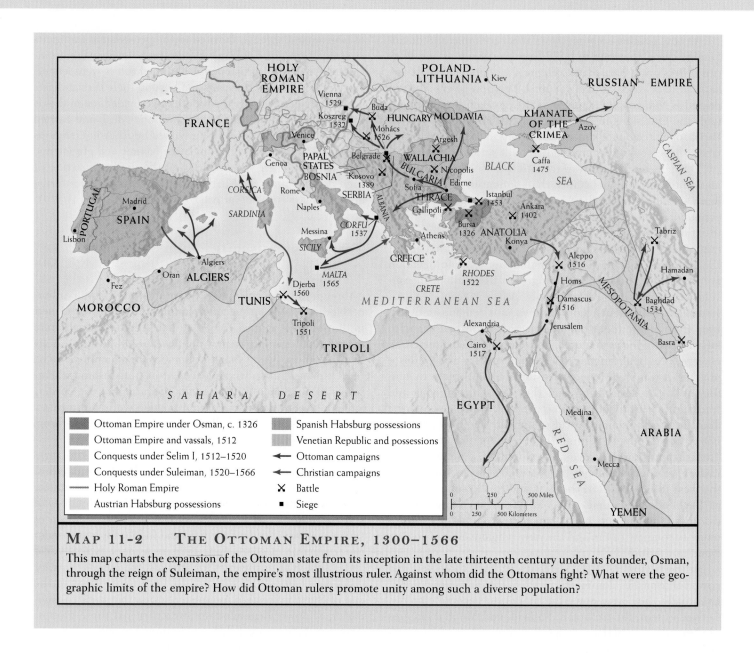

MAP 11-2   THE OTTOMAN EMPIRE, 1300–1566

This map charts the expansion of the Ottoman state from its inception in the late thirteenth century under its founder, Osman, through the reign of Suleiman, the empire's most illustrious ruler. Against whom did the Ottomans fight? What were the geographic limits of the empire? How did Ottoman rulers promote unity among such a diverse population?

THE CONQUEST OF CONSTANTINOPLE   The Ottoman Empire's spectacular expansion was first and foremost a military affair. To recruit followers, the Ottomans promised wealth and glory to new subjects. This was expensive, but territorial expansion generated vast financial and administrative rewards. Moreover, by spreading the spoils of conquest and lucrative positions in the emerging state, rulers bought off potentially discontented subordinates. Still, without military might, the Ottomans would not have enjoyed the successes of the fifteenth century that were associated with the brilliant reigns of Murad II (ruled 1421–1451) and his aptly named successor, Mehmed the Conqueror (ruled 1451–1481). Mehmed vowed, shortly after his coronation as emperor in 1451, to capture Constantinople, capital of the

Byzantine Empire and a city of strategic and commercial importance. He knew he would need a large and well-armed fighting force to take Constantinople, for the heavily fortified city had kept the Turks at bay for almost a century. First he built a fortress of his own, on the European bank of the Bosporus Strait; here he could prevent European vessels from reaching the capital. Then, by promising his soldiers free access to booty and portraying the conquest of Constantinople as a holy cause, he amassed a huge army that outnumbered the defending force of 7,000 by more than tenfold. His troops bombarded Constantinople's massive walls, with artillery that included enormous cannons built by Hungarian and Italian engineers, for forty days. On May 29, 1453, Ottoman troops overwhelmed the surviving soldiers and took the ancient

Roman and Christian capital of Byzantium, which Mehmed promptly renamed Istanbul.

Many of the Christian survivors fled the city for ports to the west, taking with them their knowledge of Greek, which had virtually died out in western Europe. Some also carried classical and Arabic manuscripts. These refugees would be instrumental in reviving the study of ancient texts in Europe. Meanwhile, Mehmed made Istanbul the Ottoman capital, adopting Byzantine bureaucrats and administrative practices to solidify his newly enlarged state. From Istanbul, Mehmed and his successors would continue their expansion, eventually seizing all of Greece and the Balkan region. Ottoman navies increasingly controlled sea lanes in the eastern Mediterranean, curtailing European access to the rich ports through which the goods of the lucrative caravan trade were traded. By the end of the fifteenth century, Ottoman forces were menacing another of Christendom's great capitals, Vienna, and European merchants had grown fearful that never again would they be able to obtain the riches of Asia by the traditional overland route.

THE TOOLS OF EMPIRE-BUILDING Having penetrated the heartland of Christian Byzantium in southeastern Europe in the fourteenth and fifteenth centuries, the Ottomans turned their expansionist designs to the Arab world in the next century. What Osman had begun, a sixteenth-century Ottoman successor, Suleiman (ruled 1520–1566), consolidated. During Suleiman's reign, the Ottomans reached the height of their territorial expansion, and the sultan himself led the army on thirteen of its major military campaigns and many of its minor engagements. An exceptional military leader, Suleiman was an equally gifted administrator. He garnered accolades from his subjects, who called him "the Lawgiver" and "the Magnificent," in recognition of the attention he lavished on civil bureaucratic efficiency and justice for his people. His fame spread to Europe, where he was known as "the Great Turk." Under Suleiman's administration, the Ottoman state ruled over some 20 to 30 million people. When Suleiman died in 1566, the Ottoman Empire bridged Europe and the Arab world. Istanbul became a busy imperial hub, dispatching bureaucrats and

The Conquest of Constantinople. In 1453, the Ottoman Turks, led by Sultan Mehmed, later called the Conqueror, broke through the defenses of the city of Constantinople and incorporated this bastion of Byzantine Christian civilization into the Ottoman Empire. They changed the city's name to Istanbul and made it their own capital.

military men from the capital to administer and control the vast domain.

Ottoman dynastic power was, however, not only military; it also rested on a religious foundation. At the center of this empire were the Ottoman sultans, who combined a warrior ethos with an unwavering devotion to Islamic beliefs. Describing themselves as the "shadow of God" on earth, sultans claimed to be caretakers for the welfare of the Islamic faith. Around the empire, the sultans devoted substantial resources to the construction of great mosques and to the support of Islamic schools. As self-appointed defenders of the faithful, the sultans assumed the role of protectors of the holy cities on the Arabian peninsula and of Jerusalem, defending the internal cohesion of the realm and defining the borders demarcating heretics and infidels. Thus the Islamic faith helped to unite a diverse and sprawling imperial populace, with the sultan's power fusing the sacred and the secular.

Suleiman and Territorial Expansion. Sultan Suleiman, at the center of this illustration, leads his army as it is about to embark on a campaign to conquer Europe.

ISTANBUL AND THE TOPKAPI PALACE   Istanbul reflected the splendor of this powerful empire. After the Ottoman conquest, the sultans' engineers rebuilt the city's crumbling walls, while their architects redesigned homes, public buildings, baths, inns, and marketplaces to display the majesty of Islam's new imperial center. To crown his achievements, Suleiman Mehmed II ordered the construction of the Suleymaniye Mosque, which sat across from Hagia Sophia, a domed Byzantine cathedral that was formerly the most sacred of the Christian cathedrals, the largest house of worship in all Christendom, but which Suleiman Mehmed II had turned into a mosque. The Ottoman dynasts welcomed, indeed, forcibly transported, thousands of Muslims and non-Muslims to the city and revived Istanbul as a major trading center. Before its conquest, the city's population had fallen to 30,000. Within twenty-five years of its conquest by the Ottomans, its population had more than tripled, and by the end of the sixteenth century Istanbul's population numbered 400,000, making it the world's largest city outside China.

Istanbul's Topkapi Palace neatly displayed the Ottomans' view of governance, the importance the sultans attached to religion, and the continuing influence of Ottoman household and familial traditions, even in the administration of a far-flung empire. Laid out by Constantinople's conqueror, Mehmed II, and largely completed by the middle of the sixteenth century, the palace complex reflected Mehmed's vision of Istanbul as the center of the world. As a way to exalt the magnificent power of the sultan, the architects designed the various palaces and courtyards so that the buildings that housed the imperial household would be nestled behind layers of outer courtyards, in a mosaic of mosques, courts, and special dwellings for the sultan's harem.

The growing importance of the Topkapi Palace as the command post of empire represented an important transition in the history of Ottoman rulers. Not only was the palace the place where future bureaucrats were trained; it was also the place where the chief bureaucrat of the realm, the grand vizier, carried out the day-to-day running of the empire. Whereas the early sultans had led their soldiers into battle personally and had met face-to-face with their kinsmen, the later rulers withdrew into the sanctity of the palace, venturing out only occasionally for grand ceremonies. Still, every Friday, subjects queued up outside the palace to introduce their petitions, ask for favors, and seek justice. If they were lucky, the sultans would be there to greet the people—but they did so behind grated glass, issuing their decisions by tapping on the window. The palace thus projected a sense of majestic, distant wonder, a home fit for semidivine rulers.

Home Topkapi was, for the increasingly sedentary sultan and his harem. Among his most cherished quarters were those set aside for women. At first, the influence of women in the Ottoman polity was slight. But as the realm consolidated, women became a powerful political force. The harem, like the rest of Ottoman society, had its own hierarchy of rank

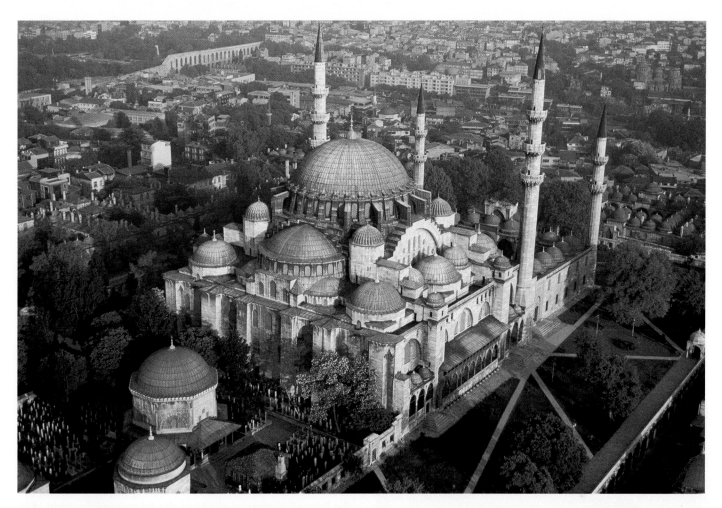

The Suleymaniye Mosque. Built by Sultan Suleiman to crown his achievements, the Suleymaniye Mosque was designed by the architect Sinan to dominate the city and to have four tall minarets from which the faithful were called to prayer.

and prestige. At the bottom were slave women; at the top were the sultan's mother and his favorite consorts. As many as 10,000 to 12,000 women lived in the palace, often in cramped quarters. Those who had the ruler's ear conspired to have him favor their own children, which made for widespread intrigue. When a sultan died the entire retinue of women would be dispatched to a distant palace poignantly called the Palace of Tears, because the women who occupied it wept at the loss of the sultan and their banishment from power.

DIVERSITY AND CONTROL IN THE OTTOMAN EMPIRE Ruling the realm through conquest and conversion did not entirely efface cultural differences in distant provinces. Take the example of the Ottomans' language policy. From the fifteenth century onward, the Ottoman Empire was more multilingual than any of its rivals. Although Ottoman Turkish was the official language of administration, Arabic was the lingua

franca of the Arab provinces, the common tongue of street life. Within the European corner of the empire, various languages also continued to be spoken.

In politics, as in language, the Ottomans showed flexibility and tolerance. The imperial bureaucracy permitted a high degree of regional autonomy. In the course of imperial expansion, the Ottoman military cadres perfected a technique for absorbing newly conquered territories into the empire by parceling out these territories as revenue-producing units among loyal followers (including Christian converts) and kin. Regional appointees could collect local taxes, part of which they earmarked for Istanbul and part of which they kept for themselves. As we shall see, this was a common administrative device for many world dynasties trying to rule extensive domains.

Like other expansive realms, the Ottoman state was perennially in danger of losing control over its provincial rulers. As provincial rulers learned to operate independently

The Topkapi Palace. A view of the inner courtyard of the seraglio, where the sultan and his harem lived.

from central authority, local authorities kept larger amounts of tax revenues than Istanbul deemed proper. To clip local autonomy, the Ottomans established a corps of infantry soldiers and bureaucrats (called janissaries) who owed direct allegiance to the sultan. The system as it operated at its high point involved a conscription of Christian youths from villages in the European lands of the empire. This conscription, called the *devshirme,* required each village to turn over to the state a certain number of young males between the ages of eight and eighteen. Uprooted from their families and villages, selected for their fine physiques and good looks, these young men were converted to Islam and were sent to farms to build up their bodies and learn Turkish. A select few were then sent to Topkapi Palace to learn Ottoman military, religious, and administrative techniques. Some of these men went on to exceptional careers in the arts and sciences, as did the architect Sinan, who designed the Suleymaniye Mosque. Recipients of the best education available in the Islamic world, trained in Ottoman ways, instructed in the use of modern weaponry, and shorn of all family connections, the boys recruited through the *devshirme* were thus prepared to serve the sultan, and the empire as a whole, rather than the interests of any particular locality or ethnic group.

The Ottomans were thus able to artfully balance the decentralizing tendencies of far-flung regions with the centralizing forces of the imperial capital. Relying on a careful mixture of faith, patronage, and tolerance, Ottoman sultans curried loyalty and secured political stability. Indeed, so strong and stable was the polity that the Ottoman Empire dominated the much coveted and highly contested crossroads between Europe and Asia for many centuries.

A Harem. An interior room of an opulent Turkish palace. This image comes from the late nineteenth century but captures the arrangements employed by wealthy and elite members of Turkish society to seclude women in their own parts of a house or a palace.

Primary Source

QALANDAR DERVISHES IN THE ISLAMIC WORLD

The Qalandar dervish order came into being in Damascus, Syria, and Egypt in the thirteenth century and spread rapidly throughout the Islamic world into Arab and Ottoman lands in reaction to the unrest of the times. Renouncing the world and engaging in highly individualistic practices as they moved from place to place, the Qalandars were condemned by the educated elite, who believed them to be ignorant hypocrites living on alms obtained from gullible common folk. Giovan Antonio Manavino, a European observer of Ottoman society in the late fifteenth century, gives an obviously biased account of the Qalandars, whom he called the torlaks.

Dressed in sheepskins, the *torlaks* [Qalandars] are otherwise naked, with no headgear. Their scalps are always clean-shaven and well rubbed with oil as a precaution against the cold. They burn their temples with an old rag so that their faces will not be damaged by sweat. Illiterate and unable to do anything manly, they live like beasts, surviving on alms only. For this reason, they are to be found around taverns and public kitchens in cities. If, while roaming the countryside, they come across a well-dressed person, they try to make him one of their own, stripping him naked. Like Gypsies in Europe, they practice chiromancy, especially for women who then provide them with bread, eggs, cheese, and other foods in return for their services. Amongst them there is usually an old man whom they revere and worship like God. When they enter a town, they gather around the best house of the town and listen in great humility to the words of this old man, who, after a spell of ecstasy, foretells the descent of a great evil upon the town. His disciples then implore him to fend off the disaster through his good services. The old man accepts the plea of his followers, though not without an initial show of reluctance, and prays to God, asking him to spare the town the imminent danger awaiting it. This time-honored trick earns them considerable sums of alms from ignorant and credulous people. The *torlaks* . . . chew hashish and sleep on the ground; they also openly practice sodomy like savage beasts.

→ *Why do you think Manavino is so critical of the Qalandars?*

→ *Why do you think the Qalanders chose individualistic practices rather than communal living?*

SOURCE: Ahmet T. Karamustafa, *God's Unruly Friends: Dervish Groups in the Islamic Later Middle Period, 1200–1550* (Salt Lake City: University of Utah Press, 1994), pp. 6–7.

THE EMERGENCE OF THE SAFAVID EMPIRE IN IRAN

The Ottoman dynasts were not the only rulers to extend the political domain of Islam in Afro-Eurasia. In Persia, too, a new empire arose in the aftermath of the Mongols. The Safavid Empire, like the Ottoman Empire, rested its legitimacy on an Islamic foundation. But the Shiism espoused by Safavid rulers was quite different from the Sunni faith of the Ottomans, and these contrasting religious visions shaped distinct political systems.

Even more so than in Anatolia, the Mongol conquest and decline brought terrible destruction and political instability to Persia. Initially, Mongol conquerors refused to embrace the Islamic faith of the majority of the area's population. Instead, from 1221 to 1295, Mongol rulers practiced a form of religious toleration. Various Mongol autocrats permitted Jews to serve the state as viziers (administrators) and employed Christians as auxiliary soldiers. But in 1295, the Great Khan of the Persian state, Ghazan, adopted Islam as the state religion. When the Mongol order slipped into decline soon after, no power arose to dominate the area. The region between Konya

The *Devshirme*. A miniature painting from 1558 depicts the *devshirme* system of taking non-Muslim children from their families in the Balkan Peninsula as a human tribute in place of cash taxes, which the poor region could not pay. The children were educated in Ottoman Muslim ways and prepared for service in the sultan's civil and military bureaucracy.

in eastern Anatolia and Tabriz in Persia and including Iraq fell into even greater disorder, with warrior chieftains fighting one another for preeminence. Adding to the volatility of the region were various populist Islamic movements that appeared at this time. Some of these urged followers to withdraw from society or encouraged devotees to parade around without clothing. Among the more prominent movements was a Sufi brotherhood led by Safi al-Din (1252–1334), which gained the backing of religious adherents and Turkish-speaking warrior bands. However, his later successors, known as Safaviyeh or Safavids, embraced Shiism.

The Safavid aspirants to power rallied support from tribal groups in badly devastated parts of Persia by promising to restore good governance to the region, and steeped themselves in the separatist sacred tradition of Shiism. As a result, of the

three great Islamic empires, the Safavid state became the most single-mindedly religious, persecuting those who did not follow its Shiite form of Islam. When in 1501 the most dynamic of Safi al-Din's successors, Ismail (ruled 1501–1524), acceded to power in Tabriz, he required that the call to prayer announce that "there is no God but Allah, that Muhammad is His prophet, and that Ali is the successor of Muhammad." Ismail rejected the pragmatic counsels of his advisers to tolerate the Sunni creed of the vast majority of the city's population and made Shiism the official religion of the Persian state. He offered the people a choice between conversion to Shiism or death, exclaiming at the moment of conquest that "with God's help, if the people utter one word of protest, I will draw the sword and leave not one of them alive." Under Ismail and his successors, the Safavid shahs succeeded in restoring Persian sovereignty over the whole of the region traditionally regarded as the homeland of Persian speakers (see Map 11-3).

In 1502, Ismail proclaimed himself the first shah of the Safavid Empire. In the hands of the Safavids, Islam assumed an extreme and often quite militant form. The Safavids revived the traditional Persian idea that rulers were ordained by God, believing the shahs to be divinely chosen. But some Shiites went so far as to affirm that there was no God but the shah. Moreover, Persian Shiism fostered an activist clergy, the so-called turbaned classes, who, in contrast to Sunni clerics, cast themselves in the role of political and religious enforcers against any heretical authority. They compelled Safavid leaders to rule with a sacred purpose. Because the Safavids did not tolerate diversity within their realm, unlike the Ottomans, they never had as expansive an empire. Whatever territories they conquered, the Safavids ruled much more directly, based on central—and theocratic—authority.

THE DELHI SULTANATE AND THE EARLY MUGHAL EMPIRE

A quarter century after the Safavids seized power in Persia, another new Islamic dynasty, the Mughals, emerged to the east in South Asia. Like the Ottomans and Safavids, the Mughals created a new regime destined to last for many centuries. But unlike those other Islamic empires, the Mughals did not replace a Mongol regime. Instead, they erected their state on the foundations of the old Delhi Sultanate, which had come into existence in 1206.

In 1303, when Mongol forces had moved toward South Asia, the Delhi Sultanate was at the height of its powers. Its formidable military force extended imperial authority to large parts of the northern Indus River valley and cast a shadow over the political map of the south. The reigning sultan, Alaud din Khalji (ruled 1296–1316), was able to raise a sufficiently powerful army to drive the Mongols, who were

MAP 11-3   THE SAFAVID EMPIRE, 1500–1722

The Safavid Empire rose to prominence alongside the Ottoman state. Where did it originate? What were the territories over which the Ottomans and Safavids battled? Did the Safavids have any other political enemies?

Legend:
- Safavid Empire, c. 1500
- Safavid Empire, 1512
- Safavid Empire, 1722
- Ottoman Empire, 1722
- Easternmost limit of area contested between Ottomans and Safavids
- Ottoman campaigns
- Uzbek invasion, 1587
- Portuguese entry into Persian Gulf
- ✕ Battle

was a force led by Timur (Tamerlane), a Turkish warrior from central Asia, whose army succeeded where the Mongols had not. Sweeping down from the northwest, Timur's army sacked Delhi in 1398 and pillaged and annexed the Punjab. Death and destruction engulfed the city and much of the northern Indus River valley. Thousands were taken prisoner and carried off as slaves. Artisans and stonemasons who had built Delhi's beautiful buildings were carted away to beautify the conqueror's city of Samarkand (in present-day Uzbekistan). Yet, as the summer of 1399 approached, a time when semi-arid Delhi gets dusty and the temperature hovers between 100 to 110 degrees, Timur abandoned the hot plains of northern India and returned home. Still, Timur's conquest accelerated the fragmentation of the Delhi Sultanate.

A wave of religious revival followed in the wake Timur's conquests. Some of the more radical movements, like Persia's Shiism, adopted an intransigent stance against central rulers and official credos. Religious reaction stood in the way of re-creating powerful state structures. Bengal broke away from Delhi and was soon engulfed in a Sufi form of mystical Islam, extolling personal union with God. Here, too, a special form of Hinduism, called Bhakti Hinduism, put down deep roots. Its devotees preached the doctrine of divine love. In the Punjab, previously a core area of the Delhi Sultanate, a new religion, Sikhism, came into being, which largely followed the teachings of Nanak (1469–1539), who while born a Hindu was inspired by Islamic ideals and called on his followers to renounce the caste system and to treat all believers as equal before God.

Following Timur's attack, rival kingdoms and sultanates asserted their independence, leaving the Delhi Sultanate a mere shadow of its former self. It became just one of several

threatening the northwestern cities of the sultanate, back toward Afghanistan. The Mongols never again disturbed the tranquility of the sultanate.

Although military strength was the foundation of the sultanate's power, it was also its Achilles' heel. Toward the close of the fourteenth century, a decline in the government's revenues, from military campaigns of conquest and plunder and tax yields from the rural economy, and a rise in expenditures, on buildings and charitable institutions, combined to reduce the resources for the military. Intrigues and quarreling among nobles further weakened the Delhi Sultanate and left it vulnerable to a new Turkish, rather than Mongol, invader. This

NANAK'S TEACHINGS IN INDIA

Nanak, generally recognized as the founder of Sikhism, lived from 1469 to 1539 in the Punjab in northern India, where he surrounded himself with disciples and participated in the religious discussions that were such a prominent feature of the fifteenth century. This was a period, much like that in western Europe and Islamic Southwest Asia, of political turmoil and intense personal introspection. As the following excerpts of hymns and poems from his writings demonstrate, Nanak exposed the failings of the age and used spiritual ideas drawn from Islamic and Hindu thought to elaborate his own unique spiritual perspective as a bulwark against the travails of the period. Nanak stressed the unity of God, an emphasis that reflected Islamic influences. Nonetheless, his insistence on the comparative unimportance of prophets ran counter to Islam, and his belief in rebirth was strictly Hindu.

There is but one God, whose name is true, the Creator, devoid of fear and enmity, immortal, unborn, self-existent; God the great and bountiful. Repeat His Name.

Numberless are the fools appallingly blind;
Numberless are the thieves and devourers of others' property;
Numberless are those who establish their sovereignty by force;
Numberless the cutthroats and murderers; Numberless the liars who roam about lying;
Numberless the filthy who enjoy filthy gain;
Numberless the slandered who carry loads of calumny on their heads;
Nanak thus described the degraded.
So lowly am I, I cannot even once be a sacrifice unto Thee. Whatever pleaseth Thee is good.
O Formless One, Thou art ever secure.

The Hindus have forgotten God, and are going the wrong way.
They worship according to the instruction of Narad.
They are blind and dumb, the blindest of the blind.
The ignorant fools take stones and worship them.
O Hindus, how shall the stone which itself sinketh carry you across?

What power hath caste? It is the reality that is tested.
Poison may be held in the hand, but man dieth if he eat it.
The sovereignty of the True One is known in every age. He who obeyeth God's order shall become a noble in His court.

Those who have meditated on God as the truest of the true have done real worship and are contented;
They have refrained from evil, done good deeds, and practiced honesty;
They have lived on a little corn and water, and burst the entanglements of the world.
Thou art the great Bestower; ever Thou givest gifts which increase a quarterfold.
Those who have magnified the great God have found Him.

→ *How does Nanak's conception of God differ from the Hindu conception?*
→ *Why does Nanak call for the end of the caste system?*

SOURCE: William Theodore de Bary, *Sources of Indian Tradition* (New York: Columbia University Press, 1958), pp. 536–38.

competing regional powers in northern India, ruled first by the Sayyids (1414–1451) and then by the Afghan dynasty of the Lodis (1451–1526). Surrounded by resurgent Hindu and Islamic polities, the truncated sultanate experienced something of a revival in the Lodi era. But the attempt by the last sultan, Ibrahim Lodi, to consolidate his power by clipping the wings of the Afghan nobility provoked the governor of the Punjab to invite the Turkish prince Babur (the "Tiger") to India in 1526. A great-grandson of Timur, Babur traced his lineage to both the Turks and the Mongols (he was said to be a descendant of Chinggis Khan). For years, Babur had longed to conquer India. So, he accepted the invitation and marched against Sultan Ibrahim. Massing an army of Turks and Afghans and armed with matchlock cannons, he easily breached the wall of elephants put together by Ibrahim. Delhi fell, and the sultanate came to an end. Babur proclaimed himself emperor (ruled 1526–1530), and he spent the next few years snuffing out the remaining resistance to his rule (see Map 11-4). Thus was laid the foundation of the Mughal Empire, the third great Islamic dynasty (discussed in detail in Chapter 12).

By the sixteenth century, then, the Islamic heartland had seen the emergence of three new empires. Although these states did not hesitate to go to war against each other, they shared similar styles of rule. All established their legitimacy by using military prowess, religious backing, and a loyal bureaucracy to balance sacred and secular authority. This combination of spiritual and military weaponry enabled emperors, carrying Muhammad's preachings across the Afro-Eurasian landmass, to lay claim to vast domains. Islam also bound rulers and ruled together and gave them a common cause and a singular view of the world. This shared Islamic religious culture fostered the movement of goods, ideas, merchants, and scholars across political boundaries, even across Islam's most divisive boundary, that along the border between Sunni Iraq and Shiite Persia.

MAP 11-4   THE MUGHAL EMPIRE, 1530

Compare the Mughal state with the other major Asian empires of this period, notably the Ming, Safavid, and Ottoman states. What distinguishes the Mughal state at this time from these others? From what part of the Afro-Eurasian landmass did the new state arise, and what effect would its place of origin have on the nature of Mughal rule? To what religious traditions did the Mughals need to be sensitive?

Raid on Delhi. Timur's swift raid on Delhi in 1398 was notable for the death and destruction it caused. This sixteenth-century miniature captures the plunder and violence.

Babur in Battle. Following his victory over the Delhi sultan, Ibrahim Lodi, in the Battle of Panipat (1526), Babur battled with Rajput chieftains in north India. Artists chronicled these events in paintings. This miniature shows Babur's army locked in fierce fight with Rana Sanga, a Rajput chief. The painting records the use of field guns, bombards (an early type of cannon, which fired stones), and swords. The red elephant head on the left may be horse armor used to trick and frighten the enemy.

 WESTERN CHRISTENDOM

> → *Why did Europe remain disunited and have difficulty recovering from the Black Death?*

On the western side of the Afro-Eurasian landmass, a period of prosperity, population growth, and cultural flowering known as the High Middle Ages ended abruptly with the coming of famine, plague, and war in the fourteenth century. The Black Death and its aftermath reversed the gains that Europe had made in the twelfth and thirteenth centuries. Between about 1100 and 1300, Europe's population had increased, and new prosperity had allowed for spectacular advances in the arts, technology, learning, building, cities, and banking. Economic and social lives focused on the family, and growing households had to crowd under the same roof. Wives worked with their husbands, especially in commerce and farming. Though excluded from many crafts and professions, women were increasingly important in retail trades, weaving, and food production.

Europe's 80 million inhabitants still resided, overwhelmingly, on rural estates, but towns and cities were growing rapidly and were allowing Europeans to widen their horizons onto the world. Between the late eleventh and early thirteenth centuries, universities had come into being in Bologna, Paris, Oxford, and Cambridge, and a few scholars began to appreciate the learning of the Arabs and the earlier achievements of the Greeks and Romans. Thomas Aquinas (1225–1274), the leading philosopher and theologian of the age, had laid out the main tenets of western Christianity and resolved questions of faith and reason to the satisfaction of clerical and secular intellectuals. New devices like mechanical clocks and the compass had improved the accuracy of measurements on sea and on land, while spinning wheels increased the pace of cloth production.

REACTIONS, REVOLTS, AND RELIGION IN EUROPE

At the beginning of the fourteenth century, Europe's rising fortunes halted, with climatic changes instigating a decline. Beginning around 1310, extremely harsh winters and rainy summers shortened the growing seasons and played havoc with harvests, especially in northern zones. Diminished and exhausted soils no longer supplied the resources to feed and clothe growing urban and rural populations. Nobles squeezed the peasantry hard in an effort to maintain their luxurious way of life. States raised taxes to keep revenues in balance with their growing expenditures. In this context, Europe endured the first of its fourteenth-century disasters: famine. Famine appeared in 1315 and did not let up until 1322, by which time millions had died of outright starvation or diseases against which the malnourished population could offer little resistance. But this would be merely the prelude to a century and more of ceaseless warfare, epidemic disease, famine, and social unrest.

In the wake of famine came the Black Death. The pandemic began around 1347, and soon ravaging the Italian peninsula moved on to France, the Low Countries, Germany, and England. Although no part of Europe was spared, the cities were particularly vulnerable because of their overcrowding and unsanitary conditions. London, with a population of about 60,000 residing within its walls and another 10,000 or 15,000 living outside, groaned under the weight of the death toll. Often in the poorer sections as many as twelve residents slept together on the floor in a single room. The disease spared few in these crowded quarters. Nor did it ignore their social betters if they hesitated to flee to their country estates.

No one had seen dying on such a scale. Anywhere from 25 to 50 percent of Europe's total population (between 19 and 38 million) perished within five years of the original outbreak. But the dying did not end then, for severe outbreaks occurred in 1361–1362, 1369, and then every five to ten years for the rest of the fourteenth century, as well as sporadically through the entire fifteenth century. The European population continued on a precipitous decline until by 1450 many areas had only one-quarter the number of people they had supported a century earlier. Indeed, it took three centuries for Europe to recover to population levels that existed prior to the Black Death.

Disaster on this scale had a number of enduring psychological, social, economic, and political effects. Many individuals, recognizing life's brevity, turned to pleasure, even debauchery, determined to enjoy themselves before it came their turn to die. Others retreated into a personal spirituality, convinced that they needed to put their lives in order before they passed on to the next life. Occasionally, like-minded individuals joined together and created eccentric groups. The Beghards or Brethren of the Free Speech claimed to be in a state of grace that allowed them to do as they pleased—from adultery, free love, and nudity to murder. By contrast, the Flagellants were so sure that man had incurred the wrath of God through his wayward ways that they whipped themselves to show their readiness to atone for human sin. But they also bullied communities that they visited, demanding to be housed, clothed, and fed in style.

For many who survived the plague, Thomas Aquinas's rational Christianity no longer appealed, and disappointment with the clergy was widespread. Famished peasants resented priests and monks for living lives of luxury in violation of church tenets. In addition, they despaired at the absence of clergy when they were so greatly needed. In fact, many clerics had perished while attending to their parishioners. Others, however, had simply deserted to rural retreats far from the ravages of the Black Death, leaving their followers to fend for themselves.

In the aftermath of famine and plague, religious authorities struggled to reclaim their power. The late medieval western church found itself divided at the top (at one point in the fourteenth century there were three popes!) and challenged from below, both by individuals pursuing alternative kinds of spirituality and by increasing demands on the clergy and church administration. In response to challenges to its right to define religious doctrine and practices, the church rigorously identified all that was suspect and demanded strict obedience to the true faith. This entailed the persecution of heretics, Jews, Muslims, homosexuals, prostitutes, and "witches." But in this period, the church was also expanding its charitable and bureaucratic functions, providing alms to the urban poor and registering births, deaths, and economic transactions.

Persecution and administration cost money. As the church had no easy way to raise new funds, the needs as well as the extravagances of the clergy spurred the undertaking of ques-

Primary Source

FLAGELLANTS IN ENGLAND

Like the Qalandar dervishes in the Islamic world, European Flagellants renounced the world and engaged in violent acts of public self-punishment in reaction to the warfare, famines, and plagues of the fourteenth century. The Flagellants carried whips (flagella) with metal pieces run through knotted thongs, which they used to beat and whip themselves until they were bruised, swollen, and bloody. Robert of Avesbury here describes the actions of Flagellants in England during the reign of King Edward III.

In that same year of 1349, about Michaelmas [29 September], more than 120 men, for the most part from Zeeland or Holland, arrived in London from Flanders. These went barefoot in procession twice a day in the sight of the people, sometimes in St Paul's church and sometimes elsewhere in the city, their bodies naked except for a linen cloth from loins to ankle. Each wore a hood painted with a red cross at front and back and carried in his right hand a whip with three thongs. Each thong had a knot in it, with something sharp, like a needle, stuck through the middle of the knot so that it stuck out on each side, and as they walked one after the other they struck themselves with these whips on their naked, bloody bodies; four of them singing in their own tongue and the rest answering in the manner of the Christian litany. Three times in each procession they would all prostrate themselves on the ground, with their arms outstretched in the shape of a cross. Still singing, and beginning with the man at the end, each in turn would step over the others, lashing the man beneath him once with his whip, until all of those lying down had gone through the same ritual. Then each one put on his usual clothes and, always with their hoods on their heads and carrying their whips, they departed to their lodgings. It was said that they performed a similar penance every night.

→ *Why do you think Flagellants whipped themselves?*
→ *How do the Flagellants differ from the Qalanders?*

SOURCE: Robertus de Avesbury de Gestis Mirabilibus Regis Edwardi Tertii, in *The Black Death*, translated and edited by Rosemary Horrox (Manchester, England: Manchester University Press, 1994), pp. 153–54.

tionable new money-making tactics. Among the most controversial of these fund-raising mechanisms was the selling of indulgences (certification that one's sins had been forgiven). This sort of unconventional fund raising, and the growing gap between the church's promises and its ability to actually bring Christianity into people's everyday lives, more than the persecutions, eventually sparked the Protestant Reformation.

Just as the mayhem of the fourteenth and fifteenth centuries unleashed a wave of popular hostility toward the church, it also undermined the legitimacy of the feudal order, especially in France and England. Since the Roman era, peasant protests and uprisings had occasionally erupted. Yet, in the wake of the catastrophes of the fourteenth century, these everyday defiances escalated into large-scale insurrections. In France and England, massive revolts broke out, in which

peasant rebels expressed their resentment against lords who failed to protect them from marauding military bands and their defiance of feudal restrictions that now seemed—for the few survivors of plague and famine—onerous. In 1358, the French revolt, or *Jacquerie*—a term derived from "Jacques Bonhomme," a name used by contemptuous masters as a blanket term for all peasants—broke out. Armed with only knives and staves, the French peasantry went on a rampage, killing a few of the hated nobles and higher clergy and burning and looting all the property they could get their hands on. At issue was the peasants' insistence that they should no longer be tied to their land or have to make payments for the tools they used in their agricultural pursuits.

A far better organized uprising took place in England in 1381. Although what became known as the English Peasants'

Peasant Revolts. Long before the French Revolution, European peasants vented their anger against their noble masters. Lacking armaments and supplies, they usually lost—as this image of the brutal suppression of the French Jacquerie of 1358 depicts.

Revolt began as a protest against a poll tax levied to raise money for a war on France, it was also fueled by post-plague labor shortages, with serfs demanding the freedom to move about and free farm workers calling for higher wages and lower rents. When landlords balked at these demands, huge numbers of aggrieved and restless peasants joined the cause, finally assembling at the gates of London. The protesters pressed for the abolition of the feudal order, but King Richard II, assembling his nobles, ruthlessly suppressed the rebellious peasants. Nonetheless, despite these defeats in both France and England, a free peasantry gradually emerged as labor shortages made it impossible to continue to bind peasants to the soil.

It took several centuries for Europe's polities to reorganize themselves into a series of centralized monarchies, interspersed with a sprinkling of city-states.

STATE-BUILDING AND ECONOMIC RECOVERY IN EUROPE

In the wake of famine, plague, and peasant uprisings, Europe's rulers (and would-be rulers) tried to rebuild their polities and consolidate their power. Their efforts at state-building, however, paled in comparison with those of the empires rising in Asia. Although one family, the Habsburgs, provided emperors for the Holy Roman Empire from 1440 to

1806, they never succeeded in restoring an integrated empire to western Europe, as Chinese dynasts had done time and again by basing their claims to legitimate rule on the universally recognized concept of the mandate of Heaven and creating a sense of a universal identity by referring to themselves as a people, the Han, or referring to their state as the Middle Kingdom. Moreover, language did not unite Europeans. While the written literary Chinese script remained a key administrative tool for the dynasts for centuries to come, and in the Islamic world Arabic was commonly accepted as the language of faith, Persian the language of poetry, and Turkish the language of administration, in Europe Latin was gradually displaced as rulers chose one of the regional dialects to be the official state language at court. In 1450, Europe had no central government, no official tongue, and only a few successful commercial centers, most of them in the Mediterranean basin. Fledgling banking systems had fallen apart during the fourteenth century's chaos. In the political sphere, feudalism had left a legacy of political fragmentation and enshrined privileges, which made the consolidation of a unified Christian Europe even more difficult to achieve.

Those who sought to rule the emerging regional states faced numerous obstacles. Feudal dues paid to other landholders in their realms made it possible for rival claimants to the throne to finance the formation of private armies. The clergy demanded and received privileges and sometimes meddled in politics themselves. The printing press became available after the 1460s, and despite governments' attempts at censorship, clandestine presses and anonymous pamphlets circulated religious and political views quite different from those championed by the king and his ministers. Some states had consultative bodies, such as the Estates General in France, the Cortès in Spain, or Parliament in England, in which princes formally asked representatives of their people for advice and, in the case of the English Parliament, for consent to new forms of taxation. Where such bodies existed, they gave no voice to most nonaristocratic men and virtually no representation to women of any social class. But they did allow for the collective expression of grievances against highhanded monarchical policies.

It took several centuries for Europe's polities to reorganize themselves into a series of centralized monarchies, interspersed with a sprinkling of city-states. Consolidation of these polities occurred sometimes as a result of strategic marital alliances but often involved warfare, both between homegrown princely families and with outsiders seeking territorial gains for themselves. Political stabilization was swiftest in southern Europe. These economies would also prove quickest to rebound, for they enjoyed unique access to the increasingly vibrant Mediterranean trade with the Levant. The stabilization of Italian city-states such as Venice and Florence and of monarchical rule in Portugal and Spain allowed for a period of Mediterranean economic and cultural flowering we know as the Renaissance (see below).

POLITICAL CONSOLIDATION AND TRADE IN PORTUGAL

The fortunes of Portugal under the House of Aviz demonstrate the ways in which political stabilization and the revival of trade were interrelated. Spain, England, and France followed the Portuguese example and established national monarchies following the chaos of the fourteenth century. In Spain and Portugal, warfare against Muslims would help unite Christian territories, and Mediterranean trade would add valuable income to state coffers. In northern Europe, by contrast, lack of access to lucrative trade routes, in addition to internal feuding, regional warfare, and after 1517, religious fragmentation, would delay recovery for decades (see Map 11-5).

Through the fourteenth century, Portuguese Christians had fought Muslim occupants of the Iberian peninsula. But in 1415, the Portuguese crossed the Strait of Gibraltar and captured the Moorish Moroccan fortresses at Ceuta, in North Africa. They could now sail between the Mediterranean and the Atlantic without Muslim interference. With the Muslim threat diminished, the enemy was now perceived to be Portugal's neighbor, Castile (part of what is now Spain). Under João (John) I (ruled 1385–1433), the Castilians were defeated, and the monarchy could now seek new territories and trading opportunities in the North Atlantic and along the coasts of West Africa.

One of João's sons, Prince Henrique (1394–1460), later known as "Henry the Navigator," never ruled as king, but he further expanded the family's domain by supporting Portuguese expeditions down the coast of Africa and offshore to the Atlantic islands of the Madeiras and the Azores. The west and central coasts of Africa and the islands of the North and South Atlantic, including the Cape Verde Islands, São Tomé, Principe, and Fernando Po, soon became Portuguese ports of call.

The Portuguese monarchs allocated the Atlantic islands to nobles, granting them as hereditary possessions on condition that the grantees colonize these new lands. Soon the colonizers were establishing lucrative sugar plantations on the islands. In gratitude, noble families and merchants threw their political weight behind the king. Subsequent monarchs continued to reduce the traditional power of local nobles and to ensure the smooth succession of members of the royal family. This political consolidation enabled Portugal to thrive in the wake of the Black Death.

DYNASTY BUILDING AND RECONQUEST IN SPAIN

The road to dynasty in Spain was arduous. Medieval Spain was fragmented into various kingdoms, each controlled by noble families that quarreled ceaselessly with each other. Nor was Spain a country of religious uniformity; Muslims, Jews, and Christians lived side by side, in relative if not perfect harmony, and Muslim armies still occupied strategic posts in the south. Over time, however, marriages and the formation of kinship ties among nobles and between royal lineages slowly allowed for the consolidation of a new political order. One by one, the major houses of the Spanish kingdoms intermarried, culminating in the most fateful wedding of Iberian royal heirs: the marriage of Isabella of Castile and Ferdinand of Aragon in 1469. Thus, Spain's two most important provinces were joined, and Spain became a state to be reckoned with.

By the time Isabella and Ferdinand married, Spain was recovering from the miserable fourteenth century. Castile and Aragon's population, for instance, rebounded from about 6 million in 1450 to 8.5 million in 1482. This was more than just a marriage of convenience. Castile was wealthy and populous; Aragon enjoyed an extended trading emporium in the Mediterranean, including access to Italian and especially Genoese financiers. Together, the new monarchs brought unruly nobles and distant towns under their domain. They topped off their achievements by marrying their children into other European royal families, especially the House of Habsburg, the most powerful dynasty in central Europe.

The new rulers also sent Christian armies south to push out Muslim forces; by the middle of the fifteenth century, only Granada, a strategic lynchpin overlooking the straits leading from the Mediterranean to the Atlantic, remained in Muslim hands. After a long and costly siege, the Christian forces entered the fortress of Granada. When Granada fell in 1492, it was a victory of enormous symbolic importance, as joyous as the fall of Constantinople was depressing. Pope Alexander recognized the triumph and praised the monarchs of Spain. In Spain many people thumped their chests in pride—unaware, or unconcerned, perhaps, that at the same time, Ottoman armies were conquering large sections of southeastern Europe.

As did the rulers of the Safavid Empire, Isabella and Ferdinand sought to eliminate all traces of heterodoxy and infidelity from Spain. Already in 1481, they had launched the Inquisition, taking aim especially against the *conversos*, converted Jews and Muslims, whom they suspected were Christians only in name. When the walls of Granada fell, the crown ordered the expulsion of all Jews from Spain. By the terms of the treaty ending the war, the Moors (a term used to denote Muslims who inhabited the western Sahara and Iberia) were allowed to remain and to practice their religion. But, in 1609, they too would be formally expelled. All told, almost half a million people were forced to pack what possessions they could carry and flee the Spanish kingdoms.

→ *Why did Europe remain disunited and have difficulty recovering from the Black Death?*

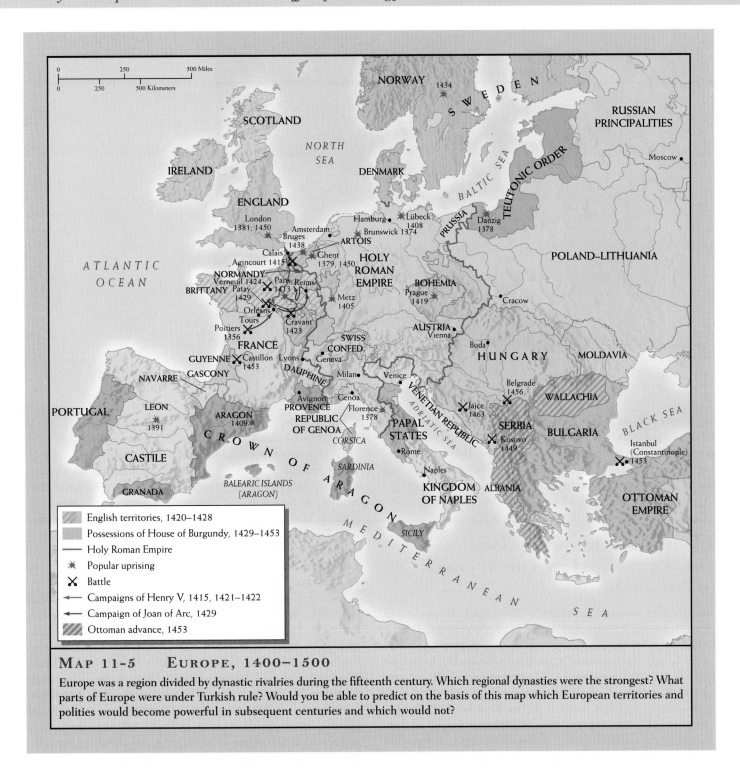

MAP 11-5   EUROPE, 1400–1500

Europe was a region divided by dynastic rivalries during the fifteenth century. Which regional dynasties were the strongest? What parts of Europe were under Turkish rule? Would you be able to predict on the basis of this map which European territories and polities would become powerful in subsequent centuries and which would not?

Those who converted and stayed behind faced torture and mass burnings before jeering crowds if they were found to be heretics or secret Jews or Muslims. Fueling this giant expulsion was a conviction that the struggle against Islam and Judaism constituted a just war.

Such was the tide of Spanish optimism and fervor by late 1491 that the monarchs listened now to a Genoese navigator whose pleas for patronage they had previously turned down. The navigator, Christopher Columbus (1451–1506), followed the Spanish monarchs to their camp below the besieged walls of Granada and promised them the riches that could pay for their military campaigns and that could bankroll a final and decisive crusade to liberate Jerusalem from Muslim hands. Off he sailed with a royal patent that guaranteed the Spanish

The Court of Spain. The court of Ferdinand and Isabella of Spain at the time of Columbus's first voyage in 1492.

monarchs a share of all he discovered. By the mid-1490s, the Spanish economy was reorienting itself toward the Atlantic, and Spain's merchants, missionaries, and soldiers were readying themselves for conquest and profiteering in what had been, just a few years before, a blank space on the map.

THE STRUGGLES OF FRANCE AND ENGLAND AND THE SUCCESS OF SMALL STATES

Warfare and strategic marriages allowed the Portuguese and Spanish monarchies to consolidate state power and to lay the foundations for the revival and flourishing of commerce. But by no means were all states immediately successful. In France and England, the great age of European monarchy had yet to dawn. When the French finally pushed the English back across the English Channel in the Hundred Years' War (1337–1453), the French House of Valois began a slow process of consolidating royal power. Once again, diplomatic marriages helped the French crown expand its domain, though the local nobility remained extremely powerful. It would take a further two centuries of royal initiatives and civil war to tame it. In England, even thirty years of civil war (1455–1485) between the houses of Lancaster and York did not settle which dynastic house would take the throne. Both families in this War of the Roses ultimately lost out to a new family, the Tudors, who seized the throne in 1485.

Even where stable states did arise, their populations remained quite small, and the boundaries of their states were fairly compact compared to the Ottoman and Ming empires. In the middle of the sixteenth century, Portugal and Spain, Europe's two most expansionist states at the time, had populations of 1 million and 9 million, respectively. England, excluding Wales, was a mere 3 million in 1550. Only France with 17 million had a population close to the Ottoman Empire's 25 million. And these numbers paled in comparison with Ming China's population of nearly 200 million in 1550 and Mughal India's 110 million in 1600.

But in Europe, small was, at least for a time, successful; Portugal's relatively small population proved an advantage, for the Portuguese nobility and crown had a less diverse population to instill with loyalty and obedience. The most successful merchants of the era were the inhabitants of the even smaller Italian city states and, a bit later, of the cities of the northern Netherlands. The Florentines developed sophisticated banking techniques and created extensive networks of agents—many of them family members—throughout Europe and the Mediterranean; intermarriage among other powerful merchant families kept the competition from getting out of hand. Venetian merchants enjoyed a unique role in the exchange of silks and spices from the eastern edge of the Mediterranean to European ports. Venice, in fact, became the leading entrepôt—a commercial hub for long-distance trade—for the flow of commodities between east and west Afro-Eurasia. It was in these small and prosperous city-states that the Renaissance began.

THE RISE OF A CHARISMATIC LEADER IN A TIME OF SOCIAL TURMOIL: JOAN OF ARC

The immense historical impact made by a French peasant girl, Joan of Arc, demonstrates the importance given to rare and charismatic individuals, even women leaders in predominantly male-dominated societies, during periods of social turmoil. Europe in the late fourteenth and early fifteenth centuries was beset by plagues, famines, and war. Its people, thus, were willing to look for help to the special talents of women, even in areas like warfare, where women had been largely excluded. Indeed, if not for Joan of Arc, the country we know today as France might not exist. Appearing on the scene in 1429, as the English seemed to have gained the upper hand in the Hundred Years' War, she rallied the French against the English occupiers and turned the tide of the war. Although by no means a patriot in the nineteenth-century sense of the term, by giving religious sanction, as well as military succor, to the Valois monarch Charles VII, she made possible the consolidation of France and left Europe an inspiring, yet enigmatic, image of the female warrior-saint.

The world of Joan's childhood was a chaotic one, in which English lords were laying claim to various French-speaking principalities. By 1420, Valois authority had been greatly eroded. Important French lords soon began to sense the wind blowing in the English direction, and English armies gradually conquered more and more French towns. In 1428, the English laid siege to Orléans, a large town in north-central France; to contemporaries, it seemed a symbolic battle: as Orléans went, they thought, so the war would go—and so would God wish it to go.

This is the point at which the paths of a seventeen-year-old peasant girl and the monarch of France crossed. Beginning at about age thirteen, the shy girl had received visions of saints who instructed her to come to rescue Orléans and conduct France's ruler to be crowned king at Reims Cathedral (he had not been crowned there, in the tradition of all French kings, because the English armies controlled Reims, Paris, and northern France). For five years, Joan resisted, but at last she agreed to obey her celestial advisers. Granted an audience with Charles VII in 1429, Joan impressed him with her piety and her passionate devotion to the Valois crown. He concluded that God really had sent her to serve France's cause—and his own. Joan was given command of 7,000 to 8,000 men and, wearing a suit of armor and brandishing a sword, she marched to relieve Orléans. Joan directed the assault with brilliance and inspired the French forces; her charisma came not only

from a tradition of female Christian "seers," but also from the peculiarity of her appearance (a young woman in male attire) and her appeal to French speakers who preferred their local French lords and customs to rule by English "outsiders." On Sunday, May 8, she drove the English from Orléans, and then pressed on to Reims; here, thanks to her military victories, Charles VII was crowned, fulfilling her visions. He was now king of France—and though the war continued, the tide now turned in favor of the French.

The tide for Joan, however, began to turn for the worse. Although she continued to direct the troops with remarkable savvy, she failed to force open the gates of Paris, and jealous courtiers around Charles began to question her divine authority. She was wounded, then taken prisoner. After a year in English captivity, she was tried by the Inquisition and found guilty—at the hands of jealous and pro-English judges—of heresy, on the grounds that her visions were false and misleading. On May 30, 1431, she was burned at the stake in the marketplace in the town of Rouen. Since that time, she has been seen as a heroic and charismatic martyr, and her name has very often been employed by the French in attempts to awaken French patriotism against foreign threats.

The fact that this young, illiterate woman played such an important role in the history of European warfare and state formation testifies to the fact that even in these spheres, male aristocrats, intellectuals, and clerics were not the only important actors. At the right place, at the right time, a woman could use courage, faith, and intelligence to make her visions prevail. Joan's followers believed that female magic could restore order to their lives, even while fearing witchcraft. They accepted her cross-dressing and personalist style of political and military leadership as proof of her calling. Yet, her death at the stake is a reminder that every charismatic heroine may be, for the opposing side, a heretic.

EUROPEAN IDENTITY AND THE RENAISSANCE

Europe's political and economic revival from the catastrophes of the fourteenth century included a powerful outpouring of cultural achievements, which was strongly linked to the rise of new polities. Much later, in the nineteenth century, scholars coined the word *Renaissance* (rebirth) to characterize the expanded cultural production of the Italian city-states, France, the Low Countries, England, and the Holy Roman Empire in the period between about 1430 and 1550. Although some Greek and Roman texts were known in Europe, and certainly had been known in the Islamic world throughout the medieval period, new ones now became accessible. Moreover, the use to which Europeans put this knowledge was new. The term *Renaissance* captures contemporaries' sense that they were making a break with the church-centered medieval world and witnessing a rebirth of classical culture. Humankind's achievements and errors in *this* world, it was now felt, were worthy of study. Looking back to ancient texts, scholars and artists found non-Christian models for geography and poetry, rhetoric and philosophy, medicine and natural history. In the process, they developed a new aesthetic and a secular foundation for elite education. The ancients became the yardstick against which modern ideas and arts could be judged, and the products of this new education, the humanists, who best knew the Latin and Greek sources, became admired authorities on subjects ranging from physiology to military operations.

Economic prosperity, the increasing pace of book circulation (after Europeans made their own printing presses in the 1460s), and interstate competition spread Renaissance culture throughout Europe by the late sixteenth century. Many princes now sought to display their wealth and power by buying paintings and sculptures. Philip II of Spain purchased more than 1,000 paintings during his reign. Courtiers followed suit, building up-to-date palaces and inviting learned scholars to live on their estates. Italian merchants, whose patronage of scholars had been very important in the Renaissance's early years, were now joined by German, French, and Dutch merchant patrons. While buying cultural goods did not make them equal to aristocrats, certainly the commercial elite was able to show, by cultivating the arts and educating its sons, that it was becoming socially influential. Even the church found Renaissance art and scholarship appealing. The artists Raphael and Michelangelo often worked for the pope; several of the great sixteenth-century humanists—such as Desiderius Erasmus (1466–1536) and Philipp Melanchthon (1497–1560)—contributed much to the launching of the Renaissance.

The relationship between Renaissance humanists and artists and their patrons in politics and the church was not always an easy one. Indeed, since political and religious power were not united in Europe, as they were in China and the

Florence. This 1480 painting of Florence shows a bird's-eye view of the city during the Renaissance. Florence expanded its territory and trade after the Black Death. Note the density of the urban area, as well as the profusion of church spires and the prominence of waterways.

Islamic world, scholars and artists had the opportunity to play one side against the other, or alternatively, to suffer both clerical and political persecution. Erasmus criticized the church, but he survived happily on the patronage of English, Dutch, and French supporters; the popes had their own, very large, stable of lawyers and humanists, who ably defended the church against critics or secular claimants to church lands. As competition grew, artists and scholars could move from state to state in search of sympathetic patrons. As they did so, the educated elite became more and more cosmopolitan, as it had in China and in the Islamic empires. Scholars met one another in royal palaces and cultural centers like Florence, Antwerp, or Amsterdam. They began to correspond, asking for specialized information or rare books.

Thus, gradually, a network of educated men and women formed that was not wholly dependent on either the church or the state, but which, increasingly, had the power to debunk old truths and create new beauties. Some families and religious institutions offered women access to the new learning, and some men encouraged their sisters, daughters, and wives to expand their horizons. The well-educated nun Caritas Pirckheimer (1467–1532) exchanged learned letters and books with important male humanists in the German states; the accomplished Latinist and moral philosopher Laura Cereta (1469–1499) composed a volume of 82 letters defending the rights of women to participate in the arts and sciences. Though Cereta's letters remained unpublished until the seventeenth century, they did circulate in manuscript form during her lifetime. If humanism often confirmed the status quo, it also would prove to be a means by which authority—political, clerical, and aesthetic—could be tested by individuals other than princes and priests.

In some cases, humanists and commercial entrepreneurs came together, creating strikingly new visions of governance. In Florence, a new self-image emerged after the devastation of the Black Death. As the plague subsided, the remaining residents devoted their skills and relatively enhanced fortunes to the expansion of Florentine territory, trade, banking networks, and textile production. They exported woolens and silks to Southwest Asia as well as to Europe and served as the bankers of preference to the popes and all major European entrepôts. Florentine citizens amassed new disposable wealth—and gladly embraced a legacy rediscovered for them by the scholarly elite. Emphasizing the city's origins in Roman Republican times and its success in commerce, Florentines pioneered a kind of secular, civic patriotism that inspired, for example, the production of the first secular histories and eloquent discourses on liberty and civic virtue. But it was also a Florentine, Niccolò Machiavelli, who wrote the most famous treatise on the maintenance of authoritarian power, *The Prince*, in 1513. He argued that political leadership was not about obeying God's rules but about mastering the amoral means of modern statecraft. Holding and exercising power could be ends in themselves.

Neither in Florence nor elsewhere did the Renaissance produce a consensus about who should rule: its artists and scholars simply reproduced (and sometimes exacerbated) rivalries between polities, between church and state, and increasingly between wealthy merchants and titled aristocrats. Instead, the Renaissance produced a culture of critics and competitive individuals, who looked to many sources of authority and power—ancient texts as well as modern princes, wealth as well as blood—for support. It also produced an image of the "good Europe," one in which all these rivalries would produce not warfare, but legitimate, stable government, not patrons who protected intellectuals because they were useful to them, but real freedom of thought. It was this dream of a good, "civilized" Europe, in combination with the crusaders' desire to spread the true faith, that would, in the following centuries, be endlessly contrasted to the "barbarism" of the rest of humankind.

MING CHINA

> → *How did the Ming centralize their authority?*

Like Europeans, people in China long conceived outsiders as barbarians, and like Europeans, the stability of the Chinese world view and political order was severely shaken by the cataclysms of human and bacterial invasions. Together, the Mongols and the Black Death upended the political and intellectual foundations of what had appeared to be the world's most integrated society. The former brought the Yuan dynasty to power; the latter devastated the Middle Kingdom and prepared the way for the emergence of the Ming dynasty in 1368.

China had been ripe for this pandemic. Its numbers had increased significantly under the Song dynasty (960–1279). Indeed, Mongol rule initially sustained Chinese prosperity and population growth. But by 1300, hunger and scarcity began to spread as resources were stretched thin. A weakened population was especially vulnerable to plague. For seventy years, the Black Death ravaged China. The death and destruction brought by the disease were unprecedented and shattered the Mongol dynasty's claim to a mandate from heaven. In 1331, the Black Death may have killed 90 percent of the population in Hebei province. From there it spread throughout the Chinese provinces, reaching Fujian and the coast at Shandong. By the 1350s, severe outbreaks occurred in most of China's large cities.

The reign of the last of the Yuan Mongol rulers, Toghon Temür (ruled 1333–1368), was a time of utter chaos. Even as the Black Death was sweeping over large parts of China, bandit groups and dissident religious sects were undercutting the power of the state. In China, as in other realms desolated by the plague, popular religious movements arose and spoke of impending doom. The most prominent of these was the Red Turban Movement, which took its name from the red headbands that its soldiers wore. The Red Turbans blended China's rich and diverse popular cultural and religious traditions, including Buddhism, Daoism, and other faiths. Its leaders imposed strict dietary restrictions on followers, engaged in penance and ceremonial rituals, in which the sexes freely mixed, and spread the belief that the world was drawing to an end.

In these chaotic times, only the emergence of a powerful military movement capable of overpowering other groups could restore order. That intervention came from a poor young man who had acquired his early training in the Red Turban Movement: Zhu Yuanzhang (ruled 1368–1398). Zhu came from the humblest of backgrounds. He was an orphan from a peasant household in an area devastated by disease and famine and a former novice at a Buddhist monastery. In 1352, the twenty-four-year-old Zhu joined the Red Turbans and rose quickly within its ranks to become a distinguished commander. Eventually, he defeated the Yuan and drove the Mongols from China.

With his ascendance, it became clear that he had a much larger design for all of China than the ambitions of most warlords. When Zhu took the important city of Nanjing in 1356, he renamed it Yingtian, meaning "In response to Heaven." With his successful military campaigns, Zhu felt strong enough by 1368 to proclaim the founding of the Ming ("brilliant") dynasty. In September of that year his troops met lit-

tle resistance when they seized the Yuan capital of Beijing. The Mongol emperor fled to his homeland in the steppe. It would, however, take Zhu close to another twenty years to reunify the entire country.

CENTRALIZATION UNDER THE MING

Zhu and successive Ming emperors had to rebuild a devastated society from the ground up. In the past, China had experienced natural catastrophes, especially flooding (see discussion on "China's Sorrow," the great flood of the Yellow River in 11 CE, in Chapter 7), depopulation, wars, and social dislocation. But the plague in the fourteenth century brought devastation on an unprecedented scale, leaving the new rulers to reconstruct the bureaucracy, rebuild the great cities, and restore respect for the ruling elites.

The rebuilding process began under Zhu, who called himself the Hongwu ("expansive and martial") Emperor and ruled in a grand style. He displayed imperial grandeur in the extravagant scale of his newly constructed capital at Nanjing. When the third emperor of the dynasty, Zhu Di, known as the Yongle Emperor (ruled 1403–1424), relocated the capital to its present-day site of Beijing, he was set on a still more grandiose style. Construction in Beijing mobilized around 100,000 artisans and 1 million laborers. The city had three separate walled enclosures. Inside the outer city walls was the section known as the imperial city; inside its walls was the palace city, often called the Forbidden City. The traffic within the walled sections navigated through boulevards lead-

The Forbidden City. The Yongle Emperor relocated the capital to Beijing, where he began the construction of the Forbidden City, or imperial palace. The palace was designed to inspire awe in all who saw it.

Chinese Irrigation. Farmers in imperial China used sophisticated devices to extract water for irrigation, as depicted in this illustration from the Yuan Mongol period.

ing to the different gates, which were marked by imposing towers. The palace compound, within which the imperial family resided, had more than 9,000 rooms. Anyone standing in the front courts, which measured more than 400 yards on a side and were adorned with marble terraces and carved railings, was struck by a sense of awesome power. That, of course, was precisely what the Ming emperors (just as the Ottoman sultans in building the Topkapi Palace) had in mind.

Marriage and kinship buttressed the power of the Ming imperial household. The founder of the dynasty married the adopted daughter of one of the leading Red Turban rebels against the Yuan Mongol regime (her father, according to legend, was a convicted murderer), thereby consolidating his power and eliminating a threat. Empress Ma, as she was known, became Hongwu's principal wife and was known for her compassion. She emerged as the kinder, gentler face of the regime, tempering the harsh and sometimes cruel disposition of her spouse.

In addition to Empress Ma, Hongwu had numerous other consorts, including Korean and Mongol women, who bore him twenty-six sons and sixteen daughters. He initially sought to rule the empire through his many kinsmen. He gave imperial princes large stipends, command of large garrisons, and significant autonomy in running their own domains. His ini-

tial idea was that kinship solidarity would provide strong support for the ruling household. But when the power of the princes became too great and threatening to the court, Hongwu cut their stipends to one-fifth, reduced their overall privileges, and took over control of their garrisons. Instead of depending on the princes, he established an imperial bureaucracy beholden to him and to his successors (as in the Ottoman Empire). These officials and bureaucrats were appointed based on their performance on a reinstated civil service examination.

The emperor put in place bureaucrats to oversee the manufacture of porcelain, cotton, and silk products, and the collection of taxes. Hongwu reestablished the Confucian school system as a means of selecting a loyal cadre of officials (not unlike the Ottoman janissaries and administrators), who would be obedient to the emperor. He also set up local networks of villages to rebuild irrigation systems and to supervise reforestation projects to prevent flooding. The amount of land reclaimed rose from 575,965 hectares in 1371 to 1,485,572 hectares in 1379. Historians estimate that about 1 billion trees were planted during Hongwu's reign, including 50 million sterculia trees, palm trees, and varnish trees in the area of the capital, Nanjing, in 1391. The products of these trees were used for building the maritime expedition fleet in the

Primary Source

THE HONGWU EMPEROR'S PROCLAMATION

This proclamation of the founding ruler of the Ming dynasty, the Hongwu Emperor (ruled 1368–1398), reveals how he envisioned the reconstruction of a devastated country as his own personal project. He distrusted his officials and berated them for their numerous shortcomings. He sought a return to a more austere world by denouncing the corrosive effect of money and material possessions on the morals of his subjects. Although frustrated in his efforts, Hongwu nonetheless set the tone for the centralization of power in the person of the emperor.

To all civil and military officials:

I have told you to refrain from evil. Doing so would enable you to bring glory to your ancestors, your wives and children, and yourselves. With your virtue, you then could assist me in my endeavors to bring good fortune and prosperity to the people. You would establish names for yourselves in Heaven and on earth, and for thousands and thousands of years, you would be praised as worthy men.

However, after assuming your posts, how many of you really followed my instructions? Those of you in charge of money and grain have stolen them yourselves; those of you in charge of criminal laws and punishments have neglected the regulations. In this way grievances are not redressed and false charges are ignored. Those with genuine grievances have nowhere to turn; even when they merely wish to state their complaints, their words never reach the higher officials. Occasionally these unjust matters come to my attention. After I discover the truth, I capture and imprison the corrupt, villainous, and oppressive officials involved. I punish them with the death penalty or forced labor or have them flogged with bamboo sticks in order to make manifest the consequences of good or evil actions. . . .

Alas, how easily money and profit can bewitch a person! With the exception of the righteous person, the true gentleman, and the sage, no one is able to avoid the temptation of money. But is it really so difficult to reject the temptation of profit? The truth is people have not really tried.

Previously, during the final years of the Yuan dynasty, there were many ambitious men competing for power who did not treasure their sons and daughters but prized jade and silk, coveted fine horses and beautiful clothes, relished drunken singing and unrestrained pleasure, and enjoyed separating people from their parents, wives, and children. I also lived in that chaotic period. How did I avoid such snares? I was able to do so because I valued my reputation and wanted to preserve my life. Therefore I did not dare to do these evil things. . . .

In order to protect my reputation and to preserve my life, I have done away with music, beautiful girls, and valuable objects. Those who love such things are usually "a success in the morning, a failure in the evening." Being aware of the fallacy of such behavior, I will not indulge such foolish fancies. It is not really that hard to do away with these tempting things.

→ *What does Hongwu's proclamation tell us about the importance of education?*
→ *Why would a Chinese emperor issue a decree that focuses on defining moral behavior?*

SOURCE: Patricia Buckley Ebrey (ed.), *Chinese Civilization: A Sourcebook*, 2nd ed., revised and expanded (New York: The Free Press, 1993), pp. 205–06.

---

early fifteenth century. For water control, 40,987 reservoirs were repaired or constructed in 1395.

Under this revamped system, the imperial palace not only projected the image of a power center, it *was* the center of power. Every official of the administration was appointed by the emperor through the Ministry of Personnel. Hongwu also eliminated the previously important post of prime minister in 1380 after he executed the man who held the post. Henceforth, Hongwu ruled directly. Ming bureaucrats literally lost their seats and had to kneel before the emperor. In one eight-day period, he reputedly reviewed over 1,600 petitions dealing with 3,392 separate matters. The drawback, of course, was that the emperor had to keep tabs on this immense system, and his bureaucrats were not always up to the task. Indeed, Hongwu constantly juggled personal and impersonal forms of authority, sometimes fortifying the administration, sometimes undermining it lest it become too autonomous. In due course, Hongwu nurtured a bureaucracy far more extensive than those of the Islamic empires. The Ming thus established the most highly centralized and rationalized system of government of all the monarchies of this period.

RELIGION UNDER THE MING

The Ming zeal to centralize and rationalize extended to the religious pantheon as well. The emperor revised and strengthened the elaborate protocol of rites and ceremonies that had undergirded dynastic power for centuries. As well as underscoring the emperor's centrality, official rituals, such as those related to the gods of soil and grain, reinforced local political and social hierarchies. Under the guise of "community" gatherings, the performance of rites and sacrifices solidified the Ming order. Ming rulers claimed to be moral and spiritual benefactors of their subjects. On at least ninety occasions each year, the emperor engaged in rites of sacrifice, providing symbolic communion between the human and the spiritual worlds. Lavish sacred festivities were occasions for the Ming rulers to reinforce their image as mediators between otherworldly affairs of their gods and worldly concerns of their subjects. The gods were on the side of the Ming household.

The emperor sanctioned official cults which were either civil or military, then further distinguished them into great, middle, or minor, as well as celestial, terrestrial, or human categories. Official cults, however, often collided with local faiths. Such conflicts revealed the limits to Ming centralism. Consider Dongyang, a small, hilly interior region of the realm. As was common in Ming China, the people of Dongyang supported Buddhist institutions. Guan Yu, a legendary martial hero killed in the year 217, was enshrined in a local Buddhist monastery. But he was also worshipped as part of a state cult. The problem was that the state cult and the Buddhist monastery were separate entities, and according to imperial law, the demands of the state cult were supposed to prevail over those of the local monastery. Local magistrates in Dongyang kept a watchful eye on local religious leaders, though they refrained from tampering directly in Dongyang's Buddhist monastery. While the dynasty insisted that people honor their contributions to the state, people in Dongyang delivered most of their funds to the Buddhist monks. So strong were local sentiments and contributions that even officials siphoned revenues to the monastery.

Ming Deities. A pantheon of deities worshipped during the Ming, demonstrating the rich religious culture of the period.

MING RULERSHIP

Overall, sacred sources of political power were comparatively less essential for the Ming dynasty than for the Islamic dynasties. Conquest and defense helped establish the realm; a bureaucracy kept it functioning. The remarkable scale of the Ming realm (see Map 11-6) meant the establishment of a complicated administration. To many outsiders, especially Europeans whose own end of Afro-Eurasia was in a state of constant war, Ming stability and centralization appeared to be political wizardry.

As we consider the structures underlying Ming power, we must not overlook the usual dynastic dilemmas. The emperor

MAP 11-6   MING CHINA, 1500s

The Ming state was one of the largest empires at the beginning of the sixteenth century and the most populous. It had a long seacoast and even longer internal borders. Does the map offer any clues as to where the Ming rulers expected the greatest threat to their security? How did the rulers enhance the security of the state against these threats? How did the Ming rulers view foreign contact and exchange during this period?

wished to be seen as the special guardian, or patriarch, of his subjects. He wanted their allegiance, as well as their taxes and their labor. During hard times, poor farmers were reluctant to provide resources—taxes or services—to distant officials. For these reasons alone, Hongwu preferred to entrust the management of the rural world to local leaders, whom he appointed as village chiefs, village elders, or tax captains. One popular Chinese proverb was: "The mountain is high and the emperor is far away." Within these village communities, the dynasty cre-

ated a social hierarchy based on age, sex, and kinship. While women's labor remained critical for the village economy, the government reinforced a gender hierarchy by promoting a cult of female chastity and constructing commemorative arches for widows who refrained from remarrying. The Ming thus produced a more elaborate system for classifying and controlling subject peoples than did the other dynasties on the Afro-Eurasian landmass, although the system began to show strains as early as the beginning of the fifteenth century.

The Ming Empire, like the European and Islamic states, also had to cope with periodic unrest and rebellions. Rebels were often inspired by their own brand of religious beliefs, just as local elites resented the encroachment of central authority. Outright terror helped stymie threats to central authority. In a massive wave of carnage, Hongwu slaughtered anyone who posed a threat to his authority, from the highest of ministers to the lowliest of scribes. From 1376 to 1393, four of his purges condemned close to 100,000 subjects to execution. Purge victims included civil and military officials, landowners, local leaders, and their families. Yet, despite the immense power of the emperor, the Ming Empire remained undergoverned; there were too few loyal officials to handle local affairs as the number of people in the realm multiplied. By the sixteenth and the early seventeenth centuries, for example, some 10,000 to 15,000 officials had responsibility for a population exceeding perhaps 200 million people. But Hongwu bequeathed a set of tools for ruling to his descendants, tools that enabled the Ming Empire to draw on the subjects' direct loyalty to the emperor and the workings of a powerful bureaucracy. This enabled his successors to balance local sources of power with centralizing ambitions. It was, of course, imperfect. But, for the times, this was a very powerful dynasty.

TRADE UNDER THE MING

In the fourteenth century, China began its economic recovery from the devastation of disease and political turmoil. Gradually, political stability allowed trade to revive. China and the new dynasty's merchants reestablished their preeminence in long-distance, commercial exchange. Chinese silk and cotton textiles, as well as fine porcelains, ranked among the most coveted luxuries in the world. Wealthy families from Lisbon to Kalabar wished to wash their hands in delicate Chinese bowls and to make fine wardrobes from bolts of Chinese dyed linens and smoothly spun silk. When a Chinese merchant ship sailed into port, local trading partners and onlookers gathered to watch the unloading of the precious cargoes. During the Ming period, Chinese maritime traders based in ports along the southern coast, in Hangzhou, Quanzhou, and Guangzhou (Canton), were as energetic as their Muslim counterparts in the Indian Ocean. These ports were home to many prosperous merchants and the point of convergence for vast sea lanes. Leaving the mainland ports, Chinese merchants carried their wares to offshore islands, the Pescadores, and Taiwan. From there, they extended their commercial activities to the ports of Kyūshū, the Ryūkyūs, Luzon, and maritime Southeast Asia. As entrepôts for global goods, East Asian ports flourished. Former fishing villages evolved into major urban centers.

The Ming dynasty viewed overseas expansion with suspicion, however. Hongwu feared that too much commerce and contact with the outside world would cause instability and undermine the authority of his rule. In fact, Hongwu banned private maritime commerce in 1371. But enforcement of this prohibition was lax, and by the late fifteenth century maritime trade along the coast once again surged. Because so much of the thriving business of the South China Sea ports was conducted in defiance of official edicts, it led to ongoing friction between government officials and maritime traders. Although the Ming government, under pressure from the mercantile communities, did relax its ban and agreed to issue

Zheng He's Ship. A testament to centuries of experience in shipbuilding and maritime activities, the largest ship in Zheng He's armada in the early fifteenth century was about five times the length of Columbus's *Santa Maria* (pictured next to Zheng's ship) and had nine times the capacity in terms of tonnage. It had nine staggered masts and twelve silk sails, all designed to demonstrate the grandeur of the Ming Empire.

licenses for overseas trade in the mid- sixteenth century, it continued to vacillate in its policies. To Ming officials, the sea ultimately represented problems of order and control rather than opportunities.

The spectacular exception to the Ming government's general attitude to maritime trade was a well-known series of officially sponsored maritime expeditions in the early fifteenth century. It was the ambitious Yongle Emperor who took the initiative. One of his loyal followers was a Muslim captured by the Ming army when he was a boy. He was castrated (as a eunuch, he could not continue his family line and so theoretically owed sole allegiance to the emperor) and sent to serve at the court. The boy, Zheng He (1371–1433), grew up to be a powerful and important military leader, entrusted by the emperor in 1405 with venturing out to trade, collect tribute, and display China's power to the world. From 1405 to 1433, Zheng He commanded the world's greatest armada and led seven naval expeditions. His larger ships reached 400 feet long (compared to Columbus's puny *Santa Maria*, which was

85 feet long), carried many hundreds of sailors on four tiers of decks, and maneuvered with sophisticated balanced rudders, nine masts, and watertight compartments. The first expedition set sail with a flotilla of 62 large ships and over 200 lesser ones. There were 28,000 men aboard, pledged to promote the cause of Ming glory.

Zheng He and his entourage aimed to establish tributary relations with far-flung territories—from Southeast Asia to the Indian Ocean ports, to the Persian Gulf, and to the east coast of Africa (see Map 11-7). A central goal of these expeditions was not territorial expansion but rather control of trade and tribute. Zheng traded for ivory, spices, ointments, exotic woods, and even some wildlife, including giraffes, zebras, and ostriches. He also used his considerable force to intervene in local affairs, exhibiting the might of China in the process. If a community refused to pay tribute to the emperor, Zheng's fleet would attack it. Rulers or envoys from Southeast Asia, India, Southwest Asia, and Africa were encouraged to visit China. When local rulers proved to be uncooperative,

MAP 11-7 VOYAGES OF ZHENG HE, 1405–1433

Compare the voyages of Zheng He with the travels of Ibn Battuta and Marco Polo described in Chapter 10 and with the voyages of the European explorers discussed in Chapter 12. What were the goals of these voyages? Did Zheng He travel across routes that were familiar to others at this time? Why did Chinese expeditions not have the same impact as European voyages of exploration toward the end of the fifteenth century?

Zheng might seize them and drag them all the way to China to face the emperor, as he did the rulers of Sumatra and Ceylon.

Although many of the items gathered on the voyages delighted the court, most were not the stuff of everyday commerce. The expeditions were, in short, glamorous but very expensive, and they came to a rather abrupt halt in 1433. Never again did the Ming undertake such large-scale maritime ventures. In fact, as early as 1424, when the Yongle Emperor died, the official expeditions had already lost their most important and enthusiastic patron. Moreover, by the mid-fifteenth century, there was a revival of military threats from the north. In 1449, the Ming court was shocked to discover that during a tour of the frontiers, the emperor had been captured and held hostage by the Mongols. Mindful of how the maritime-oriented Song dynasty had been eventually overrun by invaders from the north, officials withdrew imperial support for maritime ventures and instead devoted their energies to overland ventures and defense.

If Chinese maritime commerce continued without official patronage, the decision to abandon imperial support for oceanic exploration led to the decline of Chinese naval power and opened the way for newcomers and rivals. Southeast Asians took advantage by constructing large oceangoing vessels, known as "jong," which plied the regional trade routes from the fifteenth century to the early sixteenth century. These ships weighed an average of 350 to 500 tons, but they could be as big as 1,000 tons, with 1,000 men on board. They carried cargoes and passengers not only to southern China, but also to the Indian Ocean as far west as Calicut and the Red Sea. Muslims also occupied the vacuum left by the Chinese, sailing from ports like Calicut across the Indian Ocean west to Mombassa and Mogadishu, and east to Melaka (Malacca). In addition, Japanese pirates took over some of the trade and made the work of Chinese overseas merchants that much more difficult. The Chinese decision after 1450 to focus on internal trade and defending northern borders just at the time others began to look outward and overseas was, in its way as monumental as that of Mehmed to take Constantinople, or that of an obscure Genoese voyager, Christopher Columbus, to attempt a perilous westward voyage across "the Ocean Sea."

 CONCLUSION

Comparisons help us to understand complex institutions and historical events like those that took place in Afro-Eurasia in the two centuries after the Black Death. The ascent of new dynasties, except for the Mughals, stemmed, in the first instance, from the impact of the Mongol invasions and the Black Death. These states were shaped by varying local conditions—the ambition of a Ming warlord, the military expansionism of Turkish households on the edge of the Christian empire of Byzantium, the unifying vision of Mughal rulers in the northern part of India, and the desire of a variety of rulers to consolidate power in smaller states within Europe. But interactions between peoples also mattered. An eagerness to reestablish and expand trade networks following the Mongol invasions and the Black Death and the desire to convert unbelievers to "the true faith" set many of the peoples of the world in motion.

The great dynasties that came to the fore in this period all had to deal with a common set of problems. They had to create legitimacy for themselves, had to ensure smooth procedures of succession to the throne when a monarch died, had to come to terms with religious groups, and had to establish working relationships with the nongovernmental elements in society, especially nobles, townspeople, merchants, and peasants. Yet, the states developed distinctive traits. The new Afro-Eurasian polities were a combination of outright political innovation, the use of well-known ways of ruling handed down within their own communities, and avid borrowing from nearby polities. The monarchies of Europe were in the process of achieving a high degree of internal unity, although this unity was often brought about through warfare with neighbors and in the context of a burgeoning cultural Renaissance. The Ottoman rulers perfected techniques for ruling a far-flung and ethnically and religiously diverse empire. They were able to move military forces swiftly, to allow local communities a degree of autonomy and at the same time to train a civil and military bureaucracy dedicated to the Ottoman and Sunni Islamic way of life. The Ming fashioned an imperial system based on a Confucian-trained bureaucracy and intense subordination, if not loyalty, to the emperor so that it could cope with the mammoth task of ruling over 200 million subjects. The rising monarchies of Europe, the Shiite regime of the Safavids in Persia, and the Ottoman state were all fired by religious fervor and sought to eradicate or subordinate the beliefs of other groups.

Afro-Eurasian societies and states recovered from the Mongols and the Black Death with greater political and economic powers than before. The Islamic states, the Ming Empire, and the emerging monarchies in Europe were all founded on military prowess and keen to ensure stable hierarchies and secure borders and, if possible, to expand their domains. Each recognized the importance of vigorous commercial activity. Each used dynastic marriage and succession, religion, and administrative bureaucracies to legitimize its rule. By the sixteenth century, societies across Afro-Eurasia were seeking to expand trade with their neighbors or to conquer them. The Islamic regimes especially, and their far-flung traders, increasingly engaged in long-distance commerce, and, by conquest and conversion, extended and strengthened their holdings, especially in the eastern Mediterranean.

Ottoman conquests provoked Europeans to seek alternative trade routes to Africa and Asia. After the ravages of the plague it took more than a century for Europeans to establish new commercial connections to the east, south, and most unexpectedly, west. The consequences of their new toeholds would be momentous—just as the Chinese decision to turn *away* from overseas exploration and commerce marked a turning point in world history. Both decisions would be instrumental in determining which worlds would be brought together—and which would remain apart.

STUDY QUESTIONS

 WWNORTON.COM/STUDYSPACE

1. Explain how the Black Death, or bubonic plague, spread throughout Afro-Eurasia in the fourteenth century. What human activity facilitated the diffusion of this pathogen?
2. Describe the long-term consequences of the bubonic plague for the Afro-Eurasian world. What were the plague's social, political, and economic ramifications in the various parts of Afro-Eurasia?
3. List the Islamic dynasties that emerged in Afro-Eurasia after the bubonic plague. How were they similar, and how were they different?
4. Describe how the Ming dynasty centralized its power in China in the fourteenth and fifteenth centuries. What new political innovations did it pursue and what traditions did it sustain in the Middle Kingdom?

5. Describe the goals of the Ming dynasty's maritime exhibitions during this time. Why did the government later abandon them?
6. Explain why the bubonic plague undermined the feudal order of the Catholic church. How were regional monarchs in Europe able to capitalize on this development?
7. Analyze the connection between the rise of regional dynasties and the European Renaissance. How did regional centralization foster new modes of expression and thinking?

FURTHER READINGS

Bois, Guy, *The Crisis of Feudalism: Economy and Society in Eastern Normandy, c. 1300–1550* (1984). A good case study of a French region that illustrates the turmoil in fourteenth-century Europe.

Brook, Timothy, *Praying for Power: Buddhism and the Formation of Gentry Society in Late Ming China* (1994). An analysis of the role of a significant religious force in the political and social developments of the Ming.

Dardess, John, *A Ming Society: T'ai-ho County, Kiangsi, Fourteenth to Seventeenth Centuries* (1996). A work that covers the different changes and developments of a single locality in China through the centuries.

Dols, Michael W., *The Black Death in the Middle East* (1977). One of the few scholarly works to examine the Black Death outside Europe.

Dreyer, Edward, *Early Ming China: A Political History, 1355–1435* (1982). A useful account of the early years of the Ming dynasty

Chronology

	1300	1400
EUROPE	▪ *Famine in Europe, 1315–1322* ▪ *Hundred Years' War in France, 1337–1453* ▪ *Black Death reaches Italian port cities, 1347* ▪ *Jacquerie Revolt in France, 1358*	▪ *English Peasants' Revolt, 1381*
SOUTH ASIA	▪ *Delhi Sultanate army repulses Mongols, 1303*	▪ *Timur sacks Delhi, 1398*
EAST ASIA	▪ *Black Death begins in China, 1320* *Reign of Yongle Emperor in China, 1403–1424* ▪ *Zheng He's voyages from China, 1405–1433* ▪	▪ *Reign of Hongwu Emperor in China (Ming dynasty), 1368–1398*
THE ISLAMIC WORLD	▪ *Osman begins to build Ottoman Empire, 1299–1326*	*Murad II expands the Ottoman Empire, 1421–1451* ▪

Finkel, Caroline, *Osman's Dream: The Story of the Ottoman Empire, 1300–1923* (2005). The latest and most authoritative overview of Ottoman history.

Hale, John, *The Civilization of Europe in the Renaissance* (1994). A beautifully crafted account of the politics, economics, and culture of the Renaissance period in western Europe.

Hodgson, Marshall, *The Venture of Islam: Conscience and History in a World Civilization*, vol. 3 (1974). A good volume on the workings of the Ottoman state.

Itzkowitz, Norman, *Ottoman Empire and Islamic Tradition* (1972). Another good book on the Ottoman state.

Jackson, Peter, *The Delhi Sultanate* (1999). A meticulous, highly specialized, political and military history.

Jackson, Peter, and Lawrence Lockhart (eds.), *The Cambridge History of Iran*, vol. 6 (1986). A volume that deals with the Timurid and Safavid periods in Iran.

Jones, E. L., *The European Miracle* (1981). A provocative work on the economic and social recovery from the Black Death.

Kafadar, Cemal, *Between Two Worlds: The Construction of the Ottoman State* (1995). A thorough reconsideration of the origins of one of the world's great land empires.

Karamustafa, Ahmed, *God's Unruly Friends: Dervish Groups in the Islamic Later Middle Period, 1200–1550* (1994). A book that describes the unorthodox Islamic activities that were occurring in the Islamic world prior to and alongside the establishment of the Ottoman and Safavid empires.

Levathes, Louise, *When China Ruled the Seas: The Treasure Fleet of the Dragon Throne, 1405–33* (1994). A book that provides a lively account of the Zheng He expeditions.

Lowry, Heath W., *The Nature of the Early Ottoman State* (2003). New perspectives on the rise of the Ottomans to prominence.

McNeill, William, *Plagues and Peoples* (1976). A pathbreaking work with a highly useful chapter on the spread of the Black Death throughout the Afro-Eurasian landmass.

Morgan, David, *Medieval Persia, 1040–1797* (1988). Contains an informative discussion of the Safavid state.

Peirce, Leslie, *The Imperial Harem: Women and Sovereignty in the Ottoman Empire* (1993). A work that describes the powerful place that imperial women had in political affairs.

Pirenne, Henri, *Economic and Social History of Medieval Europe* (1937). A classic study of the economic and social recovery from the Black Death.

Reid, James J., *Tribalism and Society in Islamic Iran, 1500–1629* (1983). A useful account of how the Mongols and other nomadic steppe peoples influenced Iran in the era when the Safavids were establishing their authority.

Russell, Peter, *Prince Henry "the Navigator"* (2000). A close examination of the formation of the Portuguese kingdom of the House of Aviz.

Singman, Jeffrey L. (ed.), *Daily Life in Medieval Europe* (1999). An introductory description of the social and material world experienced by Europeans of different walks of life.

Tuchman, Barbara W., *A Distant Mirror: The Calamitous Fourteenth Century* (1978). A book that shows, in a vigorous way, how war, famine, and pestilence devastated Europeans in the fourteenth century.

Wittek, Paul, *The Rise of the Ottoman Empire* (1958). A work that contains vital insights on the emergence of the Ottoman state amid the political chaos in Anatolia.

	1500		**1600**

▌ *War of the Roses in England, 1455–1485*

  ▌ *Castile and Aragon united, 1469*

   ▌ *Tudors seize English throne, 1485*

    ▌ *Spaniards take Granada from Muslims, 1492*

      ▌ *Babur founds Mughal Empire in India, 1526*

▌ *Mehmed II expands the Ottoman Empire, 1451–1481*

▌ *Ottoman armies conquer Constantinople, 1453*

    ▌ *Shiism becomes Safavid state religion, 1501*

    ▌ *Shah Ismail reigns over Safavid Empire, 1501–1524*

      ▌ *Suleiman consolidates Ottoman Empire, 1520–1566*

Chapter

12

Contact, Commerce, and Colonization, 1450s–1600

On September 20, 1519, a fleet of five ships under the command of Ferdinand Magellan set out from the Spanish port of Sanlúcar de Barrameda. Nearly three years later, a single vessel returned home, having successfully circumnavigated the globe. This achievement had come at a high cost. Four ships had been lost, and only eighteen men, from an original complement of two hundred and sixty-five, staved off scurvy, starvation, and stormy seas to complete the journey. Magellan himself had died in a battle with inhabitants of the Philippines. But the survivors of Magellan's voyage had become the first true world travelers. In contrast to earlier adventurers who confined their primarily overland treks to Eurasia and Africa, Magellan's transoceanic passage connected these worlds with those that, from Afro-Eurasia's viewpoint, had been apart—the Americas.

Mongol armies had run up against barriers, natural and human, in their land-based expansion connecting much of Afro-Eurasia; most famously, Mongol-led forces had drowned when

511

trying to cross the sea to Japan. After the Mongol downfall, land-based interconnections persisted, but more significant were the sea-based ties that developed or deepened: across the Indian Ocean, across the Atlantic, and around the Pacific as well as the South China Sea. The voyages of Magellan and other European mariners brought westerners into contact with the already vibrant commercial networks in Asia and gave Europeans access to new resources in the region they proclaimed to be the "New World." The "discovery" of the Americas was not what Christopher Columbus had in mind when he headed west across the Atlantic looking for Asia. But his voyages did convince Europeans that there were, still, vast new territories to exploit and, if possible, convert.

In the conquest and colonization of the Americas, Europeans also drew heavily on connections with West Africa.

Spanish and Portuguese attempts to exploit African territories set the stage for experiments in the New World. African laborers became increasingly vital to agricultural production and to extracting precious metals. For European merchants, it was a lucky accident and powerful motivation that, just as they gained control over these new resources, the world's demand for silver, sugar, and (a bit later) cotton was beginning to grow. By the mid-sixteenth century, the riches of the New World were making prominent participants in the vibrant commercial circuits of Afro-Eurasia.

Through the sixteenth century, the mightiest Asian empires—the Ming (in China), the Mughal (in South Asia), and the Ottoman (straddling West Asia, North Africa, and southeastern Europe)—maintained their economic prowess and retained control over all but small pockets of their expansive realms. If, by 1600, the impact of the European conquest and colonization of the Americas was being felt around the globe, these empires still had little to fear from their upstart competitors.

THE OLD TRADE AND THE NEW

> → *What was old and what was new in sixteenth-century world trade?*

Well before the products of the Americas entered the circuits of Afro-Eurasian trade, long-distance commerce had staged an impressive recovery from the destruction wrought by the Black Death. Just as political leaders had rebuilt their states by mixing traditional ideas with innovative ones, so, too, merchant elites in Asia and Europe revived old trade patterns while establishing new networks. Increasingly, traffic across seas supplemented, if not supplanted, the overland transportation of goods across long distances. In the fifteenth century, the Indian Ocean and China Seas were the focal points of Afro-Eurasia's maritime commerce. Across these waters, an assortment of goods moved from one point to another, their shipment and exchange directed by Arab, Persian, Indian, and Chinese merchants who often settled in far-off diaspora communities and established cross-cultural liaisons.

European mariners and traders, searching for new routes to South and East Asia, began exploring the Atlantic coast of Africa. Lured by spices, silks, and slaves and aided by advances in maritime technology, Portuguese expeditions made their way around Africa and to India in the last decade of the fifteenth century. At almost the same time, neighboring monarchs in Spanish kingdoms sponsored Christopher Columbus's bid to reach Asia by sailing west across the Atlantic. Both Portuguese and Spanish ventures shared similar motivations: to convert "heathen" peoples to Christianity and to

Focus Questions CONTACT, COMMERCE, AND COLONIZATION

→ *What was old and what was new in sixteenth-century world trade?*

→ *How did the Portuguese attitude toward trade enable the Portuguese to take advantage of and dominate their trading partners?*

→ *What did European conquerors adopt and change from the New World traditions they encountered?*

→ *What military and maritime technologies advanced Portuguese exploration?*

→ *How was Europe transformed politically and spiritually?*

→ *Why did trade expand and wealth increase in sixteenth-century Asia?*

WWNORTON.COM/STUDYSPACE

reap the riches to be found in Asian ports. Although Europeans still had little to offer would-be trading partners in Asia, they did begin to develop the capability and interest in long-distance, overseas trade that would lay the foundations for a new kind of global commerce.

THE REVIVAL OF THE CHINESE ECONOMY

Crucial to Afro-Eurasia's growing economies and populations was the dynamism of China. In the fifteenth century under the Ming dynasty, commerce rebounded from the devastation of Mongol invasions and the Black Death, and the Chinese achieved impressive economic expansion. China's development, in turn, stimulated the other economies across Afro-Eurasia.

China's vast internal economy, not external trade, was the mainspring of the country's progress. The Ming dynasty transferred its capital from coastal Nanjing to the interior city of Beijing ("northern capital"), homeland of the Ming Yongle Emperor and a place better suited for defense against the Mongols. This move inland allowed Chinese merchants, artisans, and cash crop farmers to take advantage of a rapidly growing population and domestic market that had gone largely untapped when the capital and most commerce were situated on the eastern coastline of China. Over the three centuries of Ming rule, the Chinese populace doubled and increasingly congregated in large cities. The reconstruction between 1411 and 1415 of the Grand Canal, which stretched from Hangzhou in the south to Beijing in the north, opened a major artery that enabled food and riches from the lower Yangzi region to provision Beijing and the northern border cities. China's urban centers, such as Nanjing with a population approaching a million and Beijing at half a million, became massive and lucrative markets. The growth of other urban centers in the lower Yangzi area such as Suzhou and Yangzhou further challenged, and then eclipsed, Hangzhou's preeminence. Farther south, the sister cities of Guangzhou (Canton) and Foshan together had as many residents as the whole of Europe's urban population around 1600.

China's elaborate trading networks distributed silk and cotton textiles, rice, porcelain ceramics, paper, and many other products all over the country. The Ming state's concern over the autonomy of China's merchant classes did not dampen internal trade, and the dynasty's efforts to curb overseas commerce, following Zheng He's voyages (see Chapter 11), were largely unsuccessful. As long as merchants did not disturb the Ming order, they were tolerated. And in spite of the government's strictures on engaging in overseas trade, coastal cities remained active harbors (see Map 12-1).

The Chinese manufactured brocaded silks and porcelain ceramics to the highest standards of workmanship. Many Chinese cities produced silk textiles, but the city that acquired the reputation for producing the best quality was

Suzhou, south of the Yangzi River. So important were the products of the Suzhou artisans to the Ming budget that taxes on their silks often provided one-tenth of state revenues. The second of the most-prized commodities was porcelain, whose single biggest consumers, with the deepest of pockets, were the Ming rulers themselves. The great imperial ceramic works at Jingdezhen produced internationally recognized "blue on white" Ming ware depicting motifs from central Asia, Persia, and India (all of which were linked to China via enhanced trade). Potentates of the court developed an almost insatiable appetite for porcelains of high quality. With their access to the fiscal reserves of the government, courtiers purchased nearly all of its most beautiful products, leaving the rougher and more durable porcelains for less discerning foreign buyers.

Although the Chinese kept the best for themselves, their silks and porcelain were coveted by wealthy persons across Afro-Eurasia. But buyers outside China faced a severe problem: What did they have to trade with the Chinese?

The answer was silver, which became essential to the smooth functioning of the Ming monetary system. Ming predecessors had used paper money and copper coinage, but Ming consumers and traders mistrusted anything other than silver or gold for commercial transactions (coins of varying quality continued to circulate for ordinary market exchanges). Silver also became a mainstay of the Ming fiscal system. Especially once the rulers adopted the precious metal as a means of tax payment in the 1430s, silver became the predominant medium for larger commercial transactions.

But China did not produce sufficient amounts of silver for its growing needs. Indeed, silver and other precious metals were about the only commodities for which the Chinese were willing to trade their highly valued manufactures.

Chinese Porcelain Box. The shape, coloring, and texture of this Chinese porcelain writing box are a tribute to the exquisite craftsmanship that went into its production. It was also a symbol of the flourishing world trade and a typical example of what the French then called "chinoiserie," the possession of which was considered a hallmark of taste and cultivation among the rich and the status-conscious in Europe.

MAP 12-1 TRADE AND PRODUCTION IN MING CHINA

The Ming Empire at the beginning of the seventeenth century was the world's most populous state and arguably its wealthiest. What were the main items involved in China's export-import trade and who purchased Chinese exports? Why was China the world's leading importer of silver in the seventeenth and eighteenth centuries? How important was export trade to the prosperity of the empire?

Foreigners learned to exploit this need. Through most of the sixteenth century, China's main source of silver was Japan, which one Florentine merchant referred to as the "silver islands." Both Chinese and European merchants plied the routes from Japanese ports to the Chinese mainland.

After the 1570s, however, the Philippines also became a gateway for silver from the New World. The Ming had over-

seen construction of a merchant marine (using trees planted by the first Ming emperor in the 1390s), enabling Chinese merchants to ship silks, cotton, and porcelain to Manila in the Philippines in exchange for silver, as well as firearms, sugar, potatoes, and tobacco. Despite modest official attempts to control trade, China became the final repository for much of the world's silver from the beginning of the sixteenth cen-

Making and Painting Porcelain. The production of porcelain, for both domestic and external markets, became a highly sophisticated enterprise during the Ming dynasty. The most famous center was the cluster of workshops at Jingdezhen, where there was a clear division of labor among the artisans, each specializing in a particular part of the production process, including decorating and glazing porcelain cups and bowls as shown here.

tury until the end of the eighteenth century. According to one estimate, one-third of all the silver mined in the Americas wound up in Chinese hands. The influx of silver allowed China to continue its phenomenal economic expansion. New World silver also allowed Europeans to gain greater access to China's coveted goods.

REVIVAL OF INDIAN OCEAN TRADE

Chinese economic expansion took part in the broader revival of Indian Ocean trade in the fifteenth century. Many of the same merchants who sought to trade with China developed

a brisk commerce that tied the whole of the Indian Ocean together. As a result, ports in East Africa and the Red Sea were again linked with the coastal cities of India and South Asia and the Malay Peninsula. Muslims dominated the Indian Ocean trade, and Islam provided a unifying religion and a judicial system, but many merchants were Hindus.

India was the geographic and economic center of these trade routes. Its population expanded as rapidly as that of China, and it also had large cities, such as Agra, Delhi, and Lahore, each of which had nearly half a million residents. India's manufacturing center was Bengal, which exported silk and cotton textiles and rice to the rest of the subcontinent and throughout Southeast Asia. Like China, India had a favorable trade balance with Europe and West Asia, exporting textiles and pepper, the spice most coveted by Europeans, in exchange for silver.

In dealing with China, Indian merchants faced the same problem as Europeans and West Asians: they had to pay for Chinese silks and porcelains with silver. This made Indian merchants as dependent on gaining access to silver as the rest of those seeking inroads into Chinese commerce. But unlike Chinese merchants, Indian and Islamic traders in the commercial hubs from the Red Sea to Melaka did not obey a single overarching political authority. This gave them considerable autonomy from political affairs and allowed them to occupy strategic positions in the long-distance trade of Afro-Eurasia. Rulers all along the Indian Ocean flourished by taking customs duties, while they used the luxury goods from afar to flaunt their status. For glorifying sovereigns and for worshiping deities, luxuries such as silks, porcelains, ivory, bullion, diamonds, spices, frankincense, myrrh, and incense were in high demand. Thus did the Indian Ocean trade connect a vast array of consumers and producers long before Europeans arrived on the scene.

Of the many port cities that connected the peoples and commodities of the Indian Ocean, none was more important than Melaka, located at a choke point on the Malay Peninsula between the Indian Ocean and the South China Sea. Unlike other trading places in this region, Melaka had no hinterland of farmers to support it. Instead, it thrived exclusively as an emporium for world traders, thousands of whom resided in the city or passed through it. Indeed, Melaka's merchants were a microcosm of the Indian Ocean's diverse community of traders. Arabs, Indians, Armenians, Jews, East Africans, Persians, and eventually western Europeans established themselves there to participate in and profit from the commerce that moved in and out of Melaka's port.

OVERLAND COMMERCE AND OTTOMAN EXPANSION

The growth of seaborne commerce eclipsed but did not eliminate overland caravan trading. Along some routes, overland commerce thrived anew. One well-trafficked land route linked the Baltic Sea, Muscovy, the Caspian Sea, the central Asian oases, and China. Other land routes carried goods to the ports of China and the Indian Ocean, which then crossed to the Ottoman Empire's heartland and went on land farther into Europe.

Of the many great entrepôts (commercial hubs for long-distance trade) that grew up along caravan routes, none enjoyed a more spectacular economic success than Aleppo in Syria. Thanks to its prime location at the end of the caravan routes from India and Baghdad, Aleppo came to overshadow its other Syrian rivals, Damascus and Homs. A vital supply point for Anatolia and the Mediterranean cities, Aleppo by the end of the sixteenth century had become the most important commercial center, particularly for silk, in the whole of the Middle East.

Overland Caravans and Caravanserais. Muslim governments and merchants' associations constructed inns, or caravanserais, along the major trading routes. These areas were capable of accommodating a large number of traders and their animals in great comfort.

The Aleppans, like others within the Ottoman Empire, revered successful merchants. Rich merchants were extolled as "paragons" and celebrated, in popular stories such as *The Thousand and One Nights,* as shrewd men who had amassed enormous wealth by mastering the intricacies of the caravan trade. Those close to the trade recognized how difficult the merchant's task was. The caravans gathered on the edge of the city, where animals were hired, tents sewn, and saddles and packs arranged. Large caravans involved 600 to 1,000 camels and as many as 400 men; smaller parties required no more than a dozen animals. Whatever the size, a good leader was essential, for only someone who had knowledge of difficult desert routes and the confidence of the Bedouin (derived from the Arabic term for desert dweller and referring to pastoral nomads) tribes that provided safe passage for a fee could hope to make the journey profitable.

Ottoman authorities also took a keen interest in the caravan trade, since the state gained considerable revenue from taxes on it. To facilitate and secure the movement of caravans, the government maintained refreshment and military stations along the route. The largest and most ornate of these stations or caravansarais were made of stone and had individual rooms to accommodate the chief merchants. Some were so vast that they provided overnight lodging for 800 travelers and could feed and care for all their animals. Gathering so many traders, animals, and cargoes could also attract marauders, especially from among desert tribesmen. To stop the raids, authorities and merchants offered large cash payments to tribal chieftains as "protection money."

Revenue from the overland caravan trade helped finance the Ottoman Empire's expansion, underwriting the armies and allowing development of a powerful navy. The many tribes that were knitted together into Ottoman land forces by trade, plunder, and conquest had by the middle of the fifteenth century overrun the great commercial centers of the Afro-Eurasian trade.

The Muslim conquest of Constantinople, the European gateway to the east (Chapter 11), sent shock waves through Christendom. European merchants worried that the fall of Constantinople would mean that the Ottoman sultans would deprive them of safe passage through the newly named Instanbul, and that Christendom's overland route to lucrative Asian markets would be cut off. In 1560, to defend their commerce, Europeans gathered a massive armada of ninety ships and 12,000 men, but, in a naval battle that lasted only a few hours, Ottoman forces sank half of the fleet off the island of Djerba and later captured 10,000 survivors who had sought refuge on the island. The defeated soldiers were marched through the streets of Istanbul. With the Mediterranean and the overland routes to Asia increasingly in the hands of powerful Ottoman loyalists, how were the Europeans to acquire spices and textiles from Asia? Europeans would have to find alternative ways to Asian riches.

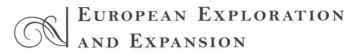

EUROPEAN EXPLORATION AND EXPANSION

> → *How did the Portuguese attitude toward trade enable the Portuguese to take advantage of and dominate their trading partners?*

Ottoman power prompted Europeans to probe unexplored links to the east. Some opted for territorial expansion against weaker neighbors. Muscovite tsars, for instance, presided over both defensive and commercial expansion across the Urals into Siberia. This stretched Christendom's eastern flank overland (see Chapter 13). Others in Europe looked south and west—and to the seas. The Portuguese were the first to see potential profits—as well as souls to be saved—across the Mediterranean, in Africa.

THE PORTUGUESE IN AFRICA AND ASIA

Europeans had long believed that Africa was a storehouse of precious metals. A fourteenth-century map, the Catalan Atlas from 1375–1380, illustrated a single black ruler, depicted as controlling a vast quantity of gold, in the interior of Africa. The fifteenth-century cartographic depiction of Africa, the so-called map of Columbus, also placed gold in the middle of the African landmass. Thus, as the price of gold skyrocketed during and after the Black Death, it made good sense, ambitious men thought, to venture southward in search of this commodity and its twin, silver.

NAVIGATION AND MILITARY DEVELOPMENTS The first Portuguese sailors had set out expecting, from stories and myths, to encounter giants and Amazons, seas of darkness, and distant lands of savages and cannibals. To some extent, these tales shaped their views of the places and peoples they encountered, which, thanks to the development of new maritime technology and the borrowing of information from other mariners, included lands around the tip of Africa and into the Indian Ocean. The Portuguese knew that great riches awaited them there.

Of the Portuguese ships, one, called a carrack, worked well on bodies of water like the Mediterranean, while a second, the caravel, was more suited for nosing in and out of estuaries and navigating unpredictable currents and winds. Often, however, their vessels blended elements of carrack and caravel, which allowed Portuguese mariners to overcome some of the hazards that oceanic voyages had always presented. Only by using highly maneuverable caravel vessels and perfecting the technique of tacking (sailing into the wind

The Catalan Atlas. This 1375 map shows the world as it was then known. Not only does it depict the location of continents and islands, it also includes information on ancient and medieval tales, regional politics, astronomy, and astrology.

rather than before it) were the Portuguese able to advance far along the West African coast. In addition, the Portuguese had become expert in the use of the compass and the astrolabe, which enabled them to determine their latitudes. The Portuguese success also owed to knowledge they had absorbed from ancient Greeks and Arabs and from the assistance they received from Muslim mariners, whom they had taken aboard and who had wide experience in Africa and the Indian Ocean.

The success of Portuguese ships in the Indian Ocean was also in part the result of a revolution in military technology and tactics that had been gathering momentum for a long time—and owed much to borrowings from Asia. This began with the adaptation of a Chinese technology: gunpowder. The Ottomans had made use of this technology to conquer Constantinople in 1453 with enormous cannons filled with gunpowder and 800-pound cannonballs. In like fashion in 1492, Christians used cannons to breach the walls of Granada. Europeans also used explosive smaller cannons, which were more mobile and could propel iron balls in relatively flat trajectories to lay ruin to old fortifications. These cannons could also be mounted against the gunwales of warships, to bombard ports and rival navies, or merchant vessels, to shift the nature of ocean commerce toward more military ends.

Within Europe, the main beneficiaries of this revolution in warfare were the dynastic rulers, who commanded the financial resources to equip large fighting forces with new armaments. In 1492, what was then a huge force of 60,000 Christian soldiers drove Islam's army out of Granada; two centuries later, such an army would have been dwarfed by the hundreds of thousands of men fielded by the most powerful European states. So, too, tactics shifted. In medieval Europe, a day of combat or a short siege of castles often settled matters. By the middle of the sixteenth century, battles often involved protracted and usually inconclusive struggles. This way of war, more costly in terms of money and manpower, gave an advantage to larger, centralized states.

SUGAR AND SLAVES Africa and the islands along its coast proved to be far more than a stop-off en route to India or a source of precious metals. Africa became a valued trading area, and its islands became prime locations in which to grow sugarcane, a crop that had exhausted the soils of Mediterranean islands where it had been cultivated since the twelfth century. Along what they called the Gold Coast, the Portuguese established many fortresses and ports of call. Having taken over islands off the West African coast, notably São Tomé, Principe, and Fernando Po, they introduced the cultivation of sugarcane on relatively large-scale plantations and used slave labor brought in from the African mainland.

The Madeira, Canary, and Cape Verde archipelagos in particular became laboratories for plantation agriculture. Their rainfall and fertile soils made these islands ideally suited for growing sugarcane. Moreover, large numbers of workers were needed to cultivate, harvest, and process the sugarcane; hence, the availability of a supply of slave labor in the vicinity enabled Portugal and Spain to build sizeable plantations in their first formal colonies. Thus, in the fifteenth century, these islands off the coast of West Africa saw the beginnings of a plantation built on a system of slavery that was to be transported across the Atlantic in the following century.

The Portuguese did not restrict the export of slaves to these West African possessions. As early as 1441, Portuguese merchants had brought a shipload of African slaves back to Portugal, where they were pressed into service as domestic workers. The slave trade to Portugal increased throughout the fifteenth and into the sixteenth century, so that by 1551 the city of Lisbon, with a population of over 100,000, was reported to have 10,000 African slaves.

COMMERCE AND CONQUEST IN THE INDIAN OCEAN
Having explored the African coast and established plantation colonies off it, Portuguese seafarers ventured into the Indian Ocean and inserted themselves into its thriving commerce (see Map 12-2). The Portuguese seaborne empire never aspired to direct rule or colonization. Rather, these Europeans

Caravels. Caravels became the classic vessel for European exploration. They combined castlelike defenses with many decks and plenty of portholes for cannon, could house a large crew, and had lots of storage for provisions, cargo, and booty.

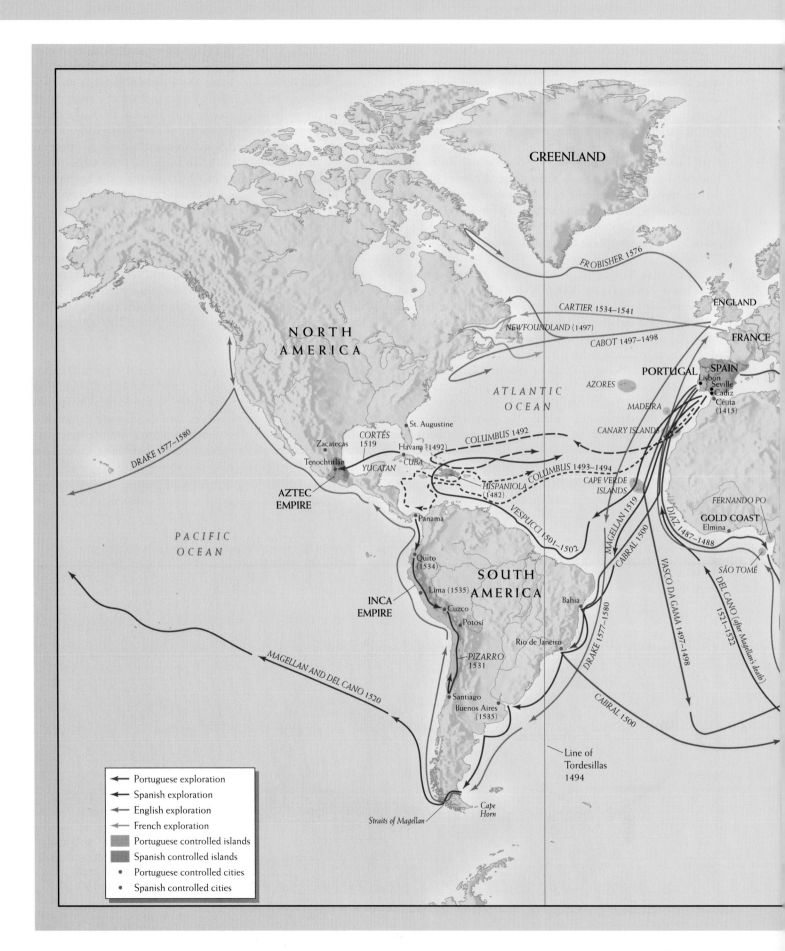

GREENLAND

FROBISHER 1576

CARTIER 1534–1541

ENGLAND

NEWFOUNDLAND (1497)

CABOT 1497–1498

FRANCE

NORTH
AMERICA

PORTUGAL SPAIN
Lisbon
Seville
Cadiz
Ceuta
(1415)

AZORES

*ATLANTIC
OCEAN*

MADEIRA

St. Augustine

COLUMBUS 1492

CANARY ISLANDS

Zacatecas

*CORTÉS
1519*

Havana (1492)

DRAKE 1577–1580

Tenochtitlán

CUBA

YUCATAN

COLUMBUS 1493–1494

*HISPANIOLA
(1492)*

*CAPE VERDE
ISLANDS*

FERNANDO PO

AZTEC
EMPIRE

VESPUCCI 1501–1502

GOLD COAST
Elmina

DIAZ 1487–1488

Panama

MAGELLAN 1519

CABRAL 1500

SÃO TOMÉ

*PACIFIC
OCEAN*

Quito
(1534)

SOUTH
AMERICA

VASCO DA GAMA 1497–1498

*DEL CANO (after Magellan's death)
1521–1522*

INCA
EMPIRE

Lima (1535)

Bahia

Cuzco

Potosí

Rio de Janeiro

DRAKE 1577–1580

*PIZARRO
1531*

MAGELLAN AND DEL CANO 1520

CABRAL 1500

Santiago

Buenos Aires
(1535)

Line of
Tordesillas
1494

Straits of Magellan

*Cape
Horn*

→ Portuguese exploration
→ Spanish exploration
→ English exploration
→ French exploration
■ Portuguese controlled islands
■ Spanish controlled islands
• Portuguese controlled cities
• Spanish controlled cities

MAP 12-2   EUROPEAN EXPLORATION, 1420–1580

In the fifteenth and sixteenth centuries, sailors from Portugal, Spain, England, and France explored and mapped the coastline of most of the world. Why did Portuguese explorers concentrate on Africa and the Indian Ocean whereas their Spanish counterparts focused on the Americas? How did each dynasty exploit its maritime and military advancements in each region? To what extent does this map preview the changes in global trade patterns that stemmed from these maritime voyages of exploration over the next century?

ARCTIC OCEAN

RUSSIAN EMPIRE

SIBERIA

Istanbul

OTTOMAN EMPIRE

Aleppo
Homs
Damascus

Isfahan

SAFAVID EMPIRE

Gombrun   Hormuz

ARABIA

Mecca

Muscat

Delhi
Agra

MUGHAL EMPIRE

Goa (1510)

Aden (1513)

COVILHÃO 1487–1489

ARABIAN SEA

AFRICA

ETHIOPIA

SWAHILI COAST

Malindi

Mombasa (1498)

Kilwa (1505)

Mozambique (1507)

Sofala (1505)

ZIMBABWE

Delagoa Bay

Cape of Good Hope

Calicut (1498)
Cochin (1502)
CEYLON (1518)

VASCO DA GAMA 1497–1498

CABRAL 1500

SEQUEIRA 1509–1510

MADAGASCAR (1500)

INDIAN OCEAN

DRAKE 1577–1580

Beijing

MING CHINA

Nanjing

Guangzhou (Canton)

Macao

JAPAN

Nagasaki (1542)

PACIFIC OCEAN

PERESTRELLO 1514–1516

Manila

PHILIPPINES

DEL CANO (after Magellan's death) 1521–1522

DRAKE 1577–1580

MALAY PENINSULA

Melaka (1511)

SUMATRA

BORNEO

ABREU 1511

MALUKU (1511)

NEW GUINEA

JAVA

AUSTRALIA

| 0 | 1000 | 2000 Miles |

| 0 | 1000 | 2000 Kilometers |

PORTUGUESE VIEWS OF THE CHINESE

When the Portuguese arrived in China in the early sixteenth century, they encountered a vast empire whose organizational structure and ideological orientation were quite different from their own. Written in 1517, this Portuguese report is replete with misrepresentations that were to characterize many Europeans' views of China for centuries to come. It also signaled a new and aggressive phase of European expansionism, in which the use of brute force was celebrated as a legitimate means to destroy and conquer those who stood in the way.

God grant that these Chinese may be fools enough to lose the country; because up to the present they have had no dominion, but little by little they have gone on taking the land from their neighbors; and for this reason the kingdom is great, because the Chinese are full of much cowardice, and hence they come to be presumptuous, arrogant, cruel; and because up to the present, being a cowardly people, they have managed without arms and without any practice of war, and have always gone on getting the land from their neighbors, and not by force but by stratagems and deceptions; and they imagine that no one can do them harm. They call every foreigner a savage; and their country they call the kingdom of God. Whoever shall come now, let it be a captain with a fleet of ten or fifteen sail. The first thing will be to destroy the fleet if they should have one, which I believe they have not; let it be by fire and blood and cruel fear for this day, without sparing the life of a single person, every junk being burnt, and no

one being taken prisoner, in order not to waste the provisions, because at all times a hundred Chinese will be found for one Portuguese. And this done, Nanto must be cleared, and at once they will have a fortress and provisions if they wish, because it will at once be in their power; and then with the whole fleet attack Aynãcha, which lies at the bar of Tãcoam, as I have already said above having a good port. Here the ships, which cannot enter the river, will be anchored, and whatever craft they may have will be burnt; and after it has been taken if it seem good the town can be burnt, in order to terrify the Chinese. . . .

→ *What do you think was the main purpose of this report?*
→ *How could this observer's views be so inaccurate?*

SOURCE: Letters from Canton, translated and edited by D. Ferguson, *The Indian Antiquary* 31 (January 1902), in J. H. Parry, *European Reconnaissance: Selected Documents* (New York: Walker, 1968), p. 140.

---

extracted benefits by exploiting Asian commercial networks and trading systems.

The first Portuguese mariner to reach the Indian Ocean was Vasco da Gama (1469–1524). Like Columbus, da Gama was a relatively unknown sailor before he commanded four ships around the Cape of Good Hope in 1497. He then spent four months exploring the east coast of Africa but did not encounter either friendly traders or great riches. What he did encounter was a vast network of existing commercial ties spanning the Indian Ocean and skilled Muslim mariners who knew the currents, winds, and ports of call. Vasco da Gama took on board a Muslim pilot at Malindi, on the coast of East Africa, to instruct da Gama on how to navigate in the winds and currents of the Indian Ocean. Da Gama then sailed straight for the Malabar coast in southern India, one of the most important trading areas in the whole region, arriving there in 1498.

To the Portuguese—who traded in the name of their crown—commercial access was worth fighting for. Da Gama was briefly taken hostage in Pantalayini, near Calicut, and though he was eventually allowed to load his ships with a valuable cargo of spices and silks, he was incensed. On his exit from southern India, da Gama roughed up whomever he came across, making sure local fishermen watched and spread the news.

On the difficult voyage back to Lisbon in 1499, da Gama lost more than half of his crew, but he had proved the feasibility—and profitability—of trade via the Indian Ocean. When da Gama returned to Calicut in 1502—with a beefed-up contingent—he asserted Portuguese supremacy by boarding the twenty ships in the harbor and cutting off the noses, ears, and hands of their sailors, then burning the ships with the mutilated sailors on board. The Portuguese repeated their shows of force throughout the region's strategic locations, especially the three great naval choke points: Aden at the base of the Red Sea, Hormuz in the Persian Gulf, and Melaka at the tip of the Malay Peninsula. Having ensconced themselves in the area's chief commercial ports, the Portuguese attempted to take over the trade themselves, or failing this, to tax local merchants. Although they failed to hold Aden for long, they did solidify their trading networks by establishing their control in Sofala, Kilwa, and other important port cities on the East African coast, Goa and Calicut in India, and Macao in southern China. From these strongholds, the Portuguese soon commanded the most active sea lanes of the Indian Ocean.

To assert their imperial domain over Indian Ocean trade (west of the Melaka Strait), the Portuguese introduced a pass system (the cartaz) that required that ships pay for cartazes, documents that stated the name of the ship's captain, size of the ship and crew, and its cargo. But some Indian Ocean rulers and merchants got cartazes for free, showing the limits of Portuguese "dominion." Others calculated it was cheaper to pay than risk losses at sea from unpredictable "retribution." Sometimes local rulers submitted to the Portuguese because it was an opportunity to free themselves of a bigger realm's rule and taxes. The big rulers, in turn, saw the Portuguese as useful for subordinating smaller fiefs. The distinctiveness of the Portuguese presence in the Indian Ocean world was that they did not interrupt the flow of luxuries among Asian and African elites—rather, they skimmed off the top.

Between 1500 and 1634, fewer than four vessels per year sailed around the Cape back to Portugal. As the products of the Indian Ocean made their way back to Lisbon, that city eclipsed the great Italian ports such as Venice that had previously been the prime entrepôts for Asian goods. Even so, spices were far less important in Europe than *within* the Indian Ocean world, where the Portuguese became an important player. Only with the discovery of the Americas and the conquest of Brazil did Portugal become an empire with large overseas colonies. For this to transpire, the Atlantic Ocean itself had to be traversed.

 THE ATLANTIC WORLD

> → *What did European conquerors adopt and change from the New World traditions they encountered?*

Western European Christendom, in opening new sea lanes in the Atlantic, set the stage for an epochal transformation in world history. New technologies certainly aided European expansion, but diseases made the difference. In their encounters with the peoples of the Americas, Europeans introduced more than new cultures to this isolated world; they also brought devastating new pathogens. The catastrophic decline of Amerindian populations enabled Europeans to colonize the Americas and reap advantage from their natural resources.

Most of the people who made the Atlantic voyage after 1500 were not Europeans but Africans. The decimation of Indians in many areas deprived Europeans of an indigenous labor force and drove them to seek workers elsewhere. As a supplier of slave labor, Africa became the third corner in a triangular order. Born of the links between the peoples and resources of Europe, Africa, and the Americas, this emerging "Atlantic Ocean system" enriched Europeans. Through conquest and resettlement in the New World, Europeans gained access to the precious metals of the Americas. New World silver provided Europeans with the means to offer something to their trading partners in Asia.

The crossing of the Atlantic Ocean was a feat of monumental importance in world history. But it was not accomplished with an aim to discover new lands; Columbus had wanted Spanish royal patronage to support a voyage into the "Ocean Sea" (the Atlantic) and to thereby open a more direct—and more lucrative—route to Japan and China. Fired by their victory at Granada, Ferdinand and Isabella had agreed to finance his trip, hoping for riches with which to bankroll a final and decisive crusade to liberate Jerusalem from Muslim hands. Just as Columbus had no idea he would find a "New World," in 1491, Spain's monarchs, not to mention its merchants, missionaries, and soldiers, never dreamed that in a few short years they would be readying themselves for conquest and profiteering in what had been, just a few years before, a blank space on the map.

Columbus's "discovery" was, therefore, something of an accident. Still, while the idea of creating an entirely new world system of trade was unintended, it took scarcely a generation for Europeans to realize the significance of their accidental discoveries. News of Columbus's voyage spread quickly through Europe, and, especially in the Iberian ports, ambitious mariners prepared their vessels to sail west. Other ships on the way to the east also found the New World by accident. For example, in 1500, Pedro Alvares Cabral and his Portuguese fleet, on a voyage originally intended for India, were blown west in the Atlantic and landed instead on the bulge of South America that is now Brazil. By 1550, all of Europe's powers were scrambling, not just for a share in the Indian Ocean action, but also for the spoils of the Atlantic. In the process, they began destroying the societies and the great dynasties of the New World. The devastation of the peoples of the Americas coincided with a sharpening of European rivalries.

WESTWARD VOYAGES OF COLUMBUS

Few figures in history have come to embody their age more than Christopher Columbus. His tiny fleet of three ships set

Columbus. As Columbus made landfall and encountered Indians, he planted a cross to indicate the spiritual purpose of the voyage and read aloud a document proclaiming the sovereign authority of the king and queen of Spain. Quickly, he learned there was barter for precious stones and metals.

sail from Spain in early 1492, stopped in the Canary Islands for supplies and repairs, and cast off into the unknown. When he walked onto the beach of San Salvador (in the Bahamas) on October 12, 1492, Columbus ushered in a new era in world history. He did not, however, return with the precious commodities of Asia that he had expected. Columbus would search in vain in three subsequent voyages for the valuable products of the South China Sea and the Indian Ocean.

It is important to see Columbus as a man of his time. Like other expansion-minded Europeans, he aimed to Christianize the world while enriching himself (and his backers). These twin goals, to save souls and to make money, drove the European colonization of the Americas and the formation of an Atlantic system. Still, it is worth reminding ourselves that Columbus's voyages aimed not to create something new but to generate revenues to pay off debts incurred in the conquest of Granada and in the reconquest of the Holy Land. To his dying day, Columbus never believed that he had discovered anything new.

FIRST ENCOUNTERS

When Columbus made landfall in the Caribbean, he unfurled the royal standard of Ferdinand and Isabella and claimed the "many islands filled with people innumerable" for Spain. Fit-

tingly, the first encounter with Caribbean inhabitants, in this case the Tainos, drew blood. As Columbus noted in his journal, "I showed them swords and they took them by the edge and through ignorance cut themselves." The Tainos certainly had their own weapons but did not forge steel—and thus such sharp edges were unknown to them.

For Columbus, the naiveté of the Tainos in grabbing his sword symbolized the child-like primitivism of these people, whom he would mislabel "Indians." In Columbus's view, the Tainos had no religion, but they did have at least some gold (found initially hanging as pendants from their noses). Likewise, Pedro Alvares Cabral wrote to his own king that the people of Brazil had all "the innocence of Adam" and were ripe for conversion, and the soils "if rightly cultivated would yield everything." But, as with Africans and Asians, Europeans also developed a contradictory view of the peoples of the Americas. From the Tainos, Columbus learned of another people, the Caribs, who, according to his informants, were savage, warlike cannibals. For centuries, these contrasting images—innocents and savages—provided the two competing visions that structured European (mis)understandings of the indigenous peoples of the Americas.

We know less about what the Indians thought of Columbus or other Europeans on their first encounters. Certainly the appearance of Europeans and their technologies often inspired awe. The Tainos of San Salvador fled into the forest at the approach of European ships, which they thought were giant monsters; others thought that approaching European ships were floating islands. European metal goods, in particular weaponry, were assumed to be otherworldly. The strangely dressed white men seemed godlike to some, although many Indians soon abandoned this view. Many found the newcomers different not for their skin color (only Europeans drew the distinction based on skin pigmentation), but for their hairiness. Indeed, the beards as well as the breath and bad manners of Europeans repulsed their Indian hosts. The inability of the Europeans to live off the fruit of the land also stood out.

In due course, the Indians realized that the strange, hairy people bearing metal weapons were not just odd trading partners, but that they meant to stay and to force the native population to labor for them. By the time Indians were aware of the dislocations and upheaval brought by the Spaniards, however, it was too late. The explorers had become conquerors (conquistadors).

FIRST CONQUESTS

After the first voyage, Columbus claimed that on the island of Hispaniola (present-day Haiti and the Dominican Republic) "he had found what he was looking for"—gold. That was sufficient inducement to persuade the Spanish crown to invest in larger, costlier expeditions. Whereas Columbus first sailed with three small ships and 87 men, ten years later the Spanish outfitted an expedition with 2,500 men.

Between 1492 and 1519, the Spanish experimented with institutions and practices of colonialism on Hispaniola, creating a model to be modified and applied in the rest of the New World colonies. Here, the Spaniards faced problems that would recur. The first was Indian resistance. As early as 1494, starving Spaniards raided and pillaged Indian villages. When the Indians revolted, Spanish soldiers replied with punitive expeditions and began enslaving the native population to work extracting gold. The crown began to systematize grants (*encomiendas*) to the conquistadors for control over Indian labor. This created a rich class of *encomenderos* who enjoyed the fruits of the system. True, the placer gold mines soon ran dry, but the model of granting favored settlers the right to co-erce Indian labor endured. In return, those granted the labor rights paid special taxes on the precious metals that were ex-tracted. Thus, both the crown and the *encomenderos* shared in the benefits of the extractive economy. The same cannot be said of the Indians, who were dying in great numbers due to disease, dislocation, malnutrition, and overwork.

> *In both Mesoamerica and the Andes, large polities began to take shape, creating the foundations of subsequent Aztec and Incan empires.*

Not surprisingly, conquests were followed by quarrels over the spoils. The family of Columbus, in particular, had been granted a commercial monopoly on his discoveries, but some of the settlers objected and challenged Columbus's authority. To prevent insurrection, the crown granted more *encomien-das* to other Spanish claimants. As special grants became a common feature of Spanish colonialism, less favored settlers grew disenchanted. When the Indians and the gold supplies began to disappear, many settlers pulled up their stakes and returned to Spain. Others looked for new untapped territories that might be rich in precious metals.

Not all joined the rush for riches or celebrated conquis-tadors and *encomenderos*. Dominican friars protested the abuse of the Indians, seeing them as potential converts, equal to the Spaniards in the eyes of God. In 1511, Father Antonio Montesinos accused the settlers of barbarity: "By what right do you wage such detestable wars on these people who lived idly and peacefully in their own lands, where you have con-sumed infinite numbers of them with unheard-of murders and desolations?" Dissent and debate would be a permanent feature of Spanish colonialism in the New World.

THE AZTEC EMPIRE AND THE SPANISH CONQUEST

As Spanish colonists saw the bounty of Hispaniola begin to dry up, they set out to discover and conquer new territories.

Finding their way to the mainlands of the American land-masses, they encountered larger, more complex, and more militarized societies than the ones they had quickly overrun in the Caribbean. On the mainland, great civilizations had arisen centuries before, boasting large cities, monumental buildings, and riches based on wealthy agrarian societies. In both Mesoamerica, starting with the Olmecs (see Chapter 5), and the Andes, somewhat later with the Chimu (see Chapter 10), large polities began to take shape, creating the foundations of subsequent Aztec and Incan empires. They were powerful. But they also represented the evolution of states and commercial systems untouched by Afro-Eurasian developments; as worlds apart, they were simply unprepared for the kind of assaults that European invaders had honed. In Mesoamerica and then the Andes, warfare was more cere-monial, less inclined to wipe out enemies than to annex them as tributary subjects. As a result, the wealth of these em-pires made them irresistible to outside conquerors they never knew, and their habits of war made them vulnerable to con-quests they could never foresee.

AZTEC SOCIETY   In Mesoamerica, the ascendant Mexi-cas (see the discussion of the Toltecs in Chapter 10) had cre-ated an empire and named it "Aztec" after the foundational story of the people who migrated from the mythic town of Aztlan. Around Lake Texcoco, Mexica cities grew and formed a three-city league in 1430, which then expanded outward through the Central Valley of Mexico to incorporate neigh-boring peoples. Over the course of the fifteenth century, the Aztec empire united numerous small, independent states under a single monarch who ruled with the help of coun-selors, military leaders, and priests. By the end of the fifteenth century, the Aztec realm may have embraced 25 million peo-ple and Tenochtitlán, the primary city, situated on an island in Lake Texcoco, ranked among the world's largest with a pop-ulation estimated at between 200,000 and 300,000.

Tenochtitlán spread in concentric circles, with the main religious and political buildings in the center and residences radiating outward. As the city was built on an immense is-land, its outskirts connected a mosaic of floating gardens pro-ducing food for urban markets. Canals constantly irrigated the land, waste was used as fertilizer, and the tremendously high yields were easily transported to markets. Entire house-holds worked: men, women, and children all had roles in Aztec agriculture.

Extended kinship provided the scaffolding for Aztec state-hood. Marriage of men and women from different villages solidified alliances and created clan-like networks. In Ten-ochtitlán, powerful families married their children to each

Tenochtitlán. At its height, the Aztec capital Tenochtitlán was as populous as Europe's largest city. (*Left*) As can be seen from this map, it spread in concentric circles, with the main religious and political buildings in the center and residences radiating outward. (*Right*) As the city was built on an immense island, its outskirts connected a mosaic of floating gardens producing food for urban markets. Canals constantly irrigated the land, waste was used as fertilizer, and the tremendously high yields were easily transported to markets. Observe how entire households worked: men, women, and children all had roles in Aztec agriculture.

other or found nuptial partners among the prominent families of other important cities. Not only did this concentrate power in the great city, it also ensured a pool of potential successors to the throne. In this fashion, a lineage emerged to create a corps of "natural" rulers. Priests legitimized the new emperor in rituals to convey for his subjects the image of a ruler close to the gods and to mark off the elite from the lower orders.

A hierarchy already present at the village level provided the bedrock for layers of increasingly centralized political authority. Local elders developed representative bodies and councils, which selected delegates to a committee responsible for electing the dominant civil authority, known as the chief speaker. As Aztec power spread, the chief speaker became a full-blown emperor. He was, however, not supreme, instead jockeying with rival religious and especially military power-wielders. At the top of the Aztec social pyramid thus stood a small but antagonistic nobility. This hierarchically organized society was held together by a shared understanding of the cosmos. The Aztecs believed that the universe was prone to unceasing cycles of disaster that would eventually end in an apocalypse. Such an unstable cosmos exposed mortals to repeated creations and destructions. The priesthood monitored the relationship between the people and their deities and balanced fatalism with a faith that the gods could be honored through rituals.

By the end of the fifteenth century, Aztec power had spread to much of Mesoamerica, but the empire's constant wars and conquests of neighboring territories deprived it of stability. In successive military campaigns, the Aztecs subjugated their neighbors, feeding off plunder and then forcing subject peoples to pay annual tribute of crops, gold, silver, textiles, and other goods that financed Aztec grandeur. Conquest of Aztec neighbors also provided imperial rulers with a constant supply of humans for sacrifice to the gods. Captives faced execution because the Aztecs believed that the great god of the sun required human hearts to keep on burning and blood to replace that given by the gods to moisten the earth through rain. Priests escorted captured warriors up the temple steps and tore out their hearts, offering their lives and blood as a sacrifice to the sun god. Allegedly, between 20,000 and 80,000 men, women, and children were slaughtered in a single ceremony in 1487, with the four-person-wide line of those who would be killed stretching for over two miles. In this marathon of bloodletting, knife-wielding priests collapsed from exhaustion and had to be replaced by fresh executioners.

The peoples the Aztecs sought to dominate did not submit peacefully. From 1440, the empire entered a state of constant turmoil as subject peoples rebelled against their oppressive Aztec overlords. Tlaxcalans and Tarascans along the Gulf of Mexico waged a relentless war for freedom, pinning down entire divisions of Aztec armies. To pacify the realm, the empire diverted more and more men and money into a mushrooming military. By the time the electoral committee chose Moctezuma II as emperor in 1502, divisions among elites and pressures from the periphery placed the Aztec Empire under stress.

CORTÉS AND CONQUEST Not long after Moctezuma became emperor, news arrived of strange sightings off the eastern coast of large floating mountains (ships) bearing pale, bearded men and monsters (horses and dogs). Moctezuma consulted with his ministers and soothsayers over the news, wondering if these men were the god Quetzalcóatl and his entourage. The people of Tenochtitlán saw omens of impending disaster. Moctezuma sank into despair, hesitating as

Aztec Sacrifice. This seventeenth-century illustration depicts the Aztec practice of sacrificing captives to the gods. Note the open chests: the hearts were cut out at the top of the temple steps before the victims were sent tumbling down.

to what course of action to take. He sent emissaries bearing jewels and prized feathers; later he sent sorcerers to confuse and bewitch the newcomers. But he did not prepare his city for any military engagement—Mesoamericans had no idea of the interlopers' destructive potential in weaponry and germs.

Aboard one of the ships was Hernán Cortés (1485–1547), a former law student from the Spanish province of Estremadura. Cortés was to become the model conquistador, just as Columbus was the model explorer. For a brief time, he was an *encomendero* in Hispaniola, but when news arrived of a potentially even more wealthy land to the west, he set sail with over 500 men, eleven ships, sixteen horses, and artillery.

When the expedition arrived near present-day Veracruz, Cortés acquired two translators, including the daughter of a local Indian noble family. The daughter, who became known

Cortés Meets Montezuma. This colonial image depicts the meeting of Cortés (second from right) and Moctezuma (seated to his left), with Doña Marina serving as an interpreter and informer for the Spanish conquistador. Notice at the bottom what are likely Aztec offerings for the newcomer.

the translators, with Moctezuma's enemies, especially the Tlaxcalans. After decades of yearning for release from the Aztec yoke, the Tlaxcalans and other Mesoamerican peoples embraced Cortés's promise of help. The Spaniards' second main advantage was their method of warfare. The Aztecs were seasoned fighters, but they fought to capture, not to kill. Nor were they familiar with gunpowder or sharp steel swords. Outnumbered, the Spaniards killed their foe with abandon, using their superior weaponry, horses, and war dogs. The Aztecs, still unsure who these strange men were, allowed Cortés to enter their city. With the aid of the Tlaxcalans and a handful of his own men, Cortés was able in 1519 to capture the Aztec ruler, Moctezuma, who became a puppet of his Spanish conqueror.

Within two years, the Aztecs realized that these newcomers were not gods and that Aztec warriors too could fight to kill. When Spanish troops massacred an unarmed crowd in Tenochtitlán's central square while Cortés was away, they provoked a massive uprising. The Spaniards led Moctezuma to one of the palace walls to plead with his people for a truce,

as Doña Marina, was a "gift" from the ruler of the region of Tabasco, a rival to the Aztecs, to the triumphant Spaniards. Fluent in several languages, Doña Marina's linguistic skills and personal charms soon brought her to the attention of Cortés. She became his lover and was to reveal several clandestine Aztec plots to wipe out the tiny Spanish force. Doña Marina subsequently bore Cortés a son, who is considered one of the first mixed-blooded Mexicans (known as mestizos).

With the assistance of Doña Marina and other native allies, Cortés marched his troops to Tenochtitlán. Entering, he gasped in wonder that "this city is so big and so remarkable" that it was "almost unbelievable." One of his soldiers wrote, "It was all so wonderful that I do not know how to describe this first glimpse of things never heard of, seen or dreamed of before."

How was this tiny force to overcome an empire of many millions with an elaborate warring tradition? Crucial to Spanish conquest was their alliance, negotiated with the help of

Cortés Meets the King of Tlaxcala. This detail from a twentieth-century Mexican mural depicts the meeting of Cortés and the king of Tlaxcala (enemy of the Aztecs). As Mexicans began to celebrate their mixed-blood heritage, Doña Marina (in the middle) became the symbolic mother of the first mestizos.

Primary Source

CORTÉS APPROACHES TENOCHTITLÁN

When the Spanish conquered the Aztec empire, they defeated a mighty power. The capital, Tenochtitlán, which was immensely rich, was probably the same size as Naples, Europe's biggest city at the time. Glimpsing the Aztec capital in 1521, Hernán Cortés marveled at the magnificence of the city. But to justify his acts, he claimed that he was bringing civilization and Christianity to the Aztecs. Note the contrast, however, between Cortés's admiration for Tenochtitlán and his condemnation of Indian beliefs and practices, as well as his claim that he abolished cannibalism, something the Aztecs did not practice (although they did sacrifice humans).

This great city of Tenochtitlán is built on the salt lake. . . . It has four approaches by means of artificial causeways. . . . The city is as large as Seville or Cordoba. Its streets . . . are very broad and straight, some of these, and all the others, are one half land, and the other half water on which they go about in canoes. . . . There are bridges, very large, strong, and well constructed, so that, over many, ten horsemen can ride abreast. . . . The city has many squares where markets are held. . . . There is one square, twice as large as that of Salamanca, all surrounded by arcades, where there are daily more than sixty thousand souls, buying and selling. . . . [I]n the service and manners of its people, their fashion of living was almost the same as in Spain, with just as much harmony and order; and considering that these people were barbarous, so cut off from the knowledge of God and other civilized peoples, it is admirable to see to what they attained in every respect. . . .

It happened . . . that a Spaniard saw an Indian . . . eating a piece of flesh taken from the body of an Indian who had been killed. . . . I had the culprit burned, explaining that the cause was his having killed that Indian and eaten him which was prohibited by Your Majesty, and by me in Your Royal name. I further made the chief understand that all the people . . . must abstain from this custom. . . . I came . . . to protect their lives as well as their property, and to teach them that they were to adore but one God . . . that they must turn from their idols, and the rites they had practised until then, for these were lies and deceptions which the devil . . . had invented. . . . I, likewise, had come to teach them that Your Majesty, by the will of Divine Providence, rules the universe, and that they also must submit themselves to the imperial yoke, and do all that we who are Your Majesty's ministers here might order them. . . .

→ *What does Cortés's report tell us about the city of Tenochtitlán?*
→ *Why does Cortés justify his actions to the degree he does?*

SOURCE: *Letters of Cortés*, translated by Francis A. MacNutt (New York: G. P. Putnam, 1908), pp. 244, 256–57.

but the Aztecs kept up their barrage of stones, spears, and arrows—striking and killing Moctezuma. Cortés returned to the city to reassert Spanish control, but realizing this was impossible, he gathered his loot and escaped. Left behind were hundreds of Spaniards, many of whom were dragged up the steps of the temple and sacrificed by Aztec priests.

With the help of the Tlaxcalans, Cortés regrouped. This time he chose to defeat the Aztecs completely. He ordered the building of boats to sail across Lake Texcoco to besiege the capital and bombard it with artillery. Even more devastating was the spread of smallpox, brought by the Spanish, which ran through the ranks of soldiers and commoners like wildfire. Still, led by a new ruler, Cuauhtémoc, the Aztecs rallied their forces and nearly drove the Spaniards from Tenochtitlán. But in the end starvation, disease, and lack of artillery ultimately vanquished the Aztec forces. More Aztecs died from disease than from fighting—the total number of casualties over two years of confrontation reached, it is said, 240,000. As Spanish troops retook the capital, they found it in ruins, with a population too weak to resist. Cuauhtémoc

The Conquest of the Aztecs. *(Left)* This is Diego Rivera's idealized account of the Spanish defeat of the Aztec warriors. It portrays Spanish soldiers with muskets and horses mowing down brave but technologically outgunned Indians. Of course, Rivera's efforts to accentuate Spanish brutality led him to exclude important factors in the fall of Tenochtitlán: Aztec rivals who joined with Spaniards, and diseases. In fact, guns and horses were important but not decisive in the Spanish conquest. *(Right)* This image of the conquest was drawn by a converted Indian later in the sixteenth century and relied on indigenous oral histories and familiar artistic forms. Observe the importance of Indians fighting Indians, and the conventional frontal images of bodies with profiles of heads.

himself was executed in 1524, thereby ending the royal Mexica lineage. The Aztecs lamented their defeat in verse: "We have pounded our hands in despair against the adobe walls, for our inheritance, our city, is lost and dead." In 1522, Cortés became the governor of the new Spanish colony which, by royal order, was renamed "New Spain." He quickly set about allocating *encomiendas* to his loyal followers and dispatching expeditions to conquer the more distant Mesoamerican provinces.

The Mexica experience taught the Spanish an important lesson: an effective conquest had to be swift—and it had to remove completely the symbols of legitimate authority. Their winning advantage, however, proved to be disease. The Spaniards unintentionally introduced germs that made their subsequent efforts at military conquests much easier.

THE INCAS

In addition to Cortés's victory over the Aztecs, the other great Spanish conquest was in the Andes, where Quechua-speaking rulers, called Incas, had established an impressive polity stretching from present-day Colombia to Argentina. From their base in the valley of Cuzco, the Incas governed an empire of 4 to 6 million. But the Incas were internally split.

Bereft of a clear inheritance system, the empire suffered repeated convulsions. In the early sixteenth century, the fight over who would succeed Huayna Capac, the Inca ruler, was especially fierce. Huascar, his "official" son, took Cuzco (the capital), while Atahualpa, his favored son, governed the province of present-day Ecuador. Open conflict might have been averted were it not for Huayna's premature death. His killer was probably smallpox, which along with other epidemics swept down the trade routes from Mesoamerica into the Andes (not unlike the bubonic plague's mid-fourteenth-century spread through the trade routes of Afro-Eurasia). With the father gone, Atahualpa declared war on his brother. After crushing his rival, Atahualpa forced him to witness the execution of all his supporters, then killed him and used his skull as a vessel for maize-beer.

When the Spaniards arrived in 1532, they ran into an empire that was already internally divided, a situation they quickly learned to exploit. Francisco Pizarro, who led the Spanish campaign, had spent time in Hispaniola and, inspired by Cortés's victory, yearned for his own glory. Pizarro commanded a force of about 600 men and invited Atahualpa to confer at the town of Cajamarca. There he laid a trap for the Inca ruler. As the columns of Inca warriors and servants covered with colorful plumage and plates of silver and gold marched into the main square of Cajamarca, the Spanish soldiers were awed. One recalled that "many of us urinated without noticing it, out of sheer terror." But Pizarro's plan worked. His guns and horses shocked the Inca forces. Atahualpa himself fell into Spanish hands, later to be decapitated. Pizarro's conquistadors overran Cuzco in 1533 and then went about mopping up the rest of the Inca forces, a process that took decades in some areas of the Andes.

In the intervening years, Spaniards began to arrive in droves, landing at the new coastal capital of Lima. They began to stake their own claims for *encomiendas,* outdoing each other with greed, and by 1538, they were at war with one another. In 1541, one armed faction managed to capture and assassinate Pizarro himself. Rival factions kept up a brutal war until the Spanish king dispatched a viceroy and issued a new set of laws in 1542 to prevent *encomiendas* from being heritable. This act was meant to prevent the establishment of a powerful aristocracy, to deter the outbreak of uncontrollable civil war, and to reinforce loyalty to Madrid, since once an *encomendero* died, his title would revert to the crown.

The defeat of the two great empires of the New World had enormous repercussions for world history. It meant first that Europeans had their way with the human and material wealth of the Americas. Second, it gave Europeans a market for their own products—goods that found little favor in Afro-Eurasia. Finally, it opened a vast new frontier, which could be colonized and made into staple-producing provinces. Now, following the Russian push into northern Asia (Siberia) and that of the Portuguese into Africa and southern Asia, the conquest of the New World introduced Europeans to a new scale of imperial expansion and enterprise—whose outcome would destabilize Europe itself.

"THE COLUMBIAN EXCHANGE"

The Spanish came to the Americas for its gold and silver, but the Indians offered Europeans a variety of hitherto unknown crops, especially potatoes and corn. Europeans also took away tomatoes, beans, cacao, peanuts, tobacco, and squash. These staples had the unexpected effect of transforming European diets and contributed to the explosion of population growth across Afro-Eurasia. In China, for example, corn could grow in areas too dry for rice and too wet for wheat.

What did the Indians get from this hemispheric transfer that historians have come to call "the Columbian exchange"? The Spanish brought wheat, grapevines, and sugarcane. But the most profound and destructive effect of the Columbian exchange was not immediately visible. For millennia, the isolated populations of the Americas had been cut off from Afro-Eurasian microbe migrations. Africans, Europeans, and Asians had long had at least some contact, even before the bubonic plague. Sharing disease pools, the peoples of Africa and Eurasia gained some immunities; in this sense, the Amerindians were indeed "worlds apart." As we saw in the last section, sickness spread from almost the moment the Spaniards arrived. One Spanish soldier noted, as he entered the Aztec capital after its fall, that "the streets were so filled with dead and sick people that our men walked over nothing but bodies." Native American accounts of the fall of Tenochtitlán recalled the epidemic of smallpox more vividly than the fighting. What made matters worse was that no sooner had smallpox done its work than Indians were visited by a second pandemic: measles. Then came pneumonic plague and influenza. As each wave retreated, it left behind a population more emaciated than before, even less prepared for the next

Disease and Decimation of Indians. The real conqueror of Native Americans was not so much guns as germs. Even before Spanish soldiers seized the Aztec capital, germs had begun decimating the population. The first big killer was in fact smallpox, recorded here by an Indian artist, covering the bodies of victims.

THE VOICE OF THE CONQUERED: GUAMAN POMA DE AYALA

After defeating the Inca armies in the sixteenth century, the Spanish conquerors tightened their hold over the central Andes. They created new political authorities, invited victors to set up silver mines and trading networks using forced native Andean laborers, and licensed missionaries to go out into Andean communities to consolidate a more difficult "spiritual conquest." In reaction, Andean peoples resisted Spanish conquerors. They fled the mines, plundered trade routes, and kept fighting, now with the use of Spanish weaponry. The conquered Andeans also used techniques of the conquerors themselves, like the Spanish language and Spanish books, to resist Spanish control.

One of the most polemical voices of the conquered was a native Andean, Felipe Guaman Poma de Ayala (c. 1535– c. 1615). His illustrated history of the Inca kingdoms, *Primer nueva crónica y bien gobierno* (c. 1615), fiercely criticized colonial rule while urging the Spanish king, Philip III, to adopt a new model of "good government." The book itself, like the idea that Spain could govern the colonized peoples benevolently, disappeared and was only discovered in a library in Copenhagen in 1908. As a polemical testimony against European conquest, however, *Primer nueva crónica* offers readers a voice of colonized peoples.

The author's native tongue was Quechua, but he was schooled, possibly by missionaries, in Spanish language and culture. With his bilingual skills, he was drafted as an interpreter in the Christian campaigns to wipe out heresy and idol worship in the Andes. In this capacity, he read books belonging to missionaries and learned of the religious, political, and historical traditions of the Spaniards.

Guaman Poma also served as an interpreter for Andeans who challenged the land claims of the conquistadors, and in this capacity he eventually earned himself a reputation as a minor nuisance and was evicted from several jurisdictions. Frustrated that the Spanish conquerors refused to live by their spiritual and political proclamations, he grew increasingly bitter and delivered his illustrated text of 1,188 pages and 398 pen-and-ink drawings to the viceroy in Lima to defend the Andeans. Rebuffed, he wrote the king on February 14, 1615. Thereafter, Guaman Poma disappeared from the historical record.

Guaman Poma narrated the history of the Inca Empire, recounted the arrival and victory of the Spanish, and then described the misery of everyday life under colonial authority. Relying on his own firsthand experiences and centuries of oral culture, the author told an epic tale— very much in a Spanish mode—of the tragic fate of a non-Spanish people. Indeed, the book accepted in many ways the Andean destiny, while denouncing colonialism. He was pro-Andean, but he celebrated Catholicism and Spanish monarchical rule.

As a chronicler of the Andean peoples before the Spanish conquest, Guaman Poma argued that his people were innocents, a Christian people, well before the conquest. They lived, according to the author, by Christian principles and knew but one God, "though they were barbarous, knowing nothing." Indeed, his history of the Incas begins with biblical creation, the arrival in South America of one of Noah's sons, and ends with the rule of Inca Huayna Capac. While much of his historical account was his own fabrication, claiming Christian roots enabled the Andean

wave. The scale of death was and remains unprecedented. Imported pathogens wiped out up to 90 percent of the Native American population, which had stood at between 80 and 100 million in 1492. A century after smallpox arrived on Hispaniola in 1519, no more than 5 to 10 percent of the island's population was left alive. Diminished and weakened by disease, Amerindians could not forestall encroachment by European settlers. Thus were Europeans the unintended beneficiaries of a horrifying catastrophe.

Environmental effects were manifold. In addition to crops, Europeans also transported livestock such as cattle,

swine, and horses to the New World. In the highland regions lying to the north of the valley of central Mexico, where Native Americans had once lived in great numbers, employing irrigation systems to support highly productive agricultural estates, Spanish settlers opened up large herding ranches. An area that had once produced maize and squash for city dwellers living to the south now had herds of sheep and cattle, the sizes of which had never before been seen in the Americas. Without natural predators, these animals reproduced with lightning speed, destroying entire landscapes with their hooves and their foraging. On the islands of the West author to denounce the conquistadors as treasonous usurpers. They had killed the natural and legitimate Inca rulers and were thus eternally doomed.

Primer nueva crónica culminated in a detailed account of everyday life in the colony. It charted the system of forced labor in the mines, the burdens of Spanish taxes, and the hypocrisy of missionaries who seized Indian property and failed to defend Indian lives. Guaman Poma wrote that the colonists violated Christian precepts of justice and their own laws. He added that, given the origins of the Andean peoples and their colonial fates, the king of Spain had a moral as well as a political duty to protect his Christian subjects in the Andes: he should free them from sinful authorities and create a sovereign Andean state as a universal Christian kingdom ruled from Madrid. Guaman Poma simultaneously denounced colonialism, while affirming his loyalty to the king.

For all his skills at crossing the large cultural and political divide between Andeans and Spaniards, conquered and conquerors, Guaman Poma was not optimistic. Near the end of his work, he asked forlornly, "Where are you, our lord king Philip?" His prose invoked many of the conventions of Spanish treatises, and his strong visual representations were meant to stir the reader's Christian sentiments. But at the same time, his images portrayed the irreconcilable differences between Spaniards and Andeans. Isolation, and not understanding, was what characterized the colonial experience for Guaman Poma. As he doubted the potential for cross-cultural communication, he concluded that "there is no resolution in this world."

Pizarro and the Incas. This illustration is by the Andean native Guaman Poma, whose c. 1587 epic of the conquest of Peru depicted many of the barbarities of the Spanish. Here we see the conquistador Pizarro and a Catholic priest appealing to Atahualpa—before betraying and then killing him.

Indies, described by Columbus as "roses of the sea," the Spanish found lush tropical and semitropical forests. The Europeans cleared the abundant trees and other vegetation for sugar plantations. This undermined the habitat of most of the large-sized mammals and many birds. By the onset of the seventeenth century, nearly all of the islands' tall trees as well as many shrubs and ground plants were gone, and residents lamented the absence of bird song. Over the ensuing centuries, the flora and fauna of the Americas took on an increasingly European appearance—a process that the historian Alfred Crosby has called ecological imperialism.

SPAIN'S TRIBUTARY EMPIRE

Like the Europeans who sailed into the Indian Ocean to tap into existing commercial systems, the Spaniards sought to exploit the wealth of indigenous empires without fully dismantling them. In Mexico and Peru, where the Inca Empire suffered the same fate as the Aztecs, Spanish conquistadors decapitated native polities but left much of their structure intact. In both the valley of Mexico and the Andes, Spanish conquerors took over existing networks of tribute. But unlike the European penetration of the Indian Ocean, the occupation

MAP 12-3   THE SPANISH AND PORTUGUESE EMPIRES IN THE AMERICAS, 1492–1750

This map examines the growth of Spanish and Portuguese empires in the Americas over two and half centuries. Why did Spaniards and Portuguese focus their empire building where they did? What were the major export commodities from these empires and how were they produced? How did the export of silver and sugar shape the labor systems that evolved in both empires?

of the New World was not restricted to control of commercial outposts. Instead, European colonialism in the Americas involved the control of large amounts of territory—and evolved into formal control over the entire landmass (see Map 12-3).

Across the heartlands of the new Spanish empire, villagers delivered goods and services to their new masters. But the Spanish authorities, as they had done in earlier conquests, also bestowed *encomiendas* on favored Spanish immigrants. Such rights enabled the *encomenderos* to demand labor from subject Indian inhabitants, for mines, landed estates, and public works. Aztec and Inca rulers had used labor conscription systems to build up their public domains; Spaniards did so for private gain.

Most Spanish migrants were men; only a few Spanish women accompanied the conquistadors and early settlers. One, Inés Suárez, reached the Indies to find her husband, who had traveled there earlier, dead. She then became the mistress of the conquistador Pedro de Valdivia, and the pair became a conquering team. Initially, she was given permission to join an expedition to conquer Chile as Valdivia's domestic servant, but she soon became much more—a nurse, caretaker, advisor, and a guard, having uncovered several plots to assassinate her lover. Suárez even served as a diplomat, shuttling between warring Indians and Spaniards in an effort to secure the conquest. Later, she helped to rule Chile as the wife of Rodrigo de Quiroga, governor of the province. Admittedly, hers was an exceptional story. More typical were female voyagers who foraged for food, tended wounded soldiers, and set up European-style settlements.

But there were always too few Spanish women to go around, and the sexual imbalance spurred Spanish men to consort with local women. Although the crown did not smile on the taking of concubines, the practice was widespread. From the onset of colonization, Spaniards also actively married into Indian families. After conquering the Incas, Francisco Pizarro wedded an Inca princess, thereby (or so he had hoped) inheriting the mantle of local dynastic rule. As a result of intermarriages, mestizos became the fastest-growing segment of the population of Spanish America.

Spanish migrants and their progeny preferred towns to the countryside. Ports (such as Veracruz, Havana, or Portobelo) excepted, the major cities of Spanish America were the former centers of Indian empires. Mexico City was built on the ruins of Tenochtitlán; Cuzco arose from the foundations of the razed Inca capital. In its architecture, its economy, and even its most intimate facets, the Spanish colonies adopted as much as they transformed the worlds they encountered.

SILVER

For the first European adventurers in the Americas, the foremost measure of wealth and power was the store of gold and silver that they could accumulate for themselves and the monarchs they served. On the surface, this seemed to benefit Spanish merchants and the Spanish crown. It was, after all, the Spanish who discovered, and then plundered, the vast

Silver. *(Left)* Silver was an important discovery for Spanish conquerors in Mesoamerica and the Andes. Conquerors expanded the customs of Inca and Aztec labor drafts to force the natives to work in mines, often in brutal conditions. *(Right)* By the middle of the sixteenth century, a vibrant trade had developed between the Americas and Asia, carrying silver, dyes, and foodstuffs. The conquest of the Americas helped give Europeans trade goods for sale in Asian markets. This image shows a fleet of Spanish galleons on the Pacific coast of Mexico as they are being loaded with the silver extracted from the mines.

Mission Sao Miguel. The Jesuits were avid missionaries in the Spanish and Portuguese empires and often tried to shelter native peoples from conquistadors and labor recruiters. Missions, like this one, in the borderlands between Brazil and Spanish colonies were targets of attack from both sides.

riches of the Aztecs and the Incas. In the twenty years after the fall of Tenochtitlán, the conquistadors took more precious metals from Mexico and the Andes than all the gold accumulated by Europeans over the previous centuries.

Having looted Indian coffers, the Spanish quickly entered the business of mining directly, opening the Andean Potosí mines in 1545. Between 1560 and 1685, Spanish America sent 25,000 to 35,000 tons of silver annually to Spain. From 1685 to 1810, this sum doubled. The two great mother lodes were Potosí in present-day Bolivia and Zacatecas in northern Mexico. Potosí was the greater fount in the sixteenth century, but the silver veins of Mexico proved the more lucrative over the centuries. Silver brought bounty not only to the crown, but also to a small coterie of families based in Spain's colonial capitals—private wealth that funded the formation of local aristocracies.

Colonial mines epitomized the new economy of the Atlantic world. They relied on an extensive network of Indian labor, at first enslaved, subsequently drafted. Here again, the Spanish adopted existing Inca and Aztec practices of requiring labor from subjugated villages. Each year, under the traditional system, village elders selected a stipulated number of men to toil in the shafts, refineries, and smelters. Under the Spanish, however, the burdens grew more onerous. The digging, hauling, and smelting of rocks taxed human limits to their capacity—and beyond. By one conservative estimate, 50,000 workers moved to Potosí each year; mortality rates were appalling. The system pumped so much silver into the networks of European commerce that it transformed Europe's relationship to all of its trading partners, especially those in China and India. It also shook up trade and politics within Europe itself.

PORTUGAL'S NEW WORLD COLONY

> → *What military and maritime technologies advanced Portuguese exploration?*

The Treaty of Tordesillas of 1494, drawn up by the pope, had foreseen that the non-European world—the Americas, Africa, and Asia—would be divided into spheres of interest between Spain and Portugal. Yet the treaty was unenforceable. No less interested in immediate riches than the Spanish, the Portuguese were disappointed by the absence of tributary populations and precious metals in the areas set aside for them. What they did find in Brazil, however, was abundant, fertile land on which favored persons received massive royal grants. These estate owners governed their plantations like fiefdoms.

COASTAL ENCLAVES

Hemmed in along the coast, the Portuguese created enclaves. By the end of the seventeenth century, Brazil's white population was 300,000. Unlike the Spanish, the Portuguese rarely intermarried with Indians, most of whom had fled or had died from imported diseases. Failing to find already established cities in Brazil, the colonists chose to remain in more dispersed settlements.

The problem for the settlers, though, was where to find the labor to work these rich lands. Unlike the Spanish in Mexico or the Andes, the Portuguese in Brazil did not encounter a centralized polity of Aztec or Inca dimensions to take over. Initially, the Portuguese tried to enlist the efforts of Brazil's fragmented and dispersed aboriginal population, but when recruitment became increasingly coercive, Indians turned on the interlopers. Some fought. Others fled to a vast interior rather than submit. Reluctant, indeed scared, to pursue the Indians inland, the Portuguese hugged their beachheads, extracting brazilwood (the source of a beautiful red dye) and sugar from their coastal enclaves.

African slaves became the solution to this labor problem. What had worked for the Portuguese on sugarcane plantations in the Azores and other Atlantic islands was now brought to their Brazilian plantations. Especially in the northeast, in the Bay of All Saints, the Atlantic world's first vast sugar emporium appeared.

SUGAR PLANTATIONS

Cultivation of sugarcane had originated in India, from where it spread to the Mediterranean region and then to the islands off the coast of West Africa. There, sugarcane plantations, tended by African slaves, flourished. This model was then transported by the Portuguese to Brazil and by other European powers to the Caribbean. By the beginning of the seventeenth century, sugar had become a major new export from the New World. By the eighteenth century, its value surpassed that of silver as an export from the Americas to Europe.

Most Brazilian sugar plantations were fairly small, employing between 60 and 100 slaves. But they were efficient enough to create an alternative model of empire, one that resulted in full-scale colonization and dislocation of the existing population. The slaves lived in wretched conditions. Their barracks were miserable, and their diets were insufficient to keep them alive under back-breaking work routines. Moreover, slaves working on Brazilian sugar plantations were disproportionately men. As the slaves rapidly died off, the only way to ensure a supply of labor for the Brazilian plantation complex was to import more Africans. This model of agrarian settlement, then, relied to a very high degree on the transatlantic flow of slaves.

BEGINNINGS OF THE TRANSATLANTIC SLAVE TRADE

The transatlantic slave trade began in a modest way in the late fifteenth century. It was inextricably linked to a single commodity, sugar. As the European demand for this commodity increased, so slavery and the slave trade expanded. From the time of Columbus until 1820, five times as many Africans as Europeans moved to the Americas. In that foundational period, approximately 2 million Europeans, voluntarily, and 10 million Africans, involuntarily, crossed the Atlantic.

First to master long-distance seafaring, the Portuguese also led the way in the taking of human cargo. The trade in slaves grew steadily through the rest of the fifteenth and sixteenth centuries, then expanded by leaps and bounds in the seventeenth and eighteenth centuries (see Chapter 13 for a map and further discussion). During the first two centuries of the slave trade, all European powers participated in the business—Portuguese, Spanish, Dutch, English, and French. Eventually, New World merchants in both North and South America also set up direct trade links with Africa.

Well before European merchants arrived off its west coast, Africa had been involved in long-distance slave trading. Owing to the long duration of this trade, the overall number of Africans sold into captivity in the Muslim world exceeded that of the Atlantic slave trade. Not only did Africans engage in long-distance slave trading, they also maintained slaves themselves. African slavery, like its American counterpart, was a response to labor scarcities. In many parts of Africa, however, slaves were not consigned to permanent servitude. Instead, slaves were assimilated into families, gradually losing their servile status and swelling the size and power of lineage groups.

With the additional European demand for slaves to work New World plantations alongside the ongoing Muslim slave trade, the pressure on the supply of African slaves intensified. Only a narrow band stretching down the spine of the African landmass in a north-south direction, from present-day Uganda and the highlands of Kenya to Zambia and Zimbabwe, escaped the impact of Asian and European slave traders.

Within Africa, the social and political consequences were not fully felt until the great age of the slave trade in the eighteenth century; but already some economic consequences were clear. The overwhelming trend was to further limit the population of Africa. African laborers fetched high enough prices to more than cover the costs of their capture and transportation across the Atlantic.

By the end of the sixteenth century, several important pieces had fallen into place to create a new Atlantic world, one that did not exist a century earlier and indeed could not have been imagined. This was a three-cornered system, with Africa supplying labor, the Americas land and minerals, and Europeans the technology and military power to keep the system together. Each part of the triangle emerged fundamentally transformed. Over the long haul, the wealth flows to Europe and the slave-based development of the Americas would alter the world balance of power.

THE TRANSFORMATION OF EUROPE

> → *How was Europe transformed politically and spiritually?*

Instead of uniting Europeans, the development of the new Atlantic system deepened the landmass's internal divisions. In particular, the growing wealth of the Spanish Empire tilted the weight of European power toward the Habsburg dynasty and toward the west. Europe was transformed by Atlantic rivalries, as well as by the Reformation, which resulted in religious divisions and led to warfare among states committed to different versions of the Christian faith.

THE HABSBURGS AND THE QUEST FOR UNIVERSAL EMPIRE IN EUROPE

The European dream of universal empire had persisted since the fall of ancient Rome and was almost realized by the Habsburg dynasts, heirs to the eastern half of Charlemagne's

Frankish empire. Here a loose confederation of principalities known as the Holy Roman Empire continued to be ruled by an emperor who was elected by an elite group of lower-level sovereigns (dukes, archbishops, and kings of individual states like Bavaria), but who, after 1273, usually came from the house of Habsburg. The emperor's dominions officially included territory now incorporated into the Netherlands, Germany, Austria, Belgium, Croatia and parts of Italy, Poland, and Switzerland; the realm was enormous, but power was never effectively centralized. Emperors were traditionally crowned by the pope in Rome, but there was persistent rivalry between the papacy and the empire, and resentment in many parts of the empire over southern Europe's hegemonic power in the church.

Charles V was the grandson of the Spanish monarchs Isabella and Ferdinand and of Maximilian I, who headed the Austrian Habsburg family and from 1493 to 1519 served as Holy Roman Emperor. In 1519, Charles was elected Holy Roman Emperor, largely because he had inherited the grandest imperial domain in European history. His realm encompassed Spain and Spain's new territories in the Americas, as well as the traditional central European holdings of the Habsburgs.

But even at its height, Charles V's loose-knit empire lacked a unified administrative structure, and religious and political divisions persisted. Moreover, Charles had to defend his eastern flank. The armies of the Ottoman Sultan Suleiman seized Habsburg Belgrade in Serbia in 1521 and Mohács in Hungary in 1526, and three years later they laid siege to Vienna but failed to capture it. Charles counterattacked in Hungary in 1531, and his successors ultimately regained Hungary from the Ottomans at the end of the seventeenth century.

Overstretched by the challenges of trying to keep such an ambitious empire intact, Charles abdicated in 1556 and formally divided his empire between his younger brother Ferdinand and his son Philip. Ferdinand (ruled 1556–1564) took the Austrian, German, and central European parts of the empire that straddled the Danube and was elected Holy Roman Emperor in 1556. The Austrian Habsburgs maintained dominance over central Europe.

Philip II (ruled Spain 1556–1598) received Spain, Belgium, the Netherlands, southern Italy, and the New World possessions. Moreover, in 1580, he inherited the Portuguese throne (his mother had been a Portuguese princess), adding Portugal and its colonial possessions to his empire; this gave him a virtual monopoly on Atlantic commerce. Yet, the Spanish Habsburgs had to defend their half of the empire against a series of Dutch revolts, beginning in 1566, as well as confront perpetual Ottoman harassment on land and at sea. Philip sent troops to subdue the Netherlands revolt—a move that ended with the massacre of civilians in the town of Antwerp—but the Spanish-Dutch war persisted. He also directed the Spanish fleet to set up defenses against the Ottomans and North African Muslim pirates in the Mediterranean Sea. In 1571, the Spanish fleet defeated the Ottoman fleet at Lepanto. But the size and wealth of Habsburg Spain continued to provoke enormous tension within Europe.

CONFLICT IN EUROPE AND THE DEMISE OF UNIVERSAL EMPIRE

French, English, and Dutch elites envied the riches of the Portuguese and Spanish colonial possessions. These rivals yearned for their own profitable colonies. But in their explorations of the New World, the French, English, and Dutch had not yet found their own mountains of gold and silver, nor had they discovered a new and easier route to Asia. Still, they were able to claim a share of the wealth of the Americas by stealing it on the high seas. Some of the plunderers were pirates, who raided for their own benefit; others were privateers, who did their stealing with official sanction and shared the profits of their thefts with their monarchs. Often the distinction between pirate and privateer was blurred.

The most famous of the raiders was Sir Francis Drake, who was commissioned by the English crown to plunder Spanish possessions. Circling the globe between 1577 and 1580, Drake plundered one Spanish port after another. His favorite hunting ground was the Caribbean, where Mesoamerican and Andean silver, loaded onto Spanish galleons (heavy, square-rigged ships used for war or commerce), made lucrative targets. Besides, the many islands provided natural shelter. While Drake's exploits were undertaken for personal gain, his monarch, Queen Elizabeth, approved of his assaults on the Spanish Empire, and rewarded him with a knighthood.

To retaliate, the Spanish sailed a mighty armada of 130 ships and almost 20,000 men into the English Channel in 1588, but England amassed 197 ships, 34 from its Royal Navy and the rest merchant vessels. The battle resulted in a devastating defeat for the Spanish fleet. In the retreat, the Spanish king lost many of his most prized battleships. The conflict between a rising England and Spain continued in other seas, and Drake returned to his career of privateering. When the news of Drake's death in the Caribbean (from yellow fever in 1596) arrived in Madrid, the Spanish court erupted in jubilation. The old, infirm King Philip declared that this news would allow him to recover quickly. Two months later, an English fleet of 40 warships and over 100 smaller vessels sailed into Spain's premier port of Cádiz and occupied the city for two weeks, burning 200 Spanish ships and seizing the massive treasure from the Indies. Spain, the powerhouse of the Atlantic world, had been severely humbled. Two years later, a despondent King Philip died. The dream of universal empire within Europe had failed, in large part because Christendom continued to be at war with itself.

Defeat of the Spanish Armada. This engraving shows the defeat of the Spanish Armada off Plymouth, England, in May of 1588.

THE REFORMATION

The same internal political conflicts and pursuit of individual aims that characterized European activities in the New World also led to the Protestant Reformation in Europe. A growing number of Europeans, like the Dutch Brethren of the Common Life in the fourteenth century, despaired of the Catholic Church's ability to satisfy longings for deeper, more individualized religious experience. Movements such as the Brethren had inspired Christians to adopt devotional practices, like the Stations of the Cross, and to form reading groups among the laity. When sixteenth-century reformers took up the call for change, they were hopeful that an already reforming church would respond to their criticisms. They had no notion that their complaints would split Christendom for good.

What seemed to reformers to be constructive criticism was, in the eyes of church officials, heresy. The clergy were right to be worried about the claims of critics like the German monk Martin Luther (1483–1546), who in 1517 proclaimed "Salvation by faith alone" and pronounced the Bible as the sole source of Christian truth. Luther circulated ninety-five "theses" for disputation with his learned colleagues. In this declaration and in subsequent debates, Luther denounced the corruptions of the church and the repression of Germanic freedoms by faraway Latin authority. In *On the Freedom of the Christian Man* (1520), he upbraided "the Roman Church, which in past ages was the holiest of all" for having "become

a den of murderers beyond all other dens of murderers, a thieves' castle beyond all other thieves' castles, the head and empire of every sin, as well as of death and damnation." His doctrine struck at both the spiritual and the social authority of the clergy over the laity, undermining the former's claims to control the channels for salvation and to determine Christian truth. He also translated the New Testament into German so that laypersons could have direct access, unmediated by the clergy, to the word of God.

Spread by printed books and ardent preachers in all the vernacular languages of Europe, Luther's doctrines won widespread support. Many of the German princes embraced the reformed faith as a means of asserting their independence from the Holy Roman Emperor. For many, the new ideas, known by 1529 as "Protestantism," promised not just the renewal of Christianity but attention to individual spiritual needs and a new moral foundation for community life. Across northern Europe, reformed ideas established a powerful presence, especially in the German states, France, Switzerland, the Low Countries, and England. The renewed Christian creed could and did appeal to commoners as well as elites. It found particular resonance among communities resentful of rule by Catholic "outsiders" (like Habsburg Philip II, who ruled the Netherlands from his palace in Spain).

Some zealous reformers, like Jean Calvin (1509–1564) in France, made their own modifications to Luther's ideas. To Luther's emphasis on the individual's relationship to God Calvin added an emphasis on moral regeneration through church discipline and the autonomy of religious communities. He laid out, and his successors underscored, the doctrine of predestination—the notion that each person was already "predestined" for damnation or salvation even before birth. The "elect," he thought, should also be free to govern themselves, a doctrine that ratified both radical political dissent (as in the case of the Puritans in England) and the rule of the clergy (as in the Swiss city-state of Geneva). Calvinism proved especially popular in Switzerland, the Netherlands, northeastern France, and Scotland (where it was called Presbyterianism).

In England, Henry VIII (ruled 1509–1547) and his daughter Elizabeth (ruled 1558–1603) crafted a moderate reformed religion—a "middle way"—called Anglicanism, which retained many Catholic practices and a hierarchy topped by bishops (hence its American followers would later call themselves Episcopalians, from the Latin word for bishop, *episcopus*). Although Anglican rule was imposed upon Ireland, most nonelite Irishmen continued to adhere to Catholicism. The Scots maintained a fierce devotion to their Presbyterian Church, ensuring a measure of religious diversity within the British Isles. In England, as with the rest of Europe, more radical sects like the Anabaptists and the Quakers survived within mainstream Protestantism. While all Protestants were opposed to Catholicism and distrustful of the papal hierarchy, members of these different communities sometimes developed animosities toward one another as well (see Map 12-4).

The Catholic Church responded to the challenges of Luther and Calvin by embarking on its own renovation, which became known as the Counter-Reformation. At the Council of Trent (1545–1563), it reaffirmed its doctrines, sacraments, the importance of acts of charity, papal supremacy, and the distinctive role of its clergy. But it also enacted reforms to answer the Protestants' assaults on clerical corruption. In contrast to many of their predecessors, the popes who headed the Catholic Church during the second half of the sixteenth century became renowned for their piety and asceticism. These pontiffs also installed bishops and abbots who generally steered clear of the unscrupulous practices that had been so fervently attacked by Protestant critics. Taking on the Protestant theological challenge, Catholicism gave greater emphasis to individual spirituality. Like Protes-

The Reformation. Reformation images played an important role in the often violent polemics of the period. In this rather tame image, Luther preaches to Christ and the godly *(left)*, while the pope *(right)* doles out indulgences to wealthy sinners.

MAP 12-4 RELIGIOUS DIVISIONS IN EUROPE AFTER THE REFORMATION, 1590

The Protestant Reformation divided Europe religiously and politically in the sixteenth century. Can you identify any geographic patterns in the distribution of Protestant communities? In what regions would you expect Protestant-Catholic tensions to be the most intense? Can you explain why Protestantism tended to triumph in the north but not in the south?

tants, reformed Catholics carried their message overseas, especially through the activities of an order established in 1534 by a former soldier named Ignatius Loyola (1491–1556). Loyola founded a brotherhood of priests, the Society of Jesus, or Jesuits, which was dedicated to the revival of the Catholic Church. From bases in Lisbon, Rome, Paris, and elsewhere in Europe, the Jesuits opened missions as far as South and North America, India, Japan, and China.

Despite these reforms, the Vatican continued to use repression and persecution to combat what it considered to be heretical beliefs. In sixteenth-century Augsburg, priests performed public exorcisms, seeking to free Protestant parishioners from the "demons" that supposedly possessed them. The Index of Prohibited Books (a list of books and theological treatises banned by the Catholic Church) and the Medieval Inquisition (from 1184) remained weapons to be used against those deemed the church's enemies. But the proliferation of printing presses and Protestantism's remarkable inroads made it impossible for the Catholic Counter-Reformation to turn back the tide leading toward increased autonomy from the papacy.

Both Catholics and Protestants persecuted witches. Between about 1500 and 1700, as many as 100,000 people, most of them women, were accused of being witches; many of them were tried, tortured, burned at the stake or hanged. Older women and widows, and women who worked as nurses were especially vulnerable to charges of having cursed or poisoned babies, causing them to become sick or die. But witches were also charged with killing livestock, causing hailstorms, or scotching marriage arrangements. The surrounding society was willing to believe that naturally weak and susceptible women might have sex with the devil or be tempted to do his bidding.

RELIGIOUS WARFARE IN EUROPE

The religious revival of the sixteenth century led Europe into another round of wars that were as disruptive and ferocious as those of the fourteenth century. Their ultimate effect was to weaken the Spanish and strengthen the English, French, and Dutch. The circulation of Luther's ideas—between 1518 and 1525, one-third of all books sold in the 300-odd German states were written by Martin Luther—precipitated a series of brutal peasant revolts across central Europe in 1524. These revolts often broke out when princes or town councils that had decided to accept or reject the Reformation tried to force religious uniformity on their subjects. Often this entailed burnings, beatings, and drownings to persuade those who were reluctant to change their beliefs. In contrast to the relatively small armies of earlier wars, in which one noble's retinue fought a rival's followers, the defense of the Catholic mass and the Protestant Bible brought a large number of simple folk to arms. In 1555, after nearly forty years of religious warfare, the Holy Roman Emperor Charles V was compelled to allow the German princes the right to choose whether Protestantism or Catholicism would be the official religion within their domains. This did not mean, however, that Europe's religious wars were over.

Religious conflicts both weakened European dynasties and made them all the more eager for conquest abroad. Spain, with its massive empire and its silver mines in the New World, spent much of its new fortune waging war in Europe. Most debilitating to Spain was its costly, and eventually futile, effort to subdue its recently acquired Dutch territories. After a series of wars that continued in fits and starts from 1566 to 1648, Catholic Spain finally conceded the Protestant Netherlands its independence.

Wars took their toll on the Spanish Empire, which was soon wallowing in debts; not even the riches of the American silver mines could bail out the court. In the late 1550s, Philip II had to renege on obligations to the empire's creditors. Within two decades, Spain was declared bankrupt three times. Spanish decline opened the way for the Dutch and the English to extend their trading networks into Asia and the New World. Competition between the latter two soon led to

St. Bartholomew's Day Massacre. An important wedding between French Catholic and Huguenot families in Paris was scheduled for August 24, 1572, St. Bartholomew's Day; but instead of reconciliation, that day saw a massacre, as Catholics tried to stamp out Protestantism in France's capital city.

trade wars, underscoring that religious differences were not the only sources of inter-European strife.

If religious conflicts drew Spain into costly struggles with the Netherlands and England, they also sparked civil wars. In France, the internal divide between Catholics and Protestants exploded in the St. Bartholomew's Day Massacre in 1572. Catholic crowds, shouting "Kill, kill, kill," rampaged through the streets of Paris murdering Huguenot (Protestant) men, women, and children and dumping their bodies into the Seine River; parades of rioters displayed the heads of Protestants on pikes. The number of dead reached 3,000 in Paris and at least 10,000 in provincial towns. Slaughter on this scale did not break the Huguenots' spirit, but it did bring more disrepute to the monarchy for failing to ensure peace. Indeed, this was the beginning of the end of the Valois dynasty. Another round of warfare exhausted the French and brought Henry of Navarre, a Protestant Bourbon prince, to the throne. To become king, Henry IV converted to Catholicism, and in 1598, he issued the Edict of Nantes. This proclamation declared France a Catholic country, but it at least temporarily diffused the tensions by tolerating some public Protestant worship.

Dynastic loyalties remained overarching, but religious ones came to the fore. As dynastic rulers sought to resolve religious questions within their own dominions—by peaceful or bloody means—and built up far larger armies than before, religious affiliations began to acquire a tinge of national identity. Religious strife propelled incipient nation formation and exacerbated still more ferocious rivalries for wealth and territory overseas. Thus, Europe entered its age of overseas exploration as a collection of increasingly powerful yet irreconcilably competitive rival states, whose differences stemmed not just from language but from the ways they worshipped the Christian God.

PROSPERITY IN ASIA

> → *Why did trade expand and wealth increase in sixteenth-century Asia?*

While Europe was beset by religious warfare, Asian empires were expanding and consolidating their power, and trade was flourishing.

MUGHAL INDIA AND COMMERCE

Illustrative of Asia's economic flourishing was the Mughal Empire, which became one of the world's wealthiest and most powerful at the very time when Europeans were establishing their first sustained connections with India. These connec-

tions, however, only touched the outer layer of Mughal India and were largely irrelevant to the emergence of one of Islam's greatest regimes. Established in 1526, the Mughal Empire was a vigorous, centralized state whose political authority extended over most of modern-day India. During the sixteenth century, its realm encompassed a population between 100 and 150 million.

The strength of the Mughals rested on their impressive military power (see Chapter 11). The dynasty's founder, Babur, brought horsemanship and, most notably, trained artillery men and field cannons from central Asia. Babur's gunpowder secured swift military victories and control over northern India. Not until the reign of his grandson, Akbar (ruled 1556–1605), however, did the empire experience a vast expansion and consolidation that would continue under Akbar's grandson Aurangzeb until the empire encompassed almost the whole of India (see Map 12-5). Known as the "Great Mughal," Akbar extended the military campaigns of his predecessors. These campaigns consolidated Akbar's control over much of the population. But the key to Akbar's success was not might alone. Akbar was a skilled practitioner of the art of alliance-making. Deals with Hindu chieftains through favors and intermarriage among notables also contributed to the growth and stability of Akbar's empire.

Mughal rulers were even more flexible in their dealings with the region's various peoples than their predecessors had been. This was especially true in spiritual affairs. Though its primary commitment to Islam was never in doubt, the imperial court patronized a variety of beliefs, earning it legitimacy in the eyes of diverse subjects. The contrast with sixteenth-century Europe, where religious differences created deep fractures within and between states, could not have been starker. Unlike European monarchs, who tried to enforce religious uniformity, whether out of their own piety or fear of instability, Akbar engaged in a systematic study and discussion of comparative religion. He hosted regular disputations in his famous *Din-i-Ilahi* (House of Worship), where Hindu, Muslim, Jain, Parsi, and Christian theologians debated the merits of different religions. Akbar had both a Hindu and a Christian wife (besides having a Muslim wife, as well as numerous concubines of many different nationalities and religions), and his palace boasted temples to each faith. Akbar's pragmatic tolerance did not always keep theologians happy—especially those who advocated orthodox beliefs—but it kept a sprawling and diverse spiritual kingdom under one political roof.

Akbar's court enjoyed the fruits of the commercial recovery and expansion in the Indian Ocean. The Mughals possessed no ocean navy, but merchants from Mughal lands used overland routes and rivers to exchange Indian cottons, tobacco, saffron, betel leaf, sugar, and indigo for Iranian melons, dried fruits, nuts, silks, carpets, and precious metals, or for Russian pelts, leathers, walrus tusks, saddles, and chainmail armor. Every year, Akbar ordered 1,000 new suits stitched of the most exquisite material. His harem was attired in fine silks dripping with gold, brocades, and pearls. Carpets,

MAP 12-5 EXPANSION OF THE MUGHAL EMPIRE, 1556–1707

Under Akbar and Aurangzeb the Mughal Empire expanded and dominated much of South Asia during this time. Yet, by looking at the trading ports along the Indian coast, one can see the growing influence of Portuguese, Dutch, French, and English interests. To what extent did these trading posts reflect a significant increase in European influence in the region? Did these European outposts play a role in shaping Mughal policies? Why did Mughal leaders tolerate this European presence?

UZBEKS

AFGHANISTAN

SAFAVIDS

Kabul · | Khyber Pass |
KABUL
KASHMIR
TIBET
Gold | LAHORE
· Lahore
MULTAN
HIMALAYAS
DELHI
· Delhi
THAR DESERT
RAJPUTS
TATTA (SIND)
AJMER
Agra ·
AWADH
BIHAR
BENGAL
Saltpetre | Dacca ·
ALLAHABAD
Sugar
Chandernagore 1673 (French) | Hooghly 1537 (Portuguese) 1640 (Dutch) 1651 (British)
AHMADABAD (GUJARAT)
Ahmadabad 1612 (British)
Calcutta 1690 (British)
Surat 1618–83 (British)
GONDWANA
Diu 1535 (Portuguese)
Daman 1558 (Portuguese)
Cotton
KHANDESH
Bombay 1661 (British)
MARATHAS
Saltpetre
AURANGABAD
Cotton
BIDAR
HYDERABAD (GOLCONDA)
Dyestuffs
Godavari R.

ARABIAN SEA

Goa 1510 (Portuguese)
BIJAPUR
Masulipatam 1570 (Portuguese) 1605 (Dutch) 1611 (British)
Bay of Bengal
Pulicat 1609 (Dutch)
Bhatkal 1637 (Dutch) 1638 (British)
Diamonds | Coffee
Madras (Ft. St. George) 1639 (British)
São Thomé c. 1520 (Portuguese)
Coffee
Tellicherry 1683 (British)
Pondicherry 1699 (French)
Calicut (Portuguese)
MALABAR COAST
Cinnamon
Nagappattinam 1658 (Dutch)
Pepper
Cochin 1503 (Portuguese) 1661 (Dutch)
Jaffna 1560 (Portuguese) 1658 (Dutch)
Pepper
Diamonds
Quilan 1512 (Portuguese) 1661 (Dutch)
Pepper
Trincomali 1639 (Dutch)
Negmobo 1640 (Dutch)
Colombo 1518 (Portuguese) 1640 (Dutch)
Galle 1518 (Portuguese) 1640 (Dutch)
CEYLON

INDIAN OCEAN

/// Babur's domain, 1526
� Akbar's domain, 1556–1605
  Areas added by Aurangzeb to 1707
■ Trading port

0   200   400 Miles
0   200   400 Kilometers

mirrors, and precious metals decorated noble households and camps, while perfume and wine flowed freely. Retainers, even horses and elephants, were garbed in elaborate attire. The splendor of the realm was perhaps most evident in the field of fine arts. In architecture, for instance, Akbar's temporary capital at Fatehpur Sikri, near Agra, combined the fort's flat stone beams and sense of immensity from the Hindu tradition with the arches and the feathery lightness of Islamic art. Indian merchant diaspora communities took root in Bukhara and Astrakhan, Isfahan and Qandahar. India's Muslim and Hindu merchants learned Persian, the key language, and some knew Turkic languages.

New western European trading connections contributed to the flow of wealth to the Mughal polity, but the latter's strength limited European incursions. Although the Portuguese occupied Goa and Bombay on the Indian coast, they had little presence beyond these ports and, in fact, they did not dare to antagonize the Mughal emperor. In 1578, Akbar recognized the credentials of a Portuguese ambassador and allowed a Jesuit missionary to enter his court. In the ensuing years, the commercial ties between the Mughals and Portuguese intensified, but the latter's merchants were still effectively confined to a few ports on the fringes of the Mughal domain. More Portuguese ships entered those harbors, but many of these were manned by Indian seamen. In addition, the Mughals ended the Portuguese monopoly on the oceanic trade with Europe. In the 1580s and 1590s, to the chagrin of the Portuguese, Dutch and English merchantmen started to arrive in Indian ports.

Akbar seized on the commercial boom to overhaul his empire's revenue system. Until the 1560s, the Mughal state, unable itself to penetrate deeply into regional societies, relied on a vast network of decentralized tribute collectors called *zamindars*. These collectors possessed rights to claim a share of the harvest from the region's peasants, while earmarking part of their earnings for the emperor. But sharing the spoils between the emperor and cooperative local leaders created underlying problems, for the Mughals did not always see their agreed share, while the high levies did not always sit well with peasants. Local populations in the periphery mounted prolonged resistance to dynastic power. But as trade flourished, the supply of money rose. Akbar's officials, and especially the Hindu revenue minister Todar Mal, monetized the tax assessment system and curbed the political and fiscal power of the *zamindars* over the peasantry. The emperor undertook a variety of other reforms that further rationalized and centralized the revenue system. The result: imperial revenues began to rise markedly, and these helped cover the cost of Akbar's military expeditions and his extravagant spending on the beautification of his court.

These fiscal policies reinforced the commercialization of the empire. To generate the cash to pay taxes, peasants had to sell their produce in the market. Market towns and ports flourished. Dealers in grain and money became more promi-

Akbar Hears a Petition. In keeping with the multiethnic and multireligious character of Akbar's empire, the image reflects the diversity of peoples seeking to have their petitions heard by the Mughal emperor.

nent in the countryside as they helped peasants get their produce to market. Between one-fifth and one-third the value of all this burgeoning rural produce flowed into state coffers. The *zamindars* evolved from private tribute lords into servants of the state, though they continued to enjoy their share of the peasants' income.

Centered in northern India, Babur and Akbar's empire seized upon the wealth of the surrounding regions and channeled resources—military, architectural, and artistic—to glorify the court. At the same time, this enhanced wealth opened potential divisions between Indian regions, and even between merchants and rulers. So long as merchants relied upon rulers for their commercial gains, and so long as rulers carefully

Primary Source

COMMENTARY ON FOREIGNERS FROM A MING OFFICIAL

Although China had a long history of both overland and maritime trade with the outside world, Ming officials were often hostile toward contact with foreigners. Urging that the foreign presence must be brought under strict government control, the bureaucrat He Ao (Ho Ao) portrayed the Europeans (whom he called Feringis) as unruly, untrustworthy, and a threat to the security of the country in this commentary from around 1520. Such sentiments were also often found among Chinese officials in subsequent centuries, even as China thrived in the growing commercial exchanges of an increasingly connected world.

The Feringis are most cruel and crafty. Their arms are superior to those of other foreigners. Some years ago they came suddenly to the city of Canton, and the noise of their cannon shook the earth [these were cannon shots fired as a salute by the fleet of Fernão Peres]. Those who remained at the post-station [places where foreigners were lodged] disobeyed the law and had intercourse with others. Those who came to the Capital were proud and struggled [among themselves?] to become head. Now if we allow them to come and go and to carry on their trade, it will inevitably lead to fighting and bloodshed, and the misfortune of our South may be boundless. In the time of our ancestors, foreigners came to bring tribute only at fixed periods, and the law provided for precautionary measures, therefore the foreigners who could come were not many. But some time ago the Provincial Treasurer, Wu T'ing-chü, saying that he needed spice to be sent to the Court, took some of their goods no matter when they came. It was due to what he did that foreigner ships have never ceased visiting our shores and that barbarians have lived scattered in our departmental cities. Prohibition and precaution having been neglected, the Feringis became more and more familiar with our fair ways. And thus availing themselves of the situation the Feringis came into our port. I pray that all the foreign junks in our bay and the foreigners who secretly live (in our territory) be driven away, that private intercourse be prohibited and that our strategical defence be close, so that that part of our country will have peace.

→ *What does this document tell us about the Chinese viewing of foreigners?*
→ *How does it compare to the earlier report from the European trader?*

SOURCE: Tien-tse Chang, *Sino-Portuguese Trade, From 1514 to 1644: A Synthesis of Portuguese and Chinese Sources* (Leyden: E. J. Brill, 1934), pp. 51–52.

balanced local and imperial interests, however, the Mughal realm remained unified and kept Europeans on the outskirts of society.

PROSPERITY IN MING CHINA

In the late sixteenth century, China's Ming dynasty also prospered from increased commerce. As with the Mughals, the Ming seemed relatively unconcerned with the now more regular appearance of foreigners, including silver-bearing European traders. As in India, the Ming retained the power to confine Europeans to port cities, while the availability of silver facilitated the spread of market activities across the Ming realm. Employers paid their workers with money rather than with produce or goods. Agriculture and handicraft production soared. The injection of money eased the constraints of borrowing and lending. Rural industries also flourished. A cotton boom, for example, helped make spinning and weaving China's largest single industry.

A clear measure of the greater prosperity under the Ming—or "the Great Ming," as the dynasty was called—was its population surge. By the middle of the seventeenth century, the Chinese population probably accounted for a higher proportion of the total world population than at any other time in the history of the world—more than one-third, or approximately 250 million out of 750 million. Although fully 90 percent of the people lived in the countryside, large numbers swelled the ranks of the urban dwellers. Beijing, the Ming capital, saw its population grow to over 1 million, and Nanjing, the secondary capital, grew to nearly the same number of inhabitants. There were another half dozen cities with populations of 500,000, and another twenty or so with 100,000 or more residents. Cities allowed urbanites of means to find all manner of diversions, ranging from literary and theatrical societies to schools of learning, religious societies, and urban associations. Here, too, the diverse manufactures from all over the Ming Empire were available to satisfy the taste of the discerning consumer. The elegance and material prosperity of Chinese cities dazzled European visitors. Matteo Ricci, a Jesuit missionary, described Nanjing in 1600 as a city that surpassed all others in the world "in beauty and grandeur. . . . It is literally filled with palaces and temples and towers and bridges. . . . There is a gaiety of spirit among the people who are well mannered and nicely spoken."

Ming urban prosperity fostered entertainment districts, charcterized by anonymity and relative freedom. Some Ming women found a place here as refined entertainers and courtesans. Others were in demand as midwives, poets, sorcerers, and matchmakers. Female painters, occasionally wives or daughters of professional painters but mostly members of scholar-official families, emulated males who used the home and garden for creative pursuits. The growth of the book trade was also particularly important for women, who were writers as well as readers, not to mention literary characters and archetypes (especially of Confucian virtues). But Chinese women played their biggest roles, and made their greatest fortunes, inside the emperor's Forbidden City, as healers, consorts, and power brokers.

By the middle of the sixteenth century, Ming rule began to stumble owing to a variety of problems, from piracy along the coasts to ineptness in the state. Some Chinese were critical of the political corruption and social decay. One critic, Wang Yangming (1472–1529), a government official and a noted scholar of Neo-Confucian thought, urged commitment to social action. He argued for the unity of knowledge and action and claimed, most importantly, that the answers to problems lay within one's own mind. Taking Wang's emphasis on the individual further, some of his more radical later followers even suggested, against orthodox belief at the time, that women were equal to men intellectually and should be fully educated, a position that led to their banishment from the elite establishment. Even as new ideas and the state's weaknesses created internal discord, the commercial vibrancy of Ming society continued. China's economic vitality also survived the fall of the dynasty in 1644, laying the foundation and providing the resources for the population growth and subsequent territorial expansion of the seventeenth and eighteenth centuries.

ASIAN RELATIONS WITH EUROPE

Europe's overseas expansion had originally been directed toward Asia. The conquest and colonization of the New World gave Europeans the means to realize some of their dreams vis-à-vis Asia. The Portuguese led the way, profiting greatly from being the first Europeans to establish themselves in the Indian Ocean. They inserted themselves into the overseas trading networks bridging East Africa to China, and within a short while they became either important commercial intermediaries or collectors of customs duties from Asian traders. In 1557, the Portuguese arrival at Macao, a port city along the southern coast of China, enabled them to penetrate

Macao. This Chinese painting depicts the Portuguese enclave of Macao on the southern border of China around 1800.

China's expanding import-export trade. By 1563, the number of Portuguese in Macao neared 1,000.

To be sure, the Portuguese contingent in Macao was dwarfed by the far larger number of Melakans, Indians, and Africans enlivening the port. Moreover, while Ming authorities had finally permitted a Portuguese presence in Macao, the court in Beijing remained unwilling to establish an official relationship with European traders there. Like the Mughals, the Ming confined Portuguese merchants to a coastal enclave. Indeed, in 1574, the Chinese built a wall at the isthmus connecting Macao with the mainland. This barrier, and the soldiers who guarded it, served to restrict the movement of the Portuguese and their access to inland trade. Restricted though their presence was, however, the Portuguese did become important shippers of China's most prized manufactures, its porcelains and silks, throughout Asia and to Europe. They also took over much of the silver trade from Japan.

Seeing how much the Portuguese were earning on Asian trade, the Spanish, English, and Dutch adventured into Asian waters. With monopolistic access to American silver, Spain enjoyed a competitive advantage. In 1565, the first Spanish trading galleon reached the Philippines, and in 1571, after the Spanish captured the city of Manila and made it a colonial capital, they established a brisk trade with China. Each year, ships from the Spanish colonies in the Americas crossed the Pacific to Manila, bearing cargoes of silver. They returned carrying vast quantities of porcelain and silks for well-to-do European consumers. Merchants of Manila also procured silks, tapestries, and feathers from the China Seas for direct shipment to the Americas, where the mining potentates waited eagerly for their imports from China.

The year 1571, therefore, proved to be a decisive date in the history of the modern world, for in that year Spain inaugurated a trade circuit that made good on Magellan's achievement of a half-century prior. As Spanish ships circumnavigated the globe from the New World to China and from China eventually back to Europe, the world was commercially interconnected. It was silver that solidified the linkage, for silver was the only foreign commodity for which the Chinese had a constant and unquenchable demand. From the massive mother lodes of the Andes and Mesoamerica, silver made the commerce of the world go round.

Other Europeans, too, wanted their share of Asia's wealth. The English and the Dutch sailed into the South China Sea in the last decade of the sixteenth century. Captain James Lancaster made the first English voyage to the East Indies between 1591 and 1594. Five years later, in 1599, 101 English subscribers pooled their funds and formed a joint-stock company (an association in which each member owned shares of capital). With an initial capital of £30,000, the English East India Company was given a royal charter the following year. The charter granted the company exclusive rights to import East Indian goods. Rapidly, the company displaced the Portuguese in the Arabian Sea and the Persian Gulf. Doing a brisk trade in indigo, saltpetre, pepper, and cotton textiles, the English East India Company would eventually acquire control in villages on both coasts of India—Fort St. George (Madras; 1639), Bombay (1661), and Calcutta (1690).

Chronology

	1500	1510	1520	1530	1540
EUROPE	▌Christians complete reconquest of Granada, 1492		▌Luther posts 95 theses, 1517 ▌Magellan's ship circumnavigates the globe, 1519–1522	▌Peasant wars in Holy Roman Empire, 1524	
AMERICAS	▌Columbus discovers the New World, 1492		▌Magellan's ship circumnavigates the globe, 1519–1522 ▌Cortés conquers the Aztecs, 1519–1522 Pizarro conquers the Incas, 1533 ▌		
SOUTH ASIA		▌Da Gama sails to the Indian Ocean, 1498 ▌Portuguese establish Indian Ocean bases, 1508–1511	▌Magellan's ship circumnavigates the globe, 1519–1522		
EAST ASIA			▌Magellan's ship circumnavigates the globe, 1519–1522		

It is tempting to see the arrival of Europeans in the waters of the South China Sea and the Indian Ocean as the beginning of the end of Asian autonomy. This was hardly the case, however. Through the sixteenth century, Europeans forged only very weak connections to Asian societies. For the moment, the increased presence of Europeans in Asia enhanced the wealth and might of Asian dynasties.

 ## CONCLUSION

In the middle of the fifteenth century, the world had many different regional trading spheres. In this sense, it was multicentered. Islam occupied a kind of pivot. In an Indian Ocean system straddling Africa, the eastern Mediterranean, and South and East Asia, merchants plied their wares along overland and increasingly seaborne routes, while intermingling in multiethnic urban centers. To the extent that Asian empires expanded, they sought tribute and trade. Exchange, or better yet, tributary relations with subject peoples drove imperial agendas.

In this multicentered world of the fifteenth century, Europe was a poor cousin. A new spirit of adventure and achievement, however, animated European peoples, stirred up by the rediscovery of antiquity (the Renaissance), the ambitions of a rising mercantile elite, and later by the spiritual fervor of the Reformation and Counter-Reformation. Learning much from Arab seamen, European sailors perfected techniques for sailing into dangerous waters. Desiring Asian goods, especially for luxury consumption, European merchants and mariners were eager to exploit existing trade routes leading eastward. But far more consequentially, Europe's location gave its people another direction into which to expand, across the still largely unknown Atlantic Ocean. With the Ottoman conquest of Constantinople and control over the eastern Mediterranean, the Atlantic sea lanes offered an alternative route to Asia. As the Europeans searched for alternative routes around Islam, they first sailed down the coast of Africa and then across the Atlantic.

Encountering the "New World" was an accident of monumental significance. In the Americas, Europeans found riches. Mountains of silver and rivers of gold gave Europeans the currency they had lacked in dealing with Asian traders. In the Americas, Europeans also found opportunities for exchange and settlement. And here, unlike in Asian empires, European rivals were able to supplement their drive for commerce with conquest and colonization. Yet, establishing these transatlantic empires heightened tensions within Europe, as rivals fought over the spoils and as a religious schism turned into a political and spiritual struggle that divided Europe. For this reason two conquests in particular characterize this age of increasing world interconnections. The Islamic conquest of Constantinople drove Europeans to search for new links to Asia and demonstrated the centrality of Islam in the making of modern world history. In turn, the conquest of Tenochtitlán, some seventy years later, gave Europeans access to silver, which enabled them to increase their presence in Asian

1550	1560	1570	1580	1590	1600

▌ *Dutch revolt against Spanish rule, 1568*

▌ *Spanish fleet defeats Ottomans at Lepanto, 1571*

▌ *English defeat Spanish Armada, 1588*

▌ *Opening of Potosí mines, 1545*

▌ *Consolidation of Mughal Empire, 1556–1605*

▌ *Portuguese arrive at Macao (China); first permanent settlement established, 1557*

▌ *Spanish capture city of Manila, 1571*

▌ *Ming erect wall to Macao to restrict European movement, 1574* trading circuits. In this era of growing interconnectedness, these two conquests were decisive turning points in the making of the modern world.

American Indians also played an important role in the making of the modern world, as Europeans sought to conquer their lands, exploit their labor, and confiscate their gold and silver. Sometimes Indians worked with Europeans, sometimes they worked under Europeans, sometimes they worked against Europeans, and sometimes none were left to work at all. In this last all-too-common case, the Europeans made Africans do what Indians could not, thereby compounding the calamity of the encounter with the tragedy of slavery. Out of the catastrophe of contact, a new oceanic system arose, linking the peoples and products of Africa, America, and Europe. This was the Atlantic world, one that gave new meaning to the notion of oceanic systems. In contrast to the tributary and trading orders of the Indian Ocean and China Seas, the Atlantic Ocean became a system of formal imperial control and settlement of distant colonies.

STUDY QUESTIONS

WWNORTON.COM/STUDYSPACE

1. Describe the new trade patterns in the Afro-Eurasian world during the fifteenth century. How similar and different were they from the Mongol period?

2. Describe the process through which Spain was able to create a vast empire in the Americas. How did the spread of lethal disease influence this outcome?

3. Explain the process involved in the "The Columbian Exchange." What consequences did this exchange (or exchanges) have on regions beyond the Atlantic world?

4. Compare and contrast Spain's "tributary empire" in the Americas with Portugal's "seaborne empire" in the Indian Ocean during the sixteenth century. Why did these empires pursue such different strategies?

5. Explain what conditions allowed for the strengthening of regional dynasties in Europe in the sixteenth century as opposed to the growth of one large European empire.

6. Explain the transformation of the African slave trade during this time period. What role did the growth of sugar plantations play in this process?

7. Analyze how the emergence of the Atlantic world in the sixteenth century transformed Europe, the Americas, and Africa. To what extent was each region transformed?

8. Compare and contrast political and commercial developments in the Mughal and Ming dynasties in Asia during the sixteenth century. How did the expansion of global commerce affect each region?

9. Evaluate to what extent an increased European presence altered the political balance of power in Asia during the

sixteenth century. How did Asian dynasties react to increased European contacts?

10. Explain the role of silver in transforming global trade patterns during the sixteenth century. Which regions and dynasties benefited from the increased use of silver for monetary transactions?

FURTHER READINGS

Axtell, James, *Beyond 1492: Encounters in Colonial North America* (1992). A wonderfully informed speculation about Indian reactions to Europeans.

Brady, Thomas A., et al. (eds.), *Handbook of European History 1400–1600: Late Middle Ages, Renaissance, and Reformation, Structures and Assertions* (1996). A good synthetic survey of recent literature and historiographical debates.

Cass, Victoria, *Dangerous Women: Warriors, Grannies, and Geishas of the Ming* (1999). An original study of Chinese female archetypes in memoirs, miscellanies, short stories, and novels.

Chaudhuri, K. N., *Trade and Civilisation in the Indian Ocean: An Economic History from the Rise of Islam to 1750* (1985). An excellent, comprehensive work that deals with the Indian Ocean economy and the appearance of European merchants there from the sixteenth century onward.

Clendinnen, Inga, *Aztecs: An Interpretation* (1991). Brilliantly reconstructs the culture of Tenochtitlán in the years before its conquest.

Crosby, Alfred W., *The Columbian Exchange: Biological and Cultural Consequences of 1492* (1972). A provocative discussion of the ecological consequences that followed the European "discovery" of the Americas.

———, *Ecological Imperialism: The Biological Expansion of Europe, 900–1900* (1986). Another important work on the ecological consequences of European expansion.

Curtin, Philip, *Cross-Cultural Trade in World History* (1984). A work stressing the role of trade and commerce in establishing cross-cultural contacts.

Febvre, Lucien, *The Problem of Unbelief in the Sixteenth Century: The Religion of Rabelais* (1982). A tour de force of intellectual history by the man who moved the study of the Reformation away from great men to the broader question of religious revival and mentalities.

Flynn, Dennis, and Arturo Giráldez (eds.), *Metals and Monies in an Emerging Global Economy* (1997). Contains several articles relating to silver and the Asian trade.

Frank, Andre Gunder, *ReOrient: Global Economy in the Asian Age* (1998). A reassessment of the role of Asia in the economic development of the world from around 1400 onward.

Gruzinski, Serge, *The Conquest of Mexico* (1993). An important work on the conquest of Mexico.

Habib, Irfan, *The Agrarian System of Mughal India* (1963). One of the best studies on the subject.

Hall, Richard Seymour, *Empires of the Monsoon: A History of the Indian Ocean and Its Invaders* (1996). A very engaging journalistic account with fabulous details.

Hodgson, Marshall, *The Venture of Islam*, vols. 2 and 3 (1974). A magisterial work that includes the Indian subcontinent in its careful study of the political and cultural history of the whole Islamic world.

Hulme, Peter, *Colonial Encounters: Europe and the Native Caribbean, 1492–1797* (1986). Presents an interesting interpretation of the encounters of Europeans and Native Americans.

Lach, Donald F., *Asia in the Making of Europe*, 5 books in 3 vols. (1965–). Perhaps the single most comprehensive and innovative guide to the European voyages of discovery.

Lockhart, James, and Stuart Schwartz, *Early Latin America* (1983). One of the finest studies of European expansion in the late fifteenth century.

Melville, Elinor G. K., *A Plague of Sheep: Environmental Consequences of the Conquest of Mexico* (1994). A history of the transformation of a valley in Mexico from the Aztec period to the era of Spanish rule.

Mignolo, Walter D., *The Darker Side of the Renaissance: Literacy, Territoriality, and Colonization* (1995). Uses literary theory and literary images to present provocative interpretations of the encounter of Europeans and Native Americans.

Pagden, Anthony, *European Encounters with the New World* (1993). A complex look at the deep and lasting imprint of the New World on its conquerors.

Parker, Geoffrey, *The Military Revolution: Military Innovation and the Rise of the West, 1500–1800* (1996). Traces the changes in technology and tactics in the early modern period and discusses the political significance of this "revolution."

Pelikan, Jaroslav, *Reformation of Church and Dogma (1300–1700)* (1988). An important overview of major religious controversies.

Phillips, William D., and Carla Rahn Phillips, *The World of Christopher Columbus* (1992). One of the finest studies of European expansion in the late fifteenth century.

Russell-Wood, A. J. R., *The Portuguese Empire, 1415–1808* (1992). An important survey of early Portuguese exploration.

Von Glahn, Richard, *Fountain of Fortune: Money and Monetary Policy in China, 1000–1700* (1996). Includes an excellent analysis of the history of silver in Ming China.

13

WORLDS ENTANGLED,
1600–1750

*I*n 1720, a devastating financial panic swept across
Europe, making rich men into paupers and ruining
many political careers. The panic was rooted in a
speculative mania surrounding anticipated high profits flowing
from trade with the Americas. A group of British merchants set up
the South Sea Trading Company to compete with French trading
firms and obtained privileged trading rights with all of Spanish
America. Most coveted of all was the exclusive right to sell African
slaves to Spanish colonies. Enthusiasm for these and other less substantial companies soared, and investors rushed in, sending share
prices skyrocketing. But rumors of fantastic spoils gave way to word
that the original investors were dumping their shares and that many
of the companies were worthless. The speculative bubble burst.
Share prices plummeted, with nearly all the companies created at
the time going bankrupt, and even many solid firms in Europe going
under. The South Sea Bubble, as it came to be called, reflected the
euphoria of overseas trading ventures and the greater interconnections across the world. But it also stood as a vivid example of
the perils that could accompany global trade and investment.

From 1600 to 1750, the circuits of world trade expanded as
commerce continued to flow across the world's oceans. Ships

laden with sugar from Brazil, spices from Southeast Asia, cotton textiles from India, silks from China, and increasingly, silver from Mesoamerica and the Andes made their way from port to port. Global trading networks emerged, and global commodities made a decisive appearance. In these new interregional trading networks, New World silver played the major role. It gave Europeans a commodity to exchange with Asian partners and began to tilt the balance of wealth and power in a westerly direction across Afro-Eurasia.

During this period, increasing economic connection along with the territorial expansion of various empires produced dramatic, if sometimes unintended, effects around the world. In the Atlantic basin, European colonial powers consolidated their control over larger portions of the Americas. England and France joined Spain and Portugal in the full-scale colonization of American possessions. Populations moved around, as peoples of European and African descent took the place of Native Americans in the New World, creating the foundations for European and African diasporic communities in the Americas. The number of African slaves shipped to the Americas rose dramatically during the seventeenth and eighteenth centuries, drawing the peoples and products of Africa, Europe, and the Americas more closely together. Extreme gender imbalances occurred in those parts of Africa that were drawn into the Atlantic slave trade as well as within the enslaved populations in the Americas. By no means was this growing expansion of empires limited to the Atlantic world. European empires also established colonies in Southeast Asia and, with New World silver, sought to extend their trade with Asian societies. At the same time, rulers in India, China, and Japan enlarged the borders of their empires, while Russia's tsars incorporated vast Siberian territories into their domain.

Predictably, economic linkages and territorial expansion were tempestuous processes. Commercial, colonial, and religious rivalries provoked bitter and bloody conflicts between and within European states. In Asia, too, increasing global trade and political expansion produced political and economic instability. In particular, the increased flow of silver posed a stiff challenge to the centralized control of the Ottoman and Mughal empires and contributed to the toppling of the Ming dynasty.

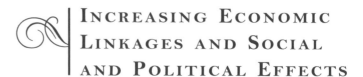

INCREASING ECONOMIC LINKAGES AND SOCIAL AND POLITICAL EFFECTS

> → *How did global economic integration affect political systems?*

Although transoceanic trade most directly affected mercantile groups and the nations who sponsored them, the deepening connections between the economies of distant places also affected both rulers and common people. Increasing economic ties brought new places and products into world markets: furs from French North America, sugar from the Caribbean, tobacco from the British mainland American colonies, and coffee from Southeast Asia and the Middle East. So important did the products of world trade become during the seventeenth and eighteenth centuries that interruptions in their availability sometimes destabilized regional economic and political systems. For example, the output of the new gold and silver mines of the Americas was vital to the commercial networks that linked the markets of the world. The supply of precious metals might fall because political disturbances brought work stoppages, or might increase greatly when new mines opened. The prices of commodities could soar or drop, bringing prosperity to some and poverty to others.

Focus Questions WORLDS ENTANGLED

→ *How did global economic integration affect political systems?*

→ *How did European mercantilism and colonialism transform the Americas?*

→ *How did the slave trade reshape African societies and polities?*

→ *How did global trade affect the Asian dynasties?*

→ *Why did the centers of European economic and political dynamism shift northward in the seventeenth century?*

 WWNORTON.COM/STUDYSPACE

STIMULANTS, SOCIABILITY, AND COFFEEHOUSES

As the world's trading networks expanded, the great merchants of Europe, Asia, Africa, and the Americas also globalized and popularized many new commodities. None were more enthusiastically received around the world than a group of stimulants—coffee, cocoa, sugar, tobacco, and tea—all of which, except for sugar, were slightly or highly addictive and had the added feature of producing a sense of well-being. Previously, many of these products had been grown in isolated parts of the world. Yemen had been the only location in the fifteenth century for the distribution of the coffee bean. Tobacco and cocoa were New World products, and sugar, while it originated in Bengal, did not become a product with a vast global market until it began to be cultivated on a large scale on American plantations. Yet, by the seventeenth century, in nearly every corner of the world, the well-to-do classes began to congregate in coffeehouses, consuming these new products and engaging in sociable activities.

Although sugar was probably consumed in larger amounts than any other product in this group, coffee and coffeehouses gained the greatest notoriety among the well-to-do. Coffeehouses everywhere served as locations for social exchange, political discussions, and business activities. Yet, they also varied from cultural area to cultural area, reflecting the values of the society in which they arose.

The coffeehouse first appeared in Islamic lands toward the end of the fifteenth century. As coffee's consumption caught on among the well-to-do and leisured classes in the Arabian Peninsula and the Ottoman Empire, local growers protected their advantage by monopolizing its cultivation and sale and refusing to allow any seeds or cuttings from the coffee tree to be taken abroad.

Despite some religious opposition, coffee spread into Egypt and throughout the Ottoman Empire in the sixteenth century. Ottoman bureaucrats, merchants, and artists assembled in coffeehouses to trade stories, to read, to listen to poetry, and to play chess and backgammon. Indeed, so deeply connected were the coffeehouses with the literary and artistic lives of

Turkish men drinking coffee at a banquet.

Drinking coffee in an English coffeehouse.

many people that they were referred to as schools of knowledge.

From the Ottoman territories, the culture of coffee drinking spread to western Europe. The first coffeehouse in London opened in 1652, and such establishments soon proliferated. By 1713, there were no fewer than 500 coffeehouses in London. The Fleet Street area of London was filled with so many of these establishments that the English essayist Charles Lamb commented "that the man must have a rare recipe for melancholy who can be dull in Fleet Street." Although the coffeehouses attracted people from all levels of society, they especially appealed to the new mercantile and professional classes as locations where stimulating beverages like coffee, cocoa, and tea easily led to lively conversations. Here, too, there were opponents, some of whom claimed that an excessive drinking of coffee destabilized the thinking processes and even resulted in conversions to Islam. But against such opposition, the pleasures of coffee, tea, and cocoa prevailed. These bitter beverages in turn required liberal doses of the sweetener, sugar. A smoke of tobacco topped off the experience. In this environment of pleasure, patrons of the coffeehouses indulged their addictions, engaged in gossip, conducted business, and talked politics.

The most ardent European exponents of coffee even suggested that its consumption would moderate another of the addictions that beset many people—the use of beer, wine, and spirits, often to excess. But this was destined not to be. Samuel Johnson, one of England's most astute observers, wryly observed that "a man is never happy in the present unless he is drunk."

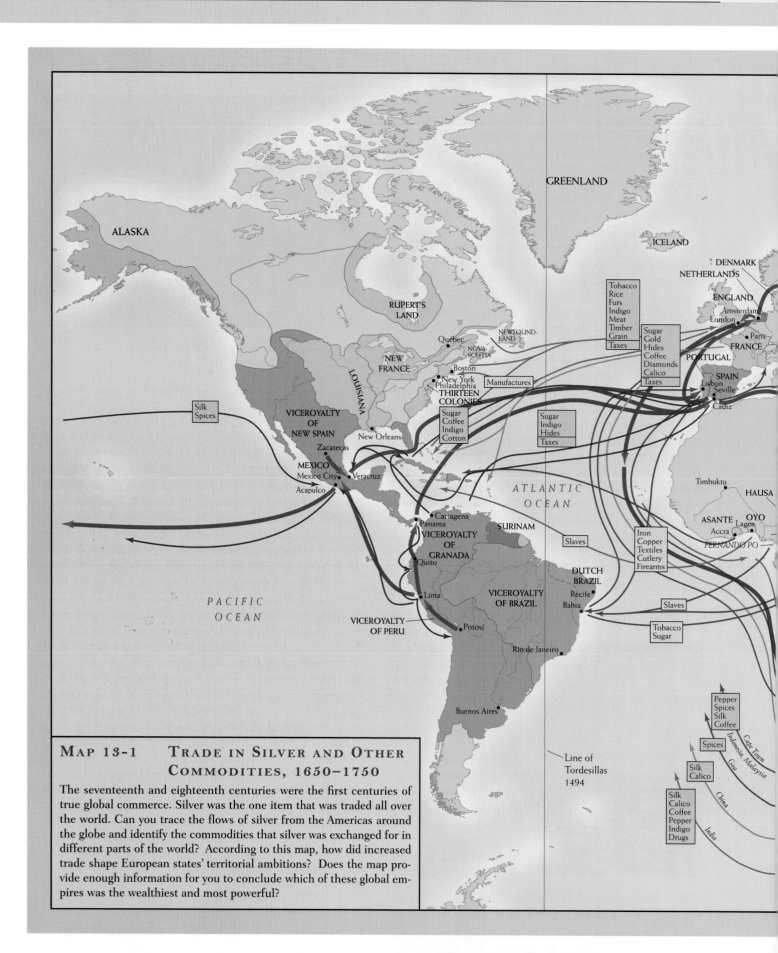

GREENLAND

ICELAND

ALASKA

DENMARK

NETHERLANDS

ENGLAND

Amsterdam

London

Paris

FRANCE

PORTUGAL

SPAIN

Lisbon

Seville

Cadiz

RUPERT'S
LAND

Québec

NEWFOUND-
LAND

NOVA
SCOTIA

NEW
FRANCE

Boston

New York

Philadelphia

THIRTEEN
COLONIES

LOUISIANA

Manufactures

Tobacco
Rice
Furs
Indigo
Meat
Timber
Grain
Taxes

Sugar
Gold
Hides
Coffee
Diamonds
Calico
Taxes

VICEROYALTY
OF
NEW SPAIN

New Orleans

Sugar
Coffee
Indigo
Cotton

Sugar
Indigo
Hides
Taxes

Silk
Spices

Zacatecas

MEXICO

Mexico City

Veracruz

Acapulco

*ATLANTIC
OCEAN*

Timbuktu

HAUSA

ASANTE

OYO

Accra

Lagos

FERNANDO PO

Cartagena

Panama

SURINAM

VICEROYALTY
OF
GRANADA

Quito

Slaves

Iron
Copper
Textiles
Cutlery
Firearms

*PACIFIC
OCEAN*

Lima

DUTCH
BRAZIL

Recife

Bahia

VICEROYALTY
OF BRAZIL

Slaves

VICEROYALTY
OF PERU

Potosí

Tobacco
Sugar

Rio de Janeiro

Buenos Aires

Line of
Tordesillas
1494

Pepper
Spices
Silk
Coffee

Spices

Indonesia, Malaysia

Cape Town

Goa

China

Silk
Calico

India

Silk
Calico
Coffee
Pepper
Indigo
Drugs

MAP 13-1   TRADE IN SILVER AND OTHER COMMODITIES, 1650–1750

The seventeenth and eighteenth centuries were the first centuries of true global commerce. Silver was the one item that was traded all over the world. Can you trace the flows of silver from the Americas around the globe and identify the commodities that silver was exchanged for in different parts of the world? According to this map, how did increased trade shape European states' territorial ambitions? Does the map provide enough information for you to conclude which of these global empires was the wealthiest and most powerful?

ARCTIC OCEAN

SWEDEN

St. Petersburg

Danzig

POLAND

AUSTRIA

RUSSIAN EMPIRE

OTTOMAN
EMPIRE

Aleppo

Baghdad

Basra

Alexandria
Suez

Hormuz

Delhi

QING CHINA

JAPAN

PACIFIC
OCEAN

ARABIA

Muscat

INDIA

Diu
Bombay
Goa
Tellicherry
Pondicherry
Cochin

Calcutta

Rangoon

ANNAM
Da Nang

Guangzhou

PHILIPPINES
Manila

ETHIOPIA

Madras

CEYLON

Melaka

BENIN

Mogadishu

Malindi
Mombasa
ZANZIBAR

Luanda

Kilwa

SUMATRA

Banten

BORNEO

MALUKU

NEW GUINEA

Batavia
JAVA

TIMOR

BANDA

Mozambique
Sofala

MADAGASCAR
MAURITIUS
RÉUNION

Delagoa Bay

INDIAN
OCEAN

Cape Town
Cape of
Good Hope

Spanish trade route	Spanish territory	Silver flow
Portuguese trade route	Portuguese territory	Export
English trade route	English territory	Import
French trade route	French territory	
Dutch trade route	Dutch territory	
	Anglo-French contested area	

0 ... 1000 ... 2000 Miles
0 ... 1000 ... 2000 Kilometers

The benefits of closer economic contact enhanced the power of some states. Increased contact bolstered the legitimacy of the rising new states of England and France, and it also encouraged local power groups to throw their weight behind new rulers, as happened in Japan and in parts of sub-Saharan Africa. In England, France, Japan, and Russia and across Africa, the linkages of the seventeenth and eighteenth centuries were accompanied by civil wars and large-scale social unrest. For other regimes and economies, the impact of trade destabilized the existing systems of rule. The Ottoman state found outlying provinces slipping from central control. To the east of the Ottoman Empire's borders, the Safavid regime foundered in 1722, and it came to an end in 1773; the once mighty Ming dynasty gave way to a new dynasty, the Qing, in 1644. In India, internal rivalries among princes and powerful merchants whittled away at the central authority of the Mughals, compounding the instability caused by peasant uprisings.

EXTRACTING WEALTH: MERCANTILISM

Transformations in relations between different parts of the world began in the Atlantic, where the extraction and shipment of gold and silver siphoned wealth from the New World to the Old. Mined by Indian and African workers and delivered into the hands of merchants and monarchs, precious metals from the Andes and Mesoamerica accounted for a rising share of the world's supply of silver. Added to the output of these regions, a boom in gold production made Brazil the world's single largest producer of that metal in the eighteenth century.

So lucrative was American mining that other European powers wanted a share in the bounty that Spain and Portugal were reaping from mineral-rich possessions. Looking for their own areas in the Americas from which to take gold and silver, a number of European rivals launched colonizing ventures in the seventeenth century. In contrast to the first century of European colonialism, latecomers failed to find much in the way of minerals. But they devised other means to extract wealth. The New World had an abundance of resources and fertile lands on which to cultivate sugarcane, cotton, tobacco, indigo, and rice, as well as fur-bearing wildlife, whose pelts were much demanded in Europe (see Map 13-1). Better still from the perspective of new colonizers, New World crops and skins could be produced and transported easily and cheaply.

If silver quickened the pace of global trade, sugar transformed the European diet. First domesticated in Polynesia, sugar was not central to the European diets, for the most part, prior to the creation of New World plantations. Previously, Europeans had sweetened their diets with honey, but they soon became the world's great consumers of sugar. Be-

Tooth Decay. The influx of New World sugar sweetened European diets—but also led to the spread of a new affliction: tooth decay.

tween 1690 and 1790, Europe imported 12 million tons of sugar, or approximately one ton for every African captive who was enslaved in the Americas. Public tooth-pulling became a popular entertainment—for the spectators!—in cities like Paris, and tooth decay became a leading cause of death for Europeans.

Whether they supplied precious metals, cotton or sweeteners, colonies were supposed to provide wealth for "mother countries," or so held exponents of mercantilism, the economic theory that drove European empire-builders in this era. Coined by a French economist in 1763, *mercantilism* described a system that had developed over several centuries. Mercantilist doctrine presumed that the world's wealth was fixed and that one country's wealth came at the expense of other countries. The system's proponents assumed that overseas possessions existed solely to enrich European motherlands. In practice, this meant that colonies should ship more value to their mother country than they received in return. In addition to creating trade surpluses, colonies were supposed to be closed to competitors, lest foreign traders drain precious resources from an empire's exclusive domain. As the mother country's monopoly over the trade of its colonial ter-

→ *How did European mercantilism and colonialism transform the Americas?*

Primary Source

THE PRINCIPLES OF MERCANTILISM

In 1757, a British commercial expert by the name of Malachy Postlewayt published a commercial dictionary, which he called The Universal Dictionary of Trade and Commerce. *Under the entry "trade," he set forth "some maxims relating to trade that should seem to be confirmed in the course of this work." The first five provide a succinct statement of the economic philosophy of mercantilism and the importance that countries attached to the acquisition of precious metals.*

I. That the lasting prosperity of the landed interest depends upon foreign commerce.

II. That the increase of the wealth, splendour, and power of Great Britain and Ireland depends upon exporting more in value of our native produce and manufactures than we import of commodities from other nations and bringing thereby money into the kingdom by means of freight by shipping.

III. That domestic and foreign trade, as they are the means of increasing national treasure, of breeding seamen, and of augmenting our mercantile and royal navies they necessarily become the means of our permanent prosperity and of the safety and preservation of our happy constitution.

IV. That the constant security of the public credit and the payment of interest and principal of the public creditors depend upon the prosperous state of our trade and navigation.

V. That gold and silver is the measure of trade, and that silver is a commodity and may be exported, especially in foreign coin as well as any other commodity.

→ *What are the key tenets of mercantilism?*
→ *Why is silver more important than gold in trade?*

SOURCE: Malachy Postlewayt, *The Universal Dictionary of Trade and Commerce*, vol. 2, p. 792.

ritories generated wealth for royal treasuries, European states acquired the wherewithal to wage almost unceasing wars against one another. Ultimately, mercantilists believed, as did Thomas Hobbes (1588–1679), that "wealth is power and power is wealth."

The mercantilist system rested on an alliance between the state and its merchants. Mercantilists believed economics and politics were interdependent, with the merchant needing the monarch to protect his interests, and the monarch relying on the merchant's trade to enrich the state's treasury. Chartered companies, such as the (English) Virginia Company or the Dutch East India Company (VOC), created by wealthy merchants and granted monopoly rights by European rulers, are ideal examples of this sort of alliance between merchants and the state.

NEW COLONIES IN THE AMERICAS

→ *How did European mercantilism and colonialism transform the Americas?*

One by one, rulers in England, France, and Holland granted monopolies to merchant companies, giving to them a monopoly over the trade and settlement of new colonies in the Americas (see Map 13-2). If old motives—finding precious metals or water routes to Asia—initiated many of these enterprises, the Dutch, French, and English learned that only

English claims 1756
French claims 1756
Spanish claims 1756
Dutch claims until 1664
English acquisitions 1763
Spanish acquisitions 1763
French possessions 1763
Anglo-French contested area

Hudson Bay

RUPERT'S LAND

NEWFOUNDLAND

Fort Albany 1670

Rupert's House 1668

Île St. Jean
Île Royale

St. Lawrence R.

Québec 1608

NOVA SCOTIA

Trois Rivières 1634

NEW FRANCE

Lake Superior

Ft. Frontenac 1673

Penobscot 1628

NH MAINE

Lake Huron

Lake Michigan

Lake Ontario Albany 1664

Boston 1630

MASSACHUSETTS

Ft. Niagara 1679

Lake Erie

Plymouth 1620
Providence 1636

RHODE ISLAND
CONNECTICUT

Mississippi R.

Ft. St. Louis 1682

PENNSYLVANIA

New Haven 1640
New York (New Amsterdam 1624–1664)

Philadelphia 1682

Hudson R.

NEW JERSEY
DELAWARE

LOUISIANA

Annapolis 1706

MARYLAND

VIRGINIA

Ohio R.

Jamestown 1607

NORTH
CAROLINA

ATLANTIC

VICEROYALTY
OF
NEW SPAIN

SOUTH
CAROLINA

OCEAN

Rio Grande

FLORIDA

Gulf of Mexico

BAHAMAS

0   100   200   300 Miles
0 100 200 300 Kilometers

MAP 13-2   COLONIES IN NORTH AMERICA, 1607–1763

France, England, and Spain laid claim to much of North America in the seventeenth and eighteenth centuries. Where was each one of these colonial powers strongest before the outbreak of the Seven Years' War in 1756? Which empire gained the most North American territory and who lost the most at the end of the war in 1763? How do you imagine that Indian peoples reacted to the territorial arrangements agreed to by Spain, France, and England at the Peace of Paris, which ended the war?

by exploiting other resources could their claims in the Americas be made into profitable colonies. That the latecomers met with New World societies very different from those in Mesoamerica or the Andes also necessitated fresh thinking about the appropriate character of colonial regimes.

HOLLAND'S TRADING COLONIES

The Dutch first established a settlement in North America at the mouth of the Hudson River. The river was named for an Englishman, Henry Hudson, who had been hired by the

Dutch East India Company to explore the Atlantic coast of North America and find a "northwest passage" to Asia. Of particular promise was the broad river, which was given Hudson's name after he entered it in 1609. When his backers realized that the Hudson River did not lead to the Pacific Ocean, however, their interest in the area diminished. Still, Dutch merchants found that the waterway did provide access

Woodlands Indians. This late-sixteenth-century drawing by John White, a pioneer settler on Roanoke Island off the coast of North Carolina, depicts the Indian village of Secoton in eastern Virginia. In contrast to the great empires that the Spanish conquered in the valley of Mexico and in the Andes, the Indians whom English, French, and Dutch colonizers encountered in the woodlands of eastern North America generally lived in villages that were politically autonomous entities.

to a region filled with fur-bearing animals and with Indian peoples, notably the Iroquois, a confederation of "five nations," living in what is now upstate New York, able to trap and ready to trade. In 1624, thirty Dutch families settled on an island at the Hudson's mouth (Manhattan); many, however, soon abandoned the town for upriver locations where they could engage in exchanges with the Iroquois.

Trading furs with Indians was not the original idea behind Dutch colonization. In the sixteenth and seventeenth centuries, the Dutch happily used their vessels to transport the cargo of other nations to any corner of the world. Dutch merchants made considerable profits from handling the slaves, spices, textiles, and silver of other colonizers. They also coveted the riches that the Spanish and Portuguese took from their possessions. Especially tempting were some of the lesser Spanish island possessions in the Caribbean. In 1621, Amsterdam merchants founded the Dutch West India Company to regulate commerce, promote settlement, and maintain the flow of slaves to the Caribbean. The Dutch laid claim to St. Eustatius and two other islands in 1632, they captured Curaçao from Spain in 1634, and a few years later claimed Aruba and St. Martin (see Map 13-3). The Dutch successfully attacked and controlled the New World's main sugar zones in Brazil starting in 1620. By 1654, however, Brazilian settlers drove out the last of the company officials, and the firm was left with the puny outpost on the South American mainland, Surinam, where it tried to introduce plantation agriculture but with only meager results. Unfortunately for the company's backers, these colonies never yielded the profits that were expected of them. By 1674 the Dutch West India Company was bankrupt.

Although the Dutch efforts to establish colonies in the Americas were largely unsuccessful, their businessmen continued to profit from financing foreign merchants, lending vessels to other nations, and handling slaves, silver, and textiles. The Dutch were, in fact, often referred to as the world's "universal carriers." The most important Dutch colonial possessions were not in the Americas. More significant for the Dutch were their lucrative colony in the East Indies and a small colonial possession in South Africa (Cape Town), which was founded in 1652 as a refreshment station for ships going between the Atlantic and Indian Oceans.

FRANCE'S FUR-TRADING EMPIRE

The French also began their colonizing exploits in North America with a search for a northern water route to the Pacific that turned into a fur-trading enterprise. The initial French explorations were conducted by Jacques Cartier (1491–1557), and the chief French route into the interior of North America was the St. Lawrence River. Sailing up the St. Lawrence, Cartier and subsequent French explorers, most notably Samuel de Champlain (1567–1635), found not a

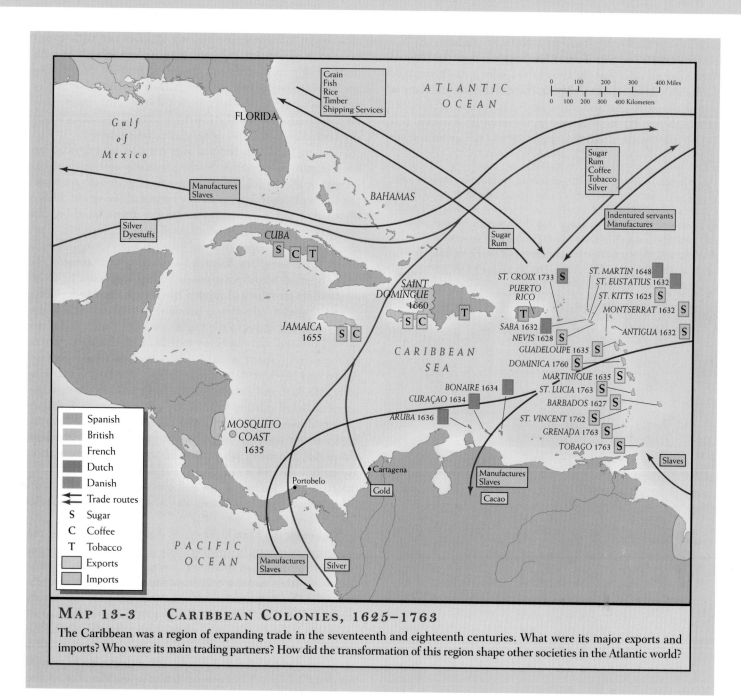

MAP 13-3 CARIBBEAN COLONIES, 1625–1763

The Caribbean was a region of expanding trade in the seventeenth and eighteenth centuries. What were its major exports and imports? Who were its main trading partners? How did the transformation of this region shape other societies in the Atlantic world?

waterway to the Pacific but huge bodies of fresh water (the Great Lakes) in the midst of a massive continent. In the wake of this discovery, Champlain founded the colony of New France, with its base in Québec, in 1608. From Québec, French traders and missionaries penetrated deep into the interior of North America, eager to engage its Indian inhabitants in commercial exchange and to convert them to the Catholic faith.

At the center of the trade between the French and the Indians in northern North America was the beaver, an animal for which Indian peoples previously had little use. But Euro-

peans coveted the barbed underfur of the beaver and were willing to give Indians a variety of goods in return. For the Indians, as one native hunter proclaimed, "the beaver does everything perfectly well; it makes kettles, hatchets, swords, knives, bread; in short it makes everything." As long as there were beavers to be trapped, trade between the French and their Indian partners flourished.

The distinctive aspect of the fur trade was the Europeans' utter dependence on Indian know-how. Trapping required close familiarity with the habits and habitats of the beaver—a form of knowledge that Europeans lacked. This reliance

The Fur Trade. For Europeans in northern North America, no commodity was as important as beaver skins. For the French especially, the fur trade determined the character of their colonial regime in North America. For Indians, it offered access to European goods, but overhunting depleted resources and provoked intertribal conflicts.

forced the French to adapt to Indian ways. Such accommodation is easily seen in the pattern of exchange. Although the French had wanted to make the export of beaver pelts a purely commercial venture, for their Indian partners exchange was governed by more than material concerns. Trade cemented familial bonds. For the most part, the French obeyed by giving gifts and partaking in Indian diplomatic rituals. To solidify their trade networks, Frenchmen often married into Indian families. As a result of these unions, *métis* (French-Indian offspring) played an important role in New France as interpreters, traders, and guides. Compared to all other empires, the French accomplished colonization without conquest, stretching their trading empire deep into North American forests.

ENGLAND'S LANDED EMPIRE

Part of the rationale for the French alliance with the Indians was strategic: the French and Indians shared a deep mistrust of the other major North American interlopers, the English. At the outset, the English, like the Spanish, sought colonies that would yield riches in the form of precious metals. But the settlements they established along the Atlantic coast of North America in the seventeenth century lacked such resources. Nor did these temperate lands boast beavers with the thick furs that French traders "mined" in lands to the north. What the English territories did have was land suitable for growing a variety of crops. And, as the population grew, English agrarian settlements expanded, encroaching

more and more on Indian lands. Accordingly, relations between English colonists and Indian inhabitants were generally far less cordial than relations between the French and their native trading partners.

Along the Atlantic seaboard, the English colonies differed from one another, but their settlers possessed a hunger for land that came at the expense of Indian inhabitants. Around Massachusetts Bay, one group of Protestant refugees (Puritans) founded a colony whose population rose substantially after 1630. As the colonial population of New England increased, so did the colonists' demand for fresh farmlands. The result was a souring of relations between natives and newcomers, which led to ferocious wars in the 1630s and 1670s.

A similar cycle unfolded farther south around Chesapeake Bay. In Virginia, the impulse for colonization was more commercial and less religious than among the Puritans of Massachusetts, but the pattern of intercultural relations was remarkably similar. The settlement at Jamestown was founded in 1607. The first disastrous winters wiped out large numbers of settlers, many of whom were gentlemen adventurers who had aimed to make money but had little interest in labor. Like the Puritans, Chesapeake colonists would not have survived their "starving times" had local Indians not provided them with food and other assistance. Within a few years, the colony began to thrive, especially once the colonists found a suitable staple that could be profitably exported. In Virginia the crop of choice was a weed that Indians cultivated called tobacco. The tobacco boom of the 1620s transformed a failing colony into a commercial phoenix. Prosperity induced thousands of English men and women to migrate to Virginia, compounding the pressures on Indian lands. As in Massachusetts, this hunger for plantations led to a series of wars and to the dispossession of Indians from their Chesapeake homelands. While the French intermixed freely with their trading partners and the Spanish married into Indian societies, English migrant communities in the New World included a larger number of women, and steered clear of marital-political alliances with natives. Instead of developing extensive trading networks, the English based their New World empire on land ownership—and did not hesitate to push the borders of European property ever deeper into Indian territory.

As Indians were evicted, European men and women, along with African slaves, occupied the Atlantic seaboard. By 1700, the European population of the English mainland colonies approached 250,000, with an additional 33,000 settled in the West Indies. At the same time, the African population of England's American possessions was close to 150,000, of whom three-quarters lived in the Caribbean islands.

THE PLANTATION COMPLEX IN THE CARIBBEAN

As late as 1670, the most populous English colony was not on the North American mainland, but on the Caribbean island of Barbados. From the mid-seventeenth century onward, the sugarcane plantations of the Portuguese in Brazil were replicated on the English- and French-controlled islands of the Caribbean. All was not sweet in the Caribbean, however. Because no colonial power held a monopoly over the sugarcane-growing islands of the Caribbean, the competition to control the region—and to profit from the production of sugar—was especially fierce. The turbulence of the Caribbean was not simply a matter of imperial rivalry. It was also the result of the labor arrangements in the colonies. The indigenous populations of the Caribbean were decimated in Columbus's wake. Bereft of a local labor force, the owners of Caribbean estates looked to Africa to obtain workers for their plantations.

Sugar, whose cultivation employed the most slaves, was a killing crop. So deadly was the tropical environment in which sugarcane flourished—hot and humid climates were as fertile for disease as they were for tropical commodities—that many sugar barons spent little time on their plantations. Management fell to overseers who supervised crop production, and in short order they worked their slaves to death. Despite having immunities to yellow fever and malaria from being raised in a similar environment, Africans could not withstand the regimen. Poor food, atrocious living conditions, and filthy sanitation added to the miseries of life on Caribbean sugarcane plantations. Here, especially, Europeans treated their slaves as nonhumans. During the first day on the plantation, all recently bought slaves were branded with the planter's seal. In

Tobacco. The cultivation of tobacco saved the Virginia colony from ruin and brought prosperity to increasing numbers of planters. The spread of tobacco plantations also pushed Indians off their lands and led planters to turn to Africa for a labor force.

Primary Source

SILVER, THE DEVIL, AND THE COCA LEAF IN THE ANDES

When the Spanish forced thousands of Andean Indians to work in the silver mines of Potosí, they also condoned the spreading habit of chewing coca leaves (which are now used to extract cocaine). Chewing the leaves gave Indians a mild "high," alleviated their hunger, and blunted the pain of hard work and deteriorating lungs. The habit also spread to some Spaniards. In this document, Bartolomé Arzáns de Orsúa y Vela, a Spaniard born in Potosí in 1676, expresses both how important coca was to Indian miners and how pernicious it was for Spaniards who fell under its spell.

I wish to declare the unhappiness and great evil that, among so many felicities, this kingdom of Peru experiences in possessing the coca herb. . . . No Indian will go into the mines or to any other labor, be it building houses or working in the fields, without taking it in his mouth, even if his life depends on it. . . .

Among the Indians (and even the Spaniards by now) the custom of not entering the mines without placing this herb in the mouth is so well established that there is a superstition that the richness of the metal will be lost if they do not do so. . . .

The Indians being accustomed to taking this herb into their mouths, there is no doubt that as long as they have it there they lose all desire to sleep, and since it is extremely warming, they say that when the weather is cold they do not feel it if they have the herb in their mouths. In addition, they also say that it increases their strength and that they feel neither hunger nor thirst; hence these Indians cannot work without it.

When the herb is ground and placed in boiling water and if a person then takes a few swallows, it opens the pores, warms the body, and shortens labor in women; and this coca herb has many other virtues besides. But human perversity has caused it to become a vice, so that the devil (that inventor of vices) has made a notable harvest of souls with it, for there are many women who have taken it—and still take it—for the sin of witchcraft, invoking the devil and using it to summon him for their evil deeds. . . .

With such ferocity has the devil seized on this coca herb that—there is no doubt about it—when it becomes an addiction it impairs or destroys the judgment of its users just as if they had drunk wine to excess and makes them see terrible visions; demons appear before their eyes in frightful forms. In this city of Potosí it is sold publicly by the Indians who work in the mines, and so the harm arising from its continued abundance cannot be corrected; but neither is that harm remediable in other large cities of this realm, where the use and sale of coca have been banned under penalties as severe as that of excommunication and yet it is secretly bought and sold and used for casting spells and other like evils.

Would that our lord the king had ordered this noxious herb pulled up by the roots wherever it is found. . . . Great good would follow were it to be extirpated from this realm: the devil would be bereft of the great harvest of souls he reaps, God would be done a great service, and vast numbers of men and women would not perish (I refer to Spaniards, for no harm comes to the Indians from it).

→ *Why would the Spaniards ban the sale of the coca herb everywhere except Potosí?*

→ *Why would Bartolomé believe that no harm would come to the Indians for taking the coca herb?*

SOURCE: Bartolomé Arzáns de Orsúa y Vela, *Tales of Potosí*, edited by R. C. Padden and translated by Frances M. López-Morillas (Providence: Brown University Press, 1975), pp. 117–20.

---

the words of one English gentleman, slaves were like cows, "as near as beasts may be, setting their souls aside."

More than disease and inadequate rations, the work process itself decimated the enslaved. The numbers are ghoulish: average life expectancy on some sugarcane plantations in the Caribbean—no matter which European power controlled the territory—was a mere three years. Six days a week, slaves rose before dawn, labored continuously until

Slaves Cutting Cane. Sugar was the preeminent agricultural export from the New World for centuries. Owners of sugarcane plantations relied almost exclusively on African slaves to produce the sweetener. Labor in the fields was especially harsh, as slaves worked in the blistering sun from dawn until dusk. This image shows how women and men toiled side by side.

noon, ate a short lunch, and then worked until dusk. At harvest time, average days of sixteen hours saw hundreds of slaves—men, women, and children alike—doubled over to cut sugarcane and transport it to large factory-like refineries, sometimes seven days per week. Under this brutal schedule, slaves occasionally dropped dead from exhaustion in the fields. Moreover, this system of production lent itself to gang labor, depriving slaves of any control over their own work.

Amidst disease and toil, the enslaved resisted as they could. The most dramatic expression of slave resistance was violent insurrection. In the early sixteenth century, slave revolts were so frequent in Panama that the crown banned the slave trade to the region altogether. In the early seventeenth century, in parts of coastal Mexico, the viceroy had to negotiate an armistice with the slaves to pacify the region. Still, these instances of large-scale uprisings were sporadic. A more common form of resistance was flight. Thousands of slaves took to the hills to seek refuge from overseers. In the remote highlands of Caribbean islands, runaway slaves found sanctuary in "maroon" communities—named after the Spanish word *cimarron,* meaning people from the heights. But the largest of these refuge havens were in Brazil, where the vast interior sheltered communities of fugitive slaves. In the group of villages that made up Palmares, for instance, there were over 20,000 Africans in the late seventeenth century. Finally, for those who remained as slaves on the plantations, by far the most common, if least dramatic, form of resistance was the everyday pattern of foot dragging, pilfering, and sabotage, which slaves employed to soften the inhumanity of their condition.

The settlements and slaveholdings of Caribbean plantations were not restricted to any single European power. But it was the latecomers, the Dutch, the English, and especially the French, who concentrated on slave plantations in the Antilles. The English took Jamaica from the Spanish and made it the premier site of Caribbean sugar by the 1740s. When the French seized half of the island of Santo Domingo in the 1660s (renaming it Saint Domingue, which is present-day Haiti), they created one of the wealthiest societies based on slavery of all time. This single French colony's exports eclipsed those of all the Spanish and English Antilles' exports combined. The capital, Port au Prince, was one of the richest cities in the Atlantic world. The great merchants and planters of Saint Domingue, known as "big whites," built immense mansions worthy of the highest of European nobles. Thus the Atlantic system transformed the lives of elite Europeans who amassed new fortunes by exploiting the natural resources of the colonies and the labor of African slaves.

THE SLAVE TRADE AND AFRICA

> → *How did the slave trade reshape African societies and polities?*

Silver and sugar were the dominant commodities flowing from west to east across the Atlantic, and slaves filled the ships on their return. During the seventeenth and eighteenth centuries, far more Africans than Europeans crossed the Atlantic. Although the beginnings of the slave trade can be traced back to the mid-fifteenth century, only in the seventeenth and eighteenth centuries did the numbers of forced human exports from Africa begin to soar (see Map 13-4). By 1800, two slaves had crossed the Atlantic for every European. Those numbers were essential to the prosperity of Europe's American colonies. At the same time, the departure of so many inhabitants depopulated parts of Africa and destabilized many of its polities.

CAPTURING AND SHIPPING SLAVES

European slave traders grafted onto an existing system of slave commerce, much of it flowing north and east to the Red Sea and toward the Swahili coast of East Africa. From these destinations, merchants, most of them Muslim but also some Hindus, shipped slaves to ports around the Indian Ocean. Although the number of these slaves was significant, it could not match the volume destined for the Americas once extensive plantation agriculture began to spread. In the western flow, 12 million Africans survived forcible enslavement and shipment to Atlantic ports from the 1440s until 1867 (when the last ship carrying slaves reached Cuba). Far more slaves were in fact loaded onto the vessels in Africa and perished en route.

Merchant capitalists in Europe and the New World prospered as the slave trade soared, but their commercial fortunes depended on alliances with African trading and political networks. Indeed, European slavers in African ports knew little if anything about the happenings in the interior. They were not themselves involved in the lucrative capture of slaves in Africa. This was a business left to their African partners and their commercial networks, which linked money-lenders and traders on the coast with their allies in the African hinterland. In the West African Bight (bay) of Biafra, for instance, English merchants relied on traditional African practices of "pawnship," the use of human "pawns" to secure European commodities in advance of the delivery of slaves. According to the custom of the region, a secret male society called Ekpe enforced payments of promised slave deliveries. If a trader failed to deliver on his promise, his pawns (quite often members of his kin group) were sold and shipped to the Americas. By the middle of the eighteenth century, Ekpe was a powerful institution with networks stretching deep into African hinterlands and supplying the expanding slave trade in the port of Old Calabar.

The slave ports along the African coast became vast, gruesome entrepôts. Indeed, the highest rates of slave mortality occurred on the African side of the shipping, with most slaves who perished doing so before ever losing sight of Africa. Stuck in vast holding camps, where disease and hunger ravaged the captives, the slaves were then forced aboard vessels in cramped and wretched conditions. These ships waited for weeks to fill their holds while their human cargoes wasted away below deck. Dead Africans were tossed overboard as other Africans were brought from the shore. When the cargo was finally complete, the ships weighed anchor and set sail. In their wake, crews continued to dump scores of dead Africans. Annual average losses on board reached 20 percent. Most died of gastrointestinal diseases, leading to dehydration. Smallpox and dysentery were also scourges. Either way, death was slow and agonizing. Because high mortality led to

Captured Africans. (*Left*) Africans were captured in the interior and then bound and marched to the coast. Note that there is only one woman among the men (and a couple of children), reflecting the gender imbalance among those captured. (*Right*) After reaching the coast, the captured Africans would be crammed into the holds of slave vessels, where they suffered grievously from overcrowding and unsanitary conditions. Long voyages were especially deadly. If the winds failed or ships had to travel longer distances than usual, many of the captives would die en route to the slave markets across the ocean.

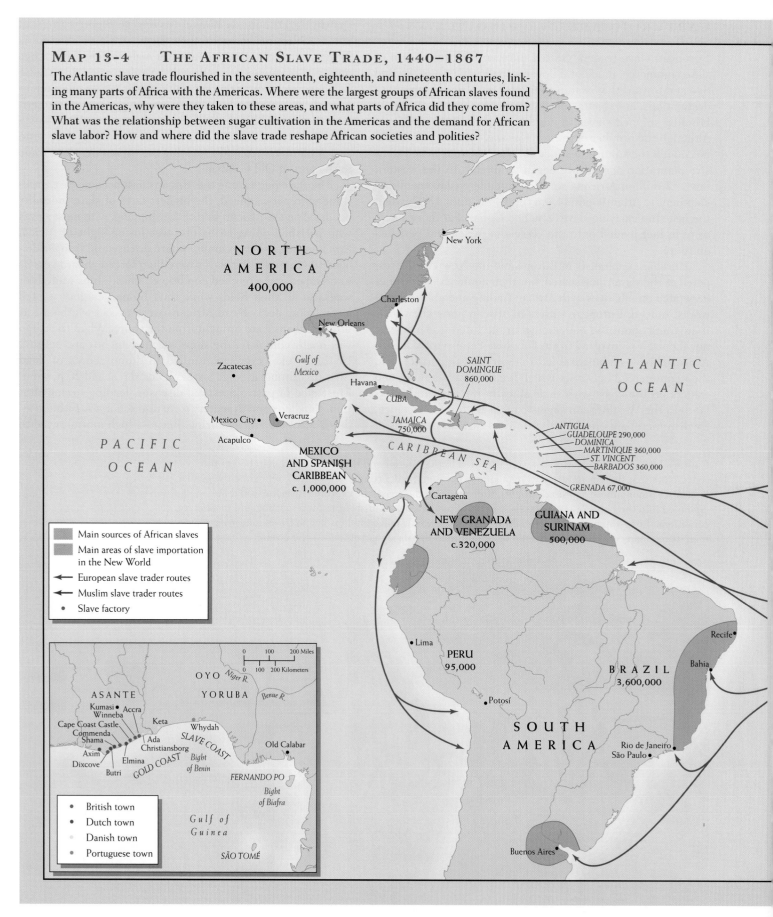

MAP 13-4   THE AFRICAN SLAVE TRADE, 1440–1867

The Atlantic slave trade flourished in the seventeenth, eighteenth, and nineteenth centuries, linking many parts of Africa with the Americas. Where were the largest groups of African slaves found in the Americas, why were they taken to these areas, and what parts of Africa did they come from? What was the relationship between sugar cultivation in the Americas and the demand for African slave labor? How and where did the slave trade reshape African societies and polities?

NORTH AMERICA 400,000

PACIFIC OCEAN

ATLANTIC OCEAN

New York

Charleston

New Orleans

Gulf of Mexico

Zacatecas

Havana

CUBA

SAINT DOMINGUE 860,000

Mexico City   Veracruz

JAMAICA 750,000

Acapulco

MEXICO AND SPANISH CARIBBEAN c. 1,000,000

ANTIGUA
GUADELOUPE 290,000
DOMINICA
MARTINIQUE 360,000
ST. VINCENT
BARBADOS 360,000

GRENADA 67,000

CARIBBEAN SEA

Cartagena

NEW GRANADA AND VENEZUELA c.320,000

GUIANA AND SURINAM 500,000

Lima

PERU 95,000

Potosí

Recife

BRAZIL 3,600,000

Bahia

SOUTH AMERICA

Rio de Janeiro
São Paulo

Buenos Aires

Legend:
- Main sources of African slaves
- Main areas of slave importation in the New World
- ← European slave trader routes
- ← Muslim slave trader routes
- • Slave factory

OYO

Niger R.

YORUBA

Benue R.

ASANTE

Kumasi • Accra
Winneba
Cape Coast Castle   Keta   Whydah
Commenda
Shama   Ada   SLAVE COAST   Old Calabar
Axim   Christiansborg   Bight of Benin
Dixcove   Elmina   GOLD COAST
Butri

FERNANDO PO

Bight of Biafra

Gulf of Guinea

SÃO TOMÉ

0   100   200 Miles
0   100   200 Kilometers

- • British town
- • Dutch town
- • Danish town
- • Portuguese town

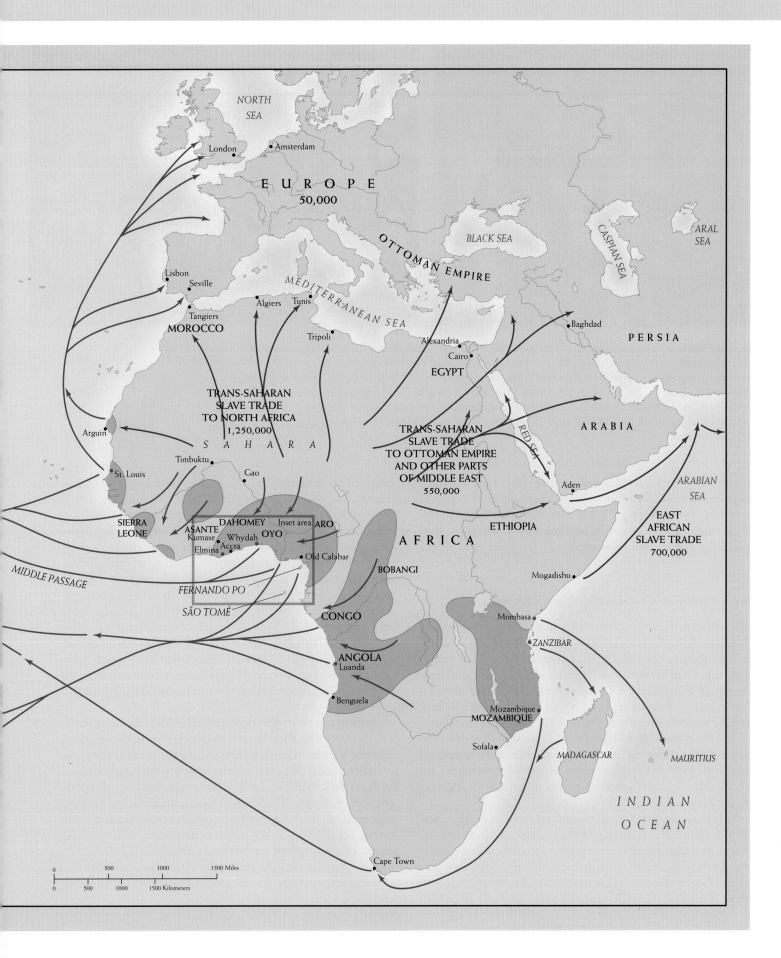

NORTH SEA

London • Amsterdam

EUROPE
50,000

BLACK SEA

CASPIAN SEA

ARAL SEA

OTTOMAN EMPIRE

Lisbon
Seville

MEDITERRANEAN SEA

Algiers • Tunis

Tangiers

MOROCCO

Tripoli

Alexandria

Cairo •

EGYPT

• Baghdad

PERSIA

TRANS-SAHARAN
SLAVE TRADE
TO NORTH AFRICA
1,250,000

SAHARA

Arguin •

TRANS-SAHARAN
SLAVE TRADE
TO OTTOMAN EMPIRE
AND OTHER PARTS
OF MIDDLE EAST
550,000

RED SEA

ARABIA

St. Louis

Timbuktu •

Gao •

Aden •

ARABIAN SEA

SIERRA
LEONE

DAHOMEY

ASANTE
Kumase
Elmina • Accra
Whydah

Inset area

OYO

ARO

Old Calabar

AFRICA

ETHIOPIA

EAST
AFRICAN
SLAVE TRADE
700,000

MIDDLE PASSAGE

FERNANDO PO

SÃO TOMÉ

BOBANGI

CONGO

Mogadishu •

Mombasa •

• ZANZIBAR

ANGOLA
Luanda •

Benguela •

Mozambique •
MOZAMBIQUE

Sofala •

MADAGASCAR

MAURITIUS

INDIAN
OCEAN

Cape Town •

0   500   1000   1500 Miles
0   500   1000   1500 Kilometers

African Trade with Europeans. (*Left*) People living along the Congo coast engaged in vigorous trade with European merchants. Portuguese slave traders are depicted on this late-sixteenth- or early-seventeenth-century plaque that decorated the doors of the Obas, or Kings, of Benin, one of the West African kingdoms deeply involved in the Atlantic slave trade. (*Right*) The kings and other high-ranking individuals in the Kongo kingdom in central Africa embraced Christianity as a result of their contacts with European traders. Here King Alvaro II, an active slave trader, is receiving a deputation of Dutch officials in 1642.

losses of profits, slavers learned to carry better food and more supplies of fresh water as the trade became more sophisticated in the eighteenth century. Mortality rates began to dip. Still, when slave ships finally reached New World ports, they reeked of disease and excrement.

SLAVERY'S GENDER IMBALANCE

The Atlantic slave trade not only moved vast numbers of Africans to the Americas; it also played havoc with sex ratios in both places. Most of the Atlantic slaves were adult men—only one-third were women and 10 percent were children. Although this reflected European preferences for male laborers, it also was the result of African slavers' desire to keep female slaves, primarily for household work. The imbalance of sex ratios made it difficult for slaves to reproduce in most places in the Americas. Accordingly, planters and slavers had to return to Africa to procure more captives, especially for the Caribbean sugar-growing islands, where the death rates of slaves were high.

Male slaves greatly outnumbered females in the New World, but in the slave-supplying regions of Africa the opposite was true—women outnumbered males in substantial numbers. African dynasties converted long-established patterns of domestic slavery (described in Chapter 10) into vast slave plantations; female captives were especially prized be-

cause of their traditional role in the production of grains, leather, and cotton. In this era Africa's female slaves served as cultivators and artisans and were more important contributors to the economy than they were on the male-dominated slave plantations in the Americas. The slave trade also reinforced the traditional practice of polygyny—allowing relatively scarce men to take several wives. But in some states, most notably the powerful slave-supplying kingdom of Dahomey on the West African coast, women were able to assert their power because of their large numbers and their heightened importance. Dahomean women became deeply involved in succession disputes, which were often violent and bloody. The intrigues of dynamic women made the difference between winning and losing political power.

Within the court the most powerful and wealthy woman was the queen mother, known as the *kpojito*. Each new ruler selected his queen mother from among the wives of his predecessors, though it is not known whether she was his actual birth mother. Because she was believed to have special powers of divination and to be in close communication with the supernatural, the King and his courtiers sought out her views before making important political decisions. The most dynamic of these queen mothers was Hwanjile (1740–1797), who was instrumental in placing king Tegbasa on the throne. Queen mothers were so influential that in reality the king and the kpojito were joint rulers.

AFRICA'S NEW SLAVE-SUPPLYING POLITIES

Africa's participation in the world economy through the slave trade profoundly reshaped its political and social structures. Africans did not stand on the sidelines, passively letting captives fall into the arms of European slave buyers. Instead, African political leaders and merchants played an active role in supplying slaves for transatlantic shipment. Their participation in the Atlantic slave trade contributed to the growth of centralized polities, particularly in the rain forest areas of West Africa. The trade also shifted control of wealth away from households that commanded large animal herds or land to those who profited from the capture and exchange of slaves—urban merchants and warrior elites. In Luanda and Benguela (in present-day Angola), where the Portuguese had established slave trading centers in 1575, African merchants erected impressive homes to emulate fashions in Lisbon.

In some parts of Africa, the booming slave trade wreaked only havoc. To get their share of the spoils, African leaders feuded over control of the traffic. In the Kongo kingdom, civil wars raged for over a century after 1665, and captured war-riors were sold as slaves. As members of the kingdom's royal family fought one another, entire provinces saw their populations vanish. Most important to the conduct of war and the control of trade were firearms and gunpowder. With this weaponry, capturing slaves became a highly efficient enterprise. Large numbers were also kidnapped. So prevalent was kidnapping in certain forest areas and among some of the stateless people that cultivators went out to their fields bearing weapons, leaving their children and wards behind in guarded stockades.

Some leaders of the kingdom of Kongo fought back against the ravages of the slave trade. The most impressive resister was Queen Nzinga (1583–1663), who was a masterful diplomat and a shrewd military planner. Converted to Christianity early in her life, she was able to keep the Portuguese slavers at bay during her long reign. Even after the Portuguese forces defeated her troops in open battle, she conducted effective guerrilla warfare, leading her troops in the field even into her sixties.

An equally powerful response to the political instability of the age was the Christian visionary Dona Beatriz Kimpa Vita, who was born in the Kingdom of Kongo in 1684 and

The Port of Loango. Partly as a result of the profits of the slave trade, African rulers and merchants were able to create large and prosperous port cities such as Loango, pictured here, which was on the west coast of south-central Africa.

baptized as a Christian. She experienced religious visions in her youth and in 1704, at the age of twenty, claimed to have received visions from St. Anthony of Padua, who then entered and took over her body. She believed that she died every Friday and was transported to heaven to converse with God, returning to earth on Monday to broadcast God's commands to the believers. Her message was directed to ending the Kongo civil wars and recreating a unified kingdom. Although she gained a large following, she failed to win the support of any of the leading political figures. In 1706 she was captured and burned at the stake.

As some African merchants and warlords became active vendors of other Africans, their commercial windfall enabled them to consolidate their political power. Through the taking and trading of slaves, West African kingdoms like the Oyo Empire in present-day Nigeria and the Asante state in present-day Ghana, as well as wealthy mercantile groups like the Aro peoples in southeastern Nigeria and the Bobangi canoemen in the Central Congo River, grew wealthy. That wealth enabled them to purchase additional weapons, with which they subdued their neighbors and extended their political control.

Among the most durable of the new polities was the Asante state, which arose in the West African tropical rain forest in 1701 and expanded through 1750. This state grew in power because of its access to gold, which its Akan speakers used to acquire firearms from European traders. They employed their arms to raid nearby communities for servile workers. At first, different village groups competed with one another for pre-eminence, but at the beginning of the eighteenth century, the Asante triumphed over their rivals. From its capital city at Kumasi, the state eventually encompassed almost the whole of present-day Ghana, an area of 250,000 square miles. A network of main roads spread out from the capital like spokes of a wheel, each of which was approximately twenty days' travel from the center. The empire thus acquired territorial definition, even clear boundary lines, which were established through the commonsense notion that the state could control territories within twenty days' march from the capital, but no more. Through the Asante trading networks, African traders bought, bartered, and sold slaves, who eventually wound up in the hands of European merchants waiting in coastal ports with vessels loaded with manufactures and weaponry.

Another regime that was active in the organization of the slave trade and enriched by it was the Yoruba-speaking Oyo Empire. The Oyo territory, which was strategically located astride the main trade routes, enjoyed easy transportation that linked tropical rain forests with interior markets of the savannah areas to the north. The king of the Oyo, called the *Alafin,* was in theory an absolute ruler, but he needed the support of powerful Yoruba families to remain in power. These families deposed or endorsed *Alafins* at will, which often led to turmoil during times of succession. The strength of the empire rested on its ability to field an impressive army bristling with weaponry secured from trade with Europeans. Straddling the boundary between the savannah and the rain forest, the Oyo used cavalry units in the savannah and infantry units in the rain forest. Military campaigns became annual incursions, only suspended so that the warriors could return for their agricultural duties. Every dry season, Oyo armies marched on their neighbors to capture entire villages.

African slavery and the emergence of new political organizations enriched and empowered some Africans, but they cost Africa dearly. For the princes, warriors, and merchants who organized the trade in Africa, their business, not unlike that of Amerindian fur suppliers, enabled them to obtain European goods, especially alcohol, tobacco, textiles, and guns. The Atlantic commercial system also tilted wealth away from rural dwellers and village elders and increasingly toward the port cities that handled the traffic in and out of Africa. Across the landmass, the slave trade thinned the population. True, Africa was spared a demographic catastrophe equal to the devastation of American Indians. The introduction of new American food crops, notably maize and cassava, capable of producing many more calories per acre than the old staples of millet and sorghum, blunted the depopulating aspects of the trade. Yet, some areas, such as Angola, suffered grievously. Three centuries of heavy involvement in the slave trade caused depopulation and disintegration in West Africa. The Atlantic slave trade enhanced the power of the warrior class, who were the vital element in carrying out raids for captives to be shipped to the Americas; the dislocations, internal power struggles, and economic hardships that followed precipitated the rise and fall of West African kingdoms.

> *Three centuries of heavy involvement in the slave trade caused depopulation and disintegration in West Africa.*

ASIA IN THE SEVENTEENTH AND EIGHTEENTH CENTURIES

> → *How did global trade affect the Asian dynasties?*

Long-distance trading networks blossomed as vigorously in Asia as they did in the Americas. In Asia, however, the Europeans were less dominant. With American silver, Europeans could open Asian markets, but they could not conquer powerful Asian empires or colonize vast portions of the region. Nor were Europeans able to enslave Asian peoples as they were enslaving Africans. The Mughals continued to expand their empire, and the Qing dynasty, which had wrested control of China from the Ming dynasty, initiated a vast expansion of the empire's borders. China remained the richest state in the world at the time. But in some places, the balance of power had begun to tilt in Europe's direction. The Ottomans experienced a contraction of their borders. Even more reflective of the tilt, by the end of the eighteenth century, Europeans had established economic and military dominance in parts of India and much of Southeast Asia.

THE DUTCH IN SOUTHEAST ASIA

In Southeast Asia the Dutch already enjoyed a dominant position by the seventeenth century. Although the Portuguese had seized the vibrant port city of Melaka in 1511 and the Spaniards had taken Manila in 1571, neither was able to monopolize the lucrative spice trade. To challenge the Portuguese and the Spaniards, the Dutch government took the initiative in persuading its merchants to charter the Dutch East India Company (abbreviated as VOC) in 1602. Making full use of Amsterdam's position as the most efficient money market with the lowest interest rates in the world, the VOC raised ten times the capital of its English counterpart—the royal chartered English East India Company, established two years earlier. The advantages of chartered companies could be seen in the VOC's scale of operation. At its peak in the 1660s, the company had 257 ships and employed 12,000 persons. In the two centuries of its existence, it sent ships manned by a

total of one million men to Asia, although the toll of the Asian trade was such that only a third of them ever returned to Europe.

Much of the impact of the VOC was felt in Southeast Asia, where spices, coffee, tea, and teak were grown and exported. The objective of the VOC was to secure a monopoly in trade wherever it could, to fix prices, and to replace the native population with Dutch planters. In 1619, under the militant leadership of Jan Pieterszoon Coen, who once said that trade could not be conducted without war nor war without trade, the Dutch swept into the Javanese port of Jakarta (renamed Batavia by the Dutch). In defiance of local rulers and English rivals, the Dutch burned all the houses, drove out the population, and proceeded to construct a fortress from which the VOC could control the Southeast Asian trade. Two years later, Coen and his fleet of twelve ships took over a cluster of five small nutmeg-producing islands known collectively as Banda. The traditional chiefs and almost the entire population of the islands, some 15,000 people, were killed outright, left to starve in isolation, or otherwise taken into slavery in Jakarta. Dutch planters and their slaves replaced the decimated local population and sent their produce to the VOC. The motive for such rapacious action was the huge profits that could be made by buying nutmeg at a small price in the Bandanese Islands and selling it at many times that price in Europe.

With their monopoly of nutmeg secured, the Dutch went after the market in cloves. The VOC's strategy was to control the clove-growing in one region and then destroy the rest, which entailed, once again, wars against both producers and traders in other areas. Portuguese Melaka fell to the Dutch in 1641 and became an outpost of the VOC. Resistance to

Batavia. At the beginning of the seventeenth century, Dutch traders established a base at the Javanese coastal settlement of Jakarta, which became Batavia, the capital of a Dutch Asian empire. The Batavian fortress projected Dutch power, as did the numerous warehouses for shipping the many riches coveted by Europeans.

Attack on Bantam. This engraving depicts a Dutch attack on Bantam in the late seventeenth century as part of the VOC's effort to expand its empire in Southeast Asia.

this aggressive Dutch expansion was widespread among the local population, as well as among Muslim, Chinese, and other European merchants involved in the Southeast Asian trade. Nevertheless, with a combination of ruthlessness and ability in taking advantage of local political divisions, the Dutch had the whole of the lucrative Moluccan spice trade in their hands by 1670.

Next, the VOC set its sights on another of the important spices of Southeast Asia, pepper, which was a rather more difficult target to monopolize because its trade was scattered across a dozen major and minor ports. In this gambit, the VOC gained control of Bantam (present-day Banten), the largest pepper-exporting port, but the Dutch could not fully reserve the commerce in this spice to themselves. Chinese and English merchants continued to be competitors. Moreover, since there was virtually no demand for European products in Asia, the Dutch were forced to become more involved in inter-Asian trade as a way to reduce their payments in bullion. They purchased, for example, calicoes in India or copper in Japan for resale in Melaka and Java. They also diversified their trade to include silk, cotton, tea, and coffee, in addition to spices.

One of the significant side effects of the Dutch enterprise, however, was reducing old cosmopolitan cities such as Bantam, which had once served as centers of political power, economic life, and cultural creativity in Southeast Asia, to a subsidiary position eclipsed by newer European outposts such as Dutch Batavia or Spanish Manila. As Europeans penetrated and competed for supremacy in the borderlands of Southeast Asia, they harnessed local societies to their commercial ambitions and began replacing traditional Afro-Eurasian networks with Europe-serving trade routes.

TRANSFORMATIONS IN ISLAM

Compared with Southeast Asia, the Islamic empires were as yet not so directly affected by European intrusion. The Islamic empires did, however, face a variety of internal difficulties. While the Ottoman and Mughal empires continued to demonstrate resilience, the Safavid Empire by the mid-eighteenth century had entered a period of chaos.

THE SAFAVID EMPIRE Challenged by neighboring powers, the Safavid Empire had always depended on a powerful, religiously inspired ruler, like the founding figure, Shah Ismail, and his most noteworthy successor, Abbas I. When such a figure was not present to enforce Shiite religious orthodoxy and to hold together the tribal, pastoral, mercantile, and agricultural factions, the state foundered. A series of weak successors to Abbas left the state in a chaotic condition. By 1722, it was under assault from within and without. Afghan clansmen, who had never been subdued by imperial armies, invaded Safavid territory. They overran the inept and divided armies and besieged Isfahan, the Safavid capital. The city's inhabitants began to perish from hunger and disease. Some survivors ate the corpses of the deceased. Finally the shah abdicated. The invading Afghan fighters executed thousands of Safavid officials and members of the royal household. The empire limped along until 1773, when a revolt toppled the last puppet ruler from the throne.

THE OTTOMAN EMPIRE The threat to the Ottomans was not as great as the threat to the Safavids, but having attained a high point in the reign of Suleiman (ruled 1520–1566), the Ottoman Empire, too, entered a period of perceived decline. Some of the Ottoman Empire's subsequent difficulties stemmed from its successes. After Suleiman's reign, Ottoman armies and navies continued to try to expand the empire's borders but were defeated. On the empire's western flank, the European Habsburgs finally reversed Ottoman military expansion. Financing military campaigns strained the realm's limited resources, as did the needs of a growing population. Already at the end of the sixteenth century, Ottoman intellectuals were concerned that the empire's glory was ebbing, comparing the military triumphs and political expansion of early sultans to the difficulties of later rulers. During the seventeenth century, the sense of decline became a preoccupation of the Ottoman elite, whose essays were increasingly devoted to identifying causes of this supposed decline and proposing remedies for it.

A series of unimpressive successors to Suleiman allowed the Ottoman Empire's strength to wane. Suleiman the Great, for example, passed the crown to Selim, whom his detractors dubbed the Sot (ruled 1566–1574). He was succeeded by a string of incompetent sultans. Indeed, of the nine individuals who became sultans in the 1600s, only three were both adults and sane when they ascended to the throne. Such were the weaknesses of monarchy.

Competent or not, seventeenth-century sultans confronted the problems of a commercially more connected world. As silver flowed from the mines of Mesoamerica and the Andes, it entered Ottoman networks of commerce and money lending and eventually destabilized the empire. The early Ottoman rulers had endeavored to create an autonomous economy that did not depend for its well-being on trade with the outside world. The lure of silver broke through state regulations, however, drawing commodities like wheat, copper, wool, and other items in demand in Europe away from Ottoman areas. Merchants sidestepped imperial regulations by establishing black markets for commodities that were paid for in silver. Because these goods were illegally exported, their sale did not generate tax revenues, which led to a shortfall in money to pay administrative and military expenses. Ottoman rulers were then forced to rely on merchant loans of silver to sustain their civilian and especially military administration. Financial dependency meant that rulers could ill afford to impose their own official rules on those who bankrolled them.

More silver and budget deficits were a recipe for inflation. Indeed, prices doubled between 1550 and 1600 and then tripled in the first half of the seventeenth century. The surge in the price of goods hit the artisans and peasants living in Anatolia especially hard. Fed up with high food prices and shortages —and increasing taxes to pay off dynastic debts—they joined together in a series of popular uprisings, called the Celali revolts, which threatened the stability of the Ottoman state between 1595 and 1610. By the time of Sultan Ibrahim's reign (1640–1648), the cycle of spending, taxing, borrowing, and inflation was so bad that his own officials toppled and murdered him.

The Ottoman Empire also faced growing pressures for commercial and political autonomy from its outlying regions.

In 1517, Egypt became the Ottoman state's greatest conquest. As the wealthiest of the Ottoman territories, it was an imperial plum for any administrator. Egypt was also a great source of revenue, and its people shouldered heavy tax burdens. Moreover, trading routes continued to run through Egypt, and as commerce grew, many merchants began to resent Ottoman control. By the seventeenth century, the Ottoman administrator of Egypt had become a mere figurehead, funneling increasingly limited revenues to Istanbul but unable to control the military groups around him. When the sultan dispatched slaves who had converted to Islam from the Caucasus to extend military and administrative rule over Egypt, the newcomers forged alliances with Egyptian merchants and catered to the Egyptian *ulama*. These military groups were known as *Mamluks*. They were taken as youths from their Christian families in the Caucasus and brought to Egypt, where they converted to Islam and learned military and administrative skills. As a new provincial ruling elite, these men kept much of the fiscal wealth for themselves, at the expense not only of imperial coffers but also of the local peasantry.

Yet, there was great resilience in the Ottoman system. Decaying leadership provoked demands for reform from administrative elites. Toward the end of the seventeenth century, the Koprulu family took control of the powerful office of

Kara Mustafa Pasha. Kara Mustafa was a reformist-minded grand vizier of the Ottoman Empire. He led the second Turkish siege of Vienna in 1683.

grand vizier and spearheaded changes to revitalize the empire. Mehmed Koprulu, the first of the family to assume office, had been born into an obscure Albanian family. Taken as a slave in the *devshirme* (see Chapter 11), he slowly made his way up the bureaucratic ladder until he became grand vizier when he was eighty years old, in 1656. Pragmatic and incorruptible, Mehmed not only rooted out his venal peers but also balanced the budget and reversed the misfortunes of the Ottoman armies. His death in 1661 did not halt the reforms, for Mehmed had groomed his son, Fazil Ahmed Koprulu, to continue them. Indeed, Fazil Ahmed was, if anything, more successful than his father. Better educated and even more shrewd, the young grand vizier continued trimming the administration and strengthening the Ottoman armies until he died after fifteen years in charge.

Known as the "Koprulu reforms," the changes in public administration gave the state a new burst of energy and enabled the military to reacquire some of its lost possessions. Thanks to these reforms, revenues again began to rise and inflation abated, reviving expansionist ambitions. Emboldened by its new energy, Istanbul decided to renew its assault on Christianity. Fazil Ahmed's brother-in-law, Kara Mustafa Pasha, rekindled old plans to seize Vienna. Outside the Habsburg capital, the Ottomans gathered between 200,000 and 500,000 soldiers in July 1683. An all-out attack on September 12, 1683, inflicted heavy losses on both sides, after which

Kara Mustafa withdrew his forces, intending to renew his assault in the spring. The sultan, however, worried about disgracing the realm, ordered his followers to have Kara Mustafa strangled. Thereafter, the Ottomans halted their military advance, never again threatening Vienna. With the end of conquest, the Ottomans were deprived of the booty that had been theirs after taking over new regions. Worse still, the Treaty of Carlowitz (1699), the result of an Ottoman military defeat following the Austro-Ottoman war of 1683–1697, resulted in the Ottoman Empire's loss of major European territorial possessions, including Hungary, prompting further soul-searching for the causes of the empire's decline.

THE MUGHAL EMPIRE In contrast to the Ottoman Empire's territorial setbacks, the Mughal Empire reached its height in the 1600s. By the end of the seventeenth century, Mughal rulers had extended their domain over almost all of India, and the Mughal Empire prospered from an increase in domestic and international trade. But as they expanded their empire, the Mughals eventually also faced the difficulties of governing dispersed and not always loyal provinces. Indeed, though nominally in control of wide areas, the Mughals had a limited impact on many villages, whose inhabitants retained their own religions and cultures.

Before the Mughals, India had never had a single political authority. Akbar conquered much territory, but expansion

Siege of Vienna. This seventeenth-century painting depicts the Turkish siege of Vienna, which began on July 14, 1683, and ended on September 12. The city might have fallen if the Polish king, John III, had not answered the pope's plea to defend Christendom and sent an army to assist German and Austrian troops in defeating the Turks.

did not stop after his death in 1605. Throughout the seventeenth century, Akbar's successors continued expanding the empire and extending administrative control over conquered territories (see Map 12-5, p. 544). With the north of India already under their jurisdiction, the Mughals turned to the south. Though the advances were slow and frustrating, the Mughals controlled most of the region by 1689. The new, outlying provinces of the empire provided the state with resources and local lords, warriors, and tributary chiefs, and the Mughal bureaucracy grew ever better at extracting services as well as taxes from the diverse inhabitants of this empire.

Mughal stability and prosperity did not depend on the revival and flourishing of the Indian Ocean trading system. Indeed, the Mughals showed little interest in becoming a naval power; they were willing to profit from seaborne trade, but they never undertook overseas expansion. The main source of their wealth remained land rents, which were increasing thanks to incentives offered to those who brought new land into cultivation; on these new farms peasants planted, in part, New World crops like maize and tobacco. But the empire's economy also benefited from the growing demand for Indian goods and services by Europeans. For example, the English East India Company's purchase of textiles rose from 4.2 million square meters in 1664 to 26.9 million square meters in 1684. Similar trends existed in the Dutch trade with India. As specie flowed in from Japan and the New World to finance this growing trade, the imperial mint struck increasing numbers of silver coins, which in turn contributed to the growth of trade and the use of specie as a medium of exchange.

To a considerable extent, the Mughals were victims of their own success. More than a century of imperial expansion, commercial prosperity, and agricultural development placed an increasing amount of resources in the hands of local and regional magnates. Using these resources, powerful local warrior elites, always looking for opportunities to evade imperial demands, became increasingly autonomous. By the late seventeenth century, many of these regional leaders were well positioned to resist Mughal authority.

As in the Ottoman Empire, then, distant provinces began to challenge central rulers. Under Aurangzeb (ruled 1658–1707), the Mughals had pushed the political frontier of the empire deep into southern India. There, however, the Mughals encountered fierce opposition from the powerful Marathas in the northwestern Deccan plateau. The military effort cost the imperial treasury a small fortune and pinned down Mughal armies. To finance these expansionist operations, Aurangzeb raised taxes on the empire's peasants. Resentment and alienation spread through the population, and even the Mughal elite grew restive at the continuing drain on imperial finances. In an effort to win the support of the orthodox *ulama,* the monarch abandoned the toleration of heterodoxy and of non-Muslims practiced by his predecessors. But ultimately only the strong hand of Aurangzeb kept order in the empire.

Indian Cotton. European traders were drawn to India by its famed cotton textiles. This image from c. 1800 shows a woman separating the cotton from the seeds; it captures the preindustrial technology of cotton production in India.

When Aurangzeb died in 1707, a war of succession broke out almost immediately. The revenue system eroded as local tax collectors kept more of the returns for themselves. Prosperous and powerful local elites used their growing fiscal autonomy to rally military forces of their own, annexing neighboring lands to their fiefdoms and chipping away at imperial authority.

Indian peasants, like their counterparts in Ming China, Safavid Persia, and the Ottoman Empire, capitalized on the breakdown in central authority to assert their independence from state authority. Many rose in rebellions; others took up banditry. Bonds of caste and religion were critical in the revolt of the Jat peasant caste in northern India in the late seventeenth century. Refusing to pay taxes, the Jat people killed a Mughal official and then seized lands and plundered the region. A half century later, peasant cultivators of the Punjab in northern India turned their closely knit community into a military power that was able to keep the Mughal forces off balance. Peasants were also critical in the rise of the Marathas of western India, whose charismatic leader, Shivaji (1627–1680), used the peasantry's hatred of imperial oppression to mount fierce resistance to Mughal hegemony.

The Mughal emperors had to reconcile themselves to their diminished power. The empire now existed as a loose

Aurangzeb. The last powerful Mughal emperor, Aurangzeb continued the conquest of the Indian subcontinent. Pictured in his old age, he is shown here with his courtiers.

The Mughals themselves paid scant attention to commercial matters, but local potentates, recognizing the benefits of exchange with foreign traders, encouraged the Europeans to establish posts at Indian ports. As more and more European ships arrived in Indian harbors, provincial magnates struck special deals with rival merchants from Portugal and increasingly from England and Holland. Some Indian merchants created trading companies of their own to control the sale of regional produce to competing Europeans; others set up vast trading networks that reached as far north as Russia, straddling west and east between Iraq and the South China Sea.

One of these companies was the house of Jagat Seths in eastern India. The Jagat Seths built a huge trading and banking empire, involving extensive shipments of Bengal cloth and commercial relations with Asian and European merchants. Increasingly, however, a large part of their business in the provinces of Bengal and Bihar was tax-farming, whereby the Jagat Seths took responsibility for collecting taxes for the imperial coffers. The Jagat Seths maintained their own retinue of agents to gather levies from farmers, while pocketing substantial profits for themselves. Thus did mercantile houses grow ever richer and gain greater political influence over financially strapped emperors. As a result, local economic and social prosperity undercut the Mughal dynasty.

FROM MING TO QING IN CHINA

China prospered enormously during the Ming period, but prosperity also led to a splintering of central control. As in Mughal India, local power holders in China often defied the authority of the Ming central government. Because Ming sovereigns turned inward and away from the possibilities of overseas commerce, forbidding the Chinese to travel abroad and prohibiting coastal shipping, the emperors did not reap the rewards of long-distance exchange. Rather, most of the profits went to traders and adventurers who successfully evaded imperial edicts. Together, the persistence of local autonomy and the challenge of defiant merchants weakened imperial structures until finally, in 1644, the Ming dynasty collapsed.

ADMINISTRATIVE PROBLEMS   How did a dynasty that in the early seventeenth century governed perhaps a third of the world's population and was the most economically advanced society fall from power? As in the Ottoman Empire, bad rulers played a big role. Take, for example, the disastrous reign of Zhu Yijun, the Wanli Emperor (ruled 1573–1620). Reputedly a precocious young boy, Wanli ascended to the throne at age nine. Like his predecessors, he grew up within the confines of the Forbidden City (see Chapter 11). The emperor was secluded despite being surrounded by a staff of 20,000 eunuchs and 3,000 women. The "Son of Heaven"

unity of provincial "successor states." While the Marathas based in Poona and the Sikhs in the Punjab stood outside the imperial system, the successor states of Bengal, Awadh, and Hyderabad accepted Mughal paramountcy in name only. They administered semiautonomous regimes based on their access to local economic, political, and cultural resources.

Although local elites hollowed out the structure of the empire, India still flourished. Imperial expansion and the rising power of landed elites brought new territories into agrarian production. Cotton, for instance, became a major staple crop to supply a thriving textile industry. In many parts of India, peasant households complemented agrarian production with weaving and artisanal cloth production. Much of this industry was destined for export as the region deepened its integration into world trading systems.

rarely ventured outside the palace compound in Ming times, and when he moved within it he was accompanied by a large retinue led by eunuchs clearing his path with whips. His day was filled with state functions, during which he had to change clothes to suit each occasion—including formal headgear with uncomfortable, curtain-like beads that forced the emperor to move solemnly and deliberately.

Ming emperors like Wanli quickly found out that while all the elaborate arrangements and ritual performances affirmed their position as the Son of Heaven, the rulers actually exercised little direct control over the vast bureaucracy. An emperor frustrated with his officials could do little more than punish them or refuse to cooperate. Unable to change or reshape the Ming administration, Wanli avoided any involvement with the administration of the realm, to the point that he refused to meet with his officials or preside over routine state ritual performances. A mountain of reports and petitions piled up in his study unattended, while some of his bureaucrats took advantage of his neglect to accumulate private wealth. During his long reign, Wanli's major claim to fame was his reputation for degrading the image of a wise and just emperor.

ECONOMIC PROBLEMS   The timing of administrative breakdown in the Ming government was unfortunate. Expanding trade induced many to circumvent official regulations. From the mid-sixteenth century, bands of supposedly Japanese pirates, or *wokou*, ravaged the Chinese coast. Indeed, the Ming government had great difficulties regulating its official trade relations with Japan. Japanese missions, often armed and several hundred people strong, raided and looted Chinese coastal villages. Yet, while Ming officials labeled all pirates as Japanese, most of the *wokou* were in fact Chinese subjects.

Operating out of coastal towns of the empire, as well as from Japanese and Southeast Asian ports, these maritime adventurers deeply disturbed Ming authorities. In tough times, pirates became roving gangs, terrorizing sea lanes and harbors. In better times, some of them functioned much like mercantile groups; their leaders often mingled with gentry elites, foreign trade representatives, and imperial officials. What made these commercial predators so resilient—and their business so lucrative—was their ability to move among the mosaic of East Asian cultures.

The Chinese economy was further stimulated and commercialized by the influx of silver from the New World and from Japan. As noted in Chapter 12, Europeans used New World silver to pay for their purchases of Chinese goods. During the second half of the sixteenth century, silver imports contributed at least eight times more bullion to China's domestic stock of money; in the first half of the seventeenth century, silver imports exceeded domestic bullion production by some twentyfold. Increasing monetization of the economy bolstered market activity and state revenues at the same time.

As silver became the primary medium of exchange in the Chinese economy, peasants came under pressure to convert the copper coins that circulated widely in the local economy into silver. With this silver, they could pay off their taxes and purchase locally traded goods. But the need to acquire silver created hardships for the peasants. When silver supplies were abundant, peasants had to deal with price inflation. When silver supplies were interrupted, peasants faced problems discharging their obligations to state officials and merchants. Peasants thus often seethed with resentment, which quickly turned to rebellion.

Market fluctuations in trading centers as far off as Mexico now also affected the Chinese economy, introducing new sources of unpredictability and instability. After 1610, Dutch and English assaults on Spanish ships headed to Asia cut down silver flows into China. Then, in 1639, Japanese authorities clamped down on foreign traders, thereby curbing the outflow of Japanese specie to China. All these blows to the Asian trading system destabilized the supply of money in China and contributed to a downturn in the Chinese economy in the 1630s and 1640s.

THE COLLAPSE OF MING AUTHORITY   By the seventeenth century, the administrative and economic difficulties of the Ming government had a visibly negative impact on the daily lives of its subjects. This became particularly evident when the regime failed to cope with the devastation caused by natural disasters in outlying regions such as the northwestern province of Shaanxi, once a center of the Chinese state and home to the capital (Chang'an) of earlier dynasties. By the late Ming, however, it had become a troubled province. Its once fertile soil lagged behind in productivity, and the center of economic activities and agrarian production gradually shifted over the centuries to the more hospitable environment and climatic conditions of the south. The decline of the region had been long in coming, but in the late 1620s the area was particularly hard hit by adverse weather conditions, resulting in protracted drought and a series of crop failures. Administrative and fiscal incompetence as well as failures to address the problems contributed to the crisis. The price of grain soared, and without relief from the government, the poor and the hungry fanned out to find food by whatever means they could muster. Officials wrote of abandoned babies and noted signs of cannibalism. Meanwhile, the financial problems of the government led to additional tax levies and cutbacks in the military budgets. A large contingent of young, mobile, and able-bodied males, including mutinous soldiers and demobilized government couriers, swelled the ranks of the desperate and the discontented. Many of them were instrumental in organizing the multitude of uprooted peasants into rebels, turning the late Ming world upside down in the process.

After 1600, increasingly large bands of dispossessed and marginalized peasants vented their anger at local tax collectors.

Primary Source

HUANG LIUHONG ON ELIMINATING AUTHORIZED SILVERSMITHS

The influx of silver into China had profound effects on its economy and government. In the seventeenth century, silver, for instance, gradually became the medium through which taxes were assessed. In his magistrate's manual from around 1694, Huang Liuhong (Huang Liu-hung) indicated the problems and abuses posed by the use of authorized silversmiths in the payment process, demonstrating clearly how silver had become an integral part of the lives of the Chinese people.

The purpose of using an authorized silversmith in the collection of tax money is twofold. First, the quality of the silver delivered by the taxpayers must be up to standard. The authorized silversmith is expected to reject any substandard silver. Second, when the silver is delivered to the provincial treasury, it should be melted and cast into ingots to avoid theft while in transit. But, to get his commission, the authorized silversmith has to pay a fee and arrange for a guarantor. In addition, he has to pay bribes to the clerks of the revenue section and to absorb the operating expenses of his shop—rent, food, coal, wages for his employees, and so on. If he does not impose a surcharge on the taxpayers, how can he maintain his business?

There are many ways for an authorized silversmith to defraud the taxpayers. First, he can declare that the quality of the silver is not up to standard and a larger amount is required. Second, he can insist that all small pieces of silver have to be melted and cast into ingots; hence there will be wastage in the process of melting. Third, he may demand that all ingots, no matter how small they are, be stamped with his seal, and of course charge a stamping fee. Fourth, he may require a fee for each melting as a legitimate charge for the service. Fifth, he can procrastinate until the taxpayer becomes impatient and is willing to double the melting fee. Last, if the taxpayer seems naive or simple minded, the smith can purposely upset the melting container and put the blame on the taxpayer. All these tricks are prevalent, and little can be done to thwart them.

When the silver ingots are delivered to the provincial treasury, few of them are up to standard. The authorized silversmith often blames the taxpayers for bringing in silver of inferior quality although it would be easy for him to reject them at the time of melting. Powerful official families and audacious licentiates often put poor quality silver in sealed envelopes, which the authorized silversmith is not empowered to examine. Therefore, the use of an authorized silversmith contributes very little to the business of tax collection; it only increases the burden of small taxpayers. . . .

→ *Why does the author suggest that the use of authorized silversmiths increases the burden of small taxpayers?*

→ *What reasons would the Chinese state have for maintaining such a "flawed" system?*

SOURCE: Huang Liu-hung, *A Complete Book Concerning Happiness and Benevolence: A Manual for Local Magistrates in Seventeenth Century China* (Tucson: University of Arizona Press, 1984), pp. 190–91.

At the core of these armed peasant bands, former soldiers and transport workers became leaders. Outlaw armies terrorized vast areas. Led by charismatic leaders whose appeals often contained messianic and religious overtones, half a dozen or so such large mobile armies—the so-called roving bandits—appeared in the 1620s. The most famous of these rebel leaders, the self-anointed "dashing prince" Li Zicheng, arrived at the outskirts of the capital, Beijing, on April 23, 1644. The capital's twenty-one miles of walls were defended by only a few companies of soldiers and a few thousand eunuchs, allowing Li Zicheng to take Beijing easily. Two days later, the emperor hanged himself. On the following day, the triumphant "dashing prince" rode into the capital and claimed the throne.

The news of the fall of the Ming capital sent shock waves around the empire. One hundred and seventy miles northeast of the capital, where northeast China meets Manchuria, the commander of the Ming army, Wu Sangui, received the news in late April of the death of the emperor and of Li Zicheng's triumph. Wu's task in the area was to defend the Ming against its increasingly menacing neighbor, a group who began to identify themselves as "Manchu" around 1635 but who were descendants of the Jurchens (see Chapter 10). In May 1644, Wu found himself in a very precarious position. Caught between an advancing rebel army on the one side, and the Manchus on the other, Wu made a fateful decision. He appealed for the cooperation of the Manchus to fight the "dashing prince," promising his newfound allies that "gold and treasure" awaited them in the capital. Thus, without shedding a drop of blood, the Manchus crossed the strategic pass and joined Wu's army. After years of coveting the Ming Empire, the Manchus were finally on their way to Beijing (see Map 13-5).

THE QING DYNASTY ASSERTS CONTROL At the time that they defeated Li Zicheng and seized power in Beijing, the Manchus numbered around 1 million. Assuming control of a domain that then included perhaps 250 million people, the conquerors were keenly aware of their minority status. Taking power, they understood, was one thing; keeping it was another. But keep it they did. In fact, in the eighteenth century, the Qing (which means "pure") dynasty (1644–1911) embarked on impressive economic expansion, incorporated new territories, and experienced substantial population growth. All this happened without provoking the kind of economic and political turmoil that rocked the societies of the Atlantic world.

The key to China's relatively stable economic and geographical expansion can be found in the shrewd and flexible policies of its rulers. The early Manchu emperors were able and diligent administrators. They also knew that to govern a sprawling and diverse population they had to adapt to local mores. To promote continuity with the earlier regime and draw upon the social and cultural practices of their predecessors, they respected Confucian ideas, codes, and ethics. The classic texts remained the basis of the prestigious civil service examinations. Social hierarchies of age, gender, and kin—indeed, the entire image of the family as the bedrock of social organization—endured. In some areas, like Taiwan, the Manchus consolidated new territories into existing provinces. Elsewhere, they gave newly acquired territories, like Mongolia, Tibet, and Xinjiang, their own distinct form of local administration. In these regions, imperial envoys presided, but they administered through staffs of locals and relied on indigenous institutions. Until the late nineteenth century, the Qing dynasty showed little interest in integrating those regions into "China proper."

At the same time, Qing rulers and their minions were determined to convey a clear sense of their own majesty and legitimacy. Rulers relentlessly promoted patriarchal values.

Widows who remained "chaste" were publicly praised, and women in general were exhorted to lead a "virtuous" life serving their male kin and family. To the majority Han, the Manchu emperor represented himself as the worthy upholder of familial values and classical Chinese civilization; to the Tibetan Buddhists, by contrast, the Manchu state offered plenty of imperial patronage. So, too, with otherwise disgruntled Islamic subjects. Although the Islamic Uighurs, as well as other Muslim subjects, might not have approved of the Manchus' easygoing religious attitude, they accepted the emperor's favors and generally endorsed his claim to rule.

But merely insinuating themselves into an existing order or simply appeasing subject peoples did not wholly satisfy the Manchu yearning to leave their imprint on the governed. They also introduced measures that extolled their authority, emphasized their distinctiveness, and ensured the submission of their mostly Han Chinese subjects. Qing officials composed or translated all important documents into Manchu and banned intermarriage between Manchu and Han (although this was difficult to enforce in practice). Other edicts imposed Manchu ways on Han subjects. The day after the Manchus entered Beijing in 1644, a decree required all Han Chinese males to follow the Manchu practice of shaving their foreheads and braiding their hair at the back in a queue. This met with immediate and vociferous protests from the Chinese and led to temporary shelving of the policy. A year later, however, feeling somewhat more secure, the new dynasty reissued the order and presented its subjects with the stark choice of cutting their hair or losing their heads. This time, the policy stuck. In a similar vein, the Qing also decreed that Han males adopt Manchu garb: instead of the loose Ming-style robes, they now had to wear high collars and tight jackets.

Although the Chinese people found ways to contest official Qing values, the Manchus sought to suppress dissent by assuming a role as guardians of moral rectitude, decrying the evidence of decadence and extravagance. Nothing earned the regime's opprobrium more than the urban elites' display of conspicuous consumption and indulgence in sensual pleasure. The Qing court regarded the "decadence" of the late Ming, symbolized by its famous actresses, as one of the latter's principal failings. In 1723, the Yongzheng emperor effectively banned female performers from the court, and the practice spread to commercial theaters, with young boys then assuming the role of females on stage. At the same time, mid-Qing prosperity created new wealth among the urban elites. They displayed their riches by becoming, for example, collectors—books, painting, calligraphy—and patrons of a vibrant public theater sector. The eighteenth century thus witnessed new dramatic forms. Merchants often traveled with their own troupes with distinctive regional styles, some of which were known for the robust sexuality of their performances. The popularity of female impersonators on stage even brought a new cachet to homosexual

MAP 13-5 FROM MING TO QING CHINA, 1644–1760

Qing China, as was the case with other dynasties during this era, expanded its territory significantly. Where did the Qing dynasty expand? How was the Qing expansion similar to and different from the expansion of European, including Russian, dynasties during this period? How did Qing expansionism reflect Qing concerns about foreign influence within the empire?

relationships, as the Qing government tried to regulate commercial theater still further by banning women from the audiences of public performances. But a gulf began to open between the government's aspirations and its ability to police

society. For example, the urban public continued to flock to performances by female impersonators in defiance of Qing efforts to ban this and other sexually provocative forms of theater.

Manchu impositions fell mostly on the peasantry, for the Qing financed their administrative edifice by extracting surpluses from peasant households through taxation and surcharges. In response, the peasants spread out to border areas to find new lands to cultivate. Often they planted these newly occupied lands with New World crops that grew well in less fertile soils. This resulted in an important change in Chinese diets. While rice was the staple diet of wealthy Chinese, peasants increasingly relied on corn and sweet potatoes for their subsistence.

EXPANSION AND TRADE UNDER THE QING Despite the public's disregard for some imperial edicts, the Qing dynasty enjoyed something of a heyday during the eighteenth century. Territorial expansion extended the realm far beyond the frontiers of the Ming into central Asia, Tibet, and Mongolia. Tributary relations were established with Korea, Vietnam, Burma, and Nepal. While officials emphasized and redoubled their reliance on their agrarian base, trade and commerce flourished as they had done in the late Ming era. Chinese merchants continued to ply the waters stretching from Southeast Asia to Japan, exchanging textiles, ceramics, and medicine for spices and rice. In the early years of the dynasty, the Qing authorities

> *By the middle of the eighteenth century, it was still clear that Europe needed China more than the other way around.*

vacillated about whether to permit trade with foreigners in China. Meanwhile, in 1720 in Canton, a group of merchants formed a monopolistic guild, known as the Cohong, to trade with European merchants, whose numbers rose as they vied for coveted Chinese goods and tried to peddle their wares to the vast Chinese market. Although the guild disbanded after a year in the face of opposition from foreign and other local merchants, it was revived after the Qing decided to restrict the Europeans to trading in Canton and ordered that Chinese merchants guarantee the good behavior and the payment of fees by the Europeans. This "Canton system," as it came to be known, would be formalized by decree of the emperor in 1759.

China, in sum, negotiated a century of upheaval without dismantling established ways of arranging politics or economics. For the peasantry, popular faiths continued to govern their belief systems, and most peasants continued to cultivate their crops and stay close to their fields and villages. Trading with the outside world was marginal to the overall commercial life of the Qing era; the Qing, like their Ming predecessors, cared more about the agrarian than the commercial health of the empire, believing the former to be the foundation of prosperity and social tranquility. As long as China's vast peasantry could keep the dynasty's coffers full, the government was content to squeeze the merchants when they needed funds. Some historians have labeled this China's

failure to adapt to a changing world order. In time, these historians assert, this left China vulnerable to outsiders, especially Europeans. But this view puts the historical cart before the horse. By the middle of the eighteenth century, it was still clear that Europe needed China more than the other way around. For the vast majority of Chinese, no superior model of belief, politics, or economics was conceivable. Indeed, although the Qing had taken over a crumbling empire in 1644, a century later China achieved a new level of prosperity.

TOKUGAWA JAPAN

Integration with the Asian trading system exposed Japan to new external pressures, even as the islands grappled with internal turmoil. But the Japanese dealt with these pressures far more successfully than did the four great mainland Asian empires (the Ottomans, the Safavid, the Mughal, and the Ming), where political fragmentation and even the overthrow of existing dynasties took place. In Japan, rivalry among powerful clans did not produce autonomous regimes. Instead, a single ruling family emerged, and this dynastic state, known as the Tokugawa Shogunate, managed to do something that eluded most of the regimes around the world at this time: regulate foreign intrusion into its islands. While Japan played a modest role in the expanding world economic system, it remained free of outside exploitation.

UNIFICATION OF JAPAN During the sixteenth century, Japan had suffered from chronic political instability, as rampant banditry and civil strife spread disorder across the countryside. Regional ruling households, called daimyos, had commanded private armies made up of skilled warriors known as samurai. The daimyos held sway over local populations and sometimes succeeded in bringing a measure of order to their domains. But no one daimyo family could establish its preeminence over others. Although Japan did have an emperor, who ruled from Kyoto, his authority did not extend beyond the court.

At the end of the sixteenth century, several military leaders attempted to unify Japan. One general loomed above his rivals: Toyotomi Hideyoshi (1535–1598). He not only conquered his rivals, but with the imprimatur of the Kyoto emperor, he became the supreme minister and proceeded to arrange marriages among the children of the local magnates to solidify political bonds. He also ordered that the wives and children of the daimyos be kept within reach as semihostages, thereby coaxing cooperation from powerful regional rulers.

Edo in the Rain. This facsimile of an *ukiyo-e* ("floating world") print by Hiroshige (1797–1858) depicts one of several bridges in the bustling city of Edo (later Tokyo), with Mount Fuji in the background.

After Hideyoshi died, one of the daimyos, Tokugawa Ieyasu (1542–1616), took power for himself. This was a decisive moment. In 1603, Ieyasu assumed the title of shogun (military ruler). He also solved the problem of succession, declaring that thereafter rulership was hereditary and that his family would be the ruling household. Ieyasu passed the shogunate to his son in 1605, though he continued to rule behind the scenes. This hereditary Tokugawa Shogunate lasted until 1867.

The source of administrative authority shifted from the imperial capital of Kyoto to the site of Ieyasu's new domain headquarters: the castle town called Edo (later renamed Tokyo). The Tokugawa built Edo out of a small earthen fortification that was in bad repair and clinging to a coastal bluff. Behind Edo lay a village in a swampy plain. In a monumental work of engineering, the rulers ordered the swamp drained, the forest cleared, many of the hills leveled, canals dredged, bridges built, the seashore extended by landfill, and a new stone castle completed. By the time Ieyasu died in 1616, Edo had a population of 150,000.

The Tokugawa shoguns ensured a flow of resources from the working population to rulers and from the provinces to the capital. Villages paid taxes to the daimyos, who in turn transferred resources to the seat of shogunate authority. No longer engaged in constant warfare, the samurai became administrators. Peace brought prosperity. Agriculture thrived. Improved farming techniques and land reclamation projects enabled the country's population to grow from 10 million in 1550 to 16 million in 1600 and 30 million by 1700.

FOREIGN AFFAIRS AND FOREIGNERS   Having consolidated a national regime based on power sharing with the regions, Japanese rulers tackled foreign affairs. The most pressing concern for Hideyoshi's successors was what to do about the intrusion of foreigners, especially Christian missionaries and European traders, who had begun to arrive in Japan at the end of the sixteenth and beginning of the seventeenth centuries. Initially, Japanese officials welcomed trade and Christianity because of their eagerness to acquire muskets, gunpowder, and other new technology. But once the ranks of the converted had swelled into the hundreds of thousands, Japanese authorities came to see that Christians were intolerant of other faiths, believed Christ to be superior to any authority, and fought among themselves. Trying to stem the tide, the shoguns issued decrees to stop conversion to Christianity and attempted to ban its practice. After a 1637 rebellion, in which peasants in southwestern Japan who had converted to Christianity rose up in protest against high rents and taxes, the government cracked down, suppressing Christianity and driving European missionaries from the country.

Even more troublesome for the shogunate was how to handle the lure of trade with Europeans, whose record of conquest of Manila and Melaka was well known. The Tokugawa knew that trading at different ports in Japan threatened to pull the commercial regions in various directions, away from the capital. When it became clear that European traders preferred the ports of Kyūshū, the shogunate restricted Europeans to trade only in ports under Edo's direct rule. Then, one by one, Japanese authorities expelled all European

MAP 13-6   TOKUGAWA JAPAN, 1603-1867

The Tokugawa Shoguns created a strong central state in Japan during the seventeenth and eighteenth centuries. According to this map, how extensive was their control? What other states challenged Tokugawa rule in this region? How did Tokugawa leaders attempt to manage relations with foreign states and entities?

Portuguese Arriving in Japan. In the 1540s, the Portuguese arrival on the islands of Japan sparked a fascination with the strange costumes and the great ships of these "southern barbarians" (so called because they had approached Japan from the south). Silk-screen paintings depicted Portuguese prowess in exaggerated form, such as in the impossible height of the fore and aft of the vessel pictured here.

competitors. Only the Protestant (and nonmissionizing) Dutch were permitted to remain in Japan, but they were confined to a small island near Nagasaki. The Dutch were allowed to unload just one ship each year, and only under strict supervision by Japanese authorities.

These measures did not close Tokugawa Japan to the outside world, however. Trade with the Chinese and Koreans flourished, and the shogun received Korean and Ryūkyū missions. Beyond these embassies, Edo gathered reports and publications about the outside world from the resident Dutch and Chinese (who included monks, physicians, and painters). A select few Japanese were permitted to learn Dutch and to learn about European technology, shipbuilding, and medicine (see Chapter 14). By setting the terms on which encounters with outsiders would occur, however, Japanese authorities ensured that foreigners would not threaten Japan's security.

Ruling over three islands, Tokugawa Japan was surrounded by "vassals" that were neither completely part of the realm nor entirely independent (see Map 13-6). The most important peripheral areas were the Ryūkyūs in the south and the island of Ezo to the north, neither of which the Japanese attempted to annex, preferring to maintain them as buffers. Establishing dependent buffer areas facilitated the strengthening of a distinct Japanese identity for all the peoples living "on the inside" and limited outside influence. When, beginning in 1697, the Russians approached Japan from the north, the Japanese rebuffed entreaties to open relations and instead sought to manage contacts with the Russians through their northern buffer zone. As the Russians became more aggressive in trying to "open" Japan to trade, the Japanese annexed and began to colonize Ezo. Ezo became Hokkaidō, the country's fourth main island, and a strong barrier to European penetration. In regulating outside contacts, Japanese rulers suppressed sources of upheaval and consolidated a dynasty that lasted well into the nineteenth century.

TRANSFORMATIONS OF EUROPE

> ➤ *Why did the centers of European economic and political dynamism shift northward in the seventeenth century?*

Between 1600 and 1750, religious conflict, commercial expansion, and the consolidation of dynastic power transformed Europe. Commercial centers shifted northward, and Spain and Portugal lost ground to England and France. Waged chiefly over religion, the Thirty Years' War (1618–1648) changed the nature of warfare and political authority.

EXPANSION AND DYNASTIC CHANGE IN RUSSIA

Untouched by the devastation of the Thirty Years' War, the Russian Empire expanded in all directions to become the world's largest-ever state, gaining positions on Europe's Baltic Sea and the Pacific Ocean. Russia established political borders with the western-expanding Qing Empire and with Japan. These momentous shifts involved the elimination of the steppe nomads, who had roamed through Russia and China, as an independent force in world history and recast the problem of the Europe-Asia frontier. For China and Japan, Europe (in the form of predominantly Christian Russia) stretched right up to their states. By contrast, western Europeans placed the geographical boundary of Europe and Asia at the Ural Mountains. Culturally, Europeans as well as Russians debated whether Russia belonged more to Europe or to Asia. The answer was both.

Muscovy, like Japan and China, used territorial expansion and extended commercial networks to consolidate a powerful political order, the Russian Empire, the new name given to Muscovy by Tsar Peter the Great around 1700. But Russia was more internally heterogeneous than its Asian neighbors, both in its core and as a result of its annexation of adjacent lands. In the four centuries after 1480, the weak principality of Muscovy, a mixture of Slavs, Finnish tribes, Turkic speakers, and many others, expanded at the rate of about fifty square miles per day. Despite setbacks and long defensive periods, this new Russian Empire grew to occupy one-sixth of the earth's land surface, spanning parts of Europe, much of northern Asia, numerous islands in the North Pacific, and even a corner of North America. Territorial expansion, together with natural population growth, increased Russia's population from about 6 million in 1550 to 20 million by 1750.

Like Japan, Russia emerged out of turmoil. Muscovy's security concerns, the ambitions of private individuals, and religious conviction inspired the regime to seize territory. For the Muscovite grand prince Ivan III (ruled 1462–1505), expansion was inseparable from security. Because the steppe, which stretches deep into Asia, remained a highway for horseriding peoples, especially descendants of the Mongols, Muscovy sought to dominate the areas south and east of Moscow.

By marrying the niece of the last Byzantine emperor, Ivan added a strong religious dimension to his expansionist claims. Now he could assert that Moscow was the center of the Byzantine faith and heir to the conquered city of Constantinople. Territorial expansion continued under Ivan III's successors, especially his grandson, Ivan IV (ruled 1533–1584), who adopted the title of tsar in 1547. To secure Muscovy's eastern borders, Ivan IV permitted private armies to extend the domain of the Russian state into Siberia. Beginning in the 1590s, Russian authorities built forts and trading posts along the great Siberian rivers for defensive purposes and to facilitate the taxation of aboriginal peoples. The rulers' efforts to control tribute and trans-Afro-Eurasian trade, however, could not prevent privateers, enticed by the large profits that could be made from the sale of furs, from pushing the Russian domain outward. In this fashion, Muscovy's frontier expanded eastward, reaching the Pacific, more than 5,000 miles from Moscow, in 1639. In just over a century, Moscow had created a landed empire straddling Eurasia from west to east, incorporating peoples of many languages and religions (see Map 13-7).

Much of this expansion occurred despite the dynastic chaos that followed the death of Ivan IV. Following what was known as the Time of Troubles, a group of prominent families gathered in 1613 to reestablish central authority and

Nenets Hunters. Hunters of the Nenets tribe in far North Asia's treeless tundra, showing off their warm animalskin clothing and self-fashioned weapons, as depicted in a 1620 engraving by Theodore de Bry, one of the first Europeans to come into contact with them.

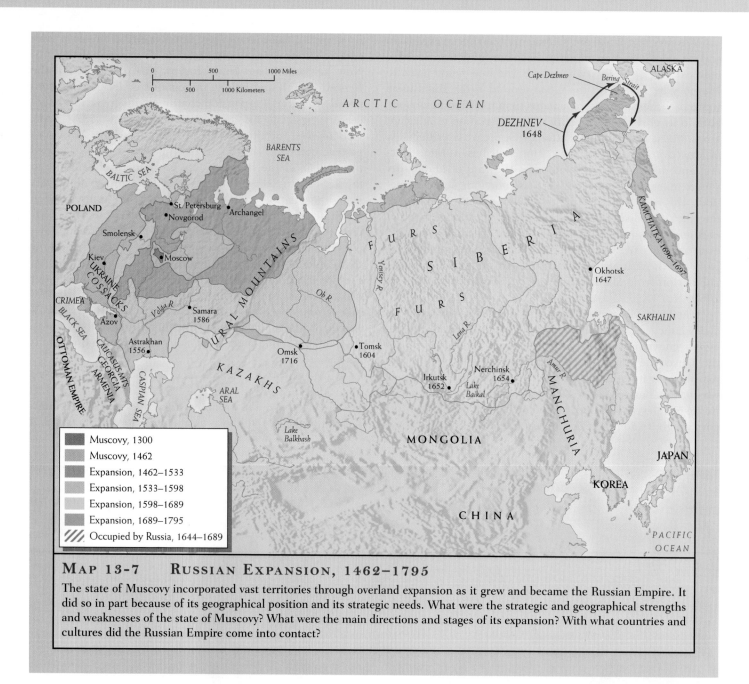

MAP 13-7   RUSSIAN EXPANSION, 1462–1795

The state of Muscovy incorporated vast territories through overland expansion as it grew and became the Russian Empire. It did so in part because of its geographical position and its strategic needs. What were the strategic and geographical strengths and weaknesses of the state of Muscovy? What were the main directions and stages of its expansion? With what countries and cultures did the Russian Empire come into contact?

threw their weight behind a new family of potentates. These were the Romanovs, court barons who set about reviving the Kremlin's fortunes. Like the Ottoman and Qing dynasts, Romanov tsars and their aristocratic supporters would retain power into the twentieth century.

In the seventeenth and eighteenth centuries, the Romanovs created an absolutist system of government, clustering power in the hands of the ruling family. The right to make war, tax, judge, and coin money was limited to the tsar and his retinue. To transcend old sources of tension and friction, the Romanovs made the nobles serve as bureaucrats. Russia, following the Byzantine preference for a monarch, embraced a despotic version of rulership. Moscow had no political assemblies for nobles or any other sectors of society. Powerful families at the court referred to themselves as "slaves of the tsar." Away from Moscow, local aristocrats exercised nearly unlimited authority in exchange for fealty and tribute to the tsar.

Russia's peasantry bore the burden of maintaining the wealth of the small nobility and the monarchy. Most of Muscovy's peasant families gathered into communes, enclosed rural worlds in which people helped each other to deal with the everyday strains of the harsh climate and the periodic travails of poor harvests and severe masters. Communes were

Celebration in Red Square. Russian nobles gathered to celebrate in Red Square, which originally meant "Beautiful Square" and was a processional and market space just outside the walls of the Kremlin fortress where the Muscovite tsars lived, ruled, and prayed. The Russian nobles wore long beards and caftans, or gowns, often lined with Siberian furs, which were much coveted both at home and abroad. Many Russian nobles were descended from Tatar (Turkish) Muslims, conquered peoples who converted to Christianity and loyally served the tsar.

not based on kinship, but they functioned like extended kin networks in that members reciprocated favors and chores for survival. Even with mutual support, the peasants lived poorly, their huts usually consisting of a single chamber heated by a wood-burning stove and no chimney. Livestock and humans often shared the same quarters. In 1649, peasants were legally bound as serfs to the nobles and the tsar, meaning they had to perform obligatory services and deliver part of their produce to their lords, who exercised almost complete command over the life and death of their minions. Serfdom grew directly out of the state's ever-increasing military ambitions and challenges.

Having consolidated an internal order, Russian leaders redoubled their pursuit of imperial expansion. Peter the Great (ruled 1682–1725) symbolized a westward push by founding, and building with forced labor, a new capital, St. Petersburg, in 1703. Under his successors, including the hard-nosed autocrat Catherine the Great (ruled 1762–1796), Russia added even more territory. In 1763, Catherine placed her former lover, Stanislaw Poniatowski, on the Polish throne, and three decades later, together with the Austrians and Prussians, carved up the great medieval state of Poland. Her armies' victories against the Ottoman Turks allowed Russia to annex the great "breadbasket" of central Europe, the Ukraine. By the late eighteenth century, Russian sovereignty stretched from the Baltic Sea through the heart of Europe, Ukraine, and the Crimea on the Black Sea and into the ancient lands of Armenia and Georgia in the Caucasus Mountains bordering on the Ottoman Empire.

With a vast territorial empire secured, more people started to migrate eastward, some to escape being serfs and to settle their own land. At the beginning of the migration eastward, more than 90 percent of Siberia's approximately 200,000 inhabitants were indigenes (natives). By 1750, the number of Slavs in Siberia had almost caught up to the native population and soon surpassed it. Battling astoundingly harsh circumstances, temperatures falling to –40 degrees centigrade and freezing artic winds, peasant migrants traveled on horseback and foot to resettle in the east. Religious schismatics, known after 1667 as Old Believers because of their refusal to accept changes in the Eastern Orthodox liturgy, were deported to uninhabited areas. But the difficulties of clearing forested lands or planting crops in boggy Siberian soils, combined with extraordinarily harsh winters, made for very high attrition among settlers. To this was added the problem of isolation. There was no established land route back to Moscow until the 1770s, when the Great Siberian Post Road finally cut through the swamps and peat bogs of western Siberia. The writer Anton Chekhov called it "the longest and ugliest road in the whole world."

Russia's territorial acquisitions produced complex, mixed societies that bridged eastern and western ends of Eurasia, producing many children of mixed parentage. Perhaps half the inhabitants of Siberia in the 1750s were runaway serfs.

Catherine the Great. Catherine the Great styled herself an enlightened despot of the baroque epoch, furthering the Russian empire's adaptation of European high culture. Her dress is adorned with the Byzantine double-headed eagle.

Russian authorities also resettled in Siberia unwanted families and people banished by the tsar because they were considered politically dangerous or undesirable. These exiles, though they never approached in number the legions of hardy peasant settlers, would later make Siberia infamous as a land for prisoners, overshadowing its reputation as a destination of freedom. "The road to Siberia is wide," went the saying, "the way back, narrow."

ECONOMIC AND POLITICAL FLUCTUATIONS IN WESTERN EUROPE

During the seventeenth and eighteenth centuries, the commercial integration of different parts of the world shook up old regimes in Mughal India, Ming China, and the Ottoman Empire, while spawning new dynasties like the Tokugawa in Japan and the Romanovs in Russia. At the same time, European economies grew and became more commercialized, es-

pecially after the devastating Thirty Years' War (1618–1648). As in Asia, developments in distant parts of the world shaped upturns and downturns in European economies. Compounding the pressures of economic change in Europe was the continuation of dynastic rivalries and religious conflicts.

THE THIRTY YEARS' WAR Over the course of the century after Martin Luther broke with the Catholic Church, religious warfare continued to rage in Europe. To these tensions were added contests for territory, power, and, increasingly, trade wars. The Thirty Years' War (1618–1648) was all three of these—a war fought between the Protestant princes and the Habsburg Catholic emperor for religious predominance in central Europe; a struggle for regional control fought between Catholic powers (the Spanish and Austrian Habsburgs and the French); and a bid for independence (from Spain) by the Dutch, who wanted the freedom to trade and worship as they liked. It was a brutal conflict, which cost the lives of many civilians as well as mercenary soldiers. Just when it seemed as if Protestantism would be wiped off the central European map, the Swedish king, Gustavus Adolphus II (ruled 1611–1632), came to the rescue. Though he died from battle wounds, his intervention allowed the Protestant forces to survive. The most notorious battle in this conflict occurred in 1631 at Magdeburg, where Catholic forces sacked and destroyed the city of 40,000. Three-quarters of the civilian inhabitants died. In total, fighting, disease, and famine wiped out a third of the urban population and two-fifths of the rural population of the German states. The war also depopulated Sweden and Poland. Exhausted from the long conflict, the primary belligerents signed the Treaty of Westphalia in 1648, agreeing, in essence, that as there was a rough balance of power between Protestant and Catholic states, they would simply have to put up with each other. The Dutch got their independence, but the enormous costs of the war proved a major source of discontent in Spain, France, and England. Central Europe was so devastated that it did not recover in economic or demographic terms for more than a century.

The Thirty Years' War did not remake Europe's religious map, but it did transform European war-making, and with it, a series of other practices. Medieval struggles had been mainly sieges between nobles, and the belligerents had fielded relatively small armies. The Thirty Years' War enhanced the powers of larger centralized states. After 1648, with the increase in the size of standing armies, rulers had to wage decisive, grand-scale campaigns. The Thirty Years' War changed the nature of being a soldier, too; as the war ground on, enlisted men who had been recruited from among the local population to defend their king, country, and faith were replaced by criminals who were forced into service or mercenaries who were hired to fight. Even officers, previously granted their stripes by purchase or royal fiat, now earned them and became more professional. Gunpowder, cannons, and handguns became standardized and more efficient. By the eighteenth century, Europe's wars were being fought by

The Thirty Years' War. The mercenary armies of the Thirty Years' War were renowned for pillaging and tormenting the civilians of central Europe. Here, the townsfolk exact revenge on some of these soldiers, hanging, as the engraving's caption claims, "damned and infamous thieves, like bad fruit, from this tree."

huge standing armies boasting a professional officer corps and bristling with effective artillery. To keep these armies going, rulers had to organize and sustain long supply lines and make sure that food and ammunition got to the front. The costs—material and human—of war in Europe began to soar. In Holland, the public debt, mostly for supporting armies, soared from 140 million guilders in 1650 to over 400 million a century later.

WESTERN EUROPEAN ECONOMIES   To finance their armies and balance the state's books, European rulers in this era, like the Mughals and Ottomans, depended chiefly on income from land—their own and that of their heavily taxed peasants. But commercial expansion had powerful effects on economic and social relations and spurred the growth of northern cities like Amsterdam and London. Here, powerful new merchant classes arose, able and willing to risk capital on new endeavors. In the meantime, some countries—especially those that had pioneered commercial connections in the fifteenth and sixteenth centuries—began to face new threats. In the seventeenth century, Spain, for example, began to lose ground to its rivals as the costs of defending the empire soared and north European merchants began to cut in on Spanish trading networks. The enormous costs of Spain's involvement in the Thirty Years' War dealt the Spanish economy a final, disastrous blow. But not only Spain felt the effects of new competition; many economies that had flourished in the sixteenth century now had difficulty adapting to the pressures of greater economic connection. The economy of Venice, which before the era of transoceanic shipping had been Europe's chief gateway to Asia, fell into decline.

During the seventeenth century, the centers of European dynamism shifted northward. The Dutch were at the forefront, creating new commercial practices and a new mercantile elite. They specialized in shipping and in financing regional and long-distance trade. Their famous *fluitschips* could carry heavy, bulky cargoes, like Baltic wood, with relatively small crews over long distances. The cost of shipping goods around the Atlantic world dropped significantly as Dutch ships transported their own goods as well as cargoes of other countries. Amsterdam's merchants founded an exchange bank in 1609 and even a rudimentary stock exchange in 1611—with a weekly publication of price quotations in 1613. They also pioneered systems of underwriting and insuring cargoes. Other mercantile centers in Europe followed suit and soon began to compete with Dutch merchants. The Dutch began to lose their share of the commercial activity and eventually fell behind the larger European commercial and military powers. But their pioneering ways set an early example for new trading and financing practices that helped integrate the Atlantic economies even further.

England and to some extent France also emerged as commercial powerhouses in the seventeenth century. Each was backed by aggressive state policies that aimed to promote national business and drive out competitors. The English Navigation Act of 1651, which stipulated that only English ships could carry goods between the mother country and its colonies, sought to protect English shipping and merchants, especially from the Dutch. The English subsequently launched a series of effective trade wars against Holland between 1652 and 1672. The French, too, especially under King Louis XIV's finance minister, Jean-Baptiste Colbert, aggressively applied mercantilist policies and joined forces with England to invade Holland in 1672. These European powers also perfected the use of official monopoly trading companies to organize commerce and drive away competitors.

Economic development was not limited to port towns. In the countryside, too, new techniques for organizing production led to breakthroughs. Most important was the expansion in the production of food. In northwestern Europe, especially, investments in water drainage, larger livestock herds, and the refinement of cultivation practices all helped farmers produce more and more food. A new four-field crop rotation, in which wheat, clover, barley, and turnips alternated, helped to keep nutrients in the soil and provided fodder for livestock year-round. This increased output supported a growing urban population. By contrast, in Spain and Italy, agricultural change came more slowly, and agrarian backwardness checked population growth.

Production rose most where farming underwent profound changes in the way rural property was organized. The sharpest transformation came in England. For generations, leading up to the end of the eighteenth century, landowners redefined their relations with their workforces. In a movement known as "enclosure," landowners took control of lands that local customs had treated as the common property of residents. Landowners now built fences, and claimed exclusive rights to these properties. They planted new crops or pastured sheep with the aim not of satisfying local needs, but of selling the products in distant markets—especially cities. At the same time, large landowners put their farms in the hands of tenants, who in turn hired wage laborers to till the land and collect harvests. In England, peasant agriculture gave way increasingly to farms run by families who made their money from buying and selling what they needed (including labor) and what they produced in the marketplace. England was not alone in this practice; it simply was at the forefront of a European-wide process of commercializing the countryside.

DYNASTIC MONARCHIES: FRANCE AND ENGLAND

European monarchs had various degrees of success in their attempts to centralize state power. Louis XIII of France (ruled 1610–1643), and especially his chief minister Cardinal Richelieu, concentrated power in the hands of the king. By the time of Louis XIV's reign (ruled 1643–1715), the Bourbon family had established a monarchy in which succession passed strictly to the oldest male in the male line. After 1614, kings refused to convene the Estates-General, a medieval advisory body. Once composed of representatives of three groups—the clergy (the First Estate, those who pray), the nobility (the Second Estate, those who fight), and the unprivileged remainder of the population (the Third Estate, those who work)—the Estates-General was seen as an obstacle to the full empowerment of the king. Instead of sharing power, the king and his counselors sought to create a monarchy that was absolute. By this they did not mean tyrannical rule, but complete and thorough rule, free of bloody disorders such as the religious wars that shattered France during the sixteenth century. The king's rule was to be lawful, but it was he, not his jurists, who dictated the last legal word. If the king made a mistake, only God could call him to account. This was the "divine right of kings."

In absolutist France, privileges and state offices flowed from the king's grace. All patronage networks, even those headed by dukes and princes, ultimately were linked to the king's grants and treasury. The great palace Louis XIV built at Versailles teemed with noblemen and noblewomen from all over France, seeking favor, dressing according to the king's expensive fashion code, and attending the latest tragedies, comedies, and concerts. Just as the Japanese shogun monitored the daimyos by keeping them in Edo, so, too, did Louis XIV and his retainers keep a watchful eye on the French nobility at Versailles.

The French dynastic monarchy provided a model of absolute rule for other European dynasts, like the Habsburgs of the Holy Roman Empire, the Hohenzollerns of Prussia, and the Romanovs of Muscovy. Public power was clustered in the hands of the king and his ministers, while the various groups in society, from the nobility to the peasantry, were deprived of formal means to represent their interests. Nonetheless, French absolutist government was not as absolute as the king would have wished. Pockets of stalwart Protestants practiced their religion secretly in the plateau villages of central France. Peasant disturbances continued. Criticism of court life and of Louis's wars and religious policies flowed from pens in anonymous printed pamphlets, jurists' notebooks, and the private journals of courtiers. The nobility also grumbled

Amsterdam Stock Exchange. Buying and selling shares in the new joint-stock companies was daily business at the Stock Exchange in seventeenth-century Amsterdam. This image depicts gentlemanly negotiations between prosperous merchants and investors, but panics could also occur, as during the South Sea Bubble.

Versailles. Louis XIV's Versailles, just southwest of Paris, was a hunting lodge that was converted at colossal cost in the 1670s–1680s into a grand royal chateau with expansive grounds. Much envied and imitated across Europe, the palace became the epicenter of a luxurious court life that included entertainments such as plays and musical offerings, state receptions, royal hunts, boating, and gambling. Thousands of nobles at Versailles vied with each other for closer proximity to the king in the performance of court rituals.

about their political misfortunes, but since the king would not call the Estates-General, they had no formal way to express their political concerns.

England might also have evolved into an absolutist regime. Queen Elizabeth (ruled 1558–1603) and her successors in the early seventeenth century employed many of the same policies of the absolute monarchy in France, such as control of patronage and elaborate court festivities. Not wishing to share her power with a man, the "Virgin Queen" never married and exerted extensive control over the church, military, and aristocracy. But there were important differences. In England, the system of succession allowed women to rule as queens in their own right. In addition, in England, Parliament remained an important force. Importantly, while the French kings did not need the consent of the Estates-General to enact taxes, the English monarchs were required to call Parliament if they wanted to raise money.

Under Elizabeth's successors, fierce quarrels broke out over taxation, religion, and royal efforts to rule without parliamentary consent. Tensions ran high between the Puritans, with their relatively simple form of worship and more egalitarian church government, and the Anglicans, supporters of the Church of England, with its more ornate ceremonies and its hierarchy of bishops and archbishops headed by the king. Social and economic grievances aggravated the unrest. Civil war erupted in the 1640s, ending in a victory for the parliamentary army (which was largely Puritan) and the beheading of King Charles I (ruled 1625–1649). Twelve years of government as a commonwealth without a king ensued, during which the middle and lower classes enjoyed political and religious power, but the commonwealth became a military dictatorship.

In 1660, the monarchy was restored, but the issues of the king's relation to Parliament and of religious tolerance were

Queen Elizabeth of England. This portrait (c. 1600) depicts an idealized Queen Elizabeth near the end of her long reign. The queen is pictured riding in a procession in the midst of an admiring crowd composed of the most important nobles of the realm.

unresolved. Charles II (ruled 1660–1685) and his successor James II (ruled 1685–1688) aroused opposition by their autocracy and clandestine efforts to bring England back into the Catholic fold. The conflict between an aspiring absolutist throne and Parliament's insistence on shared sovereignty and Protestant succession culminated in the Glorious Revolution of 1688–1689. In a bloodless upheaval, James II fled to France and Parliament offered the crown to William of Orange and his wife Mary (a Protestant daughter of James II). The outcome of the conflict established the principle that monarchs must rule in conjunction with Parliament. The Church of England was reaffirmed as the official church, but Presbyterians and Jews, though saddled with many civic disabilities (they were not welcome at the universities, for instance), could at least practice their religions. Catholic worship was still officially forbidden but was in fact tolerated as long as the Catholics kept quiet. By 1700, then, England's powerful nobility and merchant classes were permanently guaranteed a say in public affairs and ensured that state activity would operate to the advantage of propertied classes and not just the ruler.

Events in France and England stimulated much political writing. In England, Thomas Hobbes published his *Leviathan* in 1651, a reasoned defense of the absolute power of the state over all competing forces as a necessary remedy against the natural "war of all against all." Nearly forty years later, John Locke published his *Two Treatises of Civil Government,* which laid out an argument based on the natural rights to liberty and property and on the rights of peoples to agree to form a government and to disband and reform it when it did not live up to its contract. French theorists, like Jean Bodin, also wrote about new forms of conducting politics and making law. More and more, writers began to discuss the costs of

unchecked state power. What differed was the extent to which these elites could demand and win the right to check the king. As the eighteenth century unfolded, the question of where sovereignty lay grew ever more pressing.

MERCANTILIST WARS The ascendance of new powers in Europe, especially France and England, intensified commercial rivalries for control of the Atlantic system. In the eighteenth century, a new type of conflict replaced earlier religious and territorial struggles: mercantilist wars for control of commercial colonies and sea lanes. Commercial struggles, then, evolved into worldwide wars. Across the world, European empires engaged in constant skirmishing over control of trade and territory. The English and Dutch trading companies took aim at the Portuguese outposts in Asia and the Americas. Then they took aim at each other. Ports in India were the target for repeated assaults and counterassaults. In response, European powers built huge navies to protect their colonies and trade routes and to attack their rivals.

Smuggling across the mercantilist lines became rampant. English and French traders, sometimes with the open support of their political authorities, violated the sovereign claims of rival colonies. Curaçao, for instance, became an entrepôt for traders from England and the Low Countries to sell illegal goods in South America. French and English traders set up shop in southern Brazil to smuggle goods into the River Plate in return for Andean silver. All around the Gulf of Mexico and the Caribbean, merchants sought to introduce their goods into their enemies' colonies.

After 1715, mercantilist wars were mainly conducted outside Europe, as empires feuded over colonial possessions. They were especially bitter in border areas, where the lines between empires blurred. In the Caribbean and North America, in particular, mercantilist wars turned the borderlands into battlegrounds. Each round of peripheral warfare ratcheted up the scale and cost of fighting, culminating in the first world conflict, which was known as the French and Indian War in the United States but as the Seven Years' War (1756–1763) everywhere else. For the first time in history, a war was fought simultaneously across many hemispheric fronts: not just in Europe but also in India and across the Americas. American Indians, African slaves, and European settlers were all dragged into the conflict.

The Seven Years' War marked the triumph of the British Empire over its rivals, especially France and Spain. Britain captured one of Spain's prime Caribbean defensive bastions, Havana, as well as Florida and Manila, Spain's prize in Asia. Later, the British returned Havana and Manila, but they kept Florida, leaving little doubt that Spain's main rival in the New World was definitely Britain. France lost Canada and several outposts in India but hung onto its Caribbean possessions. While Britain emerged as the dominant overseas power in the world, the struggle left all the European empires in deep debt.

CONCLUSION

Between the beginning of the seventeenth century and the middle of the eighteenth century, the corners of the world went from being loosely connected to becoming more economically linked. Traders shipped ever more goods over longer distances. They exchanged a wider variety of commodities, from Baltic wood to Indian cotton. The world's commercial linkages could be seen in people wearing clothes manufactured elsewhere, consuming beverages made from products cultivated in far-off locations, and using imported guns to settle local conflicts. Colonization in the Americas provides an obvious example of this growing interdependence. European decisions to settle new colonies meant an increase in the Atlantic slave trade from Africa and the expulsion of Indians from their lands, clear cases of global connectedness—and glaring inequalities.

Economic integration had destabilizing and fragmenting political consequences for many of the great dynasties of Afro-Eurasia. The Mughals, the Ming, and the Ottomans all confronted rivals to their authority—both inside and out. Local magnates challenged the imperial centers, while European newcomers knocked with greater frequency at imperial doors, for royal favor, for rights to trade, and for permission to convert souls.

Politically, certain societies coped with increased commercial exchange more successfully than others, although everywhere greater linkages and new wealth shook up existing orders. The Safavid and Ming dynasties could not cope with these pressures; both collapsed. The Spanish and Mughal dynasts managed to survive, but they were harried by aggressive rivals. For the newcomers to the integrating world, the opportunity to trade helped create new dynasties. Japan, Russia, and England emerged on the world stage. But even in these newer regimes, competition and conflict created enormous internal pressures, some of which sparked domestic upheaval.

STUDY QUESTIONS

Ⓖ WWNORTON.COM/STUDYSPACE

1. Define mercantilism and analyze how this philosophy shaped the Atlantic world during the period covered in this chapter. How did mercantilist practices affect all regions of the Atlantic world?
2. Describe the plantation complex in the Caribbean. Why was it so valued by Europeans relative to other regions of the Americas?
3. Analyze how the Atlantic slave trade reshaped sub-Saharan African societies and polities during this era. Which regions and groups benefited from Africa's growing entanglements in global commerce?
4. Analyze how global trade affected the history of the Ottoman and Mughal empires during this era. How did each regime respond to these growing entanglements?
5. List and describe major factors that caused the end of the Ming dynasty and the rise of the Qing dynasty in China during this era. How did global trade affect this outcome? How did Qing rulers react to global commerce?
6. Analyze to what extent the Tokugawa Shogunate succeeded in creating a strong central government in Japan during this time. How did it avoid the problems associated with expanding trade faced by many other dynasties during this time period?
7. Compare and contrast the expansionist policies of the Russian state with those pursued by the British and French regimes during this time period. How were they similar and how were they different?
8. Analyze how increased global trade shaped the history of Europe during this time period. Why did Britain (England) tend to be the largest beneficiary of these trends in terms of regional dynastic rivalries? What other social and political groups were strongly affected by Europe's increased global entanglements?
9. Compare and contrast the impact of global entanglements on European and Asian dynasties during this era. Did any dynasty hold an advantage over others in terms of controlling these entanglements and using them to enrich their societies?

FURTHER READINGS

Alam, Muzaffar, *The Crisis of Empire in Mughal North India* (1993). Represents the best of the new interpretations on the subject.

Bay, Edna, *Wives of the Leopard: Gender, Politics, and Culture in the Kingdom of Dahomey* (1998). A useful treatment of gender issues in Dahomey.

Blackburn, Robin, *The Making of New World Slavery: From the Baroque to the Modern, 1492–1800* (1997). A good place to begin when studying African slavery and the Atlantic slave trade, it compares the early expansion of the plantation systems across the Atlantic and throughout the Americas.

Crossley, Pamela, *A Translucent Mirror: History and Identity in Qing Imperial Ideology* (1999). The author historicizes the formation of identities such as "Manchu" and "Chinese" during the Qing period.

Dennis, Matthew, *Cultivating a Landscape of Peace: Iroquois-European Encounters in Seventeenth-Century America* (1993). An excellent discussion of the relations of the Iroquois and the European colonists.

De Vries, Jan, *The Economy of Europe in an Age of Crisis, 1600–1750* (1976). A useful discussion of the European economy.

Dvornik, Francis, *The Slavs in European History and Civilization* (1962). Thorough analysis of Muscovy as well as other Slavic dynasties that did not achieve the power of the Russian one.

Flynn, Dennis O., and Arturo Girladez (eds.), *Metals and Money in an Emerging World Economy* (1997). A collection of articles about the place of silver in the world economy.

Forsyth, James, *A History of the Peoples of Siberia: Russia's North Asian Colony 1581–1990* (1992). A narrative overview of a violent history reminiscent of the western expansion of the United States.

Glahn, Richard von, *Fountains of Fortune: Money and Monetary Policy in China, 1000–1700* (1996). A discussion of the place of silver in the Chinese economy.

Halperin, Charles J., *Russia and the Golden Horde: The Mongol Impact on Medieval Russian History* (1985). A book on the rise of Muscovy, forebear of the Russian Empire, from within the Mongol realm.

Hattox, Ralph S., *Coffee and Coffeehouses: The Origins of a Social Beverage in the Medieval Near East* (1985). This work shows how widespread and popular coffee consumption and coffeehouses were around the world.

Huang, Ray, *1587, A Year of No Significance: The Ming Dynasty in Decline* (1981). An insightful analysis of the problems confronting the late Ming.

Katz, Stanley N., John M. Murrin, and Douglas Greenberg (eds.), *Colonial America: Essays in Politics and Social Development* (5th ed., 2001). Brings together many of the most important interpretations of seventeenth- and eighteenth-century life in North America.

Klein, Herbert S., *The Atlantic Slave Trade* (1999). A recent study of the African slave trade.

Lensen, George, *The Russian Push Toward Japan: Russo-Japanese Relations 1697–1875* (1959). A discussion of why and how Japan established its first border with another state and how Russia pursued its ambitions in the Pacific.

Lockhart, James, *The Nahuas After the Conquest* (1992). A landmark study of the social reorganization of Mesoamerican societies under Spanish rule.

Lovejoy, Paul, *Transformations in Slavery: A History of Slavery in Africa* (1983). An excellent discussion of African slavery.

Nakane, Chie, and Shinzaburo Oishi (eds.), *Tokugawa Japan: The Social and Economic Antecedents of Modern Japan* (1990). First-

Chronology

1600

THE AMERICAS
- English establish Jamestown colony, 1607
- French establish colony of New France, 1608
- Dutch settle New Amsterdam, 1624

SOUTH ASIA
- Aurangzeb expands Mughal Empire, 1658–1707

RUSSIA
- Romanov dynasty established in Russia, 1613
- Russian state's frontier reaches Pacific, 1639
- Peter the Great rules Russia, 1682–1725

EAST ASIA
- Political and economic problems in China, 1600–1640s
- Tokugawa Shogunate founded in Japan, 1603
- Japanese expel European missionaries, 1637
- Dutch seize Melaka from Portuguese, 1641
- Ming dynasty falls to the Qing, 1644

EUROPE
- English East India Company established, 1600
- Dutch East India Company established, 1602
- Thirty Years' War, 1618–1648
- Dutch West India Company founded, 1621
- English Civil War, 1642–1649
- Reign of France's Louis XIV, 1643–1715
- Glorious Revolution in England, 1688–1689

AFRICA
- Massive expansion of the Atlantic slave trade, 1600–1800
- Oyo Empire expands to coast of Africa, 1690s–1713

SOUTHWEST ASIA
- Koprulu reforms revitalize Ottoman Empire, 1656–1676

rate essays on Japanese village society, urban life, literacy, and culture.

Pamuk, Sevket, *A Monetary History of the Ottoman Empire* (2000). A discussion of the place of silver in the Ottoman Empire.

Parker, Geoffrey (ed.), *The Thirty Years' War* (1997). The standard account of the conflict and its outcomes.

Perdue, Peter C., *China Marches West: The Qing Conquest of Central Asia* (2005). This volume chronicles the expansion of the Qing Empire to its northwest, drawing comparisons to other colonial empires and their legacies.

Platonov, S. F., *Ivan the Terrible* (1986). Covers the controversies over Russia's infamous tsar.

Rawski, Evelyn, *The Last Emperors: A Social History of Qing Imperial Institutions* (1998). This volume explores the mechanisms and processes through which the Qing court negotiated its Manchu identity.

Reid, Anthony, *Charting the Shape of Early Modern Southeast Asia* (1999). A collection of articles by a leading historian of Southeast Asia.

Richter, Daniel, *The Ordeal of the Longhouse: The Peoples of the Iroquois League in the Era of European Colonization* (1992). A superb analysis of the Iroquois and their relations with Dutch, English, and French colonists.

Spence, Jonathan, and John Wills (eds.), *From Ming to Ch'ing: Conquest, Region, and Continuity in Seventeenth-Century China* (1979). Covers the various aspects of a tumultuous period of dynastic transition.

Thornton, John, *Africa and Africans in the Making of the Atlantic World, 1400–1800* (1998). A wonderful discussion of how African slaves played a large role in the formation of the Atlantic world.

Thornton, John K., *The Kongolese Saint Anthony: Dona Beatriz Kimpa Vita and the Antonian Movement, 1684–1706* (1998). An excellent monograph on religious movements in the Kongo.

Toby, Ronald P., *State and Diplomacy in Early Modern Japan: Asia in the Development of the Tokugawa Bakufu* (1984). A demolition of the myth of Japanese isolationism with a subtle alternative view.

Vilar, Pierre, *A History of Gold and Money* (1991). An excellent study of the development of the early silver and gold economies.

1700										1800

▮ *Seven Years' War, 1756–1763*

▮ *Asante state expands in Africa, 1701–1750*

▮ *Safavid Empire under assault, 1722–1773*

Chapter

14

CULTURES OF SPLENDOR AND POWER, 1500–1780

The flourishing of the Indian Ocean trade and the consolidation of empires made for considerable prosperity in Eurasia by 1500. In the seventeenth and eighteenth centuries, silver from the New World coursed through the arteries of world trade, creating new wealth, especially in western Europe. China, the Islamic empires, and Europe developed bureaucracies that could more effectively extract wealth from their lands and used their newfound prosperity to patronize the arts and sciences. Monarchs built architectural masterpieces often as a means to prove the legitimacy of their rule by displaying their taste and munificence. Book production and consumption soared, with some publications even finding their way across the world. Artists and writers in distant places reveled in their cultural attainments and celebrated the vitality of their ways of life. Experiments in religious toleration helped to foster cultural diversity, though these were often difficult to sustain.

World prosperity supported cultural splendors and fostered knowledge of foreign ways. This was an era of vastly increased cultural commerce. Europeans, the most avid observers and borrowers, invented what they believed to be universal principles. But intellectual developments still remained rooted in the cultural soil of each of the different regions of the world. In Africa, the slave trade enriched the rulers of some kingdoms, but the traditions of African sculpture and crafts developed as they had for centuries. So, too, Ottoman, Safavid, and Mughal architecture remained wedded to Islamic precepts, and Chinese writing and painting continued to be based on their particular beliefs and traditions. Muslim and Chinese scholars remained convinced that their forms of knowledge and art were superior to those of others. Even the indigenous peoples of the Americas, along with imported African slaves, tended to borrow European ideas selectively. Here, too, people ignored or rejected the universalist claims of Europeans and adhered instead to their own traditions of arts and sciences. Despite the increasing familiarity among peoples around the world, the real cultural battles of this period, like the struggles to achieve political autonomy, were waged inside polities, as centralized dynasties and new states struggled to dominate the cultural production of their intellectuals.

TRADE AND CULTURE

> → *How did world trade begin changing world cultures?*

It is not surprising that in 1500 the world's most flourishing cultures were in Asia, in the areas profiting from the Indian Ocean and China Sea trades. It was in China and the Islamic world that the spice and luxury trades first flourished; here, too, rulers had been most successful in establishing political stability and consolidating centralized control of taxation, law-making, and military force. This often entailed recruiting talented individuals, some of whom came from different religious, ethnic, or class backgrounds than did the ruling elite. It also entailed the promotion of new kinds of secular education, which sometimes flew in the face of traditional, clerical learning. Though older ways of making sense of the world and giving pleasure to its inhabitants did not die out, both trade and empire-building contributed to the diversification of global cultural production.

Of course, some rulers and some polities were more eager for change than others, and some cultures—in the Americas and the South Pacific, for example—found that conquest and trade undermined many aspects of indigenous cultural life. Although Europeans and native peoples often borrowed ideas and practices from one another, these were not free and equal exchanges. Native Americans, for example, adapted to European missionizing efforts in resourceful ways, by creating mixed forms of religious worship, but they did so in response to external pressure. And as the Europeans grew richer and swallowed new territories, it was their culture, not that of the local populations, that spread and diversified, absorbing ideas and practices from Native Americans and African slaves but offering these contributors little share of either expanding sovereignty or increasing prosperity.

European cultural flourishing after the mid-seventeenth century resulted in part, too, from the consolidation of nation-states and the centralization of wealth, administration, and military power by rulers often described as "enlightened absolutists." Europe's internal religious and political rivalries and its commercial ambitions propelled it to develop new forms of information-gathering, at home and especially

Focus Questions CULTURES OF SPLENDOR AND POWER

- → *How did world trade begin changing world cultures?*
- → *How did the Islamic empires foster vibrant and syncretic cultures?*
- → *How and why did the Chinese and Japanese governments attempt to control culture and knowledge?*
- → *What were the major tenets of Enlightenment thought?*
- → *How did global entanglements, particularly involvement in the slave trade, reshape African cultures?*
- → *How did cultural developments in the Americas reflect new global entanglements?*
- → *What role did race play in how Europeans viewed others, especially those from Oceania?*

 WWNORTON.COM/STUDYSPACE

abroad. By the eighteenth century's end, Europeans had collected information on everything from Sanskrit grammar to Polynesian wind currents. Based on the data they gathered, they created pragmatic principles for commercial and even colonial use, as well as a kind of empirical knowledge they felt could be extended to the rest of the world. In the eighteenth century, the decline of religious persecution and warfare made possible the notion that ideas and texts could and should circulate freely—though in many places, such as Tsarist Russia, this continued to be more dream than reality. The three scientific-colonizing voyages of Captain James Cook (1728–1779) in the South Pacific epitomized the search for knowledge about the unknown. In a few years, between 1768 and 1779, this virtually uncharted world suddenly became the subject of plays, poems, scientific treatises, and political rivalries. It is worth emphasizing how bizarre the desire to make this long, arduous trip would have seemed to Europeans just a few centuries earlier and how technically and fiscally impossible launching it would have been. Cook's voyages certainly signal, then, just how much Europe's wealth and aspirations had expanded.

The cultural flourishings of the sixteenth, seventeenth, and eighteenth centuries took place in a world much changed since the Mongol invasions and the Black Death. There were new dynasties. There were also many more people. By 1750, the world's population had doubled from its level in 1300. There was also a much greater volume of long-distance trade, which generated a level of prosperity that would have amazed even the wealthiest dynast 500 years earlier. Yet, despite the unifying aspects of world trade, each culture flourished in its own way and was shaped by local educational institutions and local artistic conventions. Ruling classes disseminated values that drew from their cherished classical texts, crafted their visions of the world on the basis of long-established moral and religious principles, mapped their geographies according to their traditional visions of the universe, and wrote their separate histories. They could still celebrate their achievements in politics, economics, and culture without worrying about threats from within or from without.

CULTURE IN THE ISLAMIC WORLD

> → *How did the Islamic empires foster vibrant and syncretic cultures?*

For centuries, Muslim elites had put significant resources into cultural development. As the Ottoman, the Safavid, and the Mughal empires extended their control, dominating territories from the Balkans to Bengal, new resources were available to fund cultural pursuits. Rulers used the vast agrarian

and commercial wealth at their disposal to patronize new schools and building projects, and the elite produced and consumed new books, artworks, and luxury goods. Cultural life was clearly connected to the politics of empire-building, as emperors and elites sought to gain prestige from their patronage of intellectuals and artists.

Forged under contrasting imperial auspices, the cultural and intellectual life of the Islamic world was organized in three distinct, regional worlds. In place of an earlier Islamic cosmopolitanism, a specific pattern of cultural flourishing prevailed within the boundaries of each empire. Though the Ottomans, the Safavids, and the Mughals were united by a common faith, each developed a relatively autonomous form of Muslim culture.

THE OTTOMAN CULTURAL SYNTHESIS

By the sixteenth century, the Ottoman Empire had developed a remarkably rich and syncretic culture. Its blend of ethnic, religious, and linguistic elements, in fact, exceeded in diversity and depth those of previous empires of the Islamic world. The Ottomans' creative and flexible cultural synthesis accommodated both Sufis (mystics who stressed contemplation

Suleiman the Lawgiver. The most illustrious ruler of the Ottoman Empire was Suleiman, who began his reign in 1520 and brought the empire to its military and political height. This miniature painting shows Suleiman giving advice to the crown prince.

and ecstasy through poetry, music, and dancing) and ultra-orthodox *ulama* (Islamic jurists who stressed tradition and religious law). It also balanced the interests of military men and administrators with the desires of clerics. Finally, it allowed autonomy to the minority faiths of Christianity and Judaism.

The Ottomans permitted religious diversity, allowing *dhimmis* (followers of religions permitted by law: Armenian Christians, Greek Orthodox Christians, and Jews) to organize themselves into *millets* (minority religious communities) as long as they acknowledged the political superiority of the Sunni and Sufi Muslims. Drawing on Islamic law, the Ottomans allowed the *dhimmis* to worship as they pleased, to send their children to their own religious schools, and to cultivate the arts and sciences as they wished. For this cultural autonomy, the *dhimmis* paid a special tax (*jizya*) that applied to all non-Muslims.

The Ottoman world achieved its cultural unity, above all, by what many regarded as the supreme intellectual achievement of the Ottomans, its system of administrative law, known as *kanun*. As the sultans gained control over diverse cultures and territories, they realized that the *sharia* (Islamic holy law) by itself would not suffice; it was silent on many crucial secular matters. Moreover, the far-flung Ottoman state needed a comprehensive and well-understood set of laws to bridge differences between the many different social and legal systems that had come under Ottoman rule. Mehmed II, conqueror of Constantinople, began the process of administrative reform. Mehmed recruited young boys, rather than established noblemen, to be trained as professional bureaucrats or military men, accountable directly to the sultan. Mehmed's most illustrious successor, Suleiman the Magnificent and the Lawgiver, continued his work, overseeing the codification of a comprehensive legal code. The code included laws on the rights and duties of subjects, on what clothes they could wear, and on how Muslims were to

Islamic Scientists. This fifteenth-century Persian miniature shows a group of Islamic scholars working with sophisticated navigational and astronomical instruments and reflects the importance that the educated classes in the Islamic world attached to observing and recording the regularities in the natural world. Indeed, many of Europe's advances in sailing drew upon knowledge from the Muslim world.

Ottoman Court Women. This eighteenth-century watercolor found in Topkapi Palace in Istanbul shows various musical instruments being played by court women, who were often called upon to provide entertainment.

relate to non-Muslims. The code reconciled many differences between administrative and religious law.

A highly developed educational system was crucial for the religious and intellectual integration of the Ottoman Empire. Here, too, the Ottomans displayed a talent for flexibility and showed their tolerance of difference. They encouraged three distinct educational systems that produced three streams of talent—civil and military bureaucrats, *ulama,* and Sufi masters. The Ottoman administrative elite received its training at a hierarchically organized set of schools, culminating in the palace schools at Topkapi. The young men who passed through these institutions staffed the civil and military bureaucracy of the Ottoman state and accepted posts all across the empire. In the religious sphere, an equally elaborate series of schools took students from elementary schools, where they received basic instruction in reading, writing, and numbers, on to higher schools (*madrassas*), where they learned law, religious sciences, the *Quran,* and the regular sciences. Graduates became *ulama.* Some entered the court system as *qadis* (judges); others became *muftis* (experts in religious law) or teachers. Yet another set of schools (*tekkes*) taught the devotional strategies and the religious knowledge for students to enter Sufi orders and ultimately to become masters of these brotherhoods. Each of these sets of schools created linkages between members of the Ottoman ruling elite and the orthodox religious elite that lasted throughout their lifetimes. The *tekkes* were particularly effective in promoting empire-wide social and religious solidarity and creating frameworks of integration for the Muslim peoples living under Ottoman rule.

The Ottomans attached great prestige to education and scholarship. Scholars claimed that "an hour of learning was worth more than a year of prayer." Schools stressed training in law, language, religious commentary, rhetoric, logic, and theology over the natural and mathematical sciences. Yet, teachers did not ignore the sciences, and Ottoman scholars carried out important work in astronomy and physics, as well as in history, geography, and politics.

Under the patronage of a reformist-minded grand vizier, Damat Ibrahim Pasha, Ottoman intellectuals also took an interest in works of European science, some of which appeared in Turkish translation for the first time in the eighteenth century. The most impressive of these Ottoman efforts to disseminate European knowledge occurred when a Hungarian convert to Islam, Ibrahim Muteferrika (1674–1745), set up a printing press in Istanbul in 1729. Muteferrika published works on science, history, and geography. In one of his published essays, printed in 1731, he included sections on geometry, a discussion of the works of Copernicus, Galileo, and Descartes, and a plea to the Ottoman educated classes to learn from Europe. When his patron, the grand vizier Damat Ibrahim Pasha, was killed in 1730, however, the *ulama* moved vigorously to close off this promising avenue of contact with western learning.

The Ottomans combined inherited traditions with new elements in other ways as well. The Islamic world took up portraiture after the Italian painter Gentile Bellini visited Istanbul and composed a portrait of Mehmed II. Mehmed's pious successor, Bayezid II, disapproved and sold the portrait in the bazaar, but nonetheless, the genre spread.

In some areas the Ottomans kept their own styles. The magnificent architectural monuments of the sixteenth through eighteenth centuries, including mosques, gardens, tombs, forts, and palaces, were little touched by western influence. Nor did the Ottomans show much interest in western literature or music. For the most part, they still believed God had given the Islamic world a monopoly on truth and enlightenment; their military successes proved his favor for

The Ottomans and the Tulip. From the earliest times, the Ottomans admired the beauty of the tulip. (*Left*) Sultan Mehmed II smelling a tulip, symbol of the Ottoman sultans. (*Right*) The Ottomans used tulip motifs to decorate tiles in homes and mosques and pottery wares, as on the plate shown here.

their community and culture, over and against that of the infidel.

Despite being pushed back from the gates of Vienna in 1683, the Ottomans still enjoyed a sense of well-being and prosperity during the so-called Tulip Era that followed. The Ottoman elite had long been fascinated with the bold colors and delicate blooms of the tulip. For centuries, the flower served as the symbol of the Ottoman sultans. Mehmed the Conqueror and Suleiman the Lawgiver grew tulips in the most secluded and prestigious courtyards of the Topkapi Palace in Istanbul. Many Ottoman warriors wore undergarments embroidered with tulips into battle as a means to ensure victory. But the flower's great age was the early eighteenth century, which contemporaries dubbed "the tulip period." At this time, the Ottomans developed the same sort of infatuation that the Dutch had developed a century earlier. Interest in the flower spread from the sultan and his household to the wealthy classes, and estate owners began to specialize in growing tulips. They used tulip designs to decorate tiles and fabrics and to adorn public buildings, and they celebrated the beauty of the flower every spring by holding elaborate tulip festivals.

Fascination with the tulip was one manifestation of a widespread delight in the things of this world, encouraged by Grand Vizier Damat Ibrahim (ruled 1718–1730). As well as restoring order to the empire, Ibrahim loosened customary *ulama* controls over the social activities of the people, and he sanctioned elite consumption of luxury goods. The working classes, too, were drawn into this celebration of life's pleasures as coffeehouses and taverns became centers of popular entertainment. Indeed, eighteenth-century Ottoman demand for luxury goods was so extensive—including lemons, soap, pepper, metal tools, coffee, and wine—that a well-traveled diplomat looked askance at the supposed wealth of Europe. On the contrary, he wrote, "In most of the provinces [of Europe], poverty is widespread, as a punishment for being infidels. Anyone who travels in these areas must confess that goodness and abundance are reserved for the Ottoman realms."

SAFAVID CULTURE

The Safavid Empire in Persia was not as long-lived as the Ottoman Empire, but it was significant in the history of Southeast Asia for giving the Shiite version of Islam a home base. Previously, there had been Shiite governments, the most powerful being the Fatimid state in Egypt. But once the Mamluks overthrew the Fatimids in the thirteenth century, Shiism became overwhelmingly a religion of opposition and a faith embraced by those seeking to overthrow established rulers. This, of course, made for a great dilemma for Shiite groups; once they came to power they were likely to face opposition from other dissatisfied groups—who also drew on the tenets of Shiism. Rather like Protestant sectarianism, Shiism cre-

ated a culture of criticism with the potential to undermine dynastic stability.

The Safavids faced just such dilemmas, for they owed their rise to the support of Turkish-speaking tribesmen, the *kizilbash* ("red heads," so called because of the red color of their turbans), who espoused a populist and charismatic form of Islam. In power, the Safavid shahs endeavored to cultivate the more conservative elements of Iranian society: Persian-speaking landowners and orthodox *ulama*. They turned away from the Turkish-speaking Islamic brotherhoods with their mystical and Sufi qualities, in spite of the fact that these groups had facilitated their rise to power.

Just as the great achievement of the Ottomans was the ability to blend Sufism and clerical orthodoxy, so the Safavid triumph was to create a political-religious system based on Shiism and loyalty to the Safavid royal family. Also like the Ottomans, the Safavids used well-established institutions like the *madrassas* and brotherhood lodges (*takkiyas*) and the *ulama* to inculcate the new Shiite orthodoxy. Even after the Safavids were swept from power in the eighteenth century, Shiism remained the fundamental religion of the Iranian people.

Under the Safavids' most successful and energetic ruler, Shah Abbas I (ruled 1587–1629), Persia enjoyed a cultural revival stimulated by royal patronage and the great prosperity during his reign. Once Abbas had solidified his power, he

The King's Book of Kings. The Persian poet Firdawsi (934–1020) produced an epic poem, *The King's Book of Kings,* which celebrated the long history of Persia, glorifying its pre-Islamic past. This miniature illustration from a sixteenth-century version of the book portrays life at the royal palace.

ISLAMIC VIEWS OF THE WORLD

Although maps attempt to give the impression of objectivity and geographic precision, the way in which they arrange the world, the names that they give to locations, the areas that they place in the center or at the peripheries, and the text that accompanies them show the mapmakers' view of the world around them. Thus, in most cultures, official maps located their own major administrative and religious sites at the center of the universe and reflected local elites' speculations about how the world was organized. The two maps below, which are taken from the Islamic world, are interesting in this regard. The famous map of al-Idrisi, dating from the twelfth century, was a standard one of the period. It showed the world as it was known to peoples on the Afro-Eurasian landmass at that time and thus featured only three landmasses—Africa, Asia, and Europe. The second Islamic map, made in Iran around 1700, was unabashedly Islamic, for it offered a grid that measured the distances from any location in the Islamic world to the holy city of Mecca.

Al-Idrisi map, twelfth century.

Iranian map, seventeenth century.

→ *What does each map tell us about the worldview of these Islamic societies?*

→ *What main purposes do you think each map was used for?*

sought to make a grand gesture to display his power, wealth, and artistic sensibility. In 1598 he moved the capital of the state to Isfahan and hired elite artists and architects from all corners of Persia (as well as beyond) to design a city that would dwarf even Delhi and Istanbul, the other showplaces of the Islamic world. His centerpiece was the great plaza next to his palace and the royal mosque at the heart of the capital; when completed, the plaza, surrounded by elaborate public and religious buildings, was seven times as large as that of San Marco in Venice.

Other aspects of Safavid intellectual life also reflected a culture dominated by the ideals, aspirations, and wealth of the court and of its landed and commercial classes. Safavid artists perfected the design of the illustrated book, the outstanding example being *The King's Book of Kings,* which contained 250 miniature illustrations. They mastered the technique of three-dimensional representation and were skilled in harmonizing colors. Master weavers continued to produce the silks and carpets long traded throughout the world. Artisans painted tiles in vibrant colors and created tile mosaics that adorned mosques and other buildings. The Safavids also developed an elaborate calligraphy that was the envy of artists throughout the whole Islamic world.

POWER AND CULTURE UNDER THE MUGHALS

Like the Safavids and the Ottomans, the Mughals fostered a courtly and prosperous high culture. Because the Mughals, like the Ottomans and unlike the Safavids, ruled over a large non-Muslim population, the Islamic high culture that developed in South Asia was a broad and open one. This culture

Akbar Leading Religious Discussion. This miniature painting from 1604 shows Akbar receiving Muslim theologians and Jesuits. The Jesuits (in the black robes on the left) hold a page relating, in Persian, the birth of Christ. A lively debate will follow the Jesuits' claims on behalf of Christianity.

attached high value to works of art and learning, making it possible to overlook the religious identity of non-Muslim artists and to admit them into the world of the arts and learning. Thus, while Islamic traditions were structurally dominant, the Hindus shared with the Muslims the aristocratic culture of learning, music, painting, and architecture; the realm of high culture functioned as an arena in which religious differences could be bridged by aesthetic refinement and philosophical sophistication.

The promise of an open Islamic high culture found its greatest fulfillment under the Mughal emperor Akbar (ruled 1556–1605). In addition to being a very successful military leader, Akbar was a popular ruler who allowed common people as well as nobles from all ethnic groups to converse with him at court. His quest for universal truths outside the strict limits of the *sharia* led him to develop a religion of his own, which incorporated many aspects of Hindu belief and ritual practice. His trusted advisor Abulfazl (1551–1602) encouraged Akbar's eclectic pursuits and composed a grand-scale tribute to the ruler and his predecessors that is still a major source of our knowledge of early Mughal history. In the *Akbarnamah* (the Book of Akbar), written between 1587 and 1602, Abulfazl described Akbar as a philosopher-king, someone who had received kingship as a gift from God because he was a true philosopher and who was born a perfect person in the Sufi sense. Regrettably, Akbar's son Salim was jealous of Abulfazl and arranged for his murder.

In architecture, too, the Mughals produced eclectic masterpieces. This was already evident in the combination of Persian, Indian, and Ottoman elements in the tombs and mosques built by Akbar's predecessors. But Akbar enhanced this syncretic tendency in the elaborate new city he built at Fatehpur Sikri, beginning in 1571. The buildings included residences for the nobility (whose loyalty Akbar wanted to secure), gardens, a drinking and gambling zone, and even an experimental school devoted to studying language acquisition in children. The huge complex was completed in about a decade, a much shorter time than it took for Louis XIV to build the comparable royal residence—a century later—at Versailles.

Akbar's descendant Shah Jahan (ruled 1628–1658) was also a lavish patron of architecture and the arts. In 1630, Shah Jahan ordered the building in Agra of a magnificent tomb of white marble for his beloved wife, Mumtaz Mahal, who had been—like many other women in the Mughal court—an important political counselor. Designed by an Indian architect of Persian origin, this structure, known as the Taj Mahal, took twenty years and 20,000 workers to build. The forty-two-acre complex included a main gateway, garden, minarets, and a mosque; the mausoleum for Mumtaz Mahal was built of translucent white marble and lay squarely in the middle of the structure, enclosed by four identical facades and crowned by a majestic central dome rising to 240 feet. The stone inlays of different types and hues, organized in geometrical and floral patterns, and Quranic verses inscribed in

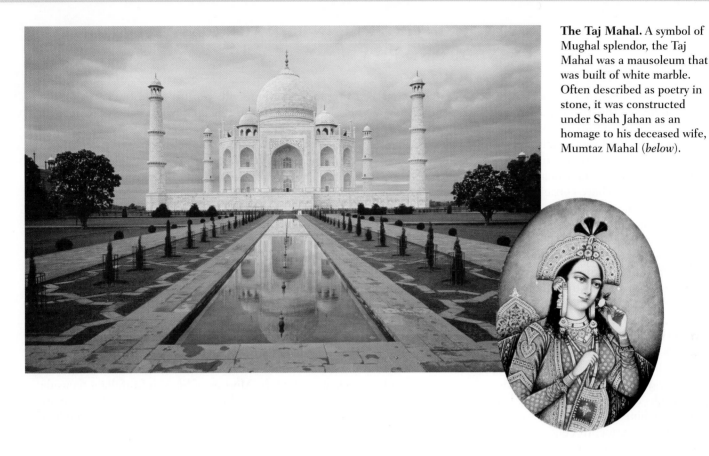

The Taj Mahal. A symbol of Mughal splendor, the Taj Mahal was a mausoleum that was built of white marble. Often described as poetry in stone, it was constructed under Shah Jahan as an homage to his deceased wife, Mumtaz Mahal (*below*).

Arabic calligraphy gave the white marble surface an appearance of delicacy and lightness. Blending Persian and Islamic design with Indian materials and motifs, this poetry in stone represented the most splendid example of Mughal cultural efflorescence and the combining of cultural traditions. Like Shah Abbas's great plaza, the Taj Mahal lent a sense of refined grandeur to this Islamic empire's formidable political, military, and economic power.

Though the brilliance of Akbar, Abulfazl, and Shah Jahan was not equaled under later emperors, Mughal culture remained vibrant. François Bernier, a seventeenth-century French traveler to the Mughal Empire, wrote admiringly of the broad philosophical interests of Danishmand Khan, a prominent intellectual whom the Emperor Aurangzeb had appointed as the governor of Delhi. According to Bernier, Khan avidly read the works of the French philosophers Gassendi and Descartes and studied Sanskrit treatises to understand different philosophical traditions. But Aurangzeb, a very pious Muslim, heavily favored Islamic arts and sciences. He dismissed many of the court's painters and musicians, and in 1669 ordered that all recently built non-Islamic places of worship be torn down. In his court, intellectuals debated whether metaphysics, astronomy, medicine, mathematics, and ethics were of any use in the practice of Islam. Clearly women, at least at court, were not discouraged from pursuing the arts; two of Aurangzeb's daughters, Zebunissa and Zinat-um-nissa, were accomplished poets.

Well into the eighteenth century, the Mughal nobility exuded confidence and lived in unrivaled luxury. The presence of foreign scholars and artists only added to the luster of courtly culture, and the elite eagerly consumed foreign luxuries. Traders who carried goods from China or Europe were welcome. Besides, foreign trade brought increasing supplies of silver to India, helping to advance the money economy and support the sumptuous urban lifestyles of the nobility. The Mughals were also quick to assimilate European military technology and resources. They hired the Europeans as gunners and sappers in their armies, employed them to forge guns, and bought guns and cannons from them. Their appreciation for European knowledge and technology, however, was limited. Thus, when Thomas Roe, the representative of the English East India Company, presented an edition of Mercator's *Maps of the World* to Emperor Jahangir in 1617, the emperor returned it a fortnight later with the remark that no one could read or understand it. Supremely confident of their own cultural world, the Mughals saw limited use for European knowledge and culture.

The cultural life of the Islamic world was centered in Istanbul, Cairo, Isfahan, and Delhi and thus drew on intellectual currents that spanned the Eurasian–North African landmass.

Global Connections & Disconnections

ROYAL ARCHITECTURE IN THE AGE OF SPLENDOR AND POWER

By the seventeenth century, all of the great imperial monarchies of the Afro-Eurasian landmass had elaborate architectural structures that projected the power and the values of their individual states. All were ornate and splendid. All were expensive to construct and involved the best craftsmen and artists available to the monarchs. While they seem not to have consciously borrowed from one another, they all arose or were elaborated on in an age when imperial and monarchical power was at a high point. In the case of the Ottoman, Safavid, and Mughal royal structures, the emperors brought in skilled artisans and craftsmen from outside their empires, and through the work of these skilled people they indirectly borrowed from the achievements of other cultures. Yet, each structure reflected unique elements of its own culture as well as the vision of the ruler or rulers who paid for its construction.

We start with the Forbidden City of Beijing, which was the earliest of these sites of royal power and, because of its worldwide reputation, an inspiration to other powerful monarchs and emperors. Beijing became the capital of a unified Chinese empire for the first time under the Mongols in the thirteenth century, although the city had enjoyed some prominence in earlier times. Chinggis Khan had razed the old city to the ground, but his successor, Kubilai Khan, restored the city and made it the capital of his empire. Kubilai Khan did more than that, however. He rebuilt the city, calling it Khanbaliq, along the lines of early imperial Chinese capitals. Following the classical ideal of a capital city, Khanbaliq was laid out on strict north-south and east-west axes. It was surrounded by high walls, and the inner part of the city housed the emperor and his court. The Ming successors, who overthrew the Mongols, first made Nanjing their capital, but the Yongle Emperor reinstated Beijing as the imperial capital. The inner areas of the city, known as the Imperial City and the Forbidden City, were aligned on a firm north-south axis and were thought to be the very center of the Chinese state and indeed of the whole universe. Here, government took place, and it was to here that those who sought the favor of the emperor journeyed. Indeed, only those who had business with the state were permitted to enter the imperial domain. They entered bowing and scraping ("kowtowing") as indications of the great respect they felt for the awesome power of the emperor. As befit a powerful figure, the ruler was expected to stay within the confines of the imperial quarters (although Qing emperors—who succeeded the Ming in the seventeenth century—did travel with more regularity) and had to rely on envoys and chief ministers for information about the rest of his kingdom and the outside world. So effective were these arrangements that the Qing rulers retained Beijing as their capital, and, despite changes and renovations, the Qing kept the Ming structures mostly in place.

The center of Safavid power in the seventeenth century was the great plaza at Isfahan, the inspiration of Shah Abbas, who ruled from 1587 to 1629. It reflected Shah Abbas's notion that trade, government, and religion should be brought together under the authority of the supreme political leader. A great public mosque, called the Shah Abbas Mosque, dominated one end of the plaza, which measured 1,667 feet by 517 feet. At the other end were the trading stalls and markets, which made Iran wealthy. On one side of the rectangular mosque were the offices of the government, and on the other side was an exquisite mosque, called the Mosque of Shaykh Lutfollah, set aside for the shah's personal use. Many of Shah Abbas's most proficient craftsmen came from India and were familiar with the architecture of the Mughal Empire.

The Palace of Versailles, which Louis XIV built in the 1660s, has many similarities with the Isfahan plaza, although the French builders had no knowledge of Isfahan. Here, too, the great royal palace opens outward onto a large courtyard. The buildings adjoining the central palace housed the great notables and clergy, whom the French monarchs wanted to keep an eye on.

The Topkapi Palace was in Istanbul, the capital of the Ottoman Empire. Topkapi began to take shape in 1458 under Mehmed II and was steadily added to over the years. As described in detail in Chapter 11, Topkapi projected royal authority in much the same way as the Forbidden City emphasized the power of the Chinese emperors. Here, too, the governing officials worked enclosed within massive walls, and the monarchs rarely went outside their inner domain. By isolating the rulers from the rest of society the Ottomans and the Chinese made even more awesome the power of their monarchs.

Yet another advocate of royal architecture was the Mughal emperor Shah Jahan, who ruled from 1628 until 1658. He is best known for his peacock throne; for the Taj Mahal, which he built as a magnificent tomb for his wife, Mumtaz Mahal; and for his building program for the state's capital at Delhi.

But from Islam's founding, Muslims had looked eastward, to India and China, not to Europe, for external inspiration. While the crusades had proved that Europeans could be worthy military rivals, most Muslims continued to regard Europeans as rude barbarians, who had little to teach Islamic scholars. Thus, the world histories that Muslim intellectuals had composed in the fourteenth century had said little about Europe, and the Islamic elites in Persia, India, and the Ottoman Empire in the seventeenth and eighteenth centuries continued to view Europeans as less than their cultural and political equals.

CULTURE AND POLITICS IN EAST ASIA

> → *How and why did the Chinese and Japanese governments attempt to control culture and knowledge?*

Like the Ottomans, Safavids, and Mughals, the Chinese did not need to prove to anyone the richness of their scholarly and artistic traditions. China had long been a venerable and renowned center of learning, its emperors and elites serving as patrons to a large number of artists, poets, musicians, scientists, and teachers. But the cultural flourishing that characterized late Ming and early Qing China owed less to imperial leadership than to a robust internal market. A growing population and extensive mercantile networks proved instrumental in enhancing the circulation and exchange of ideas as well as goods. As a result, China's cultural sphere underwent significant diversification and expansion, predating similar changes elsewhere. For the dynasty to remain at the center of this expanding cultural sphere, it had to exert increased control over new consumers and producers.

In Japan, too, economic prosperity created favorable conditions for cultural dynamism in this period. The looming presence of its giant neighbor across the sea had rendered the Japanese historically amenable to recognizing outside influences. Like the Chinese dynastic government, the ruling Tokugawa Shogunate tried to disseminate a cultural orthodoxy based on Confucian notions of order and hierarchy and to shield the country from potentially subversive ideas. But the forces that worked to undermine the government's control of knowledge in China proved stronger still in Japan. Japan's decentralized political structure facilitated the spread of different cultural currents, including European ideas and practices. By the eighteenth century, in struggling to define its own identity through these different contending currents, the cultural scene in Japan was rather more lively, open, and varied than its counterpart in China.

CHINA: THE CHALLENGE OF EXPANSION AND DIVERSITY

TRANSMISSION OF IDEAS In the sixteenth and seventeenth centuries, China witnessed significant expansion in the publication and circulation of books and ideas. The phenomenon had less to do with technological innovations—both woodblock and moveable type printing had been known in China for centuries—than with the gradual decentralization of cultural production. At the outset, the state provided the initiative for book production—sponsoring and printing editions of Confucian texts—but as the years passed, the increasing commercialization of the economy eroded governmental controls.

Schools acquired books not officially sanctioned by the state as early as the fifteenth century. As an observer proudly remarked when a school in Shanghai built a library in 1484, its collection included "the six classics, the imperially produced books issued by the Ming court, plus the philosophers of the hundred schools and the histories; there isn't a title they don't have!" The holdings, in other words, clearly exceeded the corpus of official publications. Although local magistrates still backed library expansion, seeing this as part of a government effort to control the production of knowledge, the state could not dictate the way in which all books were produced and consumed. While officials could and did clamp down on unorthodox texts, the empire had no centralized system of censorship, and many unauthorized opinions circulated freely.

By the late Ming era, a burgeoning commercial publishing sector had emerged, catering to the diverse social, cultural,

Ming Publication. A typical late Ming publication with illustrations of the lives of emperors. These images refer to the First Emperor (r. 221–210 BCE), who was said to have buried scholars alive and burned books deemed threatening to his rule.

and religious needs of the educated elites and the growing urban population. European visitors were struck by the vast collections of printed materials housed in Chinese libraries, describing them as "magnificently built" and "finely adorn'd." In fact, the latter part of the Ming was an age of collections of other sorts as well. Many members of the elite in this increasingly affluent society cultivated a passion for acquiring physical objects for display as a sign of their status, refinement, and taste. Connoisseurship of all the arts reached unprecedented levels. Consumers could build their collections by purchasing artworks from multiple sources, from roadside peddlers to monasteries to gentlemen dealers whose proclaimed love of art masked the commercial orientation of their passions.

Perhaps more importantly, books and other luxury goods were now more affordable. A low-quality commentary on the Confucian classics—the Four Books—published in Nanjing in 1615 cost only half a tael of silver (a unit of measurement based on the silver's weight). Even a low-level private tutor could earn more than forty taels from tuition in a year. Increasingly, publishers offered diverse wares: readers could purchase guidebooks for patrons of the arts, travelers, or merchants; handbooks for those performing rituals; manuals on how to choose dates for ceremonies or on how to write proper letters. Other book choices included almanacs, encyclopedias, morality books, and medical manuals. Demand was especially high for study aids for the civil service examination. By the late fifteenth century, examinees were required to submit their answers in the so-called eight-legged style, a highly structured form of essay in eight parts. Model essays, written by either examiners or successful candidates, flooded the

Chinese Civil Service Exam. Lining the sides of this Chinese examination compound were cells in which candidates sat for the examination. Other than three long boards—the highest served as a shelf, the middle one as a desk, and the lowest as a seat—the cell had neither furniture nor a door. Indeed, the cells were little more than spaces partitioned on three sides by brick walls and covered by a roof; the floors were packed dirt. Generations of candidates spent three days and two nights in succession in these cells as they strove to enter officialdom.

market. In 1595, a scandal broke out in Beijing as the second-place graduate at the metropolitan examination reproduced verbatim a series of model essays published by commercial printers. Just over twenty years later, the top graduate was found to have plagiarized a winning essay submitted years earlier. Ironically, then, the increased circulation of knowledge led critics to bemoan a decline in real learning; instead of mastering the classics, they charged, the candidates were simply memorizing the work of others.

Examination hopefuls were not the only beneficiaries of the booming book trade. Elite women also took advantage of widening access to China's literary culture. As readers, writers, and editors, educated women now assumed a limited but visible presence in what was hitherto an exclusively male domain. Anthologies of poetry produced by women were particularly popular. Besides producing for the market, some collected works of individual women were issued by their families for limited circulation to celebrate the refinement of the family. Men of letters were quick to recognize the market potential of women's writings; some also saw the less regularized style of women—who usually acquired their skills through family channels rather than through state-sponsored schools —as a means to challenge what was perceived as the stifling stylistic conformity of the sixteenth century. The promotion of new styles opened up opportunities for women writers. On rare occasions, women even served as publishers themselves.

If in this era some elite women enjoyed success in the cultural sphere, the period also brought increasing restrictions on their lives. Widow remarriage and premarital sex might have been discouraged in earlier times, but in the sixteenth, seventeenth, and eighteenth centuries they had become unthinkable for women from "good" families. The practice of footbinding, meanwhile, continued to spread among the common people; small, delicate feet signified femininity and respectability for a larger share of the population. Ironically, the thriving publishing sector produced plays and novels that helped the government's effort to promote a stricter morality for women, underscoring the fact that increasing cultural production has not always served the cause of human liberation.

POPULAR CULTURE AND RELIGION Important as the development of the book trade was, its impact on the majority of men and women in late Ming China was indirect. To those excluded from the literary culture because they could not read or could not read well, the transmission of cultural norms and values occurred through oral communication, ritual performance, and daily practices. The Ming government tried to control these channels, too. It appointed village elders as guardians of local society and instituted a system of "village compacts" to ensure communal social responsibility for proper conduct and observation of the laws.

Still, the everyday life of rural and small-town dwellers existed mostly outside these official networks. Apart from toiling in the field, the villagers' social milieu was typically shaped

Foot Binding. Two images of bound feet: (*left*) as an emblem of feminine respectability when wrapped and concealed, as on this well-to-do Chinese woman; (*right*) as an object of curiosity and condemnation when exposed for the world to see.

by a variety of popular cultural and religious practices. Most villages had shrines honoring the guardian spirits of the locality as well as Buddhist and Daoist temples, not all of which were officially approved.

Villagers often undertook group pilgrimages to religious sites. They might attend periodic markets in adjacent towns, which during good times would be filled with restaurants, brothels, and other venues of entertainment. Otherwise, their links to the outside world were forged by gathering news and gossip in the teahouses or marketplaces, listening to the tales of itinerant storytellers and traveling monks, or by watching performances by touring theater groups on portable stages or in the courtyards of temples. Despite official vigilance, the open-ended nature of such a process of cultural transmission meant that village audiences were quite capable of appropriating and reinterpreting official norms and values to serve their own purposes and to challenge the dictates of the government.

The popular religions of the late Ming period were syncretic, and religious practices remained diffuse and decentralized. Sectarian lines were usually of minimal significance;

at the grassroots level there was often little distinction between Buddhist, Daoist, and local cults. Thus, China avoided the sectarian or religious warfare of post-Reformation Europe. This was largely because the Chinese believed in cosmic unity and, although they recognized and venerated spiritual forces, they did not consider any of them a Supreme Being who favored one faction over another. It was the emperor, rather than any religious group, who was supposed to have the Mandate of Heaven. The enforcement of orthodox norms and values and the suppression of popular resistance to them were more a matter of political than of religious control. Unless sects posed an obvious threat, the emperor had no real reason to regulate their spiritual practices. This situation made for a unique kind of religious tolerance.

TECHNOLOGY AND CARTOGRAPHY Belief in cosmic unity did not prevent members of the Chinese elite from devising technologies to master and control nature's operations in this world, however. The magnetic compass, gunpowder, and the printing press were invented in China. Chinese technicians had mastered iron casting and produced mechanical clocks centuries before Europeans managed such feats. Chinese astronomers were historically the most accurate observers of celestial phenomena in the premodern period, and they had compiled records of eclipses, comets, novae, and meteors. Their interest in astronomy and calendrical science was driven in part by the needs of the emperor—it was his job as the Son of Heaven, and thus mediator between heaven and earth, to determine the dates for the beginning of the agrarian seasons, festivities, mourning periods, and judicial assizes (periodic court sessions). The Chinese believed that the very stability of the empire depended on correct calculation of these dates. Even by modern standards, the Chinese were quite precise.

European missionaries and traders who arrived in China were greatly impressed by Chinese technological expertise, eloquence, and artistic refinement. Nonetheless, convinced of the superiority of their sciences, Christian missionaries sought to impress the Chinese with their knowledge in areas such as astronomy and cartography. Possessing sophisticated sciences of their own, the Chinese were selective in their appropriation of these novel European practices. To be sure, members of the Jesuit order served in the astronomy bureau within the imperial bureaucracy. In the early eighteenth century, they also undertook a series of monumental surveys of the Qing Empire for the emperor. Taken as a whole, however, the cultural impact of the Europeans in China in this period was decidedly limited.

Nowhere was this more evident than in the realm of cartography. Here, the Chinese demonstrated most clearly their understanding of the world. Significantly, Chinese maps were meant to encompass elements of history, literature, and art, not simply to offer technical detail. It was not that the necessary "scientific" techniques were lacking; a map made as early as 1136 reveals that Chinese cartographers were fully capable of producing maps drawn to scale. Yet, operating within a cultural context in which the written text was often privileged over visual and other forms of representation, Chinese elites did not always treat geometric and mathematical precision as the principal objective of cartography. Rather, these maps offered vivid testimony to the worldview of the Chinese elites. The realm of the Chinese emperor, as the ruler of "all under Heaven," typically occupied the very center of the map surrounded by foreign countries. As such, the physical scale of China and the actual size and distances to other lands were generally distorted. Still, some of the maps do manage to cover a vast expanse of territory. One fourteenth-century map includes an area stretching from Japan to the Atlantic, encompassing Europe and Africa.

Although Europeans might understand resistance to Christianization—they had, after all, long experience with heretics, infidels, and sectarian intransigence at home—they were puzzled by the Chinese resistance to the adoption of European science. In 1583, the Jesuit missionary Matteo Ricci brought European maps to China, hoping to impress the local elite with European learning. Ricci challenged the conventional wisdom of the Chinese elites, who held that the world was flat. His maps demonstrated the spherical shape of the earth—and that China was just one country among many other similar ones. Chinese critics complained that he treated the Ming Empire as just "a small unimportant country." As a concession, Ricci modified his projection and placed China closer to the center of the maps. He also followed the practice of Chinese cartographers in providing additional textual information. Still, the long-term impact of Ricci's maps was negligible. The makers of "Complete Maps of All under Heaven," who provided Qing China's images of the world until the mid-nineteenth century, did not consider the earth's shape or precise mathematical scale particularly important.

Jesuit Missionary. Shown in the garb of a Qing official, Father Johann Adam Schall von Bell was in Beijing when the Ming fell in 1644. Recognizing his scientific expertise, the new Qing government appointed him the director of the Imperial Bureau of Astronomy. Schall von Bell was close to the young Shunzhi Emperor, who called the Jesuit "Grandpa" and regularly discussed religion and politics with him.

Primary Source

CHINESE VIEWS OF THE WORLD

The Chinese developed cartographical skills at an early stage in their history. A third-century map, no longer extant, was designed to enable the emperors to "comprehend the four corners of the world without ever having to leave their imperial quarters." *The Huayi tu* map from 1136 depicted the whole world on stone stele and included 500 place names and textual information on foreign lands. The Jesuit missionary Matteo Ricci modified his original map of the world in response to Chinese concerns and placed China more in the center. Chinese maps devoted more attention to textual explanations that carried moral and political messages than to locating places. One such map is a Chinese wheel map, which is from the 1760s and is full of textual explanations.

The *Huayi tu* map, 1136.

Chinese wheel map, 1760s.

→ *Why do you think Chinese maps included textual messages that focused on moral and political themes?*

→ *How are these maps similar to and different from the Islamic maps?*

The European regime of spatial ordering, as represented through its cartography, was rejected as mostly irrelevant.

In China, prior to the nineteenth century, knowledge regarding foreign lands, despite a long history of contacts, remained rather partial. Like many other cultures, the Chinese empire cultivated an image of its own superiority and tended to see others through its own prism. From antiquity onward, Chinese elites glorified their own "white" complexions against the dark skin of the peasants, the black, wavy-haired "devils" of Southeast Asia, and the "ash-white" pallor of the Europeans. Chinese writers often identified groups of people as oddities, to be scrutinized with a mixture of curiosity and revulsion. A Ming geographical publication, for example, portrayed the Portuguese as "seven feet tall, having eyes like a cat, a mouth like an oriole, an ash-white face, thick and curly beards like black gauze, and almost red hair." In a ten-volume compendium put together as late as the mid-eighteenth century, the authors vaguely described the "Great Western Ocean Country" as somewhere in the Atlantic region. They did not distinguish European countries from their Asian counterparts. They confused France with the Portugal known during Ming times, and they characterized England and Sweden as dependencies of Holland. During this period of cultural flourishing, in short, the Qing Empire did not yet feel any compelling reason to revise its view of the world.

CULTURAL IDENTITY AND TOKUGAWA JAPAN

Chinese cultural influence had long crossed the Sea of Japan. But during the Tokugawa Shogunate, there was also a renewed interest in a competing cultural model from Europe. Japanese interest in Europe grew via the Dutch presence in Japan and more limited contacts with Russians. In addition to such foreign influences, however, there was also a surge in "native learning," or the study of Japanese traditions and culture in the late seventeenth and especially eighteenth centuries. Thus, Tokugawa Japan found itself engaged in a three-cornered conversation among time-honored Chinese ways (transmitted via Korea), distinctly Japanese traditions, and European teachings. Increased trade, new prosperity in the land, and a long period of domestic and international peace were, in turn, accompanied by a remarkable cultural flowering that provided the background for debates over competing cultural models.

Until the sixteenth and seventeenth centuries, cultural patronage remained the preserve of the imperial court in Kyoto (which did not rule), the hereditary shogunate, religious institutions, and the upper class, about 5 percent of the population. Samurai (former warriors turned bureaucrats) and daimyo (the regional lords) favored a masked theater, called Nō, and an elegant ritual for making tea and engaging in contemplation. In their gardens, the lords built teahouses with stages for Nō drama. There arose hereditary schools of actors, tea masters, and cultivated flower arrangers. The upper classes also used the services of commoner-painters, who decorated tea utensils and other articles made of lacquer (dried sap of the sumac tree) and painted the brilliant interiors and standing screens in grand stone castles. Some upper-class men did their own painting, called literati painting, which was supposed to convey philosophical thoughts. Calligraphy was also proof of cultivation.

Alongside this elegant elite culture of theater and stylized painting arose a new, rougher urban culture, one that was patronized by artisans and especially merchants. Urban dwellers, consisting of 10 percent of the population by 1800, delighted in an array of popular entertainment; consumers could purchase works of fiction and colorful prints made from carved wood blocks—also used to make books—that were often risqué. A new class of female entertainers appeared who were known as geisha because they were artistically skilled (*gei*) in the three-stringed instrument (*shamisen*), storytelling, and performing, though some were also prostitutes. Geisha could be found in officially approved pleasure quarters of the big cities, which were famous for their geisha houses, public baths, brothels, and theaters. Kabuki, a type of theater that combined song, dance, and skillful staging to dramatize conflicts between duty and passion, became a wildly popular diversion and art form characterized by bravura acting, brilliant makeup, and sumptuous costumes. In 1629, the shogunate, concerned for public order, banned female actors, and so men began to play women's roles. These male actors sometimes maintained their impersonations of females offstage, and they inspired trends in fashion for urban women.

Much Japanese popular entertainment chronicled the world of the common people rather than politics or high society. The pleasure-oriented culture of urbanites was known

Artist and Geisha at Tea. The erotic, luxuriant atmosphere of Japan's urban pleasure quarters was captured in a new art form, the *ukiyo-e*, or "pictures from a floating world." In this image set in Tokyo's celebrated Yoshiwara district, several geisha flutter about a male artist.

Kabuki Theater. Kabuki originated among dance troupes in the environs of temples and shrines in Kyoto in the late sixteenth and early seventeenth centuries. The characters used to denote *kabuki* mean "song, dance, and skill," though some scholars believe the term derives from a related word (*kabuku*) meaning eccentric, rakish, deviant, outlandish, or erotic. As kabuki spread to the urban centers of Japan, the theater designs enabled the actors to enter and exit from many directions and to step out into the audience, lending the skillful, raucous shows great intimacy.

as "the floating world" (*ukiyo*), and the woodblock prints depicting it as *ukiyo-e* (*e* meaning picture). Here, the normal order of society was temporarily turned upside down. The wealth of the socially low-ranked merchant trumped the official highly ranked samurai. Those who were otherwise looked down upon—actors, musicians, courtesans, and rakes—became idols and objects of dedicated imitation. To a degree, upper-class samurai partook of this "lower" culture. But to enter the pleasure quarters, samurai had to leave behind their swords, a prime mark of rank, since commoners were not allowed to carry such weapons.

Literacy in Japan approached a remarkable one-third of the population (it was far higher for men). The most popular novels sold 10,000 to 12,000 copies. In the late eighteenth century, Edo had some sixty booksellers and also had hundreds of book lenders, who provided an alternative to the relatively high cost of buying books and thereby spread them to a wider public. By the late eighteenth century, as books proliferated and some criticized the government, officials made arrests and sought to exercise control over publications.

THE INFLUENCE OF CHINA AND EUROPE ON JAPAN

In the realm of higher culture, China, the largest and wealthiest of Japan's neighbors, loomed large in the Tokugawa world. Japanese scholars wrote imperial histories of Japan in the Chinese style. Chinese law codes and other books at-tracted a significant readership, and many Japanese wrote exclusively in Chinese. Some Japanese traveled south to Nagasaki just to meet Zen Buddhist masters and Chinese residents of cosmopolitan Nagasaki. Some Chinese monks were even allowed to found monasteries outside Nagasaki and to travel to Kyoto and occasionally to Edo to give lectures and construct temples.

Chinese Confucianism offered the Tokugawa Shogunate a set of politically useful teachings. Initially, Zen Buddhists and monks had nurtured the study of Confucian teachings, but in the seventeenth century, some devotees of Confucianism, encouraged by the political authorities, brought Buddhism outside monasteries and developed the doctrines into a lay school of thought. After 1640, all Japanese were required to register at a Buddhist temple.

Buddhist temples grew in number, but they did not displace the indigenous Japanese practice of ancestor veneration and worshipping gods in nature, later called Shintō (the way of the gods), which boasted an extensive network of shrines throughout the country. In Japan, the religious practices that were eventually called Shintō developed through adaptation of time-honored beliefs in spirits (*kami*) who were present in or closely associated with places (mountains, rivers, waterfalls, rocks, the moon) and activities (harvest, fertility). These spirits in nature and daily life had to be addressed for healing or other assistance. Some women under

Shintō served as *mikos*, a kind of shamaness who possessed special divinatory powers. These rituals competed with a powerful strain of neo-Confucianism that set down a set of moral and behavioral precepts. In 1762, someone compiled a "Greater Learning for Females" (*onna daigaku*), which has been attributed to the earlier writings of the botanist and thinker Kaibara Ekiken or Ekken (1630–1714) or to the record of his ideas by his wife, Kaibara Token (1652–1713), who was also a scholar. This influential text rendered the precepts of Confucianism accessible to nonscholars, while, in particular, explicitly outlining for the first time societal roles that stressed hierarchy based on age and gender as a way to ensure order. At the same time, any person's place in the social hierarchy, including a woman's, was also determined by merit, such as one's record of doing the right thing (propriety) and one's virtue.

By the early eighteenth century, neo-Confucian teachings of filial piety and loyalty to superiors had become the de facto official credo of the state. The new philosophy legitimated the social hierarchy and the absolutism of the political order, but it also instructed the shogun and the upper class to provide "benevolent administration" (*jinsei*) for the people's benefit.

In partial reaction to the official credo that adapted Chinese traditions to Japanese circumstances, but also out of a desire to venerate the greatness of Japan, some creative Japanese thinkers promoted nativist intellectual traditions drawn from Japan's past. After 1728, for example, Kada Azumamaro (1668–1736), a Shintō priest, initiated a movement stressing "native learning" and the celebration of Japanese texts. Subsequent proponents of native learning, such as Motoori Norinaga (1730–1801), emphasized Japanese uniqueness, helped codify the elements of a Japanese religious and cultural tradition, and denounced Confucianism and Buddhism as foreign contaminants from a country of disorder and deceit. A few also looked to the nonruling but uninterrupted imperial line in Kyoto for validation of Japan's intellectual lineage and cultural superiority. While some who called for the revival of rule by the dormant Japanese emperor were arrested, others went on to develop Japanese poetry, one of the art forms popular with both upper and lower social groups.

Not only did Chinese intellectual authority in Japan have to compete with a new native learning, but by the late seventeenth century, Japan was also tapping other imported sources of knowledge. In East Asia in the late seventeenth

Japanese Map of the World. Japanese maps underwent a shift in connection with their encounters with the Dutch. Here, in a map dated 1671, much information is incorporated about distant lands, both cartographically on the globe and pictorially, to the left, in two-person images representing various peoples of the world in their purported typical costumes.

century, Portuguese was the *lingua franca* (common language), and even the Dutch used it in communicating with the Japanese. By 1670, however, there was a guild of Japanese interpreters in Nagasaki who could speak and read Dutch and who accompanied Dutch merchants on trips to Edo. European knowledge also spread to high circles in Edo in 1709. In 1720, the shogunate lifted its ban on foreign books. Thereafter, European ideas, called "Dutch learning," circulated more openly. Scientific, geographical, and medical texts, such as *The New Book of Dissection,* were translated into Japanese and in some cases displaced Chinese texts, particularly for the calculation of important celestial phenomena. A Japanese-Dutch dictionary appeared in 1745, and the first official school of Dutch learning followed. Students of Dutch or European teachings remained a limited, if enthusiastic, segment of Japanese society, but the demand for translations rose appreciably.

One of the strong proponents of a European orientation was Honda Toshiaki (1744–1821), who traveled to Ezo to examine the frontier, studied European texts, and set his thoughts down in late-eighteenth-century unpublished manuscripts. Toshiaki believed that Japan should learn about and adapt European advances in science, especially geography and astronomy, which helped in ocean trade. He also praised European economic progress, while extolling the vastness and might of Japan's new neighbor to the north, the Russian Empire. For Toshiaki, the greatness of Japan depended on its ability to modernize. Nonetheless, despite his admiration for European advances, Toshiaki did not reject Confucianism, nor did he repudiate Japan's system of social ranks, based on Confucianism, and he showed Confucian contempt for unethical businessmen. What comes across most clearly in his celebrations of European prowess are his pragmatism about adaptation and his aspirations for Japan.

Japanese deliberations about what and how to borrow from the Europeans and the Chinese illustrate the vast changes that the world had undergone in the previous several centuries. A few hundred years earlier, products and ideas did travel, but they usually did not travel very far or make significant inroads into local cultural practices. By the eighteenth century, new networks of exchange and communication and new prosperity made the integration of foreign ideas into local cultures feasible and sometimes desirable. The Japanese were especially eager to choose among useful new ideas and practices and often to transform them. This selective openness to the ideas of foreigners stemmed from Japan's long historical relationship to outside influences, particularly its receptivity to Chinese thought and institutions. The Japanese did not consider embracing learning from overseas as a mark of inferiority or subordination, particularly when they knew that they could put new ideas to good use at home. This was not the case for the great Asian land-based empires, which were eager lenders but hesitant borrowers.

THE ENLIGHTENMENT IN EUROPE

> ↬ *What were the major tenets of Enlightenment thought?*

An extraordinary cultural flourishing, often defined in intellectual terms as the Enlightenment but in fact a much broader series of developments, took place in Europe in the seventeenth and eighteenth centuries. This era was unique in the history of thought, in that the individuals who championed the new ideas sought not simply to sell them to the elite but to diffuse them widely. They wanted not only to change their contemporaries' worldviews but also to transform political and social institutions. Crucial for the success of their endeavor were widening patronage networks that extended beyond the traditional ecclesiastical and monarchical supporters of arts and sciences to the lower aristocracy and members of the bureaucratic and commercial elites. Equally important was an expansion in the methods and networks of communication that now included cafes and intellectual salons, newspapers, extensive exchanges of correspondence, public theaters, and book publishing. The men and women of letters of this period, although their ideas frequently clashed, nonetheless shared a desire to "spread light" and to change the way their societies were governed.

Abandoning traditional Christian belief in original sin and God's mysterious tamperings with natural forces and human events, Enlightenment thinkers aspired to know the world in new ways. They sought universal and objective knowledge, knowledge that would not depend on the knower's religion, political views, class, or gender. Recognizing no territorial boundaries, scholars sought to formulate natural laws, which they presumed applied everywhere and to all peoples. Most of these thinkers were quite unaware of the extent to which their "objective" knowledge was colored by European, upper-class, male perspectives.

ORIGINS OF THE ENLIGHTENMENT

Well into the seventeenth century, European culture continued to be defined by two major institutions: the Catholic and Protestant churches and the dynastic court system. After the Reformation, Europeans were more divided than ever into hostile states. While the sixteenth century brought new prosperity, the seventeenth century produced grand-scale disasters: civil and religious wars, dynastic conflicts, and famine. These crises devastated central Europe and bankrupted the Spanish; they resulted in five years of chaos in France (the "Fronde"), the execution of Charles I of England, and the

EUROPEAN VIEWS OF THE WORLD

As the Europeans became world travelers and traders, they needed accurate information on places and distances that they had reached so that they could get home as well as return to these sites. This meant forsaking their own tradition of placing Jerusalem at the world's core. Europe's first printed map to show the New World, the Waldseemüller map, was produced in 1507 and portrayed the Americas as a long and narrow strip of land, its unexplored landmass dwarfed by Asia and Africa. By the mid-seventeenth century, maps were seemingly more objective, yet European maps invariably grouped the rest of the world around the European countries. Moreover, the effort to make world maps that could actually be used for navigational purposes led to certain distortions (like the stretching of the polar zones in the popular 1569 Mercator projection) that made Europe seem disproportionately large and central. Had Europeans had a map, like the Peterson projection, only developed much later, in which the landmasses of the world were in correct geographical proportion to one another, Europe would have seemed quite small. Moreover, the mapmaker decided which territories appeared at the center of the map and which appeared on the edges. Maps made in Europe invariably grouped the rest of the world around the European countries.

Waldseemüller map, 1507.

Mercator projection, 1569.

→ *What are the most striking differences between the two maps?*

→ *How are these European maps similar to and different from the Islamic and Chinese ones?*

securing of Dutch independence from Spanish control. They contributed as well to the spread of Protestantism in Europe. But they also resulted in a general revulsion toward religious strife, a widespread desire among monarchs to centralize and regularize their powers, and a longing for impersonal, useful knowledge of the world.

By 1750, the sons and daughters of the lower clergy, of the provincial nobility, of the commercial classes, and even of skilled craftsmen had begun to participate in the production and consumption of the arts and sciences. A new set of cultural ambitions emerged as this group of literate, middle-class men and women gained confidence in their own worthiness —to create art, to write books, to observe the world accurately, and perhaps even to rule their states.

To understand the development of this confidence, and of Enlightenment knowledge as a whole, it is necessary to understand the powerful effects of the Reformation and Counter-Reformation in increasing literacy and the diffusion of the new science and its premises. But it is also important to take stock of the increasing contacts between Europeans and the wider world that had taken place since the fourteenth century. Europeans had been consumers of the cultural goods of other peoples. From the trapping methods of Native Americans to the crop cultivation techniques of African slaves, from Chinese porcelain to New World tobacco and chocolate, Europe in the seventeenth and eighteenth centuries continued to be shaped by its contact with others. Yet, European intellectuals became more and more critical of other cultures —and more confident that their culture was unique and superior and that it should be the standard against which other cultures were judged.

THE NEW SCIENCE

The search for objective knowledge is most apparent in the seventeenth-century flourishing of natural science. Scientific visions of astronomers like Nicolaus Copernicus (1473–1542) and Galileo Galilei (1564–1642), once reviled by the church, now began to gain acceptance. Galileo's findings in mathematics, physics, and astronomy contradicted age-old assumptions. His belief that the earth revolved around the sun led to his publication of *Dialogue on the Two Chief Systems of the World* (1632) and to his subsequent trial (1633) for heresy. But this was a late, and much criticized, attempt to put the genie back in the bottle. By this time, a small but influential group of new scientists increasingly expected that theories were to be built on experiment and observation. The skepticism of the philosopher Sir Francis Bacon (1561–1626) became these scientists' unwritten code of conduct. According to Bacon, in such works as *The Advancement of Learning* (1605) and the *Novum Organum* (1620), the duty of the scientist was to observe and to test nature himself following the inductive method. By means of carefully controlled, empirical testing, Bacon believed that modern man could gradually comprehend the general principles of nature's manifold operations and thus bend nature to man's will. Bacon believed experiments should be conducted, samples collected,

Galileo. The Catholic Church was initially worried that the new science would undermine Christian faith. In 1633, the Italian scientist Galileo was put on trial for espousing heretical beliefs and was condemned to house arrest.

variables isolated; traditional authorities should not be trusted. Of course, Bacon was chiefly concerned that classical and medieval authorities be distrusted, but the principle would be the same when European scientists confronted traditional knowledge in the rest of the world. Confident of their own calculations, scientists like Isaac Newton (1642–1727) defined what they believed were the universal laws that applied to all matter and motion, and they disparaged all older conceptions of nature—from Aristotelian ideas to folkloric and foreign ones—as absurd and obsolete. Thus, in his *Principia Mathematica* (1687), Newton set forth the laws of motion, including the famous law of gravitation, which explained falling bodies on earth and planetary motion.

It is no longer fashionable to speak about the changing views of sixteenth- and seventeenth-century Europeans regarding nature and the universe as a scientific revolution. European thinking about nature and the universe did not change overnight. Only gradually and fitfully did a group of European thinkers come to see the natural world as operating according to inviolable laws that experimenters could fathom. But by the late seventeenth century monarchs and oligarchs, particularly in Protestant countries, had developed a new interest in science's discoveries, and many established royal academies of science to encourage local endeavors. This patronage, of course, was not purely disinterested; in incorporating the British Royal Society in 1662, for example, Charles II hoped to show not only that the crown backed scientific progress but also that England's great minds backed the crown. Similar reasoning was shown in the founding of the French Royal Academy of Sciences in 1666. Support for artistic monuments had a similar political function. In France, Louis XIV's erection of the fabulously expensive new palace complex at Versailles beginning in 1661 was meant to show not only that he had taste but also that he had power. The nobility, he meant to say, needed to look to him for both cultural and political guidance.

Gradually, science began to expand beyond court circles around 1700. By the early eighteenth century, the new science was becoming popular in elite circles; the upper-crust Marquise de Châtelet (1706–1749) built a scientific laboratory in her home and translated Newton's *Principia* into French. Groups of well-to-do landowners formed societies, like the Society for the Improvement of Knowledge in Agriculture—founded in Edinburgh in 1723—to discuss the latest methods of successful animal breeding. Military schools increasingly stressed engineering methods and thus produced graduates with refined technical skills. By about 1750, even artisans and journalists, especially in England, could be found applying Newtonian mechanics to their practical problems and inventions. In Italy, a number of female natural philosophers emerged, and the genre of scientific literature for "ladies" became popular. In 1763, the mathematician Diamante Medaglia Faini delivered an oration recommending that all women

Marquise de Chatelet-Lomont. Gabrielle-Emilie Le Tonnelier de Breteuil, Marquise de Chatelet-Lomont (1706–1749), was one of the few in her day to understand Newtonian physics. Her French translation of Newton's *Principia Mathematica* included extensive explanations of the science that informed Newton's thinking. Her lover and admirer Voltaire wrote of her, "She was a great man whose only fault was in being a woman."

seek to increase their knowledge of science. A consensus emerged among European proponents of the new science that useful knowledge came from collecting data and organizing it into universally valid systems, rather than from revered classical texts.

By no means, however, was the scientific worldview the only one held by Europeans; most still understood their relationships with God, nature, and fellow humans by reference to Christian doctrines on the one hand and local customs on the other. Although literacy was increasing, especially in northern Europe, it was by no means universal; schools remained church-governed or elite, male institutions. All governments employed censors and punished, often severely, radical thinkers; peasants still suffered under arbitrary systems of taxation, and judicial regimes had hardly improved since medieval times. It certainly cannot be said that science and rationality pervaded all spheres of European life by 1700.

Indeed, if it had been so, there would have been no need for the movement we now call the Enlightenment.

ENLIGHTENMENT THINKERS

Enlightenment thinkers like Voltaire (1694–1778), Denis Diderot (1713–1784), and Adam Smith (1723–1790) believed in the power of human reason and the perfectibility of humankind; they rejected the medieval belief in man's helplessness and God's remoteness. But while these writers affirmed the ultimate rationality of the universe, they also observed with unprecedented acuity the evils and flaws of human society in their day. Voltaire wrote scathing critiques of the torture of criminals; Diderot denounced the despotic tendencies of Louis XIV and Louis XV; Smith detailed the inefficiency of mercantile economics.

In general, Enlightenment thinkers trusted nature and individual human reason and distrusted institutions and traditions. "Man is born good," Jean-Jacques Rousseau (1712–1778) wrote in *Émile* (1762); "it is society that corrupts him." In *The Social Contract* (1762) Rousseau wrote about government as the expression of the general will and how the people could withdraw their support if the government violated this social contract. Moreover, in *Candide* (1759), Voltaire warned against undue optimism in a world suffused with stupidity, greed, and injustice. Like Rousseau and Voltaire, other Enlightenment thinkers believed that improvements could be made to human society but that there

was a great deal that needed to be altered. Their critiques of tradition, of religious and secular customs and authorities, and of barriers to social mobility were largely directed at contemporary European conditions, and they were often imprisoned or exiled as punishment for writing about what they considered to be superstitious beliefs and corrupt political structures.

The Enlightenment can be described as a pan-European movement, but the extent of its reach varied in different countries: in France and Britain, enlightened learning spread rather widely; in other places, like Spain, Poland, and Scandinavia, enlightened circles were small and had little influence either on the rulers or on the population at large. Enlightened thought flourished in commercial centers like Amsterdam and Edinburgh, and it also spread to colonial ports like Philadelphia and Boston. As education and literacy became more widespread in these commercial cities, book sales and newspaper circulation expanded. By 1770, approximately 3,500 different books and pamphlets were being produced each year in France alone, as compared to 1,000 in 1720. By 1776, about 12 million copies of newspapers were being issued in Britain.

POPULAR CULTURE   In the emerging marketplace for new books, new ideas, and new visions, some of the most popular works were not from the high intellectuals of the period. Pamphlets alleging rampant corruption circulated widely wherever reading publics flourished; charges of fraudulent stock speculation and insider trading provided raw material

Salon of Madame Geoffrin. Much of the important work—and wit—of the Enlightenment was the product of private gatherings known as salons. Often hosted, like the one depicted here, by aristocratic women, these salons also welcomed down-at-the-heels writers and artists, offering everyone, at least in theory, the opportunity to discuss the sciences, the arts, politics, and the idiocies of their fellow humans on an equal basis.

for popular literary slander. Sex, too, sold well. While the works of Voltaire, for instance, enjoyed a respectable readership among France's increasingly literate population, some of the real best-sellers of the age came from the pens of cruder and more sensationalist essayists. Works like *Venus in the Cloister or the Nun in a Nightgown* (anonymous, with at least twenty-two editions between 1682 and 1782) sold as well as many of the now-classical works of the Enlightenment and were full of bawdy and irreligious material. These vulgar best-sellers took advantage of consumer demand—but they also seized the opportunity to mock icons of authority. In many of these works, nuns often came across as lascivious, priests as fornicators. Some were daring enough to go after the royal family, portraying Louis XV as a king fond of being spanked or Marie Antoinette copulating with her court confessor. In these cases, pornography—some of it even philosophical— spilled into the literary marketplace for political satire. These works display the seamier side of the Enlightenment. But they too spoke of the willingness of intellectuals—high and low alike—to explore new and iconoclastic modes of thought.

Those who were part of the growing reading public also participated in the creation of a whole new set of cultural institutions and practices. In Britain and Germany, book clubs proliferated and coffee-houses sprang up to cater to sober men of business and learning; here, aristocrats and well-to-do commoners could read some of the first news sheets or discuss stock prices, political affairs, or technological novelties. The same sort of noncourtly socializing was available in Parisian salons, over which female aristocrats often presided. Able to speak their minds more openly in these private settings than at court or at public assemblies, women here exchanged ideas quite freely with men. The most successful salons were the ones renowned for witty gossip, but would-be philosophers and writers also attended in order to secure jobs as secretaries or to obtain commissions for their projects. Libraries began to open their doors to the public. It must be understood, however, that aristocratic, royal, and even ecclesiastical patronage remained the major source of funding for intellectuals in this age; in the German states, Enlightenment thinkers were chiefly university professors, bureaucrats, and pastors. Art collecting boomed—primarily because local aristocrats found it a means to display their good taste, wealth, and distance from the rabble.

CHALLENGES TO AUTHORITY AND TRADITION While they took the aristocracy's money, many Enlightenment thinkers nonetheless sought to overturn the status distinc-

tions that defined the worth of individuals in Europe at this time. They emphasized merit rather than birth as the basis for status. John Locke (1632–1704) claimed that man was born with a mind that was a clean slate (*tabula rasa*) and acquired all his ideas as a result of experience. Locke's *Essay Concerning Human Understanding* (1690) stressed that cultural differences were the result not of unequal natural endowments, but rather of unequal opportunities to develop men's faculties. Similarly, in *The Wealth of Nations* (1776), Adam Smith remarked that there was little difference (other than education) between a philosopher and a street porter. Both had been endowed with reason, and were (or should be) free to rise in society according to their talents. Yet, Locke and Smith still believed that a mixed set of social and political institutions would be needed to regulate relationships between ever-imperfect humans. Moreover, they did not believe that women could act as independent, rational individuals in the same way that all men, presumably, could. Although educated women like Mary Wollstonecraft and Olympe de Gouges took up the pen to protest these inequities, the Enlightenment actually did little to change the subordinate status of women in European society.

Inspired by the new science, many Enlightenment thinkers sought to discover the "laws" of human behavior, an endeavor closely bound up with criticism of existing governments. Explaining the laws of economic relations was chiefly the work of Adam Smith. His *The Wealth of Nations*, in which he described universal economic laws, was one of the most influential and long-lived of enlightened treatises. Smith claimed that unregulated markets in a laissez-faire economy best suited mankind because they allowed our "trucking and bartering" nature full expression. In Smith's view, the "invisible hand" of the market, rather than the regulations of government, would lead to general prosperity and social peace. Interestingly, Smith was quite conscious of growing economic gaps between the "civilized and thriving" and the "savage" nations, which remained so miserably poor, that in Smith's view, they were reduced to infanticide, starvation, and euthanasia. Yet, he believed that until these nations learned to play by what he called nature's laws, they could not expect a happy fate. Smith was just one of many Enlightenment thinkers to paint a picture of what they believed to be universal laws that offered non-Europeans no other solution but that of imitation.

One of the most controversial realms for the application of universal laws was that of religion. Although few Enlightenment thinkers were actually atheists, most advocated some kind of religious toleration, insisting that reason, not force,

> *Inspired by the new science, many Enlightenment thinkers sought to discover the "laws" of human behavior, an endeavor closely bound up with criticism of existing governments.*

was the means to create a community of believers and moral actors. For European audiences, these critiques of church authorities and practices were highly controversial. States often reacted to radical critiques by censoring books or exiling writers, but some princes were convinced by these arguments. In response, acts of toleration were passed in the late eighteenth century by governments from Denmark to Austria offering religious minorities some freedom of worship. Toleration did not mean, however, that full civil rights were bestowed on, for example, Catholics in England or Jews anywhere in Europe. Toleration simply meant a loosening of religious uniformity, and the population as a whole often resented even this. The "No Popery" riots in Edinburgh and Glasgow in 1779, for example, compelled the British government to withdraw its proposed moderation of restrictions on Catholics.

The Enlightenment produced numerous works that purported to encompass universal knowledge, the most important of which was the French *Encyclopedia,* which began to be published in 1751 and would run to twenty-eight volumes by 1772. Nearly 200 intellectuals, including Voltaire and Rousseau, contributed essays; it was extremely popular among the elite, despite its political, religious, and intellectual radicalism. Its purpose, claimed Diderot, its editor and energizing force, was "to collect all the knowledge scattered over the face of the earth" and to make it useful to men and women in the present and future. Indeed, the *Encyclopedia* offered a wealth of information about the rest of the world, including more than 2,300 articles (constituting 4 percent of the total word space) that treated Islam. Here, quite typically, the authors praised Arab culture for preserving and even extending Greek and Roman science, and in doing so, preparing the way for scientific advances in Europe. But predictably, too, the *Encyclopedia* writers portrayed Islam with the same malevolence that they applied to all other organized religions, condemning Muhammad as the apostle of a bloodthirsty religion and Muslim culture in general for its inability to renounce superstition.

Enlightenment thinkers also championed a new cultural hierarchy that extolled commerce and rationality and placed those regions of the world that lacked these ingredients at the bottom of the world's cultures. While praising some of the world's cultures like the Chinese for having achieved

much in these areas, Enlightenment thinkers were confident that Europe was advancing over the rest of the world in its acquisition of goods and universal knowledge.

Absolutist governments were not entirely hostile to enlightened ideas, recognizing the virtues of universality (as in a universally applicable system of taxation) and precision (as in a well-drilled army). After all, social mobility allowed more skilled bureaucrats to rise through the ranks, while commerce provided the state with new riches. Knowledge collection, too, appealed to states that had begun to exert greater and greater dominion over their subjects; Louis XIV was persuaded to establish a census, though he never carried it out, so that he could "know with certitude in what consists his grandeur, his wealth, and his strength." Some enlightened princes, like Frederick II of Prussia and Joseph II of Austria, even instituted impressive legal reforms and backed innovations in the arts and agriculture and were accordingly idolized by Enlightenment thinkers, who liked their "top down" approach

Title Page of the *Encyclopedia.* Originally published in 1751, the *Encyclopedia* was the most comprehensive work of learning of the French Enlightenment. The title page features an image of light and reason being dispersed throughout the land. The title itself identifies the work as a dictionary, based on reason, that deals not just with the sciences but also with the arts and occupations. It identifies two of the leading men of letters (*gens de lettres*), Denis Diderot and Jean le Rond d'Alembert, as the primary authors of the work.

The *Encyclopedia* on Pin Making. Contributors to the *Encyclopedia* included craftsmen as well as intellectuals. This detailed illustration of a pin factory and the processes and machinery employed in pin making is from a plate in the fourth volume of the *Encyclopedia* and demonstrates its emphasis on practical information.

to reform. The Enlightenment was responsible for spreading the idea of liberty far and wide, even to the women, lower-class men, and enslaved peoples whom European elites were less sure deserved it. But many eighteenth-century male thinkers, like their absolutist sovereigns, were quite uncomfortable with the idea of offering liberty and equality (not to mention sovereignty) to *all* the people.

AFRICAN CULTURAL FLOURISHING

> → *How did global entanglements, particularly involvement in the slave trade, reshape African cultures?*

Unbeknownst to much of the rest of the world, kingdoms throughout Africa had strong artisanal and artistic traditions dating back centuries. But as in Europe, new wealth from the slave trade gave the upper classes the ability to fund new cultural achievements. Africa was more like East Asia, however, in that it maintained local forms of cultural production, such as wood carving, weaving, and metal-working.

Cultural traditions in Africa varied by the different kingdoms, but there were patterns among them. West African ruling classes encouraged local artisans to produce carvings, statues, masks, and other objects that would extol the power and achievements of rulers, as royal patrons in Europe, Asia, and the Islamic world would do with architecture and painting. Also widespread in West African kingdoms was a belief that rulers had the blessing of the gods, and if they were not themselves descendants of the divinities, their families were thought to enjoy spiritual sanction. Arts and crafts not only glorified royal power, they were also thought to capture the energy of a universe that was believed to be suffused with spiritual beings. Starting in the 1500s and culminating in the 1700s when the slave trade reached its zenith, African rulers had even more reason—and means—to support cultural pursuits, because as destructive and debilitating as the slave trade was for the peoples of Africa, it made the most successful slave-trading states wealthy and powerful.

THE ASANTE, OYO, AND BENIN CULTURAL TRADITIONS

The kingdom of Asante, which became prominent in the slave trade in the seventeenth and eighteenth centuries, was also well known because of its access to gold. It used its gold

Asante Gold Discs. Gold discs like these were hung on chains and worn around the necks of kings' servants and often by kings themselves.

mines to celebrate its royal tradition, crafting magnificent seats or stools coated with gold as the symbols of the authority of the chiefs. The most ornate of the golden royal stools was reserved for the titular head of the Asante federation, the Asantehene, who ruled his far-flung empire from the capital city of Kumasi and who ventured out from his secluded royal palace rarely except on ceremonial and feast days. When he would emerge, he would be clad in sumptuous garments, the famed Kente cloth woven by the artisans of his state, and hold aloft maces, spears, staffs, and other symbols of power fashioned from the abundant gold supplies in the kingdom. These articles were intended to reveal his connection to the gods.

Equally resplendent were the rulers of the Oyo Empire and Benin located in the territory that now constitutes Nigeria. The bronzes of Ife, capital city of the Yoruba Oyo Empire, are among the most elegant and sophisticated pieces of art to be found anywhere in the world. According to one commentator, they were so impressive that "little that Italy or Greece or Egypt ever produced could be finer and the appeal of their beauty is immediate and universal." Although the Ife heads were not discovered until just before World War II, they mark the high point of Yoruba craft and artistic tradition that dated back to the first millennium CE. Their elegance, refinement, and repose reflected the esteem in which the Yoruba peoples held their rulers. The best known of these works were fashioned before the slave trade era in the thirteenth century, but the tradition was maintained and elaborated in the seventeenth and eighteenth centuries.

Benin has come down through the historical records as one of the most fearsome and brutal slave-trading regimes in Africa. Whether this reputation was deserved or rather part of Europe's later desire to label African rulers as "savage" in order to justify their conquest of the landmass cannot detract from the originality and beauty of the famed Benin bronzes. Many of the terra-cotta and bronze heads did not become known outside Benin until the kingdom had been conquered by a British expeditionary force in 1897. Among the finds was a remarkable brass head dating from 1515, which was worn by a ruler (the Ata of Idah) whom the Benin forces subdued at the beginning of the sixteenth century. Benin craftsmen did not confine themselves to heads. They were also expert at presenting the whole body of the ruling classes, which they clothed in the most elaborate fighting attire.

In those parts of Africa little affected by Islam entering from the north and the east and European influences operating along the slaving coasts of west, central, and east Africa, African cultural traditions developed relatively uninfluenced by outside elements throughout the seventeenth and eighteenth centuries. The magnificent artistic achievements of the tropical rainforest peoples of west and central Africa became known to the rest of the world only as a result of

Brass Oba Head. The brass head of an Oba, or king, of Benin. The kingdom's brass and bronze work was among the finest in all of Africa.

European colonial conquests in the late nineteenth and early twentieth centuries. By contrast, where the slave trade flourished, those traditions were more deeply affected, often by the transfer of craftsmen across the Atlantic as slaves. Though some African crafts would be transferred to the Americas, African artistic skills were not valued by the Europeanized elite. The colonizers in the Americas had their own aesthetic tastes, which they tended to impose on others.

HYBRID CULTURES IN THE AMERICAS

> → *How did cultural developments in the Americas reflect new global entanglements?*

In the Americas, mingling between European colonizers and native peoples (as well as African slaves) produced new, hybrid cultures. But this syncretism, or mixing, of cultures grew increasingly unbalanced as Europeans imposed their political and cultural authority over more and more of the Americas. For Native Americans, the pressure to adapt their cultures to those of the European colonists began with their first encounters (indeed, in some places, such as North America's Great Plains, where horses spread ahead of European colonizers, borrowing and cultural adaptations preceded human contacts). Over time, Indians faced mounting pressure to accept the ways of Europeans, who insisted that their conquests and colonizations were not simply military endeavors but also spiritual errands. In addition to their guns and germs, all of Europe's colonizers brought their bibles, prayerbooks, and crucifixes. With these, they set out to Christianize and "civilize" the Indian and African populations in the Americas. Still, even with the imbalance of military power, the efforts of Christian missionaries to convert Indians and slaves produced uneven and often unpredictable outcomes. Indian and African converts adopted Christian beliefs and practices, but they also often retained older religious practices.

European colonists, too, adapted to their new cultural environments, borrowing from the peoples they subjugated and enslaved. This was especially true in the sixteenth and seventeenth centuries, when the survival of Europeans in the New World often depended on such adaptations. By the middle of the eighteenth century, however, many American settlements had achieved a level of stability and prosperity, and colonists became less and less likely to admit their past dependency on others. New sorts of hierarchies emerged, and elites in Latin and North America began increasingly to set their cultural standards according to the tastes and fashions of European aristocrats. Yet, even as they imitated Old World ways, these colonials also forged identities that separated them from Europe.

SPIRITUAL ENCOUNTERS

In the New World, unlike in other European colonial outposts, settlers possessed the military and economic power to impose their culture and especially their religion on indigenous peoples on an unprecedented scale. Although the Jesuits had relatively little impact in China and the Islamic world, Christian missionaries in the Americas had armies and officials to support their insistence that indigenous peoples and African slaves abandon their own deities and spirits for Christ.

European missionaries, especially Catholics, employed a vast range of techniques to bring and keep Indians within the Christian fold. Smashing idols, razing temples, and whipping backsliders all belonged to the missionaries' arsenal. Dominicans, Jesuits, and Franciscans also learned what they could about Indian beliefs and rituals and used their knowledge in their efforts to make conversions to Christianity. Many of the missionaries found it useful to demonize native gods, subvert indigenous spiritual leaders, and transform In-

Indians Becoming Christians. This image is from a colonial chronicle, illustrated and narrated by indigenous scribes who had converted to Christianity. The picture of Indians before the conquest entering a house of prayer is intended to represent the Indians as proto-Christians.

dian iconography into Christian symbols. But historians have reason to be grateful to these missionaries, for they are responsible for preserving much of the linguistic and ethnographic information about these communities that survives. In sixteenth-century Mexico, the Dominican friar Bernardino de Sahagún compiled an immense ethnography of Mexican ways and beliefs. In seventeenth-century Canada, French Jesuits prepared dictionaries and grammars of the Iroquoian and Algonquian languages and translated Christian hymns into Amerindian tongues.

Neither gentle persuasion nor violent coercion produced the results that missionaries desired. When conversions did occur, the Christianity practiced was usually a hybrid form in which indigenous deities and rituals merged with newly adopted Christian ones. Among Andean mountain people, for example, priestesses of native cults were given the name of Maria to mask their secret worship of the traditional deities of local kinship groups. In other cases, indigenous communities made no secret of their disdain for missionaries. They simply turned their backs on Christianity and accused missionaries of bringing plague and death. New converts tended to see Christian spiritual power as an addition to, not as a replacement for, their own religions.

More distressing to missionaries than evidence of syncretic beliefs and outright defiance were the successes of Indians in converting colonists. Many Indian groups had long practiced adoption of captives. Such adoptions were a common means to replenish numbers and replace lost kin. That many colonists adjusted to their captivity and accepted their adoptions, refusing to return to colonial society even when given the chance, was deeply troubling to missionaries. So were those Europeans who chose to live among the Indians. Comparing the records of cultural conversion, one eighteenth-century colonist in British America suggested that "thousands of Europeans are Indians," yet, "we have no examples of even one of those Aborigines having from choice become European." While this calculation exaggerated the imbalance in rates of intercultural borrowing, it points to the fact that Europeans who adopted Indian culture, like Christianized Indians, lived in a mixed cultural world. Indeed, their familiarity with both Indian and European ways made them ideal cultural brokers, intermediaries who facilitated diplomatic arrangements and economic exchanges.

Beyond the attractions of Indian cultures, Europeans were inclined to mix with Indians because of the demography of colonization. Almost all of the early European traders, missionaries, and settlers were men, and the preponderance of male colonists remained true in all but the British North American settlements. In response to the scarcity of women and as a means to acculturate native peoples, the Portuguese crown authorized intermarriage between Portuguese men and local women. In truth, colonizing men needed no official encouragement to consort with native women; indeed, these relations often amounted to little more than rape. But in those places where Indians retained their independence, longer-lasting relationships were common, as among French fur traders and Indian women in Canada, the Great Lakes region, and the Mississippi Valley. Whether by coercion or consent, sexual relations between European men and native women created

Racial Mixing. (*Left*) This image shows racial mixing in colonial Mexico—the father is Spanish, the mother Indian, and the child a mestizo. This is a well-to-do family, illustrating how Europeans married into the native aristocracy. (*Right*) Here too we see a racially mixed family. The father is Spanish, the mother black or African, and the child a mulatto. Observe, however, the less aristocratic and markedly less peaceful nature of this family.

new, hybrid peoples—the mestizos of Spanish colonies and the métis of French outposts, who soon outnumbered settlers of wholly European ancestry.

The increasing numbers of Africans who were forcibly transported to the Americas added to and complicated the mix of New World cultures. In contrast with the marriages between fur traders and Indian women, in which the latter held considerable power thanks to the connections they offered to Indian trading partners, the sexual intercourse between European slaveholding men and enslaved African women almost always rested on coercion. The children who were born from such unions swelled the ranks of mixed ancestry people in the colonial population. Europeans initiated campaigns to Christianize slaves, though many slave owners expressed doubts about the wisdom of converting persons they regarded as mere property. Protestants had more difficulty than Catholics in reconciling the belief that Africans could be both slaves and Christians, and they were less aggressive than Catholics in mounting missionary efforts.

Sent forth with papal blessing, Catholic priests went to work among the slave populations of the American colonies of Portugal, Spain, and France. Employing many of the same techniques that had been used with Indian "heathens," missionaries produced similarly syncretic results. Often converts blended Islamic or indigenous African religions with Catholicism. Converted slaves wove remembered practices and beliefs into their American Christianity, transforming both along the way. In the northeast of Brazil, for example, slaves combined the Yoruba faiths of their ancestors with Catholic beliefs, and they frequently attributed powers of African deities to Christian saints. Sometimes Christian and African faiths were practiced side by side, as in the case of *candomblé,* a Yoruba-based religion in northern Brazil, where slaves from the Oyo and Dahomey kingdoms were shipped in large numbers. In Saint Domingue, slaves and free blacks practiced *vodun* (meaning "spirit" in the Dahomey tongue) and in Cuba, *santería,* a faith of similar origins.

Just as slaveholders feared, Christianity, especially in its syncretic forms, could inspire resistance, even revolt, among slaves. A major maroon (runaway slave) leader in mid-eighteenth-century Surinam was a Christian. In the English colonies, those held in bondage drew inspiration from Christian hymns that promised deliverance and embraced as their own the Old Testament's story of Moses leading the Israelites out of Egypt. By the end of the eighteenth century, freed slaves like the Methodist Olaudah Equiano were saying in their own voices that slavery was unjust and incompatible with Christian brotherhood.

> *By the latter part of the eighteenth century, creoles had become increasingly restive about the control that "peninsulars" had over colonial society.*

THE MAKING OF COLONIAL CULTURES

In Spanish America, widespread ethnic and cultural mixing led to the emergence of a powerful new class, the creoles, persons of European descent who were born in the Americas. By the latter part of the eighteenth century, creoles had become increasingly restive about the control that "peninsulars"—men and women born in Spain or Portugal—had over colonial society. Mercantilist restrictions, which gave peninsular merchants exclusive privileges and forbade creoles from trading with other colonial ports, fired local resentments. So, too, did the practice of royal ministers who dished out most official posts to peninsulars. While the Spanish and Portuguese rulers did occasionally soften the discriminatory blows for fear of angering the creoles, their reforms often aggravated tensions with peninsulars.

The growing sense of creole identity also stemmed from the dissemination of new ideas in the colonies, especially many of the notions circulating in the rest of the Atlantic world under the umbrella of the Enlightenment. Abbé Raynal's *History of the Settlements and Trade of the Europeans in the East and West Indies* (1770), for example, was one of the favorite texts among the colonial reading circles in Buenos Aires and Rio de Janeiro. As a history of colonization in the New World, it was unkind to Iberian emperors and conquerors—and often helped creoles justify their dissatisfaction. Other French works were also popular, especially those of Rousseau. So were some English texts, like Adam Smith's *The Wealth of Nations.* Although Smith's treatise was not translated into Spanish until the 1790s (the Portuguese translation came even later), educated creoles read it with ease in English. Smith's reformist spirit contributed to creole impressions that mercantilist Iberian authorities were political and economic laggards.

In many of the cities of the Spanish and Portuguese empires, reading clubs and salons provided environments where fresh ideas and concepts could be deliberated. Even among Catholic circles, Rousseau was made to fit a Christian critique of Spanish exploitation of the natives. In one university in Upper Peru, Catholic scholars taught their students that Spanish labor drafts and taxes on Andean natives were more than a violation of divine justice; they offended the natural rights of free men. The Spanish crown, recognizing the importance of printing presses in the spread of insidious ideas, strictly controlled the number and location of printers in the colonies; in Brazil, the royal authorities banned them altogether. In spite of these controls, books, pamphlets, and simple gossip allowed new notions of science, history, and politics to circulate widely among literate creoles.

Wealthy colonists in British America were similar to the creole elites in Spanish and Portuguese America. They, too, strove to emulate European ways, using their profits to construct "big houses" in Virginia modeled on the country estates of English gentlemen, to import opulent furnishings and fashions from the finest British stores, and to exercise more control over colonial assemblies. Becoming like the English also involved a solidification of patriarchal authority at all levels, but especially among the colonial elite. In seventeenth-century Virginia, men had vastly outnumbered women, which gave women a measure of power, with widows in particular gaining hold of substantial property. During the eighteenth century, however, sex ratios became more equal, and women's property rights diminished as they reverted to English norms. Symbolically, the new order was displayed in countless family portraits, where husband-patriarchs were customarily pictured above their wives and children.

Intellectually, too, British Americans were linked to Europe, importing enormous numbers of books and journals. Indeed, Americans played a significant role in the Enlightenment, serving as both producers and consumers of political pamphlets, scientific treatises, and social critiques. Drawing on the words of Montesquieu (1689–1755), Locke, and Rousseau, genteel American intellectuals created the most famous of enlightened documents, the Declaration of Independence (1776), which announced that all men were endowed with equal rights and created to pursue this worldly happiness. Here, Anglicized Americans showed themselves, like the creole elites of Latin America, to be both European and products of New World encounters.

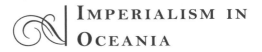

IMPERIALISM IN OCEANIA

> → *What role did race play in how Europeans viewed others, especially those from Oceania?*

Not only in Europe and the Americas, but also in the South Pacific, especially in Australia, a new, enlightened form of cultural aggrandizement was under way in the eighteenth century. Though in centuries past Hindu, Buddhist, Islamic, and Chinese missionaries and traders had brought their cultures to Malaysia and nearby islands, they had not ventured beyond Timor. Europeans began to do so in the years after 1770. Using their new wealth—public and private—to fund voyages that were both scientific and political, Europeans invaded these remaining aboriginal areas. The results were

Chronometer. In the 1760s, the English clockmaker John Harrison perfected the chronometer, a timepiece mariners could use to reckon longitude while at sea. Although the Royal Scientific Society initially refused to believe that Harrison had solved this long-standing problem, Harrison's instrument made navigation so much safer and more predictable that it became standard equipment on European ships.

mixed: while some islands maintained their autonomy, through resistance or European disinterest, the biggest prize, Australia, underwent thorough Anglicization.

Until Europeans colonized it in the late eighteenth century, Australia was truly a world apart. Separated by water and sheer distance from other regions, it was characterized primarily by its generally harsh natural conditions and sparse population. At the time of the European colonization, the island was home to around 300,000 people, mostly hunter-gatherers. While seafarers from Java, Timor, and particularly the port of Makassar were likely to have ventured into the area in the past, there was little evidence that either Chinese or Muslim merchants ever strayed that far south despite their active involvement in the Southeast Asian trade.

Europeans had visited Oceania before the eighteenth century. Spices drew the Portuguese and Dutch into the South Pacific (see Chapter 13). The Spanish had regularly plied the Pacific waters on their travels between Manila and Acapulco, but they had made habitual stops only in Guam and the Mariana Islands. In the 1670s and 1680s, they attempted to conquer these islands, and despite considerable resistance, finally succeeded in doing so by 1700. The Dutch visited Easter Island in 1722, and the French arrived in Tahiti in 1767. The Portuguese (in the sixteenth century) and the Dutch (in the seventeenth century) had seen the northern and western

MAP 14-1   SOUTHEAST ASIA

Captain Cook's voyages throughout the Pacific Ocean symbolized a new era in European exploration of other societies. Where did Cook explore and what peoples did he encounter? How did Cook's endeavors symbolize "scientific" imperialism? How are his explorations similar to those of Christopher Columbus three centuries earlier? How are they different?

   ⟵   Route of James Cook, 1768–71
   ⟵   Route of James Cook, 1772–75
   ⟵   Route of James Cook, 1776–80

coasts of Australia, but they had found only sand, flies, and Aborigines. Not until the late eighteenth century did Europeans see Australia's verdant eastern coast or find grounds for serious interest in colonization.

THE SCIENTIFIC VOYAGES OF CAPTAIN COOK

In Oceania and the South Pacific, Europeans experimented with a scientific form of imperialism. The story of the region's most famous explorer, Captain James Cook, shows how intimately related science and imperialist ventures could be and how cultural exchange became unequal even before the onset of the industrial age. As Columbus was a man of a mystical age, Cook was a man of an enlightened one—but both served the cause of European expansion. Cook's voyages and his encounter with the South Sea Islanders opened up the Pacific, and particularly Australia, to European colonizers. Captain Cook has become a legendary figure in European cultural history, portrayed as one of the saintly scientists of enlightened progress. Charged by the Royal Society with the scholarly task of observing the transit of the planet Venus from the Southern Hemisphere and by the British government with the more pragmatic, if secret, mission of finding and claiming "the southern continent" for Britain, Cook set sail for the Pacific in 1768. This voyage proved so fruitful that Cook was sent back on two more scientific-imperial adventures. The extremely popular accounts of his discoveries, and the engravings that accompanied them, opened up the exotic worlds of Tahiti, New Zealand, Australia, and Hawaii to European scrutiny. They also prepared the way for a new, more intensive sort of cultural colonization.

Cook was chosen to head the first expedition because he, like many of his British contemporaries, was scientifically inclined. Although he had little schooling, Cook had gone to sea early and, through long experience in navigating the uncharted waters of Newfoundland, had developed excellent surveying skills. Besides Cook, the Royal Society sent on the expedition one of its members, Joseph Banks, a gentlemanly but serious botanist; Daniel Solander, a doctor and student of the renowned Swedish botanist Linnaeus; and a number of artists and scientists. The crew also took along sophisticated instruments, and they were asked to keep extensive, detailed diaries. This was to be a grand data-collecting odyssey, a heroic, scientific response to recent French expeditions to the same regions.

Cook's voyages surpassed even the Royal Society's hopes. It is said that on his three voyages to the South Pacific between 1768 and 1779, the scientists made about 3,000 drawings of Pacific plants, birds, landscapes, and peoples never seen before in Europe. Naturally, the flora and fauna were described according to the new Linnaean classificatory system, and the geographical features were given English desig-

Captain James Cook. During his celebrated voyages to the South Pacific, Cook kept meticulous maps and diaries. Although he had little formal education, he became one of the great exemplars of enlightened learning through experience and experiment.

nations, like the Bay of Good Success, where Cook's ship the *Endeavour* anchored in 1769. Cook and his crew kept meticulous diaries and records, which fascinated scholars, travelers, missionaries, and government officials across Europe. Just as many poems and plays were written in celebration of the great navigator, Cook's expeditions were also considered state-of-the-art scientific practice.

More than a mere trading area, Australia was intended to supply Britain with raw materials. But the Aborigines of Australia, like the Indians of the Americas, succumbed in great numbers to new imported diseases, and survivors generally fled to escape dependency on British masters. Thus, to secure a labor force, plans were developed for grand-scale conquest and resettlement by and for British colonists. On his third voyage, Cook took with him a veritable Noah's ark of animals and plants with which to turn the South Pacific into a European-style garden. Cook's lieutenant, William Bligh, later brought apples, quinces, strawberries, and rosemary to Australia; the seventy sheep imported in 1788 laid the foundations for the region's wool-growing economy. The domestication of Australia was born from certainty about Europeans' superior know-how and a desire to make the landmass as a whole serve British interests.

In 1788, a British military expedition took official possession of the whole eastern half of Australia. The intent was, in part, to set up a prison colony far from home. This plan, too, belonged to the realm of enlightened dreams: that of ridding "civilized" society of all evils by resettling the lawbreakers among the "uncivilized" (previously convicts had been sent to Georgia in North America). Australia, too, was to be exploited for its timber and flax and used as a strategic base against Dutch and French expansion. In the next decades, immigration—free and forced—increased the Anglo-Australian population from an original 1,000 to about 1.2 million by 1860. Importing their customs and their capital, British settlers turned Australia into a frontier version of home, just as they had done in British America. Yet, as in the Americas, such large-scale immigration had disastrous consequences for the Aborigines. Like the Native Americans, the original inhabitants of Australia were decimated by diseases and increasingly forced westward by European settlement.

In one important way Cook had not departed so decisively from the practices of the past. Earlier travelers had developed an efficient means of studying foreign peoples and their languages: taking certain of them to Europe, by kidnapping if necessary. On his first voyage to the New World, Columbus captured six Amerindians and took them back to Spain, to show off these exotic people and so that they could learn Spanish and thus serve as intermediaries between the two cultures. Other explorers did the same, seizing local people, taking them to Europe, and even putting them on display. This was not the way that Europeans learned the languages of peoples they considered to be civilized, for example, the Chinese and Arabs; texts stood in for living bodies of "civilized" peoples. But exhibiting live individuals continued to be a crude means of ethnography for peoples the Europeans

Omai. Omai, the South Sea Islander brought to England by Captain Cook, was the object of much curiosity in London in the 1780s.

considered uncivilized. Through the nineteenth century, exhibitions of Laplanders, Africans, and Polynesians traveled, circus-like, from town to town through Europe. Cook himself captured and transported to England a highly skilled Polynesian navigator, Omai. Arriving in 1774, Omai quickly became the talk of London society and symbolized for some people the innocence and beauty that was being lost as Europe developed complicated machines and stock exchanges. Cook's return of Omai to his home on his third voyage was a sensation of equal proportions, seen as a colossally generous act by the revered British explorer.

Engraving from Cook's *Voyage Round the World in the Years 1768–1771*. Kangaroos were unknown in the West until Cook and his colleagues encountered (and ate) them on their first visit to Australia. This engraving of the animal (which unlike most animals, plants, and geographical features actually kept the name the Aborigines had given it) from Cook's 1773 travelogue lovingly depicts the kangaroo's environs and even emotions.

CLASSIFICATION AND "RACE"

Cook's description of the South Sea Islanders underscores the place that race had come to occupy in eighteenth-century Europeans' views of themselves and others. Previously, the word *race* referred to a swift current in a stream or a trial of speed, and on occasion meant a lineage, mainly that of a royal or noble family. By the end of the seventeenth century, a few writers were beginning to expand the definition of race to designate a European ethnic lineage, identifying, for example, the indomitable spirit and freedom-loving ethos of the Anglo-Saxon race. François Bernier, who had traveled in Asia, may have been the first European to attempt a racial division of the globe in his 1684 *New Division of the Earth by the Different Groups or Races Who Inhabit It.* Carolus Linnaeus (1707–1778); Georges Louis LeClerc, the comte de Buffon (1707–1788); and Johann Friedrich Blumenbach (1752–1840) would be the first to use racial principles to classify humankind.

Europe's most accomplished naturalist, Carolus Linnaeus, took his passion for classifying and naming all the plants and animals in the world to identify several species within the genus *Homo—Homo sapiens, Homo caudatus* (tailed man), and *Homo troglodytes*—in his *Systema Naturae* (1735). The latter two species—the tailed man and troglodyte man—were groups Linnaeus defined on the basis of classical texts, travelers' accounts, rumors, freak show exhibits, and misunderstandings. Within *Homo sapiens,* he identified five groups, or races, using a combination of physical characteristics, including skin pigmentation and social qualities. Linnaeus characterized the Europeans as light-skinned and governed by laws. In contrast with Chinese conceptions of color, by which they were of white skin, Linnaeus's scheme described the peoples of Asia as "sooty" and deemed them regulated by opinion. He said that copper-skinned, indigenous American peoples were governed by custom. He wrote that Africans, whom he consigned to the lowest rung of the human ladder, were ruled by little other than personal whim. Later eighteenth-century natural historians dismissed Linnaeus's troglodyte and tailed men, but the habit of ranking races and lumping together physical and cultural characteristics persisted. In time, some would even question the unity of the human species.

In inventorying the peoples of the world and assigning each group a place on the ladder of human achievement, the long-standing idealization of classical sculpture played a role: those who most resembled Greek nudes were believed to be the most beautiful, as well as the most civilized and suited for world power. In his *Natural History* (1750), a noted French scientist, the comte de Buffon, insisted that proper proportion for the human form had been established by classical sculptures. Having divided the human genus into distinct races, he determined white peoples to be the most admirable, and Africans the most contemptible.

The father of physical anthropology, Johann Friedrich Blumenbach, crystallized much of Enlightenment thought about race in his authoritative book *De Generis Humani Natura,* published in 1775. He divided humanity into four races: Europeans, Asians, Africans, and Americans, with these classifications based largely, although not exclusively, on physical characteristics, like skin color, cranial size, hair, and the like. Blumenbach introduced the word *Caucasian* to denote Europeans, but he believed Caucasians and "Ethiopians" (his word for Africans) belonged to the same species because they had the same physical characteristics. Blumenbach, in fact, asserted a rough racial equality, maintaining that there were beautiful Ethiopians just as there were ugly Caucasians.

Linnaeus and Classification. Linnaeus's famous system of plant and animal classifications, which depended on sexual forms (such as the stamen and pistil in plants), was in wide use by the end of the eighteenth century.

South Sea Islanders, like Omai, fell somewhere between the Caucasians and the Ethiopians. They retained an aura of mythical similarity to the Greek gods, but in succeeding decades Europeans would cease to view them as "noble savages," a phrase coined by Rousseau to describe the virtues of the uncivilized. The waning of appreciation for their innocence and simplicity may indeed have begun with the final act in the Cook legend: his killing by the Hawaiians in 1779.

In their first encounters, Cook had greatly impressed the Hawaiians; some commentators believe the Hawaiians recognized in him the embodiment of their god Lono; others simply think they treated him as an important chief. He had, in any event, deeply offended them by destroying one of their sacred shrines, ostensibly for firewood but possibly because he wished to destroy symbols of their religion. When he then tried to take several chiefs hostage in order to force the return of a boat, tensions rose. In unclear circumstances, his men killed several important Hawaiians, and the islanders, incensed and frightened by the violence, closed in on the captain, stabbing him repeatedly. The news, of course, scandalized Cook's homeland; the king himself, it is said, shed tears. Europeans began to expound upon the "darker side" of South Pacific cultures. *Ode to the Memory of the Late Captain James Cook* (1780) depicted the sullen, vengeful savage "Whose darken'd mind in mercy found no joy." A French traveler, who had seen the explorer Marion de Fresne killed by Maoris on New Zealand's coast, similarly denounced "the passions of rapacity, violence, and treachery" common to the South Pacific "Children of Nature."

CONCLUSION

New wealth produced by increasing commerce and the consolidation of polities created the conditions for a kind of global cultural renaissance in the period between 1500 and 1780, beginning in the Chinese and Islamic empires but stretching into Europe and Africa and extending into previous worlds apart in the Americas and Oceania. Experiments in religious toleration encouraged cultural exchange; book production and consumption soared; grand new monuments arose; luxury goods became available for wider enjoyment.

Perhaps the most striking thing about this cultural renaissance was its unevenness. While elites and sometimes the middle classes benefited, the poor did not. They remained illiterate, undernourished, and often subjected to brutal treatment by rulers and landowners. In Europe and China, elite women increasingly joined literate society, writing, reading, and publishing books, acting as patrons and translators, but they gained no new rights. Urban areas also profited much more from the new wealth than rural ones, and those seeking refinement flocked to the cities. Some regions, which had once been cultural meccas, like the Italian peninsula, lost their luster as new, more commercially and culturally dynamic centers took their place.

Between states, too, cultural inequalities were now glaring. Although the Islamic and Chinese worlds confidently retained their own systems of knowing, believing, and representing, the Americas and Oceania were increasingly sub-

Chronology

		1600					
THE ISLAMIC WORLD		◼ *Abulfazl's Akbarnamah in Mughal India, 1587–1602*					
		◼ *Building of palace and plaza in Isfahan, Iran, 1598–1629*					
			◼ *Building of Taj Mahal in Agra, India, 1630–1650*				
EUROPE		*Galileo Galilei's* Dialogue on the Two Chief Systems of the World, *1632* ◼					
			Building of Versailles begins outside Paris, 1661 ◼				
			Incorporation of British Royal Society, 1662 ◼				
AMERICAS		◼ *Hybrid cultures emerge in Americas, 1600s*					
AFRICA		◼ *Oyo and Asante kingdoms produce vibrant artistic work, 1600s*					
EAST ASIA		◼ *Jesuit missionary Matteo Ricci brings European cartography to China, 1583*					
		◼ *Growing circulation of books and ideas in China, 1600s*					
		◼ *Kabuki theater appears in Japan, 1600s*					

jected to European cultural pressures. Here, while syncretic practices were widespread by the later eighteenth century, clearly European ideas, beliefs, and habits had become the standards by which degrees of "civilization" were judged. African cultures were the exception in that they largely managed to escape this influence, though because of the slave trade, the peoples of that landmass certainly felt the impact of European expansionism.

As the Oceania example shows, by the late eighteenth century, Europeans had an expansive view of the world and their place in it. They were gleefully classifying the plants, animals, and peoples of the world and seeking ways to make new worlds more and more useful and comfortable for themselves. It is important to recognize, however, that Europe's categories and descriptions did not win easy acceptance beyond Europe's self-created borders. The Chinese, Ottomans, Safavids, Mughals, and Africans remained largely unaware of or unimpressed by European endeavors, and resistance from Native Americans as from South Sea Islanders remained stiff.

From a commercial standpoint, the world in the seventeenth and eighteenth centuries was more tightly integrated than ever before. Populations moved around with increasing ease and frequency, and mercantile dealings involving distant groups became more common. In general, well-established cultural groups and traditional institutions dealt effectively with these interactions and transactions.

In some respects, borrowing and exposure only reconfirmed established ways. The Chinese, for instance, still believed in the superiority of Chinese knowledge and customs and regarded those who had not mastered their ways as lesser peoples. Islamic rulers, too, claimed universality on behalf of Islam as a body of revealed, not objective, knowledge. Confident of the superiority of Islam, the dynasts allowed others to form their own—though clearly subordinate—cultural communities. At the elite level, they accommodated non-Muslim subjects and knowledge by constructing a realm of courtly culture and philosophy, where the superiority of Islam was not in question but where other systems of knowledge could be discussed and debated. Within these imperial Islamic cultures, the Europeans were useful, decorative pieces, and their knowledge, to the extent considered helpful for imperial purposes, was taken into account.

Only the Europeans were constructing knowledge that they believed was both universal and objective, a kind of knowledge that could be used to master nature and all its inhabitants. This approach to cultural differences was to prove consequential as well as controversial, in the centuries to come.

STUDY QUESTIONS

 WWNORTON.COM/STUDYSPACE

1. Explain the processes that brought forth new syncretic cultural syntheses in the three Islamic dynasties during this era. To what extent did European ideas and culture influence each empire?

1700   **1800**

❚ *Tulip Period in Ottoman Empire, 1720s*

❚ *Isaac Newton's* Principia Mathematica, *1687*   ❚ *Carolus Linnaeus's* Systema Naturae, *1735*

❚ *John Locke's* Essay Concerning Human Understanding, *1690*   ❚ *Denis Diderot's* Encyclopedia, *1751–1772*

❚ *Voyages of Captain James Cook, 1768–1779*

❚ *Adam Smith's* The Wealth of Nations, *1776*

❚ *Enlightenment philosophy introduces elite thought in American colonies, 1700s*

❚ *Shogun lifts ban on foreign books, 1720*

❚ *Movement for "native learning" begins in Japan, 1728*

2. List and describe Chinese and Japanese cultural achievements during this time period. How did foreign influences shape ideas and beliefs in each dynasty?

3. Define the term *Enlightenment* as it pertained to Europe during this time period. How did Enlightenment ideas shape European attitudes toward other cultures?

4. Explain the various factors that contributed to the growth of hybrid cultures in the Americas during this era. How similar and different were these new societies across the Americas?

5. Analyze the impact of Enlightenment ideas in the Americas. Did the spread of this new philosophy bring communities across the Atlantic together or did it drive them apart?

6. Compare and contrast European exploration of Oceania in the eighteenth century to European exploration of the Americas in the sixteenth century. How did European exploration of Oceania transform European attitudes toward non-European groups around the world?

7. Analyze how world trade changed world cultures during this time period. To what extent did a universal culture emerge?

8. Analyze to what extent dynastic rulers around the world were able to control cultural developments during this era. How did new cultural manifestations potentially undermine local governments?

FURTHER READINGS

Axtell, James, *The Invasion of America: The Contest of Cultures in Colonial North America* (1985). Discusses the strategies of Christian missionaries in converting the Indians, as well as the success of Indians in converting Europeans.

Berlin, Ira, *Many Thousands Gone: The First Two Centuries of Slavery in North America* (1998). Surveys the development of African-American culture in colonial North America.

Brook, Timothy, *The Confusions of Pleasure: Commerce and Culture in Ming China* (1999). An insightful survey of Ming society.

Clunas, Craig, *Superfluous Things: Material Culture and Social Status in Early Modern China* (1991). A good account of the late Ming elite's growing passion for material things.

Collcutt, Martin, Marius Jansen, and Isao Kumakura, *A Cultural Atlas of Japan* (1988). A sweeping look at the many different forms of Japanese cultural expression over the centuries, including the flourishing urban culture of Edo.

Darnton, Robert, *The Business of the Enlightenment: A Publishing History of the Encyclopédie, 1775–1800* (1979). The classic study of Europe's first great compendium of knowledge.

Dash, Mike, *Tulipomania: The Story of the World's Most Coveted Flower and the Extraordinary Passions It Aroused* (1999). A global perspective on and lively account of the spread of the tulip around the world as a flower signifying both beauty and status.

Elman, Benjamin A., *On Their Own Terms: Science in China, 1550–1900* (2005). A study of the development of "native" Chinese science and how the process interacted with the introduction of western science to China over the course of three and a half centuries.

Eze, Emmanuel Chukwudi (ed.), *Race and the Enlightenment: A Reader* (1997). Readings examining the idea of race in the context of the Enlightenment.

Fleischer, Cornell, *Bureaucrat and Intellectual in the Ottoman Empire: The Historian Mustafa Ali (1540–1600)* (1986). Offers good insight into the world of culture and intellectual vitality in the Ottoman Empire.

Grafton, Anthony, April Shelford, and Nancy Siraisi, *New Worlds, Ancient Texts: The Power of Tradition and the Shock of Discovery* (1995). A concise discussion of the impact of the New World on European thought.

Gutierrez, Ramon, *When Jesus Came, the Corn Mothers Went Away: Marriage, Sexuality, and Power in New Mexico, 1500–1846* (1991). A provocative dissection of the spiritual dimensions of European colonialism in the Americas.

Hannaford, Ivan, *Race: The History of an Idea in the West* (1996). A study of how race began to take on critical importance in western thinking in the seventeenth and eighteenth centuries.

Harley, J. B., and David Woodward (eds.), *The History of Cartography.* Vol. 2, Book 2: *Cartography in the Traditional East and Southeast Asian Societies* (1994). An authoritative treatment of the subject.

Horton, Robin, *Patterns of Thought in Africa and the West: Essays on Magic, Religion, and Science* (1993). Reflections on African patterns of thought and attitudes toward nature, which can help us to understand African-American religious beliefs and resistance movements.

Keene, Donald, *The Japanese Discovery of Europe: Honda Toshiaki and Other Discoverers, 1720–1798* (1952). A study of the ways Japan managed to incorporate knowledge from the outside world with the development of national traditions.

Ko, Dorothy, *Teachers of the Inner Chambers: Women and Culture in Seventeenth-Century China* (1994). Explores the lives of elite women in late Ming and early Qing China.

Lewis, Bernard, *Race and Color in Islam* (1979). Examines the Islamic attitude toward race and color.

Morgan, Philip D., *Slave Counterpoint: Black Culture in the Eighteenth-Century Chesapeake and Lowcountry* (1998). Describes the development of African-American culture in colonial North America.

Munck, Thomas, *The Enlightenment: A Comparative Social History, 1721–1794* (2000). A wonderful survey, with unusual examples from the periphery, especially from Scandinavia and the Habsburg Empire.

Necipoglu, Gulru, *Architecture, Ceremonial and Power: The Topkapi Palace in the Fifteenth and Sixteenth Centuries* (1991). A magnificently illustrated book that shows the enormous artistic talent that the Ottoman rulers poured into their imperial structure.

Publishing and the Print Culture in Late Imperial China (Special Issue). *Late Imperial China*, Vol. 17:1 (June 1996). Contains a collection of important articles with a foreword by the French cultural historian Roger Chartier.

Qaisar, Ahsan Jan, *The Indian Response to European Technology, AD 1498–1707* (1998). A meticulous, scholarly work on this little-studied subject.

Rizvi, Athar Abbas, *The Wonder That Was India.* Vol. 2: *A Survey of the History and Culture of the Indian Sub-continent from the Coming of the Muslims to the British Conquest, 1200–1700* (1987). A deeply learned work in intellectual history.

Shapin, Stephen, *The Scientific Revolution* (1998). An overview that is informed by innovative new thinking on the subject.

Smith, Bernard, *European Vision and the South Pacific* (1985). An excellent cultural history of Cook's voyages.

Smith, Richard J., *Chinese Maps: Images of "All under Heaven"* (1996). Provides a good introduction to the history of cartography in China.

Welch, Anthony, *Shah Abbas and the Arts of Isfahan* (1973). Describes the astonishing architectural and artistic renaissance of the city of Isfahan under the Safavid ruler, Shah Abbas.

Whitfield, Peter, *The Image of the World: Twenty Centuries of World Maps* (1994). A good introduction to the history of cartography in different parts of the world.

Zilfi, Madeline C., *The Politics of Piety: The Ottoman Ulema in the Post-Classical Age (1600–1800)* (1988). Explores the cultural flourishing that took place within the Islamic world in this period.

Chapter 15

REORDERING THE WORLD, 1750–1850

At the end of the eighteenth century, the commander of a French army, Napoleon Bonaparte, led an expedition to Egypt. For many Europeans, Egypt was an exalted territory—the cradle of a once-great culture, the setting for many a Biblical story, a land bridge to the Red Sea and trade with Asia, and a provincial outpost of an old rival, the Ottoman Empire. Introducing the principles of the recent French Revolution (liberty, equality, and fraternity) to distant lands would bring glory to France. Occupying the country would also represent a strategic victory over Great Britain for the control of trade routes to Asia. Most important to Napoleon, however, defeat of the Ottomans would catapult him to historic greatness.

But the revolutionary crusade of 1798 did not go as Napoleon planned. After defeating the Mamluk army of Egypt beneath the pyramids just outside Cairo, his troops bogged down in the country and faced the wrath of the local population. Eager to play a larger role in Europe, Napoleon returned to France a little more than one year after he had stepped on Egyptian soil, leaving his troops vulnerable to inevitable counterattacks. But the invasion of Egypt did shake up Ottoman rule and played a role in altering the

European balance of power. Indeed, Napoleon's actions in Africa, the Americas, and Europe combined with the principles of the French Revolution laid the foundations for the era of the nation-state. What gave these political events added impact were a number of equally disruptive changes in social and economic arrangements around the world.

The period 1750–1850 witnessed a fundamental reordering of the balance of power in the world. The reordering began in the Atlantic world, where political upheavals destroyed the colonial domains of Spain, Portugal, Britain, and France in the Americas and established a number of new nations. To these political events were added far-reaching economic changes that propelled western Europe to global preeminence. These reorderings, in turn, forced Asian and African governments to come to terms with the new economic and political might of Europe. In Egypt and the Ottoman Empire, reform-minded leaders undertook desperate modernizing efforts to deal with Europe's threatening power. In China, too, by the 1830s the ruling Manchus were faced with European gunboats insisting that the Chinese permit expanded trade with the Europeans.

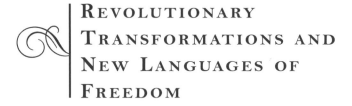

REVOLUTIONARY TRANSFORMATIONS AND NEW LANGUAGES OF FREEDOM

> → *How did Enlightenment ideas transform the world?*

In the eighteenth century, the increasing circulation of goods, people, and ideas created new pressures for reform around the Atlantic world. As economies expanded, many men and women felt that the restrictions of the mercantilist system stood in the way of their aspirations. They clamored for changes that would enable them to partake of this wealth and power. Similarly, as enlightened ideas spread through an increasingly literate public, new voices called for their states to adopt rational, humane, and just practices, including the abolition of torture and the accountability of the governors to the people they governed. Demanding more freedom to trade and more influence in governing institutions, these reformers ran up against the resistance of aristocratic elites. It is a testimony to the weakness of these elites, as well as to the power of these new forces, that those in power could not stamp out these demands before they became—in a number of places—full-scale revolutions. Reformers began to advance concepts of popular sovereignty (of power residing in the people themselves) and to argue that unregulated economies would produce more rapid economic growth. In denouncing commercial privileges and monopolies, as well as arbitrary rulers, reformers employed a rhetoric of freedom, which would alter the course of world history. They argued that free trade, free markets, and free labor would yield more just and more efficient societies. With time, proponents of the new order argued that this new social order would benefit everyone everywhere in the world.

The struggle to create new political and economic relationships offered people the opportunity to think differently about the way the world should be ordered. In this era languages of nationalism (the idea that the people who belonged to a shared community called a "nation" should enjoy sovereignty within the borders of their state) and democracy (that these people, by virtue of their membership in the nation, enjoyed public rights to representation) appealed to so many that it would be difficult afterward to restore absolute sovereignty to monarchs or lasting stability to multiethnic empires. The first expression of this new thinking occurred in thirteen of Britain's North American colonies and in France, where in the late eighteenth century the "nation" and the "people" mobilized sufficient opposition to topple old rulers.

Focus Questions   REORDERING THE WORLD

> → *How did Enlightenment ideas transform the world?*
> → *What major changes in government and society grew out of the Atlantic revolutions?*
> → *Why did the abolition of the slave trade have unintended effects on African society?*
> → *How did the industrial and commercial revolutions reorder society?*
> → *How did the Atlantic revolutions affect Afro-Eurasian societies?*

As democratic and nationalist ideas emerged in the American and French revolutions, the question arose as to how far freedom should be extended, even within the Atlantic world. Should women, Native Americans, and slaves be given the rights of citizens? Should people without property be given the vote? Moreover, should freedom be extended to non-Europeans? By and large, European and Euro-American elite groups answered no to these questions, and often they backed their answer with violence. The very same elites who championed a freer world often exploited slaves and those in the lower orders, denied women equal treatment, restricted colonial economies, and were prepared to use force to expand further the markets of Asia and Africa to European trade and investment. In Africa, the third corner of the Atlantic world, idealistic upheavals resulted not in the emergence of free and sovereign peoples but in intensified enslavement.

POLITICAL REORDERINGS

> ↦ *What major changes in government and society grew out of the Atlantic revolutions?*

The second half of the eighteenth century witnessed the spread of revolutionary ideas across the Atlantic world (see Map 15-1). In part, this spread followed the trail of Enlightenment ideas about freedom and reason. By the late eighteenth century, the number of newspapers, pamphlets, and books in circulation had soared, drawing readers in European countries and American colonies into a discussion of their society's problems—and how to fix them. Many more people began to believe that they had the right to participate in governance. Gradually and unevenly, on both sides of the Atlantic, politics became a noisier activity, involving a wider group (though chiefly of middle- and upper-class males), rather than a matter reserved for kings, court advisers, and landed magnates. Increasingly, too, those who made or wished to make political revolutions claimed that they were acting for the good of "the people."

The slogans of the era—independence, freedom, liberty, and equality—were especially powerful terms that seemed to promise an end to oppression, hardship, and inequities of all kinds. Fired by these new ideas, political revolts spread throughout the Atlantic world, starting first in Britain's North American colonies and spreading to France's absolute monarchy. In both, revolutions ultimately caused monarchies to be replaced with republics. The examples of the United States and France soon encouraged others in the Caribbean and Central and South America to seek king-less polities. In all of these revolutionary environments, new representative institutions such as permanent parliaments, enshrined in written constitutions, came into being. The rhetoric of revolution, once unleashed, proved difficult to contain in later generations.

THE NORTH AMERICAN WAR OF INDEPENDENCE, 1776–1783

By the mid-eighteenth century, Britain's mainland colonies swelled with people and prosperity. Through bustling port cities like Charleston, Philadelphia, New York, and Boston, African slaves, European migrants, and manufactured goods flowed in, while agrarian staples flowed out. A colonial "genteel" class, composed of merchants and landowning planters, came to dominate the affairs of these colonies and aspired to the status of English gentlemen. But with settlers arriving from Europe and slaves from Africa, land was a constant source of dispute. Planters collided with independent farmers (yeomen). Sons and daughters of farmers, unable to inherit or acquire real estate near their parents, spilled into the landmass's interior, and their land-seeking put them in conflict with Indian peoples. To defend their lands, many Indians allied with Britain's rival, France, but after losing the Seven Years' War (1756–1763), France ceded its Canadian colony to Britain. Without French support and overwhelmed by settlers, many Indians continued to mount a spirited resistance, but they often died in battle or of disease. A large number of survivors fled west.

By the mid-1760s, the British Empire stood supreme in eastern North America. A political revolution seemed unimaginable. And yet, a decade later, that is precisely what occurred. Why did colonists sever their ties with England? They acted, paradoxically, in defense of their rights as "freeborn Englishmen." The spark was provided by King George III, who proposed to end the policy of benign neglect of the colonies and to make the colonists pay for Britain's war with France and for the benefits of being subjects of the empire. Colonial merchants, particularly in New England, protested the Revenue Act of 1764, which sought to end lucrative smuggling by many colonists. Even more vexing to the colonists was taxation without representation, for no colonists sat in the British House of Commons, Great Britain's governing legislative body. Agitation for freedom turned to open warfare between a colonial militia and British troops at Lexington and Concord, Massachusetts, in the spring of 1775. One firebrand, Thomas Paine, a recent immigrant from England, captured the mood in a pamphlet published in January 1776, in which he argued to an increasingly literate public that it was "common sense" for people to govern themselves. Paine's pamphlet had sold more than 100,000 copies by July 1776, when the Continental Congress adapted part of it for the Declaration of Independence.

The declaration—written primarily by the Virginia tobacco planter Thomas Jefferson—drew on themes of the European Enlightenment. It championed the "natural rights"

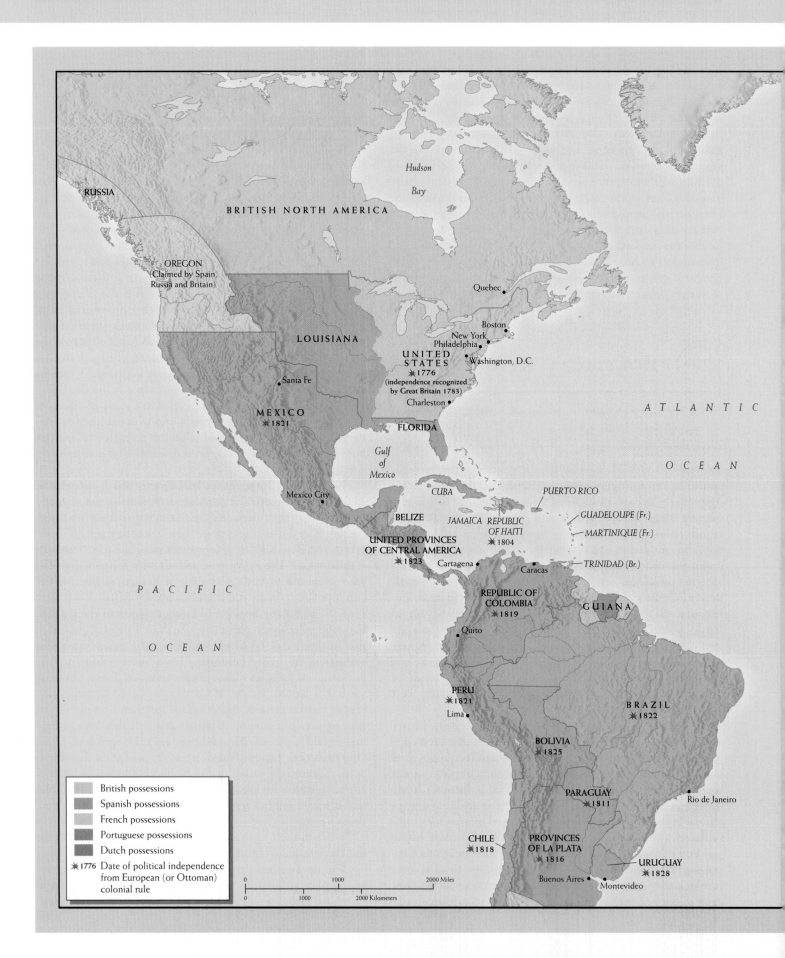

RUSSIA

Hudson Bay

BRITISH NORTH AMERICA

OREGON
(Claimed by Spain,
Russia and Britain)

Quebec

Boston
New York
Philadelphia
Washington, D.C.

LOUISIANA

UNITED
STATES
✳ 1776
(independence recognized
by Great Britain 1783)

Charleston

Santa Fe

MEXICO
✳ 1821

FLORIDA

ATLANTIC

*Gulf
of
Mexico*

OCEAN

Mexico City

CUBA

PUERTO RICO

GUADELOUPE (Fr.)

BELIZE

JAMAICA   REPUBLIC
OF HAITI
✳ 1804

MARTINIQUE (Fr.)

UNITED PROVINCES
OF CENTRAL AMERICA
✳ 1823

Cartagena

Caracas

TRINIDAD (Br.)

PACIFIC

REPUBLIC OF
COLOMBIA
✳ 1819

GUIANA

Quito

OCEAN

PERU
✳ 1821
Lima

BRAZIL
✳ 1822

BOLIVIA
✳ 1825

PARAGUAY
✳ 1811

Rio de Janeiro

CHILE
✳ 1818

PROVINCES
OF LA PLATA
✳ 1816

URUGUAY
✳ 1828

Buenos Aires
Montevideo

British possessions
Spanish possessions
French possessions
Portuguese possessions
Dutch possessions
✳ 1776 Date of political independence
from European (or Ottoman)
colonial rule

0   1000   2000 Miles
0   1000   2000 Kilometers

MAP 15-1   REVOLUTIONS OF NATIONAL INDEPENDENCE IN THE ATLANTIC WORLD, 1776–1829

Colonies gained independence from European powers (and in the case of Greece from the Ottoman Empire) in the late eighteenth and early nineteenth centuries under the influence of Enlightenment thinkers and the French Revolution. What were the first two American colonial territories to gain independence? Why was the United States reluctant to recognize the political independence of the second independent American republic? Why did colonies in Spanish and Portuguese America obtain their political independence decades after the United States gained its independence?

The Boston Massacre. Paul Revere's idealized view of the Boston Massacre of March 5, 1770. In the years after the Seven Years' War, Bostonians grew increasingly disenchanted with British efforts to enforce imperial regulations. When British troops fired on and killed several members of an angry mob in what came to be called the "Boston Massacre," the resulting frenzy stirred revolutionary sentiments among the populace.

of people to govern themselves and the idea, drawn from John Locke's political writings, that governments should be based on a social contract, according to which both the sovereign and the people are bound by the law. Locke also stipulated that the people had the right to rebel against their government if it did not obey the contract and tried to infringe on the rights of the people. "We hold these truths to be self-evident," the declaration proclaimed, "that all men are created equal, that they are endowed by their Creator with certain inalienable Rights, that among these are Life, Liberty and the Pursuit of Happiness. That to secure these rights, Governments are instituted among Men, deriving their just powers from the consent of the governed. That whenever any Form of Government becomes destructive of these ends, it is the Right of the People to alter or abolish it." Thus the Americans announced their right to rid themselves of the English king and form their own independent polity, but neither the Declaration of Independence nor *Common Sense* provided a blueprint for how a nonmonarchical government might be organized or how thirteen tenuously connected states might win a war against the world's most powerful empire.

During the War of Independence, Americans began to work out new political arrangements. Much of that work occurred in the individual states, where elections were held to select delegates to constitutional conventions. These elec-

tions were unprecedented, as was the decision to put the constitutions in writing. Constitution-writers exhibited a revolutionary faith in representative government. Dispensing with royal authority, all the new state constitutions assigned sweeping powers to legislative bodies, whose members were to be elected by "the people." But who constituted the people? No women qualified as voters. Property qualifications also continued to limit the franchise (the right to vote) to a percentage of adult white men, though the constitutions generally reduced the landholding requirements that had prevailed during the colonial era.

The notion that all men were created equal flew in the face of established hierarchies in which people supposedly knew—and kept—their place. Taking this rhetoric to heart, common men no longer automatically deferred to gentlemen of higher rank. Many women, too, claimed that their contributions to the patriots' cause, managing farms and shops in the absence of husbands, merited greater respect and equality in marital relations, including property rights. In letters to her husband, John Adams, Abigail Adams stopped referring to the family farm as "yours." In a telling substitution of pronouns, she started writing of the farm as "ours." Most revolutionary of all, tens of thousands of slaves from the Carolinas to Maryland fled plantations to join the war effort, though these runaways usually sided with the British, believing that loyalty to the crown would win them freedom from their masters.

The prospect of a social revolution of artisans, women, and slaves, rather than a narrower liberal revolution, generated a reaction against what American elites called the "excesses of democracy." Their fears grew after farmers in western Massachusetts, led by Daniel Shays, interrupted court proceedings in which the state sought to foreclose on properties for nonpayment of taxes. The farmers who joined in Shays rebellion in the fall of 1786 also denounced illegitimate taxation, this time by the American government. Massachusetts militiamen easily defeated the ragtag rebel army, but to save the nation from falling into "anarchy," propertied men convened the Constitutional Convention in Philadelphia in the summer of 1787.

Amid fierce debate among the assembled merchants, planters, physicians, governors, military officers, and lawyers (common farmers were not in attendance), the Constitutional Convention drafted a charter for a republican government. The convention looked back to the ancient Roman Republic for a model of a state ruled by representatives of the people rather than by a king. It adopted some aspects of the Roman system but also added some of its own innovations, such as the institution of a single, elected head of state: the president. The new Constitution substantially enlarged the power of the federal government and, compared to the state constitutions of a decade earlier, reduced the stature of the legislature, the branch of government most responsive to popular will. The Constitution also included a system of checks and

Abigail Adams. Abigail Adams was the wife of John Adams, a leader in the movement for American independence and later the second president of the United States. Abigail's letters to her husband testified to the ways in which revolutionary enthusiasm for liberty and equality began to reach into women's minds. While the Continental Congress was debating whether to declare independence in the spring of 1776, Abigail wrote to implore that the men in the Congress "remember the ladies, and be more generous and favorable to them than your ancestors. Do not put such unlimited power into the hands of the Husbands. Remember all Men would be tyrants if they could. If particular care and attention is not paid to the Ladies we are determined to foment a Rebellion, and will not hold ourselves bound by any Laws in which we have no voice, or Representation."

balances. These included the legislature's right to impeach the head of the executive branch (the president) and the judiciary's right to test the constitutionality of laws passed by the legislature. Thus was the Constitution designed to prevent any of the three branches of government from becoming too powerful and to deter majorities from trampling on the rights and property of a wealthier minority. Submitted to the states for approval, the Constitution proved controversial. Its critics, known as Anti-Federalists, echoing Shays, claimed to be defending the people against the growth of a potentially tyrannical federal government. Anti-Federalists also insisted

on the inclusion of the Bill of Rights to protect individual liberties from abusive government intrusions. After a series of closely contested campaigns, the Constitution won ratification, though the Bill of Rights was soon amended to it.

From the 1780s onward, the Federalists and Anti-Federalists disagreed fervently over the new design of the United States, as the new country was called, but they confined their jousting to the constitutional arena. In an uneasy truce, property owners agreed not to convert the debate over whether to abolish slavery, brewing since the 1770s, into a cause for disunion. As the frontier expanded westward, the question of which new states would allow slavery and which would not led to a series of contentious compromises. For the moment, the existence of ample land postponed a confrontation, but with ideas of the dignity and rights of free labor gaining currency in the northern states (and across the North Atlantic world), it became impossible to remove slavery, as southern slaveholders sought, from the realm of national politics. In 1800, the election of Thomas Jefferson as the third president of the United States signaled the triumph of a model of sending pioneers out to new lands to defuse conflict on old lands. In the same year, however, a Virginia slave named Gabriel Prosser hatched a plan to raise an army of slaves to seize the state capital at Richmond and win support from white artisans and laborers for a more inclusive republic. Gabriel's dream of an egalitarian revolution fell victim to white terror and black betrayal. Twenty-seven slaves, including Gabriel, went to the gallows. With them, for the moment, died the dream of a multiracial republic in which all men were truly created equal.

THE FRENCH REVOLUTION, 1789–1799

The rhetoric of freedom and rights also shook up social and political hierarchies in Europe's capitals. Partly inspired by the American Revolution, French men and women soon began to issue their own calls for liberty—and the result was a series of events that, even more than the American Revolution, shook Europe's established dynasties and social hierarchies. In France, the revolution changed its course so suddenly, involved so many participants, and was so extensively reported in books, pamphlets, journals, and songs across the globe that it had a riveting effect on all who heard of it. The revolution's powerful ideas and its violent course inspired so many other rebels around the world, and terrified so many members of the ruling classes, that it must be considered an event not only of European but also of global importance.

ORIGINS AND OUTBREAK For decades before the outbreak of the revolution, enlightened thinkers had attacked the inefficiencies, inequalities, and cruelties of France's old regime. In widely read pamphlets and books, satirists poked fun at the corruptions and prejudices of the church, the court, and the aristocracy and offered suggestions on how the system might be reformed. Their criticisms often resulted in their imprisonment or exile, but by the mid-eighteenth century, discontent with France's ruling elite had spread beyond the educated few. In the countryside, peasants grumbled about paying taxes and tithes to the church and, despite generally improved health and nutrition, suffered periods of deprivation (while the nobility and clergy paid almost no taxes). But revolutions do not occur simply because people are oppressed, hungry, and angry—as had been the case for the European peasantry for centuries—or even because some begin to imagine alternatives to the order of things. It took a unique combination of these pressures, and the opportunity provided by a fiscal crisis, to unleash the French Revolution of 1789.

Interestingly, it was the king himself who opened the door to revolution. Eager to weaken his arch-rival, England, Louis XVI (ruled 1774–1793) spent huge sums in support of the American rebels; by doing so, he greatly increased France's state debt, which consumed some 50 percent of France's national budget by 1788. In and of itself, this was not disastrous—the Dutch and the English at the time had even larger debts. But in France, the king could not raise taxes on the privileged classes without calling a meeting of the Estates-General, a medieval advisory body that had last met in 1614. Like American colonists, French nobles argued that taxation gave them the right of representation. When the king reluctantly agreed to summon the Estates-General in 1788, he still believed that his will would prevail: the delegates of the clergy (the First Estate) and the aristocracy (the Second Estate) could overrule the delegates who represented everybody else

(the Third Estate) because each estate voted as one body rather than as individuals, which meant that the Third Estate could be outvoted.

When the delegates finally assembled in the spring of 1789, the Third Estate refused to be outvoted by the other two, insisted that those who worked and paid the taxes *were* the nation, and demanded that the delegates sit together in one chamber and vote as individuals. The privileged few, some began to say, were simply parasites. As arguments raged and pamphlets poured out of Paris in the spring and early summer of 1789, peasants in the countryside began to sack castles—yet another indication that "the people" now believed the time had come to throw off the old system of inequalities. In June 1789, the delegates of the Third Estate simply declared themselves to be the "National" Assembly, the body fit to determine France's future.

On July 14, 1789, a Parisian crowd, angered at the king's dismissal of a favorite minister, attacked a medieval armory in search of weapons. Not only did this armory, the Bastille, hold gunpowder, it was also an infamous prison for political prisoners—though in 1789 it held only five forgers and two lunatics. Enraged at the commanding officer's refusal to open the doors, the crowd stormed the prison and murdered the officer, then cut off his head and paraded it through the streets of Paris, stuck on a pike. On this day, subsequently celebrated as Bastille Day, the king made the fateful decision not to call out the army, and the capital city belonged to the crowd. The news from Paris quickly spread to the countryside, emboldening peasants to burn down manor houses and destroy municipal archives, where the records of the hated feudal dues were kept. Reformist sentiment ran so high that on August 4, 1789, the deputies of the French National Assembly declared

The "Tennis Court Oath." Locked out of the chambers of the Estates General, the deputies of the Third Estates reconvened at a nearby indoor tennis court in June 1789; there they swore an oath not to disband until the king recognized the sovereignty of a National Assembly.

Women March on Versailles. On October 5, 1789, a group of market women, many of them fishwives (traditionally regarded as leaders of the poor), marched on the Paris city hall to demand bread. Quickly, their numbers grew, and they redirected their march to Versailles, some twelve miles away and the symbol of the entire political order. In response to the women, the king finally appeared on the balcony and agreed to sign the revolutionary decree and return with the women to Paris.

the abolition of the feudal privileges of the nobility and the clergy and the opening of a new era of liberty, equality, and fraternity.

REVOLUTIONARY TRANSFORMATIONS The "Declaration of the Rights of Man and Citizen" followed on August 26. Its seventeen articles echoed Jefferson's Declaration of Independence—but the grander promises of the French document and its different context made it a more radical statement. It endowed all citizens of the French nation with inviolable liberties and gave all men equality under the law. The French document also proclaimed in Article 3 that "the principle of all sovereignty rests essentially in the nation." Thus, the French Revolution not only trumpeted individual rights and the principle of equality but also connected more closely the concept of a people with a nation. Both the rhetorical and real war against feudal privileges marked the beginning of the end of dynastic and aristocratic rule in Europe.

Altering social hierarchies affected the relations among men and women. Some women felt that the new principles of citizenship should also include the rights of women. Radical republican ideology spawned an early feminist movement. In 1791, a group of women circulated a petition demanding the right to bear arms to defend the revolution, but they stopped short of demanding equal rights for both sexes. Women would become citizens by being good revolutionary wives and mothers, not by virtue of enjoying their own natural rights. In that same year, Olympe de Gouges (1748–1793) composed the "Declaration of the Rights of Woman and Citizen," in which she repeated the seventeen articles of the Rights of Man, adding to each one the word "woman," and proposed female rights to divorce, to hold property in marriage, to be educated, and to have public careers. The all-male assembly did not

take up these proposals, despite the claims that "liberty and equality" were universal rights. For them, it was self-evident that a "fraternity" of free *men* composed the nation.

As the revolution gained momentum between the fall of 1789 and the winter of 1792, the radicals gained greater power, and more and more nobles and clergy fled the country. In late 1790, all clergy were forced to take an oath of loyalty to the new state. This action created enormous opposition among pious Catholics and spurred a major counter-revolutionary movement. Meanwhile, the revolutionary ranks began to splinter, as men and women discussed the proper aims and ends of the revolution. In September 1792, a new National Convention was elected by universal manhood suffrage (the first such election in Europe), and the first French Republic was proclaimed. By early 1793, Louis XVI had been tried, found guilty of treason, and guillotined, and France was at war with many of its neighbors. The events in France, especially the execution of the king, shocked Europeans accustomed to fixed social hierarchies and a world in which the king was presumed to rule as God's representative on earth, answering to no one.

THE TERROR In the wake of the king's execution, radicals known as Jacobins, who had sought to extend the revolution beyond France's borders, launched a campaign known as the Reign of Terror to purge the nation of its enemies. Jacobin leaders, such as the lawyer Maximilien Robespierre (1758–1794), oversaw the execution of as many as 40,000 people who were judged enemies of the state—most of whom were peasants and urban laborers. The institution of universal conscription allowed radicals to create an army large enough to spread the revolution to Europe. By the spring of 1794, France's army numbered some 800,000 soldiers,

THE RIGHTS OF WOMEN

In the late eighteenth century, revolutionaries extolled the rights of "man" across the Atlantic world. But what about women? Mary Wollstonecraft (1759–1797), an English writer, teacher, editor, and proponent of spreading education, grew exasperated at her male colleagues' celebration of newfound liberties for men. In 1792, she published A Vindication of the Rights of Woman, *one of the founding works of modern feminism. In this work, she argued that the superiority of men was as arbitrary as the divine right of kings. For this, she won the opprobrium of male progressives. The author is a "hyena in petticoats," noted one critic. In fact, she was arguing that women had the same rights to be reasonable creatures as men, and that especially education should be available equally to both sexes.*

I love man as my fellow; but his sceptre, real or usurped, extends not to me, unless the reason of an individual demands my homage; and even then the submission is to reason, and not to man. In fact, the conduct of an accountable being must be regulated by the operations of its own reason; or on what foundation rests the throne of God?

It appears to me necessary to dwell on these obvious truths, because females have been insulated, as it were; and while they have been stripped of the virtues that should clothe humanity, they have been decked with artificial graces that enable them to exercise a short-lived tyranny. Love, in their bosoms, taking the place of every nobler passion, their sole ambition is to be fair, to raise emotion instead of inspiring respect; and this ignoble desire, like the servility in absolute monarchies, destroys all strength of character. Liberty is the mother of virtue, and if women be, by their very constitution, slaves, and not allowed to breathe the sharp invigorating air of freedom, they must ever languish like exotics, and be reckoned beautiful flaws in nature. Let it also be remembered, that they are the only flaw.

As to the argument respecting the subjection in which the sex has ever been held, it retorts on man. The many have always been enthralled by the few; and monsters, who scarcely have shown any discernment of human excellence, have tyrannized over thousands of their fellow-creatures. Why have men of superior endowments submitted to such degradation? For, is it not universally acknowledged that kings, viewed collectively, have ever been inferior, in abilities and virtue, to the same number of men taken from the common mass of mankind—yet have they not, and are they not still treated with a degree of reverence that is an insult to reason? China is not the only country where a living man has been made a God. *Men* have submitted to superior strength to enjoy with impunity the pleasure of the moment; *women* have only done the same, and therefore till it is proved that the courtier, who servilely resigns the birthright of a man, is not a moral agent, it cannot be demonstrated that woman is essentially inferior to man because she has always been subjugated.

Brutal force has hitherto governed the world, and that the science of politics is in its infancy, is evident from philosophers scrupling to give the knowledge most useful to man that determinate distinction.

→ *In what ways are Mary Wollstonecraft's ideas an outgrowth of Enlightenment thinking?*
→ *Do you find Wollstonecraft's arguments compelling?*

SOURCE: Mary Wollstonecraft, *A Vindication of the Rights of Woman*, edited by Miriam Brody (New York: Penguin Books, 1792/1993), pp. 122–23.

making it the world's largest. In a startling departure from older practice, most of the French officers came from the middle classes, and some even had lower-class origins; foot soldiers identified with the French *patrie,* or fatherland, and demonstrated their solidarity with revolutionary songs like "The Marseillaise," which soon became the French national anthem. This enormous conscript army also was a major means by which ordinary Frenchmen learned to identify themselves with the goals of the nation as a whole.

The revolutionaries understood that to change society fundamentally they would have to do away with the symbols and rituals of the old regime. They changed street names and took down monuments to the royal family, substituting for religious and dynastic names the names of revolutionary heroes. They adopted a new flag, eliminated titles, and insisted that everyone be addressed as "Citizen." The revolutionaries' passion for rationalizing the world and the prospect of creating a new world should not be forgotten or underestimated. Indeed, they were so exhilarated by the new world they were creating that they changed time itself. Time was now reckoned not from the birth of Christ but from the moment that the French Republic was proclaimed: September 22, 1792, became day 1 of year 1 of the new age. The new calendar boasted only ten months, which were named after natural phenomena; one of the hottest summer months, for example, was called Thermidor and the often foggy late fall month was called Brumaire (*brume* in French means mist or fog). The radicals also attempted to supplant the Catholic faith, since they believed it smacked of corruption and inequality, with a religion of Reason. The French people could, they were told, worship a rational Supreme Being on days prescribed by the state. This did not go over very well, however. In 1794, in the town of Saint Vincent, the unveiling of a statue of the Supreme Being invited characteristic derision from townspeople. The occasion was interrupted by an old woman who motioned to all the women in the crowd to rise, turn their backs to the secular altar, raise their skirts, and expose their buttocks to the Supreme Being.

By mid-1794, enthusiasm for Robespierre's measures had lost popular support, as had the perpetrators of the Terror, many of whom would lose their heads. Robespierre himself went to the guillotine on 9 Thermidor (July 28, 1794), an event that marked the end of the Terror. In 1799, following more political turmoil, a coup d'état unexpectedly resulted in the rise to power of a thirty-year-old general from the recently annexed Mediterranean island of Corsica, Napoleon Bonaparte (1769–1821).

Napoleon checked the excesses and chaos of radical rule, while letting some revolutionary changes continue. Retreating from the anti-Catholicism of the Jacobins, Napoleon signed a concordat with the Vatican in 1801, which allowed religion to be freely practiced again in France. Determined to reform France as well as win the ongoing wars with her enemies, he retreated more and more from republican principles. Napoleon first was a member of a three-man consulate, then became first consul, and in 1804 proclaimed himself emperor. But he took the title Emperor of the French, not Emperor of France, and he prepared a constitution, which he submitted to a vote of approval known as a plebiscite. Maintaining the revolution's enthusiasm for a more rational order, he centralized government administration (appointing local prefects who reported to the central government) and revamped finances by eliminating tax exemptions and centralizing tax collection. Most important, he codified the nation's laws, including those for property and contracts, thereby providing a legal framework for business and commerce. The new "Code Napoleon" eliminated a baroque system of old laws and privileges and created a uniform civil law code for all of France. By emphasizing the equality of all men and the protection of individual property across France, Napoleon's reforms revolutionized European legal history.

NAPOLEON'S EMPIRE, 1799–1815

Napoleon shared with the radicals a determination to extend the geographic reach of the French Revolution. He dreamed of reinventing the Roman Empire on new foundations. Everywhere that French armies advanced, they claimed to be introducing the principles of liberty, equality, and fraternity, and in many places local populations embraced the French, regarding them as liberators from the old order. Napoleon believed that the entire world would greet his cause with open arms. But such was not always the case, as he learned in Egypt. After defeating Ottoman troops at the Battle of the Pyramids in 1798, Napoleon soon found himself faced with uprisings by the local Egyptian population.

In Portugal, Spain, and Russia, French troops also faced fierce national resistance. Portuguese and Spanish soldiers and peasants formed bands of resisters called guerrillas (after the French word *guerre*), and they were joined by British troops to fight the French in what became known as the Peninsular War (1808–1813). In Germany and in Italy, French occupiers quickly wore out their welcome, as they plundered resources, imposed taxes, and conscripted young men. As the locals in these areas tired of being told that French ways were better in all spheres of life, many looked

Battle of the Pyramids. The French army invaded Egypt with grand ambitions and high hopes. Napoleon brought a large cadre of scholars along with his 36,000-man army, intending to win Egyptians to the cause of the French Revolution and to establish a French imperial presence on the banks of the Nile. This idealized portrait of the famous Battle of the Pyramids, fought on July 21, 1798, shows Napoleon and his forces crushing the Mamluk military forces.

backward to their past for comfort and for inspiration to oppose the French. In so doing, they discovered something that had only barely been visible before: *national* traditions, borders, and character types. It is one of the great ironies of Napoleon's attempt to bring all of Europe under French rule that it did not create a unified landmass, but rather laid the foundations for nineteenth-century nationalist strife.

The revolutionary conflicts of the 1790s became, after 1800, a world war, with armies inspired by the revolutionary message fighting in Africa, across Europe, and throughout the Americas. In Europe, Napoleon extended his empire from the Iberian Peninsula in southwestern Europe all the way to the

Austrian and Prussian borders (see Map 15-2). By 1812, when he invaded Russia, however, his forces were overstretched and lacked food supplies to survive the harsh winter. Napoleon had been aided by divisions among his enemies; only Great Britain had been continuously at war with France (except for 1803–1804). But in 1813, after Napoleon's attack on Russia, all the major European powers (Austria, Prussia, Russia, and Great Britain) united against the French. Forced to retreat from Russia and now confronted by a united force of all his enemies, Napoleon and his army were finally vanquished in Paris in 1814. Exiled to the island of Elba, Napoleon escaped to lead his troops one last time. At the Battle of Waterloo in

MAP 15-2   NAPOLEON'S EMPIRE, 1812

During the first decade of the nineteenth century, Napoleon controlled almost the whole of Europe. How did Napoleon redraw the map of Europe? How did he administer regions directly under his control? What long-term impact would his reforms have on these regions?

Belgium in 1815, however, a coalition of armies from Prussia, Austria, Russia, and Britain decisively crushed Napoleon and his troops as they made their last stand.

At the Congress of Vienna (1814–1815), convened to restore peace, the victorious European monarchies agreed to respect each other's borders and to cooperate in guarding against future revolutions and war. Delegates to the congress understood that the world had changed, but they were determined to manage those changes as best they could. France became a monarchy once more, under Louis XVIII (the Bourbon brother of executed Louis XVI). Great Britain and Russia—one a constitutional monarchy (ruled primarily by a prime minister and legislative body but with monarchical oversight), the other an autocracy in which the ruler was not bound to share power with anyone—cooperated to prevent a revival of French or other attempts to assert hegemony over the continent.

The impact of the French Revolution and Napoleon's conquests, however, proved to be far reaching. In many of the smaller German principalities (states) between Prussia and France—which Napoleon reduced from roughly 300 to around 30—the changes introduced under French revolutionary occupation, such as the abolition of serfdom, remained in place after Napoleon's defeat. Napoleon's occupation of the Italian peninsula also sparked a number of underground movements for liberty and for Italian unification, much to the chagrin of Austrian and French monarchs. These upheavals also had decisive effects on Spain and Portugal's links to their colonies in the Americas.

REVOLUTIONS IN THE CARIBBEAN AND IBERIAN AMERICA

From North America and France, revolutionary enthusiasm spread through the Caribbean and Spanish and Portuguese America. But while men of property directed the war of independence that gave birth to the United States, the political upheaval in the rest of the Americas started from the bottom up, with uprisings by subordinated people of color, whose desire for freedom from exploitation predated the French Revolution's insistence on liberty.

Even before the French Revolution, Andean Indians had risen against Spanish colonial authority to protest onerous taxes and labor obligations. In a spectacular uprising in the 1780s, Andean Indians called for freedom from the forced labor draft and compulsory consumption of Spanish wares. Led by a local political chieftain who took the name of an early anti-Spanish rebel, Tupac Amarú, an Indian army of 40,000 to 60,000 besieged the ancient capital of Cuzco and nearly vanquished Spanish armies. It took the Spanish many years to eliminate the insurgents.

This uprising shook the confidence of Iberian-American colonial elites whose fear of their Indian or slave majorities caused them to renew their loyalty to the Spanish or Portuguese crown. For a time, these elites hesitated to follow the example of independence-seeking Anglo-American colonists, lest the struggle for political power unleash a more radical and uncontrollable social revolution. Ultimately, however, the French Revolution and Napoleonic wars shattered the ties between Spain and Portugal and their colonies in the Americas. Like their counterparts in the United States, Iberian-American elites severed colonial ties, but they sought to minimize the power of lower orders by establishing regimes that interpreted the principle of liberty to mean freedom for the property-owning classes. Only in the French colony of Saint Domingue (modern-day Haiti) did slaves carry out a successful insurrection. This sent shivers down the spine of white elites throughout the Americas and made them even more determined to secure property and order.

REVOLUTION IN SAINT DOMINGUE (HAITI) The French Revolution had its most immediate reverberation in the most highly prized of all French colonies, Saint Domingue. There, it led to the loss of the colony and the emancipation of its slaves, though the road to independence and emancipation was a bloody one. The island's black slave population numbered 500,000, compared with 40,000 white French settlers and about 30,000 free "people of color" (free mulattoes, who were of mixed black and white ancestry, as well as freed black slaves). After the events of 1789 in France, white settlers in Saint Domingue campaigned for self-government, while slaves borrowed the revolutionary language to denounce their masters. As whites clashed with people of color and slaves in 1791, the island descended into civil war. Dominican slaves fought French forces dispatched

Toussaint L'Ouverture. In the 1790s, Toussaint L'Ouverture led the slaves of the French colony of Saint Domingue in the world's largest and most successful slave insurrection. Toussaint embraced the principles of the French Revolution and demanded that universal rights be applied to people of African descent.

Revolution in Saint Domingue. In 1791, slaves and people of color rose up against the white planters. This engraving was based on a contemporary German report on the uprising and depicted the fears of the whites in the face of slave rebellion as much as the actual events themselves.

in 1792 to restore order. Finally, in 1793, the National Convention in France abolished slavery. Championed by highly influential figures like Robespierre and the Marquis de Lafayette, the argument that the principles of the revolution—liberty, fraternity, and equality—should apply to the French colonies as well as to the metropole briefly won out over claims that abolition would mean economic disaster. Once liberated, the former slaves took control of the island but had to fight British and Spanish forces sent to Saint Domingue to stir up trouble. When Napoleon took power, he decided to reassert French authority on the island, and he restored slavery in 1802. Napoleon sent an army of 58,000 under his brother-in-law, General Victor-Emmanuel Leclerc, to quash the forces led by Toussaint L'Ouverture (1743–1803), a former slave. Leclerc's army, perhaps the most fearsome in Europe, was decimated by guerrilla fighters and yellow fever. After eighteen months, the French surrendered and left, having lost over 50,000 of their finest soldiers. Toussaint L'Ouverture died in a French jail, after treachery led to his capture while he was trying to negotiate a settlement. Nonetheless, in January 1804, General Jean-Jacques Dessalines declared "Haiti" independent.

The scale of the revolt had serious environmental consequences. Not only did the canefields become battlefields,

with extensive burnings and destruction that left the land smoldering in ashes, but freed slaves rushed to stake out independent plots of land for their subsistence. In some cases, old sugar plantations became peasant plots; in other cases the slaves fled to wooded hinterlands. In both places the new peasant class began to clear the land with great energy. The small country soon found itself increasingly deforested, and the intensive cultivation of small farms initiated a gradual process of erosion and soil depletion, which locked independent Haiti into a vicious cycle of environmental degradation and poverty.

Nor did independence bring the victorious Haitians international recognition from fellow revolutionaries. France's commitment to empire ultimately overrode its commitment to the ideals of republican citizenship. Toussaint (the "black Jacobin") and the slaves of Saint Domingue had shown a greater fidelity to ideals of liberty than the French themselves. Yet, Thomas Jefferson, the author of the Declaration of Independence and the U.S. president at the time, refused to recognize Haiti. Like many other American slave owners, Jefferson worried that the example of a successful slave insurrection might inspire slave revolts in the United States.

BRAZIL AND CONSTITUTIONAL MONARCHY Brazil offers an example of a colonial society whose path to independent statehood minimized political turmoil and avoided social revolution. In late 1807, French troops stormed Lisbon, but they were too late to capture the royal Braganza family. The royal family and their extensive retinue fled to Rio de Janeiro, the capital of Portugal's prize colony, Brazil. Upon arrival, they instituted reforms in administration, agriculture, and manufacturing, and established schools, hospitals, and a library. The migration of the royal family to Brazil preempted colonial claims for autonomy, for Brazil was now the center of the Portuguese empire. Further dampening revolutionary enthusiasm was the royal family's willingness to share power with the local planter aristocracy. Over the ensuing years, the economy prospered, and slavery expanded.

In 1821, the exiled Portuguese king agreed to return to Lisbon, leaving instructions to his son Pedro to preserve the family lineage in Rio de Janeiro. It did not take long, however, before Brazilian elites rejected Portugal altogether. Faced with the threat that colonists might topple the dynasty in Rio de Janeiro and concerned that such upheaval might cascade into regional disputes and rivalries, Pedro declared Brazil an independent empire that was free from Portugal in 1822. Shortly thereafter, he signed a charter establishing a constitutional monarchy that would last until the late nineteenth century.

Brazilian business elites and bureaucrats collaborated to minimize their conflicts, lest an insurrection of slaves erupt. Regional insurrections, like the creation of the fledgling Republic of the Equator in 1817, were crushed. In the south, a campaign by cowboys, known as gauchos, who wanted a

INSPIRATIONS FOR SLAVE REBELLION ON HAITI

The ideals of the French Revolution spread rapidly beyond France through the rest of Europe and even overseas. In few places did they produce a more radical effect than on the island of Saint Domingue, renamed Haiti after it acquired independence. By the 1780s, Saint Domingue was France's richest colony and its most valuable overseas trading possession. Its wealth came from sugar plantations that depended on a vast, highly coerced slave population. About 40,000 whites ruled over and ruthlessly exploited 500,000 enslaved Africans, approximately two-thirds of whom had recently arrived from Africa. The lives of the slaves were short and brutal, lasting on average only fifteen years; hence the need for the wealthy planter class to replenish their labor supplies from Africa at frequent intervals. White planters from the island had the reputation of great wealth. People who dressed ostentatiously as they strode the streets of Paris in the late eighteenth century were said to be as wealthy as a "creole," meaning a Caribbean planter. But the white planters also knew their privileges were vulnerable, which made them eager to amass quick fortunes so that they could sell out and return to France. These men and women were vastly outnumbered by the enslaved, who were seething with resentment, at a time when abolitionist sentiments were gaining ground in Europe and even circulating among the slaves in the Americas.

Yet, the planters greeted the onset of the French Revolution in 1789 with enthusiasm. They saw an opportunity to gain internal political power and to engage in wider trading contacts with North America and the rest of the world. They ignored, at their peril, the fact that the ideals of the French Revolution, and especially its slogan of liberty, equality, and fraternity, could inspire the island's free blacks, free mulattoes, and slaves. Indeed, no sooner had the white planters thrown in their lot with the Third Estate in France than a slave rebellion broke out in their midst in Saint Domingue. From its inception in August 1791, it led, after great loss of life to African slave dissidents and French soldiers, to the proclamation of an independent state in Haiti in 1804, ruled by African-Americans. Haiti became, in fact, the Americas' second independent republican government.

The revolution had many sources of inspiration. It was both French and African. According to a later West Indian scholar, a group of black Jacobins, determined to carry the ideals of the French Revolution to their logical end point—the abolition of slavery—made up the revolutionary cadre. Their undisputed leader was a freed black by the name of Toussaint L'Ouverture, who had learned about the French abolitionist writings of the age. But it is hardly surprising, given how recently most of the slaves had arrived from Africa, that African cultural and political ideals also fomented slave resistance. At a secret forest meeting held on August 14, 1791, the persons who were to lead the initial stage of the revolution gathered to affirm their commitment to one another at a voodoo ritual, presided over by a tall, black priestess, "with strange eyes and bristly hair." Voodoo was a mixture of African and New World religious beliefs that existed among slave communities in many parts of the Americas (see Chapter 14). According to one description of the forest ceremony, the priestess arrived "armed with a long pointed knife that she waved above her head [as] she performed a sinister dance singing an African song, which the others, face down against the ground, repeated as a chorus. A black pig was then dragged in front of her, and she split it open with her knife. The animal's blood was collected in a wooden bowl and served still foaming to each delegate. At a signal from the priestess, everyone threw themselves on their knees and swore blindly to obey the orders of Boukman, who had been proclaimed supreme chief of the rebellion." Boukman was a voodoo chief himself, and he initiated the revolution against the planters, though it was Toussaint L'Ouverture who later assumed leadership of the revolt.

Inspired by both voodoo and the French Revolution, the rebellion in Saint Domingue resulted in a series of dramatic ruptures. European slavery came to an end. White planters yielded to a black political elite. Hundreds of thousands of slaves and French soldiers perished or were maimed, and the old sugar export economy could no longer be sustained. No slave shipments arrived, and no sugar was exported.

decentralized federation with a great deal of autonomy, also proved to be no match for the central government's powerful army and navy. Even the largest urban slave revolt in the Americas, led by African Muslims in the Brazilian state of Bahia in 1835, was put down in a matter of days. By the 1840s, Brazil had achieved a political stability unmatched in the Americas. Indeed, Brazil's socially controlled transition from colony to nation proved to be the exception in Latin America.

The strength of the Brazilian state and its ruling elite gave tremendous impetus to the expansion of the agrarian frontier and eventually led to profound environmental degradation. Especially in the new coffee belts, landowners oversaw the clearing of old Atlantic hardwood forests, pushing the frontier inward and opening swaths of land for slaves and squatters to plant coffee trees in lieu of ancient woodlands. This was a process that had begun with coastal sugarcane but accelerated with coffee plantings, which drove the frontier into the hilly regions of São Paulo (which eventually became the world's largest single regional supplier of coffee). Coffee was a more intense threat to Brazil's great forests than any other invader in the previous 300 years. But it also created problems. Coffee trees thrived on soils that were neither soggy nor parched. But this fertile soil was also quickly depleted by the monocrop as planters razed the "virgin" balanced forest, leading within a generation to infertile soils and extensive erosion. This propelled coffee planters further into the frontier to clearcut or burn the old forest and plant coffee groves. The scale of the environmental change was monumental: between 1788 and 1888 (when slavery was abolished), Brazil produced about 10 million tons of coffee, which required the clearing or burning of 300 million tons of ancient forest biomass.

MEXICO'S INDEPENDENCE   When Napoleon occupied Spain, he sparked a crisis in the Spanish empire. Unlike the Portuguese Braganza family, which managed to elude French troops, the Spanish Bourbons fell captive to Napoleon in 1807 and spent many years under comfortable house arrest. Colonial elites in Buenos Aires, Caracas, and Mexico City, grappling with the problem of self-rule without an emperor, came to enjoy autonomy from Madrid. Creoles (American-born Spaniards) resented it when the mother country reinstated peninsulars (officials from Spain) once the Spanish Bourbons returned to power in 1814. The creoles disliked the economic regulations and taxation of the mother country and chafed under the rule of the peninsulars. Inspired by Enlightenment thinkers and revolution in North America, the creoles wished to retain their elite privileges and to rid their lands of the peninsulars.

In Mexico, the royal army prevailed as long as there was any hope that the emperor in Madrid could keep a firm grip on political authority. But from 1810 to 1813, two rural priests, Father Miguel Hidalgo (1753–1811) and Father José María Morelos (1765–1815), galvanized an insurrection that

Miguel Hidalgo y Costilla. At the center of this mural by Juan O'Gorman is the revolutionary Mexican priest Miguel Hidalgo y Costilla, who led the first uprising against Spanish rulers. This painting suggests the rebellion was a multiclass and multiethnic movement.

incorporated a broad alliance of peasants, Indians, and artisans. They advocated an end to elite abuses, denounced bad government, and called for redistribution of wealth, return of land to the Indians, and respect for the Virgin of Guadalupe (who would become Mexico's patron saint). The rebels sent shock waves across the viceroyalty and nearly encircled Mexico City itself, the capital of Spain's richest colony. This horrified peninsulars and creoles alike, who overcame internal disputes to plead with Spanish armies to rescue them from the rebels. It took years, but the royal armies eventually crushed the uprising.

Despite the military victory, the Spanish crown's hold on its colony gave way. In these years of conflict, colonists started to enjoy measures of autonomy and even began electing representatives to local assemblies. Moreover, like the creoles of South America, those of Mexico were beginning to identify themselves more as Mexicans and less as Spanish Americans. So, when Ferdinand VII, the Spanish king, appeared unable to handle affairs, not only abroad but within Spain itself, the colonists began considering home rule. The critical factor was the army, which remained faithful to the crown. When anarchy seemed to spread through Spain in 1820, however, Mexican generals, with the support of the creoles, cut their losses, proclaiming Mexican independence in 1821.

OTHER SOUTH AMERICAN REVOLUTIONS   Most political independence movements in Spanish America evolved into noisy social revolutions or civil wars. The process of uncoupling Spain's grip on mainland America was far more prolonged and militarized than was Britain's separation from its American colonies. The struggle for independence from Spain completely refashioned the nature of political leadership in South America. Venezuela's Simón Bolívar (1783–1830), the son of a wealthy merchant-planter family who was weaned on European Enlightenment texts, dreamed of a land governed by reason. In Napoleonic France, he found a compelling model of a new state, one forged by military heroism and constitutional proclamations. The same held true for the less aristocratic Argentine leader, General José de San Martín (1778–1850). Men like Bolívar, San Martín, and their many generals waged extended wars between 1810 and 1824. In some areas, like present-day Uruguay and Venezuela, the carnage depopulated entire provinces.

What in South America started as a political revolution against Bourbon authority escalated into a social struggle among Indians, mestizos, slaves, and whites. The militarized populace threatened the fortunes of planters and great merchants. Rural folk from the grasslands rode into battle against aristocratic creoles. Andean Indians fled the mines and occupied great estates. Provinces fought their neighbors. Popular armies, having defeated Spain by the 1820s, engaged in civil wars over the new postcolonial order in South America. By the 1840s and 1850s, the old viceroyalties had broken up.

Simón Bolívar. The son of a wealthy creole family, Simón Bolívar fought Spanish armies from Venezuela to Bolivia, securing the independence of five countries. Bolívar wanted to transform the former colonies into modern republics and used many of the icons of revolution from the rest of the Atlantic world—among his favorite models were George Washington and Napoleon Bonaparte. Notice how this image portrays Bolívar in a quintessential Napoleonic pose on horseback.

In Latin America, new states, common myths of sacrifice, and collective identities of nationhood emerged, but the people active in these political communities made up a narrow social elite, and the myths were contradictory. Simón Bolívar, for instance, repeatedly urged his followers to become "American," to identify with a larger, pan-creole ideal. He tried to get the liberated countries to unite into a Latin American confederation, urging Peru and Bolivia to join Venezuela, Ecuador, and Colombia in the "Gran Colombia." But the confederation quickly fell apart as local identities continued to take precedence over Spanish-American unity. Bolívar's dream of a United States of South America, possibly even governed by a hereditary king or dictator, gave way to unstable national republics. Bolívar met his end surrounded and hounded by his enemies; San Martín died in exile. The real heirs to independence were not slaves, Indians, or even republican national leaders, but local military chieftains called *caudillos,* who often forged alliances with landowners. The contradictory legacy of the revolutions of Spanish America was the triumph of wealthy and powerful elites under a banner of liberty yet often at the expense of poorer, ethnic, and mixed populations.

CHANGE AND TRADE IN AFRICA

→ *Why did the abolition of the slave trade have unintended effects on African society?*

Along with Europe and the Americas, Africa, the third corner of the Atlantic world, was also swept up in revolutionary tides. Increased domestic and world trade, particularly but not exclusively in African slaves, shifted the terms of state-building across the landmass. Around the edges of Lake Victoria, in the highlands of present-day Rwanda and Burundi, and in southern Africa, new, more powerful kingdoms emerged in the first half of the nineteenth century. Burgeoning commerce created new sources of wealth for ruling groups, who began to assert their power over other peoples. Some regimes, however, fell apart as a result of internal rivalries. The main commercial catalyst for Africa's political shake-up was the rapid growth and then the demise of the Atlantic slave trade.

ABOLITION OF THE SLAVE TRADE

Even as it enriched and empowered some Africans and many Europeans, the slave trade became a subject of fierce debate in the late eighteenth century. Some European and American revolutionaries wanted trade and production to be governed not by the laws of compulsion, but by the laws of supply and demand. Alongside these advocates of free trade emerged a small but committed group of abolitionists who insisted that traffic in slaves was immoral. In London, they created committees, often led by Quakers, to lobby Parliament for an end to the slave trade. Quakers in Philadelphia followed suit. Pamphlets, reports, and personal narratives denounced the traffic in people.

In response to abolitionist campaigns, North Atlantic powers moved to prohibit the international slave trade. Denmark acted first in 1803, Great Britain followed in 1807, and the United States banned it in 1808. Over time, the British persuaded the French and other European governments of the rightness of this position, with France abolishing the slave trade in 1814, the Netherlands in 1817, and Spain in 1845. To enforce the ban, Britain posted an anti-slave-trade naval squadron off the coast of West Africa to cut off traders operating above the equator and compelled the emperor of Brazil to respect earlier promises to end slave imports. After 1850, Atlantic slave-shipping dropped sharply. In 1867, the last slave vessel entered a New World harbor, Havana.

But until the 1860s, slavers continued to ply the waters of the West African coast to buy captives and illegally transport them as slaves. The British naval squadrons stopped as many smugglers as they could and took the captives they freed to the British base at Sierra Leone, where they were resettled. Liberia, first settled in 1821 by free black Americans, also became a refuge for freed captives and for former slaves returning to Africa from the Americas.

NEW TRADE WITH AFRICA

While eventually choking off the Atlantic slave trade, Europeans endeavored to promote new forms of commerce with Africa. European traders, who had previously thought of Africa only as a source of human captives, now wanted Africans to supply Europe with raw materials and for them to purchase European manufactures. European publicists dubbed the new trade "legitimate" commerce to distinguish it from the "illegitimate" trade in human beings. It was intended to raise the standards of living of Africans by substituting trade in produce for trade in slaves. West African cultivators responded by beginning a brisk export in palm kernels and peanuts. The real bonanza was in vegetable oils to lubricate machinery and to be made into candles, and especially palm oil to produce soap. European merchants argued that by becoming vibrant export societies, Africans would earn the wealth to become potentially profitable importers of European wares.

Arising in the age of legitimate commerce, the new palm and peanut plantations of Africa were less devastating to the environment than their predecessors in the West Indies. There forests were felled to make way for sugar estates (Chapter 12). In West Africa, where palm products became crucial exports, the palm tree had always grown wild and though some areas of intensive cultivation witnessed a degree of deforestation, the results were not comparable to the Caribbean. Especially in northwest Africa (present-day Senegal) peanuts thrive in sandy soils and their cultivation often leads to tree removal. But the great period of deforestation did not occur until the twentieth century when cultivators moved into the more arid regions. There removal of trees altered the environment and the climate, and led quickly to a process of desertification.

The gradual abolition of the slave trade and the emergence of legitimate commerce gave rise to a new generation of West African merchants. Inserting themselves between African producers in the interior or plantations on the coast, and the European export-import firms, they amassed fortunes. There were many rags-to-riches stories, like that of King Jaja of Opobo (1821–1891), who was kidnapped and

Chasing Slave Dhows. From being the major proponents of the Atlantic slave trade the British became its chief opponents, using their naval forces to suppress those European and African slave traders who attempted to subvert the injunction against slave trading. Here a British vessel chases an East African slaving dhow trying to run slaves from the island of Zanzibar.

sold into slavery as a youngster. Jaja was initially one of the many slaves who paddled the canoes that carried palm oil from inland markets to coastal ports. He rose to become the head of a coastal canoe house. As a powerful merchant-prince and chief, he founded the new port of Opobo and could summon a flotilla of war canoes on command. Another freed slave, a Yoruba, William Lewis, made his way back to Africa and settled in Sierra Leone in 1828. Starting with only a few utensils and a small plot of land, Lewis became a successful merchant who was able to send his son Samuel to England for his education. There, Samuel studied law, attended University College in London, and eventually became an important political leader in Sierra Leone. Queen Victoria recognized him with a knighthood.

Just as the slave trade shaped the rhythms of African political communities, its demise forced African polities to adjust. For some, it was a boon because it ended the constant drainage of people from an already underpopulated region. For others, especially if they had positioned themselves as the commercial brokers between African slave supply and Euro-American demand, the demise of the traffic was a disaster, cutting off income necessary to buy European arms and luxury goods. The Asante state, however, endured even as the slave trade declined and despite British military efforts to de-

stroy it. Other West African regimes, like the Yoruba kingdom, collapsed. There, civil strife broke out once chieftains could no longer use the spoils of the slave trade to support retinues and armies.

The rise of free labor in the Atlantic world and the dwindling of the foreign slave trade had another unintended and even perverse effect in Africa: it strengthened slavery in Africa

King Jaja of Opobo. Among the merchant-princes who came to prominence along the West African coast in the nineteenth century was King Jaja of Opobo, who rose out of slavery to become the head of a canoe house that transported and traded palm oil. In 1869, Jaja established an independent trading state based around the city of Opobo.

Primary Source

FREDERICK DOUGLASS ASKS,
"WHAT TO THE SLAVE IS THE FOURTH OF JULY?"

Born in 1818, Frederick Douglass spent the first twenty years of his life as a slave. After running away in 1838, Douglass toured the northern United States delivering speeches that attacked the institution of slavery. The publication of Douglass's autobiography in 1845 cemented his standing as a leading abolitionist. In the excerpt below, taken from an address delivered on July 5, 1852, Douglass contrasts the freedom and natural rights extolled in the American Declaration of Independence and celebrated on the Fourth of July with the dehumanizing condition—and lack of freedom—of African-American slaves.

Fellow-Citizens—pardon me, and allow me to ask, why am I called upon to speak here to-day? What have I, or those I represent, to do with your national independence? Are the great principles of political freedom and of natural justice, embodied in that Declaration of Independence, extended to us? and am I, therefore, called upon to bring our humble offering to the national altar, and to confess the benefits, and express devout gratitude for the blessings, resulting from your independence to us? . . .

But, such is not the state of the case. I say it with a sad sense of the disparity between us. I am not included within the pale of this glorious anniversary! Your high independence only reveals the immeasurable distance between us. The blessings in which you this day rejoice, are not enjoyed in common. The rich inheritance of justice, liberty, prosperity, and independence, bequeathed by your fathers, is shared by you, not by me. The sunlight that brought life and healing to you, has brought stripes and death to me. This Fourth of July is *yours*, not *mine. You* may rejoice, *I* must mourn. . . .

. . . Must I undertake to prove that the slave is a man? That point is conceded already. Nobody doubts it. The slaveholders themselves acknowledge it in the enactment of laws for their government. They acknowledge it when they punish disobedience on the part of the slave. There are seventy-two crimes in the state of Virginia, which, if committed by a black man (no matter how ignorant he be) subject him to the punishment of death; while only two of these same crimes will subject a white man to the like punishment. What is this but the acknowledgment that the slave is a moral, intellectual, and responsible being. The manhood of the slave is conceded. It is admitted in the fact that southern statute books are covered with enactments forbidding, under severe fines and penalties, the teaching of the slave to read or write. When you can point to any such laws, in reference to the beasts of the field, then I may consent to argue the manhood of the slave. When the dogs in your streets, when the fowls of the air, when the cattle on your hills, when the fish of the sea, and the reptiles that crawl, shall be unable to distinguish the slave from a brute, then will I argue with you that the slave is a man!

→ *How does Douglass suggest that slaves are indeed human beings?*
→ *What is the significance of the last sentence of Douglass's speech?*

SOURCE: David W. Blight (ed.), *Narrative of the Life of Frederick Douglass: An American Slave, Written by Himself* (Boston: Bedford Books, 1993), pp. 141–45.

itself. In some African locales by the mid-nineteenth century, slaves accounted for more than half of the population. No longer were slaves mainly to be found in domestic employment, sharing the same table with their masters, eating the same foods, and likely to be assimilated into that society. Instead, slaves worked on palm oil plantations or, in East Africa (especially in Zanzibar), on clove plantations owned by Arabs or Swahilis. They also served in the military forces, carried palm oil and ivory to markets as porters, or served as the oarsmen on the canoes that plied the rivers leading to the coast. In 1850, the Fulani emirates of northern Nigeria had as many as 2.5 million slaves, more than the slaves in independent Brazil and second only to the number of slaves in the United States. No longer the supplier of slaves, Africa, in the wake of Atlantic world revolutions, had turned into the largest slaveholding region.

ECONOMIC REORDERING

> → *How did the industrial and commercial revolutions reorder society?*

The political upheavals in the Atlantic world shattered the old mercantilist system and encouraged economic transformations that placed western Europe at the hub of an increasingly interconnected world economy. These economic transformations are often referred to collectively as the industrial revolution. They also marked the opening of what many scholars regard as "the great divide" in world history between the economically developed areas of the world and less developed areas. Certainly by 1850 people living in western Europe and North America were wealthier and healthier than their counterparts elsewhere—a statement that probably could not have been made about the world's population a century earlier. In addition, the western Europeans, notably the British, were able to translate their economic prowess into political power and were in the process of altering the global balance of power.

BRITAIN'S ECONOMIC LEADERSHIP

The presence of a variety of institutional and economic factors enabled the British to pioneer the innovations that have ever since characterized economic modernity. To begin with, Britain had large and accessible supplies of coal and iron, two of the most important raw materials used to produce the goods of what has conventionally been called the industrial revolution. This term has usually been employed to designate developments in Britain beginning in the second half of the eighteenth century—though historians now know that there were similar phases of development earlier, during the Song dynasty in China (960–1127 CE), for example, and that further "industrial revolutions" would later ensue in Europe and elsewhere. In addition, Britain's manufacturers benefited from a cascade of technological innovations, notably in steam power and textile production, which they put to practical use to produce cheaper goods in larger quantities. But none of these physical or technological factors alone propelled an economic revolution. What was crucial also was that political and social conditions enabled merchants and industrialists to mobilize capital for investment while expanding internal and international markets for their commodities. Finally, Britain's agrarian colonies provided it with sources of financial investment, raw materials, and markets for manufactured goods. And after the independence of most New

A Model Textile Mill. In the nineteenth century, the English industrialist and reformer Robert Owen tried to create humane factories. Worried about the terrible conditions in most textile mills, Owen created clean and orderly working environments in his mills and had the work rules posted on the walls. Owen still shared most of his contemporaries' employment of children, as can be seen in this image.

New Farming Technologies. Although new technologies only gradually transformed agriculture, the spread of more intensive cultivation led to increased yields.

World colonies in the late eighteenth and early nineteenth centuries, the commitment to free trade enabled British consumers to import cheap foodstuffs from the Americas. It is important to note that these factors were present individually elsewhere in Europe; but in Britain they converged, driving the British economy into continuous and self-sustaining economic growth and constituting a "revolution" that would transform social relations across most of the country.

A crucial aspect of economic progress also involved a remarkable expansion in agricultural production for the market, and here, too, British farmers led the way. By exploiting new lands and making existing lands more productive (through enclosing fields and pastures and draining swamp land), farmers in western Europe and North America could feed more mouths and support a large increase in population. In Great Britain, for example, the population rose from about 5 million in the early 1700s to 9 million by 1800 and to 18 million by 1851. Population growth, in turn, generated pressure on the land and forced many people to migrate to the cities, creating a supply of urban laborers for the new manufacturing industries. Also adding to the growth of the labor force was the appropriation of common lands as private property by English landowners in the eighteenth century. This threw a large number of small farmers off the land, compelling them to earn their livelihood as wage workers.

As Britain outdistanced its European rivals in manufacturing, claiming for itself the designation "the workshop of the world," a new economic world order began to emerge (see Map 15-3). Britain's industrial capitalists increased productivity by drawing on labor from around the world. British wage laborers turned the raw cotton grown by peasants in

India and slaves in North America into cloth, which was then sold in the home market or exported abroad in exchange for agricultural products from India and Argentina. Thus emerged a new organization of labor, whereby colonies and dependencies would export raw materials to industrializing states, which would then export manufactures to colonies and dependencies, all under the banner of free trade and free (wage) labor.

TRADING AND FINANCING

Economic reordering involved dramatic expansions and alterations in patterns of commerce and consumption. By the eighteenth century, sugar and silver, the pioneering commercial commodities of world trade, were joined by other products. Tea became a beverage of international commerce. Its leaves came from China, the sugar to cut its bitterness from the Caribbean, the slaves to harvest the sweetener from Africa, and the ceramics from which to drink a proper cup from the English Midlands. Soap was another truly international commodity. In the 1840s, the American entrepreneur William Colgate was importing palm oil from the slave states of West Africa, coconut oil from Malabar and Ceylon, and poppy seed oil from colonial South Asia, all to make aromatic bars of soap, which were then sold around the world.

So widespread was the economic reordering that ordinary people were able to purchase imported goods with their earnings. Thus, even the poor expanded their diets to include coffee, tea, and sugar—all tropical goods, and all goods that had to be purchased on the market with cash. European artisans as well as farmers purchased tools, furnishings, and home decorations on the market. Slaves and colonial laborers also used their meager earnings to buy imported cotton cloth made in Europe from the raw cotton they picked.

Merchants reaped the greatest rewards of international trade, earning more money than previous traders ever had and enjoying higher social status than they had under dynastic regimes. To be sure, merchants faced great risks. Bad weather, unexpected price fluctuations, and inept handling turned many promising deals into bankrupting disasters. But successful merchants accumulated immense fortunes. Also profiting were accountants and lawyers, who assisted with insurance, bookkeeping, and the recording of legal documents. The new class of commercial men and women, known as the "bourgeoisie," took up residence in thriving ports and other centers of trade. The bourgeoisie formed a new elite, not of birth and titles, but of property and capital. They increasingly assumed positions of authority to match their growing wealth. Indeed, if the bourgeoisie sometimes strove to marry their sons and daughters into old aristocratic families as a way to establish legitimacy for their new wealth, aristocrats just as often sought such marriages for the money and property they brought.

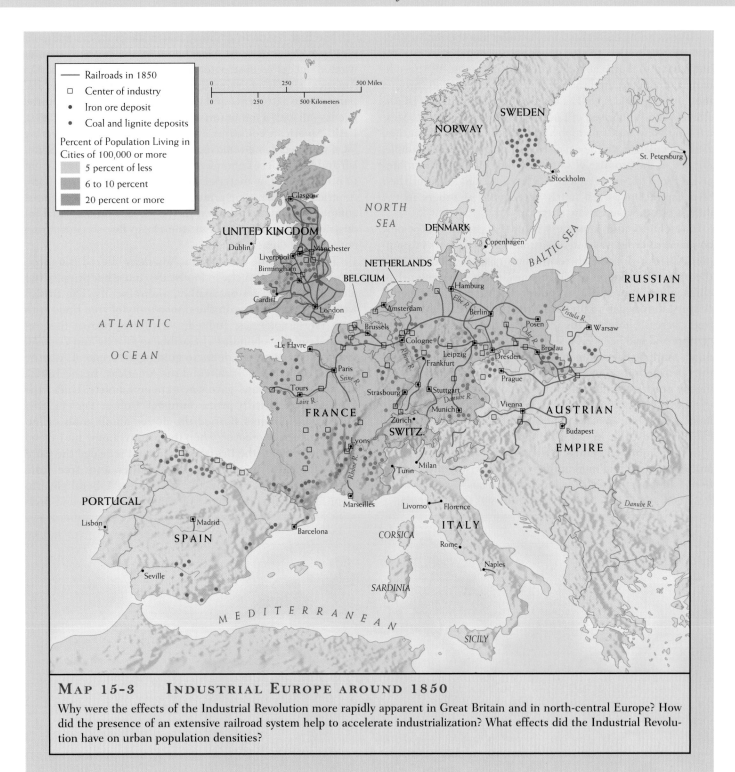

MAP 15-3   INDUSTRIAL EUROPE AROUND 1850
Why were the effects of the Industrial Revolution more rapidly apparent in Great Britain and in north-central Europe? How did the presence of an extensive railroad system help to accelerate industrialization? What effects did the Industrial Revolution have on urban population densities?

The greatest fortunes—and considerable political power—flowed to those who bankrolled world trade. Some financiers, like many merchants, emerged not from long-established noble families but from the common people. Consider, for example, Mayer Amschel Rothschild (1744–1812). Born the son of a money changer in the Jewish ghetto of Frankfurt, Rothschild expanded his activities from coin dealing to money changing, from trading textiles to lending funds to kings and governments, especially to those at war. By the time of his death, he owned the world's biggest banking operation, and his five sons were running powerful branches in London, Paris, Vienna, and Naples, as well as in Frankfurt.

By extending credit for a fee, families like the Rothschilds also enabled traders to ship goods across long distances without having to worry about immediate payment. All these financial changes eased the way for world integration through the flow of goods as well as the flow of money. In the 1820s, sizeable funds amassed in London flowed out to Egypt, Mexico, and New York to support trade, public investment, and even speculation. Some eager British financiers, for example, jumped at the promise of untold fortunes in the silver mines of La Rioja in South America. They invested some of their own capital and, even more, the capital of others in the mines, but they never saw a return.

Merchants and financiers soon recognized that a new commercial order was emerging and wanted new laws to support it. Through the eighteenth century, and especially with the political shake-up of old regimes, these emerging urban elites gained more political power. By the early nineteenth century, they began to press for free trade, the right to trade freely across borders. This idea dated back to the sixteenth century and had been extensively elaborated in the writings of Adam Smith in the eighteenth century. But it took decades for the doctrine to become practice, partly because so many domestic interests benefited from special tariff protections and exclusive access to certain markets. For example, Europe's landed interests ensured that laws obstructed the entry of cheaper foodstuffs; in Great Britain, the Corn Laws imposed a tariff on imported grain and thereby kept the price of bread artificially high. Old mercantilist laws likewise protected national shipping interests. As long as more businesses profited from commercial protection, free trade was a pipe dream.

The first region to embrace free trade practices and policies was the Americas. Merchants in the former colonies wanted access to obstructed markets. Especially in Iberian America, merchants wanted to export raw materials and import needed European, and especially British, manufactured goods—all with a minimum of hurdles and taxes. After 1810, Latin American countries abolished most tariffs protecting local producers and removed all special laws covering Spanish and Portuguese commerce. The United States also sought to promote its raw materials, but never went as far as Latin America in dismantling protection of local producers against competitive imports. Rather, in the United States, local industries clamored for laws to stop cheap British goods from entering the domestic market.

The rise of free trade in the Americas offered European consumers access to cheap foodstuffs and other primary staples, like timber, cotton, leather, and minerals. The British were the first to seize on the opportunity of free trade with New World societies. Indeed, with fewer formal ties, restricted only to a handful of Caribbean islands and Canada, free trade became the de facto guiding principle of Atlantic commerce between Britain and the Americas. In the 1840s, old protectionist laws gave way to open markets. Under the Conservative British prime minister Robert Peel (1788–1850), new budgets slashed the duties on all kinds of imported staples. Moreover, when the potato famine hit Ireland in the mid-1840s, the British government repealed the Corn Laws (in 1846) to allow grains to enter duty free from around the world. Finally, the succeeding Liberal government abolished many of the remaining obstacles and pref-

Irish Potato Famine. Victims of the Irish potato famine, winter 1849–50. By this time, hundreds of thousands of men, women, and children had already died or left Ireland for the Americas.

Primary Source

THE OTHER REVOLUTION OF 1776

The year 1776 is mainly known as the year American colonists declared their independence from the British Empire, but it also was the year of the publication of Adam Smith's An Inquiry into the Nature and Causes of the Wealth of Nations, *the most important book in the history of economic thought. Smith, a Scottish philosopher, felt that constraints on trade, by governments or private monopolies, deprived people of their ability to realize their full potential and as such impoverished nations. Although he was not opposed to colonies per se, in this short selection, he warns British authorities that the exclusions placed on their colonies, which bear the brunt of mercantilist controls, are not only unjust, they are counterproductive. Thus, "free trade" is tied up with the fate of Europe's colonies.*

The exclusive trade of the mother countries tends to diminish, or, at least, to keep down below what they would otherwise rise to, both the enjoyments and industry of all those nations in general, and of the American colonies in particular. It is a dead weight upon the action of one of the great springs which puts into motion a great part of the business of mankind. By rendering the colony produce dearer in all other countries, it lessens its consumption, and thereby cramps the industry of the colonies, and both the enjoyments and the industry of all other countries, which both enjoy less when they pay more for what they enjoy, and produce less when they get less for what they produce. By rendering the produce of all other countries dearer in the colonies, it cramps, in the same manner, the industry of all other countries, and both the enjoyments and the industry of the colonies. It is a clog which, for the supposed benefit of some particular countries, embarrasses the pleasures, and encumbers the industry of all other countries; but of the colonies more than of any other. It not only excludes, as much as possible, all other countries from one particular market; but it confines, as much as possible, the colonies to one particular market: and the difference is very great between being excluded from one particular market, when all others are open, and being confined to one particular market, when all others are shut up. The surplus produce of the colonies, however, is the original source of all that increase of enjoyments and industry which Europe derives from the discovery and colonization of America; and the exclusive trade of the mother countries tends to render this source much less abundant than it otherwise would be.

→ *According to Smith, how does exclusive trade between the north country and the colonists diminish the development of the colonies?*
→ *What historical developments in this period contributed to the growth of free trade?*

SOURCE: Adam Smith, *An Inquiry into the Nature and Causes of the Wealth of Nations*, Book 4, edited by Edwin Cannan (Chicago: The University of Chicago Press, 1776/1977), pp. 105–106.

erences, especially the Navigation Acts, which had been originally designed to prevent Dutch merchants from taking over English trade routes. Free trade then became the guiding commercial policy of Great Britain as it embraced the idea that domestic wealth depended on imports of basic goods and exports of new industrial commodities to the world's consumers.

MANUFACTURING

Bankers and merchants facilitated the development not only of trade but also of industries. Industrial development was due to several interlocking changes, however. The accumulation and diffusion of technical knowledge necessary for manufacturing began in the countryside, where handicraft operations were gradually enlarged and mechanized. Often it was small- and medium-sized producers, and the occasional crackpot in a barn, who were the inventors and innovators. Numerous little inventions, applied and diffused across the Atlantic world, gradually built up a stock of technical knowledge and practice that was widely available.

Most famous of these inventors was James Watt (1736–1819) of Scotland, who succeeded in making steam engines more efficient. Steam engines burned coal to boil water, and the resulting steam drove mechanized devices. Watt devised a way to separate steam condensers from piston cylinders so that pistons could be kept hot and therefore running constantly. This set the stage for a fuel-efficient engine. Early prototypes of Watt's engine were used to pump water out of mines. After moving to Birmingham in 1774, Watt joined forces with the industrialist Matthew Boulton (1728–1809), who marketed the steam engine, won an extension of the patent for another twenty-five years, and set up a special laboratory for Watt so that he could refine his device. Collaboration between inventors and entrepreneurs was a sign of the new times. Moreover, perhaps the most important aspect of Watt's engineering feat was that it was subject to a stream of improvement and adaptation, not just from Boulton and company, but from its competitors as well.

The steam engine, driven by burning coal, provided vastly increased power and catalyzed a revolution in transportation. Steam-powered ships and railroads, built once inventors were able to construct lighter engines that required less coal to run, slashed the time and cost of long-distance travel. Steam power's diffusion accelerated when iron-making improved, allowing for the production of railroad track and cables used to hang suspension bridges. The first public rail line opened in 1830 in England between Manchester and Liverpool. During the next twenty years, railway mileage increased from less than 100 to almost 25,000 in England, France, Russia, and the German-speaking countries. Steamships appeared in the 1780s in France, Britain, and the United States, and in 1807 Robert Fulton inaugurated the first commercially successful route between New York City and Albany on the Hudson River. A century of toying with boilers and pistons culminated in the radical reduction of distances. Steam-powered engines also improved sugar refining, pottery making, and many other industrial processes. Mechanizing processes that would have taken much longer and been subject to human error if done by hand enabled manufacturers to make more products at cheaper cost.

Textile production was one of the areas that benefited from both technical changes and the consolidation of different stages of the work in a factory. With new machinery, a single textile operator could handle many looms and spindles at once and could produce bolts of cloth with stunning efficiency. Gone were the hand tools, the family traditions, and the loosely organized and dispersed systems of households producing cloth in their homes for local merchants to carry to markets. The new material was also stronger, finer, and more uniform. Thanks to such innovations, British cotton output increased tenfold between 1770 and 1790, leading to a 90 percent decline in the price of cloth between 1782 and 1812.

Most raw cotton for the British cloth industry had come from colonial India until 1793, when the American inventor Eli Whitney (1765–1825) patented a device called a "cotton gin" that separated cotton seeds from fiber. Cotton farming quickly spread from South Carolina into Georgia, Alabama, Mississippi, and Louisiana, as the United States came to produce more than 80 percent of the world cotton supply by the

Steam Locomotive. A woodcut of a steam locomotive in Syracuse New York, c. 1850.

A Cotton Textile Mill in the 1830s. The region of Lancashire became one of the major industrial hubs for textile production in the world. By the 1830s, mills had made the shift from artisanal work to highly mechanical mass production. Among the great breakthroughs was the discovery that cloth could be printed with designs, such as paisley or calico (as in this image), and marketed to middle-class consumers.

1850s. Thus, the American South became a supplier of raw cotton to Britain. In turn, every black slave in the Americas and many Indians in British India could be consumers of cheap, British-produced cotton shirts. Between 1816 and 1848, cotton goods amounted to 40 percent of British exports.

Manufacturing was not only developing in England, however; it had a place in other western European economies as well. Coal mining and textile and iron industries could also be found in various parts of northern Europe in the middle of the nineteenth century, although only England at this time had half its labor force employed in manufacturing. In the rest of Europe, manufacturing accounted for between 5 and 10 percent of employment, most of it still in rural domestic workshops. Except for Great Britain, the quantity and quality of the agrarian harvest remained by far the primary economic concern for most people throughout the world.

WORKING AND LIVING

While the industrial revolution did not mean a wholesale shift to factory labor, industrialization did alter where people worked and how they worked. People had to work harder and had more demanding work routines. This was true in the industrializing economies of western Europe and North America and on the farms and plantations of Asia and Africa. The European side of the story is better known and more fully documented, but it had its counterpart in intensified agrarian routines throughout the rest of the world.

Increasingly, Europe's workers dwelled and made their livings in cities. London, already Europe's largest city in 1700, saw its population nearly double over the next century to almost 1 million. By the 1820s, the rate of population growth was even greater in the industrial hubs of Leeds, Glasgow, Birmingham, Liverpool, and Manchester. By contrast, in the Low Countries and France, where the pace of industrializa-

tion was more gradual and small-scale rural-based manufacturing flourished, the shift to cities was less marked.

For most urban dwellers, cities were not healthy places. No European city in the early nineteenth century had as clean a water supply as the largest towns of the ancient Roman Empire once had. Water that was used to power the mills along with chemicals used in the dyeing process were poured directly back into waterways, like Manchester's filthy Irk River, which also served as the source of drinking water for thousands of residents. Overcrowded tenements shared a very small number of outhouses; in most European cities, as late as 1850, there was no running water or garbage pickup, and underground sewers were virtually unknown. Disease, not surprisingly, was widespread.

As families moved to cities and found jobs in small and large factories, they earned wages, which they brought home and added to the family's revenues. Children, wives, and husbands, who ordinarily had worked at home and sold the goods they produced, increasingly worked outside the home for cash (though many members of most families continued to work at least part of the time at making handicrafts inside the home). Urban employers experimented with various ways of paying workers according to tasks performed or the number of goods produced per day (piece rates). To earn subsistence wages, men, women, and children frequently remained on the job for twelve or more hours. In 1851 in England, in the cotton and woolen industries, the most mechanized industries, there were 811,000 workers, about two-thirds of whom were women and children. England also had 1 million domestic servants, the large majority of whom were women, and 1.8 million agricultural laborers.

Changes in work affected the understanding of time. Whereas most farmers had adapted tasks and workloads to seasonal demands and constraints, employers and master artisans had always asked workers to obey some form of schedule. After about 1800, a more rigid concept of work discipline began to spread in industrial settings. To keep new machinery operating, factory and mill owners fastened huge clocks at the top of towers over work sites, using bells or horns to signify the beginning or end of the workday. Employers also used clocks to measure output per hour and to compare one worker's performance to that of others. Josiah Wedgwood (1730–1795), a maker of teacups and other porcelain, installed a Boulton & Watt steam engine in his manufacturing plant, and saw to it that his workers used it efficiently. He rang a bell at 5:45 in the morning so that employees could get to work as day broke. At 8:30 the bell rang for breakfast, 9:00 to call them back, and 12:00 for a half-hour lunch, and it last tolled when darkness put an end to the workday. Sometimes, however, the clocks at factories were put back in the morning and forward at night, falsely extending the workday and cheating workers. In response, some workers smashed the timekeeping instruments.

> *Periodic downturns in the economy put wageworkers, most of whom had no savings, at risk and many responded to involuntary unemployment by organizing protests.*

Industrialization meant greater levels of production, but it established numbing work routines and provided paltry wages. Real wages did not begin to rise for most workers until after 1850. Worse than the drudgery or low pay, however, was having no work at all. As families moved off farmland and became dependent on wages, being idle meant having no source of income. Periodic downturns in the economy put wageworkers, most of whom had no savings, at risk and many responded to involuntary unemployment by organizing protests. The spectacle of riotous crowds and strikers haunted Europe's propertied sectors. In 1834, the British Parliament centralized the administration of all poor relief under a national board and deprived able-bodied workers of any relief unless they joined a workhouse, where working conditions resembled those of a prison. Work routines in these houses were intended to be more heinous than working for an employer.

Even as much new literature celebrated "entrepreneurs" who accumulated private wealth through diligence and enterprise, the effects of the industrial revolution on working-class families became a cause of widespread concern. In the 1810s in England, groups of jobless craftsmen, who called themselves Luddites, smashed the machines that had rendered them unemployed. In 1849, the English novelist Charlotte Brontë published a novel, *Shirley*, which depicted the misfortunes wrought by the power loom. Yorkshire weavers lost their jobs, leading to, in Brontë's words, a moral earthquake and forcing the poor to drink the waters of affliction. Charles Dickens described a mythic Coketown to evoke pity for the proletariat in his 1854 classic, *Hard Times*. Both Elizabeth Gaskell, in England, and Emile Zola, in France, described the hardships suffered by women whose children were perpetually malnourished and forced into the workforce too early; the novels written by these two reformers also highlighted the miseries of prostitutes and widows, whose lives, like their real-life counterparts, were characterized by hunger, loneliness, and illness. These social advocates added to the pressures to promulgate protective legislation for workers, including curbing child labor, limiting the work day, and even, in some countries, legalizing prostitution so that the courtesans' health could be monitored.

Capital and Labor. By the 1840s, many people in Europe were growing worried about the effects of industrialization. This English cartoon from 1843 depicts the terrible laboring conditions for coal miners and satirizes the lazy and idle owners of mining capital. Around this time, writers invented the term *capitalist* to deride this class.

Some, however, preferred to vote with their feet rather than wait for legislative reform. The period of European industrialization was also one of the greatest periods of emigration, as unemployed workers or peasants whose lands were exhausted or enclosed abandoned their homes to seek their fortunes, especially in America, Canada, and Australia. During the Irish Potato Famine of 1845–1849, at least one million Irish men, women, and children left their country—a further million or so died (estimates range between 500,000 and two million) when fungi attacked their single subsistence crop. Irish immigrants desperate to escape starvation at home sold their belongings and booked cheap passage to North America from Liverpool. The ships they sailed on were so deadly that they were called "Coffin Ships"; often the death-rate onboard, from disease and malnutrition, exceeded one-third of the number of passengers. Those who did survive would face discrimination—many Americans feared that the mostly unskilled and Catholic Irish would drive down wages and/or create social unrest—at least until the 1880s, when a wave of new emigrants, this time chiefly from southern Europe, took their place at the bottom of the social and economic ladder.

The economic reordering of the late eighteenth and early nineteenth centuries transformed virtually all aspects of the lives of people who were caught up in it. It required people to alter the way they traded with one another and what they consumed. It also required new methods for mobilizing capital, as well as changes in the rhythms and work routines of merchants, wage laborers, and farmers. Furthermore, changes affected where people worked, where they lived, whom they married, how many children they had, and how they regarded people whose lives were different from their own. And, for many Europeans, it even meant starting life over in a different region of the world, far away from the places their parents had inhabited.

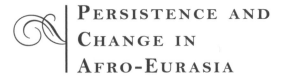

PERSISTENCE AND CHANGE IN AFRO-EURASIA

> → *How did the Atlantic revolutions affect Afro-Eurasian societies?*

While the ideas that originated in the Enlightenment and stimulated the American and French revolutions spread across the Afro-Eurasian landmass, western Europe's military might, its technological achievements, and its economic strength represented the clearest threat to the well-being of the remaining Afro-Eurasian empires. Everywhere on the Afro-Eurasian landmass, western European merchants and industrialists, often backed by military power, sought to forge tighter economic and sometimes even political ties. They did so in the name of securing "free" access to Asian markets and products. In response, ruling elites in the Russian and the Ottoman empires moved rapidly to modernize their military organizations and to emulate Europe's economic accomplishments. At the same time, they distanced themselves from the liberal, egalitarian, and democratic principles of the French Revolution. The Chinese empire, at a long distance from the revolutionary epicenter in the Atlantic world, remained largely unaffected by Europe and America's revolutionary transformations, until the first Opium War of the early 1840s forced the Chinese to face up to their military weaknesses. Thus, changes in the Atlantic world unleashed new political and economic pressures around the world, though with varying degrees of intensity.

REVAMPING THE RUSSIAN MONARCHY

Some eastern European dynasties responded to western European economic and political pressures by bolstering the strength of traditional rulers—enacting modest reforms combined with the suppression of domestic opposition. This was how Russian rulers reacted in the nineteenth century. Tsar Alexander I (ruled 1801–1825) was fortunate that Napoleon committed a number of blunders and lost the world's most modern army in the Russian snows. Yet, even though Russia was among the victors at the Congress of Vienna in 1815, the French Revolution and the massive French armies motivated by patriotism struck at the heart of Russian political institutions, which were based upon the enserfment of the peasantry. The autocratic tsars could no longer justify their absolutism by claiming that enlightened despotism was the most advanced form of government, since a new model, rooted in popular sovereignty and the concept of the nation, had taken its place. One response was to make much of the heroic resistance of the Russian people that culminated in the great victory over the French. Tsar Alexander glorified patriots who had either fought in the war or grown up hearing about it, but he offered few concessions for any new political order.

In December 1825, when Alexander died unexpectedly and childless, there was a question as to which of his brothers would be the next tsar. In the confusion, some members of the Russian officer corps launched a patriotic revolt, hoping to convince one of Alexander's brothers, Constantine, to take the throne (and to guarantee a constitution) in place of another, more conservative brother, Nicholas. The Decembrists, as they were called, came primarily from elite families. Many had first-hand knowledge of western European life and institutions, some from the campaigns against Napoleon.

Decembrists in St. Petersburg. Russians energetically participated in the coalition that defeated Napoleon, but the ideas of the French Revolution exerted great appeal to the educated upper classes, including aristocrats of the officer corps. In December 1825, at the death of Tsar Alexander I, some regimental officers staged an uprising of about 3,000 men, demanding a constitution and the end of serfdom. But Nicholas I, the new tsar, called in loyal troops and brutally dispersed the "Decembrists," executing or exiling their leaders.

A few Decembrists called for a constitutional monarchy to replace Russia's despotism; others favored a tsar-less republic and the abolition of serfdom. But they failed to win over the peasantry, who continued to believe in the divine right of the tsar to rule without constraints. Constantine supported Nicholas's claim to power. Nicholas (ruled 1825–1855) became tsar and brutally suppressed the insurrectionists. For the time being, the influence of the French Revolution was quashed.

Still, Alexander's successors had to meet the challenges of a world in which powerful European states had constitutions and national armies of citizens, not subjects. One way Russian tsars tried to reinvigorate absolute rule was by idealizing the monarch's family as the historical embodiment of the nation with direct ties to the people. But in addition to cultivating this image, Nicholas sought to keep thoughts and acts of rebellion under control by expanding the Third Section (a political police force), enforcing censorship, having his army engage in military exercises, and maintaining serfdom.

Not all subjects were susceptible to Russian national feeling or could be kept under control by the secret police, however. It took the government more than a year to suppress a revolt that began in November 1830 in the empire's Polish provinces. The special constitution granted in 1815 for Russian Poland was abolished, and Nicholas sought a closer alliance with the conservative monarchies of Austria and Prussia. In the 1830s, Nicholas introduced a conservative ideology with the slogan of "Orthodoxy, Autocracy, and Folk Nationality," which stressed religious faith, hierarchy, and obedience, and idealized but did not enfranchise the people. And while some reformers continued to call for more far-reaching changes, these as yet led nowhere.

REFORMING EGYPT AND THE OTTOMAN EMPIRE

Unlike in Russia, where Napoleon's army had reached Moscow, the Ottoman capital in Istanbul was never threatened by French troops. Still, the Napoleonic invasion of Egypt shook the Ottoman Empire and led European merchants to press Ottoman rulers for increased commercial concessions. Even before this trauma, imperial authorities faced the challenge that increased trade with Europe—and the increased presence of European merchants and missionaries—posed. Many of the non-Muslim religious communities in the sultan's empire openly looked to the European powers to advance their interests. In the wake of Napoleon, who had promised to remake Egyptian society, reformist energies swept from Egypt to the center of the Ottoman domain.

In Egypt, far-reaching changes came with Muhammad Ali (ruled 1805–1848), the most adept of the area's modernizing rulers. After the French withdrawal in 1801, Muhammad Ali emerged victorious in a chaotic struggle for supreme power in Egypt, defying Ottoman superiors and aligning himself with influential Egyptian merchant and scholarly families. Yet he looked to revolutionary France for a model of modern state-building. As with Napoleon and Simón Bolívar, the key to his rise and hold on power was the army. With the

AN EGYPTIAN INTELLECTUAL'S REACTION TO THE FRENCH OCCUPATION OF EGYPT

In the invasion of Egypt in 1798, the French commander, Napoleon Bonaparte, attempted to win rank-and-file Egyptian support against the country's Mamluk Turkish rulers by portraying himself as a liberator and by invoking the ideals of the French Revolution as he had done with great success all over Europe. His campaign did not succeed, and the French met with bitter local opposition. The Egyptian chronicler Abd al-Rahman al-Jabarti has left one of the most perceptive accounts of these years.

On Monday news arrived that the French had reached Damanhur and Rosetta [in the Nile delta]. . . . They printed a large proclamation in Arabic, calling on the people to obey them. . . . In this proclamation were inducements, warnings, all manner of wiliness and stipulations. Some copies were sent from the provinces to Cairo and its text is:

In the name of God, the Merciful, the Compassionate. There is no God but God. He has no son nor has He an associate in His Dominion.

On behalf of the French Republic which is based upon the foundation of liberty and equality, General Bonaparte, Commander-in-Chief of the French armies makes known to all the Egyptian people that for a long time the Sanjaqs [its Mamluk rulers] who lorded it over Egypt have treated the French community basely and contemptuously and have persecuted its merchants with all manner of extortion and violence. Therefore the hour of punishment has now come.

Unfortunately, this group of Mamluks, imported from the mountains of Circassia and Georgia, have acted corruptly for ages in the fairest land that is to be found upon the face of the globe. However, the Lord of the Universe, the Almighty, has decreed the end of their power.

O ye Egyptians . . . I have not come to you except for the purpose of restoring your rights from the hands of the oppressors and that I more than the Mamluks serve God. . . .

And tell them also that all people are equal in the eyes of God and the only circumstances which distinguish one from the other are reason, virtue, and knowledge. . . . Formerly, in the lands of Egypt there were great cities, and wide canals and extensive commerce and nothing ruined all this but the avarice and the tyranny of the Mamluks.

[Jabarti then undertook to challenge the arguments in the French proclamation and to portray the French as godless invaders, inspired by false ideals.] They follow this rule: great and small, high and low, male and female are all equal. Sometimes they break this rule according to their whims and inclinations or reasoning. Their women do not veil themselves and have no modesty. They do not care whether they uncover their private parts. Whenever a Frenchman has to perform an act of nature he does so where he happens to be, even in full view of people, and he goes away as he is, without washing his private parts after defecation. . . . They have intercourse with any woman who pleases them and vice versa. . . .

His saying "[all people] are equal in the eyes of God" the Almighty is a lie and stupidity. How can this be when God has made some superior to others as is testified by the dwellers in the Heavens and on Earth? . . .

So those people are opposed to both Christians and Muslims, and do not hold fast to any religion. You see that they are materialists, who deny all God's attributes. . . . May God hurry misfortune and punishment upon them, may He strike their tongues with dumbness, may He scatter their hosts, and disperse them.

→ *Why do you think Napoleon's appeals to the ideals of the French Revolution failed with Egyptians?*

→ *Why does al-Jabarti claim that the invaders are godless even though the proclamation clearly suggests otherwise?*

SOURCE: Abd al-Rahman al-Jabarti, *Napoleon in Egypt: al-Jabarti's Chronicle of the French Occupation, 1798*, translated by Shmuel Moreh (Princeton: Markus Wiener Publishing, 1993), pp. 24–29.

Muhammad Ali. The Middle Eastern ruler who most successfully assimilated the educational, technological, and economic advances of nineteenth-century Europe was Muhammad Ali, ruler of Egypt from 1805 until 1848.

help of French advisors, including one who had served with Napoleon but converted to Islam and took the name Suleiman Pasha, the Egyptian army became the most powerful fighting force in the Middle East.

Along with modernizing the military, Muhammad Ali pushed for reforms in education and agriculture. He established a school of engineering, and he opened the first modern medical school in Cairo under the supervision of a French military doctor, A. B. Clot. During an autopsy, an enraged student attacked the French doctor, claiming that the dissection of human cadavers violated Islamic norms. With time Clot accustomed his students to anatomical lessons, but he still conducted his classes in secret. In the countryside, Muhammad Ali made Egypt one of the world's leading cotton exporters and the primary region for the cultivation of the highly prized long-staple cotton. A summer crop, cotton required steady watering during the low Nile season when irrigation waters were in short supply. To meet those needs, Muhammad Ali's Public Works Department, acting under the advice of European engineers, deepened the irrigation canals and began to construct a series of dams across the Nile.

Muhammad Ali's modernizing reforms, however, disrupted the habits of the local peasantry. Incorporation into the new industrial world economy, whether as wage laborers in English factories or peasants on Egyptian cotton estates, entailed harder and more demanding work, often with little additional compensation. Because irrigation improvements permitted year-round cultivation, peasants now had to plant and harvest three crops instead of one or two. Moreover, the Egyptian state controlled the prices at which cultivators sold their products, so peasants saw little profit from their added exertions. Young men also now faced conscription into the state's enlarged army, while whole families had to engage in unpaid public works projects. Those who had to work on Egypt's irrigation canals often contracted *bilharzia*, a waterborne illness that debilitated its hosts. Egypt's ruler also designed a state-sponsored program of industrialization that would put Egypt on a par with Europe. Within the short span of a decade and a half, the state had set up textile and munitions factories that employed 200,000 workers. But Egypt had few skilled laborers or cheap sources of energy. By the time of Muhammad Ali's death in 1849, few of the factories still survived.

External forces also checked Muhammad Ali's ambitious plans. At first, his new army enjoyed spectacular success. At the bidding of the Ottoman sultan, the Egyptian military fought credibly against Greek nationalists, although Egyptian forces were unable to prevent the Greeks from acquiring independence in 1829. Egyptian soldiers also carried out conquests in the Sudan. Muhammad Ali overplayed his hand, however, when he sent his forces into Syria in the early 1830s and later in the decade when he threatened to launch expeditions into Anatolia, the heart of the Ottoman state. The prospect that an Egyptian ruler might march into Istanbul and supplant the Ottoman sultan alarmed the European powers. Led by the British foreign minister Lord Palmerston, European diplomats compelled Egypt to withdraw from Anatolia and in 1841 to reduce its army to 18,000 soldiers. In the name of free trade, European merchants pressed for unobstructed access to Egyptian markets, just as they did in Latin America and Africa.

Under political and economic pressures that were similar to those facing Muhammad Ali in Egypt, Ottoman rulers also began to change their ways. Already in the eighteenth century, the more forward-looking sultans were well aware of the rising power of Europe. Military defeats and humiliating treaties with Europe provided ample reminders of the Ottoman rulers' vulnerability. This vulnerability deepened as Europe's economic and military might increased. Stunned by Napoleon's defeat of the Egyptian Mamluks and disenchanted with conservative and privileged janissaries who resisted efforts to impose discipline and reforms, in 1805 Sultan Selim III tried to create a new and effective source of military strength. He founded the New Order infantry, trained by western European officers. But before he could bring this new force up to fighting strength, the janissaries rose in revolt, storming the palace, killing New Order officers and sticking their heads on poles outside the palace. They overturned the New Order army and deposed Selim in 1807. Over the next decades, janissary military men and clerical scholars (*ulama*) cobbled together an alliance that continuously thwarted reformers.

Why did reform falter in the Ottoman state even before it had a chance to be implemented? After all, in France and Spain, the old regimes were also inefficient and saddled with accumulated debts and military losses. But reform or revolution was only feasible if the forces of restraint—especially in the military—were weak and the reformers strong; in France, a domestic coalition toppled the ruling bloc; in Spain, colonists allied to reject absolutism and mercantilism. In the Ottoman Empire, the janissary class had grown powerful, providing the bulwark of resistance to change. Also, Ottoman authority aligned with and depended upon clerical support, and the clergy also resisted change. Blocked at the top, Ottoman rulers were loath to appeal for popular support in a struggle against anti-reformers. Such an appeal, in the new age of popular sovereignty and national feeling, was always dangerous for an unelected dynast in a multiethnic and multireligious realm.

The political deadlock was broken by Mahmud II (ruled 1808–1839), who spoke no European languages but was painfully aware of the need to deal with Europe's rising power. He was also a shrewd tactician, able to manipulate his conservative opponents. Convincing some clerics that the janissaries neglected old laws and customs of discipline and piety and promising that a new corps would pray fervently, the sultan won the support of the *ulama* and in 1826 established a new European-style army corps. When the janissaries plotted their inevitable mutiny, Mahmud rallied clerics, students, and his subjects. The schemers retreated to their barracks, only to be shelled by the sultan's artillery and then destroyed in flames. Thousands of janissaries were rounded up and executed.

The sultan was now freer to follow the example of Muhammad Ali in Egypt and pursue reform within an autocratic framework. Like Muhammad Ali, Mahmud brought in a group of European officers (in 1835) to advise his forces. Here, too, military reform spilled over into nonmilitary areas. The Ottoman modernizers created a medical college, then a school of military sciences. To understand Europe better and to create a first-rate diplomatic corps, the Ottomans schooled their officials in European languages and encouraged the translation of European classics into Turkish. Mahmud's successors kept up the reforms and extended them into civilian life. This era, referred to as the *Tanzimat*, or Reorganization period, saw legislation that guaranteed equality for all Ottoman subjects, regardless of religion.

The reforms, however, stopped well short of revolutionary change. For one thing, reform relied too much on the personal whim of rulers. The bureaucratic and religious infrastructure of the Ottoman Empire remained wedded to old ways. Moreover, any effort to reform the rural sector encountered the resistance of the landed interests. Finally, the merchant classes profited from business with a debt-ridden sultan. By staving off the fiscal collapse of the empire, the bankers alleviated the pressure for reform and removed the spark that had fired the revolutions in Europe. Together, these factors impaired the cause of reform in the Ottoman Empire. Yet, by failing to make greater reforms, the empire lost economic and military ground to its European neighbors. For centuries, European traders had needed Islam's goods and services more than the other way around. By the nineteenth century, however, the ties of trade and financial dependency bound the Ottomans to Europe on terms that the Europeans controlled.

> *By the nineteenth century, the ties of trade and financial dependency bound the Ottomans to Europe on terms that the Europeans controlled.*

COLONIAL REORDERING IN INDIA

The largest and most important of Europe's Asian colonial possessions between 1750 and 1850 was British India. Unlike in North America, the changes that the British fostered in Asia at this time did not lead to political independence. Quite the contrary, India was increasingly dominated by the East India Company, a private company that had been chartered by the crown in 1600. The company's increasing control over India's imports and exports in the eighteenth and nineteenth centuries, however, flew in the face of British professions about their allegiance to a world economic system based on "free trade."

Initially, the British, through the East India Company, sought to control the commerce of India by establishing trading posts along the coast but without taking complete political control. After conquering the princely state of Bengal in 1757 and placing a puppet on Bengal's throne, the East India Company began to fill its coffers, and company officials began to amass personal fortunes. In 1760, several senior officials were making the astonishing sum of £500,000 a year through illicit and predatory business ventures. Robert Clive, the governor of Bengal, accrued a huge private fortune by forcing the ruler to cede him a portion of the tax revenues. The unbridled abuse of power caused the Bengal ruler to initiate hostilities against the company. In 1764, the forces of the Mughal emperor and the ruler of Awadh joined with his army to battle against British troops. They were defeated, but instead of decapitating the empire, British officials elected to leave the emperor and most provincial leaders in place—at least as nominal rulers. Nonetheless, in 1765, the British extracted a proclamation from the Mughal emperor that granted the East India Company the right to collect the tax revenues in Bengal as well as in Bihar and Orissa. In addition, the company secured the right to trade free of duties throughout the Mughal territory. In return, the company agreed to pay the emperor an annual pension of £260,000. The company went on to annex other territories, bringing much of South Asia and its estimated 200 million inhabitants under company rule by the early 1800s (see Map 15-4).

To carry out its responsibilities, the East India Company needed to establish a civil administration. Rather than place Britons in these positions, the company preferred to enlist Hindu kings and Muslim princes. The company allowed them to retain their royal symbols and privileges while depriving them of their autonomy. Though the Mughal emperor proclaimed in 1765 that the East India Company was his "servant," the roles were in fact reversed. Previously weakened by the rise of provincial rulers, the emperor was now permanently under the thumb of the company's administrators. Still,

the company did not depend entirely on local leaders to enforce its dictates, for it also maintained a large standing army. By 1805, this army included 155,000 soldiers, more than a third of whom were native recruits or sepoys (a corruption of the Urdu term *sipahi* for soldier). It employed a centralized bureaucracy that by the 1780s was trained to rule colonial subjects. Together, the military force, bureaucracy, and an array of local rulers enabled the company state to maintain security and assure the stability of revenue collection.

To rule with a minimum of interference and cost, however, required knowing the conquered society. This provided the impetus for what became known as "Orientalist" scholarship. English scholar-officials wrote the first modern histories of South Asia, translated and published Sanskrit and Persian texts, identified philosophical writings, and compiled Hindu and Muslim law books. The most famous of these scholars was William Jones who, while serving as a judge in Calcutta between 1783 and 1794, founded the Asiatic Society. While Jones and like-minded Orientalists admired Sanskrit language and literature, they still approved of English colonial rule. Thanks to their efforts, the company state presented itself as a force for revitalizing authentic Hinduism and recovering India's literary and cultural treasures. Nonetheless, the views of Orientalist scholars did not always ac-

MAP 15-4 THE BRITISH IN INDIA, 1767–1857

Starting from locations in eastern and northeastern India, the British East India Company extended its authority over much of South Asia prior to the outbreak of the Indian Rebellion of 1857. Why did this process take several centuries to unfold? How did the company administer these possessions? Why did it choose a strategy of direct and indirect rule over different areas within the larger region?

Indian Resistance to Company Rule. Tipu Sultan, the Mysore ruler, put up a determined resistance against the British. This painting by Robert Home shows Cornwallis, the East India Company's governor, receiving Tipu's two sons as hostages after defeating him in the 1792 war. The boys remained in British custody for two years. Tipu returned to fighting the British and was killed in the war of 1799.

cord with the actual Indian village beliefs in local deities and the importance of local vernacular tongues.

Maintaining a sizeable military and civilian bureaucracy compelled the East India Company to intrude on the lives of Indians in many ways, especially through taxation. Land-holding arrangements were of vital importance to the company because taxes on land were its largest source of revenue. From 1793 onward, a series of land settlements bolstered state revenues and undercut the autonomy of villagers. These policies made large and small landowners responsible for paying taxes to the company—in so doing, tax policies helped spread private property at the expense of traditional landowning rights. In particular, large estate owners gained more power and joined with the company in determining who could own property. The old flexible tax system gave way to one in which all landholders had to pay, irrespective of means. When proprietors defaulted on their taxes, the company put their properties up for auction, with the firm's own employees and large estate owners often obtaining title. Some took out loans to save their property or to make rental payments, exposing themselves to rural moneylenders.

Company rule altered India's urban geography as well. By the early nineteenth century, colonial cities, like Calcutta, Madras, and Bombay, became the new and growing centers at the expense of older Mughal cities like Agra, Delhi, Murshidabad, and Hyderabad. As trade boomed, colonial cities attracted British merchants and Indian clerks, artisans, and laborers. Calcutta's population reached 350,000 in 1820, and Bombay's jumped to 200,000 by 1825. In these cities, Europeans lived in enclaves around the company's fort and trading stations, while migrants from the Indian countryside clustered in crowded quarters called "black towns."

Back in Britain, the debts of rural Indians and the conditions of black towns generated little concern. Instead, calls for reform focused on the East India Company's monopoly. Criticism of colonial methods, but not of colonialism, mounted as the company's arbitrary rule in India became better known in London. British critics of the company objected to its monopoly over access to Indian wealth, and British industrialists resented the protection afforded to the company's shareholders and investors. In 1813, the British Parliament, responding to the wishes of merchants and traders to participate in the Indian economy, abolished the East India Company's monopoly over trade with India.

No longer the preserve of a single company, India was now expected to serve the interests of an industrializing Britain. In pursuit of this goal, India became an important market for British textiles, as well as an exporter of raw cotton. This was a new trading arrangement, entailing a reversal of India's traditional trade. In the past, even under early company rule, India had been an important textile manufacturer, exporting fine cotton goods throughout the Indian Ocean and to Europe. But the Indian business elites had difficulty resisting the import of cheap British textiles. As a result, a long-term partial deindustrialization took place in the region. In addition, Indian imports of British manufactures

Primary Source

JAMES MILL ON INDIAN TRADITION

James Mill was a Scottish political economist and philosopher and a follower of Jeremy Bentham, the Utilitarian thinker. In line with Utilitarianism, Mill believed that law and government were of central importance in maximizing utility and happiness. With this idea in mind, he penned the multivolume History of British India *in 1818. He criticized India's Hindu and Muslim cultures and traditions and attributed their so-called backwardness to the absence of a strong and systematic form of law. His trenchant critique of India's traditions was also an attack on earlier British Orientalists who stressed the study of indigenous texts and noninterference in traditional practices. A year after the publication of the book, he was appointed as an official by the East India Company.*

The condition of the women is one of the most remarkable circumstances in the manners of nations. Among rude people, the women are generally degraded; among civilized people they are exalted.

———————

Nothing can exceed the habitual contempt which the Hindus entertain for their women. Hardly are they ever mentioned in their laws, or other books, but as wretches of the most base and vicious inclinations, on whose natures no virtuous or useful qualities can be engrafted. "Their husbands," says the sacred code, "should be diligently careful in guarding them: though they well know the disposition with which the lord of creation formed them; Manu allotted to such women a love of their bed, of their seat, and of ornament, impure appetites, wrath, weak flexibility, desire of mischief, and bad conduct."

———————

They are held, accordingly, in extreme degradation. They are not accounted worthy to partake of religious rites but in conjunction with their husbands. They are entirely excluded from the sacred books. . . .

———————

It is not surprising, that grossness, in ideas and language, respecting the intercourse of the sexes, is a uniform concomitant of the degraded state of the women. . . . Inquiry discovers, that grossness in this respect is a regular ingredient in the manners of a rude age; and that society, as it refines, deposits this, among its other impurities. The ancient inhabitants of our own country were as indelicate as those of the hottest regions of Asia. All European witnesses have been struck with the indelicacy of the Hindus. The gross emblems and practices of their religion are already known. To the indecent passages in the books of law, and the practices which they describe, exceedingly numerous, and exceedingly gross, we can here only allude. Both the writings and conversation of the Hindus abound with passages which are shocking to European ears.

———————

led to unfavorable trade balances that changed India from a net importer of gold and silver to an exporter of these precious metals.

Nor were the British content simply to alter the Indian economy. The colonial rulers also advocated far-reaching changes in traditional Indian society and culture so that its people would place a high value on British goods and culture. In 1817, James Mill, a philosopher and an employee of the East India Company, condemned the backwardness of indigenous social practices and cultural traditions. He and his son, John Stuart Mill, who was also employed by the company, argued that only dictatorial, illiberal rule could bring good government and economic progress to Indians, who were deemed unfit for autonomy, self-rule, or liberalism.

Evangelicals and liberal reformers also agitated for a thorough transformation of Hindu and Muslim social practices through legislation and the introduction of European education. For example, they sought to stop the practice of *sati*, wherein a woman was burned to death on the funeral pyre of her dead husband. The mood swung away from the Orientalists' respect for India's classical languages, philosophies, cultures, and texts. In 1835, Lord Macaulay, entrusted with the task of making recommendations on educational policies, declared that a single shelf in any decent western library con-

They are remarkably prone to flattery; the most prevailing mode of address from the weak to the strong, while men are still ignorant and unreflecting. The Hindus are full of dissimulation and falsehood, the universal concomitants of oppression. The vices of falsehood, indeed, they carry to a height almost unexampled among other races of men. Judicial perjury is more than common; it is almost universal.

This religion has produced a practice, which has strongly engaged the curiosity of Europeans; a superstitious care of the life of the inferior animals. A Hindu lives in perpetual terror of killing even an insect; and hardly any crime can equal that of being unintentionally the cause of death to any animal of the more sacred species. This feeble circumstance, however, is counteracted by so many gloomy and malignant principles, that their religion, instead of humanizing the character, must have had no inconsiderable effect in fostering that disposition to revenge, that insensibility to the sufferings of others, and often that active cruelty, which lurks under the smiling exterior of the Hindu.

Few nations are surpassed by the Hindus, in the total want of physical purity, in their streets, houses, and persons. Mr. Forster, whose long residence in India, and knowledge of the country, render him an excellent witness, says of the narrow streets of Benares; "In addition to the pernicious effect which must proceed from a confined atmosphere, there is, in the hot season, an intolerable stench arising from the many pieces of stagnated water dispersed in different quarters of the town. The filth also which is indiscriminately thrown into the streets, and there left exposed, (for the Hindus possess but a small portion of general cleanliness) add to the compound of ill smells so offensive to the European inhabitants of this city."

The attachment with which the Hindus, in common with all ignorant nations, bear to astrology, is a part of their manners exerting a strong influence upon the train of their actions. "The Hindus of the present age," says a partial observer, "do not undertake any affair of consequence without consulting their astrologers, who are always Brahmans." The belief of witchcraft and sorcery continues universally prevalent; and is everyday the cause of the greater enormities.

→ *What did James Mill hold to be the chief indicator of a civilization's accomplishment?*
→ *Did Mill's views on India imply a wholesale transformation of society and government?*

SOURCE: James Mill, *The History of British India* (New Delhi: Atlantic Publishers & Distributors, 1990), pp. 279, 281–82, 286–87, 288, 289, 297, 299.

tained more valuable knowledge than all the accumulated Sanskrit and Persian texts. English was to replace Persian as the language of administration, and European education was to displace training in Oriental learning. The result, reformers hoped, would be the raising of a class that was Indian in blood and color, but English in tastes and culture.

Packing Cotton Bales. This 1864 engraving of the packing of cotton bales registers the shift in cotton trade between India and Britain: from being an exporter of cotton manufactures up to the eighteenth century, India became a source of raw cotton in the nineteenth century.

This was a new colonial order, but it was not a stable one. While some European-educated Indians thanked the British rulers for their benevolent reforms, most landed magnates, facing dispossession and loss of their authority, grumbled with disaffection. Peasants, thrown to the mercy of the market, moneylenders, and landlords were in turmoil. The so-called tribals, or non-Hindu forest dwellers and shifting cultivators, faced with the hated combination of the colonial state and moneylenders, revolted. Dispossessed artisans brought unrest to towns and cities. Merchants and industrialists resented the fact that they could now make money only by working as subordinates in a British-dominated economy. Undeterred, the British persevered in extending and refining the reach of the colonial state, combining reform with autocracy, advancing free trade with colonial dictates. India participated in an increasingly interconnected world and contributed to Europe's industrialization, but it did so as a colony. Expanding freedom in Europe was paralleled by exploitation in India.

PERSISTENCE OF THE QING EMPIRE

In contrast to the declining fortunes of the other dynasts, the Qing dynasty, which had taken power in China in 1644, was still enjoying considerable economic prosperity and territorial expansion as the nineteenth century dawned. The Chinese were largely unaware of the revolutionary events taking place in North America, France, and Britain, and they felt no great compulsion to alter the fundamentals of their society. Their sense of imperial splendor continued to rest upon the political structure and social order inherited from the Ming. Although some Chinese felt that the Manchu Qing were foreign occupiers, the Qing carefully adapted Chinese institutions and philosophies. Thus, Chinese elites at court did not challenge the prerogatives of the dynasty—unlike the delegates to the Estates-General in France in 1788–1789.

EXPANSION OF THE EMPIRE   The Qing demonstrated a special talent for extending the boundaries of the empire and fostering settlement in frontier lands. Before 1750, they conquered Taiwan (the stronghold of remaining Ming forces), pushed westward into central Asia, and annexed Tibet. In the 1750s, the Qianlong Emperor (ruled 1736–1796) marched a quarter million men against the powerful West Mongol Oirats, who were utterly decimated. The Qing victory ended Russian efforts to take southern Siberia. Subsequent treaties with Russia established the limits of Chinese westward expansion into Turkic- and Mongol-speaking lands. To secure these territorial gains, the Qing encouraged settlement of western frontier lands like Xinjiang. New crops from the Americas aided this spread of China's population into recently acquired lands. Corn and sweet potatoes, which could grow well in less fertile soils, became more prominent. Crops were

seeded methodically in neat rows, unlike in Europe, where the broadcast method of seeding caused much wastage.

Thanks to rising agricultural productivity and population growth, rural life became more commercialized and state revenues increased. In the eighteenth century, rural markets multiplied, increasing the volume of interregional trade in grain, cotton, tea, and silk. Rural industries also proliferated. As in Europe, peasant households became the backbone of early manufactures, especially in textiles. The Chinese espoused an ideal in which women stayed home while men worked in the field, but in China as in Europe, relatively few rural households could afford to exclude women from fieldwork.

Like their European counterparts, Chinese peasants were on the move. Migration to frontier regions occurred in Qing China for different reasons. In the case of the westward move into Xinjiang, or "New Borderlands," the movement was state-sponsored and initiated to secure a recently pacified frontier region through military colonization, followed by civilians—peasants enticed by the offer of at least 4.5 acres of land, a set of tools, twelve pecks of seed, and a loan of two taels of silver and a horse valued at eight taels—with the objective of producing enough food grain to supply the troops as well as to relieve the pressure on the poor and arid northwestern part of the country. Perhaps as many as half a million

Rice Paddies. Farmers working in neatly planted rice paddy fields in late imperial China. The process was labor intensive, but it reduced wastage.

acres of land were brought under cultivation by 1840, fundamentally transforming the ecological and social landscape of the region.

Other migrants were on the move by their own initiative. Pushed by the ever-growing competition for land in the core areas of the country—by 1850 the Qing population had increased by 200 to 250 million since the dynasty's founding in the mid-seventeenth century—they even found themselves in areas that the Qing regime tried to restrict them from going, such as Manchuria and Taiwan. The migrants brought their agricultural techniques and settlements to those areas, reshaping the environment through their land reclamation and irrigation projects. The migrant population in Taiwan grew from around a hundred thousand in the late seventeenth century to close to a million a century later, while over two million made their way to Manchuria in the same period, with the amount of taxable land there increasing from about 9,700 acres in 1661 to over a million acres by 1820.

Even as Qing rulers recognized the problems, their ability to tackle them was limited.

PROBLEMS OF THE EMPIRE Despite their success in expanding the boundaries of the empire, the Qing faced a number of obvious problems. As a ruling minority among the vast Han Chinese majority, the Manchu Qing tended to take a conservative approach to internal innovation. Only toward the end of the eighteenth century did they grapple with problems of rapid growth in population. On the one hand, the tripling of China's population since 1300 attested to the strength and prosperity of the realm. On the other, a population that had surpassed 300 million put severe pressure on various resources, especially soil for growing crops and wood for fuel.

Even as Qing rulers recognized the problems, their ability to tackle them was limited. The taxes they levied, in comparison with those levied by European monarchs, were light. Chinese bureaucrats, who were supposed to hire and pay their underlings out of their own salaries, found themselves understaffed. As local bureaucrats introduced many ad hoc taxes, the people came to see the bureaucrats as corrupt. The Qing, however, proved unable to rationalize the taxation system or to regularize the administrative apparatus at the grassroots level. In fact, the Qing rulers could not even put an end to the corruption of their court officials. In the late eighteenth and early nineteenth centuries, the White Lotus Rebellion, a series of uprisings inspired by mystical beliefs in folk Buddhism (especially the belief that the Maitreya Buddha would appear to rescue the people from their suffering) and at times by the idea of restoring the Ming, engulfed much of northern China.

Some historians have suggested that the Qing fell into deep crisis and "failed" to seek new technologies and new systems of knowledge and rule. In time, these historians assert, that failure left China vulnerable to outsiders, especially Europeans. Yet, throughout the eighteenth century, European rulers and upper classes remained avid consumers of Chinese silks, teas, carved jade, tableware, jewelry, paper for covering walls, ceramics, and other artifacts of what the French called *chinoiserie*. The Chinese, for their part, felt little need to acquire European manufactures. In 1793, Emperor Qianlong wrote in response to a request for trade by Britain's George III that "as your ambassador can see for himself, we possess all things," adding, "I have no use for your country's manufactures."

By the mid-nineteenth century, however, the Qing had lost their ability to dismiss the Europeans and their manufactures. This resulted from the extraordinary and unforeseen changes that had made western European powers far stronger than they had ever been. The first unambiguous evidence of an altered balance of power was not the rise of Napoleon, about whom the Chinese knew little, but a British-Chinese war over a narcotic, opium. The Opium War exposed China's vulnerability in a new era of European ascendancy.

THE OPIUM WAR AND THE "OPENING" OF CHINA Europeans had been selling staples and intoxicants in China for a long time. Tobacco, a New World crop, had become a ubiquitous sight in China by the seventeenth century. Stores offered a variety of brands. While ordinary people smoked with a water pipe, members of the elite learned to use snuff. The significance of these imports was not immediately apparent. Few would have predicted that tobacco smoking would prepare the ground for the widespread use of opium, previously consumed as a medicine or an aphrodisiac. At first, crude opium was mixed with tobacco and smoked by Chinese in Southeast Asia, Taiwan, and along the southern coast of China in the seventeenth century. But the practice spread from these centers of the maritime trade to the north and the interior of the region. By the late eighteenth century, opium smokers with their long-stemmed pipes were conspicuous in every stratum of Chinese society.

The Qing banned opium imports in 1729, yet the Chinese continued to smoke the drug and illegally to import it through Portuguese and other merchants. Sensing its economic potential, the East India Company created an opium monopoly in India in 1773. The reason was a rapid growth in the company's purchase of tea. Because the Chinese showed little taste for British goods, the British had financed their tea imports with exports of silver to China. By the end of the eighteenth century, however, the quantity of its tea purchases had become too large to finance with shipments of silver. Fortunately for the company, the Chinese showed an eagerness

Opium Dens. A common sight in late Qing China were establishments catering specifically to opium smoking. Taken from a volume condemning the practice, this picture shows opium smokers idling their day away.

for Indian goods—first cotton and opium, and subsequently mostly opium—permitting the British to export very little or no silver after 1804. Given the importance of opium, the company extended its cultivation by offering loans to Indian peasants who, in return, agreed to grow opium and sell it to the company's agents at a predetermined price.

The illegal opium traffic could not have flourished without the connivance of corrupt Chinese bureaucrats and a network of local brokers and distributors. Yet, a Qing decree of 1799 reiterated the official ban. Until 1821, no more than 5,000 chests of opium per year found their way into China,

but the number increased to 16,500 chests in 1831–1832 and 40,000 in 1838–1839. The import explosion resulted primarily from an influx of private British merchants in 1834, when the British government revoked the East India Company's monopoly over trade with China, which meant that anyone could now enter the trade.

The impact of opium on the Qing's trade balance was devastating. In a clear reversal from earlier trends, silver began to flow out of instead of into China. About 2 million taels of silver left the country each year in the 1820s. The figure jumped to 9 million taels a decade later. China experienced

Opium Warehouse in India. Having established a monopoly in the 1770s over opium cultivation in India, the British greatly expanded their manufacture and export of opium to China to balance their rapidly growing import of Chinese tea and silk. This picture from the 1880s shows an opium warehouse in India where the commodity was stored before being transported to China.

Trade in Canton. In this painting, titled *A View of the Hongs,* we can see the hongs, the buildings that made up the factories, or establishments, where foreign merchants conducted their business in Canton. From the mid-eighteenth century to 1842, Canton was the only Chinese port open to European trade.

silver shortages, and ordinary peasants saw their tax burden surge (remember that taxes had to be paid in silver; see Chapter 13). Unrest in the countryside, on the rise since the 1790s, spread and gained momentum. At the Qing court, some officials wanted to legalize the opium trade to stamp out corruption and to channel revenues into the treasury (as long as it remained officially an illegal substance, the government could not tax the traffic). Others wanted stiffer prohibitions, though they did not specify how they would be enforced. The emperor followed the latter tack, and in 1838 sent a specially appointed commissioner, Lin Zexu, to the main entrepôt, Canton (now called Guangzhou, it was the only port, besides the Portuguese settlement of Macao, where foreigners could trade with the Chinese), to eradicate the influx of opium. In a letter to Queen Victoria of Britain, Lin claimed that China exported its goods such as tea and silk for no other reason than "to share the benefit with the people of the whole world," asking why the British inflicted harm on the Chinese people through opium imports.

Lin demanded that foreigners surrender their opium stocks to the Chinese government for destruction and stop the trade in opium. When British merchants in Canton balked at Lin's instructions, he ordered the arrest of Lancelot Dent, head of the second largest foreign firm in Canton and president of the British Chamber of Commerce, in March 1839. Dent refused to comply with the arrest order, and 350 foreigners were blockaded inside their own quarters. Lin scored an apparent victory when the foreign community in Canton, after forty-seven days of blockade, gave up 20,283 chests of opium, with an estimated value of $9 million, an enormous sum in those days. But merchants had overstocked their supplies in anticipation of the legalization of the trade, and the British government representative in Canton promised to compensate the merchants for their losses. For Lin, the surrendering of the opium, which the Chinese flushed out to sea, was proof that foreigners accepted submission. The Chinese victory, however, was short-lived. As a member of the British Parliament put it, the opium merchants in Canton "belonged to a country unaccustomed to defeat, to submission or to shame."

A British fleet, including four newly armed steamers, entered Chinese waters in June 1840. For the Chinese, a steam-powered battleship was a new sight. British warships bombarded Chinese coastal regions near Canton and even sailed in shallow water upriver for a short way. On land, Qing soldiers commanded by hereditary bannermen—the Chinese equivalent to the equally out-of-date Ottoman janissaries—used spears and clubs, and a few imported matchlock muskets, against the modern artillery of British troops, many of whom were Indians supplied with percussion cap rifles. Still,

Steamer *Nemesis* Destroying Junks. The Opium War was fought between a newly industrialized power and an established landed empire. One of the major disparities between the two sides was military technology. Here is a scene of a British steam-powered warship, the *Nemesis,* sailing up the Pearl River toward the city of Canton, bombarding areas along the river at will and destroying Chinese ships that attempted to block its way.

along the Yangzi River, outgunned Chinese forces fought fiercely. Rather than surrender, many Qing soldiers killed their own wives and children before committing suicide.

The British prevailed, as the Qing preferred to sue for peace rather than risk all-out war. The British seized the tiny island of Hong Kong, and with the 1842 Treaty of Nanjing they received the right to trade in five treaty ports and forced the Chinese to pay an "indemnity" for the war and compensation for the opium destroyed by Lin. British traders were now given the right to trade directly with the Chinese (and not only through the Cohong; see Chapter 13) and to reside in the treaty ports.

That the British government would go to such lengths merely to force trade struck many Chinese as barbaric. In addition, subsequent treaties guaranteed the principle of extraterritoriality, which meant that the British and other foreign nationals would be tried in their own courts for crimes, rather than in Chinese courts, and would be exempt from Chinese law. Of further threat to Chinese autonomy, the British insisted that any privileges granted to future treaty signatories would also apply to them. Accordingly, if one European country acquired special rights, others would, too, which ensured all Europeans and North Americans a privileged position in China.

Still, China did not suffer India's fate and become a formal colony. To the contrary, in the mid-nineteenth century Europeans and North Americans were trading only on the outskirts of China and restricted their presence to a few coastal cities. Most Chinese did not encounter the Euro-

Chronology

	1700							
THE AMERICAS						*American Revolution, 1776–1783* ▮		
						Haitian Rebellion, 1791–1804 ▮		
						Eli Whitney invents the cotton gin, 1793 ▮		
EUROPE					*James Watt invents steam engine, 1769* ▮			
						French Revolution, 1789–1799 ▮		
RUSSIA AND OTTOMAN EMPIRE								
AFRICA								
SOUTH ASIA					*British establish company rule in India, 1765* ▮			
EAST ASIA					▮ *Chinese expansion under Qianlong emperor, 1736–1796*			

peans, and daily life for the majority of the Chinese went on as it had before the Opium War and the Treaty of Nanjing. Only the political leaders and urban dwellers were beginning directly to feel the foreign presence and to ponder what steps, if any, China might take to acquire European technologies, goods, and learning.

 # CONCLUSION

During the second half of the eighteenth century and into the early nineteenth century, changes wrought by politics and ideas, on the one hand, and commerce, industry, and technology, on the other, resulted in unprecedented upheaval in the Atlantic world. The reordering of the Atlantic world occurred against the background of several centuries of trade and imperial conquests, and it reverberated, to varying degrees, elsewhere around the world. By 1850, the world was more integrated economically, with Europe more than ever before at the center of global affairs.

The political crises and the economic and social revolutions in western Europe and the Americas disrupted polities around the world, though less so in China than anywhere else. In the Americas, colonial ties were severed; in France, the people toppled the monarchy, and dissidents threatened the same in Russia. Political upheavals did not rewrite the rules of state completely, but they did introduce a new public vocabulary that would enjoy increasing power as the nineteenth century unfolded: the language of the nation. Equally important, they made the idea of revolution—that societies could be changed in radical ways—empowering. In the Americas and parts of Europe, nation-states, with new symbols of authority, national armies, and a mystique of self-governing communities took shape around redefined social hierarchies of class, gender, and color. Western Europe, particularly Britain and France, emerged from the political crises of the late eighteenth century with determination to expand their influence beyond their borders. Their drive forced older empires such as Russia and the Ottoman state to undertake state-led reforms.

Commerce and industrialization played a decisive role in the reshuffling of economic and political power. Through the end of the seventeenth century, commerce bridged distant cultures; thereafter, as trade deepened and diversified, it began to transform those cultures. European governments and their armies compelled various countries—including Egypt, India, and China—to expand their trade with European merchants. Ultimately this meant that these and other countries were not free to pursue whatever economic policies they wished. Rather, they were expected to participate in a European-centered economy as exporters of raw materials and importers of European manufactures.

By the 1850s, the density and strength of trading ties had helped create a more interconnected world order. More of the world's peoples produced less for themselves and more for distant markets. Thanks to changes in the organization and technology of manufacturing, some areas of the world

---

1800 | | | | | | | | | | | **1900**

■ *Robert Fulton launches first commercial steamship, 1807*
■ *Revolutions in South America, 1810–1824*
■ *Brazil declares independence, 1822*

■ *Napoleon's empire, 1804–1815*   ■ *First railway launched in England, 1830*

■ *Reign of Mahmud II, Ottoman Empire, 1808–1839*
■ *Decembrist Revolt in Russia, 1825*
■ *Greek independence, 1829*

■ *French invasion of Egypt, 1798–1801*
■ *Abolition of Atlantic slave trade, 1803–1867*
■ *Reign of Muhammad Ali, Egypt, 1805–1848*

■ *Abolition of company trade monopoly in India, 1813*

White Lotus Rebellion, China, 1796–1804   ■ *Opium War, China, 1839–1842*

also made more goods than ever before. Although the world remained multicentered, economic power in the early nineteenth century was shifting to the western end of the Afro-Eurasian landmass. With manufactures to sell in Asia and a new ideology of free trade, Europe began to force open new markets, even to the point of colonizing them. Gold and silver, which had poured into China and India in the sixteenth and seventeenth centuries, were now flowing out to pay for European-dominated products like opium and textiles.

Nonetheless, the reordering of the world did not mean that Europe's rulers had uncontested control over other people, or even over their own people. Nor did it mean that the institutions and cultures of Asia and Africa ceased to be dynamic. Some countries became informal dependencies, like the Ottomans; others, like India, became outright European colonies. China escaped colonial rule but was forced into unfavorable trade relations with the Europeans. In sum, changes in commerce, manufacturing, technology, politics, and ideas combined to unsettle systems of rulership and to alter the economic and military balance between western Europe and the rest of the world.

STUDY QUESTIONS

Ⓢ WWNORTON.COM/STUDYSPACE

1. Describe the political and social revolutions that occurred in the Atlantic world between 1750 and 1850. What ideas inspired these changes? How far did revolutionaries extend these changes?

2. Compare and contrast how Latin American peoples achieved independence to the similar process in the United States. How similar were their goals? How well did they achieve these goals?

3. Explain the role of Napoleon in spreading the ideas of the Atlantic world's political and social revolution. How did Napoleon's armies spread the concept of nationalism? How did Napoleon's military pursuits affect political and social ferment in the Americas?

4. Explain how the Atlantic world's political and social revolution led to the end of the Atlantic slave trade. What economic, social, and political consequences did this development have on sub-Saharan Africa?

5. Define industrialization. Where did it begin? What other parts of the Atlantic world did it spread to during this time?

6. Explore how industrialization altered the societies that began to industrialize during this time. What impact did this process have on the environment? How were gender roles and familial relationships altered?

7. Analyze how the two intertwined Atlantic revolutions (political and industrial) altered the global balance of power. How did the Russian, Mughal, Ottoman, and Qing dynasties respond to this change?

8. To what extent did Great Britain emerge as the leading global power between 1750 and 1850. How did the British state shape political and economic developments around the world during this era?

FURTHER READINGS

Anderson, Fred, *Crucible of War: The Seven Years' War and the Fate of Empire in British North America, 1754–1766* (2000). The best synthesis of the "great war for empire" that set the stage for the American Revolution.

Bayly, C. A., *Indian Society and the Making of the British Empire* (1998). A useful work on the early history of the British conquest of India.

Blackburn, Robin, *The Overthrow of Colonial Slavery, 1776–1848* (1988). Places the abolition of the Atlantic slave trade and colonial slavery in a large historical context.

Brook, Timothy, and Bob Tadashi Wakabayashi (eds.), *Opium Regimes: China, Britain, and Japan, 1839–1952* (2000). Examines the role of opium in the various aspects of modern Chinese history.

Cambridge History of Egypt: Modern Egypt from 1517 to the End of the Twentieth Century, Vol. 2 (1998). Volume 2 contains authoritative essays on all aspects of modern Egyptian history, including the impact of the French invasion and the rule of Muhammad Ali.

Chaudhuri, K. N., *The Trading World of Asia and the East India Company, 1660–1760* (1978). An authoritative economic history of the East India Company's operations.

Crafts, N. F. R., *British Economic Growth During the Industrial Revolution* (1985). A pioneering study that emphasizes a long-term, more gradual process of adaptation to new institutional and social circumstances.

Doyle, William, *The Oxford History of the French Revolution* (1990). A highly detailed discussion of the course of events.

Elvin, Mark, *The Retreat of the Elephants: An Environmental History of China* (2004). A study of the different ways in which China's natural environment was shaped.

Fick, Carolyn E., *The Making of Haiti: The Saint Domingue Revolution from Below* (1990). Provides a detailed account of the factors that led to the great slave rebellion on the island of Haiti at the end of the eighteenth century.

Findley, Carter, *Bureaucratic Reform in the Ottoman Empire: The Sublime Porte, 1789–1922* (1980). A useful guide to Ottoman reform efforts in the nineteenth century.

Hevia, James, *Cherishing Men from Afar: Qing Guest Ritual and the Macartney Embassy of 1793* (1995). Offers a new interpretation of the nature of Sino-British conflict in the Qing period.

Hobsbawm, Eric, *Nations and Nationalism since 1780* (1990). Charts how the French Revolution generated a tradition of imagined realities of nationhood.

Hunt, Lynn, *Politics, Culture and Class in the French Revolution* (1984). Examines the influence of sociocultural shifts as causes and consequences of the French Revolution, emphasizing the symbols and practice of politics invented during the Revolution.

Jones, E. L., *Growth Recurring* (1988). Discusses the controversy over why the industrial revolution took place in Europe, stressing the unique ecological setting that encouraged long-term investment.

Kinsbruner, Jay, *Independence in Spanish America* (1994). A fine study of the Latin American revolutions for independence that argues that the struggle was as much a civil war as a fight for national independence.

Mokyr, Joel, *The Lever of Riches* (1990). An important study of the causes of the industrial revolution that emphasizes the role of small technological and organizational breakthroughs.

Naquin, Susan, and Evelyn Rawski, *Chinese Society in the Eighteenth Century* (1987). A survey of mid-Qing society.

Neal, Larry, *The Rise of Financial Capitalism* (1990). An important study of the making of financial markets.

Nikitenko, Aleksandr, *Up from Serfdom: My Childhood and Youth in Russia, 1804–1824* (2001). One of the very few recorded life stories of a Russian serf.

Pomeranz, Kenneth, *The Great Divergence: Europe, China, and the Making of the Modern World Economy* (2000). Offers explanations of why Europe and not some other place in the world, like parts of China or India, forged ahead economically in the nineteenth century.

Rudé, George, *Europe in the Eighteenth Century* (1972). Emphasizes the rise of a new class, the bourgeoisie, against the old aristocracy, as a cause of the French Revolution.

Wakeman, Frederic, Jr., "The Canton Trade and the Opium War," in John K. Fairbank (ed.), *The Cambridge History of China*, Vol. 10 (1978), pp. 163–212. The standard account of the episode.

Wong, R. Bin, *China Transformed: Historical Change and the Limits of European Experience* (2000). Draws attention to the relative autonomy of merchant capitalists in relation to dynastic states in Europe compared to China.

Wood, Gordon, *The Radicalism of the American Revolution* (1991). Makes a persuasive case for the revolutionary consequences of American independence and nationhood.

Wortman, Richard, *Scenarios of Power: Myth and Ceremony in Russian Monarchy*, 2 vols. (1995–2000). Examines how dynastic Russia confronted the challenges of the revolutionary epoch.

Absolutism Form of government where one body, usually the monarch, controls the right to make war, tax, judge, and coin money. The term was often used to refer to state monarchies in seventeenth- and eighteenth-century Europe.

Acid rain Precipitation containing heavy doses of sulfur, mainly from coal-fired plants.

African National Congress (ANC) Multiracial organization founded in 1912 in an effort to end racial discrimination in South Africa.

Afrikaners Descendants of the original Dutch settlers of South Africa; formerly referred to as Boers.

Akbarnamah Mughal intellectual Abulfazl's *Book of Akbar*, which attempted to reconcile the traditional Sufi interest in the inner life within the worldly context of a great empire.

Allies Term used to identify those states that fought against Germany in World War I and World War II.

American Railway Union Workers' union that initiated the Pullman Strike of 1894, which led to violence and ended in the leaders' arrest.

Amnesty International Nongovernmental organization formed to defend "prisoners of conscience"—those detained for their beliefs, race, sex, ethnic origin, language, or religion.

Anarchism Political belief that society should be a free association of its members, not bound by government, laws, or the police.

Angkor Wat A magnificent Khmer Vaishnavite temple that crowned the royal palace in Angkor. It had statues representing the Hindu pantheon of gods.

Anti-Federalists Critics of the U.S. Constitution who sought to defend the people against the power of the federal government and insisted on a bill of rights to protect individual liberties from government intrusion.

Apartheid Racial segregation policy of the Afrikaner-dominated South African government. Legislated in 1948 by the Afrikaner National Party, it had existed in South Africa for many years.

Asante state Located in present-day Ghana, this state was founded by the Asantes at the end of the seventeenth century. It grew in power in the next century because of its access to gold and its involvement in the slave trade.

Asiatic Society Cultural organization founded by British Orientalists who supported native culture but still believed in colonial rule.

Atlantic system New system of trade and expansion that linked Europe, Africa, and the Americas. It emerged in the wake of European voyages across the Atlantic Ocean.

Austro-Hungarian empire Dual monarchy established by the Habsburg family in 1867; it collapsed at the end of World War I.

Authoritarianism Centralized and dictatorial form of government, proclaimed by its adherents to be superior to parliamentary democracy and especially effective at mobilizing the masses. This idea was widely accepted in parts of the world during the 1930s.

Baby boom Post–World War II upswing in U.S. birth rates; it reversed a century of decline.

Baghdad Pact (1955) Middle Eastern military alliance between countries friendly with America who were also willing to align themselves with the western countries against the Soviet Union.

Balam Na Stone temple and place of pilgrimage for the Mayan people of Mexico's Yucatan peninsula.

Balfour Declaration Letter (November 2, 1917) by Lord Arthur J. Balfour, British Foreign Secretary, that promised a homeland for the Jews in Palestine.

Battle of Adwa (1896) Battle in which the Ethiopians defeated Italian colonial forces; it inspired many of Africa's later national leaders.

Battle of Wounded Knee (1890) Bloody massacre of Sioux Ghost Dancers by U.S. armed forces.

Bay of Pigs (1961) Unsuccessful invasion of Cuba by Cuban exiles supported by the U.S. government. The invaders intended to incite an insurrection in Cuba and overthrow the Communist regime of Fidel Castro.

Bedouins Nomadic pastoralists in the deserts of the Middle East.

Beer Hall Putsch (1923) Nazi intrusion into a meeting of Bavarian leaders in a Munich beer hall; the Nazis were attempting to force support for their cause; Adolf Hitler was imprisoned for a year after the incident.

Beghards (1500s) Eccentric European group whose members claimed to be in a state of grace that allowed them to do as they pleased—from adultery, free love, and nudity to murder; also called Brethren of Free Speech.

Berlin Airlift (1948) Supply of vital necessities to West Berlin by air transport primarily under U.S. auspices. It was initiated in response to a land and water blockade of the city instituted by the Soviet Union in the hope that the Allies would be forced to abandon West Berlin.

Berlin Wall Wall built by the Communists in Berlin in 1961 to prevent citizens of East Germany from fleeing to West Germany; torn down in 1989.

Bhakti Hinduism Popular form of Hinduism that emerged in the seventh century. The religion stresses devotion (*bhakti*) to God and uses vernacular languages (not Sanskrit) spoken by the common people.

Big man Leader of the extended household communities that formed village settlements in African rain forests.

Big whites French plantation owners in Saint Domingue (present-day Haiti) who created one of the wealthiest slave societies.

Bilad al-Sudan Arabic for "the land of the blacks"; it consisted of the land lying south of the Sahara.

Bilharzia Debilitating water-borne illness. It was widespread in Egypt, where it infected peasants who worked in the irrigation canals.

Bill of Rights The first ten amendments to the U.S. Constitution; ratified in 1791.

Black Death Epidemic of the bubonic plague that ravaged Europe, East Asia, and North Africa in the fourteenth century, killing perhaps as many as one-third of the European population.

Black Jacobins Nickname for the rebels in Saint Domingue, including Toussaint L'Ouverture, a former slave who led the slaves of this French colony in the world's largest and most successful slave insurrection.

Black Panthers Radical African-American group in the 1960s and 1970s; they advocated black separatism and pan-Africanism.

Black shirts Fascist troops of Mussolini's regime; the squads received money from Italian landowners to attack socialist leaders.

Black Tuesday (October 24, 1929) Historic day when the U.S. stock market crashed, plunging the United States and international trading systems into crisis and leading the world into the "Great Depression."

Blitzkrieg "Lightning war"; type of warfare in which the Germans, during World War II, used coordinated aerial bombing campaigns along with tanks and infantryman in motorized vehicles.

Bolsheviks Former members of the Russian Social Democratic Party who advocated the destruction of capitalist political and economic institutions and started the Russian Revolution. In 1918 the Bolsheviks changed their name to the Russian Communist Party.

Bourgeoisie The middle class. In Europe, they sought to be recognized not by birth or title, but by capital and property.

Boxer Protocol Written agreement between the victors of the Boxer Uprising and the Qing Empire in 1901 that placed western troops in Beijing and required the regime to pay exorbitant damages for foreign life and property.

Boxer Uprising (1899–1900) Chinese peasant movement that opposed foreign influence, especially that of Christian missionaries; it was put down after the Boxers were defeated by an army composed mostly of Japanese, Russians, British, French, and Americans.

Brahmans Priestly caste in India.

British Commonwealth of Nations Formed in 1926, the Commonwealth conferred "dominion status" on Britain's white settler colonies in Canada, Australia, and New Zealand.

Brown shirts Troops of German men who advanced the Nazi cause by holding street marches, mass rallies, and confrontations and by beating Jews and anyone who opposed the Nazis.

Bubonic plague Acute infectious disease caused by a bacterium transmitted to humans by fleas from infected rats. It ravaged Europe and parts of Asia in the fourteenth century. Sometimes referred to as the "black death."

Buddhism One of China's major religions, it extolled the life and teachings of the Indian ascetic Siddhartha Gautama (563–483 BCE).

Cahokia A commercial center for regional and long-distance trade in precolonial North America. Its hinterlands produced staples for urban consumers. In return, its crafts were exported inland by porters and to North American markets in canoes.

Calaveras Allegorical skeleton drawings by the Mexican printmaker and artist José Guadalupe Posada. The works drew on popular themes of betrayal, death, and festivity.

Caliphs Rulers of the Islamic community and political successors to Muhammad.

Candomblé Yoruba-based religion in northern Brazil; it interwove African practices and beliefs with Christianity.

Caravans Companies of men who transported and traded goods along overland routes in North Africa and central Asia; large caravans consisted of 600–1,000 camels and as many as 400 men.

Caravansarais Inns along major trade routes that accommodated large numbers of traders, their animals, and their wares.

Caravel Sailing vessel suited for nosing in and out of estuaries and navigating in waters with unpredictable currents and winds.

Carrack Ship used on open bodies of water, such as the Mediterranean.

Caste system Hierarchical system of organizing people and distributing labor.

Caste War of Yucatan (1847–1901) Conflict between Mayan Indians and the Mexican state over Indian autonomy and legal equality, which resulted in the Mexican takeover of the Yucatan peninsula.

Catholicism Religion headed by the pope in Vatican City (Rome); worship is centered in the gospel of Jesus Christ and the sacraments.

Caudillos South American local military chieftains.

Celali revolts (1595–1610) Peasant and artisan uprisings against the Ottoman state.

Central Powers Defined in World War I as Germany and Austria-Hungary.

Chan Chan Between 850 and 900, the Moche people founded the city of Chan Chan in modern-day Peru, with a core population of 30,000 inhabitants.

Chan Santa Cruz Separate Mayan community formed as part of a crusade for spiritual salvation and the complete cultural separation of the Mayan Indians; means "little holy cross."

Chapatis Flat, unleavened Indian bread.

Chartism (1834–1848) Mass democratic movement to pass the Peoples' Charter in Britain, granting male suffrage, secret ballot, equal electoral districts, and annual Parliaments, and absolving the requirement of property ownership for members of the Parliament.

Chernobyl (1986) Site in the Soviet Union (in Ukraine) of the meltdown of a nuclear reactor.

Chimu Empire South America's first empire, it developed during the first century of the second millennium in the Moche Valley on the Pacific Ocean.

Chinampas Floating gardens used by Aztecs in the 1300s and 1400s to grow crops.

Chinoiserie Chinese silks, teas, tableware, jewelry, and paper; popular among Europeans in the seventeenth and eighteenth centuries.

Church of England The established form of Christianity in England dating from the sixteenth century.

Civil Rights Act (1964) U.S. legislation that banned segregation in public facilities, outlawed racial discrimination in employment, and marked an important step in correcting legal inequality.

Civil service examinations A set of exams for the establishment of a bureaucratic elite that was instituted by the Song (China).

Civil War, American (1861–1865) Conflict between the northern and southern states of America; this struggle led to the abolition of slavery in the United States.

Clandestine presses Small printing operations that published banned texts in the early modern era, especially in Switzerland and the Netherlands.

Cohong Chinese merchant guild that traded with Europeans under the Qing dynasty.

Cold war (1945–1990) Ideological conflict in which the Soviet Union and Eastern Europe opposed the United States and Western Europe.

Colons French settler population in Algeria.

Communist Manifesto Pamphlet published by Karl Marx and Friedrich Engels in 1848 at a time when political revolutions were sweeping Europe. It called on the workers of all nations to unite in overthrowing capitalism.

Compromise of 1867 Agreement between the Habsburgs and the peoples living in Hungarian parts of the empire that the Habsburg state would be officially known as the Austro-Hungarian empire.

Concession areas Territories, usually ports, where Chinese emperors allowed European merchants to trade and European people to settle.

Confucianism The ethics, beliefs, and practices stipulated by the Chinese philosopher Kong Qiu, or Confucius (551–479 BCE).

Congo Independent State Large colonial state in Africa created by Leopold II, king of Belgium, during the 1880s, and ruled by him alone. After rumors of mass slaughter and enslavement, the Belgian parliament took the land and formed a Belgian colony.

Congress of Vienna (1814–1815) International conference to reorganize Europe after the downfall of Napoleon. European monarchies agreed to respect each other's borders and to cooperate in guarding against future revolutions and war.

Conquistadors Spanish military leaders who led the conquest of the New World in the sixteenth century.

Constantinople Former capital of the Byzantine Empire, renamed Istanbul after its conquest by the Ottomans in 1453.

Constitutional Convention (1787) Meeting to formulate the Constitution of the United States of America.

Contra rebels Opponents of the Sandinistas in Nicaragua; they were armed and financed by the United States and other anti-Communist countries (1980).

Conversos Jewish and Muslim converts to Christianity in the Iberian peninsula and the New World.

Corn Laws Laws that imposed tariffs on grain imported to Great Britain, intended to protect British farming interests. The Corn Laws were abolished in 1846 as part of a British movement in favor of free trade.

Counter-Reformation Movement to counter the spread of the Reformation; initiated by the Catholic Church at the Council of Trent in 1545.

Coup d'état Overthrow of established state by a group of conspirators, usually from the military.

Creoles Persons of full-blooded European descent who were born in the Americas.

Crimean War (1853–1856) War waged by Russia against Great Britain and France. Spurred by Russia's encroachment on Ottoman territories, the conflict revealed Russia's military weakness when Russian forces fell to British and French troops.

Crusades (1095–1291) In the late eleventh century, western Europeans launched the wave of attacks called the Crusades. The First Crusade began in 1095, when Pope Urban II appealed to the warrior nobility of France to free Jerusalem from Muslim rule. Four Crusades were fought over the next two centuries.

Cuban Missile Crisis (1962) Diplomatic standoff between the United States and the Soviet Union that was provoked by the Soviet Union's attempt to base nuclear missiles in Cuba; it brought the world close to a nuclear war.

Daimyo Ruling lords who commanded private armies in pre-Meiji Japan.

Dar al-Islam Arabic for "the House of Islam," it describes a sense of common identity.

D-Day (June 6, 1944) Day of the Allied invasion of Normandy under General Dwight Eisenhower to liberate western Europe from German occupation.

Decembrists Russian army officers who were influenced by events in revolutionary France and formed secret societies that espoused liberal governance. They were put down by Nicholas I in December 1825.

Declaration of Independence U.S. document stating the theory of government on which America was founded.

Declaration of the Rights of Man and Citizen (1789) French charter of liberties formulated by the National Assembly that marked the end of dynastic and aristocratic rule. The seventeen articles later became the preamble to the new constitution, which the Assembly finished in 1791.

Delhi sultanate The Turkish regime of northern India, which lasted from 1206 to 1526.

Devshirme System of taking non-Muslim children in place of taxes in order to educate them in Ottoman Muslim ways and prepare them for service in the sultan's bureaucracy.

Dhimmis Followers of religions, other than Islam, that were permitted by Ottoman law: Armenian Christians, Greek Orthodox Christians, and Jews.

Dien Bien Phu (1954) Defining battle in the war between French colonialists and the Viet Minh that secured North Vietnam for Ho Chi Minh and his army and left the south to form its own government to be supported by France and the United States.

Din-I-Ilahi "House of worship" in which the Mughal emperor Akbar engaged in religious debate with Hindu, Muslim, Jain, Parsi, and Christian theologians.

Directory Temporary military committee that took over the affairs of the state of France in 1795 from the radicals and held control until the coup of Napoleon Bonaparte.

Dominion in the British Commonwealth Canadian promise to keep up the country's fealty to the British crown, even after its independence in 1867. Later applied to Australia and New Zealand.

Duma The Russian parliament.

Dutch East India Company (1600–1858) British charter company created to outperform Portuguese and Spanish traders in the Far East; in the eighteenth century the company became, in effect, the ruler of a large part of India.

Dutch learning Broad term for European teachings that were strictly regulated by the shoguns inside Japan.

Earth Summit (1992) Meeting in Rio de Janeiro between many of the world's governments in an effort to address international environmental problems.

Eastern Front Battlefront between Berlin and Moscow during World War I and World War II.

Edict of Nantes (1598) Edict issued by Henry IV to end the French Wars of Religion. The edict declared France a Catholic country, but tolerated some Protestant worship.

Eiffel Tower Completed in 1889 for the Paris Exposition, this steel monument was twice the height of any other building at the time.

Eight-legged essay Highly structured essay form with eight parts, required on Chinese civil service examinations.

Ekpe Powerful slave trade institution that organized the supply and purchase of slaves inland from the Gulf of Guinea in West Africa.

Enabling Act (1933) Emergency act passed by the Reichstag (German parliament) that helped transform Hitler from Germany's chancellor, or prime minister, into a dictator following the suspicious burning of the Reichstag building and a suspension of civil liberties.

Encomenderos Commanders of the labor services of the colonized peoples in Spanish America.

Encomiendas Grants from European Spanish governors to control the labor services of colonized people.

Endeavor Ship of Captain James Cook, whose celebrated voyages to the South Pacific in the late eighteenth century supplied Europe with information about the plants, birds, landscapes, and people of this uncharted territory.

Engels, Friedrich (1820–1895) German social and political philosopher who collaborated with Karl Marx on many publications, including *The Communist Manifesto*.

English Navigation Act of 1651 Act stipulating that only English ships could carry goods between the mother country and its colonies.

Enlightenment Intellectual movement in eighteenth-century Europe stressing natural laws and reason as the basis of authority.

Estates-General French quasi-parliamentary body called in 1789 to deal with the financial problems that afflicted France. It had not met since 1614.

Eurasia The combined area of Europe and Asia.

European Union (EU) International body organized after World War II as an attempt at reconciliation between Germany and the rest of Europe. It initially aimed to forge closer industrial cooperation. Eventually, through various treaties, many European states relinquished some of their sovereignty, and the cooperation became a full-fledged union with a single currency, the euro, and with a somewhat less powerful common European parliament.

Examination system Examinations that were open to most males and used to recruit officials and bureaucrats in imperial China.

Exclusion Act of 1882 U.S. congressional act prohibiting nearly all immigration from China to the United States; fueled by animosity toward Chinese workers in the American West.

Ezo Present-day Hokkaido, Japan's fourth main island.

Fascists Radical right-wing group of the disaffected that formed around Mussolini in 1919 and a few years later came to power in Rome.

Fatehpur Sikri Mughal emperor Akbar's temporary capital near Agra.

February Revolution (1917) The first of two uprisings of the Russian Revolution, which led to the end of the Romanov dynasty.

Federal Deposit Insurance Corporation (FDIC) Created in 1933 to guarantee all bank deposits up to $5,000 as part of the New Deal in the United States.

Federal Republic of Germany (1949–1990) Country formed of the areas occupied by the Allies after World War II. Also known as West Germany, this country experienced rapid demilitarization, democratization, and integration into the world economy.

Federal Reserve Act (1913) U.S. legislation that created a series of boards to monitor the supply and demand of the nation's money.

Federalists Supporters of the ratification of the U.S. Constitution, which was written to replace the Articles of Confederation.

Ferangi An Arabic word meaning "Frank" that was used to describe Crusaders.

Feudalism A system that developed in medieval Europe after the collapse of the Carolingian Empire (814 CE) whereby each peasant was under the authority of a lord—in effect, landowners governed the people who lived on their land.

Fiefdoms Medieval economic and political units.

First World War A total war from August 1914 to November 1918, involving the armies of Britain, France, and Russia (the Allies) against those of Germany, Austria-Hungary, and the Ottoman Empire (the Central Powers). Italy joined the Allies in 1915, and the United States joined them in 1917, helping tip the balance in favor of the Allies, who also drew upon the populations and material of their colonial possessions. Also known as the Great War and World War I.

Five-Year Plan Soviet effort launched under Stalin in 1928 to replace the market with a state-owned and state-managed economy, to promote rapid economic development over a five-year period of time and thereby "catch and overtake" the leading capitalist countries. The First Five-Year Plan was followed by the Second Five-Year Plan (1933–1937), and so on, until the collapse of the Soviet Union in 1991.

Flagellants European social group that came into existence during the bubonic plague in the fourteenth century; they believed that the plague was the wrath of God.

Fluitschips Dutch shipping vessels that could carry heavy bulky cargo with relatively small crews.

Flying cash Letters of exchange—early predecessors of paper money—first developed by guilds in the northwestern Shanxi (China).

By the thirteenth century, paper money had eclipsed coins.

Forbidden City The palace city of the Ming and Qing dynasties (China).

Force Publique Colonial army used to maintain order in the Belgian Congo; during the early stages of King Leopold's rule, it was responsible for bullying local communities.

Free Officers Movement Secret organization of Egyptian junior military officers who came to power in a coup d'état in 1952, forced King Faruq to abdicate, and consolidated their own control through dissolving the parliament, banning opposing parties, and rewriting the constitution.

Front de Libération Nationale (FLN) Algerian anti-colonial, nationalist party that waged an eight-year war against French troops, beginning in 1854, that forced nearly all of the 1,000,000 colonists to leave.

Fulani Muslim group in West Africa that carried out religious revolts at the end of the eighteenth and the beginning of the nineteenth centuries in an effort to return to the pure Islam of the past.

Fur trade The trading of animal pelts (especially beaver skins) by Indians for European goods in North America.

Gandhi, Mohandhas (1869–1948) Indian leader who led a nonviolent struggle for India's independence from Britain.

Garrisons Military bases inside cities; often used for political purposes, such as protecting rulers and putting down domestic revolts or enforcing colonial rule.

Gauchos Argentine, Brazilian, and Uruguayan cowboys who wanted a decentralized federation, with autonomy for their provinces and respect for their way of life.

Gdansk shipyard Site of mass strikes in Poland that led in 1980 to the formation of the first independent trade union, Solidarity, in the Communist bloc.

Geneva Peace Conference (1954) International conference to restore peace in Korea and Indochina. The chief participants were the United States, the Soviet Union, Great Britain, France, the People's Republic of China, North Korea, South Korea, Vietnam, the Viet Minh party, Laos, and Cambodia. The conference resulted in the division of North and South Vietnam.

Genoa In 1300 CE, Genoa and Venice were two nodes of commerce linking Europe, Africa, and Asia. Genoese ships linked the Mediterranean to the coast of Flanders through consistent routes along the Atlantic coasts of Spain, Portugal, and France.

German Democratic Republic Nation founded from the Soviet zone of occupation of Germany after World War II; also known as East Germany.

German Social Democratic Party Founded in 1875, it was the most powerful Socialist party in Europe before 1917.

Ghost Dance American Indian ritual performed in the nineteenth century in the hope of restoring the world to precolonial conditions.

Girondins Liberal revolutionary group that supported the creation of a constitutional monarchy during the early stages of the French Revolution.

Gold Coast Name that European mariners and merchants gave to that part of West Africa from which gold was exported. This area was conquered by the British in the nineteenth century and became a British colony; upon independence, it became Ghana.

Grand Canal World's longest human-made waterway, located in China and extended in the thirteenth century.

"Greased cartridge" controversy Controversy spawned by the rumor that cow and pig fat had been used to grease the shotguns of the sepoys in the British army in India. Believing that this was a British attempt to defile their religion and speed their conversion to Christianity, the sepoys mutinied against the British officers.

Great Depression Worldwide depression following the U.S. stock market crash on October 29, 1929.

Great divide The division between economically developed nations and less developed nations.

Great East Asia Co-Prosperity Sphere Term used by the Japanese during the 1930s and 1940s to refer to Hong Kong, Singapore, Malaya, Burma, and other states that they seized during their run for expansion.

Great Game Competition over areas such as Turkistan, Persia (present-day Iran), and Afghanistan. The British (in India) and the Russians believed that controlling these areas was crucial to preventing their enemies' expansion.

Great League of Peace and Power Iroquois Indian alliance that united previously warring communities.

Great Leap Forward (1958–1961) Plan devised by Mao Zedong to achieve rapid agricultural and industrial growth in China. The plan failed miserably and more than 20 million people died.

Great Proletarian Cultural Revolution (1966–1976) Mass mobilization of urban Chinese youth inaugurated by Mao Zedong in an attempt to reinvigorate the Chinese revolution and to prevent the development of a bureaucratized Soviet style of communism; with this movement, Mao turned against his longtime associates in the Communist Party.

Great Trek Afrikaner migration to the interiors of Africa after the British abolished slavery in the empire in 1833.

Great War (1914–1918) World War I.

Greenbacks Members of the American political party of the late nineteenth century that worked to advance the interest of farmers by promoting cheap money.

Griots Counselors and other officials to the royal family in African kingships. They were also responsible for the preservation and transmission of oral histories.

Group Areas Act (1950) This act divided South Africa into separate racial and tribal areas and required Africans to live in their own separate communities, including the "homelands."

Guerillas Portuguese and Spanish peasant bands who resisted the revolutionary and expansionist efforts of Napoleon; after the French word *guerre.*

Guest workers Migrants looking for temporary employment abroad.

Gulag Administrative name for the vast system of forced labor camps under the Soviet regime; it originated in a small monastery near the Arctic Circle and spread throughout the Soviet Union and to other Soviet-style socialist countries. Penal labor was required of both ordinary criminals (rapists, murderers, thieves) and those accused of political crimes (counterrevolution, anti-Soviet agitation).

Gulf War (1991) Armed conflict between Iraq and a coalition of thirty-two nations, including the United States, Britain, Egypt, France, and Saudi Arabia. It was started by Iraq's invasion of Kuwait, which it had long claimed, on August 2, 1990.

Gunpowder empires Muslim empires of the Ottomans, Safavids, and the Mughals that used cannonry and gunpowder to advance their military causes.

Guomindang Nationalist party of China, founded just before World War I by Sun Yat-sen and later led by Chiang Kai-shek.

Habsburg Empire Ruling house of Austria, which once ruled both Spain and Central Europe but came to settle in lands along the Danube River; it played a prominent role in European affairs for many centuries. In 1867, the Habsburg Empire was reorganized into the Austro-Hungarian Dual Monarchy, and in 1918 it collapsed.

Hadith Sayings attributed to the Prophet Muhammad and his early converts. Used to guide the behavior of Muslim peoples.

Hagia Sophia The largest house of worship in all of Christendom, located in Constantinople and turned into a Muslim house of worship when Constantinople fell to Ottoman forces in 1453.

Hajj The pilgrimage to Mecca; an obligation for Muslims.

Han Chinese Inhabitants of China proper who considered others to be outsiders. They felt that they were the only authentic Chinese.

Hangzhou This city and former provincial seaport became the political center of the Chinese people in their ongoing struggles with northern steppe nomads. It was also one of China's gateways to the rest of the world by way of the South China Sea.

Harem Secluded women's quarters in Muslim households.

Harlem Renaissance Cultural movement in the 1920s that was based in Harlem, a part of New York City with a large African-American population. The movement gave voice to black novelists, poets, painters, and musicians, many of whom used their art to protest racism; also referred to as the "New Negro Movement."

Haussmannization The redevelopment and beautification of urban centers; named after the city planner who "modernized" mid-nineteenth-century Paris.

Heian period The period from 794 to 1185, during which began the pattern of regents ruling Japan in the name of the sacred emperor.

Hijra Tradition of Islam, whereby one withdraws from one's community to create another, more holy, one. The practice is based on the Prophet Muhammad's withdrawal from the city of Mecca to Medina in 622 CE.

Hindu revivalism Movement to reconfigure traditional Hinduism to be less diverse and more amenable to producing a narrowed version of Indian tradition.

Hiroshima Japanese port devastated by an atomic bomb on August 6, 1945.

Holy Russia Name applied to Muscovy and then to the Russian empire by Slavic Eastern Orthodox clerics who were appalled by the Muslim conquest in 1453 of Constantinople (the capital of Byzantium and of Eastern Christianity) and who were hopeful that Russia would become the new protector of the faith.

Home charges Fees India was forced to pay to Britain as its colonial master; these fees included interest on railroad loans, salaries to colonial officers, and the maintenance of imperial troops outside India.

Homo caudatus "Tailed man," believed by some European Enlightenment thinkers to be an early species of humankind.

Homo sapiens Term created by Linnaeus in 1737 and commonly used to refer to human beings. During the Enlightenment, many thinkers believed that the human species was divided into five subgroups, or races, identified by a combination of physical characteristics, including skin pigmentation and social qualities.

Huguenots French Protestants who endured severe persecution in the sixteenth and seventeenth centuries.

Hundred Days' Reform (1898) Abortive modernizing reform program of the Qing government of China.

Il Duce Term designating the fascist Italian leader, Benito Mussolini.

Il-khanate Mongol-founded dynasty in thirteenth-century Persia.

Imam Muslim religious leader and also a politico-religious descendant of Ali; believed by some to have a special relationship with Allah.

Indian Institutes of Technology (ITT) Originally designed as engineering schools to expand knowledge and to modernize India, ITTs produced a whole generation of pioneering computer engineers, many of whom moved to the United States.

Indian National Congress Formed in 1885, this political party was deeply committed to constitutional methods, industrialization, and cultural nationalism.

Indian National Muslim League Founded in 1906, the league was dedicated to advancing the political interests of Muslims in India.

Indulgences Church-sponsored fund-raising mechanism that gave certification that one's sins had been forgiven in return for money.

Inquisition Tribunal of the Roman Catholic Church that enforced religious orthodoxy during the Protestant Reformation.

International Monetary Fund (IMF) Agency founded in 1944 to help restore financial order in Europe and the rest of the world, to revive international trade, and to support the financial concerns of Third World governments.

Invisible hand As described in Adam Smith's *The Wealth of Nations,* the idea that the operations of a free market produce economic efficiency and economic benefits for all.

Iron Curtain Term popularized by Winston Churchill after World War II to refer to a rift, or an iron curtain, that divided western Europe, under American influence, from eastern Europe, under the domination of the Soviet Union.

Jacobins Radical French political group that came into existence during the French Revolution and executed the French king and sought to remake French culture.

Jacquerie (1358) French peasant revolt in defiance of feudal restrictions.

Jagat Seths Enormous trading and banking empire in eastern India.

Janissaries Corps of infantry soldiers recruited as children from the Christian provinces of the Ottoman Empire and raised with intense loyalty to the Ottoman state. The Ottoman sultan used these forces to control local communities and as his personal bodyguards.

Jati Social groups as defined by Hinduism's caste system.

Jesuit Religious order founded by Ignatius Loyola to counter the inroads of the Protestant Reformation; the Jesuits were active in politics, education, and missionary work.

Jihad To engage in struggle and, if necessary, holy war toward the advancement of the cause of Islam.

Jih-pen Chinese for "Japan."

Jim Crow laws Laws that codified racial segregation and inequality in the southern part of the United States after the Civil War.

Jizya Special tax that non-Muslims were forced to pay to their Islamic rulers in return for which they were given security and property and granted cultural autonomy.

Jong Large oceangoing vessels built by Southeast Asians; they sailed the regional trade routes from the fifteenth century to the early sixteenth century.

Junks Trusty seafaring vessels used in the South China Seas after 1000 CE. They helped make shipping by sea less dangerous.

Kabuki Theater performance that combined song, dance, and skillful staging to dramatize conflicts between duty and passion in Tokogawa, Japan.

Kamikaze Japanese for "divine winds" or typhoons; such a storm saved Japan from a Mongol attack.

Kanun Highly detailed system of Ottoman administrative law that jurists developed to deal with matters not treated in the religious law of Islam.

Keynesian Revolution Post-Depression economic ideas developed by the British economist John Maynard Keynes, wherein the state took a greater role in managing the economy, stimulating it by increasing the money supply and creating jobs.

KGB Soviet political police and spy agency, formed as the Cheka not long after the Bolshevik coup in October 1917. Grew to more than 750,000 operatives with military rank by the 1980s.

Khanate Major political unit of the vast Mongol empire. There were four Khanates, including the Yuan empire in China, forged by Chinggis Khan's grandson Kubilai.

Khmers In what is modern-day Cambodia, the Khmers created the most powerful empire in Southwest Asia between the tenth and thirteenth centuries.

Kiev After the eleventh century, Kiev (in present-day Ukraine) became one of the great cities of Europe. It was built to be a small-scale Constantinople on the Dnieper.

Kikuyu Kenya's largest ethnic group; organizers of a revolt against the British in the 1950s.

Kingdom of Awadh One of the most prized lands for annexation, the Kingdom of Awadh was the fertile, opulent, and traditional vestige of Mughal rule in India.

Kizilbash Mystical, Turkish-speaking tribesmen who facilitated the Safavid rise to power.

Koprulu reforms Named after two grand viziers who revitalized the Ottoman Empire in the seventeenth century through administrative and budget trimming as well as by rebuilding the military.

Kremlin Once synonymous with the Soviet government, it refers to Moscow's walled city center.

Kshatriyas Warriors within the caste system of Hinduism.

Ku Klux Klan Racist organization that first emerged in the U.S. South after the Civil War and then gained national strength as a radically traditionalist movement during the 1920s.

Kulaks Originally a pejorative word used to designate better-off peasants, it was used in the late 1920s and early 1930s to refer to any peasant, rich or poor, perceived as an opponent of the Soviet regime. Russian for "fist."

Labour Party Founded in Britain in 1900, this party represented workers and was based on socialist principles.

League of Nations Organization founded after World War I to solve international disputes through arbitration; it was dissolved in 1946 and its assets were transferred to the United Nations.

Lenin, Nikolai (1870–1924) Leader of the Bolshevik Revolution in Russia and the first leader of the Soviet Union.

Liberalism Political and social theory that advocates representative government, free trade, and freedom of speech and religion.

Little Europes Between 1100 and 1200 CE, these were urban landscapes composed of castles, churches, and towns in what are today Poland, the Czech Republic, Hungary, and the Baltic States.

Long March (1934–1935) Trek of over 10,000 kilometers by Mao Zedong and his Communist followers to establish a new base of operations in northwestern China.

Lord Privileged landowner who exercised authority over the people who lived on his land.

Lost generation Refers to the 17 million former members of the Red Guard and other Chinese youth who were denied education from the late 1960s to the mid-1970s as part of the Chinese government's attempt to prevent political disruptions.

Louisiana Purchase (1803) American purchase of French territory from Napoleon, including much of the present-day United States between the Mississippi River and the Rocky Mountains.

Luftwaffe German air force.

Maastricht Treaty (1991) Treaty that formed the European Union, a fully integrated trading and financial bloc with its own bureaucracy and elected representatives.

Madrassas Higher schools of Muslim education that taught law, the Quran, religious sciences, and the regular sciences.

Mahdi The "chosen one" in Islam whose appearance was supposed to foretell the end of the world and the final day of reckoning for all people.

Maji-Maji Revolt (early 1900s) Swahili insurrection against German colonialists; inspired by the belief that those who were anointed with specially blessed water (*maji*) would be immune to bullets. It resulted in 200,000–300,000 African deaths.

Manaus Opera House Opera house built in the interior of Brazil in a lucrative rubber-growing area at the turn of the twentieth century.

Manchukuo Japanese puppet state in Manchuria in the 1930s.

Mandate of heaven Insistence that the ruling family of China belonged in power as a calling from above. The ruler could potentially lose the mandate if he did not properly discharge his duties.

Mande The Mande or Mandinka people lived in the area between the bend in the Senegal River and the bend in the Niger River east to west and from the Senegal River and Bandama River north to south. Their civilization emerged around 1100 CE.

Manifest Destiny Belief that it was God's will for the American people to expand their territory and political processes across the North American continent.

Maroon community Sanctuary for runaway slaves in the Americas.

Marshall Plan Economic aid package given by the United States to Europe after World War II in hopes of a rapid period of reconstruction and economic gain, thereby securing the countries who received the aid from a Communist takeover.

Marx, Karl (1818–1883) German philosopher and economist who created Marxism and believed that a revolution of the working classes would overthrow the capitalist order and create a classless society.

Mau-Mau Revolt (1952–1957) Uprising orchestrated by a Kenyan guerilla movement; this conflict forced the British to grant independence to the black majority in Kenya.

Maxim gun European weaponry that was capable of firing many bullets per second; it was used against Africans in the conquest of the continent.

Mayans Native American peoples whose widespread and culturally and politically sophisticated empire encompassed lands in present-day Mexico and Guatemala. The empire was flourishing when the Spanish arrived at the end of the fifteenth century.

McCarthyism Campaign by Republican senator Joseph McCarthy in the late 1940s and early 1950s to uncover closet Communists, particularly in the State Department and in Hollywood.

Meat Inspection Act (1906) Provided for government supervision of meat-packing operations; it was part of a broader "Progressive" reform movement dedicated to correcting the negative consequences of urbanization and industrialization in the United States.

Mecca Major commercial city of the Arabian Peninsula in the sixth century CE at which time the founder of Islam, Muhammad, was born and achieved prominence. With the spread of Islam, the city became the chief religious pilgrimage destination for Muslims.

Meiji Empire Empire created under the leadership of Mutsuhito, emperor of Japan from 1868 until 1912. During the Meiji period

Japan became a world industrial and naval power.

Meiji Restoration The reign of the Meiji emperor, which was characterized by a new nationalist identity, economic advances, and political transformation.

Mercantilism Belief that a country's wealth and power were based on a favorable balance of trade (more exports and imports) and the accumulation of precious metals.

Mercosur Free-trade pact between the governments of Argentina, Brazil, Paraguay, and Uruguay.

Mestizos Mixed-blood offspring of Spanish settlers and native Indians.

Métis Mixed-blood offspring of French settlers and native Indians.

Mexican Revolution (1910) Conflict fueled by the unequal distribution of land and by disgruntled workers; it erupted when political elites split over the succession of General Porfirio Díaz after decades of his rule. The fight lasted over ten years and cost one million lives, but resulted in a widespread reform and a new constitution.

Mfecane African political revolts in the first half of the nineteenth century that were caused by the expansionist methods of King Shaka of the Zulu people.

Millets Minority religious communities of the Ottoman Empire.

Minaret Slender tower within a mosque from which Muslims are called to prayer.

Minbar Pulpit inside a mosque from which Muslim religious speakers broadcast their message to the faithful.

Mission civilisatrice Term French colonizers used to refer to France's form of "rationalized" colonial rule, which attempted to bring "civilization" to the "uncivilized."

Moche At the height of the Chimu Empire, the Moche people extended their power over several valleys in what is modern-day Peru.

Model T First automobile, manufactured by the Ford Motor Company of Henry Ford, to be priced reasonably enough to be sold to the masses.

Mosque Place of worship for the people of Islam.

Mound people A name for the people of Cahokia, since its landscape was dominated by earthen monuments in the shapes of mounds. The mounds were carefully maintained and were the places from which Cahokians paid respect to spiritual forces.

Muckrakers Journalists who aimed to expose political and commercial corruption in late-nineteenth- and early-twentieth-century America.

Muftis Experts on Muslim religious law.

Muhammad (570–632 CE) The founder of Islam, he claimed to be the prophet whom God (Allah) had chosen for his final revelation to humankind.

Muhammad Ali Ruler of Egypt between 1805 and 1848, he initiated a set of modernizing reforms that sought to make Egypt competitive with the great powers.

Mullahs Religious leaders in Iran who in the 1970s led a movement opposing Shah Reza Pahlavi and denounced American materialism and secularism.

Multinational corporations Corporations based in many different countries that have global investment, trading, and distribution goals.

Mutiny of 1857 Indian rebellion against the English East India Company to bring religious purification, an egalitarian society, and local and communal solidarity without the interference of British rule.

Muslim Brotherhood Egyptian organization founded in 1938 by Hassan al-Banna. It attacked liberal democracy as a cover for middle-class, business, and land-owning interests and fought for a return to a purified Islam.

Muslim League National Muslim party of India.

Mussolini, Benito (1883–1945) Italian dictator and founder of the fascist movement in Italy.

Muwahhidin A term meaning "unitarians"; these were followers of the Wahhabi Movement that emerged in the Arabian peninsula in the eighteenth century.

Nagasaki Second Japanese city to be hit by an atomic bomb near the end of World War II.

Napoleonic Code Legal code drafted by Napoleon in 1804, it distilled different legal traditions to create one uniform law. The code confirmed the abolition of feudal privileges of all kinds and set the conditions for exercising property rights.

National Assembly of France Governing body of France that succeeded the Estates-General in 1789 during the French Revolution. It was composed of, and defined by, the delegates of the Third Estate.

National Association for the Advancement of Colored People (NAACP) Founded in 1910, this U.S. civil rights organization was dedicated to ending inequality and segregation for black Americans.

National Recovery Administration (NRA) New Deal agency created in 1933 to prepare codes of fair administration and to plan for public works. It was later declared unconstitutional.

National Socialist German Workers Party (Nazi Party) German organization dedicated to winning workers over from socialism to nationalism; the first Nazi Party platform combined nationalism with anticapitalism and anti-Semitism.

Native learning Japanese movement to promote nativist intellectual traditions and the celebration of Japanese texts.

Native paramountcy British form of "rationalized" colonial rule, which attempted to bring "civilization" to the "uncivilized" by proclaiming that when the interests of European settlers in Africa clashed with those of the African population, the latter should take precedence.

Natural rights Belief that emerged in eighteenth-century western Europe and North America that rights fundamental to human nature were discernible to reason and should be affirmed in human-made law.

Needle compass A crucial instrument made available to navigators after 1000 CE that helped guide sailors on the high seas. It was a Chinese invention.

Negritude Statement of the virtues of the black identity and the validation of African culture and the African past, even in a westernizing world. This idea was shaped by African and African-American intellectuals like Senegal's first president, Léopold Sédar Senghor.

New Deal President Franklin Delano Roosevelt's package of government reforms that were enacted during the 1930s to provide jobs for the unemployed, social welfare programs for the poor, and security to the financial markets.

New Economic Policy Enacted decrees of the Bolsheviks between 1921 and 1927 that grudgingly sanctioned private trade and private property.

New Negro Movement Cultural movement in the 1920s that gave voice to black novelists, poets, painters, and musicians, many of whom used their art to protest racism; also referred to as the "Harlem Renaissance."

Nō drama Masked theater favored by Japanese bureaucrats and regional lords during the Tokogawa period.

Nongovernmental organizations (NGOs) Term used to refer to private organizations like the Red Cross that play a large role in international affairs.

North American Free Trade Agreement (NAFTA) Treaty negotiated in the early 1990s to promote free trade between Canada, the United States, and Mexico.

North Atlantic Treaty Organization (NATO) International organization set up in 1949 to provide for the defense of western European countries and the United States from the perceived Soviet threat.

Northwest passage Long-sought marine passageway between the Atlantic and Pacific oceans.

Oceania Collective name for the lands of the Central and Southern Pacific Ocean.

Open Door Policy As European imperial powers carved out spheres of trade in late-nineteenth-century China, American leaders worried that the United States would be excluded from trade with China. To prevent this, American Secretary of State John Hay proposed a policy that would give all foreign nations equal access to trade with China.

Opium War (1839–1842) War fought between the British and Qing China over British trade in opium; resulted in the ceding of Hong Kong to the British.

Organization of Petroleum Exporting Countries (OPEC) International association established in 1960 to coordinate price and supply policies of oil-producing states.

Orientalists Western scholars who specialized in the study of the East.

Pacific War (1879–1883) War between Chile and the alliance of Bolivia and Peru.

Pan-Germanism Movement to encourage German-speaking peoples to think of themselves as members of a German race, with their identities fixed by blood and "race" rather than defined by state boundaries.

Pan-Islamism Movement to overcome political and religious differences within the Islamic world, including the divide between Sunni and Shiite Muslims, in order to make a common cause against the West.

Pan-Slavism Movement to unite all Slavs (Czech, Polish, Serbian, and Ukrainian) against their Austrian, German, and Ottoman overlords.

Pansophia Ideal republic of inquisitive Christians united in the search for knowledge of nature as a means of loving God.

Papal Of, relating to, or issued by a pope.

Patria French, meaning "fatherland."

Pax Mongolica Term that refers to the political and especially the commercial stability that the vast Mongol Empire provided for the travelers and merchants of Eurasia during the thirteenth and fourteenth centuries.

Peace Preservation Act (1925) Act instituted in Japan that specified up to ten years hard labor for any member of an organization advocating a basic change in the political system or the abolition of private property.

Pearl Harbor American naval base in Hawaii on which the Japanese launched a surprise attack on December 7, 1941, bringing the United States into World War II.

Peninsular War (1808–1814) Conflict in which the Portuguese and Spanish populations, supported by the British, resisted the French invasion under Napoleon of the Iberian peninsula.

Peninsulars Spaniards who, although born in Spain, resided in the Spanish colonial territories. They regarded themselves as superior to Spaniards born in the colonies (Creoles).

Peoples' Charter Between 1839 and 1842 over 3 million British signed this document calling for universal suffrage for adult males, the secret ballot, electoral districts, and annual parliamentary elections.

Peterloo Massacre (1819) The killing of 11 and wounding of 460 following a peaceful demonstration for political reform by workers in Manchester, England.

Phalanx Utopian-like communities, designed by Charles Fourier, where 1,500 to 1,600 people and 810 personality types would create an economic system free of middle men and full of comforts and rewards that would make working enjoyable.

Pochteca Archaic term for merchants of the Mexicos.

Polyglot communities Societies composed of diverse linguistic and ethnic groups.

Populists Members of a political movement that supported U.S. farmers in late-nineteenth-century America. The term is often used generically to refer to political groups who appeal to the majority of the population.

Potato famine (1840s) Severe famine in Ireland that led to the rise of radical political movements and the migration of large numbers of Irish to the United States.

Prague Spring (1968) Program of liberalization under a new Communist party in Czechoslovakia that strove to create a democratic and pluralist socialism.

Predestinarian Belief of many sixteenth- and seventeenth-century Protestant groups that God had foreordained the lives of individuals, including their bad and good deeds.

Primitivism Western art movement of the late-nineteenth and early-twentieth centuries that drew upon the so-called primitive art forms of Africa, Oceania, and pre-Columbian America.

Progressive movement U.S. reform movement in the early twentieth century that aimed to eliminate political corruption, improve working conditions, and regulate the power of large industrial and financial enterprises.

Prophet's Town Indian village that was burned down by American forces in the early nineteenth century.

Protestantism Division of Christianity that emerged in sixteenth-century western Europe at the time of the Reformation. It focused on individual spiritual needs and rejected the authority of the papacy and the Catholic clergy.

Pullman Strike (1894) American Railway Union strike in response to wage cuts and firings.

Puppet states Governments with little power in the international arena that follow the dictates of their more powerful neighbors or patrons.

Puritans Seventeenth-century reform group of the Church of England; also known as dissenters or nonconformists.

Qadiriyya Sufi order that facilitated the spread of Islam into West Africa.

Qadis Judges in the Ottoman Empire.

Quetzalcoatl Ancient deity and legendary ruler of Native American peoples living in Mexico.

Quran (often spelled Koran) Islam's holy book; composed of Allah's revelations.

Radicals Widely used term in nineteenth-century Europe that referred to those individuals and political organizations that favored the total reconfiguration of Europe's old state system.

Raj Referred to the British crown's administration of India following the end of the East India Company's rule after the Mutiny of 1857.

Ramadan Ninth month of the Muslim year, during which all Muslims must fast during daylight hours.

Rape of Nanjing Attack against the Chinese in which the Japanese slaughtered at least 100,000 civilians and raped thousands of women between December 1937 and February 1938.

Rashtriya Swayamsevak Sangh (**RSS**) (1925) Campaign to organize Hindus as a militant, modern community in India; translated in English as "National Volunteer Organization."

Reconquista The Spanish reconquest of territories lost to the Islamic Empire, beginning with Toledo in 1061.

Red Guards Chinese students who were the shock troopers in the early phases of Mao's Cultural Revolution in 1966–1968.

Red Lanterns Female supporters of the Chinese Boxers who rebelled against foreign intrusions in China at the turn of the twentieth century. Most were teenage girls and unmarried women and dressed in red garments.

Red Turbans Diverse religious movement in China during the fourteenth century that spread the belief that the world was drawing to an end as Mongol rule was collapsing.

Reds The Bolsheviks.

Reformation Religious and political movement in sixteenth-century Europe that led to the breakaway of Protestant groups from the Catholic Church.

Reich German empire composed of Denmark, Austria, and parts of western France.

Reichstag The German parliament.

Reign of Terror Campaign at the height of the French Revolution in the early 1790s that used violence, including systematic execution of opponents of the Revolution, to purge France of its enemies and to extend the Revolution beyond its borders; radicals executed as many as 40,000 persons who were judged enemies of the state.

Renaissance Term meaning "rebirth" that historians use to characterize the expanded cultural production of European nations between 1430 and 1550. Emphasized a break from the church-centered medieval world and a new concept of humans as the center of the world.

Restoration period (1815–1848) European movement after the defeat of Napoleon to restore Europe to its pre-French revolutionary status and to quash radical movements.

Roving bandits Large bands of dispossessed and marginalized peasants who vented their anger at tax collectors in the waning years of the Ming dynasty.

Russification Programs to assimilate people of over 146 dialects into the Russian empire.

S.S. (*Schutzstaffel*) Hitler's security police force.

Sack of Constantinople In 1204 Frankish armies sacked the capital city of Constantinople.

Sacred kingships Institutions that marked the centralized politics of West Africa. The inhabitants of these kingships believed that their kings were descendants of the gods.

Salt March (1930) A 240-mile trek to the sea in India, led by Mohandas Gandhi, to gather salt for free, thus breaking the British colonial monopoly on salt.

Samurai Japanese warriors who made up the private armies of Japanese daimyos.

Sandinista coalition Left-leaning Nicaraguan coalition of the 1970s and 1980s.

Santería African-based religion, blended with Christian influences, that was first practiced by slaves in Cuba.

Sati Hindu practice whereby a woman was burned to death on the pyre of her dead husband.

Satyagraha Moral and political philosophy of nonviolent resistance developed by Indian National Congress leader Mohandas Gandhi.

Scramble for Africa European rush to colonize parts of Africa at the end of the nineteenth century.

SEATO (Southeast Asia Treaty Organization) Military alliance of pro-American, anti-Communist states in Southeast Asia in 1954.

Second World Term invented during the cold war to refer to the Communist countries, as opposed to the West (or First World) and the former colonies (or Third World).

Second World War Worldwide war that began in September 1939 in Europe, and even earlier in Asia, and pitted Britain, the United States, and the Soviet Union (the Allies) against Nazi Germany, Japan, and Italy (the Axis).

Self-Strengthening Movement Movement in which reformist Chinese bureaucrats attempted to adopt western elements of learning and technological skill in the latter half of the nineteenth century.

Semu This term referred to "outsiders" or non-Chinese people—Mongols, Tanguts, Khitan, Jurchen, Muslims, Tibetans, Persians, Turks, Nestorians, Jews, and Armenians—who became a new ruling elite over a Han majority population in late-thirteenth-century China.

Sepoys Hindu and Muslim recruits of the East India Company's military force.

Serfs Peasants who farmed the land and paid fees to be protected and governed by lords under a system of rule called feudalism.

Seven Years' War (1756–1763) Worldwide war that ended when Prussia defeated Austria, establishing itself as a European power, and when Britain gained control of India and many of France's colonies through the Treaty of Paris.

Shah Traditional title of Persian rulers.

Shamisen Three-stringed instrument, often played by Japanese geisha.

Shanghai School Style of painting characterized by an emphasis on spontaneous brushwork, feeling, and the incorporation of western influences into classical Chinese pieces.

Sharia Laws of Islam that regulate the spiritual and secular actions of Muslims.

Sharpeville Massacre (1960) Massacre of sixty-nine black Africans when police fired upon a rally against the recently passed laws requiring non-white South Africans to carry identity papers.

Shawnees Native American tribe that inhabited the Ohio valley during the eighteenth century.

Shays's Rebellion (1786) Uprising of armed farmers when the Massachusetts state government refused to offer them economic relief.

Shiism One of the two main branches of Islam. Shiites recognize Ali, the fourth caliph, and his descendants as rightful rulers of the Islamic world; practiced in the Safavid empire.

Shinto Japan's official religion; it promoted the state and the emperor's divinity; meaning "the way of the gods."

Shogun Archaic term for the military ruler of Japan. From 1192 to 1333, the Kamakura shoguns served as military "protectors" of the ruler in the city of Heian.

Shudras Peasants and laborers in Hinduism's caste system.

Silicon Valley Valley between the California cities of San Francisco and San Jose, known for its innovative computer and high-technology industries.

Silver Islands Term used by European merchants in the sixteenth century to refer to Japan, because of its substantial trade in silver with China.

Sino-Japanese War (1894–1895) Conflict over the control of Korea in which China was forced to cede the province of Taiwan to Japan.

Sipahi Urdu for soldier.

Social Darwinism Belief that Charles Darwin's theory of evolution was applicable to humans and justified the right of the ruling classes or countries to dominate the weak.

Social Security Act (1935) New Deal act that instituted old-age pensions and insurance for the unemployed.

Socialism Political ideology that calls for a classless society with collective ownership of all property.

Solidarity The Communist bloc's first independent trade union, it was established in Poland at the Gdansk shipyard.

Song dynasty This dynasty took over the mandate of heaven for three centuries starting in 976 CE. It was an era of many economic and political successes, but the Song eventually lost northern China to nomadic tribes.

Song porcelain A type of porcelain perfected during the Song period that was light, durable, and beautiful.

South African War (1899–1902) Often called the Boer War, this conflict between the British and Dutch colonists of South Africa resulted in bringing two Afrikaner republics under the control of the British.

Soviet bloc International alliance that included the East European countries of the Warsaw Pact as well as the Soviet Union, but also came to include Cuba.

Spanish-American War (1898) War between the United States and Spain in Cuba, Puerto Rico, and the Philippines. It ended with a treaty in which the United States took over the Philippines, Guam, and Puerto Rico; Cuba won partial independence.

St. Bartholomew's Day Massacre Massacre in Paris of French Protestants by Catholics in 1572.

Stalin, Joseph (1879–1953) Leader of the Communist Party and the Soviet Union; sought to create "socialism in one country."

Strait of Malacca The seagoing gateway to Southeast and East Asia.

Strategic Defense Initiative ("Stars Wars") Master plan, championed by U.S. president Ronald Reagan in the 1980s, that envisions the deployment of satellites and space missiles to protect the United States from incoming nuclear bombs.

Suez Canal Built in 1869 across the Isthmus of Suez to connect the Mediterranean Sea with the Red Sea and to lower the costs of international trade.

Sufi brotherhoods Mystics within Islam who were responsible for the expansion of Islam into many regions of the world.

Sufism Emotional and mystical form of Islam that appealed to the common people.

Sultan An Islamic political leader. In the Ottoman Empire, the sultan combined a warrior ethos with an unwavering devotion to Islam.

Sun Yat-sen (1866–1925) Chinese revolutionary and founder of the Nationalist Party in China.

Sunni Orthodox Islam, as opposed to Shiite Islam.

Supranational organizations International organizations such as NGOs, the World Bank, and the IMF.

Survival of the fittest Charles Darwin's belief that as animal populations grew and resources became scarce, a struggle for existence arose, the outcome of which was that only the "fittest" survived.

Swadeshi Movement Voluntary organizations in India that championed the creation of indigenous manufacturing enterprises and schools of nationalist thought, in order to gain autonomy from Britain.

Syndicalism Organization of workplace associations that included unskilled labor.

Tabula rasa Term used by John Locke to describe the human mind before it begins to acquire ideas from experience; French for "clean slate."

Taiping Heavenly Kingdom (Heavenly Kingdom of Great Peace) Religious sect established by the Chinese prophet Hong Xiuquan in the mid-nineteenth century. The group struggled to "restore" the heavenly kingdom, imagined as a just and egalitarian order.

Taiping Rebellion Chinese rebellion against the Manchu leaders, led by Hong Xiuquan.

Taj Mahal Royal palace of the Mughal empire, built by Shah Jahan in the seventeenth century in homage to his wife.

Tale of Genji Written by Lady Murasaki in the eleventh century, a Japanese work that gives vivid accounts of Heian court life; Japan's first novel.

Talking cures Psychological practice developed by Sigmund Freud whereby the symptoms of neurotic and traumatized patients would decrease after regular periods of thoughtful discussion.

Tanzimat The reorganization period of the Ottoman Empire in the mid-nineteenth century; modernizing reforms affected the military, trade, foreign relations, and civilian life.

Tappers Rubber workers in Brazil, mostly either Indian or mixed-blood people.

Tarascans Mesoamerican society of the 1400s; rivals to and sometimes subjects of the Aztecs.

Tatish Ruler of Chan Santa Cruz during the Mexican Caste War; meaning "father."

Tekkes Schools that taught devotional strategies and the religious knowledge for students to enter Sufi orders and become masters of the brotherhood.

Third Estate The French people minus the clergy and the aristocracy; this term was popularized in the late eighteenth century and used to exalt the power of the bourgeoisie during the French Revolution.

Third Reich The German state from 1933 to 1945 under Adolf Hitler.

Third World Nations of the world, mostly in Asia, Latin America, and Africa, that were not highly industrialized like First World nations or tied to the Soviet Bloc (the Second World).

Thirty Years' War (1618–1648) Begun as a conflict between Protestants and Catholics in Germany, it escalated into a general European war fought against the unity and power of the Holy Roman Empire.

Tiananmen Square Largest public square in the world and site of the pro-democracy movement in 1989 that resulted in the killing of as many as a thousand protesters by the Chinese army.

Tiers monde French intellectuals coined this term meaning "Third World" to describe countries seeking a "third way" between Soviet communism and western capitalism.

Tiwanaku Another name for Tihuanaco, the first Great Andean polity, on the shores of Lake Titicaca.

Tlaxcalans A Mesoamerican society of the 1400s; these people were enemies of the powerful Aztec empire.

Tokugawa Shogunate Founded in 1603, this hereditary military administration ruled Japan while keeping the emperor as a figurehead; it was toppled in 1868 by reformers who felt that Japan should adopt, not reject, Western influences.

Toltecs By 1000, the Toltecs had filled the political vacuum created by the decline of the city of Teotihuacan.

Topkapi Palace Political headquarters of the Ottoman Empire, it was located in Istanbul.

Total war All-out war involving civilian populations as well as military forces, often used in reference to World War II.

Trans-Siberian Railroad Railroad built over very difficult terrain between 1891 and 1903, and subsequently expanded; it created an overland bridge for troops, peasant settlers, and commodities to move between Europe and the Pacific.

Treaty of Brest-Litovsk (1918) Separate peace between imperial Germany and the new Bolshevik regime in Russia. The treaty acknowledged the German victory on the Eastern Front and withdrew Russia from the war.

Treaty of Nanjing (1842) Treaty between China and Britain following the Opium War; it called for indemnities, the opening of new ports, and the cession of Hong Kong to the British.

Treaty of Tordesillas (1494) Treaty in which the pope decreed that the non-European world would be divided into spheres of trade and missionary responsibility between Spain and Portugal.

Tripartite Pact (1940) A pact that stated that Germany, Italy, and Japan would act together in all future military ventures.

Triple Entente Alliance developed before World War I that eventually included Britain, France, and Russia.

Truman Doctrine (1947) Declaration promising U.S. economic and military intervention, whenever and wherever needed, for the sake of preventing Communist expansion.

Truth and Reconciliation Commission Quasi-judicial body established after the overthrow of the apartheid system in South Africa and the election of Nelson Mandela as the country's first black president in 1994. The commission was to gather evidence about crimes committed during the apartheid years. Those who showed remorse for their actions could appeal for clemency. The South African leaders believed that an airing of the grievances from this period would promote racial harmony and reconciliation.

tsar/czar Russian word derived from the Latin "Caesar" to refer to the Russian ruler of Kiev, and eventually to all rulers in Russia.

Tula The Toltec capital city; a commercial hub and political and ceremonial center.

Uitlanders British populations living in Afrikaner republics; they were denied voting rights and subject to other forms of discrimination in the late nineteenth century; meaning "outsiders."

Ulama Scholarly class among Muslim people.

Umma Arabic for "the community of the faithful," it describes a sense of common identity among Muslims.

Universal Declaration of Human Rights (1948) United Nations declaration that laid out the rights to which all human beings are entitled.

Universitas Beginning in the late twelfth century, this term denoted scholars who came together, first in Paris. They formed a *universitas*, a term borrowed from the merchant communities, where it denoted the equivalent of the modern "union."

Upanishads Classic Hindu spiritual texts.

Utopian socialism The most visionary of all Restoration-era movements; Utopian socialists, like Charles Fourier, dreamed of transforming states, workplaces, and human relations and proposed plans to do so.

Vaishyas Merchants and artisans in the Hindu caste system.

Varna Caste system established by the Vedas in 600 BCE.

Versailles Conference (1919) Peace conference between the victors of World War I; resulted in the Treaty of Versailles, which forced Germany to pay reparations and to give up its colonies to the victors.

Viet Cong Vietnamese Communist group committed to overthrowing the government of South Vietnam and reunifying North and South Vietnam.

Viet Minh Group founded in 1941 by Ho Chi Minh to oppose the Japanese occupation of Indochina; it later fought the French colonial forces for independence. Also known as the Vietnamese Independent League.

Viziers Bureaucrats of the Ottoman Empire.

Vodun Mixed religion of African and Christian customs practiced by slaves and free blacks in the colony of Saint Domingue.

Voting Rights Act (1965) Law that granted universal suffrage in the United States.

Wafd Nationalist party that came into existence during a rebellion in Egypt in 1919 and held power sporadically after Egypt was granted limited independence from Britain in 1922.

Wahhabi Movement Early-eighteenth-century reform movement organized by Muhammad Ibn abd al-Wahhab, who preached the absolute oneness of Allah and a return to the pure Islam of Muhammad.

War of 1812 Conflict between Britain and the United States arising from U.S. grievances over oppressive British maritime practices in the Napoleonic Wars.

War on Poverty President Lyndon Johnson's push for an increased range of social programs and increased spending on social security, health, education, and assistance for the disabled.

Warsaw Pact (1955–1991) Military alliance between the Soviet Union and other Communist states that was established in response to the creation of the NATO alliance.

Weimar Republic (1919–1933) Constitutional Republic of Germany that was subverted by Hitler soon after he became chancellor.

Western Front Military front that stretched from the English Channel through Belgium and France to the Alps during World War I.

White Lotus Rebellion Series of uprisings in northern China (1790–1800s) inspired by mystical beliefs in folk Buddhism and, at times, the idea of restoring the Ming dynasty.

White Wolf Popular myth depicted this mysterious militia leader as a Chinese Robin Hood whose mission was to rid the country of the injustices of Yuan Shikai's government in the early years of the Chinese Republic (1910s).

Whites Refers to the "counterrevolutionaries" of the Bolshevik Revolution (1918–1921) who fought the Bolsheviks (the "Reds"); included former supporters of the tsar, Social Democrats, and large independent peasant armies.

Wokou Supposedly Japanese pirates, many of these thieves were actually Chinese subjects of the Ming dynasty.

Works Progress Administration (WPA) New Deal program instituted in 1935 that put nearly 3 million people to work building roads, bridges, airports, and post offices.

World Bank International agency established in 1944 to provide economic assistance to war-torn and poor countries. Its formal title is the International Bank for Reconstruction and Development.

Yalta Accords Results of the meeting between President Roosevelt, Prime Minister Churchill, and Premier Stalin that occurred in the Crimea in 1945 to plan for the postwar order.

Yellow press Newspapers that sought a mass circulation by featuring sensationalist reporting that appealed to the masses.

Young Egypt Antiliberal, fascist group that gained a large following in Egypt during the 1930s.

Young Italy Nationalist organization made up of young students and intellectuals, devoted to the unification and renewal of the Italian state.

Yuan Dynasty After the defeat of the Song, the Mongols established this dynasty, which was strong from 1280 to 1386 CE; its capital was at Dadu, or modern-day Beijing.

Yuan Mongols Mongol rulers of China who were overthrown by the Ming dynasty in 1368.

Zaibatsu Large-scale, family-owned corporations in Japan consisting of factories, import-export business, and banks that dominated the Japanese economy up until 1945.

Zamindars Archaic tax system of the Mughal empire where decentralized lords collected tribute for the emperor.

Zapatistas Group of indigenous rebels that rose up against the Mexican government in 1994 and drew inspiration from an earlier Mexican rebel, Emiliano Zapata.

Zhongguo Term originating in the ancient period and subsequently used to emphasize the central cultural and geographical location of China in the world. Meaning "Middle Kingdom."

Zionism Political movement advocating the reestablishment of a Jewish homeland in Palestine.

Zulus African tribe that, under Shaka, created a ruthless warrior state in southern Africa in the early 1800s.

Credits

World political map and world satellite map appear in the book courtesy of the National Geographic Society.

PRIMARY SOURCE DOCUMENTS

ROBERTUS AVESBURY: "Flagellants in England" from "The Black Death," *Manchester Medieval Sources*, Rosemary Horrox, trans./ed., pp. 153–54. Reprinted with permission of Manchester University Press.

PATRICIA BUCKLEY EBREY: "Proclamations of the HongWu Emperor." Reprinted with the permission of The Free Press, a division of Simon & Schuster Adult Publishing Group, from *Chinese Civilization: A Sourcebook*, Second Edition, Revised and Expanded by Patricia Buckley Ebrey. Copyright © 1993 by Patricia Buckley Ebrey. All rights reserved.

HUANG LIU-HUNG: "Elimination of Authorized Silversmiths" from *A Complete Book Concerning Happiness and Benevolence*, translated and edited by Djang Chu. Copyright © 1984 the Arizona Board of Regents. Reprinted by permission of the University of Arizona Press.

AHMET KARAMUSTAFA: "Dervish Groups in the Ottoman Empire, 1450–1550" from *God's Unruly Friends: Dervish Groups in the Islamic Later Middle Period*, pp. 6–7. Oneworld Publications, Oxford, 2006. Reprinted with the permission of Oneworld Publications.

NANAK: "Nanak's Teachings in India" from *Sources of Indian Tradition*, ed. William Theodore de Bary, © 1958 Columbia University Press. Reprinted with the permission of the publisher.

R. C. PADDEN, ED.: "Claudia the Witch," pp. 117–21, from *Tales of Potosí*. Copyright © 1975 by Brown University Press. Reprinted by permission of University Press of New England, Lebanon, NH.

ART AND PHOTOS

CHAPTER 9: pp. 366–67: Patrick Ward/Corbis; p. 373: Suhaib Salem/Reuters/Corbis; p. 375: Erich Lessing/Art Resource; p. 383 (top left): Vanni Archive/Corbis; (top right): Patrick Ward/Corbis; (bottom): The Metropolitan Museum of Art, Bequest of Cora Timken Burnett, 1956 (57.51.21) Image © The Metropolitan Museum of Art; p. 384: Bettmann/Corbis; p. 386: Gavin Hellier/JAI/Corbis; p. 388: Christine Osborne/Corbis; p. 391: akg-images/Visioars; p. 392: akg-images; p. 394: The Art Archive/British Library; p. 395 (left): Kurt Scholz/SuperStock; (right): Werner Forman/Art Resource; p. 396: Royal Ontario Museum/Corbis; p. 399: Copyright © National Land Image Information (Color Aerial Photograph), Ministry of Land, Infrastructure and Transport; p. 400: Asian Art & Archaeology, Inc./Corbis; p. 401: © The Trustees of the British Museum; p. 402: The Art Archive/Dagli Orti; p. 403: Giraudon/Bridgeman Art Library; p. 406: akg-images; p. 407 (both): Alamy; p. 408 (top): The Art Archive; (bottom): Werner Forman/Art Resource; p. 410: Alamy; p. 411: Greg Probst/Corbis.

CHAPTER 10: Pp. 416–17: Erich Lessing/Art Resource; p. 419 (top): Nik Wheeler/Corbis; (bottom): Granger Collection; p. 421: Victoria & Albert Museum, London/Art Resource; p. 425: Werner Forman/Art Resource; p. 427: HIP/Art Resource; p. 428: Colin Hoskins/Cordaiy Photo Library/Corbis; p. 429: Alamy; p. 433: Peter Guttman/Corbis; p. 434: Keren Su/Corbis; p. 436: Macduff Everton/Corbis; p. 437: The Art Archive; p. 440: Bridgeman/Giraudon/Art Resource; p. 441 (top): from *Chinese Siege Warfare: Mechanical Artillery & Siege Weapons of Antiquity* by Liang Jieming. Courtesy of the author; (bottom): Granger Collection; p. 443: akg-images/Werner Forman; p. 446: Christophe Loviny/Corbis; p. 448 (top): Erich Lessing/Art Resource; (bottom): Hubert Stadler/Corbis; p. 449: akg-images/Volker Kreidler; p. 451 (top): Paul Almasy/Corbis; (bottom): Giraudon/Art Resource; p. 452: The Art Archive; p. 456 (clockwise from left to right): Charles & Josette Lenars/Corbis; Kevin Schafer/Corbis; Alamy; p. 457 (left): Otto Lang/Corbis; (right): Alamy; p. 459: Michael S. Lewis/Corbis; p. 462: Granger Collection; p. 463: akg-images.

CHAPTER 11: pp. 472–73: Snark/Art Resource; p. 475: Granger Collection; p. 481: Scala/Art Resource; p. 482: The Topkapi Palace Museum, Istanbul, Turkey/Giraudon/Art Resource; p. 483: Yann Arthus-Bertrand/Corbis; p. 484 (top): Stapleton Collection, UK/Bridgeman Art Library; (bottom): Bibliotheque des Arts Decoratifs/Archives Charmet/Bridgeman Art Library; p. 486: Library of the Topkapi Palace Museum, folio 31b, photograph courtesy of Talat Halman; p. 490 (left): © 2007 The British Library; (right): HIP/Art Resource; p. 493: Bibliotheque Nationale de France, Paris; p. 496: Granger Collection; p. 497: Giraudon/Art Resource; p. 498: Museo di Firenze com'era Firenze/Scala/Art Resource; p. 500: Granger Collection; p. 501: The Art

Archive; **p. 503:** Réunion des Musées Nationaux/Art Resource; **p. 505:** The Jan Adkins Studio.

CHAPTER 12: pp. 510–11: Courtesy Wychwood Editions; **p. 513:** Réunion des Musées Nationaux/Art Resource, NY; **p. 515 (both):** By permission of the British Library (15226.b.19); **p. 518:** Biblioteca Estense/ScalaArt Resource, NY; **p. 519:** Historical Picture Archive/Corbis; **p. 524:** Bildarchiv Preussischer Kulturbesitz/Art Resource, NY; **p. 526 (left):** Granger Collection; **(right):** Nicolas Sapieha/Art Resource, NY; **p. 527:** Bettmann/Corbis; **p 528. (top):** Granger Collection; **(bottom):** The Art Archive/Palacio de Gobierno, Tlaxcala, Mexico; **p. 530 (left):** Schalkwijk/Art Resource, NY; **(right):** Granger Collection; **p. 533:** The Art Archive/Archaeological Museum, Lima/Dagli Orti; **p. 535 (left):** Granger Collection; **(right):** Rare Books Division, New York Public Library, Astor, Lenox and Tilden Foundations; **p. 536:** Don Klein/SuperStock; **p. 539:** The Art Archive/University Library Geneva/Dagli Orti; **p. 540:** Bildarchiv Preussischer Kulturbesitz; **p. 542:** Bridgeman Art Library; **p. 545:** Réunion des Musées Nationaux/Art Resource, NY; **p. 547:** The Art Archive/Maritime Museum Kronborg Castle, Denmark/Dagli Orti.

CHAPTER 13: pp. 552–53: Réunion de Musées Nationaux/Art Resource, NY; **p. 555 (left):** Chester Beatty Library and Gallery of Oriental Art, Dublin/Bridgeman Art Library; **(right):** British Museum, London/E.T. Archives, London/SuperStock; **p. 558:** Granger Collection; **p. 561:** Granger Collection; **p. 563:** MPI/Getty Images; **p. 564:** MPI/Getty Images; **p. 566:** Granger Collection; **p. 567 (left):** North Wind Picture Archives; **(right):** Private Collection/Bridgeman Art Library; **p. 570 (left):** Entwistle Gallery, London/Werner Forman/Art Resource; **(right):** Rare Books Division, New York Public Library, Astor, Lenox and Tilden Foundations; **p. 571:** The Newberry Library; **p. 573:** Reproduced from *Traditions and Encounters* (McGraw Hill, 2000); **p. 574:** Mary Evans Picture Library/The Image Works; **p. 575:** Imagno/Getty Images; **p. 576:** The Art Archive/Museum der Stadt Wien/Dagli Orti; **p. 577:** The British Library/Topham-HIP/The Image Works; **p. 578:** Chester Beatty Library and Gallery of Oriental Art, Dublin/The Bridgeman Art Library; **p. 584:** The Art Archive; **p. 586:** Réunion des Musées Nationaux/Art Resource, NY; **p. 587:** Chris Hellier/Corbis; **p. 589:** The British Museum/The Fotomas Index; **p. 590:** Granger Collection; **p. 591:** Anne S. K. Brown Military Collection, Brown University Library; **p. 592:** Amsterdam Historical Museum; **p. 593:** Chateau de Versailles/Bridgeman Art Library; **p. 594:** Private Collection/Bridgeman Art Library.

CHAPTER 14: pp. 598–99: Scala/Art Resource; **p. 601:** Topkapi Palace Museum, Istanbul, A3592, photograph courtesy of Talat Halman; **p. 602:** Topkapi Palace Museum, Istanbul; **p. 603 (left):** Topkapi Palace Museum, Istanbul/Werner Forman Archive/Art Resource, NY; **(right):** Victoria & Al-

bert Museum, London/Art Resource, NY; **p. 604:** Bridgeman Art Library; **p. 605 (left):** Giraudon/Art Resource; **(right):** Private Collection, courtesy of the owner and D. A. King, contributor; photo by Christie's of London; **p. 606:** Reproduced by the kind permission of the trustees of the Chester Beatty Library and Gallery of Oriental Art, Dublin; **p. 607 (clockwise from top):** Scala/Art Resource, NY; Granger Collection; Réunion des Musées Nationaux/Art Resource, NY; **p. 609:** British Library; **p. 610:** Reproduced from *World Civilizations* (Addison Wesley Longman, 2001); **p. 611 (both):** Underwood & Underwood/Corbis; **p. 612:** Courtesy Peabody Essex Museum, Salem, MA; **p. 613 (left):** The Needham Research Institute; **(right):** The British Library, London; **p. 614:** The British Library, London/ Bridgeman Art Library; **p. 615:** Réunion des Musées Nationaux/Art Resource, NY; **p. 616:** The Fotomas Index; **p. 618 (top):** Courtesy Wychwood Editions; **(bottom):** Rare Books Division, The New York Public Library, Astor, Lenox and Tilden Foundations; **p. 619:** Bridgeman Art Library; **p. 620:** Bridgeman Art Library; **p. 621:** Musée Réunion des Beaux-Arts, Rouen/Superstock; **p. 623:** Private Collection/Bridgeman Art Library; **p. 624:** Private Collection/Bridgeman Art Library; **p. 625 (top):** © The Trustees of the British Museum; **(bottom):** Image copyright © The Metropolitan Museum of Art/Art Resource, NY; **p. 626:** Bridgeman Art Library; **p. 627 (both):** Museo de America, Madrid; **p. 629:** © National Maritime Museum, London; **p. 631:** E. T. Archives, London/Superstock; **p. 632 (top):** The Art Archive/Castle Howard/Eileen Tweedy; **(bottom):** Granger Collection; **p. 633:** Natural History Museum, London/Bridgeman Art Library.

CHAPTER 15: pp. 638–39: Stefano Bianchetti/Corbis; **p. 644:** Collection of the New-York Historical Society; **p. 645:** Granger Collection; **p. 646:** Hulton Archive/Getty Images; **p. 647:** Musee de la Ville de Paris, Musee Carnavalet/Giraudon/Art Resource, NY; **p. 649:** Lauros-Giraudon/Bridgeman Art Library; **p. 652 (top):** Granger Collection; **(bottom):** North Wind Picture Archives; **p. 654:** The Art Archive/Museo Nacional de Historia, Mexico City; **p. 655:** Granger Collection; **p. 657 (top):** Private Collection/Bridgeman Art Library; **(bottom):** Reproduced from Michael Crowder's *West Africa: An Introduction to Its History* by courtesy of the publishers, Addison Wesley Longman; **p. 659:** Granger Collection; **p. 660:** Granger Collection; **p. 662:** Corbis; **p. 664:** North Wind Picture Archives; **p. 665:** Granger Collection; **p. 666:** Granger Collection; **p. 668:** Novotsi/Bridgeman Art Library; **p. 670:** Hulton/Bettmann/Corbis; **p. 673:** Courtesy of the director, National Army Museum, London; **p. 675:** Granger Collection; **p. 676:** The Art Archive; **p. 678 (top):** The British Library, London/Bridgeman Art Library; **(bottom):** North Wind Picture Archives; **p. 679:** Roy Miles Fine Paintings/Bridgeman Art Library; **p. 680:** © The National Maritime Museum Picture Library, London.

and culture, 602, 615, 616, 620
and Enlightenment, 620
and Islam, 602
see also literacy; universities; *specific nations and empires*
Edward III, king of England, 492
Egypt, 368, 421, 454, 465
agriculture in, 670
Arabia's trade with, 371
between 1600–1750, 555, 575
between 1750–1850, 639, 640, 649, *649*, 662, 668–70, *670*, 681, *681*
Black Death in, 478
bureaucracy in, 671
Christianity in, 432
and coffeehouses, 555
counter-caliphate in, 378
culture in, 604, 607, 628, 631
economy in, 662, 670
education in, 670, 671
as Islamic center, 479
Islamic conquest of, 375, 376
Mamluks in, 575, 639, 670
modernization of, 640, 668, *670*
monasticism in, 406
Napoleon in, 631, 639, 649, *649*, 668–70, *669*
as part of Ottoman empire, 575, 639
Qalandar dervish order in, 485
slaves in, 425, 428
Sunni regime in, 433
writing in, 380
see also Alexandria, Egypt
Ekken, 616
Ekpe (secret male society), 567
elections:
and American Revolution, 644
between 1750–1850, 647, 655
and French Revolution, 647
and revolutions in Caribbean and Iberian America, 655
see also voting
elephants, 402, 407–8, 423
elites:
in Americas, 627
between 1600–1750, 577, 578, 579, 581, 591, 594
between 1750–1850, 640–41, 646, 652–54, 655, 656, 660, 662, 667
and culture, 627
and dynastic monarchies, 591, 594
and economy, 660, 662
and Enlightenment, 620, 624
and French Revolution, 646
and revolutions in Caribbean and Iberian America, 652–54, 655, 656
in Soviet Russia, 667
and transformation in Atlantic world, 640–41
and war between 1600–1750, 591
Elizabeth I, queen of England, 538, 540, 593, *594*
Émile (Rousseau), 621
encomenderos, 525, 527, 530, 531, 535
Encyclopedia (Diderot and Alembert), 623, *623*, *624*, 635
England:
Black Death in, 491
feudalism in, 493
Flagellants in, 492
in Hundred Years' War, 496, 497
monarchy in, 494
Parliament in, 493

Peasants Revolt in, 493, *508*
population of, 496
Renaissance in, 498
Tudors in, 496, *508–9*
universities in, 491
see also Great Britain, British
Enlightenment:
and American Revolution, 641
and bases of new science, 619–21
between 1750–1850, 641, 654, 655
and colonial cultures, 628–29
Cook as exemplar of, 631
origins of, 617–19
and revolutions in Atlantic world, *642–43*
and revolutions in Caribbean and Iberian America, 654, 655
salons during, *621*, 622
thinkers during, 621–24
entrepôts, 421, 458, 516, 523, 567, 679
Epic of Gilgamesh, 380
Epic of Sundiata, The, 425, 426
Episcopalians, 540
equality:
and American Revolution, 644, 645
between 1750–1850, 641, 644, 645, 647, 649, 653
and French Revolution, 647, 649
and revolutions in Caribbean and Iberian America, 653
Equator, Republic of the, 652
Equiano, Olaudah, 628
Erasmus, Desiderius, 498, 499
Essay Concerning Human Understanding (Locke), 622
Estates-General, French, 592, 593, *646*, 646, 676
Ethiopia, 404
Euclid, 384
eunuchs:
Abbasid, 394–95
Tang, 394–95, *395*
Eurasia:
between 1600–1750, 554, 574, 589, 595
between 1750–1850, 667–81
and commerce and colonization between 1450–1600, 511, 512–13, 530, 531, 535–36
and culture between 1600–1780, 599, 607
persistence and change in, 667–81
population of, 531
and revival of Chinese economy, 512
and revival of trade, 512–13
and Russia between 1600–1750, 589
and Safavid Empire, 574
see also specific people, cities and regions
Europe, Europeans:
agriculture in, 370
and Americas, 566, 626–29
Asian relations with, 543, 572, 574
between 600–1000, 389, *412–13*
between 1300–1500, 490, 491, 492, 495, 507, *508–9*
between 1600–1750, 554, 558, 566, 570–72, *570*, *572*, 573, *573*, 574, 577, 578, 583, 584–94
between 1600–1780, 599, 600–601, 604, 607, 617–24, 626, 629–31, 634
between 1750–1850, 649, 650, 651–52, 653, 656, 662, 668–71, 673–81
and China, 514, 516, 545–46, 548, 583, 612, 676–81, 679

Christianity in, 401–2, 403–7, *404*, 435, 446–52, 453, 454, 466–67
and colonization between 1450–1600, 511–12, 514, 516, 517–23, *521*, 524–25, 531, 536, 537–38, 543–46
and commerce and trade, 511–12, 514, 516, 517–23, 524, 531, 536, 537–48, 656
culture in, 599, 600–601, 604, 607, 609, 612, 617–24, 627–31, 634–35
economy in, 447–48, 558, 590–94, 662, 665
and Egypt, 668–71
Enlightenment in, 617–24, 635
and exploration and expansion, 517–23, *519*
famine in, 491, *508*
and French Revolution, 649
gender in, 490–91, 499
and imperialism, 629–31, 632
Islam and, 388
and Japan, 584–86, 609, 617
map of exploration by, *520–21*
and mercantilism, 594
monarchies in, 494, 507
and Mughal empire, 543–46, 577, 578, 607
and Napoleonic empire, 650
new trade routes discovered by, 506–8
and Ottoman empire, 517, 668–71
peasant revolts in, *491*, 493, *508*
and politics, 590–94
quest for universal empire in, 538
and race, 634
religion in, 539–43
and revolutions in Caribbean and Iberian America, 651–52, 653
and Safavid Empire, 574
and slave trade, 566, 570–72, *570*, *572*, 656
and Soviet Russia, 589
study of ancient texts in, 481
trade in, 448, 452, 490–91
transformation of, 537–43, 586
universities in, 451–52, 491
see also specific nations and topics
expansionism:
Chinese, 389–91
see also colonialism; *specific empires*
extraterritoriality, in China, 680
Ezo, *see* Hokkaido, Japan

Faini, Diamante Medaglia, 620
family:
between 1600–1750, 579–81
and transition from Ming to Qing dynasty, 579–81
see also gender
famine:
between 1750–1850, 662, *662*, 667
between 1850–1914, 667
and economic reordering, 662, *662*, 667
in Europe, 491, *508*
Farabi, al-, 383–84
farmers:
and American Revolution, 641
between 1750–1850, 641, 644, 660, *660*, 665, 667
and commerce and colonization between 1450–1600, 513
and economic reordering, 660, *660*, 665, 667
see also agriculture; *specific nations and empires*
Fatehpur Sikri, 545, 606
Fatima, 387
Fatimid regime, 381, 388, *388*, *412–13*, 421, 433

Joinville, Jean de, 453
Jomon, 399
Jones, William, 672
Joseph II (Austrian ruler), 623
Journey to the West (Xuanzang), 396
Judaism, *see* Jews, Judaism
Jurchen Jin dynasty, 438, 462, 466–67
Jurchen people, 438, 438, 440, 441, 465
Jurchens, 581
Justinian, emperor of Rome, 410

kabuki, 614
kabuki theater (Japan), 614, *615, 634*
Kaibara Ekiken, 616
Kaibara Token, 616
Kaifeng, 463, 465
Kaiyuan Si, 422
Kamakura, Japan, 442, 443, *443, 466–67*
kami, 399, 400, 401
kangaroos, 632
Kanto Plain, 442
Kara Mustafa Pasha, *574,* 575, 576
karim, 419, 421, 422
Kaya, Korea, 397, 399
Kenya, 386, 537
    see also East Africa
Khadija, 379
Khalji, Alaud din, 486–87
Khan, Danishmand, 606
Khanbaliq, 608
khans, Mongol, *see specific khans*
Kharijism, 386, 388
Khitan people, 399, *412–13,* 440, 465
Khmer, 445, 446, 465, 466
Khurasan, Arabia, 368, 376, 479
Khutulun, 462
Khwarizmi, Al-, 383, *412–13*
Kiev, 410, 449, *449,* 466
Kilwa, 427, 464, 523
King Alvaro II (slave trader), 570
kings, princes, 592–94, 641
King's Book of Kings, The (Firdawsi), 434, 604, *604*
knights, *see* warriors
Koguryo, 397
Kongo kingdom, 571–72
Koprulu family, 575–76, 596
Koran, *see* Quran
Korea, Koreans, 397–99, 400
    between 1600–1750, 583, 586
    Buddhism in, 399, 400, 401
    and China, 583
    Chinese expansion into, 389, 391
    Chinese influence on, 388, 389, 396, 397, 398, 442
    and Japan, 586, 614
    Mongol invasion of, 399, 462, *466–67*
    Silla state of, *412–13*
    Three Kingdoms in, 397, *412*
Koryo kingdom, 399, *412–13,* 462, 466
    Song dynasty imitated by, 442
kpojito, 570
Kremlin (Moscow), 588, 589
Krishna, 422
Kshatriyas, 435
Kuangyin, Zhao, 437–38, 440
Kubilai Khan, 417, 422, 459, 462, *462,* 463, 465, 608
Kufic, *421*
Kumasi (Asante capital), 572, 625
Kush, Kushans, 459
Kyoto, Japan, 400, 583–84, 614, 615, 616

Kyūshū, Japan, 505, 584

labor:
    between 1600–1750, 589, 592
    between 1750–1850, 641, 651, 657, 660, 664–67, *666,* 670
    and colonization between 1450–1600, 525, 532, 535, 536, 537
    and commerce and trade, 525, 532, 535, 536, 537, 657
    and economy, 592, 660, 664–67, *666*
    in Egypt and Ottoman empire, 670
    and politics, 592
    and revolutions in Caribbean and Iberian America, 651
    and Russia, 589
    and strikes, 666
    and wages, 666, 667, 670
    working conditions of, 664–67
    see also slaves, slavery; *specific types of labor*
Lafayette, Marquis de, 652
Lahore, 515
Lake Texcoco (Mexico), 525, 529
Lake Victoria (Africa), 656
Lamb, Charles, 555
Lamu, 386
Lancashire, England, *665*
Lancaster, house of, 496
Lancaster, James, 548
land:
    and American Revolution, 644
    between 1600–1750, 592
    between 1750–1850, 641, 644
    and economic and political fluctuations in Europe, 592
    see also agriculture; farmers; peasants; planters, plantations
language:
    between 1750–1850, 672–73
    in India, 672–73
    and transformation in Atlantic world, 640
    see also writers, writing; *specific language families and languages*
L'Anse aux Meadows, 408
La Rioja mines, 662
Latin America:
    between 1750–1850, 662
    and culture, 626, 629
    and economy, 662
    and revolutions in Caribbean and Iberian America, 653
Latin American confederation, 655
Latin language, 392, 405, 493
leadership, 580
LeClerc, Georges Louis (comte de Buffon), 633
Leclerc, Victor-Emmanuel, 652
legal system, 620, 623, 641, 645, 649, 660
    see also sharia
Lelang, 397
Leo III, emperor of Constantinople, 410
Leo III, Pope, 407
Lepanto, Spanish defeat Ottomans at, 538, *549*
Leviathan (Hobbes), 594
Lewis, Samuel, 657
Lewis, William, 657
Lexington, Mass., 641
Liao dynasty, 399, 440–41
Li Bai, 397
liberalism:
    between 1750–1850, 674
    in India, 674
Liberal Party (Great Britain), 662

Liberia, 656
liberty:
    between 1750–1850, 641, 645, 647, 649, 651, 652, 653, 658
    and French Revolution, 645, 647, 649
    and revolutions in Caribbean and Iberian America, 651, 652, 653
libraries, 379, 380–81, 622
    see also books; writers, writing
Lima, Peru, 531, 532
Limpopo, 427
Linnaeus, Carolus, 631, 633, *633,* 635
Lin Zexu, 679
Lisbon, Portugal, 519, 522, 523, 571, 652
Li Shimin, 392, 393
literacy, 615, 622
    see also education
Liu Zongyuan, 397
Li Yuan, 390
Li Zicheng, 580–81
Loango (African port), *571*
Locke, John, 594, 622, 629, 635, 644
Lodi, Ibrahim, 488–89, *490*
Lodi dynasty, *436,* 488
Lodi Gardens, *436*
London, England:
    banking and finance in, 661, 662
    between 1600–1750, 555, 591
    between 1750–1850, 656, 661, 662, 665, 673
    Black Death in, 491
    coffeehouses in, 555
    and culture between 1600–1780, 632
    and economy, 591, 665
    and political fluctuations in Europe, 591
    population of, 665
    and slave trade, 656
    working and living in, 665
Louis XIII, king of France, 592
Louis XIV, king of France, 591, 592, 593, 596, 606, 608, 620, 621, 623
Louis XV, king of France, 621, 622
Louis XVI, king of France, 646, 647, 651
Louis XVIII, king of France, 651
L'Ouverture, Toussaint, *651,* 652, 653
Low Countries, 539, 594, 665
    see also specific countries
Loyola, Ignatius, 541
Luanda (slave trading center), 571
Lübceck, Germany, 448
Luddites, 666
Luoyang, China, 389, 394, 396, *396*
Luther, Martin, 537–40, *540,* 542, 548, 590

Ma, empress of China, 501
Macao, China, 523, 547–48, *547,* 549, 679
Macaulay, Lord, 674
Macedonia, Machiavelli, Niccolò, 499
Madagascar, 427, 428
Madeira Islands, 519
Madeiras, 494
Madras, 673
Madrid, Spain, 531, 533, 538, 654
Magdeburg, 590
Magellan, Ferdinand, 511–12, 548, *548*
Maghreb, 433
Mahal, Mumtaz, 606, *607*
Mahayana Buddhism, 401–2, 443
Mahmud II (Ottoman ruler), 671, *681*
Mahmud of Ghazna, 436
Maitreya Buddha, 677
maize, 421, 457, 572, 577